THE COMPLETE ILLUSTRATED HISTORY OF

AZTEC & MAYA

THE COMPLETE ILLUSTRATED HISTORY OF THE

AZTEC & MAYA

THE DEFINITIVE CHRONICLE OF THE ANCIENT PEOPLES OF CENTRAL AMERICA &
MEXICO – INCLUDING THE AZTEC, MAYA, OLMEC, MIXTEC, TOLTEC & ZAPOTEC

CHARLES PHILLIPS
CONSULTANT: DR DAVID M JONES

HERMES
HOUSE

CONTENTS

INTRODUCTION

Each year at spring and autumn equinox, people come in their thousands to the ruined ancient Mexican city of Chichén Itzá. They gather to view a remarkable solar light show on the steps of the towering Pyramid-Temple of Kukulcán, the feathered serpent god also known as Quetzalcóatl. Probably in the 10th century AD, Maya or Toltec temple builders constructed this 24m (79ft) tall, four-sided stepped pyramid in such a way that the rising and setting equinoctial sun creates a snaking pattern of light and shadow on the steps – as if the feathered serpent deity himself were manifesting at these sacredly charged times.

The beauty of the spectacle and the temple's setting in the middle of a great plaza at the heart of an evocative ruined city is matched by our sense of wonder at the extraordinary skill of these ancient builders. They also, according to recent research, engineered the acoustics of the temple so that a speaking voice on the pyramid top could be heard in the plaza far below and a handclap at ground level bounces back from the pyramid steps in an echo that mimics the call of the sacred quetzal bird, an acknowledged physical form of Kukulcán/Quetzalcóatl.

This equinoctial event at Chichén Itzá typifies the powerful attraction of Mesoamerica – the series of cultures that flourished in the lands of Central America and Mexico between the first arrival of

humans in the region in *c.*21,000BC and 1521, when invading Spanish soldiers defeated the might of the Aztec empire. At scores of ancient sites in Mexico, Guatemala, Belize and Honduras, both tourists and scholars are awestruck by the wealth of evidence left by this glittering succession of great cultures – in the form of ruined buildings and cities, beautiful wall paintings, sculptures and delicate gold and turquoise sacred artefacts.

MYSTERY AND TERROR
Mesoamerican remains have the appeal of mystery and of an exotic and terrifying religious ritual. At sites such as Tikal,

Left: The young twin gods Hunahpú and Xhalanque were Maya heroes who helped make earth and sky safe places.

Above: The Castillo is part of the northern complex of Chichén Itzá, together with the Hall of a Thousand Columns and the Temple of the Feathered Serpent.

Yaxchilán, Uaxactún and Palenque in Guatemala and Mexico, visitors view the remains of great cities built by the ancient Maya, cities that were suddenly abandoned in the 9th century AD for reasons still debated by scholars. This mysterious 'Maya Collapse' adds to the romance of these extraordinarily beautiful ruins standing amid the jungle trees and creepers that overwhelmed them after their abandonment until they were gradually rediscovered in the 18th and 19th centuries. In the ruins of the great Aztec Templo Mayor ('Great Temple') in Mexico City, and at Chichén

Above: Aztec gods of earth and fertility included Xipe Totec (left), god of spring, and Xochipilli, the flower prince.

Itzá, are the remains of religious artefacts used in sacred rituals of mass slaughter – the killing of prisoners of war and other designated victims in their thousands to appease the gods. Such bloodthirsty Mesoamerican practices – represented in surviving Aztec and Maya codices (bark-paper books) and reported with horror by the European soldiers and missionaries of the 16th century – give the ancient Mexican and Guatemalan culture a powerful, horrid allure.

The great variety of Mesoamerican sites includes La Venta and San Lorenzo, where the people of the first Mesoamerican civilization, the Olmec, built ceremonial centres in the mid-second millennium BC; Monte Albán, the mountaintop city founded in c.500BC in the Oaxaca region of Mexico; and El Tajín, where builders raised an elaborate six-tier Pyramid of the Niches, containing 365 openings – one for each day of the solar year. Perhaps the most remarkable of all is Teotihuacán – once one of the world's leading cities, now another extraordinarily evocative ruin. Laid out in the Valley of Mexico on a grid pattern with huge stepped temples including the Pyramid of the Sun and Pyramid of the Moon, Teotihuacán at its height in c.AD500 covered upwards of 20 sq km

(8 sq miles) and was home to perhaps 200,000 people. In common with other sites in Mesoamerica, it became a place of pilgrimage for later peoples; the Aztecs, who flourished in Mexico for two centuries c.1325–1521, named it 'Place of the gods' and even saw it as the arena in which the creation of the Sun and Moon had been played out at the dawn of the current world age.

ANCIENT REMAINS, LIVING CULTURE

Throughout the lands of what was once Mesoamerica the inheritance of ancient Olmec, Zapotec, Maya, Toltec and Aztec peoples interacts creatively with the long aftermath of the 16th-century Spanish conquest – as exemplified by the thrilling discovery in spring 2006 of ancient ruins beneath a site used for Roman Catholic rites on the outskirts of Mexico City. The remains were of a remarkable square pyramid measuring 18m (59ft) tall and 150m (492ft) on each side, constructed in c.AD500 by the people of Teotihuacán and abandoned in c.AD800 when the culture behind that magnificent city and trading empire mysteriously collapsed.

Subsequently the pyramid was submerged beneath a hill, which became known as Itzapalapa ('Star hill'), and since 1833 it has been the setting for a re-enactment of the Passion of Christ, begun by locals as an act of gratitude to God for delivery from a cholera epidemic but now a tourist attraction in its own right, drawing around 1 million visitors each Easter. Because of this combined ancient and modern sacred heritage, the Mexican National Institute of Anthropology and History has accepted that it cannot fully excavate these Teotihuacáno remains – to do so would destroy the setting for the Roman Catholic celebrations.

The pages that follow provide a detailed and colourful guide to the deeds, beliefs, way of life and artforms of the ancient peoples of Mesoamerica, an exploration of the enthralling cultures and remains that – as at Itzapalapa – have influenced life beneath the vibrancy of modern Mexico and Central America.

Below: One of the famous murals in the Maya city of Bonampak: musicians and priests celebrate the heir's accession.

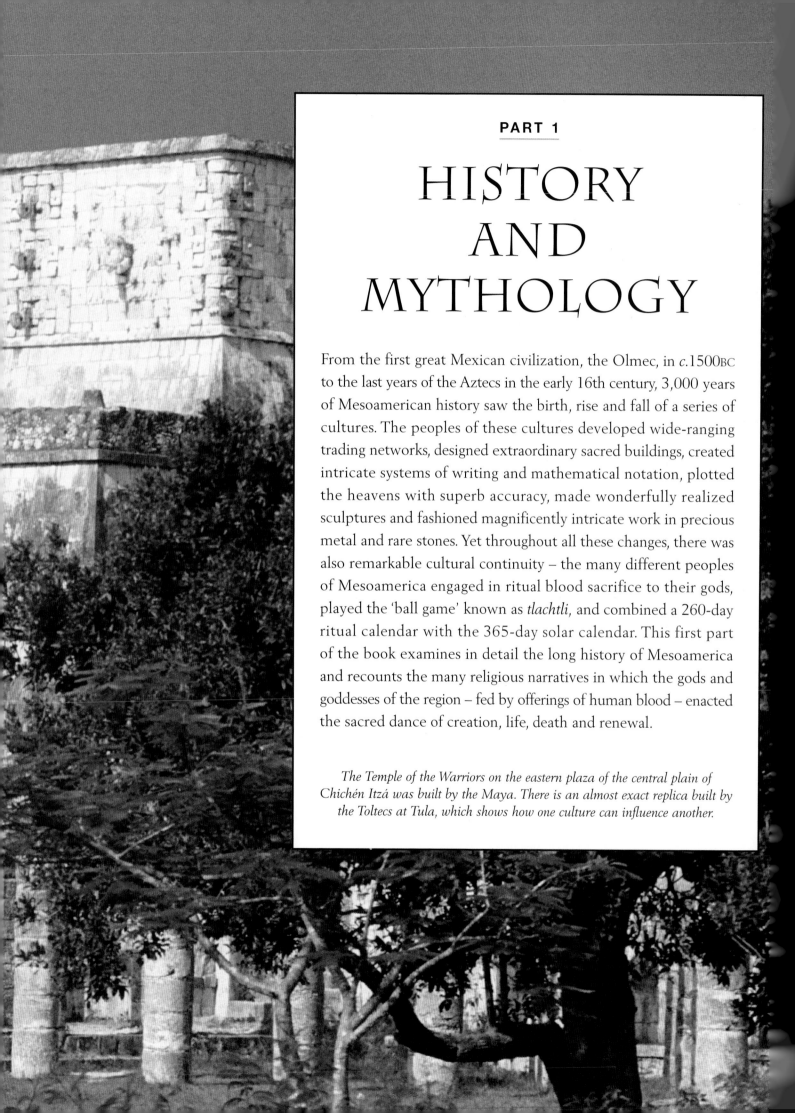

PART 1

HISTORY AND MYTHOLOGY

From the first great Mexican civilization, the Olmec, in *c.*1500BC to the last years of the Aztecs in the early 16th century, 3,000 years of Mesoamerican history saw the birth, rise and fall of a series of cultures. The peoples of these cultures developed wide-ranging trading networks, designed extraordinary sacred buildings, created intricate systems of writing and mathematical notation, plotted the heavens with superb accuracy, made wonderfully realized sculptures and fashioned magnificently intricate work in precious metal and rare stones. Yet throughout all these changes, there was also remarkable cultural continuity – the many different peoples of Mesoamerica engaged in ritual blood sacrifice to their gods, played the 'ball game' known as *tlachtli*, and combined a 260-day ritual calendar with the 365-day solar calendar. This first part of the book examines in detail the long history of Mesoamerica and recounts the many religious narratives in which the gods and goddesses of the region – fed by offerings of human blood – enacted the sacred dance of creation, life, death and renewal.

The Temple of the Warriors on the eastern plaza of the central plain of Chichén Itzá was built by the Maya. There is an almost exact replica built by the Toltecs at Tula, which shows how one culture can influence another.

THE GLORY THAT WAS MESOAMERICA

In 1519, a group of Spanish soldiers on an exploratory voyage from the Spanish colony in Cuba encountered a great civilization in full flower in the Valley of Mexico. From a cold mountain pass between the awe-inspiring snow-capped peaks of Popocatépetl and Ixtaccíhuatl, the nervous Spaniards looked down on a remarkable series of interconnected lakes in the Valley, with well-ordered towns and raised fields on the shores, and a great city built on islands and causeways towards the western edge of the largest of the lakes. They knew something of the Aztec people who built this city, Tenochtitlán, for earlier in the adventure the Spaniards had encountered the Aztecs' allies and enemies and heard tales of their vast empire. As the Spaniards marched down on to the plain and neared the city, they went across one of the causeways linking the island metropolis to the mainland and were astounded by

Below: The builders of Maya cities such as Tikal, in Guatemala, raised towering stone temples in the midst of thick jungle.

Tenochtitlán's size and beauty. The great temples and palaces rose from the water like a vision. One member of the Spanish force, Bernal Díaz del Castillo, later likened it to a city from a fairytale, a vision of enchantment.

EARLY BEGINNINGS

The city of Tenochtitlán and the culture of its Aztec builders was the product of more than 22,000 years of human activity, which stretched back to the arrival of the first hunter-gatherers in America in 21,000BC.

Descendants of these ancient settlers who left their mark in the area included the Olmec builders of the great cities of La Venta and San Lorenzo in c.1200BC, the Zapotec architects of Monte Albán in c.500BC and the Toltec founders of Tollán in AD950. They also included the Maya, who built their remarkable jungle cities in the lands to the east of the Valley of Mexico in the first centuries of the Christian era. At the time of the Conquest they were still thriving in the northern part of the Yucatán peninsula.

Above: Mictlantecuhtli, the Aztec 'Lord of the Dead', was worshipped in this form by the people of Teotihuacán in c.100BC.

WHAT WAS MESOAMERICA?

Scholars give the name Mesoamerica to this 22,000-year timespan and to the lands settled by these peoples; it is both a cultural and a geographical label. Geographically, Mesoamerica runs from the area of desert north of the Valley of Mexico across Guatemala and Honduras to western Nicaragua and Costa Rica.

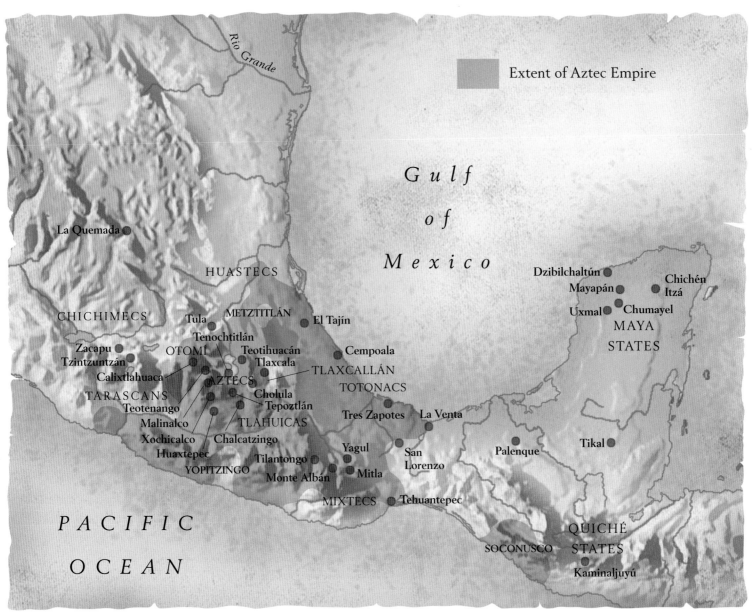

Extent of Aztec Empire

Above: Map showing the extent of the Aztec empire in 1510, and the other main Mesoamerican civilizations.

It largely coincides with what we call Middle America, including areas of some modern Central American countries. Other Central American countries, such as Panama, were not settled by Mesoamericans. Mexico, most of which was an important part of Mesoamerica, is geographically part of North America. Historically, Mesoamerica covers all events between the arrival of the first human settlers in the region in *c*.21,000BC and the Conquest of the Mesoamerican empire in 1521.

Scholars use an additional set of chronological divisions to divide Maya history. The years *c*.AD250–900 that represent the fullest flowering of Maya civilization are labelled the Classic Period. The Classic years are the ones in which the Maya set up dated stone columns celebrating the achievements of their holy kings. The 20,000-odd years before are called the Archaic (20,000–*c*.2500BC) and Preclassic (*c*.2500BC– AD250) periods. The 600-odd years after are known as the Postclassic Period (AD900–1500s).

This book covers the historical achievements and mythology of all these cultures, concentrating on the cultures of the Maya and the Aztecs because we know most about them. Succeeding cultures inherited a great deal from their predecessors.

Right: Tall stone warrior figures carved by Toltec craftsmen in the 11th century AD celebrated a fierce, militaristic culture.

Religious rituals, cultural achievements and mythological elements are common to most of the peoples of the Mesoamerican region and historical period, so that it is possible to talk of 'Mesoamerican civilization'.

CALENDARS

Foremost among these common elements was the use of a complex ritual calendar. Among the Maya and Aztecs, priests marked the passing of time and predicted

the future with two calendars, one a solar count of 365 days linked to the passing seasons, another a ritual calendar of 260 days, thought to be based on the length of a human pregnancy. The two calendars combined to make a longer measure. The period needed for a particular day in the 365-day calendar and a particular day in the 260-day calendar to coincide was 18,980 days, or 52 365-day years. This measure, called the 'bundle of years' by the Aztecs, was invested with great

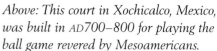

Above: This court in Xochicalco, Mexico, was built in AD700–800 for playing the ball game revered by Mesoamericans.

significance. The end of each 52-year period was seen as a moment of great danger, at which the gods might end the world. The preoccupation with measuring and recording time went far back into Mesoamerican history – the earliest surviving writing from the region may be a Zapotec calendrical note from *c.*600BC – and the calendar was very widely used throughout the region. Indeed, the scholar Michael Coe has suggested that one good way of defining Mesoamerica would be to draw a line around the area known to have used the ritual calendar.

BLOOD SACRIFICE

Another important central element of Mesoamerican civilization – at least as far back as the Olmecs in *c.*1200BC – was the use of human blood sacrifice to honour and propitiate the gods. Among the Aztecs, vast lines of prisoners of

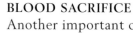

Left: The long-nosed Maya rain god Chac – carved here at Sayil, Mexico – had his counterpart in Tláloc, the Aztec god of rain.

war were paraded up steep temple pyramids to be sacrificed by having their hearts ripped from their chests. The Classic-Period Maya more commonly decapitated their victims. Both Maya and Aztec worshippers also offered their own blood to the gods. Women and men drew blood from wounds in their cheeks, ears, arms and legs while men also made cuts in the penis.

The Mesoamericans worshipped a vast pantheon of gods and goddesses in the course of their civilization. These deities often have alternative names and animal or human twin forms. The cult of one god in particular was enduringly popular across centuries and cultures. The Plumed Serpent Quetzalcóatl, known to the Maya as Kukulcán, was associated with wise rulership and revered as a creator, a wind god and as the morning star. In myth, he was said to have departed by sea on a raft of snakes, promising to return. It is a popular theory that some among the Aztecs may have interpreted the coming of Hernán Cortés and his Spanish troops in 1519 as the promised return of Quetzalcóatl from exile.

THE BALL COURT

One of the basic common elements of Mesoamerican civilization was a ball game played on a court shaped like a capital 'I'. The court, which formed part of the ritual

Above: On the steep steps of temples, the Aztecs made human sacrifices to the gods.

complex in cities, had sloping or vertical side walls. The object appears to have been to get the ball into the end sections, rather like the 'endzones' on an American football pitch or the areas where tries are scored on a British rugby pitch. Some courts had rings high on the side walls and extra points may have been scored by getting the ball through the hoop. This would have been difficult since players

Left: Tezcatlipoca played a part in the ball game as an enactment of cosmic struggles.

could not direct the ball with their feet or hands, only their hips, elbows and knees. The game seems to have been understood as an enactment of cosmic struggles; by the Aztecs as a clash between light and dark, between Quetzalcóatl and his dark brother Tezcatlipoca, by the Maya as a re-enactment of the myth cycle in which the Hero Twins go to the underworld to overcome the gods of that fearsome realm.

UNCOVERING THE SECRETS OF THE PAST

There was great excitement in Europe when the conqueror of the Aztecs, Hernán Cortés, sent a consignment of gold, featherwork and other rare treasures from Mesoamerica to the court of Charles V. The German artist Albrecht Dürer, who viewed the collection of objects, wrote in his journal, 'I have seen nothing that has so thrilled my heart as these artefacts, for I saw in them strange and wonderfully worked objects and marvelled at the subtle genius of men in far-off lands.'

Europeans had a tantalizing introduction to the 'subtle genius' of Mesoamerican civilization. Almost five centuries after Dürer wrote these words and following more than a century of excavations and interpretations, today we know much more about ancient Mesoamerican civilization. Weather and land conditions often did not favour the survival of early remains. Local practice before the Conquest meant that much of Mesoamerican mythology and history was transmitted orally from generation to generation and never written down. But the major part of the blame for the paucity of surviving remains must be shouldered by the Spanish conquerors themselves. After they had captured Tenochtitlán in 1521, they vandalized the city, breaking images of the gods, melting down treasures into ingots to be sent back to Europe, tearing down buildings and using the materials for the foundations of their colony, New Spain.

Left: The imposing Pyramid of the Moon in Teotihuacán contains a hidden burial chamber with a sacrificial victim.

FRAGMENTS OF HISTORY

The Spanish missionaries who arrived in Maya lands after the conquest of Tenochtitlán were responsible for burning many of the locals' bark-paper books or codices. One of the most enthusiastic of these was Bishop Diego de Landa, author of *Report of Things in Yucatán*, who wrote, 'These people used certain letters with which they wrote in their books about ancient subjects … We found many books written with these letters and since they held nothing that was not falsehood and the work of the evil one, we burned them all'.

THE CODICES

As far as we know, only four Maya codices survived the attentions of the monks. Three of these codices are now known after the names of the European cities in which they are kept – the Dresden, Madrid and Paris Codices – while the fourth, the *Grolier Codex*, is in North America. They contain many images of Maya deities, as well as information used by priests for divining the future, timing sacred rituals and monitoring the movements of Venus and the eclipses of the sun and moon.

THE POPOL VUH

Other surviving accounts of Maya history and mythology were written down after the Conquest. The *Popol Vuh* ('Book of Advice') was a sacred text of the Quiché, a group of southern Maya inhabiting highland Guatemala. It survived for posterity through a combination of Quiché determination and good fortune. The original book, in Maya hieroglyphs, was secretly translated into the Roman alphabet by members of the Quiché nobility in the mid-1500s. This was part of an attempt to preserve the book at a time when the Spaniards, who had conquered the region in 1523–24, were seeking to exterminate native culture. The manuscript was not found until later in the century, by which time some members of the Catholic Church had begun to see some merit in recording and preserving accounts of ancient Mesoamerican culture and history and so allowed it to be preserved. This version was discovered in 1703 by Francisco Ximenez, a Franciscan friar who could read Quiché and who was therefore able to translate the text into Spanish.

Left: This funerary urn was used by the Quiché, southern Guatemalan Maya, whose holy book, the Popol Vuh, *contains a detailed account of the creation of the world.*

Above: An unknown 4th-century Maya ruler adorns a jade belt pendant found in the Petén region.

NATIVE HISTORIES

Two other native histories survive. The first, *The Annals of the Cakchiquels*, contains entries up to 1604 and describes the history of the Cakchiquels, neighbours of the Quiché, from mythical beginnings onwards. Like the *Popol Vuh*, it was first transcribed into the Roman alphabet in the 1500s. The second, *The Books of Chilam Balam*, contains a mixture

Right: Spanish conquistadors prepare to land in Mexico in 1519. The invaders' unfortunate belief that the local books and religious rites were wicked led to a terrible cultural loss.

of prophecy and history-myth of the Maya of Yucatán. These accounts were kept from the early 16th century onwards, but were rewritten, with additions, until the 19th century. They take their name from a Maya seer who is said to have predicted the coming of 'bearded men of the east' who would bring violence and force the Maya to speak another language. Both these sources give eyewitness accounts of the Spanish conquest and the many changes that followed it.

Below: Information concerning Maya cosmology and details of the gods associated with the four principal directions are to be found in the Madrid Codex.

AZTEC HISTORY AND MYTHOLOGY

Most of the written evidence we have of Aztec customs, beliefs, history and mythology was recorded after the Conquest, in manuscript books or codices written by young natives educated in Spanish schools and in reports written by the Spanish chroniclers, based on what they saw and heard from locals.

WRITTEN SOURCES

An important example is the *Codex Mendoza*, commissioned c.1525 by the first Spanish Viceroy, Don Antonio de Mendoza. It contains an account of the growth of the Aztec empire illustrated and written by native Mesoamericans based on older pictorial records.

The movements of the México/Aztec and other tribal groups prior to the establishment of Tenochtitlán are described in 16th-century manuscripts such as the *Codex Aubin* and the *Codex Xólotl* and also in the 17th-century history recorded by Fernando de Alva Ixtlilxóchitl. All were based on oral histories and earlier codices, now lost.

Among the Spanish chroniclers' accounts is Friar Bernardino de Sahagún's compendious 12-volume *General History of the Things of New Spain*, completed in 1569. His fellow Churchman Diego Durán compiled both the *History of the Indies of New Spain* and the *Book of the Gods and Rites and the Ancient Calendar*. First-hand accounts of the Conquest itself survive in the letters written by Hernán Cortés to Charles V and in *True History of the Conquest of New Spain*, written by Bernal Díaz del Castillo, a member of Cortés' force.

Above: Serpents writhe round the neck of the Aztec earth goddess Coatlícue. Ritual victims were decapitated in her honour.

REWRITING THE PAST

Scholars treat all the surviving written evidence with caution as many accounts blend history and mythology in a dense combination that is difficult to interpret, not least because it is full of repetitions and contradictions. A good example is that of the Aztecs' treatment of Tula, which combines knowledge handed down by oral tradition of the historical city (flourished c.AD950–1150) with the myth of Tollán ('the Place of the Reeds'), home to wondrous craftsmen, where the god Quetzalcóatl ruled in the guise of the prince Topiltzin. In general, Mesoamerican peoples looked to the past for justification of the present. The

Left: The Palace of King Yaxchilán contains a sculpture honouring the 8th-century AD Maya monarch Bird Jaguar.

Above: Aztec codices are more numerous than their Maya counterparts. The Codex Magliabechano *is a late 1500s copy of a pre-Hispanic manuscript. It contains valuable information on Aztec worship and the use of the ritual calendar.*

Aztecs, for example, rewrote their own history to establish that their destiny was to dominate other peoples and expand their own territories. The Aztecs often presented events or themes that were common to many cultures as unique 'historical' happenings. The Aztecs claimed they found their origin in the 'Place of the Seven Caves', but this origin story was common to the beliefs of many Mesoamerican groups.

Yet the Mesoamericans themselves viewed these accounts as history, even though the narratives contain non-sequential episodes and metaphorical accounts of events. Because of the Mesoamericans' willingness to blend fact with what the modern mind would class as myth in historical accounts, we know nothing for certain of events that took place more than 400 years before the Conquest. All scholars can do in the circumstances is to gauge the meaning of surviving buildings and ruins in the light of the latest knowledge.

Left: Mesoamerican societies had an enduring fascination with the jaguar. This clay model was made by an Aztec artist.

STELAE

Many carved inscriptions survive in Maya lands, notably on stelae, stone columns set up during the Classic Period in the 3rd to 9th centuries AD. They bear portraits of the 'holy kings' of Maya city-states and commemorate the rulers' accessions and jubilees, battle victories and important religious sacrifices, which sometimes included the humiliation and slaughter of a rival king.

One stela, erected in honour of King Cauac Sky in Quiriguá, south-eastern Guatemala, is 10m (33ft) tall and weighs 10 tons. It was set up in AD771. The Maya stopped erecting carved stelae in the 9th century AD and scholars believe that after this point they probably kept their records in books. The books were destroyed by the Spanish, but the stelae survive, providing an invaluable source of information about Maya history and culture in the Classic Period.

19

UNLOCKING THE SECRETS OF MAYA SOCIETY

In the mid-20th century, a breakthrough in the interpretation of Maya hieroglyphs led to a major reappraisal of the very nature of Maya society. Earlier scholars thought that the hieroglyphs combined a picture-image (rebus) and a symbol representing a word or idea (logogram). But in 1952 Soviet language specialist Yuri Knorosov showed that Maya hieroglyphs were also phonetic: different signs represented combinations of vowels and consonants and were used to spell out words. Phonetic signs, he argued, were written or carved alongside logograms. Maya experts resisted Knorosov's theory for some years , but in time they came to realize that he was right. Now they could begin to read the inscriptions, with results that helped to turn our understanding of the Maya on its head.

NEW UNDERSTANDINGS

In the early 20th century, scholars had recognized that the inscriptions contained a great deal of information about the ritual calendar and astronomy. They thought the carvings on the stelae were of priests rather than kings, and that

Above: The Chiapas rainforest crowds in on the ruins at Bonampak of the court of Lord Chan Muan, who reigned AD776–795.

images of beheaded victims represented sacred rites. They argued that the Maya were a peaceful people led by priestly astronomers. However, later scholars who could read the writing began to see that the inscriptions were about events in a king's reign. They understood that the carvings were of kings and that the sacrificial victims were often rival kings put to ritual death after defeat. A new, more accurate image emerged of the Maya as a martial people living in city-states that were almost constantly at war.

Another major breakthrough in our understanding of the Maya also occurred in 1952, with the discovery of a great royal tomb beneath a mortuary monument in the Maya city of Palenque. Mexican architect Alberto Ruz Lhuillier was excavating the vast Temple of Inscriptions there when his curiosity was aroused by one of the slabs on the temple floor. This particular stone slab was cut with a double row of holes that could, he conjectured, be used as finger grips to raise the stone. When he had the stone

lifted, he discovered a narrow stairway leading downward. The stairway had been deliberately blocked with rubble, which Lhuillier painstakingly cleared over the following four years. In June 1952 he discovered the stairs led to a chamber, beyond which he found a great funerary crypt 9m long and 7m in height (30ft by 23ft). The crypt held a carved stone sarcophagus in which lay a body later identified from inscriptions as that of King Pacal, ruler of Palenque in the 7th–8th centuries AD. Prior to Lhuillier's breakthrough, scholars had generally understood that the Maya built stepped pyramids as temples, but the discovery of Pacal in his magnificent royal tomb suggested that some of the pyramids were erected primarily as funerary monuments to honour deceased monarchs.

'PAINTED WALLS'

Six years earlier, in 1946, an American photographer called Giles Healey made another remarkable discovery deep in the rainforest of the Mexican state of Chiapas. Healey, who was searching for Maya ruins in the area, was led by locals to a city they referred to as Bonampak ('Painted Walls'). There he found a three-roomed building

ARCHAEOLOGIST AND LITERARY SLEUTH

Mexican archaeologist Alfonso Caso y Andrade (1896–1970) bridged the gap between the interpreters of ancient literature and the investigators of ruined sites. Not only did Andrade decipher a number of Mixtec codices in the course of his work, he also performed a painstaking archaeological study at Monte Albán, establishing a chronology for the occupation of the site in the Oaxaca valley and demonstrating that the Mixtec people occupied Monte Albán in the wake of the Zapotecs. Andrade published the celebrated *El Mapa de Teozacaoalco* in 1949 and *Kings and Kingdoms of the Mixteca* in 1970.

Above: The murals at Bonampak depict court life and celebrations marking a battle won by Lord Chan Muan in AD790.

whose walls were decorated with a remarkable series of murals that contain vivid images of life at a Maya royal court in the 8th century AD, including royal accessions, battles, musical performances and other ceremonies. In recent years, scholars have used digital technology to enhance photographs of the images and restore their original bright colours. The natives' name stuck: the city, about 30km (18 miles) from Yaxchilán, became known as Bonampak.

Archaeological work on Tenochtitlán was complicated by the fact that the capital of the Spanish colony of New Spain and later the vast metropolis of Mexico City were built on top of Aztec ruins. Important discoveries were made in the course of building work. In 1790, workers laying flagstones in the main square of Mexico City discovered the 24-ton Sun Stone, which commemorates the five Aztecs 'suns' or ages, together with a remarkable sculpture of Coatlícue, the earth goddess. A carving of the earth lord Tlaltecuhtli was found in 1968 during

digging for a metro line. In 1978, an electrical company worker uncovered part of a 3.25m- (10ft 9in) diameter monolith depicting the dismembered goddess Coyolxauhqui, who in myth was killed by her brother Huitzilopochtli. Scholars knew that the foundations of the Aztecs' Great Pyramid were adjacent to the spot where the monolith was found. The discovery of what became known as the 'Coyolxauhqui Stone' resulted in a major excavation of the foundations of the Great Pyramid over the following years.

Archaeologists' investigations brought many valuable insights into Teotihuacán, the site in the north-east Valley of Mexico that was revered by the Aztecs as the 'place of the gods'. The city was surveyed systematically in the 1960s and 1970s by American archaeologist René Millon. One of the major breakthroughs came by accident. In 1971, digging during preparations for a *son et lumière* ('sound and light') show uncovered a cave in volcanic lava beneath the city's most sacred building, the vast Pyramid of the

Sun. Offerings found there have been dated to many centuries before the Pyramid was built in the 2nd century AD, suggesting that the city had been built on an ancient site of pilgrimage. The Aztecs frequently visited ruined sites such as Teotihuacán, sometimes taking artefacts from the site and sometimes adding others of a different period.

Right: In Mexico City the Aztec past is never far away. A subway station is home to a temple honouring the wind god Éhecatl.

HISTORY

The magnificent architectural and cultural achievements of a succession of peoples in the region historians call Mesoamerica – which encompasses parts of Mexico and of Central America – cover almost 3,000 years. These achievements range from the step pyramids and colossal stone carvings of the Olmec in *c.*1200BC to the awe-inspiring cities, vast trading networks and complex religious societies of the Aztecs and Maya, who were both conquered by Spanish invaders in the years after the arrival of Hernán Cortés in 1519. Archaeological finds and examination of surviving documents continue to enrich our understanding of Mesoamerican history and culture. They provide intriguing insights into a number of fascinating ancient civilizations that can boast pioneering successes in astronomy and the development of calendars, in mathematics, writing and the arts – as well as a severe commitment to war and an intense religious devotion to gods who demanded the blood of human sacrifice. Our survey of Mesoamerican history provides an overview of this extended chronology, a detailed look at the varied landscapes of the region and an in-depth examination of the Mesoamerican way of religion, warfare, law and order and timekeeping.

Mesoamerican achievements were built on ancient foundations. By the time of the Aztec empire, the vast and impressive ruins of the city of Teotihuacán were already 1,000 years old. The towering Pyramid of the Sun, 66m (216ft) in height, became a favourite place of pilgrimage for Aztecs.

TIMELINE: A HISTORY OF MESOAMERICA

ARCHAIC AND PRECLASSIC PERIODS TO AD250

Above: Stepped temple-pyramids at Monte Albán give on to a large plaza.

21,000BC Hunter-gatherers enter the New World across the Bering Strait and a few thousand years later live in the Valley of Mexico near where the Aztecs will build their capital, Tenochtitlán.

7000–5000BC Mesoamerican settlers develop farming skills and domesticate wild plants – including maize.

2500–1500BC The first farming villages in Mesoamerica appear. Settlers raise maize, chilli peppers, squash and cotton.

1500–1200BC Olmecs build San Lorenzo.

1350BC A major urban settlement is built at San José Mogote.

1100BC A second Olmec city is built at La Venta.

1000BC The Ocós and Cuadros village-farming cultures thrive on the Pacific coast of Guatemala.

900BC The Olmec site of San Lorenzo is destroyed.

800BC Settlers build the first villages in the lowland Maya region.

600BC Carving on a monument at San José Mogote may be the earliest Mesoamerican writing.

c.600–400BC Maya build a living and ceremonial centre at Nakbé.

c.500BC Zapotecs build Monte Albán.

c.400BC The Olmec site of La Venta, on the Gulf coast, is destroyed. In the Valley of Mexico, Cuicuilco becomes an important city.

300BC Decline sets in at Nakbé.

300BC–AD100 Maya craftsmen build ceremonial and living centres at Tikal and Uaxactún, northern Guatemala.

c.100BC Volcanic eruption drives settlers from Cuicuilco, Valley of Mexico, to the city of Teotihuacán.

36BC The earliest Pre-Maya Long Count inscription is carved at Chiapa de Corzo in the Chiapas region of southern Mexico.

AD150 The Pyramid of the Sun is built at Teotihuacán.

AD199 The Hauberg stela, the earliest piece of writing in the Maya system, is carved.

AD200 The Zapotecs are at the peak of their powers.

CLASSIC PERIOD c.AD250–900

Above: Temples at Palenque stand in the forested foothills of the Sierra Madre.

c. AD300–650 Peak of Maya building: pyramids, temples and ballcourts are put up in many Maya lowland cities.

c. AD350 Teotihuacán becomes the pre-eminent Mesoamerican city.

c. AD400 Copán expands from a farming settlement to a major city.

c. AD750 Northern tribes sack Teotihuacán.

AD700–900 Decline in Maya lowlands is perhaps caused by overpopulation.

AD799 Last stela carved in Palenque.

c. AD800 Murals painted at Bonampak.

AD820 Last dated stela is put up at Copán.

AD879 Last dated stela at Tikal.

c. AD850–950 Many Maya centres in Guatemala and Mexico are abandoned.

POSTCLASSIC PERIOD AD900–1521

AD 900–950 The Toltecs build their capital at Tula.

c.1000 Mixtec people carry out royal burials at Monte Albán.

c.1150 The city of Tula is destroyed by Chichimec tribesmen.

c.1200 The México/Aztecs make their way southward into the Valley of Mexico.

1263 The city of Mayapán is founded.

1325 The México/Aztecs found the city of Tenochtitlán.

Below: Toltec stone warriors at Tollán were originally painted in bright colours.

1375 Acamapichtli, the first historical ruler of the México/Aztecs, is elected *tlatoani* ('speaker') in Tenochtitlán.

1428 The cities of Tenochtitlán, Texcoco and Tlacopán form the Triple Alliance and begin to build the Aztec Empire.

1441 Mayapán falls and is abandoned.

1481 The Aztec Sun Stone is erected in Tenochtitlán.

1487 Ahuitzol, *tlatoani* in Tenochtitlán, oversees the rededication of the city's Great Temple.

1492 Spanish explorers land in the West Indies.

1502 Christopher Columbus meets Maya traders in the Gulf of Honduras.

1502 Moctezuma II, the last independent Aztec ruler, becomes *tlatoani* in Tenochtitlán.

1507 A new 52-year cycle begins for the Aztecs with a New Fire ceremony.

1517 The first of three Spanish exploratory missions to Mesoamerica from Cuba is led by Francisco Hernández de Córdoba.

1519 Spanish explorers, led by Hernán Cortés, land in Mexico.

1521 Tenochtitlán falls to Cortés and his Spanish troops on 13 August after a siege of 93 days.

Above: The Aztec Sun Stone is an ancient calendar revealing much about the past.

1523–4 Spanish under Pedro de Alvarado conquer southern Maya lands in the highlands of Chiapas and in southern Guatemala.

c.1550 Members of the nobility among the Quiché, a group of southern Maya, secretly translate the Maya sacred book *Popol Vuh* ('Book of Advice') into the Roman alphabet in a bid to save it from the book-burning zeal of Spanish monks.

1566 Bishop Diego de Landa completes his *Report of Things of Yucatán*.

1569 Friar Bernardino de Sahagún completes his *General History of the Things of New Spain*.

1697 The last independent Maya centre – at Tayasal, on an island in Lake Flores, Guatemala – falls to the Spanish.

1703 Quiché-speaking Franciscan friar Francisco Ximenez finds *Popol Vuh* and translates it into Spanish.

1790 The Aztec Sun Stone is discovered in Mexico City.

CHAPTER 1

3,000 YEARS OF CIVILIZATION

Civilization was born in the lands of Mesoamerica when the region's early farmers began to settle in villages around 2500–1500BC. The ancestors of these first villagers had spent perhaps 5,000 years in more or less nomadic farming and many millennia as hunter-gatherers. However, they took very quickly to the settled life and within a few centuries a major culture had arisen in the fertile, low-lying lands of Veracruz and Tabasco, adjoining the Gulf of Mexico. The creators of the Olmec civilization produced corn, squashes and other foodstuffs in such quantities that they could divert their energies into building and artistic activities. At La Venta and San Lorenzo they left behind large and impressive ceremonial centres and enigmatic carvings in stone. They laid the foundations for the great Mesoamerican civilization that would follow them: their pyramids, open plazas and rites of human sacrifice can all be found among the Zapotec, Teotihuacano, Toltec, Maya and Aztec societies that came in their wake. Other aspects of Mesoamerican religious and cultural life, including a deep reverence for the fleet-footed jaguar, were also first seen in Olmec lands. The essentials of a civilization that would endure for 3,000 years until the sudden and bloody arrival from the east of Hernán Cortés appear to have been laid in just a few hundred years by the inventive Olmec.

Left: Grass and stunted trees grow at high altitude beneath the vast, magnificent Popocatépetl. Rising 5,452m (17,900ft) above sea level, the volcano dominates the Valley of Mexico, where a succession of Mesoamerican cultures flourished.

THE BIRTH OF THE OLMEC

The first inhabitants of Mexico were probably descendants of Siberian immigrants to North America. Scholars do not know for sure when the first nomads arrived in the region we call Mesoamerica, but radiocarbon dating of bone fragments found at Tlapacoya (south-east of Mexico City) proves that by 21,000BC people were living in a region close to where the Aztecs would construct their magnificent capital city, Tenochtitlán.

EARLY INHABITANTS

For another 14,000 years, these early Mesoamericans lived as hunter-gatherers. The climate in the region was cooler than today's, and large herds of grazing animals thrived on lush grassland vegetation. Around 7000–5000BC, the settlers began to develop farming skills, gradually domesticating the plants that they had gathered in the wild. One of these in particular would become crucial to Mesoamerican civilization. A wild cereal of the region, maize, became the staple food over many centuries of selective breeding. Settlers had domesticated this grass by 5000BC.

A major climate change may have encouraged this change of lifestyle for the Mesoamerican settlers. Around 7000BC, temperatures rose worldwide and in Central America many grassland areas

Below: This Olmec stone from La Venta was probably a royal throne. The carving above the ruler's head is of a jaguar pelt.

Above: Six monoliths and 16 figures, made of jade and serpentine, were buried in this position as an offering by Olmec worshippers.

gave way either to desert or to tropical jungle. Animals were fewer and hunting became more difficult, so people turned to more intensive food cultivation.

People in the 'New World' of the Americas began to cultivate food in roughly the same era as the first farmers in the 'Old World' of the Near East and Europe, but in some ways the Mesoamericans had a harder time of it. Where the Old World farmers had cows, pigs and sheep, the peoples of Mesoamerica had only small dogs and turkeys to supplement the meat and fish they hunted. Another major difference was that the Mesoamericans had to manage without beasts of burden – they had no oxen or horses and did not even use the llamas and other camelids that were animal pack-carriers for the peoples of the central Andes who developed the Inca civilization. Partly as a result of this, Mesoamericans did not develop wheeled vehicles. Although small wheeled objects

have been found in graves, it is clear that the early Mesoamericans did not have the benefit of animal-drawn vehicles or even handcarts for moving food and materials.

Over many centuries, these early farmers gradually abandoned their nomadic existence. By the time that the first Mesoamerican villages appeared, about 2000–1500BC, the farmers were raising crops of corn, chilli peppers, squashes and cotton. They were using flint knives, stone axes and very sharp cutting blades made from the volcanic rock obsidian, inhabiting thatched cane huts, weaving cloth, making pottery and fashioning evocative female figures thought to be images of an archaic fertility goddess. They appear to have lived essentially as equals in self-contained settlements. Then, in about 1500–1200BC, the first major Mesoamerican civilization was born in the jungles of Mexico's southern Gulf coast.

THE RISE OF THE OLMEC

Labourers built awe-inspiring ceremonial centres on the banks of the region's slow-moving rivers. In the Veracruz rainforest, at San Lorenzo, men working with handbaskets raised a towering earthen platform 45m (150ft) high, topped by a cone-shaped earthen mound, by c.1200BC. At La Venta, around 50km (30 miles) downriver towards the coast, they built an earthen pyramid mound 32m (106ft) high and a ceremonial plaza in c.1000BC. The San Lorenzo complex contained the earliest stone drainage system to have been discovered in the Americas.

Craftsmen carved remarkable stone heads up to 3m (10ft) in height. These ancient works of art have characteristic flattened faces, thick lips and headgear reminiscent of a helmet. Their creation is a matter of enduring wonder. To make the carvings found at San Lorenzo, stone-cutters and labourers transported huge rocks on sledges and water-rafts over 80km (50 miles) from the Tuxtla Mountains.

The people behind these astonishing achievements lived in a more hierarchical society than their immediate ancestors. Scholars believe that the vast stone heads

Below: The priest in this Olmec carving wears a jaguar helmet. The Olmec revered the jaguar as the supreme predator.

Above: Olmec sacred buildings had a major influence on those erected by their Mesoamerican descendants, such as this pyramid at the Maya site of Uaxactún.

they carved were a homage to their rulers. Great armies of labourers were needed to build their vast ceremonial centres.

This ancient culture is now called Olmec from the Aztec word for the area in which it originated. The Olmecs developed a wide-ranging trading network. At its height, their civilization had a very wide sphere of influence. Olmec-style grave objects have been found in the north-western area of Mexico City, while stone carvings exhibiting an Olmec influence were made some 1,200km (750 miles) to the south in El Salvador. However, there is no evidence that there was an Olmec empire and the civilization gradually faded in the early part of the first millennium BC. The site at San Lorenzo was destroyed in 900BC and, within 100 years, Olmec cultural and stylistic influences began to wane, although they would continue to survive for many years. The culture's full span was probably c.1500–c.400BC.

The Olmec had lasting influence, for they bequeathed many distinctive religious ideas and practices to their descendants in the region. They developed religious rites involving human sacrifice and blood-letting, pioneered the use of ceremonial centres and invented the ball game that would remain popular right through Aztec times. They propounded the idea that the universe was divided into four directions and often carved a divine figure that combines the features of a human baby with those of a jaguar. Some scholars claim the Olmec may also have invented the writing system later developed by Mesoamerican peoples, notably the Maya. Archaeologists examining Olmec works of art have identified more than 180 symbols that may have been used as glyphs.

THE ZAPOTEC AND THE MAYA

The distinction of developing the Mesoamerican writing system is more often claimed for the Zapotec people of the Oaxaca Valley who, less than 200km (125 miles) from the centre of Olmec power, established a distinctive civilization that endured for more than 1,000 years. At the height of Olmec influence, in about 1350BC, the peoples of southern Mexico near the modern city of Oaxaca constructed a ceremonial and possibly living centre at San José Mogote. They were clearly engaged in trade with the Olmec region, for archaeologists in San José have found turtle-shell drums and conch-shell trumpets from as far north and east as the Gulf of Mexico.

DAILY LIFE
By c.1000BC, the settlement's central area covered almost 50 acres (20 hectares) and boasted imposing temples and tall platforms of stone. What we know of religious and daily life at San José

Below: The Zapotec were keen traders. This incense vase may have been made for sale or exchange with the people of Teotihuacán.

indicates that the city's inhabitants shared many features with the Olmec and engaged in practices that would characterize Mesoamerican culture for centuries to come. Finds of fish spines suggest that they practised blood sacrifice, for these objects are known to have been used at Maya sites for the sacred rites of autosacrifice – the letting of a person's own blood. They were also – like the Olmec – initiates of the cult of the jaguar. They made pottery that was decorated with the distinctive jaguar imagery that is associated with shamanism and Aztec worship of Tezcatlipoca. They understood the importance of measuring and marking the passage of time and, by c.600BC, they had begun to cut calendar symbols and early hieroglyphs at the site.

MONTE ALBÁN
Around 500BC, the peoples of the Oaxaca region built a major centre at Monte Albán. Labourers carried out vast earthworks to construct a flattened mountaintop 1km (³⁄₅ mile) in length, raising stone pyramids, temples and

Above: From early days rival Maya leaders won respect through warfare. Soldiers fought at close quarters with spears and darts.

Below: A stepped pyramid at Monte Albán gives on to a large plaza. The city has a ball court, and 170 tombs have been found there.

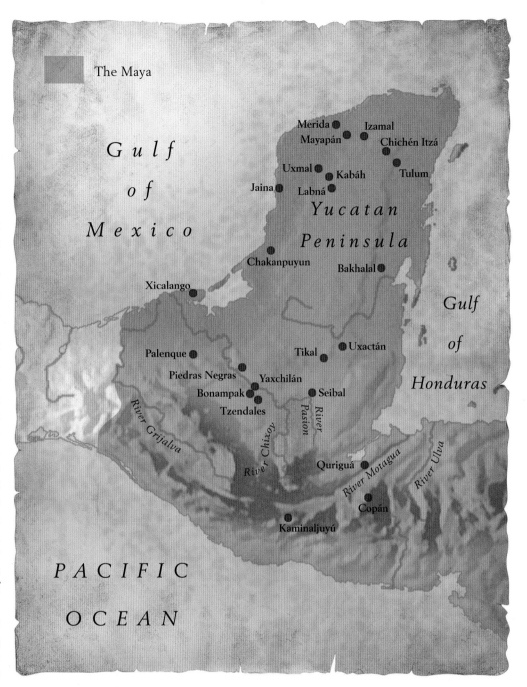

The Maya

Gulf
of
Mexico

Merida
Mayapán
Izamal
Chichén Itzá
Uxmal
Kabáh
Tulum
Jaina
Labná

Yucatan
Peninsula

Chakanpuyun
Bakhalal

Xicalango

Gulf
of
Honduras

Palenque
Tikal
Uxactán
Piedras Negras
Yaxchilán
Bonampak
Seibal
Tzendales

River Grijalva
River Chixoy
River Pasion

Quiriguá
River Motagua
River Ulva

Copán

Kaminaljuyú

PACIFIC

OCEAN

Right: In later years Maya lands stretched from Palenque in the west to Mayapán and Uxmal in the north and Copán in the east.

palaces around a vast ceremonial plaza. The site, which commands a magnificent view over the valleys below, was almost certainly built as a symbol of local power. It may have been occupied only by the political and religious elite, while the bulk of the population lived below in the valleys.

Monte Albán grew rapidly. By 200BC as many as 15,000 people lived there. Buildings spread on to painstakingly terraced lands on adjoining hills. At the height of the city's size and prestige in the period 200BC–AD200 there were 15 residential areas, each with its own plaza. Scholars do not know for sure who founded Monte Albán, but by 200BC it was occupied and controlled by the Zapotec people, who had risen to pre-eminence in the region. Monte Albán thrived as the Zapotec capital for another 1,000 years. Its people traded with the merchants of the more powerful city of Teotihuacán to the north-west.

By the 8th century AD, 25,000 people lived in Monte Albán, but in the following century the city, which had endured for more than a millennium, declined rapidly in power. The city – or its Zapotec elite – lost its hold over the people, who appear to have spread into surrounding communities.

THE MAYA

While the culture of the Olmec and Zapotec and of Teotihuacán was blooming in central Mexico, another great civilization was flowering in the jungles to the south and east, in lands that now form south-eastern and eastern Mexico, Guatemala and Belize.

Little is known of the earliest history of the Maya, partly because the tropical lands they occupied did not provide a good base in which archaeological remains could survive. But we know that village settlements with clear cultural connections to the later Maya way of life had been established by the second millennium BC on the Pacific coast of Guatemala close to the Mexican border.

Village farmers established settlements in the southern highland and central lowland regions of what were later to be the Maya homelands in the centuries after 800BC. Curiously, they do not appear to have been dominated or even influenced by the powerful Olmec culture of Mexico, perhaps because as essentially peasant villages they were not drawn into trade or cultural exchange. The Maya began to build larger ceremonial and urban settlements by c.600BC–400BC and in the four centuries after 300BC, many of the villages expanded into notable settlements as the culture thrived. A village at Tikal, in the tropical rainforest of northern Guatemala, became an important ceremonial centre. Its builders erected temples and pyramids in the years 300BC–AD100. Ceremonial buildings were also put up at Uaxactún, 20km (12 miles) to the north, before AD100. They contain giant masks that suggest a definite Olmec influence. A great city was built at El Mirador just to the north of Nakbé, with vast limestone temple pyramids on huge basalt bases.

TEOTIHUACÁN: CITY OF THE GODS

In the 1st century BC, a new power arose in the Valley of Mexico. Unknown builders laid out a magnificent city at a site 50km (30 miles) north-east of Lake Texcoco, where the Aztecs would build their capital, Tenochtitlán. The imposing ruins at Teotihuacán so overwhelmed the Aztecs that they incorporated the site into their mythology as the place where the sun and moon were created at the beginning of the current era, the 'fifth sun'. They named it Teotihuacán ('The Place of the Gods'). Historians use the name 'Teotihuacanos' for the unidentified people who built Teotihuacán.

TWO CENTRES

The inhabitants of the Valley of Mexico thrived through trade with the great Olmec civilization, exchanging highly prized local green obsidian and other goods for exotic bird feathers and sea shells. In the first millennium BC the population of the Valley grew rapidly and two centres were established, at Teotihuacán and at Cuicuilco in the south-western part of the Valley, in an area now covered by southern Mexico City.

But Cuicuilco had an unhappy destiny, for it was situated close to an active volcano. In c.100BC the volcano erupted, destroying buildings and burying the fertile agricultural lands around the city beneath rock. This natural disaster sent waves of refugees travelling north-east from the wasteland of Cuicuilco. Teotihuacán, made rich by trade in obsidian and its position on a mercantile route between the Valley of Mexico and the Gulf of Mexico, was able to take them in and the city expanded very rapidly.

PLANNED GROWTH

By AD1 Teotihuacán had upwards of 40,000 inhabitants, and it had as many as 100,000–200,000 in AD500. At this point it covered more than 20sq km (8sq miles) and was one of the largest cities in the world – far larger than the London of that era. Remarkably, its growth was not

Above: The carved head of the Plumed Serpent Quetzalcóatl adorns the pyramid built in his honour at Teotihuacán.

haphazard, for its architects followed an established layout to create a landscape of manmade foothills and mountains with a powerful symbolic meaning for Mesoamerican peoples. Scholars believe that it was built on a site of ancient

Below: The awe-inspiring Pyramid of the Moon in Teotihuacán measures 130m by 156m (426ft by 511ft) around its base.

Right: The doorway of this Maya temple at Hochob, Campeche, represents the mouth of a monster. Carvings of human figures are visible on the roof.

religious significance that may have been a place of pilgrimage long before the construction of the towering Pyramid of the Sun and Pyramid of the Moon and many centuries before the awe-inspiring Street of the Dead was laid out.

The people of Teotihuacán appear to have been cosmopolitan and to have thrived as much by trade as by war. Around two-thirds of the vast population farmed the fields that surrounded the urban development, while others worked as potters or carved tools, ornaments and weapons from the volcanic glass obsidian.

They may not have been known for their military prowess, but the Teotihuacános engaged in religious practices that were bloodthirsty in the extreme and had a lasting effect on the rites of the Maya and Aztecs. At its height, the Teotihuacános' influence was felt throughout Mesoamerica and left an enduring symbolic legacy in the creation of an evocative city of the divine that was to be a place of pilgrimage and worship for generations of Aztecs.

MAYA EXPANSION AND COLLAPSE

In this era, in the lands to the south and east of Teotihuacán's sphere of influence, the Maya continued to thrive. The 650 years after *c.*AD250 – the era dubbed the Classic Period by scholars – saw the Maya culture at its zenith. Important settlements were founded or expanded at Chichén Itzá, Copán, Uxmal and Palenque. At the height of the Classic Period of Maya civilization there were more than 40 Maya cities, with populations of between 5,000 and 50,000

Right: Maya cities such as Uxmal in Yucatán continued to thrive at the time of the great Maya 'collapse' in lands further south.

in each, giving a total of perhaps two million people. Most of these lived in the area known as the Maya lowlands, now in Guatemala.

Maya city-states existed in a state of almost constant conflict. Each had its ruling family and these dynasties made and broke alliances with rival rulers as the demands of conflict dictated. At the same time, Maya civilization produced a magnificent flowering of culture that produced imposing temples, pyramids and palaces, advanced irrigation systems, a sophisticated calendar for timekeeping, elegant mathematics, detailed astronomical science and a highly developed writing system.

Around the 9th century AD, the great Maya lowland cities were suddenly abandoned. Scholars are still debating what caused this sudden change and why Maya cities situated further north in the Yucatán peninsula such as Chichén Itzá and Uxmal continued to thrive.

THE MIXTECS AND THE TOLTECS

The glory of Teotihuacán was not destined to last forever and the city's very grandeur may have contributed to its downfall. Its inhabitants laid waste to large areas of countryside to manufacture the lime needed for the mortar and stucco used in Teotihuacán's fine buildings. This may have caused erosion and reduced the amount of land available for agriculture. When food was short, a severe drought or other natural disaster may have been enough to undermine the once-unchallengeable authority of Teotihuacán's rulers. Parts of the city's complex were torched, perhaps by angry Teotihuacanos, perhaps by outsiders. At some point in the 7th or 8th centuries AD, nomads poured south into the Valley of Mexico, probably driven by changes in the climate of northern Mesoamerica that made a farmer's lifestyle unsustainable. Teotihuacán was too weak to repel them.

A POWER VACUUM
The collapse of the city, which had stood proud and pre-eminent for many centuries, created a power vacuum in which various groups competed for position. One group, the Mixtecs, rose to prominence in the Oaxaca Valley, settling and flourishing in the Zapotecs' former centre at Monte Albán. As well as winning a reputation for martial prowess, the Mixtecs made a name as refined craftsmen, excelling as potters, mosaic artists and goldsmiths.

THE TOLTECS
To the north-west, the Toltecs became a pre-eminent group. In about AD950 they founded the city of Tollán ('the Place of the Reeds') near modern Tula, about 80km (50 miles) north of the site of the later Aztec

Above: The Plumed Serpent Quetzalcóatl, a Toltec and an Aztec deity, protects this back-shield worn by a Toltec nobleman.

Below: A beautifully fashioned gold and turquoise disc bears witness to the Mixtecs' high reputation for working precious metals.

capital of Tenochtitlán. The Aztecs later viewed the Toltecs with great reverence, mythologizing them as tall, peerless warriors, ruthless conquerors, pioneers of the finest arts and sciences, developers of the Aztec calendar and year count, writers of just and lasting laws. In the Aztec account they were led in their southward expansion by Mixcóatl ('Cloud Serpent') whose son Topiltzin became identified with the god Quetzalcóatl and presided at Tollán over a city of wonderful architecture, a peaceful golden era of magnificent artistic progress, before being tricked and driven out by the warrior devotees of the war god Tezcatlipoca.

TOLLÁN
In reality, the city of Tollán was far less grand than its predecessor Teotihuacán. The exact position of Tollán was unknown for many years – indeed the Aztecs at some points identified Teotihuacán as the urban centre of the revered Toltec forebears. However, an archaeological site near Tula was identified as the remains of the Toltecs' principal city by Mexican archaeologist Jimenez Moreno in 1941. His work and further excavations have established that Tollán grew to be a centre of great importance and some size, but even at its height it was home to no more than 30,000 people, less than one-sixth of Teotihuacán's estimated population peak of some 200,000.

A MARTIAL PEOPLE
The Toltecs engaged in trade with distant regions, notably in turquoise with parts of what is now the southern USA, but they were also a martial race who, through war, expanded their territories to include the

Above: Toltec stone warriors, which stand impressively on a pyramid in Tollán (Tula), were originally painted in bright colours.

THE COLLAPSE OF TOLLÁN

A highly competitive environment lay behind the collapse of Tollán. The city of the Toltecs was destroyed in the mid- to late 12th century in the era of a ruler called Huemac, of whose depravity and failings many tales were later told. Migrations of nomads from the north had continued and the Toltecs may have met their match. The city was sacked. According to later Aztec accounts, the roof columns were torn down from Quetzalcóatl's temple, the buildings were torched and the people driven out. Many Toltecs moved on, some settling elsewhere in the Valley of Mexico, others as far to the east as the Maya city of Chichén Itzá in northern Yucatán, where architectural details such as death's-head decorations echo those in Tollán.

Following Tollán's collapse, many nomadic groups known by the name of Chichimec ('Sons of the Dog') flooded into the Valley of Mexico, competing for the most fertile territories and for strategic positions. The myth of the Toltecs' golden achievements was amplified as competing groups claimed descent from the people of Tollán. Among these peoples was a small group, the Méxica or Aztecs, who would become celebrated in history as the builders of great Tenochtitlán and rulers of a glorious empire.

bulk of the modern Mexican state of Hidalgo and the northern areas of the Valley of Mexico. Within their empire, the Toltecs settled a number of tribute areas, where garrisons kept the peace and oversaw the collection of produce; a pioneering development from which the Aztecs would learn a good deal.

Toltec culture, religious imagery and architecture celebrated ritual bloodshed and war: the capital is filled with warlike imagery. Forbidding stone columns carved in the shape of warriors stand atop one of the pyramids at Tollán and at one time held up the roof of the temple that stood there. The walls of the city's temples are decorated with soldiers wearing armour and shields on their backs and carrying spear-throwers and clumps of darts.

The temples are also adorned with gruesome *chacmools* – reclining stone figures with a bowl on the stomach in which the heart of a sacrificial victim was flung – and also contain skull racks on which heads were displayed. Scholars see in the fiercely militaristic culture of the Toltecs a reflection of a demanding political reality; a world in which tribal groups had to compete desperately for land, scarce resources and trade.

Right: Stone carvings featuring Toltec-style death's-head decorations are found in the Maya city of Chichén Itzá in Yucatán.

THE RISE OF THE AZTECS

The details of the Aztecs' origins are shrouded in myth, for this proud people told many tales that legitimized their supremacy, their use of human sacrifice and their devotion to the tribal god Huitzilopochtli. Their mythologized history told how the first Aztecs or México found their origin in the island-town of Aztlán, from which they set off on a long, hazardous migration across northern landscapes, guided by Huitzilopochtli, before they came to the place on Lake Texcoco at which they were destined to found their capital, another island site identified by the divinely ordained vision of an eagle perched on a prickly cactus making a meal of a writhing serpent.

NAMING THE AZTECS

The founders of Tenochtitlán had three names in their original language, Nahuatl: Aztecs, México and Tenochcas. According to the chronicler Hernando Alvarado de

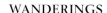

Above: A mask of Xochipilli, later worshipped by the Aztecs as the god of flowers, was found at Teotihuacán.

Tezozómoc, they were known as Aztecs because of their place of origin, the mysterious island-city of Aztlán (meaning perhaps 'White Land' or ' Land of the Cranes'), which has never been identified. The second name, México, was given to the wandering tribes by their patron god Huitzilopochtli, and scholars believe it

either comes from Méxi, one of the god's secret titles, or derives from Metzliapán ('Moon Lake'), a name for Lake Texcoco. The tribe was also called Tenochnas after Tenoch, the ruler who led it under the guidance of Huitzilopochtli in the final parts of its wandering journey. The name of their capital, Tenochtitlán, came from Tenocha while the divinely delivered appellation, the México, gave its name to the great metropolis of Mexico City that grew on that site and to the country of Mexico itself.

The founders of the empire based on Tenochtitlán called themselves 'México' and were known by this name by their Spanish conquerors. But scholars brought the name Aztec back into use in the 18th and 19th centuries and it is now the generic title for all the tribes of the Valley of Mexico in the era of the Spanish Conquest. In this book, 'México' is used where it is necessary to distinguish the people of Tenochtitlán from other tribes in the Valley of Mexico, but otherwise 'Aztec' is used to discuss the achievements and governance of the empire and the culture shared by these people.

WANDERINGS

The México wandered throughout the 12th and 13th centuries in search of a safe place to put down roots. It was a lawless time; scholars compare the southward incursions of Chichimec groups that followed the fall and collapse of Toltec civilization to the waves of barbarians that took advantage of the collapse of the western Roman empire in 5th-century Europe. A group of Chichimec – said to be led by a ruler named Xólotl, who is probably a legendary figure or a conflation of several

Left: The Toltecs cast a long shadow. Many details in the Maya city of Chichén Itzá suggest Toltec influence or conquest.

Above: The Codex Boturini, *an Aztec account of their travels, depicts ancestors leaving their original homeland, Aztlán.*

historical rulers – established themselves in the Valley of Mexico, first at Tenayuca and later at Texcoco, and formed an alliance with dispersed members of the Toltecs who were settled at Culhuacán. A group named the Tepanecs intermingled with the inhabitants of the Valley of Mexico and settled at Azcapotzalco near Lake Texcoco. The migrations of a third group, named the Acolhua, led them to eastern regions of the Valley.

The México's mythical account of their origins has it that in this period they were temporarily settled in ruins near Tula or, in some accounts, Teotihuacán. Here they learned the skills of irrigation and agriculture and developed the religious culture, including sun worship and human sacrifice, under which they later thrived. But Huitzilopochtli, diviner of the tribe's destiny, would not let them settle there and set them once more on their wanderings.

Toward the end of the 13th century, the México passed to the west of Lake Texcoco and settled at Chapultepec near some highly prized springs in a region under the control of the city of Culhuacán. The people of Azcapotzalco and Culhuacán attacked the incomers to safeguard their control of the spring waters and sacrificed the México leader. The México threw themselves on the protection of Culhuacán and were allowed to settle in the stony area of Tizapán, which was infested with poisonous snakes. Here their presence was

tolerated and they stayed for perhaps a quarter-century, using all their growing agricultural skills to raise crops in the unfriendly landscape and, according to one account, roasting the snakes to supplement their meals.

SETTLEMENT

The México intermarried with the locals and began to call themselves México-Culhua to emphasize their connection with that city's Toltec inheritance. They won honour in battle supporting the Culhua against nearby Xochimilco. However, in 1323, after a dramatic fallout with one of Culhuacán's leading nobles, they were forced to move on and to explore Lake Texcoco's marshes. Two years later, on an island around 3km (2 miles) out in the lake surrounded by marshes, they founded their new settlement, the future capital of a glorious empire that would be blessed by the bloodthirsty gods with wealth and enduring fame.

Above: The first pages of the Aztecs' Codex Boturini *detail their long migration across Mexico before founding Tenochtitlán.*

THE TWIN CITIES

Shortly after establishing Tenochtitlán, the México founded a second settlement, Tlatelolco, on another island nearby. For around 30 years, the Mexica developed their twin towns, trading with their neighbours and perfecting the science of building the *chinampa*, or artificial islands called 'floating gardens'. With careful irrigation these produced invaluable crops. The two México cities strengthened their links with the most powerful local peoples in an astute manner.

A SOCIAL CONTRACT

Tezozómoc, the brilliant Tepanec empire builder and military ruler of Azacoalco, cast a long shadow and, in the times of high tension following his death, the people of Tenochtitlán were understandably nervous about waging war against the Azcapotzalcans.

The warrior Tlacaélel delivered a declaration of war to the Azcapotzalcán leader Maxtla but, according to México accounts, the news was not well received by all at home. A public debate brought the warriors, who wished to pursue the war, into conflict with the common people, who wanted to avoid the risk of defeat. The warriors, it is said, then made a remarkable pledge in an attempt to win popular support for an attack on Maxtla. 'If we fail', they declared, 'we are yours to feast on. You will be able to slice our bodies limb from limb and eat us in your dinner pots. The war will be lost but there will be food in plenty.' This moved the people to give their agreement. 'Let it be so,' they said, 'and we will pledge that if you deliver victory in this fearful encounter we will honour you with tribute. You will be our lords. We will serve you in the sweat of our bodies and build you fine houses.'

The story legitimizes the increasing social hierarchy that accompanied changes in granting land following victory over the Azcapotzalcán leader Maxtla and the establishment of the Triple Alliance. The warriors' offer of themselves for self-sacrifice reflects the fact that it was considered an honour to be sacrificed if defeated in war and a shame to be spared or kept as a prisoner.

THE RISE OF THE AZTECS

TLATOANI 'HE WHO SPEAKS'

The chieftain at the time of the foundation of the twin cities was Tenoch. He lived for many years after 1325. He was identified as *tlatoani* ('He Who Speaks') and this was the title of the supreme ruler of the México/Aztecs until the fall of the empire. Following Tenoch's death, the México of Tenochtitlán approached the leaders of Culhuacán to ask for one of the nobles of that city, Acamapichtli, to become *tlatoani* of Tenochtitlán. There had been intermarriage between México and Culhua when the México were living near Culhualcán at Tizapán, and Acamapichtli was descended from both Culhua and México families. At the same time, the México of Tlatelolco asked for the son of a Tepanec ruler of Azcapotzalco to become their lord. Acamapichtli and the Tepanec prince were both installed as rulers with full ritual and ceremony in 1375.

A SUCCESSION OF RULERS

Under the leadership of Acamapichtli, who legitimized his rule by claiming descent from the blessed Topiltzin-Quetzalcóatl of Tollán, the México started to take a more significant part in local political events. During this period, Azcapotzalco, the Tepanec city-state, was ruled by Tezozómoc, who built up an empire through ruthless military skill and a genius for intrigue. The México people began by serving as mercenaries for Tezozómoc in his struggles against the

Above: With Huitzilopochtli and Tezcatlipoca, the Plumed Serpent Quetzalcóatl was foremost among Aztec deities.

Chichimec of Texcoco and against the Toltec of Culhualcán. In time, they built up a measure of independent power, and even expanded their territories by managing to gain *chinampa* lands in the area of Lake Xochimilco to the south of Lake Texcoco.

Acamapichtli was ruler until 1396 and he became the founder of a dynasty in Tenochtitlán,

Left: An Aztec eagle carving celebrates Tenochtitlán's foundation in 1325. The Aztecs were told they would know they had found the right spot to settle when they saw an eagle on a cactus clasping a serpent.

while his younger sons and favoured followers established a ruling class in the city. He was succeeded by his son Huitzilíhuitl although, in keeping with ancient tradition, Huitzilíhuitl was elected by a council of elders rather than simply by accession to his father's place. Huitzilíhuitl strengthened the México's ties to Tepanec by marrying a grand-daughter of Tezozómoc. They continued to fight as vassals in Tepanec wars and were rewarded with grants of land, notably after wars against Xaltocán.

In the years leading up to 1426, the México made a significant advance in power and status. They fought alongside Tezozómoc against the city-state of Texcoco. The Texcocan leader Ixtlilxóchitl was forced to abandon his city and flee to the mountains, where he was killed as his young son Netzahualcóyotl looked on.

In the same year, the death of Tezozómoc further changed the balance of power in the region. Tezozómoc was succeeded, after a reign of 55 years, by his less able son Maxtla, sparking

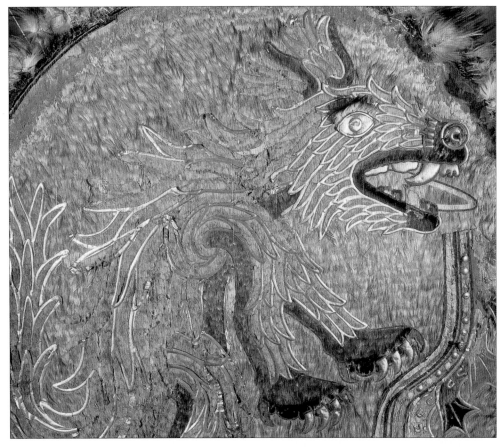

a number of conflicts between México and Tepanec that led to the assassination of Chimalpopoca, ruler of Tenochtitlán. Tensions rose to breaking point between the two cities. Maxtla prepared for war and demanded tribute from his México neighbours, while opinion was sharply divided in Tenochtitlán about the wisdom of provoking the might of Azcapotzalco.

In the end the México, now led by Itzcóatl, formed a coalition of sufficient might to let them defeat Maxtla. Netzahualcóyotl, the Texcocan prince who had witnessed the slaughter of his father was prominent in this grouping. He led a force from Huexotzingo to the southeast, where he had twice fled for his life from Tepanec attacks. Another significant coalition member was the Tepanec town of Tlacopán, which rose up and took part in the revolt against Azcapotzalco. After a siege of 114 days,

Below: The Plumed Serpent Quetzalcóatl was one of many gods the Aztecs inherited from their forerunners in Mesoamerica.

Azcapotzalco fell and Maxtla was captured. The historian Fernando de Alva Ixtlilxóchitl reports that the defeated ruler was hauled from his place of refuge in a ritual sweat-bath and handed over to Netzahualcóyotl, who dispatched him by cutting out his heart in sacrifice.

Above: The animal on this Aztec shield of c.1500 may be a coyote, a fierce creature associated with warriors and warfare.

THE TRIPLE ALLIANCE

The Tepanec empire created by Tezozómoc was no more. The three main players in the victorious coalition – Tenochtitlán, Texcoco and Tlacopán – formed a triple alliance in 1428 and divided the spoils. Tlacopán took control over land in the western region of the Valley of Mexico, Texcoco was granted much of the eastern part of the Valley, while Tenochtitlán now had power over the lands to the south and north.

This balance of power would remain essentially unchanged until the Spanish Conquest. The Aztec empire was a confederation of these three city-states, each drawing tribute from its own lands. Tenochtitlán was of prime importance: the México were the largest and most significant grouping and their capital was dominant. Next in significance was the capital of the Acolhua, Texcoco, which gained a reputation for learning, goldwork, jewellery and fine picture-manuscripts. Third, but still an enduring member of the alliance, was Tlacopán.

THE COMING OF THE SPANIARDS

Moctezuma II ruled over a great empire, but he was troubled by ill portents. In 1509, ten years before the arrival of the Spanish conquistadors, a comet appeared in the skies over Lake Texcoco. According to Friar Bernardino de Sahagún, author of *General History of the Things of New Spain*, it thrust into the sky like a tongue of flame and spilled a rain of small fiery drops as if it had broken through the canopy of the heavens. The priests and astronomers either would not or could not provide an interpretation, but the Texcocan ruler Netzahualpilli, who was believed to be able to see the future, declared that terrible events lay ahead that would usher in the destruction of the cities of the lake and of their empire. Many tales were told of unhappy omens that preceded the collapse of the Aztecs – some probably seeking with the benefit of hindsight to establish the inevitability of the Spanish triumph. Yet it appears that when the Spaniards arrived, the Aztec ruler was unsettled by doubt and ill equipped for decisive action.

REPORTS OF STRANGERS

The Aztecs must surely have known of European visitors, perhaps by word of mouth through merchants, many years before the conquistadors landed in Mexico in 1519. In 1492, the Spaniards landed in the West Indies and afterwards left their mark around the region in Hispaniola, Cuba, Venezuela and Panama. In 1502, Christopher Columbus encountered Maya traders, probably near the place now known as the Bay Islands in the Gulf of Honduras. In 1508, two Spanish sailors from Seville landed in the Maya region of Yucatán and may have inspired a drawing of what appears to be three temples borne on the sea in canoes that was seen by Moctezuma and his advisers in Tenochtitlán. Three years later, several Spanish survivors of a shipwreck off Yucatán were taken prisoner by the Maya.

In 1518, a labourer came to the imperial court reporting that he had seen mountains floating on the sea – a reference to the large Spanish ships – and Moctezuma sent advisers to the coast to investigate. They discovered reports of men with long beards and fair skin, of fishing vessels and of floating mountains.

RETURN OF THE GOD?

The most intriguing aspect of these reports was the possibility that they were portents of the return of the god Quetzalcóatl, the Plumed Serpent.

Below: Cortés and his men first explored the coast, then cut boldly inland towards Popocatépetl to find the Aztec capital.

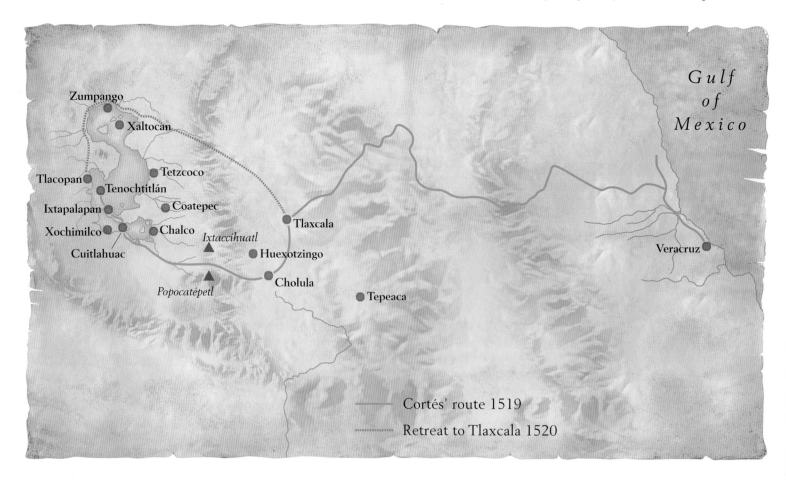

Gulf of Mexico

Zumpango
Xaltocan
Tlacopan
Tetzcoco
Tenochtitlán
Ixtapalapan
Coatepec
Xochimilco
Chalco
Cuitlahuac
Ixtaccihuatl
Tlaxcala
Huexotzingo
Popocatépetl
Cholula
Tepeaca
Veracruz

——— Cortés' route 1519

·········· Retreat to Tlaxcala 1520

Above: A lookout sees the Spaniards near landfall in what Moctezuma's informers considered to be a 'floating mountain'.

According to myth, he had departed by sea heading east following the collapse of his power in Tollán and had vowed to return from that direction in order to usher in a new age. When Moctezuma was told in April 1519 that ships belonging to these sailors had made landfall in the region that would become Veracruz, it confirmed his impression, for they landed at the exact spot where Quetzalcóatl was said to have made his departure and vowed to make his second coming, and also came in the very year (1-Reed according to the Aztec reckoning) prophesied for the Plumed Serpent's return.

WELCOME VISITORS?

The Spanish expedition was led by Hernán Cortés and came from the Spanish colony in Cuba to explore the coast of Mexico. It was in fact the third exploratory Spanish trip from Cuba; the first, in 1517, had been led by Francisco Hernández de Córdoba and the second, in 1518, by Juan de Grijalva.

Moctezuma seems to have been uncertain whether to treat the incomers with reverence, as gods, or with violence, as invaders. First he sent supplies, together with magnificent offerings including large discs of gold and silver representing the sun and moon, and ritual costumes that had been worn by performers impersonating the gods in ceremonies at Tenochtitlán. Some of the food he sent had been ceremonially doused with the blood of a sacrificial victim as was customary in the Aztec capital. Upon the rejection of his envoys by Cortés he changed his mind and dispatched sorcerers to cast spells capable of keeping the intruders in their place. However, the Spaniards proved resistant to local magic and Cortés led them inland from the coast towards the imperial capital.

He came first to the high plateau of Tlaxcala, where the locals attempted to drive the Spaniards back but were defeated. Cortés persuaded the Tlaxcaláns, who had resisted attempts to persuade them into the Aztec empire and who were determined enemies of Tenochtitlán, to join in his campaign. The invaders came next to Cholula, which was allied to the Aztecs. As part of a plan hatched by Moctezuma, the Choluláns invited the army into the city. Hidden warriors were supposed to emerge later and put the foreigners to death. The plan was revealed to the Spaniards, however, and they slaughtered the Cholulán chiefs.

When the Spanish force and its allies came to Tenochtitlán, Moctezuma went out to meet Cortés on a palanquin carried by four noblemen and greeted the Spaniard with the utmost respect.

Below: This turquoise and shell mosaic figure formed the handle of a knife used by Aztec priests to despatch sacrificial victims.

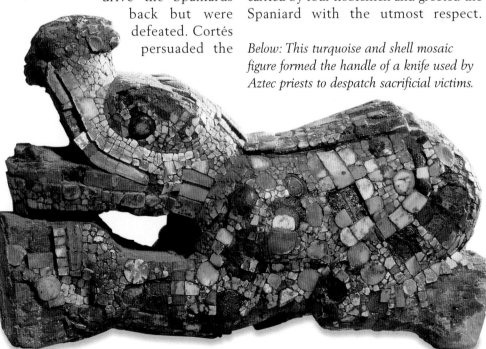

41

THE COMING OF THE SPANIARDS

Moctezuma gave Cortés a necklace of snail shells and shrimps fashioned from solid gold and in return was presented with a string of Venetian glass beads. Then, in a fateful moment, he invited the Spaniards into the Aztec capital.

HOSTILITIES BEGIN

The visitors were quartered in the palace of Axayácatl near the ritual enclosure at the heart of the city. They soon saw the need to act swiftly, and were well aware that the plot that had failed in Cholula might be tried again. In an act of great simplicity and audacity, they took the Aztec emperor prisoner and kept him in guarded apartments in their palace of Axayácatl. The Aztec nobility began to prepare for violent resistance but Moctezuma urged cooperation.

Cortés had enraged the governor of Cuba by exceeding the brief of his expedition and dealing directly with Charles V in Europe. Now he was called away from Tenochtitlán to face a Spanish force sent from Cuba to arrest him. Cortés defeated the new arrivals and he persuaded the bulk of the force to return to the Aztec capital under his command. They found the city silent, but primed for explosion. In Cortés' absence, the Spaniards had attacked and slaughtered a group of Aztec nobles in order, the officers said, to put down a conspiracy.

Desperate for revenge, the Aztecs attacked the Spanish and their allies in the palace of Axayácatl. Moctezuma was persuaded to climb on to the palace roof to call for peace, but although the Aztecs obeyed their emperor, they lost their respect for him in that moment. Shortly afterward they elected Moctezuma's brother, Cuitláhuac, *tlatoani* and attacked once more. Again Moctezuma climbed to the palace parapet to calm the enraged warriors, but this time they would not hear him. They greeted his words with

Above: Moctezuma presented Cortés with a splendid quetzal feather headdress like this. Priests wore these magnificent feathers when impersonating the gods during rites.

jeers and then with a storm of arrows and stones. He was injured and later died, either from his wounds or secretly strangled by his Spanish captors, according to differing accounts.

Afterwards the Spaniards, led by Cortés, stormed the Great Pyramid itself, set fire to the shrines and threw down the Aztecs' revered idols. At every level of the pyramid the invaders were met by

ferocious defenders, who hurled burning missiles down on their heads, but the well-organized Spanish force prevailed. To the people of Tenochtitlán, this defeat, and the sight of the column of smoke that rose mournfully from the ruined shrines above their once apparently invincible city, was the greatest of humiliations. In Mesoamerican warfare, the capture and sacking of an enemy temple was proof of total victory.

HASTY RETREAT

Another wave of Aztec violence was inevitable and Cortés decided to quit the city with his troops. Under cover of a moonless night and a storm of rain on 30 June 1520, Cortés' men attempted to retreat across the causeway that led westward to Tlacopán, but their movements were discovered and the Aztecs launched furious assaults on them.

Below: The ashes of Moctezuma's predecessor Ahuítzotl (1486–1502) were stored in this stone casket, which is carved with a relief of the Aztec rain god Tláloc.

Right: An illustration from Diego Durán's account of the Spanish invasion depicts Aztec warriors attacking beleagured Spaniards in Tenochtitlán.

The Spaniards and their allies lost many men in this bloody encounter. As dawn rose at the end of what was to become known as the *Noche Triste* ('Sad Night') the remnant of the Spanish army was left to lick its wounds as the Aztecs retreated, bearing booty and their partially restored honour, to Tenochtitlán.

FINAL ASSAULT

Cortés prepared for another assault on the Aztec capital. He made allies in Tlaxcala and Texcoco and a new contingent of Cholulans also joined his army. In the hour of their greatest need, the Aztecs' much-vaunted 'empire' fell apart. Even as Cortés had made his first approach to Tenochtitlán he had encountered subjects only too willing to overthrow the pride of Moctezuma.

Cortés planned to besiege the lake city of Tenochtitlán and so force its surrender. He placed armies at the head of each of the three causeways, while armed vessels or barques prevented the defending Tenochtitláns from using their usual shoreline landing places. Fighting was prolonged and bloody, but gradually the besiegers began to gain ground, pinning the defenders down in Tlatelolco. The Tlaxcaláns seized the opportunity to avenge themselves on the Aztecs with ferocious enthusiasm, piling up the bodies of their victims.

Finally, on 13 August 1521, after a siege of 93 days, the *tlatoani* Cuauhtemoc and his leading warriors were captured as they attempted to flee to a new base from which to carry on the fight. They made a dignified surrender. The Aztec empire was no more.

CONQUEST OF THE MAYA

The Spaniards found the more dispersed Maya a harder enemy to bring under control than the Aztecs.

Francisco Hernández de Córdoba, leader of the first exploratory expedition sent to Mesoamerican lands from the Spanish island of Cuba, died of wounds inflicted by Maya warriors in 1517 near what is now Champotón. The clash was the Maya's first encounter with gunpowder, but it was not their first contact with the Europeans, for Maya traders had met Christopher Columbus as early as 1502.

The second and third Spanish-Cuban voyages, led by Juan de Grijalva in 1518 and Hernán Cortés in 1518–19, largely bypassed Yucatán. It was not until 1528 that the Spaniards turned their attention to the 'northern Maya' of Yucatán. Francisco de Montejo, who led the campaign, faced a tough task. Cortés had succeeded against the Aztecs partly because he was able to isolate and undermine the authority of their emperor, but among the Maya there was no comparable figure of central authority. In addition, the pragmatic Maya fought a campaign reminiscent of modern guerrilla warfare, attacking by night and setting traps and ambushes in the difficult jungle terrain. It took the

Above: Hernán Cortés moved with great directness and simplicity against the Aztecs.

Spaniards 14 years to establish a colonial capital, at Mérida in 1542, and four years later they put resistant Maya tribes to the sword.

The southern Maya area, incorporating the Quiché and Cakchiquel kingdoms, was conquered by Pedro de Alvarado between 1523 and 1541. However, one pocket of Maya independence survived until 1697, when their lands were found to be in the path of a proposed roadway that would link Guatemala and Yucatán. When Martin de Ursua, Governor of Yucatán, sailed across Lake Flores to demand the surrender of the people of Tayasal, his ship was surrounded by Maya canoes, and when one of the Spanish soldiers fired his arquebus at the canoes it unleashed a hail of Spanish gunshot that crushed the Maya and terrified the remaining defenders into fleeing the city. The last pocket of Maya independence was defeated.

CHAPTER 2

DESERT, MOUNTAIN, LAKE AND JUNGLE

Mesoamerica was a region of great contrasts. Its landscapes range from the snowcapped volcanoes of Popocatépetl and Ixtaccíhuatl to the swampy Tabasco Plain that borders the Gulf of Campeche; from the dusty sagebrush of the northern Mexican plateau to the humid lowland jungles of El Petén in northern Guatemala.

Varied climates and landscapes called for different survival strategies. The northern Mexican plateau could only support bands of nomads; the southern part of the plateau in which lies the Valley of Mexico, was a well irrigated, fertile highland area of 800,000 hectares (2 million acres). Over many centuries, several major cultures established themselves in the Valley of Mexico, including the Teotihuacános and the México/Aztecs. Throughout this period, warlike northern groups were a threat to their southerly neighbours and on more than one occasion they flooded southward, either to overrun local peoples or simply to settle. The México themselves came originally from the north. According to their own account of their origins, it was only after they had come south and been settled for some time near Tollán that they picked up 'civilization' in the form of the skills needed to raise crops and to irrigate the land.

Left: Tall trees and strong tropical creeper grow on the hills surrounding the ceremonial structures at the Maya city of Palenque in Chiapas, Mexico.

MANY LANDSCAPES

The variety of the Mesoamerican landscape had a significant influence on the type of civilization that developed area by area. In many parts of the region, such as the Valley of Mexico and the tropical forests of Maya lands, the peoples of Mesoamerica were blessed with fertile soil. Fed and protected by the land, they were nevertheless always at the mercy of drought and the famines it brought. The Maya and Aztecs, and their cultural predecessors, were drawn into an intense, spiritually charged relationship with the natural world. They saw the gods everywhere: in the earth, the crops that grew from it, the rain that fed the plants, the mountains where the rainclouds gathered and the wind that carried the clouds to their fields.

TOPOGRAPHY

To the east and west of the Mexican plateau rise the great mountains of the Sierra Madre Oriental and the Sierra Madre Occidental, while to its south lie the spectacular peaks of the Transverse Volcanic Axis, including Popocatépetl, Ixtaccíhuatl and Toluca. Beyond the mountains to east and west lie coastal lowlands bordering the Pacific Ocean and the Gulf of Mexico. Further south of the plateau lie more mountains, the Southern Highlands, which include the ranges of the Sierra Madre del Sur. These run down

Below: In the rainforests of Veracruz, bordering the Gulf of Mexico, the Olmec set up basalt columns to mark sacred places.

Above: In the tropical woodlands of El Petén in Guatemala, Maya cities such as Tikal and Uaxactún once defied the dense jungle.

almost to the coast of the Pacific Ocean. To their east lies the lowland area of the Isthmus of Tehuantepec, beyond which the land rises to the south-east in the Sierra Madre de Chiapas and runs to the north-east into the Tabasco Plain, filled with swamps and slow-moving rivers.

MAYA LANDS

The highlands of Chiapas run eastward, linking up with the volcanic mountains in Guatemala that form the southern limit of the territories occupied by the Maya. In these uplands, where the volcanic soil is highly fertile, the Maya raised their crops with comparative ease. They also found materials that were highly valuable both for trade and their own use. These included obsidian, the hard volcanic glass used throughout Mesoamerica for the blades of knives and spears, flint and jade, the latter prized as a precious stone and often found in grave offerings. The Maya also mined basalt, which they used to make grinding stones for processing maize. In the mountain forests they

tracked the quetzal bird, whose long green feathers were worn in costumes and headdresses by kings and priests.

To the north of the volcanic mountains, the land runs down to the lowlands of El Petén, where the first Maya settlers encountered areas of highly fertile

Below: Despite the harsh terrain of the mountainous landscape of Oaxaca's peaks, the Zapotec built a great civilization there.

Map labels:

Sonoran Desert
Baja California
SIERRA MADRE OCCIDENTAL
Mexican Plain
SIERRA MADRE ORIENTAL
Sinaloa River
Río Grande
Gulf of Mexico
La Quemada
Pánuco River
Chichén Itzá
Yucatán Peninsula
Lake Chapala
Lake Cuitzco
Tula
Teotihuacán
Lake Texcoco
Lake Pátzcuaro
Mt Tlaloc
Tenochtitlán
Citlaitepetl
Yucatán Basin
Popocatepetl
Balsas River
La Venta
Usumacinta River
PACIFIC OCEAN
Monte Albán
Palenque
Tikal
SIERRA MADRE DEL SUR
Kaminaljuyú
Motagua River
Copán

- - - - - Boundary of Mesoamerican cultural region

tropical forest interspersed with low-lying seasonal swamps and areas of tall bush. In this unlikely setting they built the early ceremonial centre of Nakbé and the great cities of Calakmul, Tikal, Uaxactún and Yaxchilán. Here they felled great cedar trees that were carved into canoes 24m (80ft) in length that carried traders as far as Panama, a distance of 2,400 sea miles. They found brazil wood, which they processed as a dye for staining cloth, and collected copal, a resin exuded by tropical trees, which was burned in religious ceremonies.

Further north, Maya settlers found that the land spread out in a flat expanse covered with scrub forest, which is now known as the northern Yucatán peninsula. The name came originally from a misunderstanding, for when early

Spanish explorers from Cuba first asked the Maya what their country was called, the natives replied 'Ci-u-than' ('We cannot understand you'), which in time became 'Yucatán'. According to Bernal Díaz del Castillo, at the time of the Conquest the Maya had accepted the use of Yucatán but among themselves still called the land by its old name, which he reports was 'Land of the Deer and the Turkey'.

On the north-western edge of the lower Yucatán peninsula is a forested region known as Campeche, and to its west, bordering the Gulf of Campeche, lies the tropical area of Tabasco, filled with swamps and sluggish rivers. Here the Maya grew cacao, which was very highly prized and traded as a luxury item throughout Mesoamerica.

Above: A map of Mesoamerican terrains indicates how mountains and expanses of ocean hem in areas of very fertile land.

AREAS OF OCCUPATION

Scholars identify three areas of Maya occupation. The 'Southern Maya' were those living in the volcanic mountains of Guatemala and the highlands of Chiapas. The 'Central Maya' occupied the region stretching from Tabasco and the southern part of the Campeche through the lowlands of El Petén to Belize and part of western Honduras. This is the area largely abandoned in the 'Maya collapse' of the 9th century. The 'Northern Maya' lived in northern Campeche and towards the tip of the Yucatán peninsula. This region includes great settlements such as Chichén Itzá, Uxmal and Mayapán.

JUNGLE CITIES OF THE MAYA

We cannot know why the Maya built their cities where they did. Some are close to rivers, lakes or waterholes, but many are far from natural water sources. The lands of El Petén, which had thick tropical growth, high bush and seasonal marshes, would appear to present a daunting challenge to builders, but it was here that the first ceremonial centres and cities of the emerging Maya civilization were built. It may be that the sites were chosen by priests claiming divine inspiration; with the Aztecs and the founding mythology of their capital, Tenochtitlán, the city rose in the place that had been chosen by the gods.

Differences in farming techniques and attitudes to land between the lowlands of El Petén and the highland southern Maya regions may have had a significant impact on the types of settlement and kinds of rule that developed in the two places.

THE FARMER'S FIELD

The sacred book of the Quiché Maya, the *Popol Vuh*, tells how the sky and sea gods brought the Earth into being from the primordial waters at the dawn of time. They had only to speak the word 'Earth' and it rose up like a great mist, unfurling

Left: The great heights to which Maya builders aspired in cities such as Tikal outdid even the towering jungle trees.

and clearing to reveal the mountains and the plain. Dense vegetation spread over the terrain. The holy text likens the miraculous event to the process a Maya farmer followed to measure out a field. This was a 'fourfold siding, fourfold cornering, measuring, fourfold staking, halving the cord, stretching the cord, in the sky, on the earth, the four sides, the four corners.' Farmers across the Maya realm used a measuring technique like this, but they cleared and used the land differently in the Guatemalan highlands where the Quiché lived and the jungle-covered lowlands of El Petén, with corresponding effects on their feeling for the land and perhaps also their loyalty to their ruler.

SETTLEMENT PATTERNS

In the jungle, farmers traditionally practised 'slash and burn' agriculture. During the dry season, a farmer would use a stone axe to clear the dense growth of trees and set them ablaze. He would measure out his plot with the fourfold cornering and plant seeds of maize and other crops in the ash-enriched earth in good time for the beginning of the rainy season in May or early June. Ten years or so would usually exhaust the land on a particular plot, so after that period the farmer would move on to clear and burn another area of jungle.

In the highlands the volcanic earth was deeper and richer and farmers did not need to move their fields periodically.

Left: Shrieking monkeys were the Mayas' neighbours in the Guatemalan jungle. This pot dates from around the 9th century AD.

There, settlements were more rooted; in the jungle, farmers did not feel themselves tied to a particular piece of the land in the same way. Scholars believe that this contributed to the long-term instability of the jungle city-states. The cities were close together, often no more than a day's march apart. As farmers moved further away from the stone towers of their own settlement, they may have felt increasingly vulnerable to interference or attack.

Kings commanded loyalty by military ability, charisma and their capacity to demonstrate power through great public sacrificial rituals on the temple-pyramids of their ancestors. This type of loyalty could quickly melt away if a king was defeated, captured and sacrificed – and the next member of his dynasty was weak. The result was that a succession of kingdoms rose to brief pre-eminence, then were conquered or faded away.

INTENSE COMPETITION

Recent archaeological work has transformed our idea of what the jungle and the jungle cities would have looked like in the 8th or 9th centuries AD. At one

time, scholars thought that the Maya of the lowland jungles were relatively few in number and that there was plenty of land for clearance and sowing. But the latest evidence indicates that in the 8th century the Maya population in the jungle lowlands was extremely high and that the Maya at this time were farming the land intensively. We now know the Maya jungle farmers cleared slopes and built terraced fields and even constructed raised fields in the region's low-lying swamps.

It appears that by the 8th century the Maya had cleared the jungle almost completely. The lush vegetation that now almost swamps many of the jungle cities is secondary rather than primary growth. Modern tourists climb the towering

Below: In the mid-20th century the lush forest of El Petén swamped Tikal. Clearing work, beginning in 1956, uncovered the city.

pyramids of sites such as Tikal and look down beyond the city limits on the tall green towers of the forest, but a Maya priest in the same position in the 8th century would have looked down on land that had been cleared and set aside for farming.

Many scholars now believe that this state of affairs holds the key to the 'Maya collapse' – the abandonment of the cities of the region in the 9th century that

Above: The temples of Palenque stand on the densely forested foothills of the Sierra Madre, overlooking the plain of Chiapas.

marks the end of the Classic Period. They argue that the overuse of the land caused an ecological catastrophe. There was no longer enough land to go round and what territory there was was not highly fertile. The Maya city-states fought bitterly over the last available areas of good land.

SACRED MOUNTAINS IN THE JUNGLE

Mountains were revered throughout Mesoamerica. To the Maya, they were the place where deceased ancestors lived on and even today the Maya peoples of the Chiapas region hold to this belief. The architects of the El Petén region and northern Yucatán lived many miles north of the Chiapas highlands and the volcanic mountains of southern Guatemala, but in cities such as Tikal, Palenque and Uxmal they created their own sacred mountains in the form of the stepped stone pyramids that today still tower above great ceremonial plazas.

THE PYRAMIDS

Pyramids were identified by the word *witz*, which could also mean 'mountain'. A pyramid was a sacred building with a temple at its summit, used for ceremonial processions and religious rituals. However, they were also, and perhaps primarily, mortuary monuments, erected to honour the memory of a dead king. Both

Below: The ceremonial centre at Uxmal, in Yucatán, is bounded to the right by the soaring Pyramid of the Magician.

Above: Access to the Temple of the Masks, Tikal, at the top of the staircase and halfway to heaven, was restricted to the priesthood.

symbolically (as a stone mountain) and literally (as a giant tomb) they were homes to deified royal ancestors.

It may be that the temples on top of the pyramids were architectural versions of the natural caves in which Mesoamericans had left offerings from time immemorial. Some – such as those at Tikal and Yaxchilán, for example – had large vertical roofcombs that reinforced the impression that they were openings in a rockface close to the sacred sky. Many of the pyramids, like mountains, presented a forbidding challenge to those seeking to climb them. They towered to great heights, their stepped sides were very steep and the steps themselves so narrow that the members of the religious procession mounting to the holy places on high would have had to put their feet sideways on each step.

SACRED STRUCTURES

Other architectural elements of the Maya city were representations in stone of the sacred structures of the universe and of the natural world around them. In Maya culture, water was linked to the underworld; a number of surviving carvings represent royal passengers in a canoe on their final voyage to the spirit world. Scholars believe the great ceremonial plazas of Maya cities represented lakes or

suggest the nine regions of the underworld the king encounters as his soul makes its voyage through the spirit realm. One construction at Tikal, Temple II, has three layers. At Izapa, in the Pacific coastal region of Chiapas, a plaza contains three pillars, each 1.3m (4ft 3in) tall and supporting a circular stone. Both the Tikal temple and Izapa pillars are symbolic references to the three hearthstones of the Maya creation myth, which the Maya believed were visible in the night sky as the three stars in Orion's belt.

In man-made versions of natural holy places, the gods could be honoured with sacrifices designed to recycle spiritual and cosmic energy (largely in the form of life-blood) on behalf of the city state. Maya kings, priests and people hoped that the sacrifices would safeguard the flow of divine power needed to keep the natural world functioning; the sun rising, the rain clouds forming and unloading their cargo, the land giving birth to maize plants.

Below: At Cobá, in Quintana Roo, a rounded pyramid rises like a natural mountain peak from the jungle floor.

Above: The steep incline of the steps – as here at Palenque – made it a demanding task to climb to the holy places above.

seas that offered a way to the underworld. Some scholars believe the Maya thought the ball court, specifically, represented an entry to the underworld, while the ball used in the game represented the sun. Even the stone columns or stelae on which rulers recorded their dates of accession, anniversaries of their rule and political or military triumphs were associated with the natural world. The Maya word for the stela was *te tun* ('tree rock'). The stelae at Yaxchilán, for example, rise toward the sacred sky in the same way as the trees of the forest in which the city stands.

UNDERWORLDS AND HEARTHSTONES

The structures of pyramids, temples and plazas had detailed religious and mythic significance. For example, temples at Palenque and Tikal with nine levels

WATER: A SCARCE RESOURCE

Because of the physical characteristics of their lands, the Maya often had to come up with ingenious solutions to provide water for their cities and their people.

Below: Some cenotes *or underground waterholes, such as this well at Dzitnup, are accessible only through a small opening.*

FRESH WATER

In the northern part of the Yucatán peninsula there are no large rivers and early in the dry season, which can last six months, all streams disappear. The land is porous limestone; water runs through the rock and collects below ground. In places, the land has collapsed, forming

Above: The city of Tulum on the cliffs of eastern Yucatán is battered by ocean winds and washed by Caribbean spray.

vast holes – some 60m (200ft across) and 30m (100ft) deep – which are fed by underground rivers. These holes, called *cenotes*, are used as wells.

CENOTES

Chichén Itzá was built around two *cenotes*. The earliest settlers constructed the city in the 5th century around the southernmost of the two wells. They built two stairways of masonry 20m (65ft) down to the water. The city was 'refounded' by the Itzá in the years after AD987, based on a second *cenote* further north. This second well is around 60m (200ft) across, while its rim is 22m (73ft) above the surface of the water. While they continued to use the southern *cenote* for drawing water, they used the northern one for religious rituals. A sacred causeway 275m (900ft) in length runs from the Great Plaza northward to the 'Well of Sacrifice'.

According to Bishop de Landa, the Maya held sacrifices to the rain god Chac during droughts, in which priests threw

Right: With two wells, Chichén Itzá had a plentiful water supply. This is the northern waterhole, set aside for religious rites.

human victims into the well with offerings of precious gold and jade. De Landa suggests that the Maya did not think that the victims died, although they did not see them again once they had been cast into the well. A colourful 19th-century addition to the folklore surrounding the sacred well suggested that beautiful virgins were cast into its water to please Chac. Edward Thompson, US Consul to Merida, bought the site of Chichén Itzá in 1901 and had the well dredged, turning up precious offerings and the remains of human sacrifices. Biological anthropologist Ernest Hooton examined skulls found in the well and found them to include skulls of men, women and children.

Another celebrated *cenote* existed at Bolonchen ('Nine Wells') in the Campeche, where water lies 135m (450ft) below the surface. The American traveller and archaeologist John Lloyd Stephens, author of *Incidents of Travel in Central America, Chiapas, and Yucatán* (1841), visited the site and described how, by the light of pine torches, the Maya descended over crumbling rock deep into the earth using a long ladder made from

Below: At Labná, near Uxmal in the Puuc region of Yucatán, rainwater was collected in a specially constructed cistern.

great planks of wood lashed together, with earthen pots for carrying the water tied to their backs and heads. His companion Frederick Catherwood made a celebrated lithograph of the Bolonchen well in use, showing heavily laden natives clambering down to the water and up to the light.

RESERVOIRS AND RIVERS

In some places the Maya made their own reservoirs. The city of Tikal had no access to water from springs, rivers or wells but rainfall was plentiful. Its inhabitants relied on the water collected in a great reservoir situated just off the city's ceremonial centre. Its builders lined two natural ravines with clay and left them to dry in the sun, thus creating a water-tight area. They added a causeway across the reservoir that also functioned as a dam. Rainwater could flow in freely from the ceremonial area: the builders laid the plaza so that its surface tilted at an angle of five degrees from level to encourage water-flow into the reservoir. The Maya also built wells that collected rainwater as it ran off the roofs of houses and ceremonial buildings. The wells had their own roofs to limit evaporation of the precious liquid during hot weather.

Some Maya cities were built within convenient reach of water. Yaxchilán and Piedras Negras, for example, were built alongside the River Usumacinta. At Palenque, which lies just above the floodplain of the Usumacinta, the River Otulum runs right through the site: here the builders diverted the river into an artificial waterway that passes beneath the palace. Cobá, in north-eastern Yucatán, was situated between two lakes.

SALT WATER

Some Maya cities were built on the coast, facing the ocean. The builders of Tulum erected their city atop a 12m (40ft) limestone cliff on the coast of eastern Yucatán looking down on the Caribbean Sea. Built in the 6th century AD, it was still occupied by the Maya at the time of the Conquest. The city's name means 'fence' or 'wall' and came into use after the arrival of Europeans because Tulum is enclosed on its inland sides by high walls. Its ancient name may have been Zama ('dawn') because it faces east to greet the jaguar sun god each morning on his emergence from the underworld.

Tulum greatly impressed Europeans when they first encountered it. The 1518 Spanish exploratory mission led by Juan de Grijalva sailed down the coast and Juan Díaz, the mission chaplain, reported he had seen three great towns, one as large as Seville with a great tower. Tulum contains a tall building known as El Castillo ('the castle'), with a temple on its top. The city was connected by a stone causeway which led to Xelha and to Chichén Itzá.

CITY OF AWE: TEOTIHUACÁN

The impressive setting, the towering architecture and the vast grid layout of Teotihuacán struck awe into Aztec hearts. They knew nothing of the historically distant peoples who erected this symbolic urban landscape and became convinced that its architects must have been the gods themselves.

CITY OF THE GODS

Teotihuacán lies in a side valley running off the Valley of Mexico, around 50km (30 miles) north-east of the Aztec capital Tenochtitlán. Its unknown founders may have chosen the setting because of its proximity to a rich source of the highly prized volcanic glass obsidian and to the San Juan river, which provided water for agriculture. The site also lay on a significant trade route that ran to the Gulf Coast from the Valley of Mexico.

The Aztecs were deeply impressed by the architecture and stylized grid pattern of Teotihuacán. Their powerful mythological imagination saw in the Pyramids of the Sun and Moon the setting for the divine rituals that set the modern

Above: Goggle eyes and fanged mouth identify this Teotihuacán carving as the rain god. The Aztecs worshipped him as Tláloc.

era in motion and raised the life-giving sun and his pale companion the moon in the skies. However, to the Aztecs who made pilgrimages to the site to gaze in awe at the vast buildings, to make sacrifices and offerings to the gods, to consult oracles and to put criminals to a bloody death, this city of man-made mountains laid out against a backdrop of natural peaks was

a deeply moving statement of religious devotion and its power to safeguard a world that could at any moment be brought to an abrupt end by the gods.

SITE OF ANCIENT PILGRIMAGE

As well as being the imagined setting for primal mythological events, Teotihuacán had other deeply seated religious and spiritual associations. At some points in their history, the Aztecs identified Teotihuacán with the revered civilization of Tollán, whose golden age of fertile lands, divine leaders and just laws represented an earthly paradise. The Aztecs believed that the people of Tollán had flourished in the era immediately before their own rise in the 14th century, and so imagined the flowering of Teotihuacán to have taken place more than 500 years after the city's actual primacy (c.100BC–AD650).

Moreover, the great Pyramid of the Sun was erected atop a natural cave that was a site of ancient religious observance. The cave, discovered during architectural investigations in 1971, contains remains of religious offerings made many centuries before the pyramid was raised in honour of the gods in around AD150. From time immemorial, Mesoamerican peoples saw caves as gateways to the world of spirit; scholars suggest that these offerings may have been part of rituals that were based on archaic shamanistic practice and that the cave and surrounding area may long have been an area visited by the devout. This holy site was the natural spot for the construction of the Pyramid of the Sun, the most sacred of the buildings in Teotihuacán.

SACRED LANDSCAPE

The Pyramid of the Sun stands 66m (216ft) high, a great man-made mountain containing 765 cubic metres (1,000 cubic

Left: Priests standing atop the Pyramid of the Moon would have been able to look directly down the 'Street of the Dead'.

Above: Teotihuacán made an evocative setting for Aztec religious rites. The moon hangs above the wide 'Street of the Dead'.

yards) of laboriously quarried rock that dominates the centre of the city. It stands to the east of the ceremonial roadway that was dubbed the 'Street of the Dead' by the Aztecs. This roadway, 40m (130ft) wide, runs for 2.4km (1.5 miles) and lies 16 degrees to the east of true north, so that it runs exactly towards Cerro Gordo, an extinct volcano revered as a sacred mountain. The road, which forms the basis of the city's grid pattern, is lined with lower buildings that the Aztecs believed were the tombs of ancient kings, but which are now known to have been palace residences. At the northern end of the road, situated so that it is framed by Cerro Gordo, stands the city's second largest construction, the Pyramid of the Moon, 43m (140ft) tall. The pyramid's main stairway gives directly on to the Street of the Dead. The Pyramid of the Sun and the Pyramid of the Moon probably had temples on their flattened tops.

The southern part of the Street of the Dead gives to the east on to a 15-hectare (38-acre) sunken square courtyard called the Citadel, which contains the temple of Quetzalcóatl, a stepped pyramid-platform whose decorated walls bear numerous stone sculptures representing Quetzalcóatl and Tláloc. Many burials have been found near the temple, including a ceremonial interment dated to AD200 of 18 men, probably captured soldiers put to sacrificial death.

The vast city of Teotihuacán amazes even the modern visitor with its grandeur and scale. The city contained 2,000 apartment buildings, 600 pyramids and many other temples, plazas, administrative buildings and palaces used by nobles and priests. There were 500 areas of workshops where craftsmen made pots or worked in obsidian and a vast market-place served by merchants from many parts of central America. Its construction must have been the work of generations

Right: Heads of Quetzalcóatl flank the steep stairs of a Teotihuacán temple. One of the god's aspects was as the wind deity Éhecatl.

of Teotihuacános and is an astonishing, enduring proclamation of the power of the city's rulers. The city's great stone peaks honour and echo the natural mountains that range against the sky behind them. It is not difficult to understand the Aztecs' reverence for its architects.

'WATER MOUNTAIN': TENOCHTITLÁN

The Spanish conquistadors encountered Tenochtitlán at the height of its glory, a vast metropolis on the water with more than 150,000 and perhaps as many as 300,000 inhabitants. They were moved to compare it to the Italian city of canals, Venice, or even to the enchanted cities described so colourfully in medieval chivalric romances. Yet the Aztecs constructed what appeared to be a city of dreams from the most unlikely of beginnings.

FOUNDING OF A CITY

The México/Aztec incomers who founded Tenochtitlán were latecomers in the Chichimec incursions that followed the collapse of Toltec power in the 12th century. When they arrived in the Valley of Mexico in the mid-13th century, the best territories had already been settled and the México were not made welcome by the Alcohua, Tepanec and other groups who had already made their homes there. Moreover, the newcomers were driven out of the places where they did settle. When they finally brought their wanderings to an end in 1325, the México

had to take what lands they could get. The twin islands on which they were to found their great city were some of the least attractive lands in the vicinity, so unpromising that none of the three powers in the region of Lake Texcoco – Texcoco to the east, Azcapotzalco to the west and Culhuacán to the south – had bothered to lay claim to them.

The city had to be designed to fit the setting and its island situation and marshy surroundings were crucial shaping factors from the start. Certainly there were some benefits to the site. For food, the settlers had their pick of the fish, birds and plentiful waterlife. Indeed, the Aztecs came to view the lake as a mother who had given them refuge at her breast. In fertility rites held on the lake each year, the water was addressed as Tonanueyatl ('Mother Vast Water'). The watery setting was also an advantage in terms of transport. In a country where men and

Left: 'Floating fields' such as these created in Lake Xochimilco were needed to support the burgeoning population of Tenochtitlán.

Above: The Aztecs' reliance on causeway or boat to connect to the lake's shore is clear in this schematic image of Tenochtitlán.

women made no use of beasts of burden or wheeled carts, it was easier to move things by canoe. The islands were also in a central position, within a triangle formed by the lake's three foremost cities. This was important strategically and was also of benefit to the México when they established marketplaces in Tenochtitlán and Tlatelolco.

LAYOUT AND DESIGN

The Aztecs laid their city out in four quarters to match the four cardinal directions and built a sacred precinct at its centre. Each of the *capultin* or tribal clans was assigned its own area and its own temple within the city; the clans held their land communally. The Great Pyramid and ritual precincts that developed here were understood by the Aztecs to be the centre of the universe. The pyramid itself was a holy mountain, a reproduction within the city of

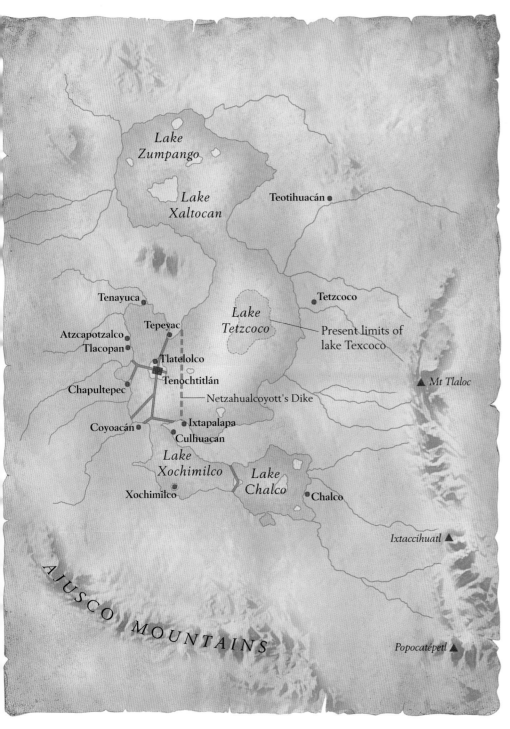

in pairs with a central footpath and canals on either side from which the farmers could draw water to irrigate the crops. Canoes used the canals to transport goods. *Chinampa* varied in size from 100sq m to 850sq m (1,100 to 9,000 sq ft). A typical *chinampa* might be farmed by 10–15 people. The available land was greatly increased after the Aztec under Itzcóatl took control in 1428 of the large *chinampa* plantations in the freshwater lakes of Xochimilco and Chalco that lay to the south of Lake Texcoco.

The city's location and design made it vulnerable. It could easily be flooded. A flood in 1500 destroyed many houses. Netzahualpilli, son of Netzahualcóyotl of Texcoco, told the Aztec *tlatoani* Ahuítzotl that the gods must be enraged. A great reconstruction project was launched: the nobles built palaces, dykes were strengthened and willows and poplars planted along the canals. The second, ultimately disastrous, drawback was that the city was not self-sufficient and could be cut off, making it vulnerable to siege. Sadly for the Aztecs, Hernán Cortés saw this. He blocked the three causeways and used a fleet of armed barges to prevent food being brought in any other way. The three-month siege led to the city's fall and the end of the Aztec empire.

Above: Netzahualcóyotl built a 16-km- (10-mile) dyke to seal off the freshwater part of the lake containing Tenochtitlán.

the sacred heights of Popocatépetl, Ixtaccíhuatl and Mount Tláloc. The city itself was a mountain on the lake – indeed the Nahuatl word for 'city', *atl tepetl*, translates as 'water mountain'. They built three long causeways, said by Hernán Cortés to be 3.5m (12ft) wide, to link the islands to the mainland. An aqueduct carried water in from mainland springs at Chapultepec hill.

CHINAMPA

Agricultural land was initially in short supply until the Aztecs developed their own *chinampa* or 'floating fields'. In shallow water, these fields were built up in the lake bed with layers of mud and plants, fixed in place by tall posts. In deeper water, fields were made by filling 'floating' reed-beds with earth and anchoring them to the lake bed. The plots were laid out

Right: An illustration from the manuscript of the Codex Mendoza *(c.1541) represents Tenochtitlán as a city founded on water.*

ON THE EDGE: COPÁN AND JAINA ISLAND

The city of Copán, which lay close to the Guatemala–Honduras border, was the most easterly of the large Maya cities. For the Maya, Copán lay at the eastern limits of their civilization.

The site at Copán was occupied from 1000BC onwards, but for many centuries it was only a small farming settlement. Copán developed into a major city c.AD400, when a group of public buildings and a ball court were erected.

OPENING TO THE UNDERWORLD

By the 9th century, the city had as many as 20,000 inhabitants. It covered 100 hectares (250 acres) and contained two large pyramids, as well as several plazas, stairways and stone temples, most arranged on a central raised platform called the Acropolis by archaeologists. In the 7th century, King Smoke Imix made the city a leading power in the world of the Maya.

Through architecture, the king also sanctified Copán: the arrangement of his

Left: King 18 Rabbit, subject of several stelae at Copán, oversaw a major building programme in the city in the early AD700s.

Above: These figures on Altar Q at Copán represent Yax Pak (centre) receiving a sceptre from his ancestor Yax K'uk Mo'.

stelae in the city and the valley around it identify the place as a sacred opening to the underworld. His descendant Smoke Shell built a magnificent dynastic stairway 15m (50ft) wide and with 1,250 hieroglyphs on the risers of its 72 steps, from which scholars have been able to trace a dynasty of 16 kings who ruled the city from Yax K'uk Mo' ('Blue Quetzal Macaw') in c.AD435 to Yax Pak ('First Sunrise') in AD820.

For many years, scholars believed that the city had a special significance for Maya civilization as a centre for study of astronomy and astrology. There is no doubt that astronomy fed strongly into the city's development. Many of the buildings and stelae erected in the reign of the 9th-century monarch King 18 Rabbit are arranged to mirror the sacred patternings of the sky. The stelae bear many detailed carvings of the king. One shows him as both a young man and an

older king, while another depicts him wearing both the jaguar-skin garment associated with kings and a beaded dress of the kind usually seen in depictions of women. As Maya scholar John S. Henderson has noted, the images, their positioning and the hieroglyphic inscriptions suggest a number of highly significant symbolic oppositions, including left–right, young–old and female–male – as well as the three realms sky–world–underworld and the four directions east–north–west–south.

ALTAR Q

Much of the scholarly debate about the significance of Copán was generated by misinterpretation of a square structure with 16 figures carved on its sides. The object, called Altar Q by archaeologists, was built by King Yax Pak in the 9th century. Historians used to believe that the figures on the altar were those of

Above: A stela honouring King Smoke Imix, 12th ruler in Yax K'uk Mo's dynasty, overlooks part of the ball court at Copán.

Below: This figurine from Jaina Island wears a fine cotton blouse, suggesting that she is a woman of high rank.

astronomers called to Copán to adjust the Maya calendar. We now know that the individuals are Yax Pak and his 15 ancestors in the dynasty of Yax K'uk Mo'. Copán might have been at the limit of Maya realms, but it had dynastic links with other Maya cities. Scholars believe that the dynasty descended from Yax K'uk Mo' had connections among the royal family at Tikal – the Copán emblem glyph has been found in texts at Tikal. The mother of the dynasty's final king, Yax Pak, was from Palenque.

At the other end of the Maya realm lay the enigmatic Jaina, a limestone island off the coast of Campeche that the Maya used as a burial ground in the late Classic Period (during the 7th–9th centuries AD) and where archaeologists have found a wealth of small clay figurines in graves. The island's westerly location made it a natural choice for a cemetery. Viewed from the mainland, the sun would have set behind Jaina on its nightly journey to the spirit realm. Its setting in the ocean also made it appropriate, for lakes, seas and expanses of water were considered to offer a passage to Xibalba. The clay figures represent women and men of different social levels and may be portraits of the deceased. Some of them certainly depict deities, notably the sun and moon gods, who in mythology survived the frightful realm of the underworld to rise immortal into the sky.

THE JEWEL OF THE CEREN

To the south of Copán lies a farming village that was of little importance in Maya times, but which is of great interest to archaeologists because a volcanic eruption in c.AD590 buried its buildings in ash, so preserving them in perfect condition for future generations to explore and analyse.

The village, now known as Joya del Ceren ('Jewel of the Ceren'), was discovered in 1976 by the American anthropology professor Payson D. Sheets. It appears that the inhabitants of the village were able to flee the disaster, but they left behind a treasure trove of tools, materials, household furniture and even food, enabling Professor Sheets and other scholars to build up a convincing picture of life in a Maya farming village during the Classic Period. Surviving structures include adobe houses, public and religious buildings and a communal bathhouse.

CHAPTER 3

APPEASING THE GODS

In 1428, Maxtla, ruler of the once-dominant Tepanec city of Azcapotzalco, was decisively defeated by a coalition of Tenochtitlán, Texcoco and Tlacopán. He was taken prisoner and put to ritual death in a ceremony that is revealing of the many ways in which war and blood sacrifice served to legitimize political power and safeguard the natural order in Mesoamerica.

The ceremony was a graphic demonstration of the triumph of the new Triple Alliance of Tenochtitlán, Texcoco and Tlacopán at the expense of the waning Tepanec empire. Maxtla's sacrifice was also a symbolic appropriation of Tepanec lands into the domain of the Triple Alliance and an expression of Netzahualcóyotl's primacy in his own city-state; he would become ruler of Texcoco three years later. However, the sacrifice had a number of more general, and more significant, symbolic meanings. First was its link to fertility. Netzahualcóyotl and all those present trusted that the offering of the victim's lifeblood would safeguard the richness of the soils, guarantee the return of the rains and therefore promote a good harvest. Second, the ritual was a renewal of the state itself, validating the power of the ruler and the war that was his weapon, keeping chaos and dissolution at bay. Third, the killing of Maxtla was an act of respect, for Mesoamericans considered it shameful for a warrior or ruler to be captured and kept alive and believed it was an honourable fate to be despatched as a human sacrifice.

Left: In sacrificial rites, the victim's heart was flung into the container on the flat belly of a chacmool *figure. This* chacmool *reclines outside the Temple of the Warriors in Chichén Itzá.*

MANY TYPES OF BLOOD OFFERING

For Mesoamerican peoples, offering human blood in sacrifice was a religious duty, necessary to sustain the world by maintaining the fertility of the land and the power of the ruler. It was also vital for satisfying the gods, who might at any moment determine to bring the present age to a violent end. Humans, gods and the natural world were part of a cosmic pattern of energy in which ritual and sacrifice were the means by which energy was recycled or passed on. Among the Aztecs, the two most common forms of sacrifice were extracting the victim's heart from his chest and burning to death.

REMOVING THE HEART

The extraction of the heart was performed with great ceremony on a special sacrificial block known as a *quauhxicalli* ('Stone of the Eagle'). The stone was pointed in the centre, so that a victim thrown down on it would be forced to arch his back and so thrust up his chest ready for the sacrificial knife.

Post-Conquest Spanish accounts report that naked victims were grouped at the foot of the temple steps as a priest descended from the sacred heights of the temple with an image of the god in whose honour the sacrifice was to be made. He showed the divinity to each victim, saying, 'this is your god', before the victims were led up to the sacrificial stone. Six priests of the highest rank (*chachalmua*) performed each sacrifice: four to hold the victim's feet, one to hold his throat and one to cut his chest. The foremost of these priests, dressed in a splendid red tunic and his head adorned with a helmet of yellow and green feathers, sliced the victim's chest with a flint knife known as a *técpatl*. He tore the heart from the chest, held it up to the sun, then cast it steaming before the image of the god. The six priests together pushed the corpse off the sacrificial stone and down the bloodstained temple

steps. Bodies gathered at the foot of the steps in a bloody pile. Later on, they were collected, prepared and eaten in a respectful and devout ritual.

BURNING

Sacrifice by burning was mainly reserved for ceremonies in honour of the fire god Xiuhtecuhtli, who was sometimes worshipped as Huehuetéotl ('The Old

Above: In a carved lintel at Yaxchilán, King Shield Jaguar's wife Lady Xoc draws a blood offering from her tongue.

God'). The rite represented the rebirth of the god, the rising of new life from death in the same way the sun was born when the god Nanahuatzin cast himself into the flames in an act of divine self-sacrifice. Other sacrificial methods were similarly

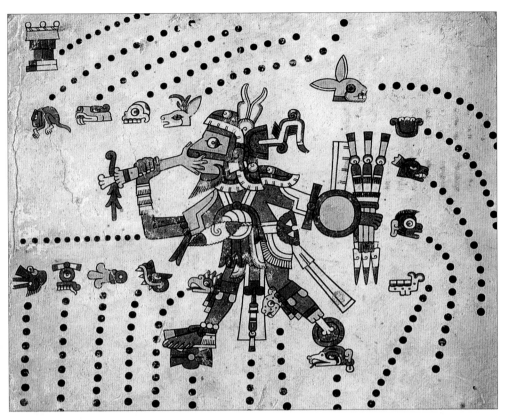

Above: A 16th-century codex illustration depicts Tezcatlipoca, dark lord of fate, feasting on the body of a sacrificed prisoner.

associated with particular gods. Victims killed in honour of Xipe Totec, the god of planting and vegetation, were shot with arrows so that their blood flowed into the earth like life-giving waters. Indeed, the Aztecs called human blood *chalchiuatl* ('precious water'). The corpse was then flayed and a priest would wear the skin in honour of the god, who was known as 'Our Lord the Flayed One'. The rite was a celebration of the splitting of seeds that makes possible the growth of new vegetation each spring.

MAYA METHODS

The Maya also used the primary Aztec method of slicing the victim's chest and extracting his dripping heart to offer to the gods. The priest oversaw the rite. Four aged men, called *chacs* in honour of the Maya rain god, were positioned to hold the body of the victim on the sacrificial stone while a specialist named the *nacom* cut open the victim's chest. In the Classic Period, however, many Maya sacrificers preferred to decapitate their victims. They also cast victims into the waters of their sacred wells or *cenotes* to drown. The

American archaeologist Edward H. Thompson found the skeletons of many men, women and children in the *cenote* at Chichén Itzá.

Autosacrifice or offering one's own blood to the gods was practised. The Maya used a string threaded with thorns to cut their cheeks, lower lips, ears and tongues. They collected blood and then smeared it on images of the god or on their own body or hair. Men also used sharp knives or the spines of stingrays to cut and draw blood from their penises for offering in the same way. Among the Maya, ritual bloodletting of this kind was considered a privilege and was performed by members of the nobility. At important times, such as the passing from one calendrical cycle to another, the king and his family would perform the ritual in honour of his ancestors and on behalf of himself, the city-state and his people. There are also illustrations in Maya codices, on door lintels and on ceramics, of the gods themselves letting their blood in this way. A vase unearthed

at Cahal Pech near Belize depicts a figure with the appearance of the sun god drawing blood from his penis.

Among the Aztecs, the offering of one's own blood was the preserve of priests. They would perform the rite prior to important state events and at auspicious and inauspicious dates in the calendar. They used maguey spines or blades of the volcanic glass obsidian to cut their earlobes and prick their legs and arms, or would run a thorned cord across their tongue or penis. In the rites prior to investiture as *tlatoani*, the new ruler would offer his own blood – drawn in this way from his earlobes, calves or arms – before the shrine of Huitzilopochtli atop the Great Temple in Tenochtitlán.

Animal sacrifices were also made. The Aztecs slaughtered many quails, ripping their heads off before images of the gods. Quails were associated with the myth of Quetzalcóatl, in which the Plumed Serpent descended to the underworld at the end of the previous age of the world, in order to take the bones of a previous race of men and use them to create a new tribe of humans to inhabit the current age. The underworld god Mictlantecuhtli was angry and ordered quails to chase him. Both Aztecs and Maya also sacrificed turkeys, dogs and, on special religious or state events, jaguars. In the Maya city-state of Copán, 16 jaguars were killed to mark the accession of the 16th king, Yax Pak. The bones of a jaguar were also placed among the foundations of the Great Temple in Tenochtitlán.

Left: An elaborate knife such as this was used to dispatch sacrificial victims. The handle of this weapon represents a warrior.

MESOAMERICAN DIVINITIES

CREATORS

AZTEC

Ometecuhtli, dual nature male and female as Ometeotl and Omecihuatl. Also took form of Tonacatecuhtli and Tonacacihuatl.

Tezcatlipoca, sometimes seen as supreme creator god.

MAYA

Itzamná, also known as Hunab Ku. In *Popol Vuh* Huracán (Hurricane or Sky Heart, sky god creator) and Gucumatz or Kukulcán (Sovereign Plumed Serpent, sea god creator). Kukulcán is the Maya equivalent of the Aztec god Quetzalcóatl.

Tezcatlipoca   *Itzamna*

SUN, MOON AND VENUS

AZTEC

Tonatiuh, sun god.
Metzli, moon god.
Tlahuizcalpantecuhtli (god of dawn, Venus as Morning Star), a form of Quetzalcóatl.
Xólotl (double of Quetzalcóatl), associated with Venus as Evening Star.

MAYA

Kinich Ahau, sun god by day. Jaguar god of the Underworld, sun god by night.
Ix Chel (Goddess Rainbow), goddess of the moon.
Lahun Chan, god of Venus.

Xipe Totec   *Xochipilli*

EARTH AND FERTILITY

AZTEC

Xipe Totec (god of vegetation and spring, transitions and oppositions) also known as Red Tezcatlipoca, linked with east.
Chicomecóatl, maize goddess.
Cihuacóatl, fertility goddess.
Cintéotl, maize god.
Coatlícue, earth goddess.
Tlatecuhtli, earth god/goddess.
Xilonen, maize goddess.
Xochipilli, the flower prince.
Xochiquetzal, flower goddess, also goddess of weaving.
Toci, earth goddess, also childbirth.
Teteoinnan, earth goddess.
Mayahuel, maguey plant goddess.
Ilamatecuhtli, ancient mother goddess.
Tepeyollotl, regeneration.
Tonantzin, mother goddess.
Tlazoltéotl, goddess of love and filth.

Kinich Ahau   *Ix Chel*

MAYA

Yum Caax, sometimes Young Maize God; in *Popol Vuh*, One Hunahpú.

DEATH AND DESTINY

AZTEC

Tezcatlipoca, god of night and destiny, also associated with kingship, creation, destruction, deception, war.

MAYA

Ah Puch, death god.

Tlazolteotl   *Yum Caax*

Ixtab, goddess of suicide.

MOUNTAINS

AZTEC

Popocatépetl.
Ixtaccíhuatl.
Mount Tláloc.
Tetzcotzingo.
Matlalcueye.

ANIMAL/BIRD DEITIES

AZTEC

Xólotl, dog-double of Quetzalcóatl.

MAYA

Hun Batz and **Hun Chouen**, Monkey-man gods, half-brothers of Hero Twins.
Vulture god.
Fox god.
Rabbit god.
Jaguar god figures worshipped from Olmec times onward.

Tláloc

Chalchiúhtlicue   *Chac*

Yacatecuhtli

Seven Macaw.
Zotz, bat god.
RAINS, WINDS, WATERS
AZTEC
Tláloc, rain god.
Tlaloques, rain gods.
Quetzalcóatl, storms and wind, also known as White Tezcatlipoca, linked with west, amid many other attributes.
Tepictoton, rain god.
Éhecatl, wind god, form of Quetzalcóatl.
Chalchiúhtlicue, goddess of springs, rivers and the sea.
Huixtocíhuatl, salt goddess.
Atl, god of water.

MAYA
Chac, rain god.

HUNTING
AZTEC

Camaxtli, hunt god.
Mixcóatl, ancient hunt god.

FIRE
AZTEC
Huehuetéotl, old fire god.
Xiuhtecuhtli, fire god.
Chantico, earth goddess.

WAR
Huitzilopochtli, México tribal god, also associated with sun and war. Also known as Blue Tezcatlipoca, linked with south.
Tezcatlipoca, associated with north.

TRADERS
AZTEC
Yacatecuhtli, god of traders and travellers.

MAYA
Ek Chuah, god of merchants.

ANCESTRAL GODS/CULTURE HEROES ETC
AZTEC
Quetzalcóatl-Topiltzin, god of storms, wind and rain, among many other attributes.
Huitzilopochtli, tribal god of México.
Mixcóatl, hunt god worshipped in both Huexotzingo and Tlaxcala.
Camaxtli, hunt god of Chichimec origin, worshipped particularly in Huexotzingo.

MAYA
Hero Twins Hunahpú and **Xbalanqué.**
MEDICINE AND FOODS
AZTEC
Octli, deities of pulque drink.
Patécatl, medicine god.

MAYA
Ix Chel, moon goddess, also goddess of medicine.

UNDERWORLD
AZTEC
Mictlantecuhtli, god of underworld or Mictlán.
Mictlantecacihuatl, goddess of underworld or Mictlán.

Huitzilopochtli   *Quetzalcóatl*

Hero Twins Hunahpú and Xbalanqué

ONE ABOVE ALL OTHERS: THE SUPREME GOD?

Mesoamericans worshipped a bewildering number of gods. Each deity could simultaneously take many forms. For example, a Maya divinity might be old and young, male and female, have both spiritual and bodily forms and have animal, human and divine characteristics.

WHY SO MANY GODS?

Mesoamericans happily took on the forms of worship of previous generations. Peoples did this partly in order to legitimize their own standing. The México, for example, were keen to associate themselves with the deities and achievements of their Toltec forerunners. In addition, new gods regularly joined the pantheon. The idea of converting new worshippers to the faith, so central to Christianity, was alien to Mesoamerican thought. When the Aztecs conquered lands during the expansion of their empire, they did not suppress the gods of the native peoples. They would occasionally impose the worship of their

Below: Builders of Classic Maya cities paid frequent homage to Chac, god of rain, as here in the 'nunnery quadrangle' at Uxmal.

Right: Itzamná, the supreme Maya god, holds a vision serpent in this limestone tablet, c.100BC–AD250.

own warlike tribal god Huitzilopochtli, but they usually let their new subjects to continue their traditional forms of worship.

Many deities of the Aztecs and Maya had their origins far in the distant Mesoamerican past. The Aztec cult of the earth mother, worshipped as Tonantzin ('Our Sacred Mother') and Toci ('Our Grandmother'), might have grown from ancient rites in honour of figures of fertility goddesses, which have been found in many parts of the Mesoamerican region and dated to as far back as *c.*2000BC. In the era of the Olmec civilization (*c.*1500–400BC) Mesoamericans were already worshipping primitive forms of Tláloc (the Aztec rain god), Tezcatlipoca (the Aztec god of night and bringer of discord), Quetzalcóatl (the Aztec Plumed Serpent, known as

Kukulcán to the Maya) and Huehuetéotl (the Aztec fire god). The Olmec were devotees of a cult of the jaguar that seems to have been associated both with fertility and royalty and which had a major influence on Maya and Aztec religion. The jaguar was later a major manifestation of Tezcatlipoca.

The builders of Teotihuacán, the city so revered by the Aztecs, worshipped Quetzalcóatl, Tláloc and the rain god's consort Chalchiúhtlicue. The cult of the rain god was also strong among the Zapotec, who worshipped him as Cocijo; the Preclassic Maya knew him as Chac.

A SUPREME DIVINITY?

Certain Maya and Aztec traditions held that a supreme creator existed behind the massed ranks of the gods. According to some Maya sources, the supreme god was Itzamná ('Lizard House'), sometimes

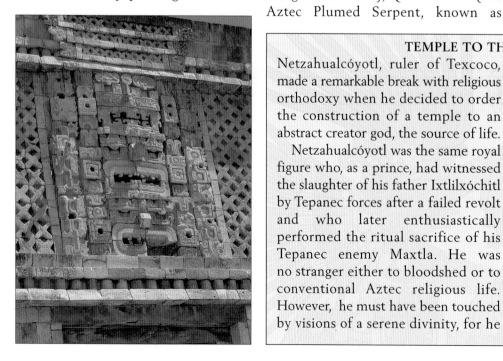

TEMPLE TO THE HIDDEN GOD

Netzahualcóyotl, ruler of Texcoco, made a remarkable break with religious orthodoxy when he decided to order the construction of a temple to an abstract creator god, the source of life.

Netzahualcóyotl was the same royal figure who, as a prince, had witnessed the slaughter of his father Ixtlilxóchitl by Tepanec forces after a failed revolt and who later enthusiastically performed the ritual sacrifice of his Tepanec enemy Maxtla. He was no stranger either to bloodshed or to conventional Aztec religious life. However, he must have been touched by visions of a serene divinity, for he

built in his city-state a nine-storey temple to an abstract god he named Ipalnemoani ('The One By Which We Live') or Tloquenahuaque ('The One Who is Always Near').

The shrine to this deity, situated at the top of the temple, was empty of statues or other conventional decoration, for the Texcocan ruler believed the god he wished to celebrate could not be ascribed a visible form. Netzahualcóyotl showed a typically Mesoamerican openness to divergent religious approaches by allowing the other major Aztec gods to be worshipped on the lower levels of his temple.

known also as Hunab Ku ('Only Spirit'). He was depicted as a great sky serpent or as an old man, toothless and with a hooked nose, and was believed to be patron of writing and divination. His consort was Ix Chel ('Lady Rainbow'), goddess of childbirth, medicine and weaving.

Similarly, one Aztec creation myth told of a supreme creator, Ometéotl, who brought the Earth into being. Ometéotl had dual male-female aspects, was known as 'Lord of Duality' and could manifest as separate deities, Tonacatecuhtli ('Lord of Our Sustenance') and Tonacacíhuatl ('Lady of Our Sustenance'), who were entwined in a fruitful embrace. In different versions of the myth, either Ometéotl created the family of Aztec gods or Tonacatecuhtli made the Plumed Serpent Quetzalcóatl from his breath.

Another prominent Aztec ruler, Netzahualcóyotl, King of Texcoco, is reported to have been drawn to the worship of an abstract and supreme deity. However, both cultures were, in general, polytheistic. The concept of one god above or encompassing all others was largely foreign to the Mesoamerican imagination.

CHANGING SIGNIFICANCE
Scholars have shown the Maya worshipped different supreme deities in different eras and perhaps different groups.

Left: A Zapotec gold pendant depicts (top to bottom) the ball game; the sun; a knife representing the moon and an early form of Tlaltecuhtli, the Earth Monster of Aztec myth.

Right: Scholars often identify this basalt deity as Ometéotl, the Aztec 'Lord of Duality'.

Itzamná and the bird deity Seven Macaw were revered as the highest of gods in the early days of Maya civilization, but later on Seven Macaw alone was worshipped in this way. Yet in the *Popol Vuh* of the Quiché Maya, Seven Macaw is no more than a boastful fraud and the Quiché acclaim the one-legged fire god Tohil as the supreme divinity.

A variant Aztec creation legend tells the story of how a multiplicity of gods was born. A primeval goddess gave birth to a *técpatl* or sacrificial knife, which fell on to the northern plains that were the land of origin of the Aztecs' Chichimec ancestors. As it hit the hard ground in that inhospitable desert place, gods beyond number were born and spread out to fill the earth.

THE BLOOD OF MANY

One of the most important religious ceremonies of the year in Tenochtitlán was Panquetzalíztli, held to honour Huitzilopochtli, the divine leader of the Aztec state and unique to the México. Panquetzalíztli was held after the harvest, when the nation readied itself for war.

BATHED SLAVES

Many captive warriors of subject peoples were put to the knife before the shrine of Huitzilopochtli. Other victims were so-called 'bathed slaves', who had been purchased at market by successful merchants and offered for sacrifice in the hope of winning divine blessing. The slaves were often picked for their good looks and musical or dancing ability, for in the build-up to the festival they had to entertain guests at magnificent feasts thrown by the merchant for senior traders and noblemen. Nine days before Panquetzalíztli, the slaves were washed in a spring sacred to Huitzilopochtli and began religious preparation for their own

Below: A tzompantli *or skull rack for displaying victims' heads stood atop the Great Pyramid in Tenochtitlán.*

sacrifice. On the day of the festival, the slaves were led four times around the Great Temple then, in the company of the merchant-donor, they climbed the temple's steep steps to the shrine of Huitzilopochtli at the top. There, a priest dressed as Huitzilopochtli dispatched them. They were spreadeagled across the sacrificial stone, the chest was sliced open and the heart torn from its cavity. The merchant was awarded the bodies, and afterwards he would take them back to his house to be consumed with maize in a cannibalistic banquet.

VICTIMS BECOME GODS

Each of the Aztec months was sacred to a particular deity and, at the end of each month, victims dressed as the god in question were respectfully slaughtered. The victims, known as *ixiptla* ('in the god's image'), became the gods they honoured and were treated with the greatest reverence and ceremony. They were said to hold the fire of the god in

Left: This wooden handle from a sacrificial knife is covered with a mosaic of turquoise, malachite, shell and mother-of-pearl.

their bodies, and when they were slaughtered this divine flame was set free to take residence in the body of a victim marked for sacrifice in a year's time.

Perhaps the most remarkable of these ceremonies was that held to honour Tezcatlipoca. Each year, at the close of the month holy to Tezcatlipoca, a young man of intelligence and good looks was selected to represent the god and for a year was treated as his embodiment. By day, he lived in the god's temple, where he learned to play the flute and dance steps sacred to the 'Lord of the Smoking Mirror'. By night, he was sent out into the city, accompanied by a guard of eight warriors. In every quarter he visited he played evocative tunes on his flute, shaking the rattles tied to his legs and arms as he danced to signal his coming. The people of Tenochtitlán would nod reverently and sometimes carry out sick children to be blessed and cured by the passing god.

As the year drew to an end, the preparations for the sacrifice intensified. The Emperor visited Tezcatlipoca's temple and dressed the young man in the costume sacred to the god.

The god-victim was given four young wives, embodiments of significant goddesses. With five days to go to the sacrifice, the *tlatoani* or ruler went into devout retreat and the people understood that Tezcatlipoca was governing the Aztec capital of Tenochtitlán.

Above: Worshippers gaze reverently up the pyramid's steep steps as a victim's warm heart is flung skywards to honour the gods.

On the final day of the month, the youth was led with full ritual to Tezcatlipoca's shrine on the Great Pyramid. There he said goodbye to his four divine consorts, was placed over the sacrificial stone and his heart was pulled from his body. His corpse was taken down the steps and a meal of his cooked flesh served to the *tlatoani* and most prominent of the city's nobility and military elite. One of those in the select company was the young man who had been chosen to carry Tezcatlipoca's sacred flame within his body for the following 20 Aztec months – and be slaughtered in the god's name on the same day the following year.

Solar eclipses were terrifying times for the Aztecs, suggesting the unnatural encroachment of night into day, and *tzitzimime*, vengeful female spirits associated with darkness, were believed to rise in power. They could send sickness epidemics and were expected to play a part in the destruction of the Fifth Sun at the end of the current age. At times of eclipse, Aztecs made offerings of their own blood to persuade the god to sustain the sun and life on Earth. People with fair complexions were said to be full of light and were sacrificed to strengthen the sun in its struggle against darkness.

The Aztecs also held frequent sacrifices in the name of the rain gods, the *tláloques*. The gods cruelly required the blood of young children. As they were led to their deaths, the children would weep and the onlookers understood the tears that fell would become the rain they prayed for.

Right: On a pre-Toltec stela carved at the Maya site of Santa Lucia, Guatemala, a priest holds a severed head that drips blood.

COMMUNION WITH THE DIVINE

Sacrificial victims were treated with the greatest reverence. When an Aztec warrior captured a prisoner who would be taken to a ritual death, he treated him with solemnity and respect, declaring, 'Here I find my well-loved son'. A prisoner taken in this way was also said to take a grim satisfaction in the event and to declare, 'Here I encounter my well-respected father.' The only honourable fate for a warrior was to kill or be killed in battle or, if captured alive, to be taken to the temple for ritual death.

TLAHUICOLE

The story of the Tlaxcaltec warrior named Tlahuicole graphically demonstrates this concept. So great was Tlahuicole's renown in battle that, when he was captured by Aztec warriors, the *tlatoani* decided to spare his life and give him command of the Aztec army in a campaign against the Tarascans. Tlahuicole took on the command as he was ordered, but when he returned from the field he asked to be put to ritual death, for he felt that living on in captivity shamed him, whereas his sacrifice would restore the honour he had laboured so hard to win.

Below: A Yaxchilán lintel shows Lady Xoc having an ecstatic encounter with the Vision Serpent after sacrificing her own blood.

Above: Sacrificial rituals presented a magnificent spectacle, with sacred music and extravagant costumes on display.

MESSENGERS TO THE GODS

Those killed in ritual sacrifice were seen as messengers to the gods or were sometimes understood to become the very gods in whose honour they were put to death. Both priests and victims sometimes dressed as the gods they honoured and, among the Aztecs, victims were sometimes declared to be *ixiptla* ('in the god's image'). In this sense, the sacrificial ritual was a way of honouring and renewing the divine presence on Earth. The gods entered and united with the bodies of the victims and so were made manifest before the watching crowds.

The sacrifices presented a magnificent spectacle. Priests were bedecked in splendid costumes and feather headdresses and flowers adorned the temples. Musicians performed on conch-shell trumpets, flutes made from bones or reeds, drums and rattles. Dancers wore gold and silver bells that made a high ringing sound and blood flowed in a bright river from the steep temple steps to the bodies of the slain piled high at the temple front.

CANNIBALISM

Among the Aztecs it was common practice for the warriors who captured prisoners in battle to feed and care for them in captivity before the sacrifice. After the ritual, the bodies were decapitated and the heads put on display on the skull rack. The cannibalistic rite in which the victorious warriors would eat the bodies particularly shocked the Spanish conquistadors. However, if we understand that the Aztecs saw the victims as touched by or even embodying the gods, then we can see the act of cannibalism as a religious ritual, an act of communion with the divine. By eating the flesh of the victim, the warriors were able to share in the offering made to Huitzilopochtli at the summit of the temple-pyramid.

RELIGIOUS ECSTASY

Maya bloodletting was sometimes seen as a mystical act, an attempt to enter an ecstatic state in which a worshipper could communicate with ancestors or gods. Celebrated carvings in the Maya city of Yaxchilán show Lady Xoc, wife of King Shield Jaguar, in a bloodletting ritual.

In the first carving, Lady Xoc is shown drawing her own blood by pulling a thorned cord across her tongue, while her husband holds a flaming torch above her head. The second carving shows that her devotions deliver her to a visionary state. The blood she has produced has been collected on a piece of bark paper and set alight, producing a swirl of smoke in whose coils she can see the awesome Vision Serpent who commands the gateway through which the supernatural becomes visible in the natural realm.

The serpent has two jaws through which ancestors or deities can make themselves known in the world of men. From one peers the head of the war god, while from the other emerges the founder of the great Yaxchilán dynasty, Yat Balam ('Jaguar Penis'). Lady Xoc is asking for the help of Jaguar Penis and the war god in a military campaign which her husband, Jaguar Shield, is preparing. The inscription alongside the carvings dates the events shown to *c.* AD724–726.

Religious sacrificial ritual was not intended to bring the divine from another place into the physical world. The universe was filled with spiritual presence and the many gods, with their defined powers and roles, were everywhere. The sacrificial ritual celebrated this ever-present divine power in magnificent and devout spectacle.

Below: Masked dancers, priests and musicians congregate for a sacrificial ceremony in the Maya city of Bonampak.

REACHING FOR THE SKY

To Mesoamericans, the sky was a sacred place. The rising of Venus or of the sun and the movements of the stars played out the events of mythology and the deeds of the gods. The holiest places were those such as mountain peaks or the tops of temple pyramids that were nearest to the sky. At the climax of religious festivals, reverent processions would make the steep climb to the top of the pyramids to honour the gods high above the earth.

Many Aztec pyramids had temples at many levels, with the shrines of the most revered deities situated in the holiest of places at the top. The Great Temple at Tenochtitlán, which was inaugurated with such fervour by Emperor Ahuítzotl, had twin shrines to Huitzilopochtli (decorated with white and red symbols of war) and to Tláloc (coloured with white and blue symbols of water and rain) on its summit. There were areas sacred to other deities lower down the temple.

Above: The eastern stairs on the Pyramid of the Magician at the Maya site of Uxmal climb directly from ground to sanctuary.

Below: Cortés struck a blow to Aztec hearts when his men captured and wrecked the sacred arena on top of the Great Pyramid.

HUMILIATING AZTEC DEFEAT

At the time of the Conquest, this temple-top area, the most sacred place in the entire Aztec realm, was effectively appropriated for Spain and for Christianity by Hernán Cortés in an act of astonishing bravado and symbolic weight.

After the Spaniards had taken Moctezuma captive, when the Aztec leader was still nominally in control of his empire, Cortés demanded that a place of Christian worship be established on the highest level of the Great Temple. Moctezuma, fearful for his life and playing for time in case he could affect an escape, had no choice but to agree.

A Christian cross and an image of the Virgin Mary were placed at the summit of the temple, which could be viewed from all over Tenochtitlán and could even be seen from the shores of Lake Texcoco. Beneath these sacred icons, Cortés and the most prominent of the Spanish party held a Christian Mass, while the Aztecs looked on in dismay and rising fury.

In the wake of this event, the Aztec warriors and nobility attacked the Spaniards in the Europeans' compound. Subsequently, Cortés and his conquistadors added insult to injury by storming and destroying the upper levels of the Great Temple, throwing down and burning Tláloc's and Huitzilopochtli's shrines.

ycq̃tla tí tetʒavitl
yn mal ques.

Above: The main pyramid at Cobá rises to 42m (138ft). A sacred way (sacbé) runs from its base towards Chichén Itzá.

MAN-MADE MOUNTAINS

Throughout Mesoamerica, mountains were important religious symbols and sometimes also the settings for sacred rites. The Maya believed that the souls of their dead ancestors found a dwelling place in the rocky heights of mountains.

The Maya living in lowland regions erected their own peaks in the form of the steep-sided temples that dominate the magnificent ruins of Maya cities. Some of these man-made mountains were royal mausoleums as well as temples; like the pyramids of ancient Egypt, they were built primarily to house the tombs of great kings. The Aztec peoples of the Triple Alliance built shrines and celebrated important religious fertility festivals on the hills of Huixachtlán and Tetzcotzingo and on Mount Tláloc. Like the Maya, they viewed their pyramid temples as sacred peaks.

Huixachtlán ('Place of the Thorn Trees') is an extinct volcano that stands between Lakes Xochimilco and Texcoco. It was a sacred place long before the México made their way into the Valley of Mexico in the 13th century. On a temple

Right: This clay temple was probably sacred to Quetzalcóatl-Éhecatl and may have been used as a household shrine.

platform high on Huixachtlán, the Aztecs celebrated the human sacrifice that was the central event in the New Fire rites that marked the end of one 52-year cycle and the beginning of the next.

Mount Tláloc, the highest peak on the eastern rim of the Valley of Mexico, rises well above 4,000m (13,000ft) and commands awe-inspiring views of the volcanoes Popocatépetl and Ixtaccíhuatl. It, too, was a sacred spot from ancient times. The México and their allies in the Triple Alliance maintained a temple on the mountain-top where they celebrated an annual fertility rite. The rulers of Tenochtitlán, Texcoco, Tlacopán and Xochimilco made a pilgrimage to the

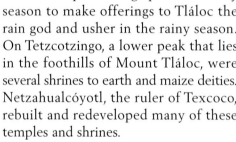

mountain-top at the high point of the dry season to make offerings to Tláloc the rain god and usher in the rainy season. On Tetzcotzingo, a lower peak that lies in the foothills of Mount Tláloc, were several shrines to earth and maize deities. Netzahualcóyotl, the ruler of Texcoco, rebuilt and redeveloped many of these temples and shrines.

THE GREATEST OF AZTEC TEMPLES

In 1487, Emperor Ahuítzotl inaugurated El Templo Mayor, the Great Temple in Tenochtitlán, with an immense ritual sacrifice described by the chronicler Fernando de Alva Ixtlilxóchitl as, 'butchery ... without equal in human history'.

Work on the Great Temple had begun many years earlier under Moctezuma I (1440–68). To the warrior leader Ahuítzotl fell the task of dedicating a temple worthy of the gods who had delivered such a great empire to the Aztecs.

Ahuítzotl had become emperor only the previous year, in 1486, and had spent the first year of his reign in military campaigns against rebel provinces. They must have furnished many prisoners of war. Back in Tenochtitlán, the festival in honour of the Great Temple lasted for four days.

According to some sources, as many as 80,000 victims were sacrificed during the festival. From all points of the compass, seemingly endless lines of captives were led towards the temple and up its steep sides to their deaths. In the sacred area at the top, Ahuítzotl stood waiting, attended by the rulers of his imperial allies Texcoco and Tlacopán. Ahuítzotl himself made the first sacrifice, plunging his obsidian knife into the chest of the victim on the sacrifical stone, then holding the heart up to the sacred sky before making obeisances to the new shrine of Huitzilopochtli. An army of priests was ready to take over in the emperor's wake. Bodies almost beyond counting were flung down the temple steps, staining them with the blood that the Aztecs understood to be the water of life, the offering sweetest to their gods.

SPIRIT JAGUARS: SHAMANS

The religious life of Mesoamericans went beyond the public rites of sacrifice conducted by the emperor, the warrior elite and the priests in temples. The people had a strong and enduring belief in shamans. These were people gifted with visionary and religious powers who were capable of making journeys of collective psychic discovery on behalf of the tribe, who could conjure the powers of the spirit world and influence the destiny of individuals and of the city-state itself.

JAGUAR IMAGERY

Belief in shamans in the region of Mexico and Guatemala dates back at least to the Olmec civilization of c.1500–400BC and probably much earlier still, into the Siberian past of Mesoamerican peoples. Shamans are still active among certain Siberian and Arctic peoples, the descendants of contemporaries of the first nomads who made the trek across the Bering landmass to North America as long as 23,000 years ago.

Jaguar imagery used by Olmec craftsmen is thought to honour the shape-shifting shamans. The jaguar's furtive behaviour and deadly capacity to hunt in the hours of darkness made it one of the key allies of the shaman in his demanding spirit-journeys. Shamans were said to be able to transform themselves into these majestic creatures during their trances.

The jaguar later became the principal animal form of the god Tezcatlipoca, the patron deity of shamans and the god of night among many other things. According to the Franciscan friar Diego Durán, a polished obsidian statue of Tezcatlipoca stood in the temple dedicated to

Left: This obsidian mirror sacred to Tezcatlipoca, god of shamans, was probably part of the treasure Cortés sent to Europe.

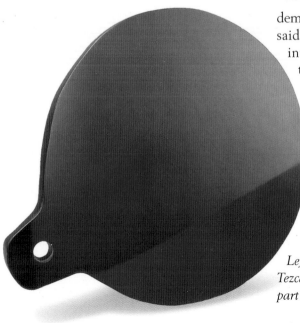

Above: According to myth, the Maya god Itzamná built the great Pyramid of the Magician, Uxmal, in a single night.

the god on the Great Pyramid at Tenochtitlán. The god Tezcatlipoca's image held a gold mirror, indicating that he saw everything that happened. The builders of Teotihuacán almost certainly practised shamanism like their forebears of the Olmec civilization and their cultural descendants among the Aztecs. A carving of a jaguar or other feline emerging from a doorway decorated with starfish and zigzag markings symbolic of light was found in excavations at Teotihuacán in 2001.

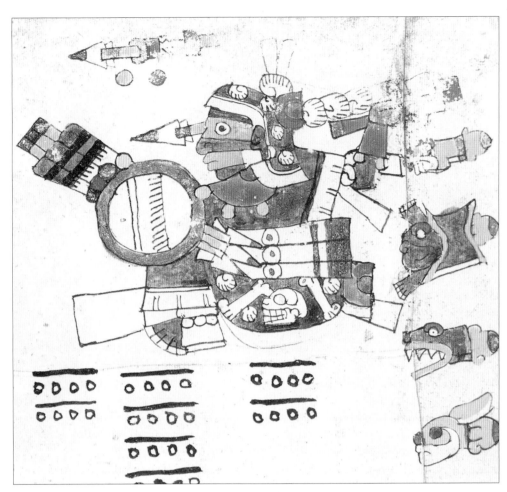

Right: An image from the Codex Cospi *(c.1350–1500) depicts the 'black aspect' of Tezcatlipoca, associated with sorcery.*

The carving is thought to represent the shaman-jaguar emerging from the spirit world on his return to the world of men after a journey. It was uncovered in the ruins that scholars believe were once a large palace, just north of the Pyramid of the Sun.

ANIMAL DOUBLES

Many Aztec gods had the capacity to appear in animal, human or other form. Tezcatlipoca, the deceiver and sower of discord, was said to appear as a coyote, a monkey or a skunk in addition to his more princely jaguar form. Moreover, Mesoamericans believed animal doubles were not the sole preserve of the gods. Each person had an animal form, a kind of animal familiar, which functioned as a protector. In the Aztecs' Nahuatl language, the animal form was called *tonal*. The word *nahual* was used to refer to the secret ability to shift shape and to the shamans who could practise it.

TRANCES AND VISIONS

From far back in Mesoamerican history, shamans took hallucinogenic substances to induce trances and visions. They made narcotic substances for ritual use from the toxin that toads make and store in small bumps on their head, as well as from the seeds of morning glory, from the peyote cactus and from various hallucinogenic mushrooms.

Some shamans were also temple priests, while others were not part of the traditional religious hierarchy. A shaman played an important role within the temple functions among the Maya. Known as a *chilam*, he was a man believed to be gifted with visionary powers. He would enter a visionary trance, after ritual bloodletting from his cheeks, earlobes or penis, and in the trance would receive and transmit messages from the gods. Other priests gathered round to translate his divinely inspired speech.

Some shamans offered to cure sickness using herbs and healing plants or native rites of magic. Others practised black magic and were deeply feared. One group of magicians known as 'sleep throwers' claimed that, through spells involving the arm of a woman who had died in childbirth, they could ensure that victims would be asleep so that a passer-by could steal from them. Other unscrupulous lay-priests promised to bring harm to enemies by burning tiny effigies of them.

THE SERPENT'S DOUBLE

Among the Aztecs, the god Xólotl's ability to change shape made him a patron of magicians and sorcerers.

In one version of the Aztec myth of the birth of the sun and moon, the assembled gods chose to sacrifice themselves in order to make these celestial bodies begin their cycle of movements across the sky. But one god, Xólotl, refused to give himself up. In his attempts to escape he transformed himself into a double ear of maize, a double maguey plant and a fish before he was caught and the gods' collective will was carried out.

Xólotl was god of monsters and of twins and other dual manifestations. He was associated with dogs, especially with the hairless dogs known as *xoloitzcuintli* by the Aztecs. Xólotl was celebrated also as the dog-double of the Plumed Serpent Quetzalcóatl and in this guise travelled with Quetzalcóatl into the underworld, Mictlán, where they succeeded in collecting the bones of past generations of humans. They later used the bones to create a human race for the new age of the world. Quetzalcóatl, of many attributes, was associated with the planet Venus and, in his form as Xólotl, was Venus rising as the evening star. Scholars believe that Xólotl was originally an independent Mesoamerican god of monsters who became associated with Quetzalcóatl in the Postclassic Period.

READING THE FUTURE

Mesoamericans believed that time was sacred, part of the substance of the gods themselves, and that those skilled in sacred rites could read the events of the future. One of the priest's key roles among both Maya and Aztecs was as a diviner of what was to come. This mystical activity had its full complement of practical applications on the level both of the city-state and of the humble farmer or merchant.

Such was the demand for information about the future that, as well as trusting in their priests, Mesoamericans also turned to a range of lay figures who offered access to arcane knowledge. Some claimed to be able to decipher patterns of future events in the shifting of light on an obsidian mirror or on water in a pot. Others could see what was to come in the lines made by a handful of maize grains when they were flung down on a cloak.

Right: A priest makes an offering. This Classic Maya stone disc (c.AD600–700) was found at Tonina in Chiapas, Mexico.

SACRED BUNDLES

Some aspects of religious life in Mesoamerica were distinctly different from the public ritual of major human sacrifices. One example is the Aztec and Maya practice of worshipping bundles that contained objects holy to a god or ancestor. This tradition may have dated back to the ancient days of migration, when nomads packed up their gods when they raised camp to move on. According to the *Popol Vuh*, the Quiché Maya brought a holy parcel with them on their migrations and worshipped it in honour of a revered ancestor, and the México and other Chichimec groups are also known to have carried sacred bundles held holy to forebears. Among the México, sacred bundles were carried by special priests named 'god-bearers'. The bundles were said to contain the mantles of the gods, which were left at the dawn of this era when the deities sacrificed themselves to give motion to the sun and moon, as well as jaguar skins, pieces of jade, jewels and other precious items. Maya of all social ranks kept life-sized clay idols for use in religious rites in the home.

RITUALS OF ATONEMENT

The need to propitiate and satisfy the gods could go beyond ritual sacrifice, whether of humans, animals or the worshippers' own blood. There were several established rituals among Mesoamericans for atonement, confession or mortification of the self. The Aztecs allowed men to make amends for sexual wrongdoing by

---

AFTER THE CONQUEST

The shapeshifting gods of Mesoamerica lived on after the conquistadors imposed Christian culture and doctrines.

The Mesoamericans were quick to take to the new faith of Christianity. They appear to have seen in the worship of Jesus Christ a similarity to the cult of the Plumed Serpent Quetzalcóatl. Jesus's teachings on brotherly love were in harmony with Topiltzin-Quetzalcóatl's pious and peaceful government, while the Christian idea of the second coming clearly resonated with the ancient Mesoamerican myth of Quetzalcóatl's departure and promised return. In an unlikely marriage of faiths, the Plumed Serpent became closely associated with Christ.

The Mesoamericans also adapted Roman Catholic Christian practices to the old faiths and continued to follow aspects of the old religion under the noses of the Christian monks. Among both Maya and Aztecs, for example, old gods were linked to Christian saints: Tláloc the rain god was revered under the guise of St John the Baptist. At the same time, traditional practices were aligned with Christian festivals: the yearly visit to the graves of the ancestors was carried out on All Souls' Day. In 1531, a peasant named Juan Diego had a vision of a dark-skinned Virgin Mary near a temple to the ancient Earth goddess Tonantzin. Under the name of the Black Virgin of Guadelupe, this hybrid Mesoamerican-Christian deity became Mexico's patron saint.

The way in which Aztecs and Maya accepted Christian practices while also maintaining the ways of the old faith is typical of Mesoamericans' approach to religion. They were generally willing to accept that new gods and new practices were an extension of what they already knew, rather than a completely new departure, and built upon existing practices and pantheons rather than replacing them.

Above: The Aztecs made regular devotions at household shrines containing clay temples and models of the gods and goddesses.

abasement before Tlazoltéotl, a fertility goddess associated with filth, excrement and sex. The individual would take his confession to a priest dressed as Tlazoltéotl and would be allowed freedom from his past deeds in return for faithful performance of penitential acts.

The Zapotecs made the rite of ritual bloodletting an occasion for confession. After making cuts in their cheeks and arms, they would let the blood flow on to husks of maize while they made a solemn statement of their evildoing.

The Maya had a scapegoat tradition, in which an individual took on the punishment for a whole community's wrongdoing. The villagers would choose one person, often an elderly woman, who would listen as each person recounted how they had shamed themselves or the group. The scapegoat would then be put to death by stoning.

Right: Fertility goddess Tlazoltéotl had the power to wipe away sexual wrongdoing. Her image is from the Codex Rios *(c.1570–95).*

DEATH AND THE AFTERLIFE

Mesoamericans had a highly developed awareness of death and its proximity. Life expectancy was low, child mortality was high, wars were frequent, if not almost continuous, and religion called for a steady stream of human victims for sacrificial rituals. Death, its rituals and speculation about a human's fate after this life inspired intriguing narratives in both Aztec and Maya mythology. Ancient Mesoamerican beliefs associated with death, sacrifice and the afterlife are as profound as those of other major civilizations. Their investigation of the human spirit's destiny after death ranks alongside the ancient Egyptian and Tibetan Books of the Dead.

Below: These solid clay figurines of elegantly attired members of the Maya nobility were left in graves on Jaina Island.

COSMOLOGY

The cosmology of both Aztec and Maya envisaged a many-layered universe, with thirteen tiers of heaven rising above the Earth and nine levels of Mictlán, a sinister underworld beneath. To the Aztecs, the underworld was a place of darkness and fear, of endless misfortune. Its rulers were the skeleton god Mictlantecuhtli, Lord of the Dead, and his serpent-skirted spouse Mictecacíhuatl.

According to the Aztecs, a select few were bound for the happy realms above. What was decisive was not how individuals lived but how they died. Those who died a natural death were bound for the underworld, but warriors killed in battle, women who died in childbirth and even those who took their own lives were spared the lower realms. Warriors who

Above: Among the Aztecs, the corpse was tied in a squatting pose prior to cremation or, for richer people, burial with grave goods.

died on the battlefield became *cuauhteca* ('Eagle Companions') and could enter the eastern paradise Tonatiuhichán. They were destined to join the entourage of the great sun himself in the form of hummingbirds or butterflies.

One tradition told that the souls of these great men were responsible for the daily miracle of the sun's return. At dawn and throughout the morning hours, the spirits of warriors slain on the battlefield hauled the sun up from its nightly residence in the underworld to its position at its zenith in the sky. Those who died by water or in storms – for example, by drowning or by lightning – were said to be destined for Tlalocán, a paradise presided over by the great rain god Tláloc, where life-giving waters fell in a constant light drizzle and flowers, fruit and delectable foods grew abundantly without need for the human labour of irrigation, digging and planting.

The Maya also believed that some would progress to a life of heavenly ease. Shaded by the strong boughs of the world's first tree, they would enjoy their leisure drinking chocolate. However, the

great majority were destined for the dark and dangerous realms of the underworld. The Maya called this dread place Xibalba ('Realm of Fright'). Here the dead would have to undergo many trials at the hands of foul and sadistic divinities.

FUNERARY RITES

Both rich and poor were buried with supplies to help them on this afterlife voyage. Poorer Maya were laid beneath the floors of their house. People were buried with the tools of the trade they followed. For example, hunters would be interred with their spears and fishermen with their harpoons and nets. The dead were also supplied with pottery containers of water and food supplies. Most would also have a little ground maize placed in their mouth and a handful of jade beads for use as money in the world after death. After an entire generation of burials, the house would no longer be used for daily living and would be kept as an ancestral shrine.

Below: A tomb in the Maya city of Uxmal marks the spot at which the deceased noble began his journey to the underworld.

Nobles, royalty and the priestly elite were buried in splendid tombs with generous supplies and even helpers. A Maya nobleman buried at Tikal was surrounded by fine ceramic vessels that contained maize stew and chocolate drink. He was accompanied by the bodies of nine servants who had been sacrificed at his death. Many took worldly wealth with them on their journey, presumably in the hope of using it during their underworld ordeals. A priest buried at Chichén Itzá was adorned with a splendid necklace of pearls that may have been brought from as far away as Venezuela by traders. The rulers and nobility were buried in the great plazas of the Maya cities. The Maya understood that the voyage to the underworld began by water, and nobles were often depicted travelling to the lands below by canoe. The great plazas were seen as symbolic lakes that gave access to the land of the dead below.

In Yucatán, some members of the nobility were cremated. Their ashes were placed in pottery or wooden urns carved with the dead person's features.

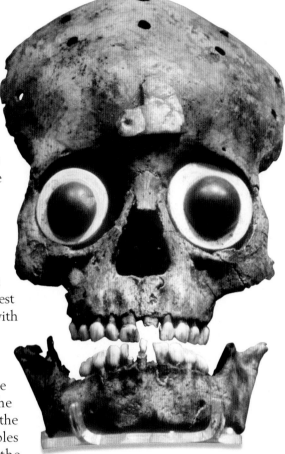

Above: To the Aztecs, death was a frequent visitor. This decorated child's skull was offered to Mictlantecuhtli, god of the dead.

Sometimes portrait statues were commissioned. These were left with a hollow space in the back of the head in which to place the ashes.

Most Aztecs were cremated. The corpse was dressed in his or her best clothes, then tied in a squatting pose and wrapped in cloth before being set alight. Interment in stone vaults was reserved for prominent members of the nobility and rulers. As among the Maya, a notable man might have a number of servants and even wives killed on his death so that they could accompany him to the underworld.

Among both Aztecs and Maya, a dead man was sometimes buried with his dog to provide a companion and protector-guide on his journey. The custom had religious and mythological resonance, for the revered deity Quetzalcóatl was accompanied by his dog-twin Xólotl on his journey to the underworld.

CHAPTER 4

WARFARE AND MILITARY LIFE

War was a way of life for Mesoamericans. The Aztecs waged war for practical gain to secure resources, raw materials and slave labour. They also understood that to wage war was to be intimately connected with the religious duty to return energy to the cosmos and to make devotions to the gods through offerings of lifeblood. Military might was an instrument of empire, used to conquer territory and deter rebellion, and also a means of capturing victims for the sacrificial knife. Some Aztec campaigns were conducted for this purpose above all others. It was not markedly different among the Maya. Classic-Period inscriptions and surviving texts suggest rival Maya city-states were almost constantly in conflict. Like the Aztecs, the Maya were hungry for live prisoners; ordinary folk were earmarked as slave labourers and the nobles among the captives were destined for sacrifice on the temple-pyramids.

War was therefore understood as a natural condition by both the Aztecs and the Maya. The great god Huitzilopochtli leapt from his mother Coatlícue's body fully armed and immediately began to wield his weapons, slaughtering his sister Coyolxauhqui, the moon goddess, and hundreds of his brothers in the first moments of his life. The Aztecs saw their male offspring in Huitzilopochtli's image, envisaging them as warriors from the day of their birth, or even before. Women who died in childbirth were understood to have perished at the hands of their unborn offspring.

Left: Toltec stone warriors at Tula stand 4.6m (15ft) tall. Ready for battle, each carries an atlatl *spear-thrower.*

THE FLOWER WARS

Some Aztec military campaigns were planned in advance and carried out with the agreement of both sides as a testing ground on which warriors could capture prisoners for religious sacrifice. Such a battle was known as *xochiyaóyotl* ('war of flowers') in reference to the magnificently dressed warriors rounded up and carried home like a garland of blooms.

Some scholars believe that the practice originated in the distant Mesoamerican past, but no examples have yet been found of Toltec or earlier wars conducted solely to capture live prisoners. Among the earliest known instances of *xochiyaóyotl* is the war between the México/Tepanecs and the Chalca, which began in 1376 and which is believed to have started as a 'flower war'.

BUYING FOOD AT MARKET

In the 1400s, the city-states of the Triple Alliance conducted regular campaigns of this kind against Atlixco, Huexotzingo and other cities. Tlacaélel, brother of Moctezuma I Ilhuicamina (1440–1468), likened the gathering of victims through war to buying food at market.

Discussing plans for the inauguration of the Great Temple in Tenochtitlán and the constant need for a plentiful supply of sacrificial victims, Tlacaélel declared that there was no actual need for their war god Huitzilopochtli to wait for an insult, diplomatic quarrel or some other conventional reason to start a war: he should simply find and enter a convenient 'market' for

Above: Images of soldiers at Bonampak show that fighting was at close quarters using spears.

the food he needed. At this market, Tlacaélel said, Huitzilopochtli and his army could gather victims like so many tortillas. The market should be nearby, because the flesh of distant peoples might not be to his liking.

Rather than fight in such distant realms as the lands of the Huastecs, the army should take their war to the conveniently situated cities of Atlixco, Tecoac, Cholula, Huexotzingo, Tlaxcala and Tliluhquitepec. The war against local enemies should not be decisive. Fighting must always continue or be easily renewed, so that Huitzilopochtli would have the victims for whom he hungered within easy reach. Huitzilopochtli would feed on them with pleasure, as a man enjoys a tortilla warm from the oven.

Right: A Totonac carving from east-central Mexico shows a prisoner of war bound hand and foot.

ESCAPE TO VICTORY

On the night of 30 June 1520, canoe-borne Aztec warriors swarmed around Spanish conquistadors as the Europeans attempted to flee Tenochtitlán along one of the many causeways that connected the city to the mainland. The Aztecs had the Spaniards at their mercy, but they did not finish them off. Instead, they allowed the surviving conquistadors to proceed on to Tlaxcalán and once there prepare for a renewed assault on Tenochtitlán.

In the darkness of the *Noche Triste* ('sad night') on 30 June, the Aztecs were in familiar surroundings while the invaders were panicking on the narrow causeway in driving rain. The defenders of Tenochtitlán had the chance to exterminate the Spaniards. Instead, they directed their attention to seizing booty and capturing prisoners. Their decision would lead to the collapse of their empire, the end of their Mesoamerican world.

Above: Battling for honour and to feed the gods, Aztec soldiers round up prisoners destined for sacrifice in Tenochtitlán.

A WAR GAME?

Some scholars suggest that the flower wars of the Aztecs might have had their origins in a kind of war game, a substitute for full conflict in which the contestants would put their fates in the hands of the gods. Historians have compared the practice to the ball game. This distinctive sport, which was practised throughout the Mesoamerican region, was seen, among other things, as a ritual enactment of cosmic struggles between good and evil or light and darkness; a kind of mythic encounter between Quetzalcóatl and his dark brother Tezcatlipoca and also between the Hero Twins and the lords of Xibalba.

Given the demand for sacrificial victims, the war game of the flower wars might have grown into a major military event, regularly conducted and leading to the deaths of thousands of warriors. Other experts suggest that the flower wars had a political and a religious dimension and were an important instrument of government. According to this theory, the wars maintained control over enemies by capturing and eliminating the leading warriors and nobles in the enemy group. It might be that in some flower wars, military and strategic aims existed alongside religious and ritual ones. Certainly, the demonstration of the Triple Alliance's military might can only have helped to discourage rebellion among subject peoples.

The flower wars took place alongside other more conventional types of conflict. The Triple Alliance regularly used its military might to extend the territory of the empire by winning land, enforcing alliances and also ensuring tribute payments were made. The religious and ritual elements so evident in the flower wars informed the Aztec approach to all types of conflict. Some historians have even suggested that the Mesoamerican understanding that ritual triumph was more important than all-out victory, was a major reason why the Aztecs were ultimately undone by Cortés's small force of conquistadors.

Below: Prisoners of the flower wars knew they had no chance of escape, but they were treated with respect. The illustration is from the Florentine Codex *(1575–77).*

CHAIN OF COMMAND: THE AZTEC ARMY

The *tlatoani* or ruler was the chief army commander. He was expected to demonstrate his own battlefield prowess by leading a military campaign as part of his coronation celebrations. His chief adviser on military matters was the *cihuacóatl* ('female serpent'). This was a position of supreme importance. Tlacaélel, the brother of Moctezuma I Ilhuicamina – who made such an eloquent statement of the values lying behind the flower wars – was *cihuacóatl* to five successive rulers of Tenochtitlán: Itzcóatl, Moctezuma I Ilhuicamina, Axayácatl, Tizoc and Ahuítzotl.

Next in command was a council of four noblemen: the *tlacochcalcatl*, the *tlaccatecatl*, the *tillancalqui* and the

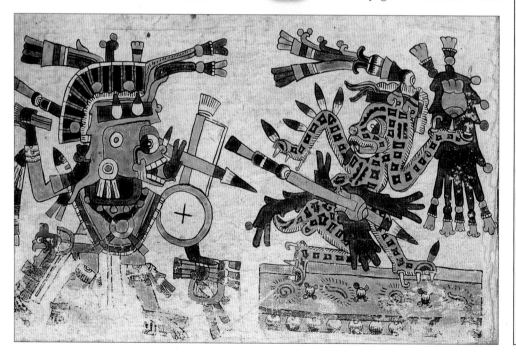

Right: The ocelot, a native wild cat, was the symbol adopted by one group of Aztec warriors.

Below: In a violent phase of its cycle, the planet Venus shoots an ocelot-warrior. This detail is from a Mixtec document, the Codex Cospi.

etzhuanhuanco. They were usually brothers or near relatives of the *tlatoani* himself. Top-ranking warriors reported directly to the council members.

MILITARY ORDERS

The military was the prime promoter of social mobility among the Aztecs. A warrior from the common ranks could rise to all but the very highest army positions by dint of bravery and success in battle. The two supreme orders of warriors were the *cuauhchique* ('Shaved Ones') and the *otontin* ('Otomies'). To be admitted, a warrior must have carried out 20 or more deeds of remarkable bravery and, naturally, also have brought home a great number of prisoners for sacrifice. The elite groups of the jaguar-warriors and the eagle-warriors were members of these top-ranking groups. These elites made the most of their right to wear the feathers, jewellery and cloaks that were emblems of their high standing. In Tenochtitlán, the eagle- and jaguar-warriors had meeting houses within the temple precincts. Here, young boys were initiated into the military way of life from an early age. While still at school, the boys were taught how to handle their weapons, march on campaign and manoeuvre in battle. They learned the importance of discipline and obedience to the military hierarchy and practised using the clubs, shields, darts and spears that were used on the battlefield. The impressively dressed elite warriors mingled with them, sharing tales of their exploits on campaign and cementing the boys' love of army life. Later the boys would compete for the chance to carry equipment and other loads into battle for the elite warriors.

DUTY TO THE EMPIRE

The Aztecs had no standing army; the military hierarchy called up warriors for campaigns as necessary. Each *capultin* – a town or area of a city, based on old tribal clans – was required to provide a unit of around 400 men. They were commanded by a local leader and marched under their

Right: An Aztec terracotta statue shows an eagle-warrior ready for combat. Eagle-warriors were dedicated to 'feeding' the sun with the blood of prisoners.

own standard, but were also grouped in larger divisions of around 8,000 warriors. As many as 25 divisions would be sent on longer campaigns, making a total of 200,000 fighting men.

Before a campaign began, the supreme council dispatched orders for supplies to be collected. Tribute-paying areas had to provide beans, salt, pumpkin seeds, maize meal and maize cakes to feed the army. Army porters carried these supplies.

ON CAMPAIGN

The army would march in a long, ordered procession along the narrow roads of the Aztec empire on its campaigns. Leading the way were the army's barelegged scouts, identifiable by their simple loin-cloths and shirts of white cotton, faces painted with yellow ochre and long hair tied with red ribbons. They were armed with spears and carried conch-shell trumpets, which they used when they needed to send messages to the main ranks of the army behind. With them marched the warrior-priests carrying images of Huitzilopochtli, the martial god in whose name the empire's wars were waged. They were followed by the top warriors and members of the military elite. This group would include the *tlatoani* himself, if he were leading the campaign, together with members of the supreme council.

The army units from Tenochtitlán came next in the train, followed by troops from Tlatelolco, Texcoco and Tlacopán and any other currently allied cities. In the rearguard, many miles down the road from the beginning of the procession, came the troops provided by subject cities of the empire as part of their tribute payment. So narrow were the tracks the army followed that an army unit of 8,000 men might stretch out for as much as 25km (15 miles), according to leading historians.

Left: An illustration from the Codex Mendoza *(c.1541) represents six triumphs in the career of a successful warrior.*

85

INTO BATTLE

Ordinary members of the Aztec army wore a simple wrapping around their thighs and loins and were given a mantle or overgarment of maguey cloth. Some went barefoot into battle adorned with body paint.

HOW THEY FOUGHT

Aztec warriors fought hand-to-hand with stabbing javelins and clubs fitted with blades of the volcanic glass obsidian, protecting themselves with leather-fringed shields. Some of the older or elite warriors wore wooden helmets carved with the symbols of the order to which they belonged. They also used the *atlatl* or spear-thrower, a spear carved with a holding place for a dart. With practice, a warrior could send these darts over great distances with deadly accuracy. The *atlatl* was usually a functional object, made from plain wood for use in battle. But it also had ceremonial uses, and archaeologists have found splendid carved and painted, even gold-covered, spear-throwers. These were probably used by priests impersonating the gods during religious ceremonies.

In a typical battle, the two armies lined up opposite one another on the battlefield. There would have been a blaze of colour as the light caught on plumes and the spears waved by warriors dressed in bright animal skins. The men demonstrated their

Above: *These two magnificent examples of the Aztec warrior's* atlatl, *or spear-thrower, are covered with gold and carved with scenes depicting ritual sacrifices.*

GLADIATORIAL SACRIFICE

A sacrificial ritual celebrating the power of the Aztec warrior was the climax of the festival of Tlacaxipehualiztli ('Flaying of men')held in honour of Xipe Totec, 'Our Lord, the Flayed One', god of spring and vegetation.

In the rite, which the Spanish called 'gladiatorial sacrifice', five prisoners of war were put to death by elite Aztec warriors in a staged conflict. The prisoners, treated as always among the Aztecs with the greatest respect and even reverence as divine offerings, were dressed in a costume that identified them as Xipe Totec and tied to a sacrificial stone. They were given a club covered with feathers with which to defend themselves. Five warriors – two eagle-warriors, two jaguar-warriors and a fifth of either order who was left-handed – were set loose upon them. The battle must have been short, for the warriors fought fiercely with *macáhuitl* (clubs with obsidian blades). The blood of the sacrificed prisoners fed the earth. The Tlacaxipehualiztli festival took place in the build-up to the rainy season. Also as part of Tlacaxipehualiztli, a group of prisoners were slain by the usual method of having their heart ripped from their chest. The bodies were then stripped of their skin. Priests wore the flayed skin in honour of Xipe Totec for 20 days.

Right: A detail from the delicate carving on an Aztec huehuetl, *or wooden drum, represents a jaguar-warrior in his finery.*

---

fearlessness by urging the enemy to do their worst or by dashing out from their own ranks to adopt a threatening or insulting pose. Excitement built as the men's voices rose to a steady roar. The blowing of the conch-shell trumpets

Right: Unlike Cortés and his men, the Aztecs did not have iron armour. A ceramic model gives a detailed impression of the protective jerkins worn by Aztec warriors.

spilled forth and the warriors burst forward, screeching and whooping with bloodlust. They hurled stones into the enemy ranks and let loose the darts from their spear-throwers, roaring as opposing warriors fell, clutching their heads or sides. When the two advancing forces met in hand-to-hand combat, warriors fought desperately with obsidian-bladed clubs which inflicted terrible slicing wounds.

REWARDS FOR VALOUR

An Aztec warrior could express his devotion to the gods through valour in battle, but there were also many worldly incentives to urge soldiers to high achievements. Those who impressed in war and won significant numbers of sacrificial captives were presented with suits of animal skin. These soldiers could win the right to drink the favourite Aztec alcoholic drink, *pulque*, in public places, to dine in the royal palaces and to keep concubines for their pleasure. Warriors who particularly distinguished themselves, by repeatedly proving their bravery or by taking captive many scores of prisoners, might be admitted to one of the elite companies of warriors such as the jaguar- or eagle-warriors. They had the right to wear sumptuous feather headdresses, leather bracelets, jewellery and cloaks adorned with feathers and were given their marks of rank at special presentation ceremonies, often in the presence of the *tlatoani* himself. The jaguar-warriors had the right to wear a jaguar skin over their cotton body armour, while eagle-warriors wore an eagle-head helmet.

Left: A detail from the Florentine Codex *(1575–7) shows a prisoner of war making a show of defiance when surrounded by four jaguar-warriors in a gladiatorial sacrifice.*

87

RUNNING THE AZTEC EMPIRE

The capture of the city of Azcapotzalco and the ritual slaughter of its ruler, Maxtla, in 1428, marked the end of the Tepanec empire and the establishment of the Triple Alliance of Tenochtitlán, Texcoco and Tlacopán that was the driving force behind Aztec expansion.

Below: This stone standard-bearer was found at the heart of the Aztec empire, the Great Pyramid in Tenochtitlán. He carried a banner outside a temple honouring Huitzilopochtli, Tláloc or another major Aztec deity.

These three independent city-states shared both in the military activity needed to conquer and control the lands of the Aztec empire and in the inflow of tribute that was its reward.

CONSOLIDATION

Following the defeat of Azcapotzalco, Itzcóatl, who was the *tlatoani* or ruler of Tenochtitlán, wasted no time in attempting to consolidate the position of his city-state and of the alliance. With the assistance of forces from Texcoco and Tlacopán, Itzcóatl led a campaign to conquer the agricultural settlements of Cuitlahuac, Culhuacán, Mixquic and Xochimilco on Lake Xochimilco to the south of Tenochtitlán.

Netzahualcóyotl, the exiled prince of Texcoco who had led the capture of Azcapotzalco, had then to attend to unfinished local business, for he was not yet established as ruler of his city-state. His father, Ixtlilxóchitl, had been ruler of that city, but in 1418 had been killed in the course of a failed war against the Tepanec warrior leader Tezozómoc. For some years Netzahualcóyotl, who had witnessed his father's death, lived in hiding, but in time he won the support of his uncle, the México leader Itzcóatl, and played a major part in the war against Azcapotzalco. Now, with Itzcóatl's backing, he eliminated elements hostile to his position and re-established his family's rule in Texcoco.

EXPANSION

The armies of the Triple Alliance looked further afield and prepared for a major campaign to conquer the fertile Tlalhuica territories that lay beyond the Ajusco Mountains, well to the south of Lake Xochimilco. They raised a vast army that marched behind a company of scouts and priests across the forest-covered Ajusco range and down to the plain beyond. The tramping soldiers carried their weapons and battle-costumes, while companies of porters transported food and other supplies. They took their objective, Cuauhnahuac, the main town of the region, and returned in triumph, carrying booty and leading prisoners for sacrifice. The Tlalhuica lands had been a valuable possession of the Tepanecs, the previous imperial power. In taking them, the Triple Alliance widened its horizons, seeking to establish itself on an equal footing with the great Tepanec state established by Tezozómoc.

The Aztec empire was a network of dependencies paying tribute to the cities of the Triple Alliance but otherwise retaining a sense of their own independence. As they acquired new territories, it was the Aztecs' policy to leave the conquered rulers in place, as long as the arranged tribute was provided on time. The initial plan, formed in the reign of Itzcóatl, was to replace local rulers with centrally appointed ones. However, Netzahualcóyotl, who had first-hand experience of the intrigues and plotting of royal factions in Texcoco, argued that leaving rulers nominally in control of their domains would reduce ill-feeling and the likelihood of revolt. Itzcóatl saw the success of Netzahualcóyotl's policy in the lands controlled by Texcoco and adopted the practice himself.

SUCCESSION

Itzcóatl's successor, Moctezuma I Ilhuicamina, consolidated the gains that had been made before embarking, in 1458, on a series of military campaigns that greatly expanded the imperial possessions. He was succeeded by his grandson Axayácatl who, in a reign of 13 years (1469–81), further expanded the empire, conquering 37 towns

Above: A battle scene from the Codex Tlaxcala *shows conquistadors overcoming Aztec resistance in the region of Culhuacán.*

in the Toluca Valley, the Gulf Coast, the Puebla Valley, Guerrero and to the north of the Valley of Mexico. He was a skilled leader and soldier, who succeeded in putting down a rebellion by Tenochtitlán's neighbouring sister-city, Tlatelolco, in 1473.

SETBACKS

Axayácatl's reign was marred six years later by a major defeat, when the Tarascans of Michoacán humbled the imperial army. In two disastrous engagements near Taximaloyán (modern Charo), the 32,000-strong Aztec army was crushed. Only 200 Méxica warriors limped home to Tenochtitlán, accompanied by fewer than 2,000 comrades from Texcoco, Xochimilco and other imperial cities. Axayácatl put this defeat behind him and led a successful campaign to put down rebellions on the Gulf Coast.

Axayácatl's brother, Tizoc, became ruler of Tenochtitlán in 1481, but his reign was a military disaster. A *tlatoani* had to lead a war as part of his coronation rites: the campaign was expected to be a triumphant procession, culminating in a magnificent sacrifice of legions of newly captured victims. In Tizoc's case, the coronation war was a near-defeat that produced only 40 prisoners. He failed to build on Axayácatl's expansionist triumphs, merely putting down revolts in already conquered parts of the empire. Rebellions became more frequent as his weakness became obvious and his reign was brought to a premature end, probably by poisoning, in 1486. Despite its military failure, Tizoc's reign produced a magnificent celebration in stone of the empire and its divine mandate.

Tizoc was succeeded by his brother Ahuítzotl. A natural leader and fearless warrior, he restored the pride of the imperial army. He led a renewed expansion, capturing 45 towns and adding great sweeps of territory to the empire, notably

Oaxaca, rich in gold, painted cotton and cochineal. Under his rule, the empire stretched from the land of the Huastecs in the north to Xoconochco in the south-east and Itzapán in the south-west.

In 1502, Ahuítzotl was succeeded by Moctezuma II Xocoyotzin, the last independent ruler of the Aztec empire. Moctezuma II further expanded the empire and consolidated it by conquering territories and countries within the imperial boundaries that had not been subjugated by his predecessors. He fought wars against Tlaxcala and Huexotzingo without marked success but with the unfortunate effect of generating a profound hatred for the Aztecs in those cities. When Hernán Cortés arrived there he found willing and unexpected allies for a war against Tenochtitlán. Overall, however, his campaigns were successful. At the time of Cortés' arrival in 1519, the empire's influence covered almost 200,000sq km (77,000sq miles) and was still growing. Moctezuma believed himself to be 'master of the world'.

Below: Aztec military might was the key to enforcing the obedience and cooperation of fellow Mesoamericans within the empire.

TRIBUTE AND TRADE

Each of the three city-states of the Triple Alliance had its own tributary areas within the empire. When they fought together on joint campaigns, tribute was divided along agreed lines: 40 per cent each for Tenochtitlán and Texcoco and 20 per cent for Tlacopán. Usually, the entire tribute would be despatched to Tenochtitlán and then sorted for redistribution. On occasion, one city agreed to assign tribute from within its tributary area to another of the allies: for example, Texcoco arranged for tribute from Tepetlaoztoc, within the Texcocan region of dependency, to be paid to Tenochtitlán as a reward for military support during the Texcocan leader Netzahualcóyotl's rise to power.

Tribute was paid to individuals as well as to cities: a ruler would often reward his committed followers with the promise of tribute payments. The wealth of many prominent lords was boosted by deliveries of rare goods from distant territories.

Left: Scholars believe that this stone warrior once stood in a building celebrating the Aztecs' divinely ordained power.

TRIBUTE PAYMENTS

Once a city or chiefdom had accepted defeat in battle, its rulers were required to agree payment of set amounts of tribute to a fixed schedule. The Aztec conquerors would usually appoint a tribute collector to see that regular payment was made. The use or threat of violence kept tribute flowing for, if payment of tribute stopped, the armies of the Triple Alliance were mobilized to enforce the tribute agreement.

Tribute payments ranged from basic produce such as maize, beans, chillies and cotton clothing to rarer and more valuable items such as jaguar skins, gold or jade ornaments, cacao beans and brightly coloured feathers. Pages from the *Codex Mendoza* detail the tribute required of particular provinces and the schedule for its delivery. For example, Cuauhnahuac was required to send

Above: In an image from the Florentine Codex, *Moctezuma II watches serenely as tribute offerings are arrayed before him.*

tribute of skirts, loincloths and cloaks every six months and war costumes and decorated shields once each year.

WEALTH OF THE EMPIRE

Diego Durán's 1581 work, *History of the Indies of New Spain*, lists the great variety of tribute paid to the lords of Tenochtitlán. This included feathers and decorated blankets, mats and seats, painted cotton clothes, and also parrots, eagles and geese.

Some tributary areas sent live lions and tigers in cages, while others sent deer, quails and rabbits. Some tributary areas sent insects, including spiders, scorpions and bees in their hives. From the coastal dependencies there came seashells, coloured stones, pearls and turtleshells, and from the city workshops came metalwork in the shape of cups and bowls and plates.

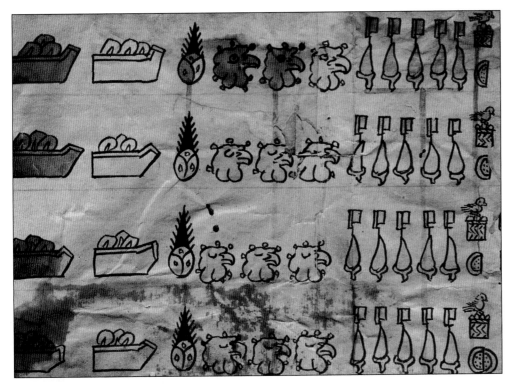

Left: Tribute exacted by the Aztec imperial power from villages within the empire included corn and trees.

routes, were engaged in alliances cemented by marriage or other ties of kinship. While their rulers remained nominally in power, some of their prominent relatives and allies were required to live at court in Tenochtitlán or Texcoco and pay homage to the *tlatoani* during state celebrations. Any goods they sent to Tenochtitlán or the other cities of the Triple Alliance were treated as gifts. Itzcóatl, Netzahualcóyotl and Moctezuma I built a series of alliances through negotiation and marriage.

Below: In Tenochtitlán towering architecture and imposing statues impressed on imperial subjects the invincibility and power of the Aztecs.

The wives and courtesans of prominent Tenochtitláns benefited from tribute payments of women's blouses and elegant skirts decorated in coloured thread with designs of roses, eagles and feathers, while other tributes included the white cotton shifts worn by women who served in the temples and the plain clothing worn by servants. Forested areas, Durán wrote, were required to send in wood, charcoal and the bark of trees for use as fuel. Food tribute included maize, beans and chillies, potatoes, avocados, bananas, pineapples, plums and honey. Rose flowers and bushes were provided for the gardens of Tenochtitlán nobles. Some provinces paid tribute in war materials: padded cotton armour, wooden shields, bows and arrows, flint arrowheads, darts, slings and stones. Some areas sent building materials such as stone and lime, while the poorer provinces, which were not able to provide worthy tribute, sent women, girls and boys to be shared among the nobility as concubines and slaves.

THE FLOW OF TRIBUTE

Demand for tribute was meticulously planned to meet needs in the cities of the Triple Alliance. In the latter years of the empire, the amount of elite produce, such as jaguar skins or golden ornaments used in warrior or priestly costumes, rose as a proportion of total tribute, reflecting an increased number of far-flung provinces able to provide such goods and a growth in the nobility's taste for extravagant display.

The flow of tribute was essential to the great religious sacrifices held in cities of the Triple Alliance. Feathers and materials were used in costumes, and tributary provinces provided the building materials and labourers used to construct the temples of Tenochtitlán.

The movement of high-quality tribute goods took place alongside commercial trading by merchants. Some combined trade with information-gathering in the marketplaces of potentially rebellious cities, working as undercover spies. Merchants working on behalf of the emperor, seeking or selling elite goods, could gather important information or make significant friendships that might facilitate political alliances within the empire.

Some provinces were not required to pay tribute to a set schedule. Instead, these cities or chiefdoms, usually situated in strategic areas such as border regions or at important sites on trade

CAMPAIGNS OF MOCTEZUMA I

Moctezuma I Ilhuicamina is celebrated as the 'father of empire' who greatly expanded the Aztec lands. However, he did not begin significant campaigns of distant conquest until 18 years after his coronation in 1440. He spent those first years building and strengthening alliances within regions already conquered by Tenochtitlán and fighting a long, intermittent war against Chalco at the eastern end of Lake Chalco that ended in victory in the mid-1450s. He also faced a series of devastating famines in the years 1450–54. These ended, presumably thanks to the gods' blessing, following the New Fire Ceremony over which the emperor presided at the close of the 52-year cycle in 1454 and the rebuilding work he began on the Great Pyramid in Tenochtitlán.

THE TIZOC AND SUN STONES

The carving known as the Stone of Tizoc, found in Tenochtitlán's ruins in 1790, projects the empire of the Triple Alliance as an enduring achievement heroically inspired by the *tlatoani* and supported by the gods of Sun and Earth.

The cylindrical stone is carved on its upper face with a sun-disc that sends rays to east, west, north and south and, at the rim, a string of all-seeing stars. On the cylinder's bottom rim four faces of the earth-goddess Tlaltecuhtli represent the land on which the Aztec army marches, balancing the upper sun image associated with Huitzilopochtli, in whose honour the armies conquer the enemy. Around the side of the stone, Aztec soldiers are represented holding prisoners from captured cities by the hair, proudly surveyed by the *tlatoani*, Tizoc, who is dressed in the regalia of the gods Huitzilopochtli and Tezcatlipoca.

Another great carved cylinder bearing an image of the sun god – known to scholars as the Sun Stone – was carved in the era of Moctezuma I and subsequently found close to the ruins of the Great Pyramid.

EARLY CAMPAIGNS

The ruler's first major campaign was into the Huastec region in the Gulf of Mexico, an area rich in natural resources. The army coped impressively with the logistical difficulties of the long march needed to take war to the northern coast and used canny tactics in pretending to retreat in order to lure local forces into a trap. After a triumphant return to Tenochtitlán, the next move was to the south-east to capture the trading centre of Coixtlahuaca in the forbidding mountain valleys of the Mixtec lands. The pretext for war was that Aztec merchants had reported being both insulted and attacked in Coixtlahuaca,

Right: This exquisite Mixtec pectoral ornament, made of gold and turquoise, represents a warrior's shield and arrows.

although the main attraction was the tribute that might be exacted from an area celebrated for its manuscript work, weaving, gold- and metalwork, and ceramics. Following careful preparations, an army of some 200,000 troops left the city of Tenochtitlán and headed south, accompanied by 100,000 porters bearing supplies. In the rugged land around Coixtlahuaca, this great force came face to face with the Mixtecs and their Huexotzingan and Tlaxcalán allies. Hostilities began with taunts, then spear-throwers and slings were brought to bear before the two armies charged. The Aztecs broke the Mixtec line, and pursued them mercilessly through the streets of Coixtlahuaca. Eventually they reached the temple pyramid, which they climbed and torched to signal their triumph. Any Mixtec warriors who escaped fled in despair to the hills, while their brothers were rounded up.

Right: The Mixtecs conquered by Moctezuma I's great army were celebrated for their metalworking. This Mixtec eagle's head, of solid gold, was intended to be worn as a lip ornament.

As the dust settled, a group of Mixtec chieftains agreed to pay tribute as a dependency of Tenochtitlán. Their ruler, Atonal, was strangled and his relatives were taken into slavery but, in the usual Aztec procedure, the other local chiefs were permitted to remain in power so long as tribute was forthcoming on the agreed schedule. The rewards for the Aztec victory included tribute of blankets, greenstone beads, feathers, gold dust, red dye, cotton, chillies and salt.

The conquerors also took home whatever they could plunder from the town, a long line of prisoners for sacrifice and religious statues from the sacked Mixtec temple. The worshippers of Huitzilopochtli would keep enemy idols 'captive' within the ceremonial area in the city of Tenochtitlán as one more sign of Aztec supremacy. Moctezuma's army returned in triumph to its homeland, its soldiers hailed as heroes by cheering crowds. The long lines of prisoners were led up the steep sides of the Great Pyramid to be dispatched in Huitzilopochtli's honour on the sacrificial stone.

Below: A detail from the Stone of Tizoc, carved during the rule of Tizoc (1469–81), shows Aztec victories over the Mixtecs.

EXTENDING THE EMPIRE

These were the first of many famous victories for Moctezuma I Ilhuicamina. The following year he sent the army eastwards to the town of Cosamaloapán, and afterwards to Ahuilzapán and Cuetlachtlán. Each time they returned in triumph, bearing tribute and plunder, having extended the might and influence of the empire and secured strategic settlements on trading routes.

When Moctezuma I Ilhuicamina's fruitful reign came to an end with the ruler's death in 1469, the Aztec lands stretched north-east to Xilotepec, east to Cosamaloapán and south to Oaxaca.

CITY-STATES IN CONSTANT CONFLICT

There was no Maya empire. Throughout the Classic Period (*c.*250BC–AD900), the city-states of the Maya lands were almost constantly at war, but no one central state emerged to establish rule over the others. Scholars liken the Maya cities to the city-states of ancient Greece: all shared a common language, religion and group of cultural assumptions, but all were strongly independent and often at each other's throats. To judge from surviving inscriptions, the dynastic ruler of a Maya state gained great prestige if he could capture a rival king, hold him captive, inflict punishing tortures on him and finally decapitate him. In the Classic Period at least, he appears not to have set much store by capturing land for himself or his subjects. The boundaries between the city-states remained largely unchanged over many years that were marked by great bloodshed.

It might be that some city-states were more powerful than others. In recent years, some scholars have suggested that

Below: Facial paint and helmet feathers impress this Maya warrior's importance and aggressive intent on his enemies.

Above: An image from a Maya codex depicts the disruption and misery of war. Two prisoners are marched into captivity.

the more powerful cities held the weaker ones in a client relationship that can be likened to the relationship between tribute-paying cities and the Triple Alliance in the Aztec empire. One of these powerful Maya cities was Calakmul. In the mid-6th century AD and afterwards it had control over Naranjo, Dos Pilas, El Perú and Cancuén. Calakmul had a great rival in Tikal and the two cities endured a long and bitter conflict.

There is also evidence that Maya cities built alliances by forging links through dynastic marriage in the same way as the Aztecs. The daughters of the nobility at Tikal, for example, appear to have made marriages with members of the ruling dynasty at Copán, Yaxchilán and Naranjo. The children of such marriages would have had strong links through their maternal family to Tikal. Scholars have demonstrated from surviving inscriptions that a noble bride from Tikal who married into the dynasty of Naranjo had a son known as Scroll Squirrel, who in turn made his wedding with a bride from Tikal, further strengthening the alliance.

HOW AND WHY THEY FOUGHT

The high-ranking Maya warrior went into battle gloriously attired. He wore a wooden helmet with brightly coloured quetzal or parrot feathers that fell across his shoulders, and painted his face with war paint. Jade jewellery around his neck and on his wrists added to the dazzling image. Maya soldiers, like the Aztecs, wore quilted jackets of cotton body armour that had been soaked in salt water to make it tougher. The Spaniards were so impressed with the effectiveness of this body protector that they adopted it in place of their own steel armour.

The principal Maya tactic was to take the enemy by surprise. The Spaniards found that Maya tactics of ambush and raiding made them a troublesome enemy. Campaigns often began with a stealthy raid into the enemy lands to seize captives. Once battle was joined, fighting was fierce, accompanied by a musical cacophony produced by the beating of drums and the blowing of whistles and conch shells. The war leaders and priests carrying divine images would occupy the centre of the battle line and were flanked by groups of foot soldiers.

Like the Aztec soldier, the Maya warrior fought mainly with a war club fitted with obsidian blades and a spear-thrower that could send darts flying over great distances when handled with skill. He also used a sling and large stones. Some accounts report that the Maya attacked by throwing fire or the nests of hornets and other stinging insects into the enemy ranks. For close-quarters fighting, the Maya warrior also had distinctive weapons in the shape of a three-pronged knife made from shell and another knife with a broad flint blade.

As among the Aztecs, warriors fought less to inflict violence than to seize booty and capture prisoners. The top prize was the ruler of a rival city. If he were

Below: A lintel at Yaxchilán shows King Shield Jaguar receiving his war gear from his wife Lady Xoc prior to battle in AD724.

captured and his capture was made known, the battle was at an end. His warriors fled if they could escape. The king faced torture and sacrificial death.

WHEN THEY FOUGHT

The fighting season was kept separate from the times of planting and harvest. Campaigns often took place in October. If they went on too long, they might well fail. There are reports of Maya campaigns fading away as the farmers fled the army to attend to their fields.

Although war was effectively continuous in that there were no prolonged periods of peace, campaigns did not need to be of particularly long duration. The Maya

Above: A Classic Maya vase (AD600–900) shows a well-equipped warrior preparing to use his spear-thrower.

city-states were small and in stark contrast to the great distances covered by the army of the Triple Alliance, a Maya force often needed to march for no more than one day to reach its enemy.

The city-states of the Maya lowlands in the Classic Period were each ruled by a dynasty that claimed descent from a historical founder and – usually – also from the gods. Each dynasty was identified by its own emblem, which would be written in inscriptions after the personal name of the ruler and his consorts.

WAR BETWEEN MAYAPÁN AND CHICHÉN ITZÁ

According to Spanish and native accounts, in the 13th and 14th centuries Mayapán was the capital of a league of city-states in northern Yucatán that also included Chichén Itzá and Uxmal. The dominant city, Mayapán, was destroyed in the 20-year period 1441–61 at the close of a struggle between tribal dynasties that had begun 250 years earlier. The dating is that given in the *Books of Chilam Balam,* which identifies events according to the Maya Short Count. (This is a variant of the Maya Long Count. The Short Count places events in 20-year periods within a cycle of 256¼ years.) The two dynasties that came head to head were members of the Itzá people.

Below: This unsettling face was created for an incense vase found at the Itzá city of Mayapán, home to the Cocom dynasty.

WHO WERE THE ITZÁ?

In the Maya chronicles, these incomers to Yucatán are described in contemptuous terms as 'lewd ones', 'tricksters' and 'those without mothers and fathers'. They clearly did not speak the local language, because the chroniclers also called them 'people who use our tongue brokenly'. Scholars believe that the Itzá were a group of Maya who came north from the Tabasco region between Yucatán and central Mexico. The chronicles describe how they lived in the city of Chakanputún (perhaps Champotón in the coastal area of Campeche), but were driven from that place by force *c.*AD1200 and made their way north into Yucatán. They settled the city of Chichén Itzá in the period 1224–44. The Itzá renamed the city, originally called *Uucil-abnal* ('Seven Bushes'). Its new name meant 'Openings

Above: A stucco mural at Mayapán includes space for the insertion of the skull of a slaughtered prisoner of war.

of the Wells of Itzá'. They promoted the worship of the sacred well or *cenote* in the city, where offerings have been found by archaeologists. The Itzá also appear to have been devout worshippers of Ix Chel, consort of the supreme Maya deity Itzamná, in her guise as goddess of medicine.

The coming of the Itzá might have been the second settlement by Mexican incomers. Traditional histories suggest that Chichén Itzá was taken over by Toltec emigrants from Tula in AD967–987, perhaps even led by the historical prince Topiltzin who was associated with the god Quetzalcóatl. There is strong evidence of Toltec style at Chichén Itzá dating from this period. However, many archaeologists doubt whether this points to a Toltec invasion and argue that it simply represents the strength of Toltec religious and archaeological influence spread by trading contacts.

Above: The Group of the Thousand Columns was erected to surround the Temple of the Warriors at Chichén Itzá.

STRUGGLE FOR POWER

The Itzá founded Mayapán in 1263–83, leaving some of the tribe in charge at Chichén Itzá. In about 1283 the vicious quarrel between Itzá dynasties that would result in the city's downfall began. (An added complication of the dating given in the *Books of Chilam Balam* is that events are identified by their place within a 256¼-year cycle, but there is no information as to which 256¼-year period is meant. As a result, there is disagreement among scholars as to when the Itzá refounded Chichén Itzá. Some authorities believe that they settled Chichén Itzá and founded Mayapán within an earlier time cycle almost 300 years before, in AD967–87.)

The Cocom dynasty of the Itzá in Mayapán seized power from the Tutul Xiu dynasty in Chichén Itzá. The leader of the Cocom dynasty hired a mercenary army from Tabasco to enforce his will.

These soldiers, who were perhaps Toltec emigrants, swept all before them with their superior weapons. They came armed with bows and arrows, perhaps bringing them for the first time into Yucatán. Their skill with the *atlatl* or spear-thrower was extraordinary and they fought fiercely at close quarters with the spear.

The capture of the city of Chichén Itzá by this Mexican force was depicted on frescoes in Chichén Itzá and in carvings on gold discs thrown as offerings into the *cenote*. There is a marked contrast between Mexican and Maya weapons and appearance in these images. The Cocom rebuilt

Right: A clay warrior left as a grave offering on Jaina Island wears quilted cotton armour.

Chichén Itzá. The Tutul Xiu princes were driven from their city, but they did not give up. They settled near the ruins of Uxmal and nursed their hatred in exile from generation to generation, awaiting their chance. The Cocoms finally met their end in the era 1441–61.

Conspiracy made Tutul Xiu revenge possible. A Tutal Xiu chief by the name of Ah Xupán plotted with nobles in Mayapán to rise up against the Cocom chiefs. All of the Cocom princes and nobles were slaughtered. The dynasty was no more and the city of Mayapán was destroyed and left to decay.

Some Itzá exiles, however, made an enduring new home. They founded the city of Tayasal on an island in the Lake Petén Itzá in northern Guatemala. Here they survived until 1697, when they were finally conquered by the invading Spaniards.

THE MAYA COLLAPSE

In the 9th century AD, the cities of the Southern Maya Lowlands began to be abandoned. The jungle vegetation that the Maya farmers had tamed grew back and, in time, even swamped the great temples and plazas where priests and kings had celebrated royal power. Further to the north, in the Puuc Hills and towards the tip of the Yucatán peninsula, cities such as Mayapán, Uxmal, Labná and Chichén Itzá were thriving, making the decline of the lowland settlements all the more puzzling.

A HUGE HUMAN TRAGEDY

This was undoubtedly a human tragedy on a vast scale. Within four or five generations, a great civilization faded. Archaeologists and historians dubbed this remarkable development 'the Maya collapse' and for years speculated as to its causes. Why would a determined people abandon these great constructions of stone, which had been laboriously erected over many years in honour of their ancestors and gods?

THE END OF THE CLASSIC MAYA

In the years before they were left to the jungle, the Southern Lowland Maya cities one by one ended their established practice of erecting stone columns carved with the dates in the Maya Long Count of their ruling dynasties and their kings' battle victories and religious sacrifices. In archaeological terms, the Classic Period of ancient Maya civilization (c.AD250–900) is demarcated as the years during which the cities carved these stelae. The final Classic Period Maya inscription was cut in AD909.

In the cities of Yucatán in the north, meanwhile, craftsmen continued to carve inscriptions, but they did not celebrate dynastic achivements.

Above: This detail from a mural at Bonampak depicts the Maya warrior's jaguar-skin costume and feathered helmet.

Left: One of many figures of Maya warriors left in graves at Jaina Island appears serene before battle.

DIFFERING THEORIES

Archaeological evidence shows that the Maya population in the Southern Lowlands collapsed in the 9th century AD. Between AD830 and AD930, numbers fell by one third. Some writers suggested the Maya were undone by an epidemic of disease, a natural disaster such as an earthquake or hurricane, or even by an invasion.

One simplified theory is that the Maya people effectively wiped one another out in the lowlands. Centuries of almost incessant fighting between the city-states led to severe damage to the environment and greatly depleted the population. In time, the combination of falling numbers and inadequate food supply meant that the cities could not be maintained and so the cities were gradually abandoned. The latest scholarly thinking is broadly in agreement with this picture, although it makes significant changes to the causal links of the argument. The consensus is that the trigger for the 'Maya collapse' was over- rather than under-population. The Classic Maya civilization was so successful that its population grew beyond

Above: Over-population followed by intensive farming seems to have been the cause of the southern Maya collapse.

Right: In a Bonampak mural the halach uinic (lord) and lieutenants, standing, watch as prisoners have their nails torn out.

the point at which the land could support it. The farmers turned to highly intensive methods of cultivation, which disturbed the ecological balance and in time this led to severe environmental damage. Disease may also have contributed. Now the population began to fall, as evidenced in the archaeological record. Rising levels of hunger and fear over future shortages fuelled ever-more violent exchanges between city-states, which competed for the fertile land available. Finally, the area was abandoned.

Throughout the previous centuries, when the Maya cities were locked in almost continuous conflict, there had been few changes in the boundaries of the city-states. Wars were conducted in large part in search of royal or noble captives for sacrifice and for common soldiers to be sold as slaves. But there is evidence from the last of the carved stelae (see box) that in the final years, lowland Maya cities were seeking to expand in an entirely new way, fighting for land more than for honour.

The modern scholarly argument therefore suggests that intensifying war between the city-states was a symptom rather than a cause of the collapse of the southern Maya region. The Maya fought themselves to a standstill as they competed for land – and perhaps also sought to capture armies of prisoners in order to mount lavish sacrifices that might be enough to bring back times of plenty.

CHAPTER 5

ROYAL POWER, LAW AND ORDER

In the Maya city of Palenque, in northern Chiapas, three temple-pyramids known to archaeologists as the Temple of the Cross, the Temple of the Foliated Cross and the Temple of the Sun contain stone panels carved with images and hieroglyphic inscriptions that establish an ancestral line for the dynasty of Palenque's most celebrated ruler, Lord Pacal. The images present the royal ruler as a link to the realm of the gods and ancestors, as the guarantor of fertility, rain and crops, and as a warrior, powerful in battle. These were the three key roles performed by the Maya ruler to justify his pre-eminent position.

The Aztec *tlatoani*, or ruler of each city-state, was understood to be both a promoter of fertility and a great warrior prince. His ritual names included *inan* and *ita altepetl* ('Mother and Father of the City') and he took the role of rainbringer in an important fertility ceremony conducted each year on Mount Tláloc. He was essentially the chief priest, conducting certain sacrificial rites himself, and was understood to assume divine power during his complex coronation rites. The power of the gods burned in him and was refreshed from time to time in ritual sacrifices. He was the living image of the warrior god Huitzilopochtli and the army's commander-in-chief. As part of the coronation rituals he had to conduct a military campaign to celebrate his divinely ordained election to the post.

Left: At Palenque, city of King Pacal, a wooded hill looms behind the raised Temple of the Foliated Cross (left).

STRUCTURES OF POWER

The rulers of Classic Period Maya states were dynastic leaders revered by their people as 'holy kings'. A man such as King Chan Muwan of Bonampak held sway, from a canopied throne protected by a curtain and sometimes covered with jaguar skins, over a large palace retinue that included his extended family, military staff, kitchen workers, dancers with a band of musicians and the *ak k'u hun* (chief scribe), himself in charge of a team of artists, sculptors and scribes. The important position of *sahal*, head of the military staff, was usually filled by a close relative of the king. A *sahal* could be dispatched to govern a provincial town.

The Spanish conquistadors encountered a similar situation in 16th-century Yucatán. Each state was governed by a ruler known as *halach uinic* ('true man'), who governed with the support of a council that was doubtless appointed from his blood relatives. He lived in great splendour in the state's main city at the head of an impressive retinue, receiving the highly prized cacao and other produce from the lands he governed and setting himself apart by the magnificence of his appearance and many layers of ritual. Like the Aztec *tlatoani*, the *halach uinic* was viewed in a paternal light; the Spaniards said he was 'father' and 'lord' of the city. He appointed officials known as batabs whose job was to govern provincial towns, with the support of a council. Batabs were magistrates and war leaders as well as administrators.

The Maya ruler took one legitimate wife, but also kept concubines. His wife was greatly revered and, on the evidence of the Bonampak murals, she cut a truly magnificent figure. She is depicted at Bonampak as wearing a necklace and earrings, with swirling hair tied up and a red stole on her arm, setting off the fine white dress that she wears.

STONE RECORDS

In the Classic Period, the holy kings of Maya cities such as Piedras Negras, Tikal, Yaxchilán, Quiriguá and Palenque erected inscribed stelae, thrones, wall panels,

Left: A cylindrical vessel left in a tomb in the Maya city of Tikal represents a splendidly attired lord receiving a visitor.

Left: One of the kings of Copán adorns the lid of a ceramic vase left as a mortuary offering c.AD650–800.

door lintels and other monuments recording their accession and its major anniversaries, together with the duration and major military triumphs of their reign and significant ritual sacrifices. At Piedras Negras, for example, each king appears to have set up a monument celebrating his accession on its fifth anniversary. The inscriptions record the anniversary, the date the ruler came to the throne and an earlier date that scholars suggest may be his date of birth or the date on which he was named. The ruler then set up new monuments every five years for as long as his reign lasted. These monuments were carved with an 'accession motif', identified by Tatiana Proskouriakoff. It shows a figure seated on a throne at the top of a ladder, with footsteps visible on a mat over the ladder, indicating the ruler had climbed to his position of royal pre-eminence.

MODES OF SUCCESSION

In the Classic Period, royal power was almost always inherited from father to son, but there is evidence that the line could pass through the daughter in some instances. At Tikal, the daughter of King Kan Boar was given a remarkably rich burial that included valuable imported oyster shell and the skeleton of a spider monkey. Kan Boar's daughter, who is known to archaeologists as 'the Lady of Tikal', is shown on a lintel standing at the right hand of her husband, who succeeded her father as king.

The evidence suggests that a woman could succeed her father in the royal palace only as a wife. Her husband would be 'adopted' by her father and become the rightful heir in her place. Their children would then inherit the throne. In some cases, the son of a royal marriage was not considered fit to rule and power might be passed to his brother, or, if no male member of the immediate family was available, to a more distant relative from the ruling council.

Among the Aztecs, succession was not hereditary. An election was held among the nobles of the highest ranks to determine who should succeed the *tlatoani* and the new ruler was then blessed, following complex coronation rites, by the high priest. However, the election was essentially token. The old

Above: This shell, delicately carved with the prominent nose and features of a Maya nobleman, was worn as a pendant.

ruler would nominate a successor and it would usually have been clear who this would be, for the ruler-in-waiting generally filled the role of *tlaccatecatl* on the elite military council. The appointment was then approved by the nobles' council, although sometimes the leaders of Texcoco and Tlacopán were asked for their input. The successor generally came from among the ruler's close blood relatives. At Tenochtitlán, three grandsons of Moctezuma I Ilhuicamina took power in turn; Axayácatl, Tizoc and Ahuítzotl. In Texcoco, sons usually succeeded fathers.

Left: Moctezuma II prepares for coronation as tlatoani *in an illustration from the* Codex Durán *(1579–81).*

THE POWER OF APPEARANCE

Both Maya kings and Aztec rulers dressed in great splendour as a mark of status and to associate themselves with the gods whose authority they claimed.

THE COSTUME OF KINGS

Classic Period Maya kings wore racks on their backs to support large headdress frames that sometimes rose a metre or more above the brow. The rack and the headdress frame, both made of wood, were covered with elaborate decorative designs which used shells, carved jade,

---

MAYA KINGSHIP

The magnificent appearance of the Young Maize God in ceramic and other imagery made him a fitting representative of Maya kingship.

The Young Maize God, mythical father of the Hero Twins Hunahpú and Xbalanqué, was patron deity of scribes, as well as a divine embodiment of Maya royalty. He is depicted with splendid jewellery, a royal headdress and a long, tonsured head whose shape represents that of an ear of maize. Sometimes, his fine headdress contains an image of a jester god. On ceramics, the Young Maize God is often shown twice or as one of a pair of twins, reflecting the fact that the father of the Hero Twins, One Hunahpú, descended to Xibalba with his twin brother Seven Hunahpú to play the ball game with the gods of that frightful place. Scholars can only speculate why the Young Maize God should be a patron of scribes. They point to the fact that the paper used for Maya books was made by soaking bark in the same way that maize was treated to make dough, usually using the same water that had been used for the maize.

---

feathers and textiles. The long, bright green plumes of the quetzal bird were the most highly prized. The headdress often contained the mask of the rain god Chac or the sun god Ahau Kin.

Some kings wore the stick bundles of the scribe in their headdress, indicating both the high status of the scribe and the fact that the king was literate. The king wore his hair long and wove jewellery and ornaments into it. He built his nose up into a great beak, using putty, wore large ornaments in the enlarged lobes of his ears and had his teeth filed and inlays of jade added.

The king dressed in specific and different costumes when performing his various roles as priest, war leader and civil ruler. In each case, the king carried a symbol of his authority. Along with leading nobles, the king wore a ceremonial version of the costume worn by players of the ball game. This must have been donned for rites associated with the game.

Below: Scholars identify this figure from a Maya vase as a palace dignitary attendant on the king.

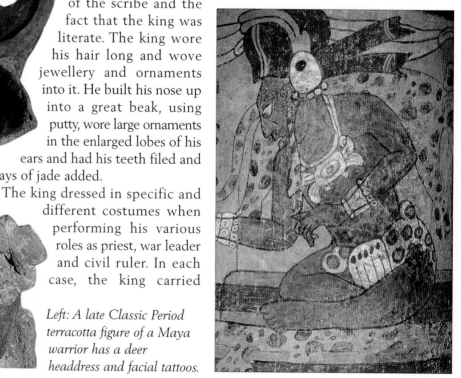

Left: A late Classic Period terracotta figure of a Maya warrior has a deer headdress and facial tattoos.

New World, and it is now held by the Museum für Völkerkunde, Vienna. Scholars believe that this particular headdress, which contains 450 quetzal feathers, was worn by priests, possibly when representing Quetzalcóatl himself in temple rites.

Below: A late Classic Period figurine represents a Maya king as both a warrior, with a shield, and a ball player, with a padded protective belt. He is also associated with the rain god Chac.

Above: The decoration on a cylindrical vase grave offering from Tikal depicts a noble with elongated earlobes and large earrings.

Maya kings also appear to have played the ball game, and carvings survive showing kings in the protective costumes worn for the game. A stone panel from La Amelia, Guatemala, depicts the King of Dos Pilas performing a dance of triumph or ritual importance in his game clothes, with a belt and kneepads.

SYMBOLS OF AUTHORITY

In Aztec lands, only the *tlatoani* was permitted to wear the *xicolli*, a decorated waistcoat, and Aztec rulers marked their status by wearing rich jewellery and ornaments made of rock-crystal and jade. The plumes of the quetzal were also used as a symbol of kingly authority. The quetzal was understood to be an important *nahualli* or animal form of the god Quetzalcóatl, the Plumed Serpent who was identified with the wise ruler and high priest of Tollán, Topiltzin. Aztec rulers wore green quetzal feathers or green stones as a mark of sovereignty. When Moctezuma II sent an offering of gifts to Hernán Cortés shortly after the Spaniards landed in April 1519, he included a headdress of green feathers. Cortés sent it on to his lord, Charles V, in a consignment of treasures from the

CORONATION SPECTACLE

The power of the ruler in both Maya and Aztec realms was often expressed through public ceremony. The vast temple rituals that culminated in human sacrifices impressed not only the rulers' subjects but also outsiders, including both allies and enemies.

VISIBLE MIGHT

The Aztecs required the lords of some allied states to live in Tenochtitlán. Here they witnessed spectacular demonstrations of Aztec might and authority on the steps

and at the summit of the Great Pyramid. Ahuítzotl's rededication of the Great Temple in 1487, in which as many as 80,000 victims may have been sacrificed, was a dramatic expression of his power as recently installed *tlatoani* and of the Aztecs' pre-eminence, as well as of his people's devotion to their gods.

Another public statement of the Aztec ruler's might was his complex coronation ceremony. In Tenochtitlán, the council's approval of the appointment of a new ruler was the start of a prolonged coronation ceremony, a powerful religious drama of several days' duration in which the whole state took part.

RETREAT

The rites began with a sober period of retreat. Following the death of the previous *tlatoani*, his elected successor was publicly stripped of all finery and symbols of status. Before the Great Pyramid in the centre of Tenochtitlán, he stood before the silent crowd dressed only in a loincloth, before being led by the rulers of the allied cities Texcoco and Tlacopán up the steep side of the pyramid to the shrine of the god Huitzilopochtli. There he was given a robe of dark green marked

Left: The splendour of Maya royal ceremony is celebrated in this image on a polychrome vase buried at Uaxactún near Tikal.

with the image of skulls. He burned incense in honour of the god. Afterwards, he descended the pyramid with a company of nobles and began a retreat lasting four days and nights in the military headquarters (*tlacochcalco*) within the ceremonial precinct. Every 12 hours, at noon and midnight, he climbed once more to the shrine of Huitzilopochtli and made offerings of his own blood, pricked from his ears, lower legs or arms.

ROBING AND ENTHRONEMENT

Following the sombre retreat, the second stage, a magnificent robing and enthronement, was full of colour. The new ruler and the company of penitent nobles processed from the *tlacochcalco* to one of the city's great palaces. The *tlatoani* of Texcoco dressed the new ruler in a robe of shining fabric with a glistening waistband, solemnly placed a greenstone crown on his head and adorned him with fabulous jewellery, including emerald earrings and nosepiece, gold armbands and anklets, and jaguar-skin sandals. He led him to a splendid throne covered with jaguar skins and eagle feathers.

This enthronement was followed by a public ceremony. The new ruler was carried on a litter to the Great Pyramid, where, before the sacred shrine of Huitzilopochtli, he used jaguar claws to let his own blood for a sacrificial offering and made a sacrifice of quails. He was then taken to a place containing either a sunstone or an eagle vessel, according to differing accounts, to make further blood sacrifices in honour of the sun.

Next, the new ruler made a stately progress, still carried on his litter, to the *coateocalli*, the building within the ritual enclosure where the Aztecs kept the captured gods of conquered peoples, some of which were accepted into the Aztec pantheon. Here he made further offerings of his blood to signify his devotion to the religious calendar, before proceeding to an earth temple used in spring planting

and other agricultural festivals. He made offerings to the sacred earth, validating his succession as ruler of the land.

The public ceremonial of enthronement was concluded when the king returned to the palace in the company of leading nobles for a series of speeches. He was informed that he was now greater than his fellow men, for his sacred role as leader gave him the power to speak to the gods and made him the deities' embodiment on Earth. The divinities filled him and were within him, they were his eyes, his tongue, his ears; symbolically, they were his claws and his sharp jaguar teeth.

BLESSED BY THE GODS
The new ruler now called on his people to follow him to war, for the next stage of his coronation ceremony required that he lead a military campaign to prove that the gods blessed him in battle. When Moctezuma I Ilhuicamina's grandson Tizoc led a dismal failure of a coronation campaign to Metztitlán following his accession in 1481, the people saw his poor performance in the field as a very bad omen for the reign that he had been seeking to celebrate. However, the campaign was judged a success and a propitious omen when the new ruler returned laden with booty and leading ranks of prisoners for sacrifice. This was the judgement made of Tizoc's successor, his brother Ahuítzotl, upon his return from his coronation campaign.

CONFIRMATION
The final stage of the sequence of rituals was a great public celebration known as confirmation, in which allies and even enemy states were expected to send offerings of tribute and the new *tlatoani* gave feasts in Tenochtitlán. On the first day, the new ruler made public demonstration of the primacy of Tenochtitlán within the Triple Alliance, when he presented the leaders of Texcoco and Tlacopán with their symbols of status. Afterwards, the allied rulers led a 2,000-strong company of nobles and warriors in a stately dance.

Above: Elite warriors donned ceremonial finery including feathered helmets and decorated armour for the coronation.

The new ruler of Tenochtitlán then made a triumphant entrance wearing a magnificent costume adorned with quetzal feathers and laden with jewellery, and the dancing group made a circle around him. He made a formal presentation of the insignia of office to the gathered ranks of Aztec society, so that his authority and pre-eminent status were clear to all. The ceremony had a bloody ending in a vast public sacrifice of the prisoners brought back from the coronation campaign.

The ritual coronation was a means of reaffirming and celebrating the many aspects of the Aztec ruler's greatness as the chief figure of the leading city of the mighty Aztec empire.

Below: Members of the Aztec nobility and imperial bureaucracy received official recognition of their status from the new tlatoani *in a palace ceremony.*

SUN KING: THE GLORY OF KING PACAL

The greatness of King Pacal of Palenque can be judged from his magnificent funerary crypt, rich grave offerings and towering sepulchral monument, the Temple of the Inscriptions, which stands atop a 20m (65ft) stepped pyramid. His city-state, Palenque, stands in a striking position, beneath a line of hills thick with rainforest, at the edge of the Usumacinta River floodplain, looking toward the Gulf of Mexico.

SPLENDOUR IN DEATH

The crypt, accessed by a long stairway leading downwards from the Temple of the Inscriptions, lies some 24m (80ft) below the temple floor. Within the crypt, the king's body was laid in a sarcophagus of red-painted stone, wearing a collar of precious jade, a green headband, several jade necklaces and mother-of-pearl sand jade earpieces. Over his face was a lifelike mask fashioned from jade, obsidian and shells. The outside of the sarcophagus was carved with images of the king's ancestors, while nine stucco figures around the walls of the crypt repre-sented the main gods of the underworld. In the corridors of the Temple of the Inscriptions

Right: Pacal's jade mosaic funeral mask has eyes of shell, mother of pearl and obsidian. A T-shaped amulet provides magical protection for the mouth.

were stone slabs carved with lists of kings. From these, together with accompanying lists commissioned by Pacal's son Chan-Bahlum, scholars have been able to construct a succession of 12 rulers. Together with the list from Copán, these are among the most detailed and complete dynastic lists of any ruling family in the Maya realm.

WHO WAS HE?

The remarkable King Pacal reigned at Palenque for 68 years. From carvings in the temple and an inscription that runs along the edge of the lid of his sarcophagus, we know that he was born on 24 March in AD603, acceded to the throne on 27 July AD615 and died, aged 81, on 29 September AD684. Scholars have identified his name, which is written both with the image of a small warshield and the hieroglyphs that made the sounds *pa*, *ca* and *la* – spelling *pacal*, which was the word for 'shield'. His full name was K'inich Janaa' Pakal ('Lord Great Sun Shield').

King Pacal is also a most unusual ruler in that the king apparently inherited the throne through his mother's line rather than by the more usual patrilineal descent, as was expected among the Maya. His mother, Lady Zac-Kuk, was ruler herself for a period. Pacal inherited the throne in her name when he

Above: This Palenque relief depicts the ceremony transferring power from Lady Zac-Kuk to her 12-year-old son Pacal.

was 12, but she lived for a further 25 years and may have been the power behind the throne. Only after she died in AD640 did Pacal begin to have significant inscriptions carved to justify his rule.

In Pacal's reign, Palenque became the dominant city in the region. As its ruler, Pacal controlled a large area: Palenque made marriage and other alliances with Tikal, Pomoná and Tortuguero. The city appears to have been at war with Toniná, for in the 8th century, a king of Toniná captured Kan Xul, one of Pacal's sons.

LEARNING FROM BURIAL RITES

The details of Pacal's burial rites show that both he and his subjects expected the deceased ruler to live on as a god after his death. When the great king was buried, five of his subjects were sacrificed so that they could accompany him on his journey to the underworld. The burial also shows that Pacal claimed authority

Above: Palenque's Temple of the Count pyramid (right) commands a view of the Temple of the Inscriptions (upper left).

for his dynasty by associating his ancestors and descendants with the sun god. The lid of his sarcophagus, which shows him descending the length of the world tree to the underworld, also depicts the sun moving between death and life. At his side within the sarcophagus was a jade figure of the sun god, suggesting that the king would rise again into the eastern sky after his underworld trials. The royal succession from Pacal to his descendants was symbolically blessed by the sun.

PASSING ON ROYAL POWER

Pacal's son, Chan-Bahlum, succeeded his father in AD684. He built the Temples of the Sun, the Cross and the Foliated Cross to celebrate his succession. The relation of this group to the main Temple of the Inscriptions confirms the sun god's approval. Once in every year, at sunset on the winter

solstice, the Maya understood the sun to undergo a symbolic death. The setting sun would shine through a dip in the ridge behind the Temple of the Inscriptions and fall on the carved scenes in the Temple of the Cross that celebrate Pacal passing his

royal power to Chan-Bahlum. As the sun set, its light would travel down the stair to King Pacal's tomb, symbolically entering the underworld with the king, prior to its rebirth the next morning.

Scholars believe that Pacal ordered the construction of the Temple of the Inscriptions as his own mortuary monument when he reached his seventies and understood that he was nearing the close of his long reign. The temple pyramid was completed after Pacal's death by Chan-Bahlum. The discovery of Pacal's tomb by Mexican archaeologist Albert Ruz in 1952 entirely changed the way that scholars view Maya temple pyramids, for it was the first evidence to emerge that some of these great constructions were essentially mortuary monuments.

Left: Pacal's final home, the Temple of the Inscriptions pyramid, has nine levels. Its stairway climbs to a five-bay sanctuary. The secret staircase to Pacal's crypt within the pyramid begins inside the sanctuary.

MOCTEZUMA II IN HIS POMP

Remembered primarily today as the last independent Aztec leader, Moctezuma II is the ruler who was ignominiously captured by the Spaniards and who apparently lost the confidence of his people; the man who lived to see the

Below and far right: 17th-century Spanish artists Miguel and Juan Gonzalez show Cortés riding to meet Moctezuma II.

empire of the Triple Alliance swept away by a small band of invaders like a spider's web in the wind. However, at the time of the Spanish Conquest, the empire was still expanding and apparently healthy.

HIERARCHY AND ETIQUETTE
Moctezuma II ruled with great pomp and absolute authority over Tenochtitlán and the Aztec empire. One of his first

Above: This later portrait of Moctezuma II presents a Europeanized view of the last Aztec leader's magnificent appearance.

endeavours, after his coronation war and the celebration of his confirmation rites, was to boost his own status and reinforce the standing of the nobility by introducing new court etiquette. He brought in laws on clothing and behaviour that set the *pipiltin* or nobility apart from the *macehuales* or commoners. For example, he stripped commoner-warriors who had excelled in battle of their much-valued privilege of wearing special clothes and insignia and insisted that they dress like the other members of their caste. He also introduced elaborate court ritual that underlined his own standing as an absolute ruler, the living image of the god Huitzilopochtli.

To further boost his authority, Moctezuma II brought his own men into government and the palace hierarchy. In the inner circle, he removed the officials

THE RAIN MAN

An annual ceremony held on Mount Tláloc cast the *tlatoani* in the role of rainmaker and illustrates how the cult of the Aztec ruler reflected his dual status as a warrior-leader and a fertility lord.

The ceremony was held in April or May, during the dry season, to draw the rain out from within the mountain. The rulers of Tenochtitlán, Texcoco, Tlacopán and Xochimilco made a pilgrimage to a temple high on Mount Tláloc. The temple was roofless, but built with high walls that cut off the view of the surrounding countryside. Within were rocks set out to echo the arrangement of peaks normally visible from the mountaintop, which included the divine mountains Popocatépetl and Ixtaccíhuatl.

The rulers carried gifts for the mountain-gods into the temple, then dressed the rock-idols in magnificent costumes. They left the temple but re-entered with offerings including food and the blood of a male infant. Afterwards, the rulers themselves feasted with their retinue on the open mountaintop.

Scholars interpret the ceremony as an act of fertilization, likening the rock temple to a cave, which the Aztecs understood to be a way into the spiritual world. This mountaintop cave was a place of opposites, where the earth met the sky and the spirit world met the physical world. The rulers' offering, like the large human sacrifices in city temples, was intended to recycle energy within the cosmos.

In the weeks after the ceremony, the dry season would come to an end. The first sign of the change would be rain clouds collecting around the summit of Mount Tláloc.

appointed by his predecessor, Ahuítzotl, and replaced them with his own close relatives and followers. (In some accounts, he ruthlessly had Ahuítzotl's men put to death.) He even removed the servants from the palaces of Tenochtitlán. In a canny move, he brought junior nobles from provincial cities of the empire and put them to work in the palaces. He calculated that the rulers of those cities would not consider revolt while their children were under his control in Tenochtitlán.

When Hernán Cortés and the Spaniards first encountered Moctezuma II at the entrance to Tenochtitlán, the Aztec leader emerged from the city borne on a litter by four noblemen and surrounded by a great number of slaves carrying goods to be offered to the gods. Moctezuma wore golden jewellery, a diadem encrusted with turquoise and the brilliant green feathers of the quetzal bird. He dismounted and walked forward supported by two nobles of the inner circle in a ceremonial manner of walking that showed great respect for the visitor. When Cortés approached to make a gift of Venetian pearls he was prevented from touching the Aztec ruler. After both had made speeches, Moctezuma led the visitors into a temple where he called on the god Huitzilopochtli, calling him his 'father', and received offerings from the rulers of Tacuba and Texcoco. At one point Moctezuma, the living embodiment of the Aztecs' principal god, lifted his clothes to show Cortés his arms and torso, saying, 'Look, I am only flesh and blood, like you'.

Moctezuma's quasi-divine standing played a significant part both in his own downfall and in that of the Aztec empire. His capture by the Spaniards was only possible because the Aztecs could not imagine that anyone would dare to manhandle this imperial figure and hold him to ransom. A Spanish delegation led by Cortés merely asked for an audience,

Above: Moctezuma II approaches his fateful first meeting with Cortés, carried out from Tenochtitlán in great style on a litter.

claiming that they wanted to complain of a supposed Aztec plan for a military action against the Spanish garrison at Veracruz. They were admitted and, finding no precautions to safeguard the emperor's person, seized him. Moctezuma had to cooperate, for his own survival. In captivity, and pleading for the Aztecs not to attack the Spanish compound, Moctezuma found that his authority was melting away.

On a larger scale, the Spaniards benefited from the fact that so much power was concentrated in one man. By eliminating him, they created a power vacuum that they were able to exploit to their advantage. The conquistadors certainly found that among the Maya, where there was no single figure to be eliminated at a stroke, conquest was a more difficult and challenging undertaking.

WISE GOVERNANCE, STRICT PUNISHMENT

The rulers of the Triple Alliance developed a legal code that defined the punishments for a range of misdemeanours and crimes, as well as set solutions for particular types of dispute. The code was used as a unifying factor and was strictly applied throughout the empire, without allowance for local differences or the details of a case.

THE BASIS OF THE LEGAL CODE

Scholars are unsure whether the code was based on ancient Mesoamerican tradition, as Netzahualcóyotl of Texcoco claimed, or whether it was developed specifically to deal with the difficulties of keeping law and order across the empire, with its many different terrains and complex mix of urban and rural peoples. The code was certainly a valued tool of central control, for it eliminated the risk of provincial lords undermining Aztec authority by developing their own legal system or list of punishments.

SON OF THE GODS

The Aztec legal system is said to have been devised by Netzahualcóyotl, the remarkable ruler of Texcoco who as a youth witnessed the killing of his father Ixtlilxóchitl and fled into exile before returning many years later to take power in the city of his birth.

Netzahualcóyotl was both a skilled politician and also a brilliant ruler who presided over his city for 41 years (1431–72) and won a glittering reputation for himself as a builder, poet, philosopher and legislator.

In part, perhaps, because of the dramatic events of his youth, an aura built around him and his life became enshrouded in myth. The story was told that he was son of the gods themselves, and that he would never taste death.

The chronicler Fernando de Alva Ixtlilxóchitl even suggested that Netzahualcóyotl had an understanding of divine reality that went far beyond that of his contemporaries, grasping the possibility of a single supreme creator deity rather than a multiplicity of many-faceted gods. He was the *tlatoani* who built a temple to an abstract god named Tloquenahuaque ('The One Who is Always Near').

Part of Netzahualcóyotl's brilliance may have lain in the fact that he constructed this godlike image for himself. He lent authority to the legal system he created by claiming to have revived the laws of Quetzalcóatl-Topiltzin, wise and fair ruler of Tula, in days of yore.

Aztecs were generally agreed as to what constituted good behaviour. According to Bernardino de Sahagún, author of *General History of the Things of New Spain*, virtuous Aztecs were obedient and honest, treating their fellows with respect and showing discretion in their dealings with others. Virtuous men and women worked hard, whether in the fields, at their sewing, preparing food, in an artisan's workshop, or in the marketplace. They brought energy to their work, without overindulging in sleep but rising early and labouring for long hours. They ate and drank in moderation; drunkenness was particularly frowned upon. They did not make a great noise when eating, thought carefully before speaking and were circumspect in what they said. They dressed and behaved with modesty. Children were raised to understand and follow this code.

Left: Although drunkenness was not encouraged, large amounts of pulque *were drunk during religious festivals.*

Below: A bronze image of Netzahualcóyotl seeks to capture his character as wise governor and deliverer of laws.

Above: A Florentine Codex *image shows judgement passed and punishment meted out under the Aztec law and order system.*

The *Codex Mendoza* contains a visual record of the trial and execution of the Mixtec leader of Coixtlahuaca, whose people attacked some Aztec merchants. This event was used by Moctezuma I Ilhuicamina as the pretext for a war that brought the Mixtecs to their knees and resulted in the payment of rich tribute into Aztec coffers. The codex image shows the merchants being killed and the arrival of Aztec emissaries to administer justice. They deliver a symbolic headdress, which indicates that the chief faces severe punishment. One of their number delivers a judgement on the ruler, who is put to death by strangulation while his child and principal wife are tied up roughly with slave collars around their necks.

The Mapa Quinatzin depicts legal process in Texcoco, whose ruler Netzahualcóyotl was famed as a legislator. A provincial chieftain who has had the temerity to rebel is warned, like the ruler of Coixtlahuaca, by being presented with a symbolic headdress. Then he is executed. Judges are depicted being put to death by strangulation because they have failed to follow required procedures and heard cases in their private lodgings.

PUNISHMENT

Punishments for wrongdoers included jailing and execution by strangulation, at the stake, or stoning. Theft was punished by strangulation. Drunks was strictly punished, with a sliding scale of penalties. The alcoholic drink *pulque* was only allowed for nobles, those who were sick and those aged over 52 years, although warriors could win the right to drink *pulque* as a reward for great bravery in battle. Those found drunk would have their heads shaved on the first occasion, on the second they would suffer the additional penalty of having their house knocked down. People found drunk on a third occasion would be put to death.

Right: Among the Aztecs, the rabbit was associated with the strong alcoholic drink pulque *and with drunkenness.*

113

THE MAYA LAW CODE

The Maya imposed severe penalties on those people who threatened social cohesion by committing crimes such as murder or adultery.

DIVINE PLAN

The Maya did not accept that bad things could happen by accident, for they viewed every event as the fulfilment of patterns that could be read in the stars and perhaps in the past, and which were set in motion by the gods. A hunter who killed another man by accident in the forest was just as guilty of murder as a man who killed another before witnesses in a quarrel over food. The unfortunate hunter must have been chosen by the gods to meet this end. Similarly, a person who lost or damaged someone else's belongings by accident was treated as if he or she had done it with intent and was required to compensate the unfortunate victim. Those who had no wealth of their own with which to pay compensation,

Above: Punishments for adultery were very severe and the man was executed. This clay couple was found in a Jaina Island grave.

nor wealthy relatives to provide help, faced slavery. They would be freed once they had worked off the money they owed to the victim.

PUNISHMENT

The punishment for murder was death. According to Bishop Diego de Landa, the murderer was placed in stocks and put to death by the relatives of the person he had killed. It appears that killing an animal for no reason was seen as akin to murder and the perpetrator might be severely disciplined for having brought shame on his patrilineal or matrilineal social group. Maya hunters were very serious about their responsibility to respect the animals on which they relied. They

Left: The figure on this Maya vase appears to be giving instruction or delivering a judgement on a question of law.

Right: Royal anniversaries were a time of clemency. A king of Copán wears a headdress celebrating the rain god Chac.

would make ritual atonement after killing an animal by sprinkling blood drawn from the penis or tongue on to a part of the creature.

When couples were caught committing adultery, the man was punished with death. If the couple were caught *in flagrante*, the man would be taken from the bed and bound hand and foot, humiliated and dragged before the judges. After hearing the case and declaring his guilt, the victim would be handed to the husband, who was permitted to exact revenge by taking the other's life. The usual method of execution, or so Bishop de Landa reports, was to crush the adulterer's head by dropping a heavy rock on it from a height.

Theft was also considered a serious offence. The Maya did not add doors to their houses, so that there was no way of barring entry to passers-by; many people hung a bell-string in the doorway that would sound when someone entered and alert whoever was at home. A person caught stealing would be thrown into slavery. He would often be given a set period of time in which to work off the cost of his crime, after which he could return to free society. However, if the members of his patriarchal or matriarchal social group were wealthy, they would pay compensation to the person he stole from and he would be free to go.

The Maya did not put thieves, murderers or adulterers in jail. The only people they kept in captivity were the captives they brought home in triumph from war who were kept for sacrifice on festival days or at the celebration of a king's anniversary. These victims-in-waiting were treated with respect until the time for sacrifice came, when they might be subjected to severe physical indignities in the name of the ancestor-gods.

Below: Maya merchants traded near and far. This Preclassic vase (c.900–200BC) is from the Sula Valley, Honduras.

TRADE AND ENFORCEMENT

Maya merchants were a privileged class known as *ppolms*, some trading by sea in great fleets of canoes, others carrying goods along trails and roadways.

A merchant god, Ek Chuah, presided over the transactions of the land traders. It was a religious duty to act with honour, but such was the wealth involved in large transactions for precious cargoes of cacao or greenstones that sometimes greed got the better of individuals and sharp practice crept in.

Maya merchants did not make written deals. Instead, they would come to a verbal agreement, which was usually signalled by drinking a toast in public. These deals were then considered binding. If a merchant refused to honour the terms of a deal, his deceit might be considered justification enough to launch a war. The end result might be wealth far greater than that involved in the deal in the form of booty, slaves and tribute.

However, while sometimes a cause of war, Maya trade may have been a source of peace in one important respect. The success of Maya merchants may have saved their people from attack by the land-hungry armies of the Aztec empire. The Maya traded regularly with the peoples of the Triple Alliance, exchanging salt, cacao beans and the highly prized green plumes of the quetzal bird for ornaments and tools in copper. The success of these trading links perhaps served to deter the Aztecs from launching military campaigns in Yucatán.

CLANS AND POWER: MAYA SOCIAL GROUPS

Each Maya belonged to two blood groups: the matrilineal group, descended from the mother, and the patrilineal group, descended from the father. Each individual had both a name given by and inherited from the mother and another taken from the father.

PATRIMONY

Property could only be inherited from the father. Like the king's crown, belongings only passed down the patrilineal line. Members of a patrilineal group were expected to help one another in times of need. For example, they would buy out a relative who had been thrown into slavery because of debt or crime. The patrilineal group also held lands in common.

According to Bishop de Landa, each family among the common people was allocated 37sq m (400sq ft) of land to farm. This unit of land was known as a *hun uinic*. Scholars believe the matrilineal and patrilineal groupings were also used

Below: The 'Nunnery' at Uxmal may have been occupied by members of one social class or worshippers of a particular god.

to control marriage between relatives. For example, a man might marry his mother's brother's daughter or his father's sister's daughter, but he would be barred from making other particular marriages.

CLASS DIVISIONS

Alongside and cutting across these blood groupings there were strong class divisions. It was extremely prestigious to be able to trace your lineage on both your mother's and father's side back across many generations to a noble family. Indeed, the word for a noble, *almehen*, translates as 'a man whose bloodline can be read on both sides'. Among members of the nobility were wealthy farmers who owned their own land, prosperous merchants, priests, leading warriors and priests. All those who held office within the political hierarchy, including councillors, judges and governors, were members of the nobility. The most important positions were filled by close members of the ruler's own blood group. The chiefs were carried in a litter decorated with plumes and borne on the shoulders of strong men.

Above: Members of the Maya nobility refashioned their looks by using clay to join the bridge of the nose to the forehead.

Scribes also occupied an elevated social position. They were leading members of the king's retinue. Most cities probably had a school for scribes, where royal and noble children such as the younger sons and daughters of the king or his children by secondary wives and concubines would learn the complex skills of reading and writing Maya hieroglyphs.

LITERACY AND CLASS

Literacy was probably not widespread among the general population. Scholars estimate that perhaps one in four of the Maya could read, and probably far fewer could write. Archaeologists have found attempts at writing by non-elite scribes at minor settlements or on the bricks that were fired at Comacalco, but these are

not comprehensible because those responsible had clearly not mastered the difficult technique required. All they could manage was a crude imitation of the fine calligraphy found on carvings and ceramics produced by the elite scribes.

Beneath the nobility were the free workers, those who were allotted the *hun uinic* on which to grow their maize. They were liable to pay taxes in the form of crops to a tax collector. The priests who played such a vital role in reading the stars and patterns of history to determine the correct planting times were supported with crops from the field. The farmers probably saw the food sent to the temple as a gift to the gods, eaten by the priesthood on their behalf.

SLAVES

Some of the men worked the lands on behalf of the wealthy. There was also a large class of slaves. Many were men and women captured in war for, in general, only the more noble among the captives were sacrificed while the poorer prisoners were put into slavery. Others were individuals from Maya homelands who had been brought to slavery by wrongdoing or by poverty. Slaves were also traded across the vast network of routes that crisscrossed the Maya lands. For most, there was no way out of their condition and their children also would be slaves, although it was possible to buy individuals out of slavery.

Female slaves worked drawing water from wells, dyeing cloth and grinding maize. Male slaves were put to work as labourers, fishermen and carriers of cargo for merchants. The males were given an ill-kempt appearance, with ragged clothing and roughly cut short hair.

Maya architecture and city planning reflected and reinforced these class divisions. In general, the king, his retinue and the nobility lived close to the centre of the city. The Maya city was usually centred on the temple complex and its fine plazas. Around this were grouped the palaces and homes of the elite nobles, with the merchants and other professionals living in smaller dwellings beyond them and the humble homes of the working people more distant still.

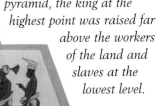

Above: Maya rulers are regularly modelled or depicted on vases occupying the throne that symbolizes their power.

Left: In the Maya social pyramid, the king at the highest point was raised far above the workers of the land and slaves at the lowest level.

THE MANY LEVELS OF AZTEC SOCIETY

Aztec society was highly stratified. The most important division was between the *pipiltin*, or nobles, and the *macehuales* or commoners. These two social groups were essentially castes; there was no possibility of a man of humble birth rising to join the nobility. A boy's destiny was determined not just by his date of birth in the ritual calendar, but also by his caste. To be born on the date 1-Alligator was a good omen: the priests promised that a noble's son born on this day could expect to become a wealthy ruler of men. The

Below: An image from the Florentine Codex *shows an Aztec metalworker making objects of gold for the wealthiest of the nobility.*

best they could promise a farmer's son born on the same day, however, was that he might become a valiant warrior in the service of the city-state.

THE NOBILITY

Nobles often received income from land holdings. They had access to prestigious positions in the priesthood and in the highest ranks of the army. Some served in the civil administration as provincial governors and judges, ambassadors and tax-collectors. Those of the highest rank were advisers to the *tlatoani*. Other nobles of lesser standing might become scribes and teachers. They had many privileges. The men were

Left: Gazing upwards, this life-size clay figure may represent a learned astronomer-priest.

allowed to take several wives and build houses of two storeys. They sent their children to *calmecac* or priestly schools. Here they learned to read and write, and to study the ritual calendar and its meaning. They also learned battlefield strategy, history and mythology, and practised martial arts.

THE COMMONERS

Commoners were primarily farmers, fishermen and soldiers. Members of the tribal clan or *calpulli* held land in common and most farmers worked the land or water owned by their clan grouping. They were liable to pay tax to the *tlatoani* and could be called on to serve in the army or to work on construction projects. If a man neglected his area or died without having children, the clan would reassign that particular piece of land to another member of the blood grouping. Another type of farmer, known as *mayeque*, worked land owned by nobles.

Soldiers had the best chance of rising through the social ranks. There were many rewards for bravery in battle, including social privileges. But there was no way into the highest positions in the army, which were reserved for members of the nobility.

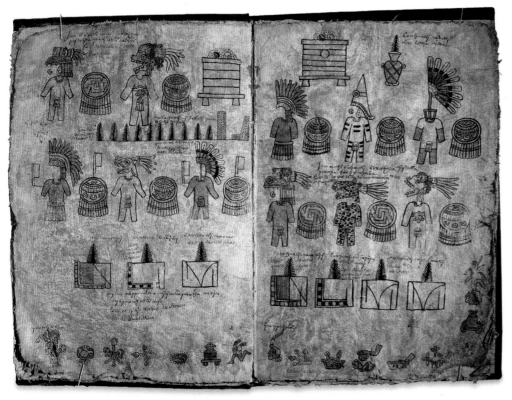

Above: Some of the many Aztec styles of clothing, headdresses and jewellery are detailed in the Codex Mendoza *(c.1541).*

Some men and women became slaves. People could volunteer for slavery if they were destitute and could become free again if circumstances improved; perhaps if clan members aided them. The children of slaves were not considered slaves.

ARTISANS

Some commoners achieved a measure of wealth by working as professional merchants (*pochteca*) or as artisans. Both groups lived in their own quarters in Aztec cities. Merchants were usually their own masters: they travelled widely throughout the empire, some trading on behalf of the ruler as well as carrying their own goods. They brought to the Aztec lands many of the raw materials such as precious metals and quetzal feathers needed by the artisans in their work. Some were secret agents, used to spy on allies and enemies and to listen out for whispers of impending revolts and other trouble. If prominent merchants were attacked or killed abroad, the *tlatoani* was quick to send the army to exact retribution. The Aztecs had a very high regard for the work of the skilled artisans who produced precious jewellery, feathered

headdresses, fine costumes and stone ornaments. They honoured their craftsmen with the name *tolteca*, a reference to the ancient Toltecs whom the Aztecs revered. Some artisans were employed by individual nobles but others were free agents, producing artefacts as required. The more successful merchants and artisans became wealthy but they could never cross the caste line to become members of the nobility.

As the empire grew, divisions in Aztec society blurred and private ownership of land increased. When Tenochtitlán was founded, most land was held by tribal clans or *calpulli*. By the time of the Spanish Conquest, there were two types of landholding nobles. At the highest level stood a small group of nobles of ancient families directly related to the *tlatoani*, who owned territories that were worked on their behalf by farmers legally tied to the soil. At a lower level were warriors who had gained land as a reward for military achievement. These awards were normally for one generation, but in practice warriors tended to be allowed to leave land to their offspring. For this reason, Moctezuma II reinforced the distinction between nobility and commoners. He enforced strict laws on the dress code permitted for the castes and introduced ceremonial procedures that further set nobility apart.

Below: This illustration from the Codex Mendoza *(c.1541) presents the stages in the career of an Aztec imperial officer.*

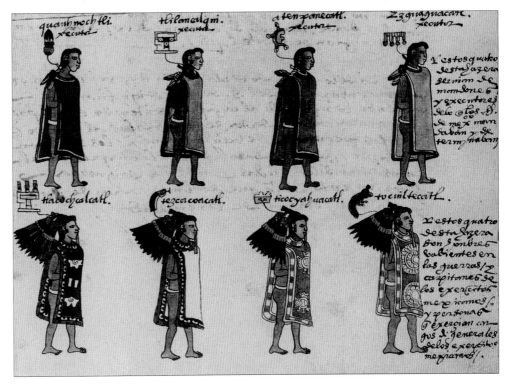

CHAPTER 6

PAST, PRESENT AND FUTURE

Mesoamericans did not understand time to be an orderly procession from the past to the future, from the beginnings of the world to its end. For one thing, they believed time to be cyclical. The Aztecs, for example, believed that we live in the Fifth Sun or 'age' and that our age would be brought to a sudden end, as had its predecessors. They also believed that time was sacred, charged with the power of the gods. Its movements could be fluid and unpredictable as the gods chose. Mesoamerican deities could take many forms simultaneously and one of these forms was time itself. In any moment there were divine influences at work for good and bad and the people relied on priestly diviners to interpret time.

A 52-year time span was produced by the intersection of the two calendars used by the Aztecs and their Mesoamerican cousins. Mesoamericans separated by centuries and by miles – perhaps from as early as the Olmec civilization in the first millennium BC to the Maya and Aztecs at the time of the Conquest, and from the Teotihuacános in the north to the inhabitants of Copán in the south-east – used a 365-day solar calendar to plot religious festivals alongside a 260-day calendar for divining the future. The first day of the 365-day calendar and the first day of the 260-day calendar intersected only once every 52 years. The Aztecs called this time span a 'bundle of years' while the Maya version is usually 'the Calendar Round'.

Left: Hunting god Mixcóatl slays a feline predator. In one Aztec creation myth, Mixcóatl hunted down earth goddess Cihuacóatl for love. Their union produced Quetzalcóatl, the great Plumed Serpent himself, bringer of winds and light.

STARTING FROM ZERO: MATHEMATICS

The Maya used a sophisticated mathematical notation that enabled them to write very large numbers in their carved inscriptions and in codices. They were among the first peoples – along with the ancient Babylonians, the Chinese and the Hindus of India – to develop the concept of zero and a symbol for it. Among the Maya, zero was represented not by an empty circle (0), but by a stylized image of a shell.

DOTS AND BARS

The Maya did not have the familiar decimal system, based on 10, but instead a count based on 20 (called a vigesimal system). Scholars suggest that the unit of 20 may have been used because it matches the number of fingers and toes in the human body. The Maya scribes and craftsmen wrote the numbers 1 to 4 with simple dots. One dot meant 1, two dots 2 and so on. The number 5 was written with a horizontal bar, and 6 was a single bar with a dot above it. They were able to write numbers up to 19 with a combination of horizontal bars and dots. For example, 17 was written with three bars, making 15, and two dots.

To write larger numbers they used these same symbols arranged in vertical columns. The bottom line showed units (1 to 19), the line above it numbers of twenties, the line above it numbers

Below: This detail from the Postclassic Madrid Codex shows the bar and dot symbols used by the Maya in counting.

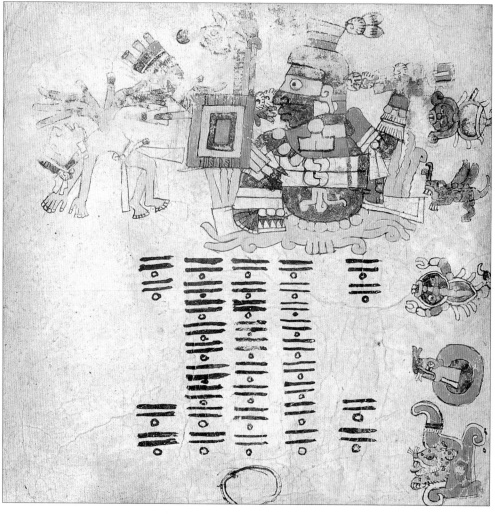

Above: The Aztec bar and dot counting system can be read in this page from the Codex Cospi (c.1350–1500). Tezcatlipoca, lord of night and fate, is in warrior garb and equipped with weapons. The images to his right are symbols for calendrical dates.

of 400s (20 units of 20), the line above that numbers of 8000s (20 units of 400) and so on. A single bar in the first line, with a dot in the line above, two bars in the line above and one bar in the line above would represent (1×5) plus (1×20) plus (10×400) plus (5×8000), which makes 5+20+4000+40,000=44,025.

The first breakthrough in deciphering the Maya bar and dot system was made in 1832 by Constantine Rafinesque (1783–1840), a brilliant naturalist and traveller-writer. Noticing the frequent use of bars and dots in the *Dresden Codex*, he surmised that these symbols were being used as numbers. He saw that the dots never appeared in groups of more than four and guessed that the bar stood for 5 and the dots for single units. Subsequently

Ernst Förstemann, archivist at Dresden where the codex was kept, discovered the Maya scribes' use of the shell symbol to stand for 0.

This system was used primarily to mark and record dates. However, the Maya apparently also used this positional mathematics for practical calculation. According to Diego de Landa, Maya merchants negotiating a deal would use grains of maize or cacao beans spread out on the dry ground or a flat rock to reckon

Above: The profiles of gods' heads carved on this Yaxchilán lintel stand for numbers. The inscribed date is 11 February AD526.

even large numbers. The writers of codices generally used the simple bar-and-dot system for writing dates, but the craftsmen who carved the Classic Period stelae sometimes produced a more elaborate version. Each number from 0 to 19 had its own patron divinity and stonemasons began to carve heads or full images of these gods to represent particular numbers. This practice was particularly common among the sculptors who produced the elegant stelae at Quiriguá and Copán. A well-known example is found on the east side of Stela D at Quiriguá, where the god of the number 7 (Uuk) is carved in place of the number. Another example, on a lintel at Yaxchilán, is illustrated above – gods' heads representing numbers are combined with animal carvings standing for cycles of time.

AZTEC NUMBERS

The Aztecs also used the bar and dot system. Some scholars believe the system to have been an ancient part of the shared

Right: Aztec numbers, from top left – 1, 2, 3, 4, 5, 6, 7, 8, 9, 10, 11, 12, 13, 14, 15, 16, 17, 18, 19, 20, 21, 22, 23, 24, 25, 29, 30, 40, 50, 55, 100, 101, 104, 114, 154, 600, 618, 1500 and 25,000.

Mesoamerican culture, possibly dating as far back back as the Olmec era (*c.*1500 –400BC). Like the Maya, the Aztecs seem to have been happy to use bars and dots to record dates in manuscripts and on monuments. However, because their growing empire drew in vast quantities of tribute from dependent territories, they also developed a system of number glyphs for use in accounting.

The newer system was still based on units of 20. A feather glyph meant 20, a flag glyph stood for 400 and a symbol representing a bag of incense was 8000 (20×400). A scribe who wanted to note receipt of 540 items of produce would draw one flag and seven feathers – 400 plus (7×20) = 540. He would generally draw a line alongside the glyphs to indicate they should be read in conjunction, then draw an image of the item received – say, a bag of cacao beans – and make a second line connecting the bag to the number. The readers of the tribute list would then understand that 540 bags of cacao beans had been received, counted and stored. Scholars would be able to decipher the system of number glyphs by

Above: The date carved on Lintel 26 at Yaxchilán marks the day on which King Shield Jaguar received his battle equipment from his wife: 9.14.12.6.12 in the Maya Long Count, or 12 February AD724.

examining the *Codex Mendoza* (*c.*1541). Part of this document comprises a detailed list of the tribute paid to Moctezuma II by subject towns and regions of the empire. It also has glosses in Spanish, written by an interpreter who understood the Nahuatl language and the Aztec system of numbers.

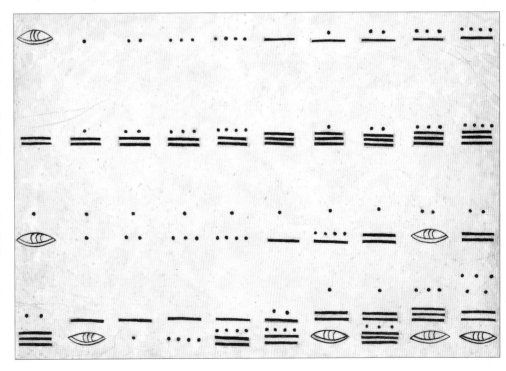

THREE INTO ONE: INTERLOCKING CALENDARS

The Aztec 365-day cycle contained 18 'months' of 20 days, plus five days at the year's end that were considered a time of ill omen. The 365-day count was called *xiuhpohualli* ('counting of the years') and was used for plotting religious festivals and for marking the seasons. The Aztec 260-day calendar combined the numbers 1–13 with 20 names of creatures, objects or forces such as crocodile, house, wind, flint knife, jaguar and reed. When the calendar was written down, each day name was denoted by a hieroglyph showing the object, animal or force, while each number was shown by dots. The cycle was called *tonalpohualli* ('the counting of the

Below: A Codex Borbonicus *image shows the deities Ometecuhtli and Omecihuatl creating the divinely ordained calendar.*

days'). It began with 1-Crocodile, 2-Wind and 3-House. The thirteenth and fourteenth names in the cycle were reed and jaguar, but there was no fourteen in the number sequence, so after 13-Reed the *tonalpohualli* proceeded to 1-Jaguar,

Above: This Aztec carving represents a 52-year cycle or 'bundle of years'. A bundle of sticks was burned to celebrate a new cycle.

and then carried on through the day names while prefixing the numbers 2, 3, 4 and so on. The cycle was therefore divided into 20 'weeks' of 13 days, which the Spanish called *trecena*.

Together, the *tonalpohualli* or day count and the *xiuhpohualli* or year count produced 18,980 unique combinations before repeating the same intersection of days in the two calendars. This was the equivalent of 73 years in the *tonalpohualli* calendar or 52 years – the 'bundle of years' – in the *xiuhpohualli* calendar.

RELIGIOUS FESTIVALS

In the year calendar, each 20-day month was associated with a religious festival. Most were linked to the agricultural year and there were three principal kinds. One group honoured the sun, the land and maize. A second included offerings to mountains and sources of water, while a third paid homage to patron deities.

Some of the days of the calendar marked religious festivals, but priestly ceremonies were usually timed according to the year calendar. Priestly astronomers also looked to the heavens, in particular to the movements of the moon and Venus, when attempting to divine the events of the future.

Above: On the Aztec Sun Stone, the glyphs in the enclosed circle surrounding the sun god are those of the 20 days of the week.

The five-day period at year's end, the *nemontemi*, was a time of withdrawal. People did not carry out their normal activities. Fields were left untended and markets were deserted. Householders broke their plates and utensils, fasted and let their fires go out. They even refrained from talking. One ritual looked to the new beginning the Aztecs hoped would follow the New Fire rites: a pregnant woman was locked in a granary in the hope that her fertility would be transferred to the corn.

The patterns of intersection between the two calendars meant that a new year in the *xiuhpohualli* could only begin on one of four possible names from the *tonalpohualli*. These were rabbit, reed, flint knife and house. Each year took its

Below: The 20 Aztec day names are (from top left) flower, rain, flint knife, movement, vulture, eagle, jaguar, reed, grass, monkey, dog, water, rabbit, deer, death, serpent, lizard, house, wind and crocodile.

name from the 'year bearer', whichever one of these four day-names fell on the first day of the new year. Within a 52-year cycle, the year bearers were numbered 1 to 13 in succession – 1-Rabbit, 2-Reed, 3-House, 4-Flint-knife, 5-Rabbit, 6-Reed, 7-House, 8-Flint-knife, 9-Rabbit, 10-Reed, 11-House, 12-Flint-knife, 13-Rabbit, 1-Reed, 2-House and so on.

Because there were 20 days in each month of the *xiuhpohualli* and a recurring pattern of 20 day-signs in the *tonalpohualli*, each month in the *tonalpohualli* began with the same day-sign as the year. That is, the year-bearer was also the 'month-bearer'. The year-bearer was also celebrated repeatedly throughout the year.

Among the Aztecs, the 52-year cycles were not differentiated from each other. The date system could specify that an event took place on a particular day in a particular year within a 52-year cycle, but not in which 52-year cycle it happened. This presented significant

problems in long cycles of time. The problem was solved by the 'Long Count', which marked time from a year zero in the distant past. Scholars believe the Long Count was widely used in Mesoamerica in early times, but that it fell into disuse in all except Maya lands, where it was developed into a sophisticated system.

THE MAYA CALENDAR

The Maya used the same combination of a 260-day ritual count with 13 20-day cycles and a 365-day solar count with 18 20-day months and a five-day unlucky period at year's end. The Maya called the 260-day calendar the *tzolkin*, and the 365-day calendar the *haab*. Scholars sometimes call the 365-day measure the 'Vague Year' because Mesoamericans did not take account of the fact that a solar year lasts slightly more than 365 days and add an extra day every four years. Nor did they make any of the other sophisticated adjustments of the Gregorian calendar now widely used in the West. Over time, their solar year must have dragged behind the movements of the stars and sun.

Bishop Diego de Landa gave a detailed description of the Maya calendars and made careful note of the glyphs used by the Maya for day-signs and months. To give a day its full Maya calendrical date would require the *tzolkin* date and the *haab* date. For example, 13 Ahau 18 Cumku. This date would have been towards the close of the final month before the unlucky five-day period (*uayeb*) at the end of the year.

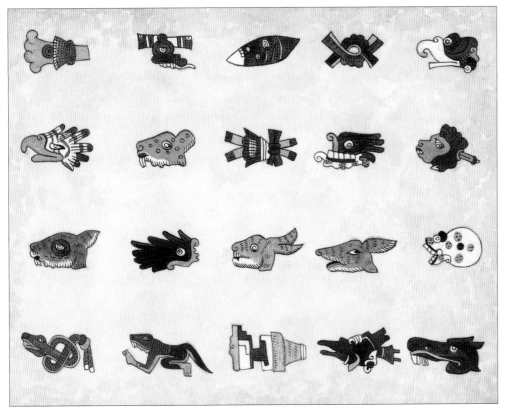

COUNTING THE DAYS

Scholars cannot agree why the early Mesoamericans first fixed on 260 days as a useful unit for measuring time. Some have argued that it was based on observation of the movements of Venus and of the sun in our skies. The 260-day period roughly corresponds to the gap between the appearance of Venus as the evening star and its emergence as the morning star. There is also an interval of 260 days between the sun's annual southward movement and its northward return when viewed from a latitude close to Copán. This celestial observation might have been used to time planting and harvest and over centuries it could have become a hallowed measurement strongly associated with divine rhythms underlying fertility.

HUMAN RHYTHMS
Most modern scholars argue that the 260-day cycle is based on human rhythms. Midwives may have used the measure, counting forward 260 days

Above: At El Tajin, Mexico, the Pyramid of the Niches has 365 niches, supposedly one for each day of the solar year.

from the date of a woman's last menstrual period, to predict when a baby would be likely to be born, as do the modern Maya still living in the mountains of southern Guatemala. The 260-day calendar has proved a most enduring invention. It is still used among the Quiché inhabitants of the tropical mountains of southern Guatemala.

THE MAYA LONG COUNT
In addition to the twinned 260-day and 365-day calendars, the Maya people greatly refined a much longer-running measuring system, the 'Long Count', which is known to have been used in many parts of Mesoamerica at the start of the first millennium BC. During the Classic Period (c.AD250–900), the Maya dated their monuments using the Long Count to record births, deaths, royal accessions and anniversaries, the dates of ritual sacrifices and battle

Left: The 20 Maya day names include Imix (top left), Akbal (centre top), Etznab (centre bottom) and Ahau (bottom right).

triumphs. This system counted forward from a zero date of 4 Ahua 8 Cumku, equivalent to 11 August 3114BC in the Gregorian calendar.

The Maya Long Count counted days in units of 20 and used a 'year' of 360 days. Its five units were the *baktun* (144,000 days), the *katun* (7,200 days), the *tun* (360 days), the *uinal* (20 days) and the *kin* (1 day). Dates were carved in this order, with units separated by full points. For example, the date 3.3.2.1.1 would be three *baktuns* (432,000 days), three *katuns* (21,600 days), 2 *tuns* (720 days), one *uinal* (20 days) and 1 *kin* (1 day), making a total of 454,341 days after the zero date of 11 August 3114BC.

The earliest Maya Long Count inscription is from El Baúl on the Pacific coast in the southern Maya or highland Maya region and dates to AD37.

A date carved on a *stela* gave the Long Count followed by the position in the Calendar Round (the combination of

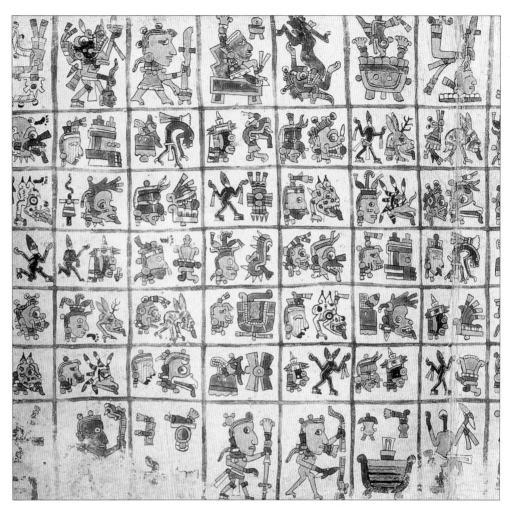

Above: The Mixtec Codex Cospi (c.1350–1500) contains a ritual calendar and a detailed survey of the movements of Venus.

the *haab* calendar and the *tzolkin* calendar). Because there are so very many dates on stelae, early scholars thought that the Maya worshipped time itself. However, breakthroughs in understanding hieroglyphics enabled the successors of those scholars to grasp that the dates were provided to set in time the image carved beneath them of a king's accession or triumph over a rival ruler.

The Long Count date is usually only carved once on a stela: dates given later for the ruler's birth-date or accession are almost invariably given only in the *tzolkin* calendar because the larger context of the Long Count date has already been established. Dates on stelae also often provide information about the moon. Scholars call the Long Count and Calendar Round dates, which come first in inscriptions, the 'Initial Series' and the information on the moon cycle the 'Lunar Series'.

Left: The glyphs for the 19 Maya months include Pop (top left), Zotz (top, fourth from left), Pax (bottom left) and Uayeb (last).

MAJOR AZTEC FESTIVALS

AZTEC MONTH 1
Western dates 14 February–5 March
Festival name Atlcaualo (The Ending of Water), Cuauhitleua (The Lifting of Trees)
Gods/goddesses honoured Tláloc (rain and fertility god), Chalchiúhtlicue (goddess of springs, rivers and the sea), Chicomecóatl (maize goddess), Xilonen (maize goddess), Quetzalcóatl (storms, wind and rain god)
Rites Offerings to maize divinities, including the sacrifice of children; banners erected in homes and temples.

AZTEC MONTH 2
Western dates 6–25 March
Festival name Tlacaxipehualiztli (Skinning of the Men)
Gods/goddesses honoured Xipe Totec (god of vegetation and spring, patron of goldworkers)
Rites Victims slaughtered, priests wear their skin over their face and body; five prisoners of war killed in staged combat; *tlatoani* takes part in dance and military ritual.

AZTEC MONTH 3
Western dates 26 March–14 April
Festival name Tozoztontli (Minor Vigil), Xochimanaloya (Presentation of flowers)
Gods/goddesses honoured Tláloc (rain and fertility god), Chalchiúhtlicue (goddess of springs, rivers and the sea), Centéotl (maize god), Coatlícue (earth goddess)
Rites Ceremonial planting of seeds; donations of flowers to the festival deities; priests made offering of flayed skins.

AZTEC MONTH 4
Western dates 15 April–4 May (End of dry season)
Festival name Huey Tozoztli (Major Vigil)
Gods/goddesses honoured Tláloc (rain and fertility god), Chalchiúhtlicue (goddess of springs, rivers and the sea), Centéotl (maize god), Coatlícue (earth goddess), Chicomecóatl (maize goddess), Xilonen (maize goddess), Quetzalcóatl (storms, wind and rain god)
Rites Rulers of Tenochtitlán, Texcoco, Tlacopán and Xochimilco made sacrifices to the earth; a girl impersonating Chalchiúhtlicue was sacrificed and her blood poured on Lake Texcoco; priestesses of Chicomecóatl bless farmers' seed supplies.

AZTEC MONTH 5
Western dates 5–22 May
Festival name Tóxcatl (Drought)
Gods/goddesses honoured Tezcatlipoca (god of fate, kingship and other attributes), Huitzilopochtli (México tribal god, also god of war and associated with the sun), Mixcóatl (hunt god), Camaxtli (hunt god)
Rites Youth who has impersonated Tezcatlipoca for a year sacrificed on the Great Pyramid in Tenochtitlán; impersonators of Huitzilopochtli, Mixcóatl and Camaxtli sacrificed separately.

AZTEC MONTH 6
Western dates 23 May–13 June (Start of rainy season)
Festival name Etzalcualiztli (Meal of Maize and Beans)
Gods/goddesses honoured Tláloc (rain and fertility god), Chalchiúhtlicue (goddess of waters), Quetzalcóatl (wind and rain god)
Rites Priests held vigils and fasts, praying for a cloudburst; noblemen danced with maize stalks; new reeds harvested on the lake; meals of maize and beans served.

AZTEC MONTH 7
Western dates 14 June–3 July
Festival name Tecuilhuitontli (Minor Festival of the Lords)
Gods/goddesses honoured Xochipilli (god of flowers, song and dance), Huixtocíhuatl (goddess of salt)
Rites *Tlatoani* dance in public and hand out gifts to the people; nobility hold feasts open to commoners; sacrifices made to salt goddess and to Xochipilli.

AZTEC MONTH 8
Western dates 4–23 July
Festival name Huey Tecuilhuitl (Major Festival of the Lords)
Gods/goddesses honoured Xilonen (maize goddess), Cihuacóatl (fertility goddess)
Rites *Tlatoani* dance and hand out gifts; nobility hold feasts for commoners to celebrate the appearance of the first maize shoots; offerings made to a girl who is impersonating Xilonen.

AZTEC MONTH 9
Western dates 24 July–12 August
Festival name Miccailhuitontli (Minor Festival of the Dead), Tlaxochimaco (Emergence of Flowers)
Gods/goddesses honoured Tezcatlipoca (god of fate, kingship, darkness, masculinity and many other attributes), Huitzilopochtli (México tribal god, also god of war and associated with the sun), ancestor gods
Rites Sacrifices to Huitzilopochtli in his guise as the ancestral leader of the migrating México; offerings made to the dead; feasts and dances held in their honour.

AZTEC MONTH 10

Western dates 13 August–1 September

Festival name Huey Miccailhuitl (Major Festival of the Dead), Xocotlhuetzi (Ripening of the Xocotl fruit)

Gods/goddesses honoured Huehuetéotl (old fire god), Xiuhtecuhtli (fire god), Yacatecuhtli (trader's god)

Rites Fire sacrifices; offerings made to ancestors.

AZTEC MONTH 11

Western dates 2–21 September (Start of harvest)

Festival name Ochpaniztli (Clearing)

Gods/goddesses honoured Toci (earth goddess), Tlazoltéotl (goddess of love and filth), Teteoinnan (earth goddess), Coatlícue (earth goddess), Cinteotl (maize goddess), Chicomecóatl (maize goddess)

Rites Female sacrificial victim beheaded and flayed by priestess of Xilonen-Chicomecóatl, who then wore her skin; corn seeds thrown to the people; cleaning and repairs carried out. Preparations for the approaching season of war included military manoeuvres; *tlatoani* gives insignia to soldiers. Priests started a major fast that ran until the Festival of Panquetzalitzli.

AZTEC MONTH 12

Western dates 22 September–11 October (Harvest)

Festival name Teotleco (Coming of the Gods and Goddesses)

Gods/goddesses honoured All

Rites General festivities included dancing and feasting; footprint made at midnight in a bowl of maize flour in the temple signified the coming of the gods and the goddesses.

AZTEC MONTH 13

Western dates 12–31 October

Festival name Tepeilhuitl (Festival of the Mountains)

Gods/goddesses honoured Tláloc (rain god), *Tlaloque* (rain god's assistants), Tepictoton (rain god), Octli (deities of *pulque* drink), Xochiquetzal (flower goddess) and divine mountains Popocatépetl, Ixtaccihuatl (Mount) Tlaloc and Matlalcueye

Rites Ritual offerings made at mountain sanctuaries.

AZTEC MONTH 14

Western dates 1–20 November

Festival name Quecholli (Treasured Feather)

Gods/goddesses honoured Mixcóatl (hunt god), Camaxtli (hunt god)

Rites Hunting competitions held; prisoners dressed as deer sacrificed in honour of the hunt gods; soldiers fast in preparation for war; weapons made for battle and hunting.

AZTEC MONTH 15

Western dates 21 November–10 December

Festival name Panquetzalitzi (Lifting of the Banners)

Gods/goddesses honoured Tezcatlipoca (god of fate, kingship, darkness, masculinity and many other attributes), Huitzilopochtli (México tribal god, also god of war and associated with the sun)

Rites Major sacrifices of prisoners of war, including sacrifice of the 'bathed slaves'; sacred procession from the Great Pyramid to Tlatelolco, Chapultepec and Coyoacan, then back to the sacred precinct at Tenochtitlán; paper banners hung on houses and in fruit trees.

AZTEC MONTH 16

Western dates 11–30 December

Festival name Atemoztli (Coming Down of Waters)

Gods/goddesses honoured Tláloque (rain god's assistants) and divine mountains Popocatépetl, Ixtaccihuatl (Mount) Tláloc and Matlalcueye

Rites Ceremonies held in honour of the mountains.

AZTEC MONTH 17

Western dates 31 December–19 January

Festival name Tititl (Stretching)

Gods/goddesses honoured Cihuacóatl (fertility goddess), Ilamatecuhtli (ancient mother goddess), Tonantzin (mother goddess), Yacatecuhtli (god of traders and travellers)

Rites Merchants offer slave sacrifices to Yacatecuhtli; weavers made offerings to Ilamatecuhtli; public dancing involving priests, nobility and the *tlatoani*.

AZTEC MONTH 18

Western dates 20 January–8 February

Festival name Izcalli (Growing)

Gods/goddesses honoured Xiuhtecuhtli (fire god), Tláloc (rain god), Chalchiúhtlicue (water goddess)

Rites Animal sacrifices to the fire god; corn toasted and tamales served with greens; dough effigies of Xiuhtecuhtli made.

The five days at the end of the year (9–13 February) were a time for doing as little as possible to avoid ill fortune. People stayed at home and did not do any business.

DIVINING THE FUTURE

Priests used the ritual calendar to divine the future. Aztec priests consulted long screenfold books called *tonalamatl*. In these books, which were made from bark paper coated with a white mineral paste, scribes recorded the calendar and the many meanings of its cycles.

ARCANE MEANINGS

The calendars contained a rich blend of arcane meanings. Each number in the *tonalpohualli* was under a divine influence. Each of the 13 lords of the day was associated with a butterfly or bird. Each of the day-names also had its associated deity (see chart). A further cycle of nine lords of the night cast its influence over the calendar. The influences that were in place at the start of each 13-day period remained a powerful force throughout.

Below: A priest on this pre-Toltec stela from Santa Lucia Cotzumalhuapa uses a staff to help make an astronomical observation.

	AZTEC DAY GODS IN THE *TONALPOHUALLI*	
Day	Symbol	God
1	Crocodile (cipactli)	Tonacatecuhtli (Creator god)
2	Wind (éhecatl)	Quetzalcóatl (Storm/wind god among many other attributes)
3	House (calli)	Tepeyolohtli (God of regeneration)
4	Lizard (cuetzpallin)	Huehuecóyotl (Old Old Coyote, a trickster god)
5	Serpent (cóatl)	Chalchiúhtlicue (Water goddess)
6	Death (miquiztli)	Tecciztécatl (Moon god)
7	Deer (mázatl)	Tláloc (Rain god)
8	Rabbit (tochtli)	Mayáhuel (Maguey plant goddess)
9	Water (atl)	Xiuhtecuhtli (Fire god)
10	Dog (izcuintli)	Mictlantecuhtli (Lord of the underworld)
11	Monkey (ozomatli)	Xochipilli (God of flowers, song and dance)
12	Grass (malinalli)	Patécatl (Medicine god)
13	Reed (ácatl)	Tezcatlipoca (God of night and destiny, among many other attributes)
14	Jaguar (océlotl)	Tlazoltéotl (Goddess of filth and love)
15	Eagle (cuauhtli)	Xipe Totec (Vegetation god)
16	Vulture (cozcacuauhtli)	Itzapapálotl (A form of Coatlícue, an earth goddess)
17	Motion (ollin)	Xólotl (double of Quetzalcóatl)
18	Flint (técpatl)	Tezcatlipoca
19	Rain (quiáhuitl)	Chantico (Hearth goddess)
20	Flower (xóchitl)	Xochiquetzal (Flower goddess)

The Maya understood that the last day of each solar month fell under the influence of the month that was about to begin. The 20th day of Zotz, for example, was influenced by the next month, Tzec, and was said to be 'the seating of Tzec'. The following day was 1-Tzec. A baby's destiny might be read in the influences prevalent on its birthday. Parents whose child was born on an ill-omened day could improve his or her chances by holding a naming ceremony on a day that carried positive associations.

Priests consulted the movements of celestial bodies. Priest-astrologer-diviners would plot the best days for planting, harvesting and other daily activities. For example, Maya planting books instructed farmers on which days to plant during the months of Chen and Yax.

Below: Priests determined the auspicious date for ceremonies. This marker from the Maya city of Chinkultic says that the ball court was dedicated on 21 May AD591.

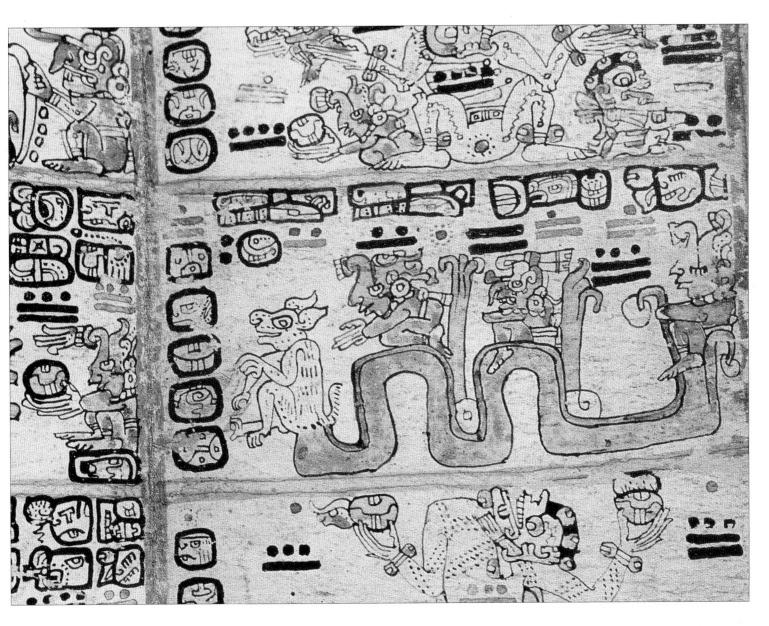

Above: The Madrid Codex *contains almanacs used by priests for timing religious rites and plotting astronomical movements.*

Merchants would take diviners' advice when planning their departure and return dates for journeys. In the Maya realms, rulers would visit the astronomer-priests to check on celestial movements: they often launched attacks to coincide with the rising of the malign planet Venus. Fittingly, the Maya hieroglyph for war consists of the logograph for Venus (one image representing the whole word) combined with another sign.

Among the Aztecs, the *tlatoani* himself and his advisers would take account of the meanings of the calendars and the heavens when plotting military campaigns. Indeed, it was one of the *tlatoani*'s duties to scan the heavens for guidance.

DAYKEEPERS AND MODERN DIVINING

Anthropologists have discovered modern diviners at work using the 260-day calendar in Guatemala.

Shaman-priests who are known as 'daykeepers' work among the Quiché people of Momostenango in Guatemala, using the ritual calendar to divine solutions for people's problems. Burning copal incense, they take a handful of coral seeds and count them out in piles of four. The number left over at the end provides information about the problem. The priest then counts the number of piles and counts back the same number of days through the 260-day round to give an indication of when the problem began. He or she may feel a 'lightning' in the blood when counting past a particular day, which gives further information to be interpreted. At this moment, the priest's body becomes an image of the universe in microcosm. The sensations he or she feels have meaning in a larger context. The priest makes use of the many associations of each day-sign to intuit the arrangements of cosmic energy around the individual and his or her difficulty, and so work out a possible response to the problem.

The Momostenango Quiché have safeguarded many traditional Maya religious practices. They hold a celebrated religious festival in which new daykeepers are initiated on the day 8-Monkey in the 260-day calendar.

READING THE STARS

In Mesoamerican societies, priests were guardians of time. As well as computing the calendar and keeping track of festivals and necessary religious ceremonies, they watched the movements of the stars and planets for bad omens or propitious dates. By interpreting the movements of the celestial bodies, priests could gain knowledge of the divinely inspired future. Among the Maya, the priest was known as Ah Kin ('Servant of the Sun'), making clear his connection to both astronomy and the calendar. As timekeeper, the Maya priest-scribe was also in charge of the genealogies of the city-state.

UNIVERSAL FORCES

Just as the priests understood the pattern of days and weeks in the ritual and solar calendars to be full of divine energy and meaning, so they saw the orbits and phases of the planets and the movements of stars to be a manifestation of

Below: The circular Venus observatory in Chichén Itzá was built to let astronomers observe the four phases of the planet Venus.

universal forces that impacted upon the lives of men. The movements of the planet Venus were considered of great importance. In Mesoamerican latitudes, Venus shines brilliantly in the morning sky, as large as a tennis ball. The planet assumed an important role in religion and mythology.

Venus follows a near-circular orbit around the sun: one orbit takes 225 days. Like the moon, Venus goes through a number of phases: one cycle of phases takes 584 days. The Mesoamerican astronomers knew about this because they had measured it from observatory-towers such as the ones in the Maya cities of Mayapán and Chichén Itzá. They knew that Venus goes through four phases. It rises first in the morning sky

Left: The standing figure on this terracotta incense burner from Palenque may be the Maya sun god.

and is visible as the morning star for 236 days. Thereafter it disappears into the light of the sun and is lost to sight for 90 days. At the end of this period it rises in the evening sky and is visible as the evening star for 250 days. In its fourth phase, it is invisible for eight days before reappearing as the morning star.

PHASES OF VENUS

The Maya associated the 'invisible phases' of Venus, when the planet disappears from view, with voyages to the spirit realm of the underworld. Quetzalcóatl's descent to the underworld to claim the bones of fish-men, the 'people' of a previous world-age, was understood to take place during the eight-day phase when Venus is invisible. When Quetzalcóatl returned successfully from his task, he rose into the heavens as the morning star. Every Maya ruler was thought to travel to the underworld after death and, if he passed successfully through the trials he encountered there, would rise into the skies as Venus.

In another tradition Quetzalcóatl-Topiltzin, overcome with shame after being outwitted by his dark double Tezcatlipoca and brought to sleep with his sister, takes his own life on a blazing pyre. From the flames his heart rises as Venus the morning star.

The appearance of Venus as the morning star would appear to be a reminder of the king's immortality and a celebration of the victory of Quetzalcóatl over the lords of the spirit realm and over death. Yet Venus did not generally have positive

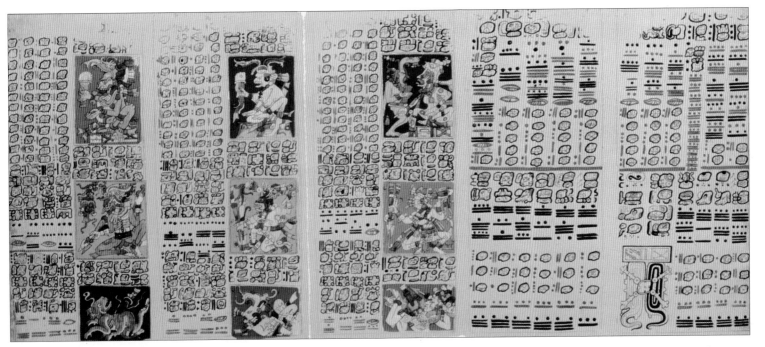

Above: Priests used the information in these pages from the Dresden Codex *to calculate the future cycles of the planet Venus.*

associations in the Mesoamerican mind. The planet was believed to have a negative influence on earthly affairs.

MAYA OBSERVATORIES

Maya star-watchers, who had no specialized astronomical equipment, predicted the rising of Venus as morning star and evening star with astonishing accuracy; to within one day in 6,000 years. The tower-observatory in the Maya city of Chichén Itzá tells of the dedication with which Maya priests plotted celestial movements. The tower is known in modern times as the Caracol, from the Spanish for snail, because it has spiral passageways. It was built for observation of Venus. Three passages leaving the Caracol line up precisely with the spots in the western sky where Venus can be seen as the evening star, among them the most northerly and southerly point at which it sets. At Palenque, the square tower that rises above the palace is decorated with a Venus glyph and appears to have been used as an observatory for plotting the planet's movements, while at Uxmal, the Governor's Palace must have been used for astronomical observation. It is aligned with a mound above which Venus would have risen at the most southerly point in its cycle.

Priests also relied on books to plot celestial movements. The *Grolier Codex* of *c.*1230 consists of around half of a table for predicting the Venus cycle over 104 years. The *Dresden Codex*, which dates to just before the Spanish Conquest, contains tables for plotting the Venus and Mars cycles and solar eclipses, as well as details of rites and deities associated with the 260-day calendar. Both these books contain eight-year Venus tables which show that the Maya understood how, after five 584-day Venus cycles and eight 365-day solar cycles, the two met ($5 \times 584 = 2920$ days $= 8 \times 365$).

GODS AND ANIMALS: THE MAYA ZODIAC

There is disagreement among scholars over whether the Maya had a zodiac of star-signs like that developed by Western astrologers.

Some authors believe that there is evidence for a Maya zodiac on a badly damaged page of the *Paris Codex*, which shows animals hanging from a band thought to represent the heavens. The *Paris Codex* animals are a scorpion, a turtle and a rattlesnake. We know that the Maya saw a constellation in the night sky by the name of *tzab* ('rattlesnake rattle') where in the western tradition we see the Pleiades.

It is likely that a Maya zodiac would contain the turtle, because that creature plays an important role in Maya creation stories. In some accounts, the world was said to be lying atop a giant turtle; there is also an image on a surviving Maya pot of the maize god rising from the broken earth, which is represented by a broken turtle shell.

Scholars believe that the Maya may have associated the stars of our constellation Orion with a turtle. In one of the murals at Bonampak a turtle is shown with the three stars from Orion's belt adorning its shell.

Among the Aztecs, most of the gods had equivalents among the stars. Tezcatlipoca was associated with the Great Bear. The jaguar skin that he was often shown wearing was an Aztec image for the night sky itself. Aztecs believed that the Great Bear's descent into the waters of the ocean was a re-enactment of the myth in which Tezcatlipoca loses his foot while he is fighting the Earth Monster. Quetzalcóatl was Venus as the morning star and the same planet as the evening star was Quetzalcóatl's double, Xólotl, who travelled with the Plumed Serpent to the underworld when he went to outwit the underworld lords and launch the current world-age.

WRITTEN RECORDS

The Olmec peoples who flourished on the Gulf Coast of Mexico c.1500–400 BC are accorded the honour of being the first Mesoamerican people to develop a written script by some scholars. On one end of a basalt column from the Olmec site at La Venta, a craftsman carved the relief of a walking man with a beard and beside the man's head cut three signs that

Below: A scribe incised Maya glyphs into this jade pendant in the 5th century AD. Added red colour makes reading easier.

look like hieroglyphs. Experts have been unable to decipher the signs, but suggest that one of the glyph-like images, which looks like a bird's head, probably represents the man's name.

Other examples of Olmec hieroglyph-like images are found on pots and celts of jade and serpentine. But most scholars now argue that while the Olmec certainly used symbols to communicate meaning, their carvings cannot be called writing because the symbols do not refer to the sounds of a language. They are symbols purely and simply. Like road signs, they carry meaning, but do not represent sounds or words.

FIRST BOOKS

Intriguingly, it appears that the Olmec might already have been using screenfold books made from *amate* bark. A ceramic bowl that might be dated as early as 1200 BC is carved with two objects that resemble this kind of book. The Olmec appear to have had a working system of written communication even if it was not writing as we define it.

Following the collapse of Olmec culture, the Zapotec craftsmen of Monte Albán in c.600–200 BC were the next to develop the art of writing in Mesoamerica. They carved images of male figures in the Temple of the Danzantes at Monte Albán alongside hieroglyphic signs that appear to represent the figures' names.

The men depicted were once thought to be dancers (*danzantes*) but are now believed to be sacrificed war captives. Later Zapotec monuments bear longer texts that include dates in the Calendar Round, cut with year signs, glyphs for days and months and bar-and-dot numbers. As with the Olmec inscriptions, scholars have been unable to decipher these carvings, apart from the dates. The earliest example of Zapotec writing is probably the stone called Monument 3 from San José Mogote in the Oaxaca Valley. It depicts a slain captive with

Above: The top section of this carving shows Aztec rulers Tizoc and Ahuítzotl. Beneath are the glyphs representing the date 8-Reed.

blood pouring from his chest and gives the Calendar date 1-Earthquake – perhaps his day-name. It has been dated to c.600 BC.

Some scholars claim this as the earliest example of Mesoamerican writing and argue that other forms derived from the Zapotec, but other authorities suggest that this was just one of several scripts that the inventive Mesoamericans developed independently in the years after the decline of the Olmec. Two monuments carved with Long Count dates survive from c.30 BC, one in Chiapas and one in Veracruz. Neither has an accompanying hieroglyphic text, so it is impossible to judge the development of writing locally at that stage.

THE ISTHMIAN SCRIPT

A writing system known as the 'Isthmian script' appears to have been used in southern Veracruz in the 2nd century AD.

Only four objects carved with this script survive. The most important are a jade figure known as the Tuxtla statuette, now in the Smithsonian Institution, Washington, DC, and a basalt stela found in 1986 at La Mojarra in Veracruz. The script used only 150 signs, so scholars argue these signs probably represented whole words rather than phonetic elements (the distinctive sounds of a language). Some of the signs used bear superficial resemblance to later Maya signs, but experts believe the Isthmian script was not a close relative of early Maya writing. Maya writing was read in double columns from left to right and also top to bottom. However, the Isthmian script does not link its columns in twos and may not have been read left to right, for the glyphs appear to face towards a standing figure in the centre of the carving.

Below: This stone calendar, inscribed with glyphs, was carved by a craftsman of the Huastec culture in north-eastern Mexico.

Carving found on a stone stela at Kaminaljuyú (near modern Guatemala City) from around the same time appears to have a much greater similarity to Maya scripts. The inscription does use paired columns as in Maya writing, and it may contain some of the same glyphs. Indeed, the carving may even be in Maya writing, but is too fragmentary to provide definitive evidence.

The earliest surviving piece definitely identified in the Maya writing system is the Hauberg stela of AD199. The stela shows a king wearing the mask of the rain god Chac and the two-headed

Above: In the intriguing Zapotec carvings that depict war sacrifices at Monte Albán, a number of early glyphs are believed to give the victims' names.

serpent that indicates royal standing. The dating inscription does not include a Long Count date, but the scholar Linda Schele has interpreted the given date to be AD199. The inscription uses the emblem glyph, which is commonly found in Maya inscriptions. The emblem glyph generally identifies the ruler as *k'ul ahaw* ('holy king') of a particular city, in this case, puzzlingly, the 'holy king of Fire'.

ROYAL SCRIBES AND CODICES

Scribes were members of the Maya elite. They were usually the sons and daughters of nobles or even royalty. A late Classic Period vase thought to have been made at Naranjo was signed by the artist Ah Maxam, who wrote that he was the son of a king of Naranjo and a princess from Yaxhá. Many kings appear to have been scribes. They are shown on vases wearing a bundle of pens in their hair, which was an accepted mark of high-ranking scribal office. Royal sons and daughters were doubtless educated in scribal schools.

The most important scribe in the Classic Period Maya city state was the *ak k'u hun* ('guardian of the sacred books').

Below: A skilled Maya stonecutter incised 32 hieroglyphs on this lintel at Yaxchilán. The work is dated AD534.

THE DUTIES OF SCRIBES

From the evidence of images on Maya vases in murals, the chief scribe or *ak k'u hun* had many courtly jobs in addition to artistic endeavours. He or she was expected to arrange royal ceremonies, was a negotiator of royal marriages and a record-keeper responsible for recording offerings of tribute from client states or allies and keeping royal genealogical lists. He or she may also have taught in scribal schools.

The Maya scribe probably painted the images that accompanied his words. Both calligraphers and painters were given the title *ah ts'ib* ('he of the writing'). Those who produced hieroglyphic inscriptions and images in stone were accorded the honour of being named *yuxul* ('sculptor'). Both women and men – although probably more men than women – were scribes. The titles *ah ts'ib* and *ak k'u hun* were given to women and men.

Above: Maya scribes also cut glyphs in wood, but little of their work has survived. This is a lintel from Temple IV at Tikal.

Students at scribe schools must have followed long and demanding courses of study, for reading and writing Maya hieroglyphs required great knowledge and skill. A scribe had many choices when writing. He or she could write the same phrase in a number of ways. Some logographs (images representing whole words) could also be used as phonetic signs (symbols representing spoken sounds). Scribes sometimes used both the logograph for a name or word and the phonetic signs that would spell out that name. An example often given by Maya experts is that the word *balam* ('jaguar'), could be written with a single logograph representing the head of a jaguar, with the logograph and

136

GODS OF THE SCRIBES

One 8th-century AD Maya vase depicts a rabbit deity writing in a screenfold book. The creature is one of the large number of gods who are associated with Maya scribes.

Itzamná, the supreme Maya god, was believed to be the creator of writing, and is shown as a scribe in the *Madrid Codex*. Itzamná's animal form was a bearded dragon: carvings at Copán show scribes emerging from the mouth of this creature. Another high-ranking Maya god, Pawahtún, was often shown in images of scribes and on one vase is seen teaching novice scribes in an elite school. The Monkey-men, half-brothers of the Hero Twins in the *Popol Vuh* cycle, are often portrayed with writing implements or working at codices. Both the Hero Twins' father, the Young Maize God, and Hunahpú, one of the Twins, were associated with kingship and writing. They, too, were often shown with quill pens working at calligraphy. The rabbit deity was linked to the moon goddess. Mesoamericans thought they saw a rabbit in the face of the moon whereas in Western tradition we think we see a man's figure or a man's face.

Right: A terracotta figure left as an offering on Jaina Island represents a noble or perhaps princely scribe at work.

column, second line/second column etc. Some shorter pieces of writing on monuments and on ceramic objects and carved bones or shells were arranged differently; sometimes as horizontal lines, sometimes as vertical lines. An intriguing variation, found on the markers of ball courts and on some altars, was for the text to be arranged in a circle; the reader would know by a marker in the text (usually a date) where to begin reading. At Quiriguá and Copán, hieroglyphs are sometimes written on monuments in a complex criss-cross pattern to resemble a woven mat. In a very few cases – for example, Lintel 25 at Yaxchilán and on four pages of the *Paris Codex* – the hieroglyphs were inscribed to be read from right to left.

MAYA WRITING

Surviving Maya writing is of various kinds. The stelae of Classic Period Maya cities such as Yaxchilán, Tikal and Copán celebrate the achievements of holy kings and the dynasties to which they belonged. However, the northern Maya cities such as Uxmal and Chichén Itzá that continued to thrive after the 'Maya Collapse' in the lowlands left few stelae from this Postclassic Period. Surviving inscriptions tend to be on stone lintels and wall panels. They do not portray great kings and tell their life histories. Instead, they use few pictures and celebrate fire rites and the dedication of buildings. It seems there was not any dynasty to celebrate.

These inscriptions refer to shared rule by a council of up to four people.

The writing in the four surviving Maya codices mainly concerns priestly rituals and tables for calculating astronomical events. Writing on carved bones and jade and on the pots and other ceramic goods left with deceased royals and nobles in their graves mostly gives the name and titles of the deceased and sometimes also contains dedications to the gods. Some also name the artist who drew them.

Below: Maya stonecut glyphs from stele M at Copán. It honours the city's 15th king, Smoke Shell, who completed Copán's Hieroglyphic Stairway. The stair has 2,500 glyphs listing the kings of the ruling dynasty.

some phonetic signs, and also with the three phonetic signs that spelled *ba*, *la* and *ma*.

Some signs were both logographs and phonetic signs. To help readers know in which way a sign was being used, scribes often used additional phonetic signs alongside the logographs.

On most Classic Period Maya monuments, the hieroglyphs are written to be read in paired columns from left to right and also from top to bottom: you read the first line/first column, first line/second column, then second line/first

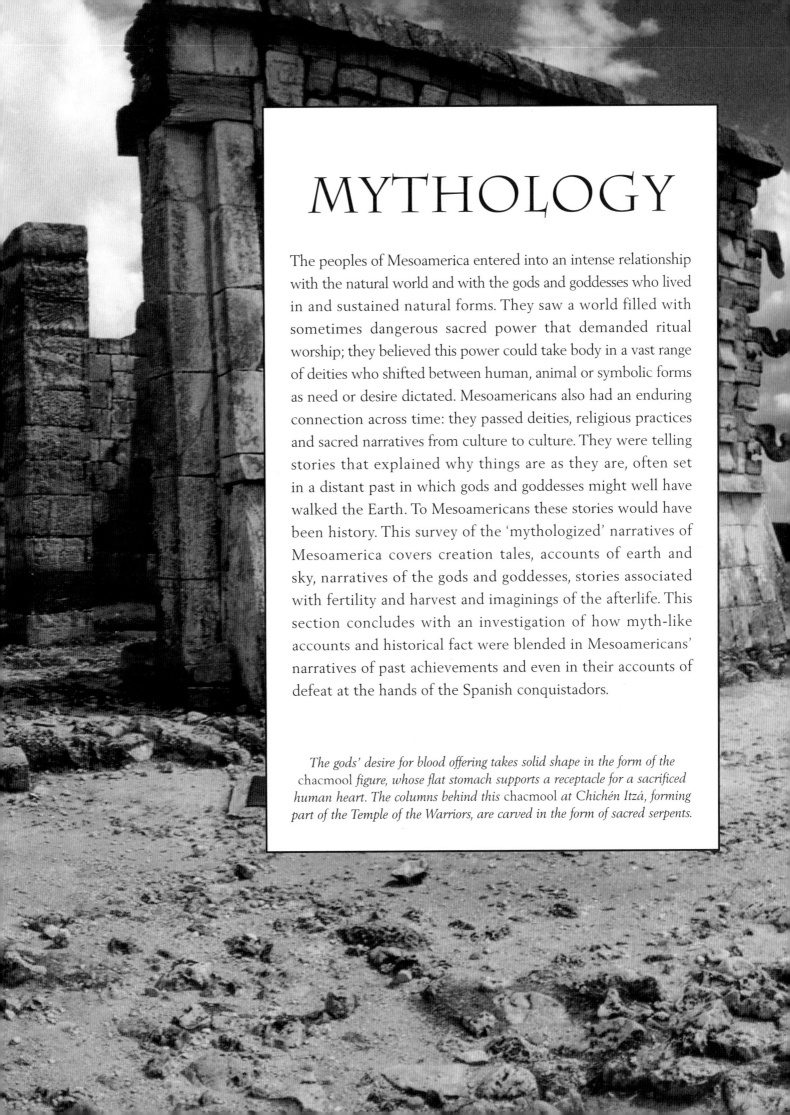

MYTHOLOGY

The peoples of Mesoamerica entered into an intense relationship with the natural world and with the gods and goddesses who lived in and sustained natural forms. They saw a world filled with sometimes dangerous sacred power that demanded ritual worship; they believed this power could take body in a vast range of deities who shifted between human, animal or symbolic forms as need or desire dictated. Mesoamericans also had an enduring connection across time: they passed deities, religious practices and sacred narratives from culture to culture. They were telling stories that explained why things are as they are, often set in a distant past in which gods and goddesses might well have walked the Earth. To Mesoamericans these stories would have been history. This survey of the 'mythologized' narratives of Mesoamerica covers creation tales, accounts of earth and sky, narratives of the gods and goddesses, stories associated with fertility and harvest and imaginings of the afterlife. This section concludes with an investigation of how myth-like accounts and historical fact were blended in Mesoamericans' narratives of past achievements and even in their accounts of defeat at the hands of the Spanish conquistadors.

The gods' desire for blood offering takes solid shape in the form of the chacmool *figure, whose flat stomach supports a receptacle for a sacrificed human heart. The columns behind this* chacmool *at Chichén Itzá, forming part of the Temple of the Warriors, are carved in the form of sacred serpents.*

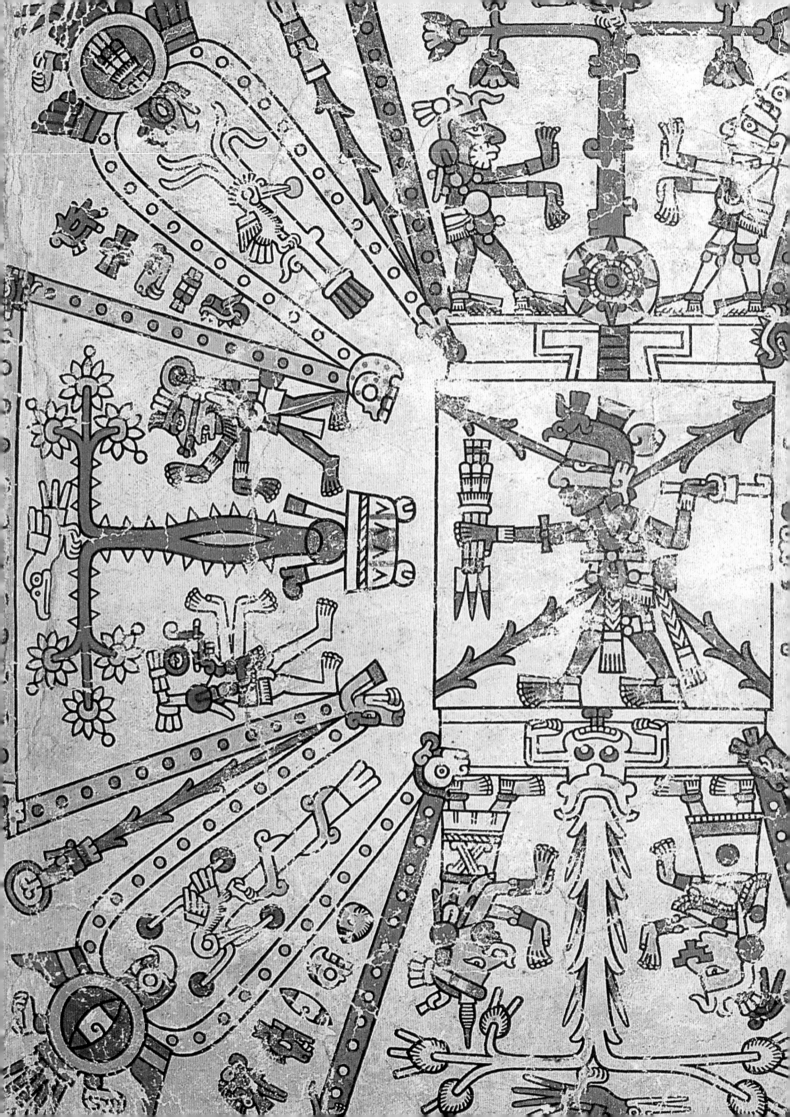

CHAPTER 7

CREATION AND THE FIRST PEOPLES

The Aztecs understood both time and space in terms of four cardinal directions and a central anchoring point. They believed that the Great Pyramid in Tenochtitlán was the centre of the Earth, which spread in a vast flat expanse to east and west and north and south. Four gods and their directions were also associated with the four 'suns' or ages that had preceded the current era on Earth. The first age was associated with Tezcatlipoca and with the north. The second was under the control of Quetzalcóatl, and linked to the west, while the third was governed by the rain god Tláloc and connected to the south. The fourth age was presided over by Tláloc's consort Chalchiúhtlicue and connected to the east. The fifth 'sun' or contemporary age was linked to the centre because the number of the centre is five; it was under the control of the fire god Xiuhtecuhtli.

According to Aztec cosmology, above the flat Earth rose thirteen layers of heaven, where Ometeotl, the supreme creator, dwelt. Beneath the earth were nine levels of the underworld or Mictlán, presided over by Mictlantecuhtli, god of that realm, with his consort Mictecacíhuatl. In some accounts, waters encircled the Earth at the farthest reaches of north, south, east and west and curved up above the land to make the sky. If the gods decreed, the sky waters could fall to wipe out men and all their achievements in one cataclysmic flood.

Left: An illustration from the Mixtec-Aztec Codex Fejérváry-Mayer *depicts the fire god Xiuhtecuhtli at the centre of the universe with four directions emanating outwards.*

THE POWER IN THE CENTRE: COSMOLOGY

At north, south, east and west of the Mesoamerican universe stood four pillars, or trees, that both supported and connected the three levels of the cosmos. In the centre was a fifth tree, whose roots were in the underworld but whose topmost branches touched the very highest of the celestial planes. The four other trees at the points of the compass were in fact outgrowths of the main cosmic tree. The trees stood on hollow hills and were themselves hollow, and within them the power of the underworld and of the heavens was always flowing, powering the repeating movements of time, of the seasons, of the sun, moon, stars and planets and of the energy recycled in acts of blood sacrifice. Only after the creation of the four trees of north, south, east and west could time be measured and sacred events honoured through use of the ritual calendar.

THE FOUR GODS

In one Aztec myth, four gods were born, sometimes known as the four Tezcatlipocas after the god of night and destiny, the sons of the supreme creator Ometeotl in his dual male-female forms Ometecuhtli and Omecíhuatl. According to this tradition, all was chaos in the first days until the four sons agreed to separate heaven and earth and take the form of the four world trees at the four cardinal points. Their act of separation created a space in which the new world could be made.

Right: This stela, carved in c.1250, shows the Earth Monster Tlaltecuhtli, ravenous for human heart blood.

A developed iconography was associated with these myths. Each of the four points of the compass was associated with a god, a glyph, at least one colour and a plant. For example, the glyph for north – the direction of Tezcatlipoca – represented a *técpatl*, the knife used for sacrificing victims; its colours were yellow and black. North was associated with the xerophyte tree, which naturally grew in northern regions of Mesoamerica. Death and cold were linked to the region, which was known as Mictlampa (the land of death). Dampness was associated with the south, where Huitzilopochtli held sway. The glyph for south represented the rabbit; the region was linked to the colour blue. The west was governed by Quetzalcóatl. Its glyph represented a house and its colour was white. The east was associated with Xipe Totec and its glyph showed a reed. Its colour was red.

Sometimes the Aztecs likened the Earth to a flower with four petals, one for each quadrant. One interpretation of the myth of the four suns or ages is that in each successive age one of the four quadrants and its tree or pillar was created and that in the fifth (current) age, the centre – that is, the Templo Mayor at the Great Pyramid in Tenochtitlán – came into being.

THE WORLD TREE

This basic cosmology was common in Mesoamerica. The Maya also told of a vast flat earth, with thirteen levels of heaven rising above and nine layers of under-world beneath. The Quiché Maya told in the *Popol Vuh* how, in the first hours of

Above: A Maya priest ceremonially plants corn. Maintaining the Earth's fertility was a focus of Mesoamerican religious life.

creation, the earth and sky emerged following a 'fourfold cornering [and] measuring', a process analogous to the one used by Maya farmers to plot their fields. The Maya also understood that in each of the four corners of creation grew a tree, supporting the sky in that place, and that in the centre rose a greater world tree, which connected the realms of earth, heaven and the underworld. The Maya king Pacal, ruler of Palenque, is depicted on the lid of his magnificent sarcophagus travelling down to the underworld along the trunk of this great cosmic tree.

In some accounts of Maya cosmography, the four supporting structures are not trees but giants called bacabs who, curiously, were patrons of beekeepers. A depiction of the bacabs survives on an 8th–9th

Right: A mural from a residential building in Teotihuacán represents the Earth Mother (centre) supporting a great cosmic tree.

century building at Chichén Itzá that was called the *Iglesia* ('church') by the Spaniards. Their names were Mulac (associated with the north and with white), Kan (linked to the east and yellow), Ix (connected to the west and to black) and Cauac (associated with the south and red). Like the Aztecs, the Maya linked colours to the four directions, but

Below: Xipe Totec (left), god of the east, confronts western deity Quetzalcóatl in an image from the Aztec Codex Borbonicus.

the associations of particular colours were different in the two traditions. For example, white was the colour of the west for the Aztecs but of the north for the Maya. According to the *Books of Chilam Balam*, which contain the legends of the Maya of Yucatán, the four trees at the four corners of the Earth were created in the first moments of each new age.

Below: The ancient rain god worshipped by the Maya as Chac was sometimes said to have power over the cardinal directions.

143

THE MAKING OF THE EARTH

The Mixtec people who made their home in former Zapotec lands in the Oaxaca Valley left a distinctive creation mythology in the images and words of their codices. They told that life began in the union of a nameless couple who lived before time. In the darkness of the unborn world, this pair of gods gave birth to another divine couple named Lord One Deer and Lady One Deer, and they in turn produced many children. Two of Lord and Lady One Deer's offspring pleased their parents by creating a sweet-smelling garden retreat, where flowers bloomed in the gentle shade of magical trees. The first of the Mixtec race climbed from a hole in the trunk of one these remarkable trees. In another account, the Mixtecs were born in a tree that grew in Mexico in Apoala, where a river fed an oasis that

Below: In this Codex Fejérváry-Mayer *image, Tezcatlipoca loses his right foot to the ravening Earth Monster Tlaltecuhtli.*

kept the desert at bay. The men and women went from this place to the four corners of the flat earth, establishing settlements in which to grow crops, raise children and worship the gods. The tree must be a representation of the world tree that Mesoamericans believed linked the spirit realms of the underworld and the many-layered heaven to the earth. It may suggest the family tree of many generations of revered ancestors.

Another version of Mixtec creation mythology told of a primordial era when earth and sky were not separated in complementary opposition as they are now, but were mixed in wetness and darkness. The earth was no more than waterlogged, muddy slime.

Left: This cedar-wood fertility goddess was still receiving offerings when it was discovered in Veracruz in the 19th century.

Then a creator god named Lord Nine Wind arose from the dark and separated the waters from the earth, raising the waters up to form the sky. Mist engulfed the earth, but from the shadowy half-light a divine couple emerged: they were Lord One Deer Jaguar-Serpent and Lady One Deer Jaguar-Serpent. As the sky perfectly complements the earth, so this god and goddess matched one another. They were two separate beings but also at the same time were one divinity encompassing male and female. Their union was fruitful: they created all the other gods of the Mixtec pantheon and built a palace on earth near Apoala. Apoala is well known, but the palace has never been found. It is said that if a mortal man could find this palace, he would discover that on its roof was set a great axe of copper, its blade facing up to and supporting the overarching sky.

CONNECTING STORIES

Lord Nine Wind is a version of the Plumed Serpent god worshipped by the Aztecs as Quetzalcóatl and by the Maya as Kukulcán. In the Quiché Maya creation myth, this same deity is a god of the sea, Sovereign Plumed Serpent, who joins with a sky god to create the unity of sky and earth.

Quetzalcóatl is also a creator-protagonist in the ancient Mexican myth of the Earth Monster Tlaltecuhtli. The Aztecs told the myth, which they had inherited from earlier cultures in the Mexican region, to glorify the gods Quetzalcóatl and Tezcatlipoca. These normally

Above: Ancestors of the Mixtecs depicted in these codex images believed they were born from a tree trunk in a garden paradise.

implacable foes decided to join forces to curb Tlaltecuhtli's power when they saw her spreading terror as she walked on the sea. The Earth Monster, like many Mesoamerican deities, was sometimes described as male and sometimes as female; she had a gaping mouth not only on her face but also at her knees, elbows and other joints.

Quetzalcóatl and Tezcatlipoca approached in the form of great, slithering serpents, muscles rippling in their strong shoulders and thighs, their eyes flashing, their long tongues darting from their mouths. Their power was wild as they seized Tlaltecuhtli. One took her left arm and right foot, the other took her right arm and left foot and together they tore her into two great pieces. The first they hurled upwards to make the sky. The second they laid out in four directions to make the flat expanse of the earth. In some accounts Tezcatlipoca fought the

Right: Quetzalcóatl is born from the Earth as Venus the morning star in this carving from a Santa Lucia Cotzumalhuapa stela.

Earth Monster in his usual form rather than as a serpent and in the course of the great battle lost one of his feet, explaining his one-legged appearance.

The other gods were not pleased to see this violence done to their sister Tlaltecuhtli. Angrily they addressed Quetzalcóatl and Tezcatlipoca, declaring that although she had been torn in pieces, her earthly part would form the basis of future life. They made herbs, flowers and trees grow from her hair, while grasses and sweet-smelling flowers issued from her skin. The life-giving waters of springs and wells were made from her eyes; her mouth made rivers and larger caverns. Her nose gave rise to tall snow-capped mountains and the deep valleys of the sierras where the air is thin. Men and women have grown used to walking on the body of Tlaltecuhtli.

145

ORDER FROM CHAOS: MAYA CREATION STORIES

The Quiché Maya give a detailed account of the creation of the world, and also of the gods' efforts to make the first humans, in their sacred book the *Popol Vuh* ('Book of Advice').

CONVERSATION OF THE GODS

The book tells how the earth was born from the conversation of the gods. Before time began, the waters stretched out endlessly in all directions beneath a blank sky and nothing existed in all the universe except these gathered waters and the sky above. There were no animals or fish, no birds or plants, no rocks and no people. There was not even the potential for life hidden in the waters or the half-darkness of the sky, waiting to be brought to life. Yet the waters did contain the sea god, Gucumatz or 'Sovereign Plumed Serpent', and so despite the near-darkness there was a stirring in the sea, a glittering like blue-green quetzal feathers. His presence was echoed and balanced high above by the sky god Huracán or Heart of Sky.

Huracán came down to meet the sea god and these two divinities, who were deep thinkers and possessed of profound knowledge, started a conversation. Their words brought life into being. The discussion was not easy. They were troubled because they could not at first be sure of the right way to proceed. However, in the course of their debate they created a vision of how life should be in the world, how the trees and bushes should grow and how the people should walk among them. As they talked, it was like the time just before dawn. They discussed how the 'sowing' and the 'dawning' should be brought about. First they decided that the waters should be cleared so that the earth could rise up, and then life could be sown in the earth and in the sky. But they knew that people were needed for this world. The sky and sea gods wanted praise for their work, and they understood that they would not receive this until they created a people capable of keeping track of time and expressing wonder and worship on the appointed days.

The words they used in their discussion had concrete effect. The waters fell away and the earth rose up, just as they said. Mountains appeared and wide forests of pine and cypress trees covered their sides. Waters collected in great lakes and ran on the mountainsides in streams. The gods were pleased. Gucumatz said to Huracán that it was a good thing that the sky god had come down to the sea and

Above: Gods above and below – the god depicted on the lower half of this Maya vessel appears to be Chac-Xib-Chac, known for his power to raise hurricanes.

that they had begun their conversation. He had seen from the beginning of their work that it would turn out well. Now they turned to creating animals and people to inhabit the good world.

The *Popol Vuh* account of creation is dense and highly allusive. The scholar and translator of the *Popol Vuh*, Dennis Tedlock, provides many helpful explanations gleaned from his training as a 'daykeeper' or shaman-priest among the contemporary Maya in the region of Momostenango in Guatemala. He states that the 'sowing and dawning' discussed by Huracán and Gucumatz can be understood in terms of the planting and growing of plants, the life cycle of humans and the movements of the planets in the sky. Plant seeds are sown in the earth and 'dawn' by emerging from the ground as

Left: This Classic Maya stone carving represents the Plumed Serpent god feared and worshipped across eras and cultures by Mesoamericans under such names as Quetzalcóatl, Kukulcán and Gucumatz.

Above: Tezcatlipoca, unpredictable Aztec god, had counterparts among storm deities elsewhere in Mesoamerica.

crops. Similarly, humans are 'sown' in the womb during sexual relations, then 'dawn' nine months later when they emerge screaming into the world. They are also 'sown' in the earth when they are buried after the body's death, but 'dawn' again

as spirits after death, taking the form of celestial lights or stars in the sky. The sun, the moon, Venus and other planets disappear in their own form of 'sowing' when they appear to sink into the earth at the horizon, but they rise again at the appointed time of their dawning.

LORDS OF CREATION

The creator gods are versions of major Mesoamerican deities. Hurakán's name can be understood as 'one-leg' and he is associated with the Classic Period Maya deity Tahil ('Obsidian Mirror' or 'Torch Mirror'), a one-legged god who was honoured in carving at the city of Palenque. Through this connection, Hurakán can be identified with the Aztec god Tezcatlipoca ('Lord of the Smoking Mirror') who, among many attributes, was a divinity of hurricanes, wore an obsidian mirror and was said to be one-legged (in some accounts, because he lost a leg while fighting the Earth Monster Tlaltecuhtli).

Tezcatlipoca was also a god of rains and Huracán's name is linked linguistically with the words used by the Quiché Maya to describe the very large raindrops that come before and after thunderstorms. Sovereign Plumed Serpent or Gucumatz is more obviously a version of the feathered serpent deity Quetzalcóatl, and is also known as Kukulcán by the Yucatec-speaking Maya.

Left: This powerful but simple Maya mask was fashioned from jade to be worn as an ornament on the chest or a belt.

Above: This Classic Maya terracotta vase (c.AD650–950) bears the face of a sky god, perhaps the sun god Ah Kin Chil.

The *Popol Vuh* creation story describes these creator gods both as individuals and as members of a group. The group of sky gods includes Newborn Thunderbolt, Raw Thunderbolt and Heart of Earth. The collection of sea gods includes Heart of the Sea and Heart of the Lake, as well as gods named Begetter, Modeller, Bearer and Maker. This willingness to allow seemingly contradictory things to be true, in this case to allow each creator god to be both individual and also a group of many, is typical of Mesoamerican thought and mythology.

147

BOTH ONE AND TWO: AZTEC CREATION STORIES

The Plumed Serpent god played an important role in creation mythology of the Aztecs. He was not the Aztecs' primal or original creator, but he was one of the active deities who carried out the work of creation. According to the peoples of the Valley of Mexico, the supreme creator was Ometeotl, a god of duality

Below: This Aztec wooden mask depicts either rain god Tláloc or Quetzalcóatl as Éhecatl, lord of the winds.

Right: A terracotta image from Veracruz (c.AD500) represents a gruesome rite in honour of Xipe Totec, 'Our Flayed Lord'.

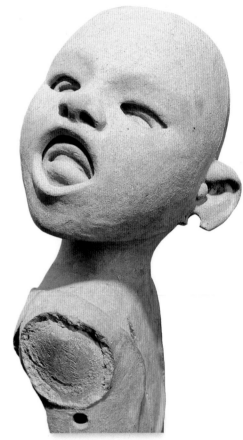

who existed in both male and female forms as Ometecuhtli and Omecíhuatl, twin gods who were also known as Tonacatecuhtli ('Lord of our Sustaining') and Tonacacíhuatl ('Lady of our Sustaining'). They lived in the thirteenth and highest level of the Aztec heaven, called Omeyocán.

BIRTH OF THE GODS

In one account, Tonacatecuhtli used his divine breath to bring life to a universe that was bathed in darkness. From his breath Quetzalcóatl was born, the Plumed Serpent as associated with the wind, particularly in his guise as Éhecatl. In another version, Omecíhuatl gave birth to all the gods and goddesses. In still another myth, the primal couple Ometecuhtli and Omecíhuatl gave birth to four gods, who they charged with the job of creating other deities, the world and the human race. They were the four Tezcatlipocas, each associated with a direction and a colour and some later identified with other gods.

Red Tezcatlipoca, connected to the east, was later identified as Xipe Totec, the god of vegetation and new life. Black Tezcatlipoca, associated with the night sky and the north, was later known simply as Tezcatlipoca. White Tezcatlipoca, associated with the west, was later known as Quetzalcóatl, while Blue Tezcatlipoca, linked to the south, was later Huitzilopochtli, the Aztec tribal god.

For six hundred years the four Tezcatlipocas delayed, then at last two of the gods, White Tezcatlipoca (Quetzalcóatl) and Blue Tezcatlipoca (Huitzilopochtli), began the ordained

Right: Chalchiúhtlicue, river goddess and consort of the rain god Tláloc, was praised for her power over the waters of spring.

work of creation. First they created fire and raised a forerunner of our sun in the sky. After this, they created the first human couple, Oxomoco and Cipactonal. They made the earth from a primal crocodile, the same creature later

identified as the Earth Monster Tlaltecuhtli. From the crocodile's body they also fashioned the rain god Tláloc and his female counterpart Chalchiúhtlicue and they must also have made the underworld region of Mictlán, for the myth says they gave life to Mictlantecuhtli and Mictecacíhuatl, the god and goddess of the underworld. At this time they fixed the sacred calendar of the 260-day count. They also created Xochiquetzal ('Flower Feather'), goddess of flowers and the earth and of dance and love.

THE FIRST HUMANS AS GODS

Oxomoco and Cipactonal gave birth to a son named Piltzintecuhtli. He was the first human to enjoy the pleasures and duties of marriage, for he took as his wife a beautiful American maiden created by

Right: This intricately finished ornament, thought to represent an early version of the Mesoamerican sun god, was found at the Zapotec site of Monte Albán.

Below: Images of Quetzalcóatl as the wind god Éhecatl characteristically have a bird-like mask on the lower face.

the great gods from the hair of Xochiquetzal. The first human husband is sometimes identified as a god, and his consort is seen by some as a human incarnation of Xochiquetzal. After this creation, the gods began the four ages or 'suns' of the Earth's history.

Oxomoco and Cipactonal, the first humans, are similarly often viewed as gods. They played an important role in the myth that details the discovery and spread of the Mesoamericans' staple maize plant. According to this myth, the red ants had hidden maize deep inside Mount Tonacatépetl but Quetzalcóatl, bringer of so many good things to the human race, intuited that the ants' mountain store contained something of great value and transformed himself into a black ant to investigate. On the mountainside he tried out the limitations of his new body, clambering over rocks and into crevices, then followed the line of red ants along narrow paths within the mountain to

their hidden store. He found great piles of cereal there and carried some back to his brother gods. They tasted it and found it good, so they ground it up to make meal and placed some in the mouths of human babies. The babies thrived on this new food and the gods decreed that the maize should be shared with humans across the lands of Mesoamerica. But how would they free it from its hiding place? First Quetzalcóatl tied a great rope around the mountain and attempted to split the hard rock. But even the Plumed Serpent was not strong enough to bring down the mountain. The gods then turned to Oxomoco and Cipactonal for advice. The divine human couple consulted with one another and at last declared that the task should be entrusted to Nanahuatzin, the unappealing god who had become the Fifth Sun. He split the mountain and the rain god spirits or *tláloque*s spread the maize far and wide.

THE ANGER OF THE GODS

The *Popol Vuh* of the Quiché Maya begins the tale of creation by describing the establishment of the fertile lands of the Earth, the gathering of the lakes and rivers that feed the soil and the springing to life of forests and life-giving plants. The account continues with the decision by the creator gods Huracán and Gucumatz to fill the Earth with animals and the first people.

They made animals to inhabit the mountains and forests, including deer and jaguars, snakes, pumas and birds. They appointed the creatures to their rightful places in the world, telling the deer to live in canyons along the banks of rivers and to roam freely in the fields and forests, while telling the birds to nest in the branches of trees and the safety of thick bushes. Then the creators called on the animals to speak to them and honour the gods who had given life to the forests and mountains. There were many names to choose from: Heart of Sky, Raw Thunderbolt, Hurricane, Plumed Serpent, Begetter, Maker, Modeller. But the animals could not speak a single name; all they could utter were wild cries, screeching and squawking. The gods were

Below: The toad was among the creatures created before the first people. This Classic Period Maya offering vessel dates from AD250–600.

not pleased, for what they wanted was a creature who was capable of keeping count of days and offering praise and sacrifices. They told the animals and birds that they would become food for each other and for the people whom the gods hoped to create.

MAN OF MUD?

Next the creators tried to make a human being from mud. However, try as they might, they could not make the body hold together: it kept sliding apart and dissolving into a watery mess. Its face was not pleasing, because it had a lopsided look and although the creature could speak, its words made no sense. The gods agreed to let the body dissolve. The man of mud was a false start and they decided to let it be a thought that led nowhere. However, they were determined to keep trying to create a human being. They decided next to consult an ancient pair of deities, divine equivalents of the

Above: This image of the Plumed Serpent god dates from 1300–1500. He was held in awe for his power to unleash floods.

'daykeepers' or shaman-diviners of the Quiché Maya. The couple were called Xpiyacoc and Xmucané. Huracán and Gucumatz addressed the couple as grandfather-grandmother, matchmaker-midwife, makers of jewellery and incense, carpenters and craftsmen.

MAN OF WOOD?

Huracán and Gucumatz asked the diviners whether human beings could be made from wood. The grandfather and grandmother performed a divination using kernels of corn and coral seeds and declared that wood was a suitable material for making people. They also warned Huracán against trying to trick Gucumatz. This aside perhaps reflects the gods' associations with forms of the Aztec deities Tezcatlipoca, linked to Huracán and always connected with deception and trickery, and Quetzalcóatl, linked to Gucumatz and in many myths the victim of Tezcatlipoca's plotting. Dennis Tedlock, the translator of the *Popol Vuh* and an

initiated diviner, points out that Maya priests expect some trickery from the gods and will sometimes warn them in this way not to give a false answer during a divination.

Huracán and Gucumatz listened to the grandparents' reply and decided at once to fill the Earth with wooden people. 'Let it be so', they said, and their words were enough to make it happen; wooden people spread across the lands of America, the men made from the wood of the coral tree and the women made from the core of bulrushes. The people formed families and multiplied, but although they could speak, their hearts and minds were empty. They did not remember their creators or

Below: This late Classic Maya Period painted ceramic bowl decorated with a resting deer was found in El Petén, Guatemala.

count the days and honour the gods at the appropriate times. Moreover, although the people could walk and behave much like human beings, their skin was dry and flaky because they had no sweat, and their bodies warped in the heat because they had no blood to keep them moist.

AN UNMAKING
The gods determined to do away with this race of wooden people. Huracán sent powerful rainstorms that produced a vast flood and many people were drowned. To deal with the survivors, Huracán sent terrifying monsters, including Gouger of Faces, who carved out eyeballs, and Sudden Bloodletter, who pulled off their heads. The natural order the gods had established unravelled. Animals left their appointed places in the forests and on the mountains and invaded the houses

Above: Images of the Maya creator god Itzamná were often shown with crossed eyes.

of the people. The grinding stones, tortilla griddles and cooking pots rose up in violence and smashed the faces of the terrified people. The dogs they had kept attacked them. Even the hearthstones in the family fireplaces leapt out and set about the people's heads.

MONKEYS
The few survivors of the failed creation of the wooden people had battered heads and faces, but still looked a little like human beings. They were allowed to live on in the world in the form of monkeys. For this reason, the monkeys and apes of the forest resemble people. They are a reminder of a less than perfect creation. If humans forget their duty to mark the days, offer praise to the gods and seek the divine patterns in their lives, then they have become little better than the wooden people whose hearts and minds were empty.

Huracán and Gucumatz had now made three failed attempts to create a being capable of marking sacred days with a calendar and offering praise to the creators. They were still determined to keep trying, and their next attempt was destined to succeed.

THE HERO TWINS AND SEVEN MACAW

The *Popol Vuh* account digresses from the creation attempts of Huracán and Gucumatz in order to describe the valiant work of the divine Hero Twins in making earth and sky safe places. These events took place during the era of the wooden people.

A BID FOR POWER

In those days there was no day or night as we know it now, but only a long, unchanging twilight. Then a vain and boastful god called Seven Macaw tried to set himself up as supreme deity. He was a macaw and lived in a tree nest high above the earth of the wooden people. He had eyes of metal and teeth encrusted with turquoise and jewels, a great shiny nose and a nest of metal. Preening high

Below: An earthenware vase from Teotihuacán shows a quetzal bird in a cacao tree.

Below: Mesoamericans revered the tobacco plant and shredded its leaves to smoke in pipes such as this ceramic parrot.

in his tree, he declared that the light reflecting off his teeth was the blue of the sky while his nose could shine as brightly as the moon. He was also the sun, he said. When he came out in front of his shiny nest he gave light to the people below and his face shone far into the distance. The diviner-narrators of the *Popol Vuh* comment that, in truth Seven Macaw was none of these things, for as yet there was no sun or moon and the whole of creation existed in a half-light.

HERO TWINS

The young twin gods known as the Hero Twins, Hunahpú and Xbalanqué, discussed the behaviour of Seven Macaw and agreed that it was unacceptable for this vainglorious bird to puff himself up and claim to be greater than Gucumatz and Huracán, the wise modellers and makers who had created the world by the power of their spoken word. The twins were the children of the god Hun Hunahpú and Blood Moon, a maiden of

the underworld. Both the twins were skilled hunters and went far and wide shooting birds and animals with their blowpipes. They decided to use their hunting skills to puncture Seven Macaw's pride. One morning the twins lay in wait for Seven Macaw beneath a tree where the bird came each day to feed. Hunahpú waited until the macaw was busy eating, then used his blowpipe to deliver an accurate shot that broke Seven Macaw's jaw. The bird fell from the tree and Hunahpú ran across the ground to seize it but, just as he arrived, Seven Macaw caught hold of his arm and wrenched it from its socket. Hunahpú was left in agony, with blood pouring from his wound, while Seven Macaw went slowly home, ruminating over the damage to his jaw. His wife Chimalmat greeted him, expressing surprise at his appearance, and he described the sudden attack that had broken his jaw and given him an almighty toothache. However, he had a trophy from the conflict, he said, and held up Hunahpú's arm. He hung the arm above his fire and declared that the trickster twins could come and get it if they wanted it.

PUNCTURED PRIDE

Hunahpú and Xbalanqué now devised a plan for outwitting Seven Macaw. They approached Great White Peccary and Great White Tapir, a wise grandfather and grandmother, for help. The twins proposed that the old couple should approach the boastful macaw pretending to be travelling medics and offer to ease his pain. Hunahpú and Xbalanqué would travel with them in the guise of their grandchildren. The bird would probably beg for help and then, once his guard was down, the elderly couple and the twins could strip him of his finery and retrieve

Above: This detail of a clay vase dating from c.AD200–400 shows Seven Macaw wearing a necklace that denotes his power.

Hunahpú's arm. Great White Peccary and Great White Tapir agreed to the deception and they went, with the twins in tow, to Seven Macaw's splendid home.

The plan worked exactly as the twins had hoped. The grandparents persuaded Seven Macaw his toothache was caused by worms gnawing in his mouth and that it would ease if he let them extract his jewel-entrusted teeth and replace them with new ones of the finest ground bone. But the 'teeth' they put in his mouth were just corn kernels. Next, while he was still under their control, they removed the precious metal from around his eyes.

The battle was now won. Seven Macaw grew weaker and weaker as his finery was stripped from him and at last he died. His wife Chimalmat, who was seemingly weakened by his decline, expired at his side. It was a simple task for Great White Peccary and Great White Tapir and the Hero Twins to retrieve Hunahpú's arm from Seven Macaw's fireplace. The aged couple then proved that they did have genuine medical skill by putting Hunahpú's arm back in place so that it was perfectly healed.

Seven Macaw's likeness can still be seen on Earth in the scarlet macaw, which has a strangely shaped beak with a larger upper part and smaller lower part, suggesting the image of the dislocated jaw. It also has featherless patches around the eyes, which resemble the bare region surrounding the god's eyes after his face had been stripped of its shining metals.

Left: A late Classic Period Maya censer, sanctified by the face of the sun god, from the Temple of the Cross, Palenque.

153

THE TRIUMPH OF THE HERO TWINS

Seven Macaw had two sons, boys who were as self-deceiving and boastful as their father. One, Zipacná, named himself 'Maker of Mountains' and claimed to have raised the great peaks of the early world that had in fact been created by Huracán and Gucumatz. The second son, Earthquake, said he could unseat the foundations of the world and bring everything crashing down in an avalanche of earth. The Hero Twins, having dealt with Seven Macaw, decided to rid the world of his arrogant offspring too.

ZIPACNÁ'S DOWNFALL

The Hero Twins made their move against Zipacná at a time when the Maker of Mountains had not eaten for several days. In normal times, Zipacná's favourite diet was crabs and fish and he spent his hours trawling the waters and lifting huge rocks – even mountains – to see if any crabs were underneath. The Twins built a mechanical crab from flowers and a rock and placed it in a crevice beneath a great

Below: A Maya polychrome vase depicts the Hero Twin Hunahpú with stern expression, magnificent headdress and regal bearing.

GODS OF DRUNKENNESS

Before the Hero Twins turned their attention to Zipacná, the 'Maker of Mountains' had a bruising encounter with the Four Hundred Boys, the gods of a strong alcoholic drink called *quii* by the Quiché Maya.

The Four Hundred Boys met Zipacná on the seashore as they were dragging along a huge log which they had cut to use as a doorpost for their house. Zipacná offered to help and lifted the great trunk on his own, carrying it all the way to the house. The Four Hundred Boys asked him to stay with them to help them the next day, but secretly they plotted to kill him, for they were frightened by his enormous strength and guessed that they could not trust him.

The Four Hundred Boys dug a deep hole and enticed Zipacná into it. When he was at the bottom, they dropped a log on top of him. They thought they had killed him and rejoiced, planning a great celebration with the *quii* drink. They would wait, they said, for two days. When ants swarmed in the hole and carried parts of Zipacná's body to the surface they would know for certain that he was dead and they would have their party.

However, Zipacná had scrambled out of the way of the log and lay at the bottom of the hole listening to their every word. Two days later, when the ants came to investigate, Zipacná handed them tufts of his hair and pieces of his nails and told them to carry them to the surface. The Four Hundred Boys saw the ants and whooped for joy. They went into their new house and toasted their own bravery, jeering at Zipacná. Soon they all became very drunk and unruly. Zipacná crept from the hole and knocked the house down around the drunkards. Every one of the Four Hundred Boys was killed and Zipacná had his revenge.

The Four Hundred Boys, who were revered as the gods of drunkenness, rose into the sky and became the constellation of the Pleiades.

mountain, then casually approached Zipacná on the beach. When he complained of his hunger, they mentioned that they had seen the biggest of crabs in the crevice nearby. He followed them and went eagerly into the crevice in search of his next meal. However, try as he might he could not reach the crab until he turned over on to his back. At this point, with the mechanical crab on his chest, he suddenly expired and his body turned to stone. For all his bravado and undoubted strength, the genius of the Hero Twins had brought him low.

EARTHQUAKE'S UNDOING

Next, the sky god Huracán talked to the Hero Twins, asking them to deal with Zipacná's brother Earthquake. When

Above: Scholars believe that this stone carving of a macaw's head was used as a ball court marker. It is from Xochicalco.

mountains rose up by the word of Huracán and Gucumatz, Earthquake had the power to bring them down again. He tapped his foot on the ground and even the greatest of mountains came tumbling down. Huracán said that this was not right; the Twins should lure him into lying down in a grave in the east, where he could cause no more trouble in the creation.

The Twins approached Earthquake on a forest path and told him of a vast new mountain they had seen in the east. They told him that they had heard he boasted of destroying mountains, but that he must have missed this one. Earthquake asked to go with them to see the mountain. He would show them his powers, opening up the foundations of the land and making the mountain collapse. So they went eastward in single file along the narrow track, Earthquake walking between the twins. He was impressed by their skill with the blowpipe, for they brought birds down from the trees to left and to right. After a while, the travellers halted to cook some of the birds. Now the Twins used a sacred spell in their cooking that was to be the

undoing of Earthquake. They coated one of the birds in plaster made from rocks and told one another that as their companion ate this, so his body would end up in a rocky grave.

Earthquake was hungry and ate the bird enthusiastically. The threesome went on their way to the east, but when they came to the foot of the new mountain Earthquake found that his strength was gone from him. The magic of the Twins' spell had worked. He fell helpless to the ground at their feet and died.

Hunahpú and Xbalanqué bound him, tying his hands behind his back and his ankles to his wrists, and then they cast him into a grave as Huracán had demanded. In this way, the Hero Twins saved the world in its early days from the threat presented by the false-talking and vainglorious trio of Seven Macaw, Zipacná and Earthquake. They brought Earthquake to his rightful place, in the earth, where

Below: These Plumed Serpent carvings overlook the ball court at Chichén Itzá.

Above: The Hero Twins were a popular choice for decorations on Maya ceramics. This vase dates from c.AD600–700.

his strength holds up the mountains rather than destroying them. From time to time, though, he shifts and it is at these times that the surface of the earth moves dangerously.

THE PEOPLE OF CORN

The Quiché Maya account of creation in the *Popol Vuh* concludes with the sky and sea gods' third and finally successful attempt to make the first human beings. Huracán and Gucumatz were not happy with their attempts to make people from mud or wood, but when they tried using the maize plant they found it was the right material for fashioning a human.

MAN OF MAIZE

The world was still laid out beneath half-light. Animals and birds followed their paths through the forests and valleys, in the thin air above the high peaks. The gods knew that the dawn was coming soon, when the sun, moon and stars would appear in the sky. They knew that one piece was still missing from the creation: a human capable of offering praise and keeping track of time.

The creators were alerted to the presence of maize by four animals, which came to them with news of a spot in the mountains named Bitter Water Place, where they had found an abundance of growing things, including cacao beans and many fruits as well as the yellow and white corn. The animals – a crow, a parrot, a fox and a coyote – all became known as corn-eaters. They knew that what they had found was good and brought some ears of maize to the creators. Huracán and Gucumatz then gave the maize to Xmucané, the grandmother goddess and sage who had performed a divination rite to determine whether the creators should try making humans from wood. Xmucané washed her hands in cold, bright spring water and ground the ears nine times. She mixed the flour with

Left: The Plumed Serpent god was associated with the Sun among both Aztec and Maya.

the water in which she had washed her hands and made a paste. Huracán and Gucumatz used the paste to make the living, breathing flesh of human beings and with the remaining water they made the blood that flows in our veins. The process was like modelling in clay.

THE GRANDFATHERS

The creators made four males, who became the founding fathers of the principal Quiché Maya lineages. Their names were Jaguar Quitze, Jaguar Night, Mahucutah and True Jaguar. At last the creators had made men capable of pleasing them. They could talk clearly, walk smoothly over the uneven land and work hard with their hands. Their hearing was sharp and they could see far and wide, even into the hidden meanings of things. The creators addressed them, asking, 'Isn't this good, the power we have given you to see and walk and work hard? Try out your gifts.' The first men gave thanks to Huracán and Gucumatz, calling them grandfather-grandmother,

and also acknowledging that humankind had been perfectly made. The men reported that they could see everything, even the hidden structures and meanings of the universe, and that they understood it all perfectly.

The creators were unsettled by this and decided that they had given their creatures too many powers; the first men were in all respects the equals of the sky god and the sea god. Therefore Huracán and Gucumatz took away the clear vision of the early humans. This process was exactly like breathing on a mirror. The gods clouded men's vision so that the human forefathers could only see what was near at hand.

THE GRANDMOTHERS

Afterwards the gods made four women as wives for the grandfathers. Jaguar Quitze had Celebrated Seahorse as his spouse; Jaguar Night wed Prawn House,

Below: The bird's head on this Maya bowl suggests the all-seeing gaze of the first people in the Quiché Maya creation tale.

Above: In the top two panels of this codex image, rain god Tláloc blesses the corn, which is represented as his consort Chalchiúhtlicue (right), while Xipe Totec (left) brings his power to bear.

Mahucutah settled with Hummingbird House and True Jaguar married Macaw House. These maidens were as intelligent, lithe and fine-looking as their husbands and brought great joy to the men. They were the grandmothers of the great Quiché lineages.

The creation was now complete: all was now ready for the dawn of the very first sun. The first Quiché embarked on many wanderings as they awaited the first light.

There were a number of variant Mesoamerican myths explaining the creation of early humans. In the Mixtec tradition, the first people were sometimes said to have climbed from a great tree in a desert oasis. In Aztec mythology the first men were created by the Plumed Serpent Quetzalcóatl and his double Xólotl at the beginning of the fifth 'sun', the current world age, from the bones of a previous race he had rescued from the underworld realm. In some Aztec accounts the divine couple Oxomoco and Cipactonal were the first humans and were ancestors of the common people or *macehuatlin*.

Right: Quetzalcóatl had malign influence in his guise as a form of the planet Venus.

CHAPTER 8

EARTH
AND SKY

Mesoamericans believed that the age we live in was not the first in the history of the world. Just as the Quiché Maya told that there had been other, failed creations before the making of the first people by the sky god Huracán and the sea god Gucumatz, so the Aztecs held that there had been previous world ages before our own. The current age, in the Aztec view, was the fifth.

Each of these five eras had its own sun, was associated with one of the elements and was presided over by a different god. The celebrated Aztec Sun Stone, discovered in the late 18th century beneath Mexico City's central plaza, depicts each of the five 'suns'. Its main face, 3.6m (almost 12ft) in diameter, has a head in the centre, representing either the ancient sun god Tonatiuh or the Earth Monster Tlaltecuhtli. Around this face in the central circle are four images in square frames. The one to the upper right represents the first sun, that of the jaguar, while the one to the upper left shows the second sun, that of the wind. The one to the lower left is for the third sun, of rain, and the one to the lower right refers to the fourth sun, of water. The central face celebrates the current sun or world age in which the Aztecs had risen to such glory. Scholars also link the four suns to the four directions of Aztec cosmology. According to this theory, the Fifth Sun represents the centre.

Left: The Sun Stone was probably carved during the rule of Axayácatl (1469–81), with the aim of validating Aztec rule. The 'people of the sun' were divinely sanctioned to govern.

LIFE UNDER THE FOUR SUNS

In the primordial era, Black Tezcatlipoca decided to set himself up as the sun. This god was one of the 'four Tezcatlipocas' associated with the primal creation, each of whom was linked to a god in the Aztec pantheon. He was linked to the god of night and destiny later worshipped as Tezcatlipoca. His age, or sun, began after the time of the initial creation, when White Tezcatlipoca (Quetzalcóatl) and Blue Tezcatlipoca (Huitzilopochtli) made fire, the first human couple and several of the other gods.

THE JAGUAR SUN

Black Tezcatlipoca rose into the sky. His era was associated with the element of earth. There were no humans; instead the lands of Mesoamerica were filled by a race of giants. These towering creatures were so strong they could rip trees from the rocky mountain ground and hurl them through the air down on to the dusty plain below. But they were not bloodthirsty and lived on a vegetarian diet of acorns. Black Tezcatlipoca's era lasted 676 years. It ended in a cataclysm when Quetzalcóatl grew displeased at seeing Tezcatlipoca in the height of the sacred sky. He used his staff to knock his rival down into the seas that lay at the farthest extremes of the flat earth.

In his anger, Black Tezcatlipoca rose from the salt waters in the form of a powerful jaguar. The sun was down and darkness covered the land. Tezcatlipoca, god of night, raced on to the plains and mountains of Mesoamerica and suddenly jaguars were running everywhere. A plague of the fierce night predators howled for blood. The jaguars hunted down the giants and killed every one. According to the Aztecs' complex calendar, this carnage occurred on the day 4-Jaguar in the year 1-Reed.

Because jaguars brought the age or sun to an end, it is usually named the 'Jaguar Sun' (*Nahui Ocelotl*); it is also sometimes called the '4-Jaguar Sun' after the day on

which it ended. All the four suns would end in a cataclysm of violence and death and each one was named after the terrible event that brought it to an end. Tezcatlipoca himself leapt into the sky, still in his jaguar form, and there made the constellation of the Great Bear.

THE WIND SUN

Quetzalcóatl created the second sun, which provided light for the next age of the world.

This era was associated with the air and Quetzalcóatl took his form as the wind god Éhecatl to perform the creation. The inhabitants of Mesoamerica in this age were more like modern humans than their primitive predecessors. They also followed a vegetarian diet, eating the seeds of the mesquite tree. The second age lasted 364 years. Tezcatlipoca

Above: A detail from an Aztec stone column depicts the head of Tláloc, rain god and creator of the third sun.

revenged himself on his great cosmic rival by bringing this age to an end. He used his dark power to overwhelm the wind god by launching a great hurricane that swept the sun from the sky and the people from the earth. Darkness fell once more on the lands of Mesoamerica and after the hurricane everything was suddenly still. The survivors clambered up into the branches of the few trees that were still standing after the storm. They were no longer people but had become monkeys and they chattered and called in the echoing dark. The era ended on the day 4-Wind in the year 1-Flint. The sun or world age is known as the 'Wind Sun' (*Nahui Éhecatl*) or 'Sun 4-Wind'. The

Aztec myth parallels the account of the Quiché Maya in the *Popol Vuh*, in which the survivors of a failed creation, the wooden people, were the ancestors of the monkeys of the forest.

THE RAIN SUN

After the hurricane, the fertility and rain god Tláloc took charge of creation. His era was associated with the element of fire. In some accounts, the people of this age made one of the great breakthroughs in human history by discovering the skills of agriculture and began to cultivate a form of maize. In other versions, however, the people lived entirely on a wild water-based plant like the water lily. Then they were transformed from human form into turkeys, dogs and butterflies.

Tláloc's era lasted 312 years before Quetzalcóatl again turned destroyer. This time, he sent a rain of fire that poured destruction on the earth for a whole day. The inferno of flame swept the sun from the sky. The inhabitants were burned up, but some must have hidden from the fire, for their descendants are the dogs, butterflies and turkeys of today. The destruction came on the day 4-Rain in the year 1-Flint. This sun or age is called 'Rain Sun' (*Nahui Quiahuitl*) or 'Sun

Left: Images of the rain god Tláloc are usually identifiable from their 'goggle' eyes and fang-like teeth.

Right: A wooden inlaid mask honours Chalchiúhtlicue, creator of the fourth world age.

4-Rain', but is also sometimes called the 'Fire Sun' because this era of creation ended in a firestorm. The coming of fire from the sky was an appropriate ending for Tláloc's era, for this god, in addition to being the deity of rain, was associated with lightning – a form of celestial fire.

THE WATER SUN

Tláloc's consort Chalchiúhtlicue, goddess of lakes, oceans, streams and rivers, created a new sun. The people of the age of water lived on the seeds of a wild plant. Chalchiúhtlicue's era lasted 676 years, as long as the previous two eras combined, and was the first of the world ages in which the presiding deity herself brought creation to an end.

The Aztecs believed that the waters of the oceans enclosed the lands on all four sides and also rose up into the sky above. In one account, Chalchiúhtlicue made these sky waters break so that they crashed down and obliterated life on earth. In another version, she made the underground waters rise up, gushing from natural wells and bursting from solid rock. Either way, a great flood covered the land. The people adapted, turning into fish, whales and other inhabitants of the deep.

The flood lasted for an entire 'bundle' of 52 years. Even the mountains were swept away, as water covered the entire creation. The flood came on the day 4-Water in the year 1-House. The era was therefore called 'Water Sun' (*Nahui Atl*) or 'Sun 4-Water'.

There is some disagreement in different sources over the order in which the suns or ages occurred. The sequence given here of Jaguar, Wind, Rain and Water is that depicted in the carvings on the Aztec Sun Stone, a 3.6m- (almost 12ft-) wide carved stone found in Mexico City in the 18th century. Some other sources report that the Water Sun came first and that the other three followed in the sequence Jaguar, Rain, Wind. The end of the fourth sun was the occasion for the creation of the current world age, the fifth sun, the time in which the Aztecs, their revered Toltec ancestors and modern Mexicans all live.

The Quiché Maya account of creation also included the notion that previous creations had their own suns that lapsed when the creation failed. For example, the vain bird Seven Macaw who was outwitted and defeated by the Hero Twins Hunahpú and Xbalanqué was the Sun in the era of the wooden people.

DAWN OF THE FIFTH SUN

Following the end of the fourth sun or age in a great earthquake, Tezcatlipoca and Quetzalcóatl had to fashion the Earth anew. They encountered the Earth Monster Tlaltecuhtli swimming in the waters of the great flood and by tearing apart her body they made a new sky and a new earth.

A period of 26 years passed between the creation of a new world for the fifth sun and the creation of the sun and moon that ushered in the age in which we live.

Below: The ancient fire god Xiuhtecuhtli was generally depicted without eyes, seated with arms crossed on his knees.

Like the four previous ages, the fifth era was named after the cataclysm that would bring it to an end. The Aztecs believed that the current age would end in earthquakes; they also said that the current sun began moving on the day 4-Ollin (4-Earthquake or 4-Movement), and that the world would end on the day 4-Earthquake. On that fateful day the god Tezcatlipoca would once more fulfil his dark destiny as a destroyer, sending earthquakes that would bring the mountains low and cause a famine in which all creatures would die. The Aztecs named the age in which we live after this day of destruction, 4-Ollin.

CREATION OF THE SUN AND THE MOON

The Aztec myth of the creation of the sun and moon tells how the gods gathered in darkness at Teotihuacán. There was no light on the earth, for the fourth sun had been destroyed in the watery cataclysm that brought an end to Chalchiúhtlicue's era. The gods were voices in the blank darkness. They agreed that what was most necessary for the creation was a new sun and a moon to provide light when the sun did not.

The god Tecuciztécatl ('He of the Sea Stone') stepped forward and volunteered to be the sun. But a second deity also volunteered. This was the small and humble god Nanahuatzin, whose

Above: Some scholars identify this Aztec stone carving as an image of a priest in the service of the fire god Xiuhtecuhtli.

face was disfigured by pimples and sores. These two began to prepare themselves for the honour of lighting the world with rites of penitence and self-discipline like those of a new Aztec *tlatoani* or ruler before he took power. Nanahuatzin and Tecuciztécatl prepared for four days and nights. When they were finished, they saw that the other gods had lit a vast pyre on the hard ground at Teotihuacán. The orange flames threw unsettling shadows all around that holy place.

Nanahuatzin and Tecuciztécatl made offerings: the self-regarding Tecuciztécatl, dressed in splendid robes, offered fine goods such as quetzal feathers, stone flints and coral incense, while the humble and self-effacing Nanahuatzin laid out simple reeds, cactus thorns he had used to make an offering of his own blood and, instead of incense, the scabs from his pimples. They approached the sacred fire. Tecuciztécatl went first, but was driven back by the heat. He tried again, and a second time did not have the courage or resolve to carry through his intention of entering the flames. In all, he approached the fire and turned back four times. Then Nanahuatzin stepped forward. He shut his eyes and steadied his nerves with deep breaths, then went fearlessly into the flames. The other gods watched in awe as his body caught, crackled and burned fast. At last, inspired by his rival, Tecuciztécatl rushed into the flames. An eagle and a jaguar followed the two gods into the flames, so gaining their distinctive markings and their reputation for fearlessness and power.

A NEW AGE

The sacrifice was complete. The other gods waited for the first day of the new age to begin. In one account, the proud

Below: The Cerro Gordo peak behind gives Teotihuacán's Pyramid of the Moon the look of a natural formation.

but fearful Tecuciztécatl rose first into the sky in the form of the moon, shining very brilliantly. He was followed by Nanahuatzin, the new sun. In another version, the new sun and moon rose together. In both accounts the light of the moon was too bright and cancelled out that of the sun. One of the gods on the ground threw a rabbit up at the moon's face, giving the moon its distinctive markings, in which Mesoamericans saw the shape of a rabbit.

The sun and moon hung in the sky, motionless and lifeless. This was not as it should be. How could time progress and the seasons be measured if there were no movements in the heavens? Nanahuatzin made an announcement

Left: All life came from the gods' initial sacrifice. This sacrificial knife, made of wood and flint, dates from c.1500.

from his position at his zenith in the sky. He would consent to follow the required daily motions of the sun, but only if the other gods offered their hearts and lifeblood in sacrifice, as he had made an offering of his earthly body. At first the gods on the ground were outraged and one, the morning star, attacked Nanahuatzin, but then they agreed to make the first of the many blood sacrifices that maintained the flow of life-energy in the Mesoamerican cosmos. They cut their own bodies and offered their hearts to the sun. The sun began to move and the moon sank behind the Earth's horizon.

THE CELESTIAL WEAVING GIRL

Other Mesoamerican myths explain how the sky and earth were separated and the moon and sun were brought into being. A Mixtec tale recounted that Lord Nine Wind, a god associated with the Aztec deity Quetzalcóatl, separated the waters and the Earth, using the waters to make a sky that would arch over and contain the land.

PARALLELS

Quiché Maya mythology in the *Popol Vuh* tells that water and sky were always already separate: the sky god and the sea god cooperated to make the earth after a

Below: Mesoamerican myths told that the sun, here honoured on a Maya pyramid, first rose above a well-established Earth.

Right: This terracotta mask may represent the ancient Maya counterpart to the Aztec fire god.

fruitful discussion of what would be right. In the Quiché tradition, the sun and moon were created later, when the Hero Twins Hunahpú and Xbalanqué rose up into the heavens after their successful mission to the underworld. The Quiché Maya and Aztec creation myths therefore both put some time between the creation of the Earth in its current age and the rising of the sun and moon to give light.

THE EARTH MONSTER'S BODY

In the Aztec myth, Quetzalcóatl and Tezcatlipoca made the Earth from the Earth Monster's body and Quetzalcóatl made the first people some time before the sun and moon were made by the gods' sacrifice at Teotihuacán. In one version of the Aztec myth there were 26 years between the creation of the Earth and the first appearance of the sun.

This myth explains that the waters of the heavens fell, unleashing the great flood that swept away the fourth sun in the year 1-Toctli (1-Rabbit), which was associated with the south. Quetzalcóatl and Tezcatlipoca made the Earth and then Tezcatlipoca assumed a new identity as Mixcóatl, an ancient hunt god sometimes said to be god of the north. This happened in the year (2-Ácatl) 2-Reed. In the diviners' calendar, the day named 2-Reed was sacred to Tezcatlipoca. The next period began on the year 1-Ácatl (1-Reed). It was sacred to Quetzalcóatl, one of whose attributes was as god of the east. The gods made the sun 13 years

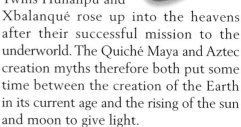

afterwards, in 13-Ácatl (13-Reed). This sequence suggests how Mesoamerican myths are intimately connected to the day-names, year-names and other timings of the sacred calendar, as well as to the movements of the stars and planets.

A LOVE STORY

A different Maya tradition explained the relationship between the sun and moon and their ascension to the sky in terms of an earthly love story and explains thereby the origins of human sexual relations. At one time, according to this story, the sun and moon lived on Earth: Sun was a sturdy young hunter and Moon a fair maiden who earned her corn bread by working as a weaver. Sun fell for the pale, luminous beauty of Moon the moment he first saw her and he was drawn back to her grandfather's house again and again to try to catch a glimpse of her peaceful face. Every morning Sun arrived at the house, carrying a vast deer carcass on his shoulders in an attempt to impress the maiden with his strength and hunting prowess. But although Moon was pleased by the attention and began to have feelings for the hunter, her grandfather was against the relationship and did all he could to prevent it flowering into love.

Now Sun had magical powers as well as virile strength and he transformed himself into a hummingbird. In this shape he

could come and go as he pleased without the maiden's grandfather seeing, and he loved to haunt the garden behind the old man's house, where tobacco plants grew. The maiden, either displeased by the attentions of the hummingbird or guessing its true identity, had her grandfather shoot the swift-winged bird in flight. In the moment he was shot, the hummingbird reverted back into human form. The moon-maiden then nursed Sun back to health, keeping his identity secret from her grandfather. When Sun was well again, she fled with him.

PREVENTING AN ELOPEMENT

Now other gods joined in to try and prevent the elopement. Spying them in a canoe on the river far below, the rain god hurled a thunderbolt at the pair. Sun changed himself into a turtle and Moon transformed herself into a crab, but for Moon it was too late. She was broken into many pieces and died.

Grieving, Sun collected the remains of his love and, with the help of a band of dragonflies, stored them in thirteen hollow logs. He waited for thirteen days,

Left: Mixtecs, proud of their creative skills, believed that from the beginning their gods were blessed with genius in fine arts, metalworking and other crafts.

Above: The Zapotecs, makers of the enigmatic figures thought to be slain war captives at Monte Albán, taught that there were separate creators of animals (made by Cozaana) and men (made by Huichaana).

then opened the logs. The first twelve logs were filled with poisonous snakes and angry insects, which fled into the world and have been an unpleasant and sometimes deadly presence ever since. But in the thirteenth log, by a thoroughly breathtaking miracle, he found the Moon maiden, restored to life. Now a deer was passing and stamped on the moon through the log, creating the very first female sexual organ. Sun and Moon then had sexual relations. This was the first time male and female had combined in this perfect complementarity.

Once again the lovers were united. They lived for many more years on Earth but Sun discovered that he could not trust his love, who had a carnal nature. She took many lovers when his attention was elsewhere and in his anger and desperate, continuing love he took her with him into exile in the sky. In one tradition, his anger and fear of her sexual happiness made him attack her, blinding her in one eye. For this reason the light given by the moon is weaker by far than that given by the sun.

MYTHS OF THE NIGHT SKY

The gods and heroes of Mesoamerican mythology were visible in the night sky. The movements of the stars and planets gave solid form to the repeating cycles of the myths. The stories of many deities ended with their ascension to the night sky to take the form of this or that group of stars, and the rising, falling and other movements of the constellations were a regular reminder of the truth of the myths and of the divine transactions that sustained life.

ASTRONOMY AND THE GODS
The movements of the stars were also connected to farmers' cycles of planting and reaping, for astronomical phenomena were used to time the agricultural cycle. For example, in the Quiché Maya *Popol Vuh* cycle, the early humans known as the Four Hundred Boys were killed by Zipacná, son of the boastful solar deity Seven Macaw. At their death they rose into the sky to become the Pleiades

Above: One face of the Aztec altar of the nocturnal animals shows an owl. The other sides depict a bat, a scorpion and a spider.

constellation. In Quiché lore, the Pleiades were associated with a handful of seeds. Dennis Tedlock, translator of the *Popol Vuh*, points out that the period in March when high-altitude farmers plant maize is marked by the setting of the Pleiades in the evening. When the lower altitude maize is planted in May, the Pleiades are completely invisible. The disappearance of the Four Hundred Boys of the Pleiades marks the time when the maize seeds 'disappear' into the earth and later the constellation is visible again as the seeds 'dawn' in the form of plants.

Seven Macaw became the seven stars that make up the Plough or Big Dipper. In the latitude of the Quiché Maya, the seasonal disappearance of this constellation appears to usher in the rainy storms of the hurricane season. In mid-July, at the

start of the hurricane season, the Plough can be seen descending at twilight and afterwards disappears for much of the night. In mid-October the reappearance of all seven stars of the constellation before dawn marks the end of the hurricanes and the start of the dry season. In the myth, the god's fall from the tree when he is shot by Hunahpú occurs just before the great flood that is sent against the wooden people. In the same way, the descent of Seven Macaw's constellation brings the waters of the rainy hurricane season.

CYCLICAL MOVEMENTS
The *Popol Vuh* cycle is entirely built on the cyclical movements of the stars and planets – especially the Venus cycle – and on the sacred calendar that is derived from them. Before the Hero Twins are born, their father and uncle One and Seven Hunahpú are summoned to the underworld because their playing of the Mesoamerican ball game makes such a racket that it annoys the underworld lords. This corresponds to a day named Hunahpú in the calendar and to the rising of Venus as the morning star in the eastern sky. One and Seven Hunahpú then descend to the underworld, where they play ball against the underworld

Below: This vast Aztec stone head is of the moon goddess Coyolxauhqui, with her characteristic lunar nose pendant.

Above: Quetzalcóatl descends to Earth in his most familiar guise, as the Plumed Serpent.

lords. This corresponds to the time in the Venus cycle when the planet is not visible. When One Hunahpú is killed, this equates to the reappearance of Venus as the evening star. When an underworld maiden, Blood Woman, becomes pregnant with One Hunahpú's sons (the Hero Twins) and climbs to the Earth's surface, she convinces One Hunahpú's mother, Xmucané, that she has come from the underworld pregnant with the sons of One Hunahpú. This corresponds to the new rising of Venus as the morning star. In addition, One Monkey and One Artisan, the half-brothers of the Hero Twins, correspond to the planet Mars. Their names are both associated with the day in the diviners' calendar when Mars becomes visible.

Aztec myths were similarly tied into astronomical movements. Tezcatlipoca brought the first sun or world age to an end by unleashing the rage of the night predator, the jaguar. He then rose in the sky in the form of a great celestial jaguar and became the Great Bear constellation. When the Great Bear dips into the sea, Aztec stargazers understood it to mark the moment in the cosmic myth of the world's creation when Tezcatlipoca lost a foot in his struggle with the Earth Monster, Tlaltecuhtli.

Quetzalcóatl's myth closely parallels the Venus cycle. In one tradition, after being outwitted by the followers of Tezcatlipoca in Tollán and subsequently disgraced, he sacrificed himself on a pyre and his soul rose as Venus. In this guise he was known as Ce Ácatl and Tlahuizcalpantecuhtli (Dawn), and understood to be an enemy of the sun. When Quetzalcóatl made a voyage to the underworld to collect the bones of the fish-men of the fourth world age, he was Venus during its invisible phase and when he returned in triumph with the bones to make a new race of men he was Venus rising again as the morning star.

Right: This small clay idol may be Xólotl, Quetzalcóatl's form as Venus the evening star.

MANY FACES OF THE SUN GOD

The Aztecs thought of themselves as the people of the sun. At Teotihuacán, the gods had performed the first blood sacrifice to set the sun and moon in motion in the sky, but the ritual did not prove sufficient to feed the blood-hungry sun. Fortunately, the Aztec people and their neighbours were able to take on the task of feeding the sun and maintaining its daily movements through war and blood sacrifice.

AZTEC DAWN

Each dawn was a time of trepidation. The moment of transition between dark and light might be the world's last, for if the sun refused to move across the sky then there would be no day, no time and no seasons to mark with the calendar. To ensure that the sun was sufficiently nourished, Aztec priests had to follow the religious calendar with the utmost devotion and make all the appropriate sacrifices at the right time.

The Aztecs believed that the sun took different forms at different times of day and night. An ancient god named Tonatiuh was the sun by day. Each dawn, as he rose from the eastern horizon, he was born anew of the earth goddess Coatlícue. In one tradition he was hauled up to the zenith of the sky by the souls of brave warriors who had died in battle. For this honour the souls took the form of hummingbirds. The Aztecs saw Tonatiuh as a strong, vibrant young man with an ochre and yellow-painted face and a red-painted body. He was guided across the sky by a great fire-serpent called the *xiuhcóatl*.

Some accounts say that at its zenith, when the sun is most powerful, it changed from Tonatiuh to the Aztec tribal god Huitzilopochtli. At noon, beneath the brilliance of Huitzilopochtli, darkness

Left: This clay pipe with its eagle's head celebrates the daily triumph of the sun god. The Aztecs thought tobacco – which they called yetl *– was sacred. Pipes in the image of the sun god were probably used by his priests.*

was entirely vanquished. With the sun directly overhead there were not even any shadows to remind men of the encroaching coldness and the many demons of night.

After noon, as the sun descended towards his nightly disappearance at dusk, he was pulled down the length of sky by the *cilhuateteo*, the souls of women who had died in childbirth, slain by unborn warriors in the womb. At dusk, as he sank beyond the horizon, he was understood to be devoured by the Earth Monster Tlaltecuhtli.

A JAGUAR BY NIGHT

By night, the sun travelled through the dread realms of the underworld, Mictlán. During these hours, Tonatiuh took the shape of Tepeyolohtli, a jaguar named 'Heart of the Hard Mountain'. The roaring of this great beast, who was caged within the mountain, could be heard in the thundering of avalanches and the noisy eruption of volcanic lava.

The jaguar was a night predator, capable of striking suddenly and fatally in the blackness of the wild countryside and so the jaguar was naturally associated with the night and with the dark underworld. In some traditions, the sun defeated his enemies in the underworld each night with the *xiuhcóatl* or fire-serpent.

Left: An Aztec codex depicts preparations for a sacrifice in the sun god's honour at the pyramid-top temple halfway to the sky.

Right: The Maya sun god Kinich Ahau was the husband of the moon goddess Ix Chel. At night, as he travelled through the underworld, it was believed that he turned into a jaguar.

The Classic Period Maya also believed that the sun became a jaguar by night. By day they thought the life-giving star was a male god named Kinich Ahau ('Sun-faced Lord'), a fresh-faced young man at dawn who aged during the long day and who, by dusk, had an old man's face and beard. In carvings and pictures, he is depicted with a fierce face and a single front tooth. On his forehead is often carved the four-petalled glyph for *kin*, which means 'day' or 'sun'. A fine stucco mask of the god survives among the remains of the main pyramid at the Maya site of Kohunlich in the Mexican state of Quintana Roo.

After dusk, the Maya sun god was reborn in the first moments of night as a jaguar who travelled through the underworld, where he had to do battle – like the Hero Twins and the souls of the dead – with the lords of Xibalba. Some images of Kinich Ahau prefigure this night-time transformation by depicting the day-sun god with the characteristics or features of a jaguar. A number of representations of the jaguar god of the underworld show him with the *kin* glyph ('sun' or 'day') on his sleek stomach.

DARKNESS AND LIGHT

Night was also a time to be feared. The Aztecs believed that Tezcatlipoca was at large in the hours of darkness, sometimes taking the form of a headless demon called Night Axe, sometimes of a wandering demon who approached travellers at the crossroads. It was also the time and the realm of the demons called *tzitimime*, female spirits who sparkled with malevolence like stars in the blue darkness. They were responsible for unleashing many of the ills that afflicted humankind, such as the epidemics that

swept through the Valley of Mexico after the Spanish Conquest. Their power was at its height when night encroached upon day in the form of a solar eclipse. At these times the Aztecs made sacrifices of fair-skinned victims to fortify Tonatiuh in his weakness.

The opposition between darkness and light was central to Mesoamerican mythology. Whereas Tezcatlipoca was associated with dark, his eternal rival and counterpart Quetzalcóatl was linked to dawn. Quetzalcóatl was associated with the east and, in his aspect as Tlahuizcalpantecuhtli, with Venus as the morning star that heralded the sunrise. His rising symbolized resurrection while the darkness of Tezcatlipoca stood for death. The ball game played throughout Mesoamerica may have been seen as a re-enactment of the struggles between Tezcatlipoca and Quetzalcóatl that were such an important part of the myth of the four suns before our own; of struggles in the Aztecs' lives between darkness and light, between death and life. The balance between light and dark also corresponded to the opposition between dryness and dampness, height and smallness and, in some instances, between masculinity and femininity.

Below: An image from the Codex Borbonicus *shows the sun god (left) in the form he assumed by night.*

BRINGERS OF RAIN

One version of the Aztec myth of the creation of the sun and moon gave a vital role to Éhecatl, the wind god who was an aspect of Quetzalcóatl. After the gods Nanahuatzin and Tecucitztécatl had thrown themselves on to the sacrificial pyre and ascended into the sky as sun and moon, they hung motionless above the Earth. In this tradition, it was Éhecatl who initiated their movements. He blew on them with all the strength of his breath. At first, only the sun moved and the moon remained stationary, but when the sun set at last in the west the moon was drawn into his proper cycle, which complements that of the sun.

Below: At Chichén Itzá, the ruined tower of the Caracol – perhaps a temple to wind god Kukulcán as well as an astronomical observatory – contained a spiral corridor.

In contrast to other gods, who were generally associated with a particular point of the compass, Éhecatl was linked to all four directions because the wind blows from the north, south, east and west. Temples built to honour the god were partly circular in form. A circular temple to Éhecatl-Quetzalcóatl reputedly stood opposite the great temple of the Aztecs in Tenochtitlán. Éhecatl was associated with, and at times represented as, a spider monkey, a duck, a spider and a snail. Statues of him often wear a half-mask with the appearance of a duck's bill, open to allow the tongue to show.

Left: This stone carving of Éhecatl-Quetzalcóatl has obsidian eyes. The god blew through his beak to make the winds.

Scholars believe the Aztecs associated the spider monkey with the wind because of its great speed and agility when swinging through the trees. Another connection is that, at the end of the fourth age, humans were destroyed by a great wind and turned into monkeys. Quetzalcóatl in the guise of Éhecatl was patron of the second day in the Aztecs' day-count calendar.

An Aztec sculpture also depicts Quetzalcóatl rising, serpentine, from the earth-mother to connect with the rain god Tláloc above. It was all part of the Aztecs' cosmological view that the rains were present in the sky above because the sea that lay at the far extremes of the earth curved up to join over it.

The connection provided between the earth and the sky by Éhecatl-Quetzalcóatl was necessary to provide a conduit or pathway by which the waters could return to the earth in the form of windblown rainclouds.

KUKULCÁN-QUETZALCÓATL

The wind god was worshipped as Kukulcán by the central and northern Maya, while the southern Maya knew him as Gucumatz. The wind god was associated with the rain god Chac as bringer of fertility.

Some scholars believe that the circular Caracol at Chichén Itzá, while certainly an astronomical observatory, may also have served as a temple to the god Kukulcán-Quetzalcóatl. Its circular shape means that the building was probably sacred to the wind god aspect of the Plumed Serpent.

Like Quetzalcóatl, Kukulcán had many other attributes as a creator, a god of new life and as a cultural hero who taught the ancestors skills such as farming in ancient times. In the Maya realms, his cult appears to have been an aristocratic one and he was particularly associated with lords and nobles. The cult of Kukulcán-Quetzalcóatl was very strong under the Toltecs, but temples in his honour were built much earlier at Teotihuacán and Tikal.

According to the Quiché Maya, the sky god was one of the two primal creators. He was associated with wind and rain, thunder and storms. The many names and identities he could adopt included Hurricane, Raw Thunderbolt and Newborn Thunderbolt. This associated him with the Aztec god Tezcatlipoca, who was also linked to hurricanes and rainstorms. The Aztec thunder god was Tláloc, bringer of rains.

Left: Éhecatl-Quetzalcóatl's breath brought the rains that fed the plants. Here the god carries five maize cobs on his back.

Above: This dancing monkey honours the power of the wind god Éhecatl-Quetzalcóatl. The snake suggests the whirlwinds with which Éhecatl ushered in the rainy season.

THE BREATH OF LIFE

The wind unleashed by Éhecatl-Quetzalcóatl was the breath of life itself for, without the setting and rising of the sun, there would be no seasons, no cycles of planting and harvesting, no crops and no life in Mesoamerica. The god blew the damp winds that carried rain clouds to the grateful farmers at the start of the rainy season. He also unleashed whirl-winds that cleared the skies for the clouds. For this reason the Aztecs called him 'the *tláloques*' road-sweeper' – a reference to the little rain gods who were assistants to the main rain deity, Tláloc.

An illustration in the *Vienna Codex* shows Éhecatl connecting earth and sky and supporting the clouds above.

DELUGE: THE UNIVERSAL FLOOD

In both Aztec and Maya traditions there are myths of terrible destruction wrought by a great flood. According to the Quiché Maya, the failed creation of the wooden people was swept away by a universal flood sent by Huracán, who is associated with Tezcatlipoca. The Aztecs told that the fourth sun or world age was ended by a destructive flood sent by its ruling deity Chalchiúhtlicue, the goddess of oceans, lakes, rivers and streams.

THE WATERS UNLEASHED

In the version found in the late 16th-century *Codex Chimalpopoca*, one woman and one man were given the chance to survive the cataclysm in a story that is strikingly similar in some ways to the biblical narrative of Noah.

As the era reached its end, a man and woman named Nata and Nena were forewarned by the god Tezcatlipoca, who came to them and called them away from their activities. Nata was making the

Below: This image of a beast in floodwater was carved on a stone box that held the ashes of the Aztec tlatoani *Ahuítzotl.*

strong alcoholic drink *pulque*, but the god told him to put it aside and to go quickly to cut and hollow out a great cypress tree. In this makeshift boat Nata was to build a covered cabin in which to shelter from water, for at the end of the month of Tozoztli the waters that rise over the earth in the arc of the sky were going to be unleashed. The earth would be swamped. Just before this time, Nata and Nena should clamber into the cypress boat and wait. They should take with them just one ear of corn each and eat no more than that.

The couple did what they were told and they were thankful for, when the waters came, the flood submerged even the highest mountains in a single day. Death was everywhere, because there was no escaping from the water's awesome power.

Left: This intriguing stone lizard was carved by a Totonac craftsman in the period 1200–1300.

However, the two human survivors were soon hungry, for their corn was quickly gone. They clambered on to the roof of their makeshift cabin and looked around them. They realized that the great population of Mesoamerica had not been entirely wiped out for the people that Nata and Nena left behind had turned into fish, dolphins, whales and other sea creatures. The water was thick with marine life.

DISOBEDIENCE

Nata cried happily to his wife that they need not go hungry: the waters were teeming. They had a few sticks laid by in the cabin and with one of these Nata began to fish, while with some others Nena made a fire. Soon the smoke was rising in the sky and four meaty fish were roasting on the sticks above the fire. The sole human survivors ate them greedily, crying with joy that they had banished their hunger pains.

They did not look up to see that the smoke from their fire was rising to the thirteen layers of the heavens. Two gods – named in this source as Citlalícue and Citlatona – were angered by the smell and complained to Tezcatlipoca. He went quickly down to confront Nata and Nena, who had disobeyed his command that they should eat no more than one ear of corn each. He punished them for their greed. He took the fish Nata had caught and fashioned a long nose for their heads, with lithe legs and a tail for their

hindquarters. The fish were transformed into dogs, which barked at the sky. They had no more escaped the flood than their fellows who had been transformed into fish. The flood lasted for a total of 52 years before the creation of the new world by Tezcatlipoca and his divine ally-rival the Plumed Serpent.

FISH, FLOODS AND FERTILITY

The Aztecs associated fish and waters with fertility. Fish were linked with the deities Chalchiúhtlicue, Xochiquetzal, Xochipilli, Mayáhuel, Quetzalcóatl and Cipactli. Fish from the lakes of Mexico were a staple food for the Aztecs. The majority of the offerings that have been found at the Great Pyramid in Tenochtitlán contained fish, but curiously there are few surviving representations of fish in Aztec art.

Below: Images of Tláloc's consort Chalchiúhtlicue often show her kneeling and wearing long ear tassels.

In view of its watery setting, the lake-city of Tenochtitlán must always have been vulnerable to flooding. The Spanish chronicler Diego Durán describes in his *History of the Indies of New Spain* describes how the *tlatoani* Ahuítzotl, his priests and people would perform obsequious offerings to the water goddess Chalchiúhtlicue in order to drive back a flood.

Left: The Aztecs removed masks such as this from Teotihuacán and used them as offerings at the Great Pyramid. This ritual mask may once have formed part of an incense burner used in religious ceremonies.

THE UNIVERSAL FLOOD: A RACE MEMORY?

Myths of a destructive universal flood are common in the traditions of diverse peoples across the world. In the Judaeo-Christian tradition there is the familiar tale of Noah, in which God sends a flood but saves Noah and his ark of animals and that of Gilgamesh in ancient Sumer.

Hindu religious mythology describes cycles of destruction and new life and tells how the universal waters cover the earth at the end of each age, before a new creation begins.

In Australia, the Worora aboriginals said that ancestral spirits once sent a vast flood to make space for the current world.

At the other end of the Earth, in the Arctic, the Inuit report that a previous world age knew no death, so that the world became dangerously overcrowded until a great flood swept the majority of people away, leaving a sustainable number, who were thereafter subject to death.

The myths are so common that some scholars have speculated there may once have been a great flood that brought near-universal destruction and that the memory of this cataclysm, buried deep in our subconscious, has inspired strikingly similar tales in cultures that have had no contact with one another.

However, in all likelihood the stories arose because flooding – whether by rivers and lakes or by the sea breaking through dykes and defensive walls – was common in so many places. Floodwaters brought death but also fertility. In the mythological imagination of early peoples, they became associated with the end of eras and the commencement of a new creation.

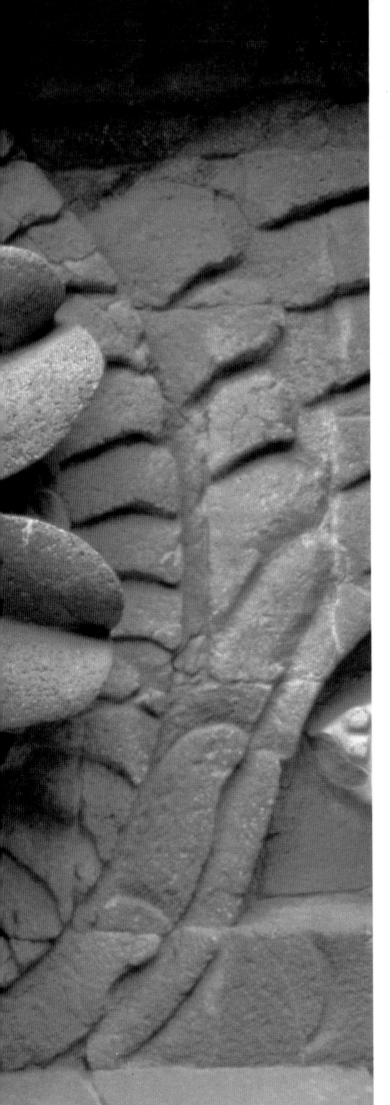

CHAPTER 9

TALES OF THE GODS

In considering their gods, Mesoamericans were happy to combine the concepts of 'many' and 'one'. The Quiché Maya creators Huracán and Gucumatz were each both an individual and also a group of cooperating gods. The Aztecs simultaneously believed in many gods and one god. They knew of Ometeotl, the primeval god and first cause of creation. The god was both male and female, taking the forms Ometecuhtli and Omecihuatl. They were mother and father deities, seen as the creative essence of the primeval god.

In general the primeval deity was inactive in his own guise: other gods issued from Ometeotl through Ometecuhtli and Omecihuatl and were engaged in action. One story tells that Omecihuatl was wandering above the dry plains of the north, and felt a movement within her like the turning of a child in a woman's womb. She squatted there to give birth: a sacrificial knife of obsidian emerged from her, fell to the plain below and gave issue to 1,600 gods and goddesses. The number 1,600 is intended to mean 'beyond counting' – and suggests the myth confirms both the primacy of sacrifice and of the multiplicity of the gods. And just as the gods coexisted as 'one' and 'many', so each individual deity could take many forms without losing his or her essential identity. The ancient god Quetzalcóatl, for instance, could be known as the celebrated Plumed Serpent, the princely priest Topiltzin, the wind god Éhecatl and the planet Venus, among many other forms.

Left: A temple to the Plumed Serpent stood in the revered city of Teotihuacán. This image of the god greeted worshippers.

A CROWDED PANTHEON

The Aztecs' primeval deity, Ometeotl, does not appear to have been carved or otherwise represented: although one surviving Aztec sculpture *c.*1350 showing a seated god has been identified by some scholars as an image of the primeval god, other historians consider it to be Quetzalcóatl or the old god Huehuetéotl. The Aztecs did produce images of Ometeotl's constituent parts, Ometecuhtli/Tonacatecuhtli and Omecihuatl/Tonacacihuatl. They were often given rich clothes, perhaps intended to associate them with light.

GOD OF TWO FACES

Artists and craftsmen also made more abstract attempts to represent the primeval deities. As early as the 8th century BC Mesoamericans produced intriguing two-faced or twin-headed figures thought by historians to represent the force of duality that was strongly present in the culture. The idea of duality, which holds opposites such as life/death or wet/dry in equilibrium, takes solid form in mythology in

Right: This Zapotec idol is of the goddess of the thirteen serpents, perhaps a version of the Aztec fertility goddess Cihuacóatl.

two-as-one deities such as Ometecuhtli/ Omecihuatl. Two-faced statues dating to this era have been found at Tlatilco. Scholars cite an Aztec mask that is half bare and half covered in skin as another representation of the same concept.

The Maya also believed in a creator deity, called Itzamná or Hunab Ku. In one version of the creation, Hunab Ku made the world three times: the first world contained dwarfs; the second contained a mysterious race called 'the offenders'; the third was the world of our era, inhabited by the Maya and their Aztec neighbours. Each of the first two creations was wiped out by a deluge and our own third age, too, was destined to end in the destruction of a universal flood. Sometimes Hunab Ku was seen, like Ometeotl, to be largely inactive in his own guise – but at the same time he was understood to be the father of Itzamná, who was moon god and bringer of culture to the people.

SERPENT IMAGERY

Itzamná taught the Maya how to write and use the sacred calendar, and he brought them knowledge of the maize and cacao plants.

As bringer of writing, Itzamná was the patron of scribes and priests. He is shown as a scribe in several illustrations to the *Madrid Codex*. He is usually shown as an old man seated on a throne, with a lined forehead and hollow cheeks, and because he was the moon god his headdress or forehead carries the glyph for night. He was also connected with new life, and linked to the snail – which was associated with childbirth. But his principal animal form was the serpent or dragon. A carved bone discovered in a tomb at Tikal shows a scribe's hand emerging from the mouth of a dragon that represents Itzamná.

Itzamná's consort was Ix Chel, the moon goddess. They were the parents of the bacabs, the giants who supported the heavens, separating earth and sky, in the four corners of creation.

Left: Carved snakes' heads guarded the steps of the pyramid temples at Tenochtitlán.

The prevalence of serpent imagery among the attributes and associations of quite different gods is suggestive of the fact that many of the deities were very closely connected, almost interchangeable. Mesoamericans believed that the divine essence was fluid and that it could take many associated forms. For the Classic-era Maya, Itzamná was linked to the serpent, and his consort Ix Chel was often shown with a snake hair-band. Itzamná was considered to be a creator, as was the sea god Sovereign Plumed Serpent by the Quiché Maya of the *Popol Vuh*.

The snake was also associated with spirit journeys and religious experience. The Maya developed the notion of the vision serpent, along whose coils the individual could travel to the spirit world or within which humans could encounter the gods. In Aztec carvings and art the open mouth of the serpent represents the cave Mesoamericans widely understood to be an entrance to the spirit world or to the underworld Mictlán.

Below: The Maya god Ix Chel was often depicted as a clawed goddess with a writhing serpent on her head and embroidered crossbones on her skirt.

Above: This large carved head at the Maya city of Copán is thought to represent the god Itzamná, culture-giver and scribes' patron.

The Aztecs (and the Toltecs before them) worshipped the snake in the form of the bird-serpent Quetzalcóatl, but the Aztecs also considered the earth goddess Coatlícue to have snake petticoats. The earth and sky were made from the dismembered body of a serpentine monster: sometimes the top layer of the earth was said to be composed of a carpet of interconnected serpents from which men, plants and animals had grown; the double-headed serpent represented in Aztec jewellery and art stood for the sky. One version of the myth of Topiltzin-Quetzalcóatl told how the god departed Mexico on a raft made of serpents.

Huitzilopochtli, sun deity and the Aztecs' tribal god, wielded a weapon called the *xiuhcóatl* or fire-snake to kill his countless brothers in the moments after his birth. In his form as Tonatiuh, the sun was led across the sky by the *xiuhcóatl* and by night fought in the underworld using the fire-snake as a weapon.

In one celebrated carving of Coatlícue, snakes represent the flow of blood from her cut arms and head. A sacrificial stone found in the Gulf of Mexico coastal region in the 19th century was carved in the shape of a two-headed snake, with a raised back on which the victim was pressed down while his heart was carved from his chest. Carvings of snakes-heads are known to have decorated the stairs on the Great Pyramid in Tenochtitlán.

Tláloc the rain and thunder god had a snake mask and was often depicted carrying a snake sceptre – driving rain was sometimes seen as a storm of water-snakes. In both Mesoamerican mythology and religion, the serpent was associated with the sun's rays, with rain, fertility and the earth, skill and power, the waters of the sea, human sexuality and rebirth.

LORD OF THE SMOKING MIRROR

Tezcatlipoca, the god of fate and bringer of discord and vice, was likened by Bernardino de Sahagún to the Christian devil. Tezcatlipoca had great powers and creative aspects but often put them to negative use, just like the angel Lucifer in the Christian tradition. Tezcatlipoca was a creator deity and shared the credit with Quetzalcóatl for the creation of the world from the body of the Earth Monster. However, whereas Quetzalcóatl was a civilizing cultural hero who introduced mankind to maize, Tezcatlipoca was a god of war who brought men into a cycle of destruction and new creation.

THE CULT OF TEZCATLIPOCA

Tezcatlipoca's cult went back at least as far as the Toltecs. They told a tale of a mirror of dark obsidian glass that could predict famine. At a time of great need, when people were starving in the land, Tezcatlipoca found and hid this mirror in order to prolong the people's suffering.

The 'Lord of the Smoking Mirror', Tezcatlipoca, was believed to wear a mirror of the volcanic glass obsidian in the back of his head. Sometimes he was also said to have a mirror in place of one of his feet. Traditions vary as to whether Tezcatlipoca lost his foot when he and Quetzalcóatl were fighting the Earth Monster in order to create the earth and sky, or when he was flung out of the thirteenth heaven as punishment for misusing his dark power to seduce a fair goddess. Often he was depicted simply with a missing foot, his leg ending in the shinbone.

The glass he wore was said to be a 'smoking mirror' because it was made of obsidian, which characteristically gives a distorted reflection that is coloured green, grey or golden depending on the type used. Sometimes the glass was said to reflect the night even in full day; obsidian was linked in the Aztec imagination with cold and with the night, as was Tezcatlipoca himself. It was also associated with death and with the rain of windblown knives that travellers to the underworld of Mictlán had to pass through. According to the Franciscan friar Diego Durán, the author of *The History of the Indies of New Spain*, there was a religious statue made wholly of obsidian in the Templo Mayor or the sacred precinct in Tenochtitlán.

Left: This Tezcatlipoca mask was probably worn on a priest's waist. It was made from the front of a human skull.

Above: An Aztec potter-artist painted his clay pot to make a wild-eyed likeness of all-seeing Tezcatlipoca.

The statue held a golden mirror. Using his shadowy mirror, Tezcatlipoca could see the patterns of the future and the private imaginings of people's hearts.

REFLECTING THE DARK SIDE

As the god of night, Tezcatlipoca was patron of hidden nocturnal activities, often shameful or wicked ones such as adultery and stealing. Sometimes he was depicted carrying a *tlachialoni*, a sceptre concealing a hole through which he could see the hidden side of people and their motives. The smoking mirror gave him access to the dark side, not only of people but also of the wider creation. He had within his control the forces of destruction as well as those of creation.

Above: The jaguar, a fierce aspect of Tezcatlipoca, was viewed with religious awe in Mesoamerica. These ravening cats are part of a mural from Teotihuacán.

DEATH EVERYWHERE

Tezcatlipoca was everywhere, invisible yet ubiquitous. Like the cold night sky, he was found in the north, south, east and west, although north was his particular direction. He resided in all the levels of the universe at once, even the underworld. He was also a god of the air, and of violent tempests, particularly hurricanes: he was associated with the Maya god Tahil.

Tezcatlipoca was also the coming destruction, for he would unleash the inevitable cataclysm destined to wipe away the current creation.

Tezcatlipoca was said to carry a sacrificial knife made of obsidian that symbolized a black wind devoid of life. Sacrificial knives were found in many of the offerings uncovered by archaeologists at the Templo Mayor in Tenochtitlán. In many, the knives are inserted into the nose or mouth of a skull mask. This symbolized the black wind that delivers death by stopping the flow of air, in contrast to the bright wind that is the breath of life.

LIFE AFTER CONQUEST

Obsidian, the volcanic glass associated so widely with Tezcatlipoca, was used by Spanish priests in a way that may have given Aztec onlookers secret amusement or satisfaction.

Archaeologists and historians have uncovered a number of obsidian blocks set in wood dating from the post-Conquest colonial period. Some are carved with Christian symbolism. Although some were doubtless used as mirrors, scholars believe that others were put to use as portable altars by travelling priests. To an Aztec, the 'smoking glass' obsidian would at once have suggested Tezcatlipoca. The god's association with shamanism, sorcery and treachery made his glass an unlikely material for priests to use for celebrating Mass. The great majority of the priests were probably ignorant of this powerful hidden association.

THE ORIGINATOR OF WAR

Alongside Huitzilopochtli, Tezcatlipoca was one of the Aztecs' principal warrior gods. A round shield called the *chimalli*, which was a symbol for battle conflict, was one of his accoutrements. In his human form, Tezcatlipoca was as youthful, virile and energetic as any eagle or jaguar warrior. The sacrifice of young victims at

Below: The Maya also worshipped the underworld jaguar god. This image is from the Temple of the Jaguar at Tikal.

the year's end granted the god eternal youthfulness. In this guise Tezcatlipoca was sometimes known as Telpochtli ('Young Warrior') and worshipped by a band of young devotees called the *telpochtiliztli*. A splendid funerary urn probably containing the ashes of a great warrior was found in the Templo Mayor in Tenochtitlán during excavations in 1978–82. It depicts Tezcatlipoca as a young warrior, carrying spears and an *atálatl* spear-thrower, wearing an

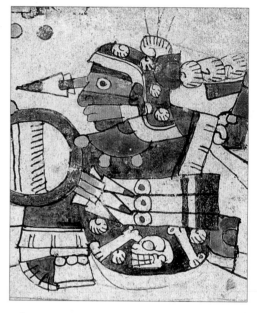

Above: In this image from the Codex Cospi *(c.1350–1500), Tezcatlipoca is in his black aspect, linked to the north and to death.*

eagle-feather headdress and spearhead nose-ring. In the Aztec codices he is also usually depicted as a soldier, carrying an *atlatl*, shield and darts and wearing two heron feathers in his hair to signify his status among the most elite groups of knights. His body is often painted black.

YÁOTL, THE ENEMY

Tezcatlipoca was the bringer of war, always at work stirring up conflict. In this guise, he was known as Yáotl ('the Enemy'). His presence was felt on the battlefield, although not as a protector. He presided over the give and take of war and decided when warriors should succeed and when they should fall. On his jacket were the skull and crossbones.

Tezcatlipoca loved and desired conflict for its own sake, but there was a positive side-effect to his stirring of wars, for on the battlefield the Aztecs gathered prisoners to carry home for sacrifice in the sacred precinct in Tenochtitlán. In this sense, his promotion of war was less a malign activity and more a valuable contribution to the religious cycle of sacrifice.

Above: This codex image depicts the dark lord Tezcatlipoca as a virile warrior, equipped with shield and weapon.

ANIMAL FORMS

All Aztec gods had one or more animal forms. Tezcatlipoca was associated particularly with the jaguar, which was like the god in that it was fierce, unpredictable and favoured the night.

The Lord of the Smoking Mirror was believed to roam the earth in the dark hours, sometimes in the form of this stealthy, keen-visioned predator. As the jaguar, Tezcatlipoca was associated with the sun during its night-time passage through the dangerous regions of the underworld. In one version of the myth describing the end of the current creation, it is told how, in that era, Tezcatlipoca would steal the sun, so bringing the world, gods and men to black nothingness.

Among his other animal forms were the deceitful skunk, the mischievous monkey and the sly coyote. Aztecs thought the coyote had particular sexual potency and Tezcatlipoca's association with him was located in the god's aspect as a deity of masculinity.

NEGATIVE AND POSITIVE POWER

Tezcatlipoca had many other attributes, always combining negative and positive aspects. His connection to the night and to the jaguar made him god of sorcerer-shamans. He was said to be 'the Left-handed One', suggesting that he was never to be trusted and that he would come at men unexpectedly. He was understood to be mocking mankind, binding them with evil. If a man or woman endured great humiliation it was understood by all to be the work of Tezcatlipoca.

Tezcatlipoca was also associated with rulers and kingly qualities; the coronation preparations of the Aztec *tlatoani* included rites in Tezcatlipoca's honour. According to one tradition, it was Tezcatlipoca, alongside Huitzilopochtli, who guided the México/Aztecs on their journey to find a place to settle. He is said to have inspired the travelling tribe by recounting the marvellous vision of their future riches and dominance that he could see in his shadow-mirror.

Some of the priests of Tenochtitlán painted their bodies black in honour of Tezcatlipoca, using a dark paste made from ground mushrooms, snake skin and tobacco. Tezcatlipoca helped the Aztecs

Above: An image from Bernardino de Sahagún's Florentine Codex (1575–7) shows a sacrifice in honour of Tezcatlipoca.

in their divinely ordained mission to provide blood nourishment for the gods. The religious festival of Tóxcatl in May, when a youthful representative of Tezcatlipoca was sacrificed in the dark lord's honour, was one of the major festivals of the Aztec year. As the youth was led to sacrifice up the temple steps, the earthly form of Tezcatlipoca would play mournfully on a thin flute that was carved in the likeness of a flower at its end.

Tezcatlipoca's feast day was 1-Death in the sixth thirteen-day 'month' of the 260-day calendar. At the festival of Teotleco (Coming of the Gods and Goddesses), a bowl of maize flour was laid in the temple and a night vigil was kept until a footprint in the bowl was hailed as the sign that the gods had come. According to some accounts, this footprint was understood to be that of Tezcatlipoca, leading the main group of gods and goddesses. He was not the first to arrive, however. This was always the youngest and fastest god, Tlamatzincatl.

DARK CHALLENGER BY NIGHT

Tezcatlipoca was a constant danger by night. A man out alone on night roads might expect to be challenged by the dark god, who was believed to roam the country looking for victims. If Tezcatlipoca met a traveller, he would challenge him to a bout of wrestling. A mortal who defeated the god could ask for anything he pleased and know that it would be granted. In this guise, Tezcatlipoca was associated with the night wind. Stone benches were built alongside the more important roadways to provide a resting place for this most unpredictable of gods;

Below: Tezcatlipoca's reputation for virility associated him with the coyote, believed by Aztecs to be sexually powerful.

Above: An unknown deity emerges from the mouth of the divine jaguar in a terracotta piece from the Zapotec city of Monte Albán.

unfortunately he often used these as sites for his ambushes. Some nights he sent thieves to do his work for him.

DANGEROUS ENERGY

A body of myths recounted how Tezcatlipoca's dangerous energy caused havoc among the Toltec people of Tollán at the time when the priest Topiltzin-Quetzalcóatl was at the height of his powers there. Tezcatlipoca travelled there to cause trouble, scantily clad with his almost naked body painted green, posing as a salesman of green paint. He knew that Huemac, who served Quetzalcóatl by governing Tollán, had a daughter whose beauty was the talk of the whole Valley of Mexico, for her appearance was more wonderful even than that of Mount

Ixtaccíhuatl. Many Toltecs longed to marry her. Tezcatlipoca made sure that he passed close to her bedchamber for he hoped to arouse strong desires in her soul. His plan worked, as he knew it would.

The princess saw the vigorous body and bright flashing eyes of the wandering salesman and fell deeply in love. She took to her bed, pining for love, and her father became worried. When he asked her handmaidens what the matter was, they explained that a passing stranger had undone his daughter, arousing passions in her that would give her no rest. Huemac summoned the

Below: An enigmatic Aztec figure (c.1200–1500) combines the features of the living (right) and the fleshless dead (left).

stranger to his court and asked him his business. Tezcatlipoca was casual. He explained that he went almost naked because it was the custom where he came from and said that his life was not of great importance to him. The king could kill him, if he pleased, to punish him for stealing his daughter's heart. However, Huemac knew that if he sacrificed the young man it would be the death of his lovelorn daughter, so instead he commanded the handsome stranger to marry the beautiful princess.

This caused great upset among the people of Tollán, but the king launched a war in order to distract them.

Tezcatlipoca went unannounced among the troops, but some soldiers recognized him as the stranger who had stolen the princess from them. They tricked him into occupying a vulnerable position on the battle-field, where they hoped he would be slain. When the moment came, however, he fought with the greatest valour and won a fine reputation.

A DEADLY DANCE

Back in Tollán, Tezcatlipoca was the toast of the city. He could do no wrong and was cheered wherever he went, attired in warrior's garb, with his beautiful wife on his arm. Now he unleashed the full force of his power on the unsuspecting people. He announced that there would be a public feast and celebration and at the appointed time the Toltecs crowded enthusiastically into the main plaza. Then he began to sing and made the people dance to his song. Faster he sang, and faster, and the people had to fling themselves into the

steps to stay ahead of the music. Faster still and faster he sang, until the dance was unbearable for the assembled crowd.

The people could no longer keep their footing, and they fell helplessly into a ravine that the god had made in the solid earth. They tumbled down the steep sides like so many rocks. It was over – they were dead.

A GOD AVENGES HIS OWN DEATH

Another tale told how Tezcatlipoca invited all the people of Tollán to meet him in the city's fair flower gardens. He hid himself in the shade, then leapt out on his victims, killing many with a simple hoe, while others fled in panic, trampling one another. Many hundreds of innocents died.

Another story told how Tezcatlipoca punished the Toltecs for his own death. He was again entertaining the people in the main plaza, this time by displaying a child dancing in his hand, who was in truth, the warlike Aztec deity Huitzilopochtli. By using fantastic magic Tezcatlipoca made the child appear to dance on his outstretched palm. The people crowded urgently around, creating such a crush that many people were killed. This unleashed the fury of the survivors and they turned on the gods Tezcatlipoca and Huitzilopochtli, pummelling them until they died.

The gods' death was not the end of the affair. Their corpses began to leak a hideous-smelling liquid and gave off a gas so foul that any who smelled it died instantly. A few came in masks to drag the pestilential corpses away, but they found that the divine bodies were far too heavy to shift. They tied them up with strong cords and gathered a huge crowd to pull, but the ropes broke and the people tumbled in a great heap, one suffocating the next. In the end the entire population died.

Left: This elaborate funerary urn was found in Teotihuacán, revered by the Aztecs as perhaps the site of the Tollán of myth.

183

THE PLUMED SERPENT

Quetzalcóatl's name has two meanings. In itself, it comprises two Nahuatl words, each of which also has two meanings. *Quetzal* can mean 'green feather' or 'precious' and *cóatl* can mean 'serpent' or 'twin'. The elements of the name taken together can therefore mean 'Plumed Serpent' or 'Precious Twin'. Each name evokes an aspect or role played by Quetzalcóatl in the Mesoamerican pantheon. Such dual meaning also

Below: A 4th-century homage to the Plumed Serpent is suggestive of the god's possible origins in an ancient dragon deity.

demonstrates the concept of duality so characteristic of Mesoamerican deities and religion in general.

A HUMAN AVATAR

Quetzalcóatl was the only one of the Aztec gods to have had a human avatar in the person of Topiltzin, the priestly ruler of Tollán. In addition, because of his association with wise governance and kingly qualities, many earthly rulers took his name and wore the green feathers of his animal familiar, the quetzal bird. These rulers may have been understood to be representatives of the god on Earth. Quetzalcóatl was a protector of rulers and their families. He was also a great cultural hero, inventor of the ritual calendar, teacher of farming skills and protector of craftsmen. In the form of an ant, he was responsible for bringing the maize plant to humans.

TWIN FORMS

God and man, man and serpent, the 'Precious Twin' was a god of duality; of twin forms. His cult goes far back into Mesoamerican history. The oldest

Above: This magnificent double-headed serpent pectoral may have been part of the treasure sent to Cortés by Moctezuma II.

surviving image of Quetzalcóatl, found at Tlatilco, dates to *c*.800 BC, while a pyramid temple to the god was built at Teotihuacán in the 3rd century AD. His cult probably grew from that of an ancient Mesoamerican sky god, a dragon who was also worshipped as a fertility and agricultural deity because of his ability to deliver fresh winds and life-giving rains. However, he was also seen as a god of land-level waters – in the *Popol Vuh* the Plumed Serpent is the sea god – and among his myriad attributes he had the power to unleash floods. When the Spanish conquistadors came to Cholula, the priests there tried to provoke the anger of Quetzalcóatl as god of the waters. They encouraged the invaders to desecrate the temple of the Plumed Serpent in the hope that the god would send a flood to drive the Europeans back. However, the plan misfired because Quetzalcóatl did not respond to their insults.

CONNECTIONS TO FERTILITY

The Plumed Serpent's connections to fertility were made clear in one Aztec myth of his conception and birth. According to this tale, Quetzalcóatl was the daughter of Cihuacóatl, a fertility and earth goddess whose name means 'Woman Serpent'. Cihuacóatl often took the shape of a deer. In early times, long before the México travelled south from the northern steppes in which they originated, she roamed the earth as a two-headed deer. In this form she attracted the attention of the hunting god Mixcóatl ('Cloud Serpent'), who pursued her through steep valleys and across wide plains, and all along the shores of the lakes, until he had her in his sights. With one well-aimed dart he brought her low. However, in that same instant he also lost her, for before his eyes the beast transformed into a woman of surpassing beauty. Now the hunt was on again. Mixcóatl pursued this maiden across the landscape until he caught her. Then they had sexual relations. The fruit of their lovemaking was the Plumed Serpent Quetzalcóatl.

Above: Another view of the shell-mosaic piece of Quetzalcóatl, in human form. Bursting forth from the jaws of a coyote, he represents life springing from the Earth.

Quetzalcóatl was also associated with a range of attributes and natural states that were in opposition to those of his ancient rival and foe Tezcatlipoca. Tezcatlipoca was associated with night, deception and cycles of violence, whereas Quetzalcóatl was linked to daylight, clear thinking and a good life. Both gods were associated with the winds, but while Tezcatlipoca was the god of night winds and hurricanes, Quetzalcóatl-Éhecatl was lord of the morning winds that bring light to the fields. Some scholars understand the ancient image of the sky serpent – often represented with its tail in its mouth – as a homage to the sun, and Quetzalcóatl had some connection to the Earth's star. Indeed, many Aztec gods had solar aspects.

Priests of Quetzalcóatl wore a conch shell whose patterning represented the movement of the wind and honoured the

Left: Some 14cm (6in) tall, this shell-mosaic piece dates from the Toltec period and may once have graced a palace in Tula.

god in his guise as the wind god Éhecatl. Quetzalcóatl was particularly associated with the priesthood and he was regarded as the protector of the priestly school in Tenochtitlán. The two foremost members of the priestly hierarchy were called 'Quetzalcóatl' as part of their title, despite the fact that they presided over the worship of other gods.

In his guise as a priestly patron, Quetzalcóatl was represented as a man with skin painted black and a long beard. In this role and in his form as the wind god, Éhecatl, Quetzalcóatl is often shown wearing a conical hat. The Maya of Yucatán worshipped the Plumed Serpent as Kukulcán, god of wind, light and waters with some solar characteristics. Among the Maya he was particularly revered as a thunder god.

QUETZALCÓATL AND THE RAFT OF SNAKES

Many myths tell of Quetzalcóatl's enduring conflict with the dark lord Tezcatlipoca. In his guise as the historical-mythical Toltec ruler Topiltzin, Quetzalcóatl was decisively defeated by his opponent and forced to leave the city of Tollán. So ended a golden era of peace and wonderful artistic achievement. There are various versions of his downfall, but according to one, the formerly pure-minded priest-king was tricked by Tezcatlipoca into becoming drunk on the strong liquor known as *pulque* and disgraced himself by seducing his own sister. He left in shame.

Topiltzin-Quetzalcóatl determined to sacrifice himself as a mark of his penitence. He dressed himself in his purest finery, including the kingly mask of turquoise, and built a pyre of great tree-trunks. Then he stepped on to the bonfire and lit it himself. He did not flinch at the touch of fire, just as the god Nanahuatzin, who became the sun, went

Below: A figurine from Teotihuacán shows Quetzalcóatl in human form but with a serpent's divided tongue.

unflinching into the flames. The flames roared. In an instant, all the king's finery and his royal body were ash. His soul became a spark that rose to the sky and settled in the form of Venus, the morning star. In this guise, Quetzalcóatl was known as Ce Ácatl or Tlahuizcalpantecuhtli: he was a malign force, the enemy of the sun. He was also feared and revered – in the form of Xólotl – as Venus the evening star.

THE END OF TOLLÁN

Another version of the myth describes how Topiltzin-Quetzalcóatl left the city, made a penitential procession to the seacoast and departed on a raft made of snakes, bound for the land of Tlapallán, whence he had originally come. First he burned the splendid buildings of Tollán, then buried the great treasures and artworks for which his reign was famous in the deep mountain valleys nearby. He transformed the cacao trees that had grown in the city into mesquites and commanded the beautiful bird that had graced Tollán to depart a great distance. Tollán was bereft of its leader and of its beauty. An era had ended.

Topiltzin-Quetzalcóatl departed, with a troop of palace assistants and pages following in his footsteps. After some hours of walking and exhausted by grief, he stopped at a place called Quauhtitlán. He asked his assistant to hand him a mirror and, examining his reflection, sighed deeply. 'I am old,' he said quietly, and handed the mirror back to his assistant. The pages were weeping, because of the king's inexplicable wrongdoing and

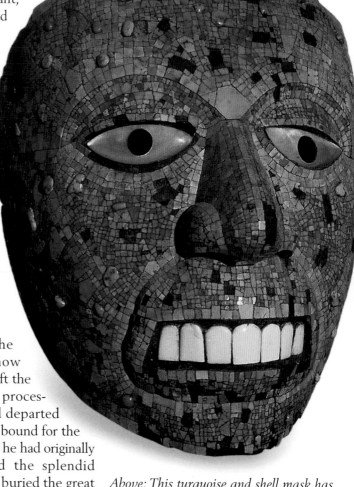

Above: This turquoise and shell mask has holes in the eyes to allow the wearer to see and was probably worn by a priest.

because they understood that, in this time-bound physical world, what is perfect and true, like the era of Topiltzin-Quetzalcóatl's rule in Tollán, cannot endure for ever. The dark shadow of Tezcatlipoca is behind every beam of light. The place was ever afterwards known as Huehuequauhtitlán ('Old Quauhtitlán') because the king saw his aged face there and was saddened. They went on then, with one of the palace musicians playing a mournful air on the flute like the victim who impersonated Tezcatlipoca in the festival of Tóxcatl. When Topiltzin-Quetzalcóatl was too tired to go further, he sat on a roadside

QUETZALCÓATL AND THE RAFT OF SNAKES

rock, again sighing deeply. The god-prince left the mark of his hands in this stone, and the place was afterwards known as Temacpalco ('The Imprint of Hands').

They went on again when Topiltzin-Quetzalcóatl was rested. At Coaapán they met a group of Aztec deities who asked the god-prince where he was going and for what reason. He replied that he was going back to his place of origin, Tlapallán, because his father the sun had called him home. The gods allowed him to pass, but demanded that Quetzalcóatl deliver the secrets of his divine magic; the supreme spells that lay behind the creation of the wonders of his rule in Tollán. Topiltzin-Quetzalcóatl refused and threw all his spells into the fountain named Cozcaapa.

The procession of penitents came to a high pass close to a volcano in the Sierra Nevada mountains. It was too cold in this forlorn spot for mere mortals and all of the palace followers died, leaving

Below: A 3rd-century BC *bas-relief celebrates the life-giving force and regal power of the ancient Plumed Serpent.*

Above: This powerful statue of Quetzalcóatl in his guise as Éhecatl, lord of the winds, was found in Calixtlahuaca, Mexico.

Topiltzin-Quetzalcóatl to mourn them with singing and flute-playing of the most exquisite beauty. He climbed to the peak of Mount Poyauhtécatl, then went down to the far side by sliding. He came at last, and alone, to the shore of the Eastern Sea (which today is known as the Gulf of Mexico) and here summoned the snakes of the entire coastal region. From them he made a raft and then he threw the magical vessel made of snakes on to the waters. He departed for Tlapallán on his snake raft. Those who await his return know that he will come back in the same way, by sea, to found anew the glorious kingdom of Tollán.

It has often been suggested that Moctezuma believed Hernán Cortés to be the returning divinity Topiltzin-Quetzalcóatl and that it was for this reason he treated the Spanish conquistadors with reverence rather than

the suspicion they merited. It was a happy coincidence for the Spanish invaders that they arrived in the year 1-Reed, which had been prophesied as the year in which the god would return, and that the first encounter between Cortés and Moctezuma took place on Quetzalcóatl's name day. The *tlatoani* received a gift of wine and biscuits from Cortés, but refused them and sent them to be buried in the temple of Quetzalcóatl at Tollán in honour of the god 'whose sons have arrived'. According to Bernardino de Sahagún, when Moctezuma greeted Cortés with a splendid speech at the gates of Tenochtitlán, he declared that the arriving leader had come from the 'unknown…a place of mystery'.

187

THE TRIBAL WAR GOD

The Aztecs' patron god, deity of war and of the sun, was a fierce warrior from the first moment of his life. According to the myth of his birth, Huitzilopochtli came from his mother's womb fully armed. His mother was the earth goddess Coatlícue, who in one account also mothered Quetzalcóatl. Coatlícue was priestess of a shrine high on the mountain at Coatepec, near the Toltec capital of Tollán or Tula. One day, as she was cleaning the shrine, she saw a ball of brightly coloured feathers descend on to her breast. She thought little of it, but rather than discard the feathers she placed them in her belt. However, when she next looked she found out that the ball had disappeared and soon afterwards she discovered the feathers had miraculously made her pregnant.

A PROTECTIVE SON

Coatlícue's existing children included one daughter, the moon goddess Coyolxauhqui, and sons almost beyond counting, the Centzonhuitznahuac ('The Four Hundred Southerners'). When they saw their mother was pregnant they were angry, for they were suspicious of her claim that the pregnancy was a miracle and suspected that she had been

Below: The xiuhcóatl *or fire-serpent brandished by Huitzilopochtli forms the motif on this mosaic disc from Chichén Itzá.*

Above: Huitzilopochtli's mother Coatlícue represents the surface of the Earth and its power to bring life from the death of winter.

promiscuous. The children gathered at the foot of the mountain and Coyolxauhqui convinced her brothers to punish their mother by putting her to death. High above in her mountain shrine, Coatlícue heard their raised voices and knew what they were planning. She shivered with fear, but then heard a voice issuing from her womb: she must not be afraid, the voice said, for her new child would protect her.

When Coyolxauhqui and the Four Hundred Southerners arrived to launch their attack, Huitzilopochtli emerged to repel them. His skin was painted blue and he wore the body armour that would later be adopted by Aztec warriors. The bright feathers of the hummingbird – the same feathers that had fallen in a ball on to the chest of Coatlícue – covered his left leg. This justified his name of

'Hummingbird of the Left'. With the *xiuhcóatl* or fire-serpent he held in his hand, he cut Coyolxauhqui into many pieces. These fell down the mountainside and landed, all jumbled up, on the plain below. Then he killed his brothers, left and right, allowing a few bedraggled survivors to escape to the south.

VICTORY FOR THE SUN

The myth proclaims the primacy of the sun, represented by Huitzilopochtli, over his moon sister Coyolxauhqui. The weapon the sun god used was the fire-serpent which was believed to guide the sun across the sky by day. His mother is the serpent-skirted earth from which the sun appears to issue each dawn, and the Four Hundred Southerners are the southern stars of the night sky that are routed every morning as the light of the sun spreads far and wide.

This victory was commemorated in a celebrated sculpture of Coyolxauhqui's dismembered body that lay at the foot of the steps of the Great Pyramid in Tenochtitlán, where the bodies of sacrificial victims landed. The tale of sun and moon deities Huizilopochtli and Coyolxauhqui is therefore a variation on the myth of the creation of the sun and

Below: This sculpture of Coyolxauhqui's massacred body received the blood of many victims that poured off the Great Pyramid.

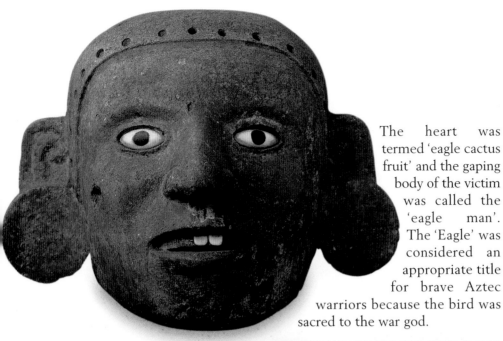

Above: Made from stone, with shell eyes and obsidian for the eyeballs, this arresting mask evokes qualities of youthful vigour.

The heart was termed 'eagle cactus fruit' and the gaping body of the victim was called the 'eagle man'. The 'Eagle' was considered an appropriate title for brave Aztec warriors because the bird was sacred to the war god.

A surviving Aztec hymn to Huitzilopochtli praises him as a young warrior dressed in yellow feathers who makes the sun appear. It praises the god for moving the sun across the heavens and associates him with the god Nanahuatzin when it declares, 'Here he comes forward, one well dressed in paper, who lives in the place that burns.'

Below: The fire serpent is celebrated in this Aztec sculpture at Tenayuca.

moon at Teotihuacán and of the enmity born there between the sun, Nanahuatzin and the moon, Tecuciztécatl. The story of Huitzilopochtli's birth also celebrates and establishes the Aztec tradition of martial vigour, conflict and bloodletting.

Spanish chroniclers have likened Huitzilopochtli to Hercules, the mythical Greek hero who performed twelve wondrous 'labours' or feats of strength and bravery. Huitzilopochtli was usually depicted wearing a plume of humming-bird feathers on his head, with his face, arms and legs painted with blue stripes. He carried four spears in one hand and a reed shield bearing five tufts of eagle's down on his other arm. The spears had eagle's down rather than the usual hard flint at their tips.

EAGLE IMAGERY

The eagle was principal among the creatures associated with the war and sun god, and eagle imagery played a major part in acts of ritual human sacrifice performed in Huitzilopochtli's honour in which the human heart was torn out. When the priest removed the heart from the victim's flayed chest, he held it up to the sun in triumphant dedication, then flung it into one of the *cuauhxicalli* ('eagle vessels') placed nearby.

HUMMINGBIRD OF THE LEFT

Huitzilopochtli, the Aztecs' war and sun god, had no antecedents among the deities of earlier Mesoamerican peoples. According to their own origin myths, Huitzilopochtli travelled south with the México or Aztecs when they entered the Valley of Mexico from the less hospitable lands to the north. In some accounts he led the tribe on its migration, in others his idol was carried by a group of four priests and made several divine prophecies of their coming greatness.

DUALITY OF LIFE AND DEATH

The Aztecs took care to establish their god's standing alongside older Mesoamerican deities. At the top of the Great Pyramid in Tenochtitlán, a shrine to Huitzilopochtli stood alongside one to the rain god Tláloc, one of the oldest gods of the region. In Huitzilopochtli's temple a sacred flame burned that had to be kept alight at all costs. The Aztecs understood that if it were allowed to die then their power and ascendancy over the other peoples of the region would abruptly come to an end. Twin temples to a rain god and a war god symbolized the duality of life and death. It also symbolized the incompatible opposition of water and fire, which the Aztecs used as an image for war. The Great Pyramid in the sacred complex

Right: The god Huitzilopochtli's mother, Coatlícue, was believed to take the bodies of the dead.

at Tenochtitlán was intended as a recreation in stone of the hill of Coatepec ('Serpent Mountain'), where the tribal god was born, and of Mount Tonacatépetl, where the staple food maize was discovered, as well as of Mount Tláloc, the peak sacred to the rain god, on which important fertility and rain festivals were held.

Huitzilopochtli's own standing was further bolstered by the god's identification with south, the sacred direction of Blue Tezcatlipoca, one of the four creator-sons of the lord of duality Ometeotl.

HUMMINGBIRDS

Huitzilopochtli's name means 'Hummingbird of the Left'. Left was used in the Aztecs' Nahuatl tongue to refer to south, the region with which hummingbirds were associated. Hummingbirds were connected to blood sacrifice, for the blood let by the priest from his own body or that of a sacrificial victim was compared to the nectar drawn by a hummingbird from a flower. The birds also became connected to war. The souls of warriors killed in battle were said to take the form of hummingbirds and to accompany the sun in its climb each morning from the dawn horizon to its zenith.

Huitzilopochtli occupied a primary position in Aztec religious life. The festival of Panquetzalíztli ('Lifting of the

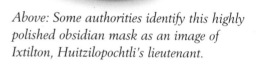

Above: Some authorities identify this highly polished obsidian mask as an image of Ixtilton, Huitzilopochtli's lieutenant.

Banners'), which was held in November and December in Huitzilopochtli's honour, was one of the most important of the Aztec year. Although none survives, we know from documentary evidence that major statues of Huitzilopochtli stood in the sacred precinct of Tenochtitlán and in the main religious areas of Texcoco and Tlatelolco.

LADY OF DISCORD

Huitzilopochtli was thirsty for human blood and many thousands of human victims were slain in his honour by the Aztecs. The majority were prisoners of the wars that the god promoted, but on occasion he demanded other victims.

A tale recounted by Fray Diego Durán in *The History of the Indies of New Spain* paints a vivid picture of the personal horror associated with these religious rites. Before they reached Tenochtitlán, the México/Aztecs were living near Culhuacán. Durán reports that Huitzilopochtli wanted to foster discord, so he declared that he required the princess of Culhuacán to serve him. Her honouring of the god would provoke unrest between the Aztecs and the uolhua and she would become known as 'Lady of Discord'.

The Aztecs went faithfully to the ruler of Culhuacán, Achitometl, and declared that his daughter had been chosen by the Aztecs' ruling deity to be his bride, to rule as a living goddess. Achitometl agreed, because he was dazzled by the prospect of having a goddess as a daughter. The Aztecs then took the princess to their temple, where, following Huitzilopochtli's urging, they sacrificed her. They flayed her, then dressed one of the priests in her skin and arrayed her in royal garments. They then asked Achitometl to come to see his daughter in her guise as a living goddess. The king was proud and came with many of the leading men and women of Culhuacán to see his daughter and make sacrifices to her.

He went gladly into the temple and made many sacrifices before the altar. The atmosphere was gloomy

Above: The Codex Tudela *(c.1550) graphically illustrates a priest tearing open a victim's chest and wrenching out his heart as blood flows down the temple steps.*

and the king could not see far beyond his hands, which were busy preparing quails for sacrifice. But when he threw incense into the fire, the flames flared up suddenly and

he saw a truly horrific sight: his daughter's skin ripped from her body and worn as a cloak by a priest who was sitting just a few feet away beside the altar. Achitometl ran from the temple, maddened with grief, and calling on his kinsmen to avenge the cruel slaughter of his daughter. They drove the Aztecs out. The travellers continued their search for a permanent home.

Left: Symbol of the sun and of a warrior elite, the eagle received the blood of sacrifice. Stone eagle vessels were used to store victims' hearts and blood.

DIVINE CREATURES

Animals were revered as manifestations of divine power from the first days of Mesoamerican civilization. From the time of the Olmecs in *c.*1500BC the fearsome jaguar was a cult object and its features were carved on sacred sculptures. The unknown builders of Teotihuacán in *c.*100BC decorated a temple with jaguar images. In the Classic Maya Period the jaguar had divine and regal associations and many Maya kings took the name jaguar as part of their title.

ANIMALS AND GODS

Mesoamerican deities took several guises simultaneously and many had more than one animal form. The Plumed Serpent Quetzalcóatl could be a brilliantly feathered quetzal bird or a serpent, but equally he was associated with the dog in his form as Xólotl, the god of monsters and twin forms; Tezcatlipoca could roam the earth as a jaguar and he was often depicted wearing a spotted jaguar skin, but he was also at

Below: Deer and jaguar were among the first creatures made in the Popol Vuh. *A Maya deer pot was found in El Petén.*

times the coyote, an animal associated by the Aztecs with sexual potency – the 'Lord of the Smoking Mirror' assumed this form in his guise as a patron god of males. Moreover, just as a god could take the form of more than one animal, so an animal could be associated with more than one god. The coyote was also Huehuecóyotl ('Old Old Coyote'): men prayed to this deity to be granted health and virility and to enjoy a long life.

For the Aztecs the serpent was a profoundly important religious symbol: of fertility and life-giving waters, of sacrificial blood, of skill and cunning. The Maya held the turtle in high regard: some creation myths told that the earth floated on the back of a great turtle and in some images from painted vases the turtle represents the earth.

The Aztecs worshipped and feared rabbit gods as the patrons of drunkenness. According to Aztec myth, a rabbit discovered the intoxicating secrets of the alcoholic drink *pulque* when it bit into the maguey cactus from which the liquor was made. A god known by the date name 2-rabbit was one of the patrons of *pulque*, while the members of the group known as the 'Four Hundred Rabbits' were the gods of drunkenness. In the *Popol Vuh* of the Quiché Maya these same deities were not rabbits, but an early form of humans: known as the Four Hundred Boys, they were defeated and killed by Zipacná, Maker of Mountains, then rose to become the Pleiades constellation.

Below: The knotted form of this Aztec stone snake (c.1500) is suggestive of vitality.

The Quiché Maya envisaged One Monkey and One Artisan, the divine half-brothers of the Hero Twins Hunahpú and Xbalanqué, as monkeys. When the Hero Twins were first born, One Monkey and One Artisan treated their new brothers cruelly, but the new arrivals got their revenge by tricking their older siblings into climbing a tree, marooning them there and turning them into monkeys. One Monkey and One Artisan were linked to the arts and sedentary pursuits while the Hero Twins – expert hunters with their blowpipes – were keen outdoorsmen. Classic-Period Maya vases and codices often represent deities with human bodies and monkey heads, who are regularly shown writing in or reading from codices; they have been identified as patron gods not only of the Maya scribes, but also of other artists such as musicians, dancers and painters.

The power of the great predator cats is attributed to the Hero Twins – it is fitting that such celebrated hunters should be honoured for having the attributes of the animals they had to mimic in order to understand and kill. Maya vases generally show Hunahpú with spotted skin and Xbalanqué with patches of jaguar pelt on his skin.

Other animal deities depicted on Classic Maya vases and in codices were the vulture god and the fox god. The vulture god seems to have been a patron deity of Maya rulers and scribes – his head is used in inscriptions as a substitute for the word 'king', while in several codex illustrations scribes with the vulture god's face are depicted at work on bark books or holding pens. The fox god might have been a divine guide for those making pots and related wares – he is shown with implements suitable for carving in clay protruding from his headdress where scribes normally kept their pens. Curiously a rabbit god also appears to have been associated with scribes and book-making and in this Maya context had none of the animal's associations with drunkenness found elsewhere in Mesoamerica. The Mesoamericans believed they saw a rabbit in the markings on the face of the Moon and the animal was often depicted with the Maya moon goddess Ix Chel – a carving from Copán shows the goddess holding a crouching rabbit deity in her arms.

BIRDS

The hummingbird and eagle were both forms of Huitzilopochtli and other birds had powerful divine associations. The Aztecs associated owls with Tezcatlipoca, with night and sorcery; among the Maya the owl was also a bird of ill omen and was sometimes a guise of the god of death.

The quetzal was a form of the Plumed Serpent, and was associated with regal bearing and wise rulership. The bird's highly prized feathers were worn by many rulers. The loud macaw reminded the Maya of the boastful sun god who was brought down to earth by the Hero Twins in the *Popol Vuh*. The falcon was associated with Hunahpú.

BATS AND THE UNDERWORLD

The Maya associated bats with the frightful scenes of the underworld. When One and Seven Hunahpú and later on the Hero Twins, Hunahpú and Xbalanqué, descend to the underworld of Xibalba in the *Popol Vuh*, they have to pass through a series of tests – one of which is entering the bat house, a dwelling dark and empty of anything save bats flying hither and thither, filling the air with their terrible shrieks. The Hero Twins spend the night in the company of the bats, waiting for dawn: and one of the shrieking

Above: These Aztec images of a dog (left) and a monkey are taken from a codex illustration of the days of the month.

bats rips off Hunahpú's head, which rolls on to the underworld ballcourt. These terrible creatures were often represented on Maya funerary vases of the Classic Period.

FISH

Among favourite offerings in Aztec religious rituals were fish and representations of fish. Their symbolic power derived from their association with the lakes and seas, which were presided over by Chalchiúhtlicue. Death by drowning or by diseases associated with water could carry the deceased directly to the heaven ruled by rain god Tláloc.

Right: An Aztec craftsman made this ocarina, a small wind-pipe with mouthpiece and fingerholes, in the form of a bright-eyed turtle.

CHAPTER 10

WATERS, FERTILITY AND HARVEST

In ancient times, long before the Aztecs worshipped their hummingbird war god Huitzilopochtli, Mesoamerican farmers made regular offerings to fertility and water gods hoping to secure frequent rains and a bumper harvest. Major gods of the Aztec period, such as the Plumed Serpent, Quetzalcóatl, and Lord of the Smoking Mirror, Tezcatlipoca, developed from primordial deities whose powers were primarily over rain, waters and the fertility of the land – sky gods with the power to deliver wet winds, storms, lightning and thunderbolts. The cult of the Aztec rain god Tláloc and the Maya rain god Chac can be traced back to the Olmec civilization at La Venta in 800BC.

In the Aztec era, worshippers at the *Templo Mayor* within the sacred precinct in Tenochtitlán brought varied offerings to many gods, especially Huitzilopochtli and Tláloc, whose temples had the prime positions at the top of the pyramid, closest to the sacred sky. But while the two gods shared centre stage in the imperial capital, in most areas – particularly in agricultural communities – worshippers felt more attached to the older cult of the rain god and his associated fertility deities than to the worship of Huitzilopochtli, patron of the war-driven Aztec state and empire.

Left: The Aztec cult of Xochiquetzal – goddess of beauty, love, flowers and the domestic arts – was one of many that grew from ancient Mesoamerican worship of fertility goddesses. This image of Xochiquetzal is from the Codex Vaticanus.

THE SACRIFICE OF BLOOD AND WATER

The cult of the rain god was crucial to Mesoamerican religion. In the *Codex Borgia*, for example, the Aztec universe is represented with five figures of Tláloc, Aztec god of rains; one stands in the east, one in the north, one in the south and one in the west, with a fifth in the centre. This cosmic map is comparable to other similar representations of the Earth divided into four quarters and a centre. In other versions of the map, each place is associated with a different god and also with a different one of the five suns or world ages. In the Borgia version, each of the Tláloc figures is standing on an image

Below: The temples of the ancient god Tláloc and the Aztec tribal deity Huitzilopochtli stand side by side at the Templo Mayor *in Tenochtitlán, in this fanciful print by Fumagalli.*

of the earth goddess suggesting that, in every place and in every age, the relationship between the fields and the clouds, the land and the sky, the earth and the rain, is of prime importance.

FERTILITY FOR THE EARTH

Even the demand for sacrificial human blood by Huitzilopochtli and other deities was driven by the desire to guarantee the fertility of the earth. The Aztecs equated blood and water: human blood was the precious liquid that sustained life as water was to the earth. This religious understanding was given symbolic form in sacrifices to the Aztec spring and vegetation god Xipe Totec, whose victims were often shot with arrows rather than despatched by another method of sacrifice. They were tied to frames and as the blood

Above: A priestly coat of shells must have made as much an audible impression as a visual impact during religious ceremonies.

flowed from their wounds it dripped on to a stone that symbolically stood for the thirsty earth, just as the rains fed new growth each spring for Xipe Totec. Similarly, the reclining *chacmool* figures on which priests placed the hearts of sacrificial victims were representations of Tláloc. The mask visible over the eyes and mouth on the *chacmools* identifies them as images of the rain god.

THE ENDING OF WATER

Tláloc was honoured with human blood sacrifice in the festival of Atlcahualo ('The Ending of Water'), which took place in the first month of the Aztec year (14 February–5 March in the Western calendar). Children and young people were sacrificed in his honour and that of his consort Chalchiúhtlicue. The rain god's cult was strongly associated with the fertility of the land. The importance of rain to farmers meant that priests of

Above: Water goddess Chalchiúhtlicue is missing her face and hands because she was deliberately damaged by zealous Spaniards.

Tláloc played a crucial role in agricultural and fertility festivals such as Ochpaniztli ('Clearing'), which took place in September. The priests would make obeisances before Tláloc's image while wearing an elaborate costume. This included a Tláloc serpent mask and a cone-shaped headdress decorated with bark paper strips, a snake sceptre and a bag of copal.

Tláloc's name derives from Nahuatl *tlalli* ('the earth') and *oc*, used as a suffix to denote something settling above or on the surface of an object. At the start of the rainy season clouds collected above the surface of the earth, rising from the canyons and floating up to jostle one another in the thin air around the mountain peaks. At shrines to Tláloc and Chalchiúhtlicue, piles of boulders represented the deities, who were associated with the mountaintops that appeared to summon the long-awaited rain-clouds.

ANNUAL PILGRIMAGE FOR WATER

One of the peaks visible from Tenochtitlán was named in Tláloc's honour and the rulers of the Valley's principal cities made an annual pilgrimage to a shrine on the mountain in the dry season of April and May. Offerings to Tláloc and Chalchiúhtlicue were regularly made in sacred caves high on the mountainsides. For example, a figure of Tláloc fashioned from sticks and covered in resin and copal was found in a cavern on the volcano Ixtaccíhuatl. Scholars believe that figures such as this would normally have been burned at the ends of the rituals and worshippers might have believed that the dark, holy smoke made by the resin and copal had the power to 'blacken' the clouds, turning windblown white travellers into dark clouds laden with rain.

NECESSARY EQUILIBRIUM

Tláloc did not always hold droughts at bay. The forces of dryness and wetness, rains and drought were balanced in a proper equilibrium. Blood sacrifices were necessary, not to propitiate the rain god or ease his anger, but to maintain this equilibrium. An intriguing greenstone figure discovered at Tlatilco and dating to *c.*1500 appears to be a three-dimensional representation of this concept. The figure's face is divided in two down the middle: one half wears the distinctive 'goggles' of Tláloc and has that god's snake-fang

Right: Chacmool figures are sacred to Tláloc. The goggle eyes and mouth ornament link them to the rain god.

Above: Images of Xipe Totec, the god presiding over the germination of seeds, often show him with a crenellated headdress.

mouth, while the other suggests a smooth-faced young man, thought to represent drought. Together the two halves suggest the proper balance of the seasons in the Mesoamerican farming year. So long as the balance of the seasons held, all was well. If calamity struck it was not because part of the year was dry but because the drought did not end; because the equilibrium had been disturbed. Sacrifice was needed to maintain the flow of divine energy in the cosmos.

ANCIENT LIFEGIVERS

Worship of the rain god probably went back to the dawn of Mesoamerican civilization. From the earliest settlements, farmers feared the long and harsh droughts that periodically afflicted the region, bringing humankind's best efforts to nothing. They fervently worshipped the rain god to bring the end of drought and to provide lush crops. He was revered under various names by different peoples and in different periods. To the Maya he was Chac; to the Zapotecs he was Cocijo; to the Totonacs he was Tajín and to the Aztecs he was Tláloc. He was generally regarded as chief of the fertility gods, with dominion over lesser deities of the fields, flowers and crops, including maize.

FOUR GREAT JARS

Like many Aztec gods, Tláloc had a dual nature, bringing both good and bad. He could deliver drought and frosts as well as fertilizing downpours and brought welcome and unwelcome forms of rain – the gentler rains that fed the land and the torrential storms that made the lands flood and spoiled the crops where they stood in the fields. He governed lightning strikes and could also send disease. The Aztecs believed that Tláloc had four great jars, one for each of the four cardinal points. From the jar of the east he brought fruitful rains to Mesoamerica but from the others he unleashed disease, freezing conditions and drought.

The Aztecs also believed that Tláloc stored rainwater in the mountains that towered over the Valley of Mexico and that he was the god of running waters in the mountains. One myth tells how he sends his helpers, the *tláloques*, to collect water from the mountains in sacred vessels. With their way cleared by the wind god Éhecatl-Quetzalcóatl, they carry the water to the vault of the sky where it forms into rain-bearing clouds.

The *tláloques* could bring five types of rain. In addition to life-giving rain to nourish the crops, they also brought

Above: This figure of the Aztec rain god Tláloc wears the very large ear decorations usually associated with the god.

unwanted storms whose winds and lashing rains flattened plants, fungal rain that caused diseases in the maize, flint rain (probably hail or hard driving rain) that pummelled plants, and fire rain, which probably referred to the rain that accompanies lightning storms or to the absence of rain in times of drought.

The serpent imagery, so important in Mesoamerica, was powerfully connected to fertility and was central to the cult of Tláloc. The god's face was often depicted made of snakes, with two curled

Right: A figurine of the Maya rain god Chac has the god's characteristic prominent nose.

serpents representing the eyes and joining in the centre as the nose and a snake 'moustache' above the mouth. Two large serpent fangs usually appeared from his mouth. He always wore outsize ear ornaments and usually had a hat with several points that stood for the mountains in which he stored water.

CHAC, THE MAYA RAIN GOD

The Maya rain god Chac shared many characteristics with the Aztec Tláloc. It is thought the 'two' gods had a common ancestor in Olmec religion and even earlier worship.

Left: Stylized forms of toads flank an abstract image of the rain god Chac on a terracotta plate found at Tikal.

in the Maya pantheon. Kings often wore the rain-god's mask in the Classic Period. The Hauberg stela of AD199, the earliest surviving artefact to bear writing in the Maya system, depicts a king wearing the mask of Chac.

THE RAIN GOD'S HELPERS

The rain god's helpers, the *chacs*, were assigned one to each of the four cardinal points. They are often depicted in Maya codices pouring out the waters of life from heavy vessels. Among the Yucatec Maya *chacs* were considered to be old men.

The *chacs* were also gods of thunder and stone axes were believed to be their thunderbolts. As among the Aztecs, worshippers burned copal resin incense – called *pom* by the Maya – to create black clouds of smoke that they believed had the power to call forth the larger rain-bearing black clouds in the sky.

Like Tláloc, Chac was god of lightning and mountain streams as well as of rains, and had helpers (called the *chacs* by the Maya) to assist him in his work. Chac was shown with a long nose, like a spout for pouring rainwater over the thirsty earth. He often had T-shaped eyes, representing rain falling from the sky. A remarkable homage to Chac was carved at Kabah (near Uxmal), where the building known as the Temple of the Masks is covered

along its 50m (150ft) length with long-snouted faces of the rain god. The worship of the rain god was popular everywhere among the Maya. At Chichén Itzá, many offerings thrown into the sacred well (*cenote*) were made to Chac. The god is probably the most frequently represented

Right: Tláloc images characteristically have protruding fangs. This squat green stone vessel dates from c.AD200.

RAIN SUN AND WATER SUN

In one version of the Aztec creation story, the rain god Tláloc and his consort Chalchiúhtlicue were created by White Tezcatlipoca (Quetzalcóatl) and by Blue Tezcatlipoca (Huitzilopochtli) from parts of the body of the Earth Monster. Other parts were used to create the sky and earth. Tláloc then presided over the third sun or world age, the 'Rain Sun' (*Nahui Quiahuitl*). Chalchiúhtlicue was in charge of the fourth age, the 'Water Sun' (*Nahui Atl*). Tláloc also presided over one of the Aztec heavens: Tlalocán, a place of bliss where drought was not known, where waters and foods were plentiful and cocoa drinks could be made and enjoyed at leisure.

GODDESS OF THE WATERS

The goddess Chalchiúhtlicue was the deity of lakes, the ocean, rivers and streams. She was often represented wearing green or blue-and-white clothes

Left: This vast statue of water goddess Chalchiúhtlicue dates from c. AD150–450, the era of Teotihuacán.

and a hairband or crown of blue reeds. She was usually said to be Tláloc's wife, but was sometimes identified as his daughter or sister.

Chalchiúhtlicue was hailed as 'Mistress of the Jade Skirt' and 'Lady of the Lakes and Ocean' and sometimes wore seashells on her blue dresses. A necklace made of precious stones – usually jade beads – adorned her neck and she often wore either a delicate mosaic of turquoise over her ears or circular earrings. She also often wore a turquoise nose-ring. The Aztecs associated turquoise with the sky and the ocean and so held it particularly sacred to Tláloc and Chalchiúhtlicue. Members of the Aztec *pipiltin* (nobility) wore turquoise ornaments to signal their devotion to Tláloc and his consort.

Chalchiúhtlicue's connection to the expanses of water made her the patron goddess of fishermen and of water-carriers. Many Aztec images of Tláloc were carved of green jadeite, which the Aztecs called *chalchiuitl*.

Images of Chalchiúhtlicue sometimes represent her as a frog, a creature sacred to and specially protected by Tláloc. On the rain god's festival day, priests would leap into Lake Texcoco, calling and kicking like frogs.

More commonly, Tláloc's impersonator-priests would wear his easily recognizable mask, with goggle eyes, an upper lip ornament and fanged mouth, and sport a fine headdress of heron feathers.

Left: This Tláloc pot was deposited as an offering to the rain god facing his temple in Tenochtitlán.

They would carry a stalk of corn or a rod to symbolize the lightning that the rain god also controlled. In the mountains, where he was known to store his rain-waters, he could be seen in the form of tall-standing boulders. Tláloc's helpers, the *tlaloques*, were sometimes said to be the rain god's children by his emerald consort. After Tláloc and the *tlaloques* had done their work in the rainy season, the streams controlled by the water goddess rose. Precious water rushed between narrow banks in torrents that made the bare river beds of the dry season a distant memory. Chalchiúhtlicue was also associated with racing streams and whirlpools and was sometimes called 'The Foaming One'. She was represented sitting on a regal throne with water gushing forth about her.

SACRIFICE OF FROGS

In some accounts, Chalchiúhtlicue also had power over strong winds. Out of a clear sky she could summon hurricanes and whirlwinds with a destructive power to equal that of any flash flood. Like Tláloc, the goddess was associated with the fertility of the land, which was facilitated by the waters she controlled. She was also one of the goddesses of the maize plant. In her honour, a frog was sacrificed during the festival of the maize goddess Chicomecóatl. The creature was cooked and placed with a cornstalk and some ground maize before images of the maize goddess to represent the free-flowing waters that were so necessary if the maize was to flourish.

Chalchiúhtlicue's shrines were built alongside streams, rivers and lakes. Her most important place of worship was at Pantitlán, a spot in the middle of Lake Texcoco marked by banners, where a young woman or girl impersonating the goddess was sacrificed during the festival of Huey Tozoztli ('Major Vigil') in the fourth Aztec month (15 April–4 May). The goddess's links to fertility are made clear by this celebration. A tree named Tota ('Father') was carried to Pantitlán on a raft and set up at that spot to symbolize new life and regeneration in the fields surrounding the lake. The 'precious

Below: The bulk of this Tláloc statue, found in Mexico City, is suggestive of the awesome power of the storms he controls.

water' of the sacrificial victim's blood was then poured on to the surface of the lake, which the Aztecs hailed as Tonanhueyatl ('Mother Vast Water').

Chalchiúhtlicue was envisaged as a beautiful young woman, symbolizing the purity of the water in springs and fast-flowing streams or rivers. Her priestess took the central role in rites that early Spanish missionaries likened to Christian baptism for, among the Aztecs, new parents would take their baby to the priestess of Chalchiúhtlicue, who sprinkled the infant with spring water and dedicated him or her to the goddess.

SACRED ANIMALS

According to some accounts, during the celebration of the festival of Atlcahualo ('The Ending of Water') Tláloc's priests leapt into the waters of Lake Texcoco imitating the movements and calls of the frog, a creature sacred to Tláloc and Chalchiúhtlicue.

Above: In an image from the Codex Borbonicus, *Tláloc unleashes the rainwaters that the farmers long for.*

The duck was also a holy form of Tláloc. Like Tláloc, it can fly, swim and walk on land, is at home in the air (where Tláloc has power over rains and winds), in the water (where the rain god controls streams, rivers, lakes and oceans through his female counterpart Chalchiúhtlicue) and in the earth (where the rain god's fertilizing waters awaken the life held in the seeds of plants and make possible the germination of life).

Nappatecuhtli was a god associated with Tláloc and Chalchiúhtlicue. He was lord and patron of the respected craftsmen who made mats and thrones from reeds. Nappatecuhtli was depicted wearing a tall headdress decorated with quetzal feathers and strips of bark paper. He was shown holding a reed stick in one hand and a snake sceptre in the other.

201

THE FLAYED LORD

Above: Moctezuma receives ambassadors under the watchful eye of a Xipe Totec priest wearing a victim's flayed skin.

Like Tláloc, the Aztec god of vegetation and seeds, Xipe Totec was an ancient deity whose worship was inherited by the Aztecs from earlier Mesoamericans. He was revered by the Zapotec builders of Monte Albán, where images of 'The Flayed Lord' have been found in tombs, and was also worshipped at Teotihuacán.

In Aztec belief, Xipe Totec was one of the four primary gods who were born from the union of Ometecuhtli and Omecíhuatl before the dawn of time. He was the oldest of the four, revered as Red Tezcatlipoca and associated with the east, where the new sun rises. He was the god of new shoots in spring and of the first growth of the maize plant.

FLAYING OF THE MEN

Xipe Totec was honoured with some distinctive and gruesome rites during the Tlacaxipehualiztli festival ('Flaying of the Men'), which was held in the second month of the Aztec year (6–25 March). This marked the start of the agricultural season, when seeds were germinating.

Sacrificial victims to Xipe Totec were shot to death with arrows so that the flow of their blood could symbolically represent the flow of rain on to the fields to nourish the seeds. At the festival's beginning, prisoners of war dressed as Xipe Totec were tied to a sacrificial stone and forced to defend themselves with mock weapons against fully armed warriors. After their death, the victims were flayed from head to toe. Priests then wore the skins over their own bodies for the entire month. Many sculptures of Xipe Totec show him wearing a flayed skin, drawn over his face and body and stitched up at the back. The mask of skin over the face usually allows the mouth and eyes of the wearer to show through.

This gruesome practice was a symbolic celebration of the splitting of seeds in the earth, which is a necessary part of their germination. The essence of plant life within the seed was likened to the essence of Xipe Totec in the sacrificial skin. The rite offered life to the gods to celebrate the renewal of life. Flaying may also have been practised on animals, for archaeologists have found statues of a coyote and a jaguar with their skin flayed along the backbone.

At the end of the festival, the priests divested themselves of the skins and stored them in a chamber within the sacred precinct in Tenochtitlán. For this purpose they used fired-clay bowls decorated with bobbles to suggest the puckered appearance of flayed skin. The bowls had tight-fitting lids to contain the smell of the rotting flesh.

Right: This image, found in an offering to Xipe Totec at Tepeji el Viejo, represents a priest wearing a flayed skin.

Above: In some accounts, the god of vegetation is said to have invented the arts of war by which the Aztecs thrived.

germination. According to some accounts, sky gods such as Quetzalcóatl and Huitzilopochtli also carried the staff. In bringing maize and other plants to harvest, Xipe Totec had to work in tandem with deities of water such as Chalchiúhtlicue and with sun gods such as Huitzilopochtli.

Mesoamerican gods always had more than one aspect. Just as Tláloc brought both life-giving rain and its opposite, drought, so Xipe Totec gave people the maize crops but also brought diseases such as blindness or the plague.

LOST-WAX GOLD CASTING
Xipe Totec was also the patron god of goldsmiths. Gold objects were often made using the lost-wax casting method and the details of the method explain the god's connection to the craft. First the craftsman made a clay core in the desired shape, then he covered the core with wax before laying another layer of clay on top of the wax. Once the clay was set, two holes were made in the outer clay layer and the molten gold was poured in. As it filled the space between the two layers of clay, it forced the wax out through the other hole. The outer and inner clay layers were then destroyed and the object was revealed.

Scholars believe that this method was associated in the Aztec mind with the layers of earth, then shoots, then taller plants, then full-grown plants that they observed in the maize fields and therefore that Xipe Totec was an appropriate patron for the goldsmiths. Mesoamericans did not view gold as the most precious of all

substances as people generally do in the Western tradition, for in their eyes such gold ornaments were no more valuable than the feathers of the quetzal bird or objects made from greenstone, both of which were important symbols of water and life.

Below: A priest wears a sacrificial victim's skin to honour Xipe Totec in the festival of Tlacaxipehualiztli. The hands dangle at the wrists where the priest's arms protrude.

A chamber within the temple complex was sacred to Xipe Totec. Called Yopico, it was a man-made cave that had been built to resemble the natural caverns that Mesoamericans understood to be openings to the spirit world and in which they had left religious offerings since time immemorial. Offerings to Xipe Totec were left in Yopico, particularly during the Tlacaxipehualiztli festival. A newly elected *tlatoani* would visit the Yopico temple as part of his coronation rites.

Xipe Totec was often represented holding a *chicahuaztli*, a pointed, hollow staff containing seeds. The staff represented the rays of the sun as they descended from the wide sky to the earth to promote the growth of maize plants. The *chicahuaztli* was also carried by Tláloc's consort Chalchiúhtlicue and by the flower goddess Xochiquetzal, who were both linked to fertility and

MOTHER EARTH AND HER FLOWERS

Mesoamericans worshipped the fertile earth from the time of their first farming settlements in 7000–5000BC. The earth goddess, provider of food crops, cotton clothes and building materials, was also associated with death, decay and regeneration. She had many names.

Tonantzin was worshipped as a mother of all and associated with the moon. After the Spanish Conquest her cult appears to have been merged with that of the Blessed Virgin Mary. Tonantzin was also known as 'Our Lady' and 'Our Holy Mother'. Indeed, many historians argue that in Mexico's patron saint, the 'Black Virgin of Guadelupe', Tonantzin has survived into the 21st century. Following the peasant Juan Diego's vision of a dark-skinned divinity in 1531 near Mexico City, the Basilica de Guadelupe was built on the very spot where Tonantzin's shrine once stood.

NAMES OF THE MOTHER
The mother goddess was also known under the name Teteoinnan-Toci ('Mother of the Gods and Goddesses' – 'Our Grandmother'). She was depicted with a calm and serene expression and a plaited cotton headdress. She was one of the main deities honoured in the festival of Ochpaniztli ('Clearing') at the start of the harvest season. Ochpaniztli also included the gruesome sacrifice of a young woman to maize goddesses Xilonen and Chicomecóatl.

Another aspect of the earth-mother goddess was Coatlícue ('Serpent-skirted'), who was particularly honoured by the Aztecs as the mother of their tribal god Huitzilopochtli and of the moon goddess Coyolxauhqui. In this form, the goddess made a regular connection with the sky realm since she was believed to give birth each morning to the sun on the eastern horizon in a blaze of red light.

RAPE IN THE UNDERWORLD
The fertility goddess was also the beautiful flower princess Xochiquetzal, who in some accounts was the twin sister of the god of flowers, Xochipilli. She was associated with love and lovemaking and with games, dancing and art as well as the

Above: Flower goddess Xochiquetzal was celebrated for her fresh-faced beauty and her patronage of the fine arts.

fair flowers of the field. She was the patron of weavers, silversmiths, painters, sculptors and embroiderers, and she was also associated with sexuality, prostitutes, pregnancy and childbirth.

In another account the goddess Xochiquetzal was married to Tláloc, the god of rains. The divine couple lived in great happiness in the Aztec heavens of Tamoanchán, where Xochiquetzal was mistress, and in Tlalocán, where her husband presided over life after death. However, the shadow god Tezcatlipoca, sower of wicked deeds and lord of the night, was taken with her delicate good looks, the freshness of her appearance in the first light, her innocence and charm. He tried to dazzle her with his dark good looks, but Xochiquetzal only turned lightly away to look for her husband. Then Tezcatlipoca seized the goddess and carried her off to the underworld. The awful skeletal rulers of that realm, Mictlantecuhtli and Mictecacíhuatl, turned a blind eye when, in a wicked hour, Tezcatlipoca forced himself on the flower goddess. Afterwards he was weakened by his lust and Xochiquetzal was able to escape her captor to return

Left: Ancient Mesoamerican religious life was founded in the cult of fertility. This fertility icon was carved by a skilled craftsman of the Huastec culture.

Above: Xochiquetzal was goddess of sexual beauty and lovemaking as well as being the princess of the Aztec heaven Tamoanchán.

to her abodes in the earth and sky above. Scholars suggest that the ravishing of Xochiquetzal in the underworld is a narrative representation of the seeming death of plants and flowers in winter that is followed by new life in the spring.

Although Xochiquetzal was said to be mistress of Tamoanchán, she was still subject to higher authority in the form of the supreme lord Ometeotl. One story tells that Xochiquetzal was banished from heaven when she broke an interdiction against touching a flowering tree in the midst of that realm. After that sad event she was sent to earth and known as Ixnextli ('Ash Eyes').

GODDESS OF FILTH AND PURIFICATION

The goddess Tlazoltéotl embodied unsettling dual aspects of the fertility-mother goddess. She was both the goddess of filth and the patron deity of childbirth, an all-encompassing mother figure and sponsor of sexual excess, associated not only with lustful degradation but also with purification. A celebrated statuette (*c.*1300–1500) depicts her in the act of giving birth, the

pain and exhilaration of the experience making an ecstatic mask of her face as the baby appears between her legs.

Tlazoltéotl struck men and women with the diseases associated with sexual promiscuity, yet the goddess was also associated with purification and with new beginnings. Her priestess would hear the confessions of penitents and prescribe rites of self-sacrifice and self-abnegation to guarantee forgiveness and a new beginning.

In some accounts, Tlazoltéotl was the mother of the flower goddess Xochiquetzal and of the maize god Centéotl. This aspect of the mother goddess was imported to Aztec territories: Tlazoltéotl was originally the mother goddess of the Huastec people from the lands bordering the Gulf of Mexico.

In the form of Yohualtecuhtli, the mother goddess was patron of sweatbaths. These were tiny buildings built alongside a cold pool. Users would dash water scented with herbs on to hot stones, creating a sweet-smelling steam. After sweating for a while and also performing ritual incantations, they would leave the building and take a cold plunge in the pool.

Below: Xochipilli, the flower prince, is depicted fishing for a jewel in this image from the Codex Vaticanus.

THE GODS OF MAIZE

The 'Young Maize God', a youthful figure with an elongated head in the shape of an ear of maize, makes frequent appearances on Classic Period Maya vases, usually in the company of an identical twin. These gods have been identified as Classic Period equivalents of One Hunahpú and Seven Hunahpú, the father and uncle respectively of the Hero Twins of the *Popol Vuh*.

RAISING THE WORLD TREE

Among the Maya, the maize god was a deity of supreme importance, sometimes perhaps even the creator. Scholars who have attempted to piece together Classic Period Maya creation narratives from finds at Tikal, Izapa, Palenque and Quirigua suggest that in these myths the maize god descended to the underworld and was reborn as the creator of the current world age. He rose into the sky and raised the world tree that holds the centre of

Below: Yum Caax, or the 'Master of the Fields in Harvest', was the Maya god of the maize.

the earth and anchors the four directions. In this guise he is probably the god referred to at Quirigua as Wak-Chan Ahaw ('Lord of the Lifted-up Sky'), for Palenque inscriptions call the World Tree Wakah Chan ('Lifted-up Sky'). At times the Maya envisaged the world tree itself as a maize plant. The carvings at Palenque show both the world tree and a second tree, the tree of the foliated cross, which has images of the maize god's head in its branches.

THE STUFF OF LIFE

The Maya maize god was also known as Yum Caax, 'Master of the Fields in Harvest'. A magnificent and floridly carved stone head found at Copán represents either Yum Caax or a king dressed in his guise. At Palenque he was referred to as Hun-Nal-Ye ('One Revealed Sprouting'). He was patron of the number 8 and of the day Kan.

Left: A brazier that was found in Tlatelolco honours Xilonen, goddess of maize.

Maize was the Maya's staple food and the very stuff of life. In the *Popol Vuh*, the perfect ancestors of modern humans, who could see and understand all things, were made from maize.

The attributes of the Young Maize God and his twin indicate that they were among the patrons of writing as well as of corn. The twins are often represented at work on codices and with pens and other scribal equipment in their headgear. Scholars suggest that there is an association linking the maize god to writing and that it developed because the bark paper used by scribes was made by soaking bark fibres in just the same way that maize kernels were soaked before being made into dough.

206

DEITIES FOR DIFFERENT STAGES

The Aztecs worshipped a number of maize deities, some linked to different stages of the maize plant's development. Xilonen ('Young Ear of Maize') was goddess of the tender first shoots of corn, while Chicomecóatl ('Seven Snake') was linked to the two ends of the sowing and harvesting process; the carefully stored seeds and the joyously harvested plants.

A fine statue of Xilonen found at Teloluapan (in modern Guerrero state in Mexico) shows the goddess as a young woman dressed in a cotton headdress and holding two corn-cobs in each hand. In Chicomecóatl's temple in Tenochtitlán, the statue of the goddess shows her as an adolescent girl with arms wide open. Other images show her wearing a vast rectangular headdress or *amacalli* ('paper

Above: A celebrated image from the Codex Fejérváry-Mayer *depicts four trees, at the four points of the compass, and a fifth in the centre. Each point is associated with a deity. The south is the realm of the vegetation god Xipe Totec; the fire god holds the centre.*

Below: This ceramic whistle (c.AD300–900) represents a dancer taking part in a ceremony in honour of the maize deities.

house') made from twigs and bark paper or holding a *chicahuaztli*, a staff filled with seeds, which celebrated the power of the sun, water and vegetation deities to bring life to maize seeds. This seed-filled *chicahuaztli* doubled as a musical instrument during fertility rites.

FLOWER GODS AND GODDESSES

Both Xilonen and Chicomecóatl were associated with the flowers that bloom at the start of the rainy season. Chicomecóatl was honoured in the festival of Huey Tozoztli ('Major Vigil') held in the fourth Aztec month (15 April–4 May). The Aztecs decorated their domestic altars with ears of corn for the festival and the goddess's priests blessed supplies of maize seeds in the temples.

Another maize deity was the god Centéotl, represented as a young man bearing maize in his headgear, his appearance usually dominated by the colour yellow. According to one story, maize, cotton, the sweet potato and other useful plants sprang forth from his buried body. Centéotl was closely linked to Xochipilli, god of plants and flowers, who

was also associated with the joyful celebration of life in dance and song. Alongside Xipe Totec, Xochipilli was a divine embodiment of nature's powerful forces of regeneration, the drive that sends green shoots upwards to defeat winter each spring.

A celebrated statue of Xochipilli, found at Tlamanalco on the lower slopes of the great volcano Ixtaccíhuatl, shows him seated cross-legged on a flower-throne with four flowers emanating in the four directions of the universe. Like the Maya maize god, he is depicted holding the centre, embodying the flowering of life in the universe.

Another god who was linked to maize was Xólotl, god of monsters and twins and a twin manifestation of Quetzalcóatl. When the gods elected to sacrifice themselves to bring movement to the newly created sun, Xólotl tried to escape and disguised himself as a double ear of corn.

THE GIFT OF *PULQUE*

The Four Hundred Boys who were defeated and killed by the Hero Twins in the tale told in the *Popol Vuh* had their counterpart among the Aztecs in the Centzóntotochtin (Four Hundred Rabbits). Both groups were makers and lovers of strong alcoholic drink, were worshipped as gods of drunkenness and they were associated with celestial phenomena. Among the Maya, the Four Hundred Boys were connected to the Pleiades constellation, while the Aztecs linked the Four Hundred Rabbits to the southern stars of the night sky.

In the ritual calendar, the eighth day, *tochtli* ('rabbit'), had associations with drunkenness. The leader of the Four Hundred Rabbits was Ome Tochtli (2-Rabbit) and was known as a god of drunkenness. Other gods among his troupe were Techalotl, Patécatl and Tezcatzontécatl. The deities of drunkenness were particularly associated with the strong alcoholic drink *pulque*, which was made from the fermented sap of the

Below: The connection of uncontrollable rabbits to the wildness of drunken behaviour is easy to comprehend.

Below: The bowl bears the wind serpent symbol. The pulque *cups have the Earth Monster's eye.*

maguey cactus and the root of a bush called 'pulque wood' (or 'wood of the evil one'). Images of *pulque* gods characteristically show them wearing a *yacameztli* ('nose moon'); a nose-ring in the shape of a half-moon that is connected to Tlazoltéotl, the goddess of filth and of sexual lust. They were associated thereby with promiscuous behaviour driven by drunkenness – and associated with rabbits – and also with the lunar cycles of woman's fertility.

RABBIT IN THE MOON
Rabbits were widely linked to the moon in Mesoamerican culture. The markings on the moon's face were thought to resemble a rabbit. One story of how the rabbit came to live on the moon tells that the moon god Tecuciztécatl shone too brightly in the first nights after the creation of the sun and moon and that the gods threw a rabbit up at his face to prevent him outshining the new sun. According to another version, the gods felt that Tecuciztécatl deserved to be punished, for when the time came for him to sacrifice himself and so create the sun he was fearful and refused three times to enter the fire. In the end, the unappealing god Nanahuatzin performed the sacrifice and became the sun, while

Tecuciztécatl was relegated to the role of the moon. The other gods therefore punished Tecuciztécatl by casting a rabbit shadow across his face to dim the glory of his light by night.

THE ORIGINS OF SACRED *PULQUE*
Pulque was highly prized for its use as a sacred intoxicant in religious ritual. Its consumption in everyday life was strictly controlled and public drunkenness was fiercely punished. The patron deity of the *tochtli* day and of the maguey cactus that was used to make *pulque* was the goddess Mayáhuel.

A myth explains the origin of *pulque*. In the first days of the current world age, the great Plumed Serpent Quetzalcóatl watched men and women going about their daily tasks and saw that once the working day was done they did not dance or sing. This great god, who gave humankind so many good things, determined to provide people with a stimulating fermented drink that would quicken their spirits for dancing and joyful celebrations.

In the thirteen tall heavens Quetzalcóatl encountered Mayáhuel, a goddess of enchanting beauty who was the granddaughter of one of the wicked *tzitzimime* night-demons. The pair fell quickly in love and Quetzalcóatl led Mayáhuel to Mesoamerica, where the two deities expressed their deep mutual devotion by making themselves into a great two-forked tree. However, Mayáhuel's grandmother was burning with anger and followed the couple to earth with a full complement of her fellow *tzitzimime* demons, bringers of sickness and woe. The night-demons swept into the blue sky like a sudden storm and travelled faster than light,

Below: This Codex Vaticanus *image depicts Mayáhuel (right), goddess of the maguey cactus from which* pulque *was made.*

following paths of darkness laid down by Tezcatlipoca. At long last they found the bodies of Quetzalcóatl and Mayáhuel entwined in a tree at the heart of a lush oasis. As they swooped down upon the tree it split into its two constituent halves. The sky was yawning wide as the *tzitzimime* poured down to get their revenge. Mayáhuel was torn to pieces by her grandmother and the *tzitzimime* gorged themselves on her flesh. Then, as quickly as they had come, they were gone.

Left: This exquisitely carved image of the Plumed Serpent is made from the fine-grained volcanic rock andesite.

Sorrowfully, Quetzalcóatl gathered the few remains of the goddess he had briefly loved and buried her far beyond the oasis. As he walked, he wept tears of grief that fed the earth. In time, the remnants of the beautiful Mayáhuel grew from the ground in the form of the maguey cactus. Many years passed and men and women learned to make the wonderful *pulque* drink from its sap. And in this way Quetzalcóatl's original purpose was fulfilled.

209

HOW MAIZE WAS TAMED

One of the many interpretations of the Quiché Maya *Popol Vuh* narrative is that it is a mythical representation of the domestication of maize and the planting of corn in the agricultural cycle. The twin maize gods, One Hunahpú and Seven Hunahpú, went down under the ground into the underworld like seeds of maize.

DIVINE GARDENERS

Another sequence of the cycle tells how the Hero Twins Hunahpú and Xbalanqué became the first inhabitants of Earth to tend the land and raise plants. The episode occurred after the Hero Twins turned their elder brothers One Monkey and One Artisan into monkeys, and these two swung away screeching into the trees. Then Hunahpú and Xbalanqué told their grandmother that they were off to tend the garden. They took their gardening tools with them, and asked their grandmother to bring food for them to eat at lunchtime. Such was their stature as divine groundbreakers that they did not have to sweat and labour over the land as humans later did. They simply stuck their hoes into the

Left: This Huastec statue depicts Chicomecóatl, the goddess of maize.

Left: An image of the rain god adorns this colourfully painted vessel of the early Classic Period.

ground and their axes into the tree trunks and sat back: the tools set to work, clearing great swathes of forest, levelling mounds of earth, and creating workable fields from the raw jungle.

The Twins relied on their magic to clear a great plot of land while they spent their time practising their shooting, using the blowpipes they had employed to strike down the boastful Seven Macaw. However, they did not want their grandmother to discover that they were not really labouring over the land, for then she might refuse to give them their food. They asked a dove to call out when it saw the old woman coming.

When the dove uttered its mournful call, the Twins dropped their pipes and picked up their agricultural implements. One took the hoe and rubbed dirt on his face and hands; the other took the axe and liberally sprinkled his hair with woodchips. When the old woman arrived, she suspected nothing and gave them a hearty meal to eat. When she left they dropped their work implements and returned to shooting with their blowpipes.

That evening when they returned home the Twins made a great fuss, complaining of aching limbs and blistered hands and regaling their grandmother with extravagant accounts of how hard

they had had to work to clear the land. However, the joke was shortly to rebound on the Twins.

When they returned to their little farm plot the next day they found that the jungle had grown back in a single night and thick vegetation covered their carefully cut and terraced mountainside fields. So they set their tools to work again and cleared a new plot – and that night lay in wait to see what magic had caused the plants to grow so fast.

They discovered that the animals of the place were calling up new jungle growth like a thick cloth to cover the nakedness of the earth. The puma, the jaguar, the rabbit, the deer, the fox, the coyote, the peccary and the rat were responsible for the trick. They sang in the night, 'Rise up and grow tall, trees and bushes, cover the land.'

The Twins tried to catch the creatures. The puma and the jaguar were far too fast and they escaped in a flash. In awe Hunahpú and Xbalanqué watched them go by moonlight. Next came the deer and the rabbit. The Twins did manage to catch these two by the tail for a moment but

Above: An illustration from Bernardino de Sahagún's Florentine Codex *shows an Aztec planting the staple food maize.*

and Cipactonal, lived in great happiness with his beautiful wife Xochiquetzal. They had a son, who was named Centéotl. He was of earthy complexion and had ruddy good looks, full of the energy of the land. But despite his apparent good health Centéotl died suddenly and inexplicably – just as winter shrouds the land in lifeless cold. Then Piltzintecuhtli found no comfort in the beauty of his wife Xochiquetzal. He mourned his son long and loudly.

The gods themselves came down from the thirteen heavens and visited the grave of this fine young man. By their great goodness they caused his body to give issue to foods and useful plants, as the earth pushes up plants in spring: maize came from his fingernails and the sweet potato from his fingers, while cotton grew from his hair and other plants of great usefulness sprang from his body. And afterwards Centéotl was one of the many gods of maize revered by the Aztecs. In some versions of the myth Centéotl was the son of the Mesoamerican earth mother. She was known by the names of Teteoinnan or Tocitzin. In yet another account, he and flower goddess Xochiquetzal were the two children of Tlazoltéotl, goddess of childbirth, lust and dirt. Centéotl was also linked to Xochipilli, the flower god; both were strong young men with an abundance of creative energy.

Left: A Zapotec funerary urn, found at Monte Albán, honours the maize god.

the animals were strong and broke away, each leaving part of its tail in the Twins' hands. For this reason those creatures have little or no tail. The only creature the boys did manage to corner was the rat. They caught him in a net and burned him over a fire to make him talk; ever afterwards the rat had no hairs on its tail.

The rat told the Twins that the field-clearing and farming techniques they had pioneered were not for them to develop and that they had a different destiny. They must follow the twin maize gods One Hunahpú and Seven Hunahpú to the underworld and tame the lords of that dark place. Some scholars believe this narrative to be a dramatization of the necessary move from a purely hunting lifestyle to a form of subsistence that relied both on hunting and domesticated food plants grown in laboriously cleared jungle fields.

CENTÉOTL AND DOMESTICATED MAIZE

The Aztecs had two main versions of the myth that described the discovery and first use of the domesticated maize plant. In one account the Plumed Serpent, Quetzalcóatl, transformed himself into an ant and brought the foodstuff back from the heart of 'food mountain', but in the variant myth the maize god Centéotl was the source of the staple food. The myth described how in the first years of the current world age Piltzintecuhtli, the son of the original human couple Oxomoco

SEX, PREGNANCY AND BIRTH

The flower goddess Xochiquetzal was patron of love and lovemaking, and she was also strongly associated with pregnancy and childbirth. According to one myth, she performed the first act of sexual congress, and in another account she was the first woman to give birth to twins.

Xochiquetzal was the archetype of youthful femininity, a young woman of great beauty and voluptuousness, with plentiful sexual allure. Her followers took the form of birds and butterflies. She was also embodied on earth in the first woman, who was fashioned from her hair in order to marry Piltzintecuhtli, the son of the primal couple Oxomoco and Cipactonal. The first woman took the goddess's name and had a son with Piltzintecuhtli named Centéotl, who after his death gave issue to the maize plant and was honoured as the maize god.

Xochiquetzal was the patron goddess of prostitutes. She protected the *ahuianime*, the city prostitutes, and the *maqui*, the priestess-prostitutes who attended to young single warriors and accompanied the soldiers on to the battlefield, where they willingly gave their lives. In some accounts, Xochiquetzal was the first woman to be sacrificed in battle. Her image in the *Codex Cospi* shows her in battle array, carrying a shield and arrows and wearing a warband as well as a garland of corn flowers.

The beautiful goddess enriched the world of men and women by giving flowers to grow on the side of the roadway and the steep mountain paths. These flowers were made from her vulva. In one myth

Below: This Olmec terracotta figure of a baby is from the dawn of Mesoamerican culture.

she was wife to Quetzalcóatl or the Plumed Serpent. One day as he was washing himself he allowed his hands to move over his penis and the seeds that spilled forth became the first bat. The gods sent this creature to visit the bountiful Xochiquetzal. It bit the goddess in her vulva and carried a piece of flesh away to the other gods. They made roses from the bat's gift, but these flowers did not smell good. The bat repeated his visit to Xochiquetzal and this time took the flesh to Mictlantecuhtli, the lord of the underworld. This time the roses were as sweet-smelling and beautiful as anyone could wish. These marvellous flowers were the gift of the goddess Xochiquetzal to the peoples of the world.

TLAZOLTÉOTL

The form of the mother-fertility goddess most powerfully connected to childbirth was Tlazoltéotl, the goddess of filth, excrement and sexual lust. She was often depicted squatting in the position that Mesoamerican women usually adopted for childbirth. Tlazoltéotl was associated with penitential rites, including the

Left: Tlazoltéotl, squatting in the typical Mesoamerican childbirth position, is a goddess of opposites, associated both with the noise of lust and the quiet of penitence. The image is from the Codex Vaticanus.

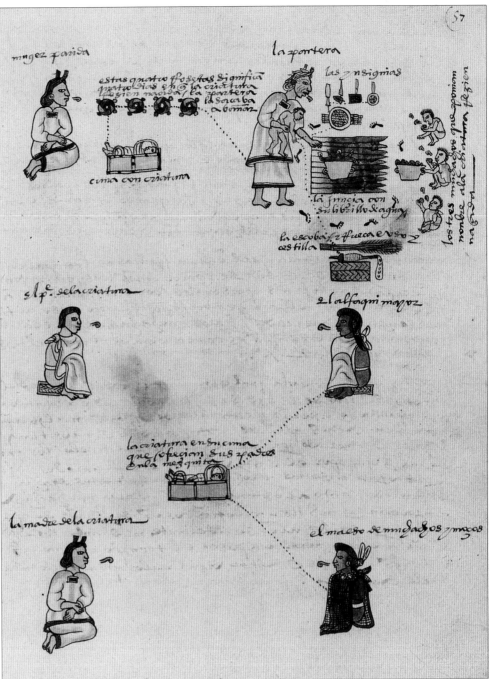

confession of sins. In one myth she was also a great temptress, who used her sexual power to unpick the virtue of a pious man.

This man was determined to win the gods' favour and took himself away from family life to settle on a rocky promontory in the northern desert. The gods wanted to probe the man's commitment, so they despatched the demon Yáotl ('The Enemy'), a much-feared manifestation of Tezcatlipoca, to test him. Yáotl the seducer brought forth a parade of the world's most beautiful women who called up to the pilgrim and tried to tempt him down, if only for a short break from his demanding religious observance. Backwards and forwards they went on the rocky ground, calling up to him and seductively singing the latest songs from the brothels of Tenochtitlán. However, the man refused to look at them and turned back to his sacred rites.

Viewing this from afar, Tlazoltéotl was determined to join in. She came to that inhospitable windswept place dressed in her finest and most seductive outfit and called up sweetly to the man, asking

Below: Tlazoltéotl rides the snake of sexuality and a broom with which she sweeps away the sins of the sorrowful.

to be allowed to climb the rock for a conversation: perhaps she could learn something from him? Such was her appeal that he agreed to allow her to climb up. When she arrived there beside him she was to him as a breeze to a soldier in the desert, like a sweet and suddenly attainable dream to a man cursed by insomnia, and he succumbed to temptation.

Yáotl then appeared beside the couple and turned the man into a scorpion. Afterwards he fetched the man's wife and brought her to the place, told her the full story of her husband's disgrace and turned her into a scorpion

Above: A page from the Codex Mendoza *illustrates the rites and experiences that fill the first months of an Aztec baby's life.*

too. They lived on in the desert under a rock and produced many generations of scorpions.

Another Aztec goddess associated with childbirth was Chalchiúhtlicue, wife of Tláloc. She was a patron of newly born children and was believed to protect virtuous married couples and honourable loves. Among the Maya, the goddess Ix Chel, consort of the supreme god Itzamná, was considered to be a protectress of women in childbirth.

CHAPTER 11

AFTER DEATH

From his place at the summit of the thirteen Aztec heavens, the primeval being Ometeotl, lord of duality, sent forth the souls of human babies about to be born. Ometeotl lived in his dual forms as Ometecuhtli and Omecíhuatl in the twelfth and thirteenth layers of heaven, in a place called Omeyocán. Here also lived the souls of babies who had died before their time and without cause, and those who had died inexplicably in their sleep. They expected a new life in a world freshly made after the cataclysmic end of the fifth sun or world age in a great earthquake. In Omeyocán a fork of the cosmic tree provided sweet milk for the nourishment of these babies' souls and the spirits newly made by Ometeotl.

The duality embodied by Ometeotl informed every particle of the sacred Mesoamerican universe. For the Aztecs and Maya, darkness was everywhere balanced by its opposite, light, night by day, dampness by dryness, feminine by masculine, death by life, the shadowy underworld by the bright heavens. The cosmic tree that held the centre grew both in heaven and on the earth, both on the earth and in the underworld. The level of the flat earth or Tlalticpac was the first plane of the nine underworld realms and also the first plane of the thirteen celestial realms. It was both celestial and terrestrial and also both terrestrial and infernal. Everywhere, two was also one: so darkness and light were both one and differentiated. Nothing was purely good or bad, for the good lay within the bad and vice versa; the gods possessed duality and had positive and negative attributes.

Left: The nine levels of the Temple of the Inscriptions at Palenque symbolize the nine levels of the underworld.

THE PARADISE OF THE FLOWER GODDESS

Tamoanchán, the level of the thirteen Aztec heavens presided over by the beautiful flower goddess Xochiquetzal, was imagined as an earthly paradise. There the branches of the cosmic tree were heavily laden with blossoms and fruit and released sweet perfume into the sunlit air. In some accounts, Tamoanchán was literally an earthly place, hidden near the holy peak of a mythical mountain in the far, far south, the region of Huitzilopochtli, where the air was thin and delightfully cool and the rocks rose almost to the moon herself. However, it was usually said to be high above the earth where the heavens climbed to a different sphere of reality.

RAW MATERIAL FOR HUMAN CREATION

Quetzalcóatl and Xólotl brought the bones they rescued from the underworld to Tamoanchán at the start of the fifth world age. In this fertile paradise they

Below: An Aztec relief carving shows four-toothed Tláloc with the skulls of people whose death has given them access to his heaven.

presented the raw material for a new human creation to the other gods. The deities gathered in the sweet air of the flower goddess's paradise to provide blood to mix with the ground bones and so make a paste with which to form the first boy and girl. These first humans were nurtured in Tamoanchán, but the human race would never be permitted to return to that place. It was an abode of the gods.

FALL OF THE GODDESS

Meanwhile in Tamoanchán, Xochiquetzal passed her time weaving wonderful textiles in inspirational colours and patterns. She had many loyal maidens to keep her company and from time to time they would pause in their work to laugh at the antics of entertainers. Tamoanchán was a happy home for the goddess but, according to one of the myths, Xochiquetzal was thrown out of the restful paradise and made to spend the full expanse of time on the Earth.

According to this tale, the fruits and blossom on the tree that perfumed Tamoanchán were sweet and tempting to anyone curious, whether divine or human. The creator lord Ometeotl had decreed that this tree should not be touched. It was permitted, however, for the birds of Tamoanchán to alight on its branches and fill them with sweet song and for other animals to scamper up the trunk and leap hither and thither, but the gods and goddesses must not taste the fruits or pick the flowers.

Left: Heavenly flower goddess Xochiquetzal was associated with nose-rings shaped like a butterfly.

Xochiquetzal was captivated by the tree's beauty, which balanced and mirrored her own. Temptation got the better of her on a day when heady delight drove her from her sense of what is right. She picked a garland of flowers for her perfumed hair and stole and tasted one of the ripe red fruits of the tree. She thought that no one would know. What could be the harm, when the tree had so many blossoms, fruits and flowers on its heavy branches? However, in the instant that she violated the supreme lord's command, the tree began to shudder and then cracked and fell into two great pieces, just like the tree made from the entwined bodies of Quetzalcóatl and Mayáhuel in another place. Blood oozed from the spot where she had plucked the fruit and from the place where the two halves had split.

Restrained in his anger but determined to uphold the sanctity of his commands, Ometeotl told Xochiquetzal of her fate. She would be sent down to the mountains and dry plains of earth and live in that place, mourning her loss. She would weep as she passed and touched the flowers and blossoms and she would henceforth be known as Ixnextli ('Ash Eyes'). Xochiquetzal's enjoyment of beauty, of the flowers that she gave to men and women, would be limited because her vision would be blurred by ever-flowing tears.

Left: Xochipilli and Xochiquetzal are usually considered brother and sister. Xochiquetzal is often shown with quetzal feathers in her headdress.

PASSAGE TO THE HEAVENS

According to the Aztecs, only the souls of those who died in particular ways found passage to the heavens. The spirits of warriors who died in the heat of battle – a dart piercing their neck, their last breath escaping in desperation – would wake in the heaven presided over by Tonatiuh, an aspect of the sun god.

They were joined in this blessed place by the souls of women who died during or after desperate labours, their infant warrior-sons having – like Huitzilopochtli – delivered death at the beginning of life. Tonatiuh's heaven was called Ilhuicatl Tonatiuh ('Sun Heaven') or Tonatiuichan. The souls of sacrificial victims also passed after death to Tonatiuh's heaven.

The souls of those who drowned in a sudden flood or when a canoe capsized, the souls of unfortunates who had been stricken by illnesses associated with water, and the souls of people caught in a violent storm or struck by lightning would find themselves in Tláloc's heaven, Tlalocán. This was a realm blessed with the utmost fertility, a land where water gently touched the brow in a light, warm drizzle that pleased the plants and encouraged them to deliver cacao beans and the finest fruits in abundance.

Below: This wall painting at Teotihuacán may represent inhabitants of Tlalocán, the paradise of the rain god.

THE BACABS AND THE COSMIC TREE

Like the Aztecs, the Maya also believed that in the centre of the universe the world tree linked the heavens, the earth and the underworld. According to one tradition of Maya cosmology, four giants named the bacabs, the sons of the supreme lord Itzamná and his goddess Ix Chel, upheld the four corners of the world in the north, south, east and west. The splendid sarcophagus of King Pacal at Palenque depicts the king's spirit making the journey downwards from the terrestrial level to the underworld along the length of the world tree.

ACCESS TO SPIRIT REALMS

The world tree could also serve as a conduit for spirits to access the realms above and below during this life. It delivered worshippers to a paradise of ecstatic spiritual experience through shamanistic voyaging. In this guise, the tree might be associated with the Vision Serpent. The Maya summoned the Vision Serpent during the solemn rites of autosacrifice

Below: This three-faced Maya brazier is from the Postclassic Period. Psychedelic substances powered Maya spirit journeys.

in which worshippers cut themselves and offered the blood of their own wounds to the gods. The intricate carvings of Lady Xoc, wife of Shield Jaguar, at Yaxchilán, show her gaining access to a heightened state brought on by rites of bloodletting to the Vision Serpent. Through the jaws of the Serpent she connects to the sacred ancestors and the gods.

The psychedelic mushroom *Psilocybe aztecorum* also provided access to spirit realms and may sometimes have been identified with the world tree. A striking ceramic discovered at Colima, in Mexico, depicts religious celebrants dancing around a central column with an umbrella-like top, which apparently represented either the world tree or the mushroom.

Maya priests and worshippers took the *Psilocybe aztecorum* mushroom to induce a religious trance. Throughout the Maya region, archaeologists have discovered stone effigies of mushrooms set up in the period 1000BC–AD500. It was highly valued – and perhaps even worshipped – alongside tobacco flowers and morning glory flowers, for its hallucinogenic properties. Scholars believe that the Maya gained their knowledge of the bright celestial realms and of the dark underworld in the course of spirit journeys brought about through the use of psychedelic substances. Paintings on Classic Period Maya ceramics reveal that Maya nobles and priests took ritual enemas of liquids containing the peyote cactus to bring on visions.

A LUXURIOUS AFTERLIFE

Some Maya traditions held that a few lucky souls would be admitted to a heavenly realm rather similar to the Tamoanchán of the Aztecs. There they would not need to perform backbreaking work cutting terraced fields from mountainsides or thick jungle, but could rest from the hunt or the long trading journeys they had made in their lifetimes

Above: A stone depicts King Pacal's journey to the underworld in this reconstruction of his crypt at Palenque.

and simply find luxury all about them. They could lie in the sweet shade provided by the cosmic tree. When they were thirsty they could gather some cacao beans, to make chocolate drink.

THE WAY TO PARADISE THROUGH THE UNDERWORLD

Most souls were destined for the underworld. Mythical narratives such as the account in the Quiché Maya *Popol Vuh* of the Hero Twins' descent to the underworld dramatized the many tests that the spirit would have to go through there. The *Popol Vuh* tale and the Classic Period myths on which it was based were a kind of guidebook to the afterlife.

The Hero Twins' narrative ends with Hunahpú and Xbalanqué defeating death in the form of the underworld lords and rising triumphant to the heavens. It was generally understood that their triumph in the underworld paved the way for those who came after them. A tablet at Palenque shows a ruler emerging from

Above: This mask of the sun god is from an Early Classic Maya pyramid at Kohunlich, Quintana Roo.

the underworld in the appearance of the jaguar god of that realm and being greeted with an offering by his mother. Death could not hold him and that cold ogre could not expect to contain any of the ruler's descendants.

According to some scholars, the Maya believed that only the noble elite would proceed to an afterlife by way of the tests in the underworld. Other authorities argue such a religion would not have been generally sustainable and that people at all levels of society must have believed that their ancestors had somehow triumphed over death and that they themselves might do the same.

In its celebration of new life out of death the story informs a splendid late Classic Period tripod plate (*c.*AD600–900) that depicts the father of the Hero Twins' One Hunahpú being born from the cracked back of a great turtle.

According to the version given in the *Popol Vuh*, One Hunahpú is unable to leave the underworld. On this plate, however, and perhaps also in the Classic Period version of the myth, he is given new life by his sons. The Maya saw the turtle as an image of the earth and identified One Hunahpú as the Young Maize God, so the image on the plate emphasizes the myth's meaning as a celebration of the life-cycle of the maize plant. However, the plate is also a truly joyful celebration of the defeat of darkness and death and of the spirit's rebirth into light and life.

Left: A clay censer found in Yucatán bears the face of a little known Maya deity who was patron of bee-keepers.

THE JOURNEY TO MICTLÁN

Above: This jade, coral, obsidian and turquoise mosaic mask is a funerary ornament from Texmilincan, Mexico.

one's consciousness lived; and the liver, home to the spirit. The liver was associated with Mictlán, realm of the spirits, by ancient Aztec tradition. Mictlantecuhtli wore sandals as a sign of his lordly standing. His consort, Mictecacíhuatl, had a fearsome skull for her face, and her thin breasts sagged despairingly. Her skirt was made of flailing fork-tongued serpents.

The underworld was the particular realm of dogs. Mictlantecuhtli was patron of the day *itzcuintli* ('dog'). Dogs were often sacrificed on their master's death and laid in his tomb, for the animals were expected to guide their masters through the ordeal after death. An underworld dog appeared to help new arrivals across the first hazard they faced.

The dead were buried with equipment to help them on their journey. They were given gifts for Mictlantecuhtli and Mictecacíhuatl, as well as paper clothes, food, water, blankets and a jade bead to serve as a replacement heart.

Below: With saucer eyes and terrible teeth, Mictecacíhuatl makes a suitably grim consort for the lord of the underworld.

In the Aztec underworld, the god Mictlantecuhtli enjoyed his power in dampness and darkness. Everything in the universe had its balancing double, the other half of a perfect duality. Mictlantecuhtli and his consort Mictecacíhuatl were the underworld equivalents of Ometecuhtli and Omecíhuatl in the uppermost layers of the Aztec heaven.

THE UNDERWORLD GOD

The underworld god was skeletal because he had lost half his flesh, and his black curly hair sparkled with stars. He was often depicted dressed in clothes made from strips of bark paper. He had enormous, clawlike hands capable of tearing the underworld spirits limb from limb and was happy to see others suffer.

Mictlantecuhtli was essentially a personification of death. His liver hung from a gaping hole in his stomach. The Aztecs believed that the body had three principal parts: the head, where a person's destiny was housed; the heart, where

TESTING THE DEAD

The soul had to negotiate different hazards at each of the nine levels of the underworld. The first was to find a way over a raging river torrent. Here a yellow or red dog appeared as a guide. The second test was to pass between towering mountains that would suddenly and terrifyingly crash together, with the noise of countless jaguars roaring as if preparing to rip flesh from bone.

The pilgrim went on through a demanding range of tests. He had to climb a mountain made of dark obsidian, the shadowy 'smoking' glass worn by the dark lord Tezcatlipoca, then survive an icy northern wind cold enough to peel the skin from the cheeks of a living man. Next he had to defeat a ravening snake, then a dread alligator, before crossing eight deserts and climbing eight great mountains. Exhaustion threatened the

Below: A gruesome Mixtec drinking cup from Zaachila, Mexico, is intended to remind drinkers of their mortality.

poor spirit, but then came a biting wind to drive him on. This gale was filled with knives of obsidian, the blades so sharp that they could slice through solid rock as easily as cut up a tortilla. Next he faced a demon named Izpuzteque, with dreadful backwards-facing legs, and then another foe who tried to blind the spirit traveller by throwing handfuls of ash in his eyes. Finally, he came face to face with Mictlantecuhtli and Mictecacíhuatl and made offerings to them. Mictlantecuhtli would rip the poor pilgrim's spirit-body to pieces. This did not end the soul's existence, for he lived on in the domain of Mictlantecuhtli and Mictecacíhuatl, in dampness and darkness, with only his companions and friends among those who had died before him to give him any pleasure or comfort. However, once a year he was permitted to return to the lands of living Mesoamerica, where his relatives would lay out earthly foods for his pleasure.

Sometimes the Aztecs located Mictlán in the far north, a desolate, dry place of dreadful famines and cold winds, associated with the colours yellow and black, with the sacrificial knife and with the dark lord Tezcatlipoca. A realm of endless fear and ill-fortune, it was the northern pole balancing the mountaintop heaven situated in the far south. It was known as Mictlampa ('Abode of the Dead'), or as Tlalxicco ('Earth's Navel'). More usually it was understood to be below the earth.

Mictlán was the place where the gods stored the bones of past generations, both from this age and from previous eras. At the beginning of the current world age, Quetzalcóatl visited the underworld in the company of his dog aspect Xólotl to gather these bones in order to fashion the first people. The Aztecs' understanding of duality meant that death always included life and

Above: Mictlantecuhtli, sunken-cheeked and horribly grimacing, keeps watch over the cold, famine-ravaged realm of the dead.

new beginnings. The seeds of future creation lay in the underworld, just as the seeds of future plants could be buried unseen in the earth. For this reason, skull masks used in religious rites and placed as offerings usually had bright shining eyes. These masks are usually now missing their eyes because the precious materials used have been stripped by the conquistadors or other gold diggers.

BEYOND THE WATER

The Maya underworld was ruled by the lords One Death and Seven Death. Its inhabitants roamed the underground kingdom desperately, their bodies disintegrating as they went. Images of Xibalba in codices and on Classic Period vases show spirit forms with horribly distended bellies and eyes hanging on cords from their sockets. Like Mictlantecuhtli, they found their flesh falling from their bones, allowing their stomach, liver and other organs to tumble out hideously. They could not control their bodily functions and streams of excrement and wind burst out. Some wore necklaces made from the fallen eyeballs of other poor souls.

LORDS OF THE UNDERWORLD

According to the account in the *Popol Vuh*, the Maya underworld lords had blood-chilling names and specialities. Jaundice Demon was master of that disease and climbed to earth to make people sicken, while Pus Demon followed in his footsteps and would cause people's limbs to swell and poison to seep from their bandaged wounds.

Below: This monstrous serpent appears on a late Classic Period Maya drinking cup from Motagua Valley, Guatemala.

Above: Bats were frequent tormentors of the spirit traveller in the Maya 'Place of Fright'. This urn was made in the Toltec period.

Two other lords were Bone Sceptre and Skull Sceptre, who carried bare human bones as staffs of authority and brought wasting diseases in their train; illnesses that caused the flesh to fall away until sufferers were good for nothing but a lonely death.

House Corner and Blood Gatherer were hungry for blood, like vampire bats or leeches. Humans could not relax in their presence, for they would come out of the shadows with their sharp teeth bared to assault the soft neck and other vulnerable parts of a man or woman's body.

The Lord of Rubbish and the Stabbing Lord were found in places where people had left remains of their meals or other activities lying around the homes. These dark gods would attack from the blind side and bring their victims low with sharp stabbing pains and fierce strikes. Packstrap and Wing trailed the roads like the Aztec god Tezcatlipoca, seeking the unwary. When they struck they caused sudden death. The victim's mouth would flood and bright blood would run on to his chin, stain his chest and gush on to the ground when he collapsed. The victim would die in the roadway, alone, like a diseased dog, with the dark wind blowing desolately past.

The aged god Pauahtun, one of many patron gods of scribes, was also strongly associated with the underworld. His old and sunken face surrounded a gap-toothed mouth and Pauahtun also wore a net head-wrapping in which the tools of his scribal arts sometimes appear. According to one tradition, Pauahtun supported the weight of the earth above him and so he was from time to time depicted with one hand above his head.

CHALLENGES FOR THE DEAD

Like the Aztecs, the Maya believed that the road to the underworld was full of challenges for the spirits of the deceased. When One Hunahpú and Seven Hunahpú, the father and uncle of the Hero Twins, made their descent to Xibalba in the *Popol Vuh*, they began by going down a sheer rockface. Then they came to a roaring torrent of water where a great river ran through a narrow canyon. They made a makeshift bridge to get across, but were no sooner safely over than they came to another waterway. This river was made up of spinning knives. Because they were such agile sportsmen, highly practised players of the ball game, they managed to get across to the far bank without being cut to pieces. Next they came to yet another river, this one filled with blood. They swam across, taking care not to drink, then came to a stream of pus. They made it across this as well and went on their way. When they came then to a place called the Crossroads, four ways beckoned: one red road, one yellow, one white and one black. They took the black road.

WATER IMAGERY

Images on Classic Period vases and in codices make it clear the Maya associated Xibalba with water. Fish, water lilies, shells and sea creatures appear as decorative features in representations of the underworld. The Maya also connected the moment of death with sinking into water. A carved bone found at Tikal depicts a canoe paddled by two gods with an important passenger and four

Right: This late Classic Period Maya vase shows gods in a boat, symbolically bound for the underworld.

animal companions; an iguana, a parrot, a spider and a dog. The passenger, who may be either a ruler of Tikal or the Young Maize God himself, holds his hand extended flat in front of his forehead in a way that represents approaching death. The image on a second carved bone shows the canoe sinking into the water as the travellers make the descent towards Xibalba.

Although it was a liquid realm, Xibalba also contained buildings, trees and solid ball courts like the world above. Once spirit travellers reached the land of One Death and Seven Death, they had to brave houses containing terrifying conditions or hungry armies of predators.

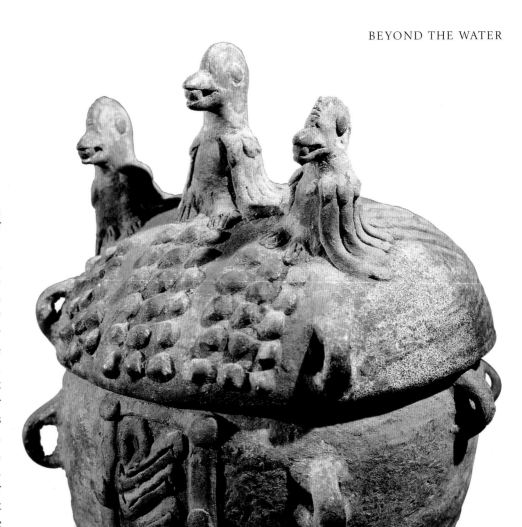

Above: Quetzal feathers, emblems of kingship, decorate the lid of a Classic Maya funerary urn from El Quiche, Guatemala.

One house was filled with the deepest, blackest darkness. Those forced to spend time there soon lost all sense of their bearings and began to despair of ever seeing light again. Another building swamped people with cold rather than darkness. Those forced into this place shivered and tried vainly to escape drafts and the sudden lashing showers of hail that somehow managed to fall indoors. A third house was full of fierce and restless jaguars, whose slavering jaws were wet with the blood of their victims. Another was filled from top to bottom with screeching bats. The air inside a fifth building was thick with blades moving everywhere, sharp enough to cut out the heart or skin their victims. Only the Hero Twins Hunahpú and Xbalanqué knew how to tame these terrors.

THE HERO TWINS AND THE UNDERWORLD

The Quiché Maya sacred book the *Popol Vuh* relates how the terrifying lords of Xibalba were no match for the Hero Twins Hunahpú and Xbalanqué. The Hero Twins descended into the underworld to avenge the deaths there of their father One Hunahpú and their uncle Seven Hunahpú.

ONE DEATH AND SEVEN DEATH ARE ANNOYED

The primal couple Xpiyacoc and Xmucané, the grandfather and grandmother diviners who approved Huracán and Gucumatz's plan to make people from wood in an earlier age, had two children, One Hunahpú and Seven Hunahpú. They were great gamblers who loved throwing dice, but their main passion in life was the Mesoamerican ball game. They practised for long hours until they could stun onlookers with their skill. One frequent visitor to the court was a falcon, a messenger of the great god Huracán.

Below: This ceramic vessel from El Petén is delicately painted with birds. They play an important messenger role in the Popol Vuh.

In time, One Hunahpú married a longhaired maiden of striking beauty named Xbaquiyalo and the couple had a pair of twins, One Monkey and One Artisan. These boys enjoyed learning the ball game from their father, but they devoted most of their time to the arts, becoming proficient at singing, playing the flute, making jewellery, carving wood and working metal. Their grandfather died and then their mother Xbaquiyalo also died, so the boys had only Xmucané, their grandmother, to provide a woman's guidance.

One Monkey and One Artisan grew very close to their widowed grandmother, because after Xbaquiyalo had died they did not see very much of their father. He spent more and more of his time playing the ball game with his brother at their court on the far eastern rim of the flat earth, in a place called Great Abyss. Their incessant playing made a thumping noise that reverberated through the earth and made the very foundations of Xibalba shake. This annoyed the underworld lords One Death and Seven Death.

The lords of the underworld decided the time had come to take on these terrestrial athletes on the Xibalba ball court, so they sent four hideous owls from the shadowy dark places to issue a challenge. 'Come down below and show your mettle', the birds sang, 'our masters summon you; bring your equipment, your ball, your yokes and your armguard down with you.'

One Hunahpú and Seven Hunahpú agreed to come, but first they went home to tell their grandmother Xmucané of their departure. As she wept, they told her they would return to see her and that they were not going down to the underworld to die.

Above: A ball player decorates this black jug from Copán (c.AD600–900).

One Hunahpú and Seven Hunahpú cannily decided not to take their own ball game equipment with them and instead hid it under the rafters of Xmucané's home. They told One Monkey and One Artisan to use their artistic skills to soothe Xmucané's spirits, then they departed, following the owl-messengers down to the lower realms.

ONE HUNAHPÚ AND SEVEN HUNAHPÚ ARE DOOMED

The brothers went down a steep cliff face and across a number of rivers, then chose the black road at the crossroads. They came at last to the council rooms of Xibalba and entered the presence of two august lords. One Hunahpú and Seven Hunahpú assumed that these people must be the rulers of Xibalba and they greeted them by name. 'Hail, One Death', 'Greetings, Seven Death.' But the figures were lifeless, mere wood carvings set there as a trick. The true underworld lords then emerged,

Above: The Maya goddess of the night takes the form of an owl, watcher and predator in the dark hours of silence.

the roadside, while the remainder of his corpse was buried with the body of his brother Seven Hunahpú. This tree flourished. One Death and Seven Death were astounded to see that the tree was suddenly covered with so many calabashes that the head was no longer visible. They decreed that no one in all of Xibalba should go near this miraculous tree. However, one young maiden broke this rule and her act of disobedience made possible the ultimate defeat of the dark powers of the underworld.

Below: The maize god celebrated so beautifully in stone at Copán has now been identified as the father of the Hero Twins, One Hunahpú.

roaring with laughter, delighted to have won the first victory against One Hunahpú and Seven Hunahpú.

Next the underworld lords offered One Hunahpú and Seven Hunahpú seats on a bench in the room. The two visitors sat, and immediately leapt up again, clasping their bottoms, for the bench was burning hot. It was another low trick. The underworld lords were almost helpless with laughter, wheezing and gasping in a way that seemed to unpeel the flesh from their bodies, allowing the blood and skeleton to show through. They laughed and laughed, congratulating one another on their trickery.

One Hunahpú and Seven Hunahpú were next ushered into a house filled to the beams with darkness. Meanwhile the lords of Xibalba were plotting. They decided that they should play the ball game with their guests on the next day using the fearsome White Dagger ball, a sphere of hard bone concealing a lethal blade. The game would be quickly over;

their guests would be dead in an instant. They sent two lighted cigars and a burning torch to cheer One Hunahpú and Seven Hunahpú in the Dark House. However, they said that the guests must return the lighted cigars and the flaming torch entirely unchanged on the following day. They could not put them out and they could not let them burn down.

Of course, the torch and the cigars burned down and One Hunahpú and Seven Hunahpú were defeated again. When they went to see One Death and Seven Death the following morning they had nothing to show them except the sooty remnants of the torch and the tiny stubs of the smoked cigars. They had failed and One Death and Seven Death declared that they must be put to death. The two ball players had promised Xmucané that they would return, but they were doomed.

The underworld lords sent One Hunahpú and Seven Hunahpú to be executed. One Hunahpú had his head cut off and placed in the fork of a tree growing by

225

RISEN FROM THE UNDERWORLD

The underworld lord Blood Gatherer had a fair daughter named Blood Maiden. She was curious to taste the fruit of the calabash tree, which had suddenly flowered after the head of the terrestrial ball player One Hunahpú was put in its branches. She knew that the lords One Death and Seven Death had forbidden all the inhabitants of Xibalba to touch the tree, but she went to look at it anyway.

A MIRACULOUS CONCEPTION

One Hunahpú's head was still among the branches, hidden by the great number of calabashes. When Blood Maiden stretched out to reach the fruit, the head of One Hunahpú spat in her palm. She felt the spittle land there and pulled her hand away, but when she looked at it she could see nothing unusual. Her hand looked exactly as it always did. Then One Hunahpú spoke to her, explaining that even though he was nothing more than a bare skull, his likeness would soon return to life in the face of his son.

Blood Maiden went away and soon afterwards discovered that she had become pregnant. There was no other possible father: it must be the spittle of One Hunahpú that lived in her. When Blood Maiden's father Blood Gatherer

Above: The Hero Twins made monkeys of their brothers and the survivors of the wooden people took monkey form.

discovered that she was with child, he was angry and asked her who the father was. She denied that she was pregnant. Blood Gatherer sent her away to be executed, instructing the owl messengers to kill her and bring back her heart in a bowl. However, on the way Blood Maiden explained to the executioners that they must not kill her, for the child in her belly had been miraculously conceived. She fashioned a block of red sap from a croton tree into the shape of a human heart and gave it to the executioners to carry back to Blood Gatherer.

One Death, Seven Death and Blood Gatherer inspected the object and appeared satisfied that it was the girl's heart. They hung it over the fire and stood round expectantly as it cooked, savouring the aroma. Meanwhile, the owls flitted away and guided Blood Maiden to the surface of the earth. It was a fateful moment when she escaped from the plots and tricks of One Death and Seven Death, because the children she would bear on the earth's surface would be the undoing of those underworld lords.

A SUSPICIOUS GRANDMOTHER

Blood Maiden came to the house of the grandmother Xmucané to explain who she was and why she had climbed to the earth's surface. At first Xmucané would not believe that Blood Maiden was pregnant with One Hunahpú's children. As a test, the grandmother sent Blood Maiden to gather a netful of food in the farm-plot kept by One Monkey and One Artisan. When Blood Maiden arrived there she found only one clump of corn plants and despaired: how would she fill a large net with corn? However, she did not give up. She began a magic song, calling on the patrons of food, Harvest Lady, Cornmeal Lady and Cacao Lady, to help her. The corn plants miraculously provided her with enough corn to fill her net.

When Blood Maiden returned with so much food, Xmucané was suspicious. She hurried to the garden to see how the underworld maiden had gathered so much food there. The grandmother found things just as they should be and saw an imprint of the net in the mud. This

Below: The calabash, fruit of a tropical American tree, grows large enough to be likened to a human head.

convinced her that Blood Maiden was mother of her new grandchildren. This element in the story appears to be a pun on one of the Maya day names, 'net'. The story is an embodiment of the cycle of Venus and this event corresponds to the rising of Venus as evening star, which should take place, according to the almanac, on the day 'net'.

BIRTH OF THE HERO TWINS
Blood Maiden gave birth to twin boys, Hunahpú and Xbalanqué, in the mountains and carried them down to Xmucané's house. The babies cried loudly by day and night and Xmucané banished them from the house. Blood Maiden made a soft bed for them, first on an anthill and then in some brambles. The twins made their own good luck by fitting in and making the best of what life offered.

Below: A ceramic vase identified by scholars only as an 'aged god' (c.AD450) was found in the jungle city of Tikal.

SIBLING RIVALRY
The twins received little love from either their grandmother or from their elder brothers One Monkey and One Artisan. The elder boys were very wise, great artists and seers. From the first day, the elder brothers could see that Hunahpú and Xbalanqué had a wonderful destiny and they became wildly jealous of their younger brothers.

While One Monkey and One Artisan stayed home practising their music and fine art, the younger twins went hunting for meat with their blowpipes. Before they had grown beards, they were already bringing home great sacks full of birds for the family pot. Xmucané, One Monkey and One Artisan just accepted it. They treated Hunahpú and Xbalanqué almost like slaves.

Finally, Hunahpú and Xbalanqué got their own back. They tricked One Monkey and One Artisan into climbing a tree to fetch food, and then turned them into monkeys. Hunahpú and Xbalanqué told Xmucané what had

Above: A late Classic Maya painted earthenware vase depicts waterbirds and their hunter – perhaps one of the Hero Twins.

happened: her favourite grandsons had abandoned the family home for a life in the trees as monkeys. The boys offered to tempt One Monkey and One Artisan back with music.

So Hunahpú and Xbalanqué took their flutes and drums and played a lively song that brought the monkey men back. They looked so funny, with their long tails and little bellies that Xmucané could not help laughing. At once the monkeys fled. Three more times Hunahpú and Xbalanqué tried the music and twice more the monkeys returned, but Xmucané could not keep a straight face and the monkeys left again. The last time the monkeys would not return. They disappeared into the forest. Now the younger twins Hunahpú and Xbalanqué were ready to fulfil their destiny by returning to the underworld realm in which their father had died.

RETURN TO XIBALBA

The Hero Twins Hunahpú and Xbalanqué found their father's ball game equipment hidden under the rafters of Xmucané's house. A rat they had caught in their farmfield told them where to find it and helped them to get it down. They went to play on their father's favourite court, out at the far eastern edge of the earth. They had a good game there. All the patience, trickery and athleticism they had developed as hunters served them well on the ball court.

ONE DEATH AND SEVEN DEATH ARE ANNOYED AGAIN

Just as before, when their father had played, the game disturbed the underworld lords One Death and Seven Death. They sent their messengers once again to deliver a summons. The messengers followed the path that led them directly to the Hero Twins' house, so the challenge was delivered to Xmucané while the boys were away playing. The underworld lords expected the ball game players to come to Xibalba within seven days.

Xmucané was very upset. Although she had never shown any affection to the Hero Twins, she loved them very deeply and could not bear for them to follow in

Above: This arresting, lifelike head (c.AD700–900) is from Copán, a centre for gifted sculptors for many years.

Below: Twin dancers and a Plumed Serpent are delicately rendered on this terracotta vase from Ulua, Honduras (AD600–900).

their father's footsteps down to the dark underworld. Nevertheless, she passed the message on. She gave it to a louse she found on her arm. The louse set off for the eastern rim of the earth bearing the message. On the road he met a toad who swallowed him and continued on the way to the eastern ball court himself. After a little while the toad was swallowed by a long snake, who went on with the journey. High in the mountains, close to the ball court, the snake was eaten by a laughing falcon, who made the last part of the journey to the place where Hunahpú and Xbalanqué were playing.

The laughing falcon flew over the court. When they heard its cry, the Hero Twins threw down their gaming equipment and took up their blowpipes. One shot was all they needed to shoot it in the eye. They ran over to where the falcon lay and asked it its business. 'I will tell you if you heal my wounded eye', said the bird. So the Twins picked some rubber off their ball and used it to heal the bird. For this reason it has a patch of black around its eye.

Then the falcon spat out the snake. The Twins asked the snake what it wanted and the snake spat out the toad. Again the Twins asked the purpose of the creature's visit. The toad tried to vomit the louse, but his belly was empty. The Twins pried open his mouth and eventually found the louse, stuck fast in the toad's teeth. The louse delivered the message exactly as he had been told.

The Twins went home to Xmucané and made their farewells, then travelled to the underworld. They passed safely across the rivers of water, spinning knives and blood and pus, then paused at the

Below: Two go as one – a Maya whistle is carved in the form of a couple with linked hands.

crossroads. They sent a mosquito ahead of them to investigate. They told it to bite any underworld lords it met. Its reward was that ever afterwards it could suck the blood of travellers and those out at dusk. The Hero Twins followed the mosquito and witnessed everything that happened. It bit all the 14 underworld lords who had gathered to play tricks on the new arrivals. Two lords, of course, did not respond. The Hero Twins could see that these were mere wooden mannequins, so they did not fall for the trick that had caught their father out. All the other lords were unsettled by the mosquito's bite and addressed one another by name. The Hero Twins listened carefully and afterwards they introduced themselves to the lords one by one.

One Death and Seven Death then tried to trick the twins into sitting on the red-hot bench that had discomfited their father, but the trickster boys refused to sit. They had the upper hand and the underworld lords were as good as beaten already. Dispirited, they led the twins into the Dark House and set them the same task that had been the undoing of One Hunahpú and Seven Hunahpú. The Hero Twins must return two newly lit cigars and a freshly burning torch in the morning.

The Hero Twins were equal to this test as well. They put a red macaw tail on the end of the torch in place of the flame and a firefly at the tip of each cigar. When they returned the cigars and torch in the morning, all three appeared to have been freshly lit. The underworld lords were really troubled now. These newcomers seemed different in appearance and in their hearts from any who had come down from the earth before.

The next challenge was to play the ball game. Hunahpú and Xbalanqué came into the court against the top Xibalban players. They agreed to use the Xibalbans'

Above: A jaguar head on this Maya terracotta incense burner might summon the jaguar god of the underworld.

own ball, which they could tell was no more than a human skull. As soon as the skull-ball was in play, it split open and the Xibalbans' sacrificial knife, the White Dagger, came shooting out. The knife whirled around the court, seeking to strike and kill the Twins, but they managed to stay out of its way.

The Hero Twins now put their own ball into play. The Xibalbans and the Twins played a close game, but in the end Hunahpú and Xbalanqué allowed themselves to be defeated. They knew where their destiny lay and that there would be more tests to undergo.

XIBALBA TAMED

After the ball game, the Hero Twins Hunahpú and Xbalanqué were shown into a house filled with flying razors. It was a fearsome place indeed, for the air was thick with blades. However, the Twins tamed the flying razors by promising them the flesh of animals to slice, from that day forward and for all time.

FINDING THE PRIZE

The Twins owed the Xibalban lords the prize that had been agreed for the ball game of four bowls of flowers. How could they find these when they were stuck in the Razor House?

They summoned the ants from the fields of Xibalba to do the job on their behalf. They sent the labouring creatures to snip the flowers from the gardens of the underworld lords. That night, while the lords were enjoying the evening air in their gardens and the Hero Twins were confined in the Razor House, the ants

Below: Scholars have not determined whether the face on this Maya incense burner is of a deity or a common man.

Above: This Classic Period Maya painted terracotta vase from Travesia in Honduras depicts dancing twins.

nibbled away enough flowers to fill the four bowls required. The lords One Death and Seven Death had set some birds – the poorwills and whippoorwills – to guard their gardens, but the birds took no notice as the ants did their work.

The next morning, Hunahpú and Xbalanqué sent the four bowls of flowers to the lords One Death and Seven Death. It was obvious where the flowers had come from. It was another embarrassing defeat for these proud underworld rulers to be presented with the flowers from their own gardens as the prize. The underworld lords punished the birds who had proved such inattentive sentries by splitting their beaks, and ever afterwards poorwills and whippoorwills have had a wide open mouth.

MORE TESTS FOR THE TWINS

The Twins were sent to the Cold House but they were so full of vitality and energy that they survived a night in that freezing place. They spent the next night in the Jaguar House, but tamed the

ferocious beasts by scattering bones on the floor. The following dusk saw them entering the House of Fire, but they survived the inferno and were safe and well the next morning.

The next test was the Bat House, which was full of shrieking bats. The Twins survived most of the night by hiding inside their blowpipe, but after waiting through many hours of darkness, Hunahpú grew impatient and stuck his head out to see if it was dawn. In that moment, a bat snatched off his head, which rolled on the hard floor of the house, out of the door and on to the underworld ball court. The underworld lords called for a game, excited that they had finally won a victory over the Twins.

SUN, MOON AND VENUS

The *Popol Vuh* stories might reflect Spanish influence and distort earlier Maya tradition.

Some scholars believe that the older Maya tales described the Twins as rising to become the sun and the planet Venus, who were regarded as brothers.

In the great majority of Maya stories, the moon is regarded as female. The male moon of the *Popol Vuh* could be a misrepresentation of the older tradition. These scholars generally identify Xbalanqué with the sun and Hunahpú with Venus.

However, the Twins go through many transformations in the course of their heroic lives and it might be that the Maya did not narrowly identify them with a particular heavenly body but rather with different phases or apparent movements of Venus, the moon and the sun.

One alternative theory is that Hunahpú became the sun by day and Xbalanqué the sun by night, when it travels through the underworld.

ANOTHER BALL GAME

One Death and Seven Death wanted to use Hunahpú's head as the ball. Then Xbalanqué called on the animals of the world to bring their foodstuffs for him. When the coati, a mammal like a raccoon, brought a squash, Xbalanqué saw that he could use it to fashion a new head for Hunahpú. Equipped with his makeshift head, Hunahpú came on to the ball court with Xbalanqué ready for a new game.

The first time they used Hunahpú's real head, Xbalanqué hit it so hard that it flew out of the ball court into a stand of oak trees alongside. A rabbit burst out of the trees, distracting the underworld lords, and Xbalanqué and Hunahpú were able to switch the squash head for the real head.

The Twins called back the underworld lords and the game began again, this time using the squash as the ball. After a couple of hits, the squash began to break up and its seeds flew out. The lords could see that they had been outwitted again by the trickster Twins.

VICTORY OVER DEATH

The Twins were put through many more underworld tests, but were victorious every time, exhausting the ingenuity of One Death and Seven Death. They decided to demonstrate their victory over death by returning from annihilation. Invited to a feast by the Xibalban lords, the Twins leapt into the oven and were burned alive. The Xibalbans were beside themselves with delight at this unexpected victory. They hauled the Twins' bones out of the ashes, ground them up and sprinkled them on the waters of the underworld river.

Just five days later, the Twins returned, in the form of twin catfish. The Xibalbans saw them and were amazed. The following day, the Twins came once more in human form, pretending to be travelling entertainers. They performed several tricks, the most dramatic when Xbalanqué performed the rites of human sacrifice on Hunahpú then brought him back to life. He took off Hunahpú's head, rolled it out of the door and tore out his heart. The next moment Hunahpú stood there, whole and well. One Death and Seven Death were in a frenzy of delight and asked the twins to perform the magic on them. This time, however, the sacrifice was made for real. The twins sacrificed One Death and Seven Death. All the other Xibalbans fled in terror. The twins' victory in the underworld was complete. They told the Xibalbans that from this day they would not receive human hearts and blood in sacrifice, only sap from the croton tree and the flesh of forest animals.

Before the twins left the underworld, they reassembled the butchered body of their father. He would remain in Xibalba, they told him, and would be honoured by men for all time. Then the Twins rose into the sky. They became the sun and the moon and they light human activities by day and by night. At this time the Four Hundred Boys also appeared in the sky as the Pleiades constellation.

Right: Like the Hero Twins, Quetzalcóatl rose from the underworld to the night sky. In this late Classic Period carving (c.AD600– 900), a priest of Quetzalcóatl emerges from the jaws of the Plumed Serpent.

QUETZALCÓATL AND HIS TWIN IN MICTLÁN

The Plumed Serpent Quetzalcóatl braved the trials of the Aztec underworld, Mictlán, to gather the raw materials for the creation of the human race. He returned with the bones of the pre-human ancestors and shed his lifeblood to make the flesh of humans.

SEARCHING FOR OLD BONES

These events took place after the fourth world age, *Nahui Atl* ('Water Sun'), had been destroyed in a great flood by the goddess Chalchiúhtlicue. Quetzalcóatl and Tezcatlipoca set about creating a new world. First they made the earth and the heavens from the body of the Earth Monster Tlaltecuhtli. Then Quetzalcóatl voyaged to the underworld to search for the bones of the previous race to have inhabited the earth; the fish and many other water creatures that lived in Chalchiúhtlicue's creation. In some versions he was accompanied by his twin aspect Xólotl, who was god of monsters and who often took dog form.

Below: The Plumed Serpent, depicted here in a Maya codex, underwent many trials to make the creation of humans possible.

Quetzalcóatl went through many tests in the underworld, Mictlán. According to the pictorial account in the *Codex Borgia*, the god entered Mictlán through the body of the earth goddess Coatlícue. He is depicted being burned to death in the east on a pyre, the windblown ashes of his body transforming into swift, strong-winged birds. This refers to the Quetzalcóatl story in which the god was identified as prince Topiltzin, the wise ruler of Tollán who was disgraced, who left the city heading east and who offered himself in penitential sacrifice.

In the south, the Place of Thorns, he faced the threat of dismemberment or beheading, but passed unscathed through the body of Tlazoltéotl. In the west, he encountered a temple, honouring the souls of women killed by their unborn warrior-sons in childbirth. In the east he found a temple that was a tribute to the heroes of the battlefield. Here he passed through the body of the Earth Monster, Tlaltecuhtli, emerging in twin forms as Red Tezcatlipoca and Black Tezcatlipoca. In the north, Black Tezcatlipoca made a sacrifice of his red twin then cast himself on to a pyre. He rose from the pyre as Venus the morning star.

AN IMPOSSIBLE TASK

Quetzalcóatl held to his human form when he met the underworld lord Mictlantecuhtli. The north was the darkest, foulest part of Mictlán and here Quetzalcóatl discovered the skeletal lord with his consort Mictecacíhuatl. The Plumed Serpent asked Mictlantecuhtli for the bones of the previous earth-race of fish and water mammals. The dark lord was unwilling to let the materials go, so he set what he considered to be an impossible task: Quetzalcóatl must travel

Above: These flint and shellfish votive offerings were used in Aztec religious rites as sacrificial knives.

four times around the underworld while trumpeting on a conch shell that had no holes drilled in it. Quetzalcóatl proved equal to the test. He summoned underworld worms to drill the holes he needed to make the conch shell sound and then made a swarm of bees enter the shell. The buzzing made a satisfying song.

Mictlantecuhtli had to hand over the bones, but he bitterly resented it, so he ordered his subjects to dig a hole in Quetzalcóatl's path. When the Plumed Serpent arrived at the place, a flock of quails swept at his face, startling him and making him fall into the hole and drop the bones. He recovered in time to gather the bones and effect his escape from Mictlán. However, because he dropped the bones, they were broken. It is for this reason that the people later made from them came in a variety of shapes and sizes.

Above: In an image from the Codex Vaticanus, Quetzalcóatl in Plumed Serpent *form rides the sky as Venus.*

A NEW CREATION

Quetzalcóatl took the bones to the gods assembled in the heaven of Tamoanchán. He gave them to the mother goddess, who ground them into a powder and asked the other deities to provide some of their blood so that a paste could be made from the bones. They gathered around and performed autosacrifice, passing thorns through their tongue or earlobes to drip blood on to the mixture. According to one version, it was Quetzalcóatl alone who provided the blood for the mixing of the paste. The gods waited and watched. They needed to be patient. After four days a male human child emerged from the paste and after four more days a girl appeared.

Another of the *Codex Borgia* images shows Quetzalcóatl as the wind god Éhecatl sitting back to back with the underworld lord Mictlantecuhtli, suggesting the duality of life and death. The tale of the god's movement through the underworld also celebrates the religious understanding that life is given meaning and context by death. The accounts of Quetzalcóatl's heroic travels end with the god rising to become Venus. The cycles of that planet repeat and celebrate Quetzalcóatl's descent to the realm of death, his outwitting of the underworld lord and his ascension in life to create the human race.

Like the *Popol Vuh* of the Quiché Maya, the tale is a celebration of the underground germination of the maize plant and its journey to the light in spring. Some scholars also see an account of the travails that await each human spirit after death in the myth of Quetzalcóatl's descent to the underworld: a sacred myth comparable to the accounts of the afterlife in the holy books of ancient Egypt, Tibetan Buddhism and the Judaeo-Christian tradition.

Below: A detail of a mural of c.AD900 from Cacaxtla shows the head of the Plumed Serpent Quetzalcóatl.

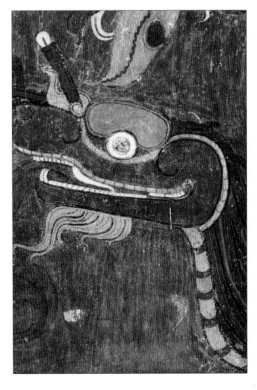

CHAPTER 12

MYTHS AND HISTORY

Mesoamericans created narratives not only about the world's beginnings and the deeds of the gods, but also about the origins of their own people and the history of the tribe. Indeed the Aztecs and other Mesoamericans often took a creative approach to history, blending fact and narratives of the past in a way designed to establish political and religious points in the present.

According to an origin narrative shared by the Aztecs and many of their neighbours, the earliest human ancestors emerged from a collection of sacred caverns known as Chicomoztoc ('Seven Caves'). The Aztecs believed that the seven womb-like caves radiated out from a central chamber and that one people or tribe emerged from each cave.

Chicomoztoc was generally understood to be in the north and was associated with dryness, darkness, barrenness and lack of civilization; it was a good place to leave behind. Several attempts have been made to identify both this place of origin and the place known as Aztlán ('Land of the Cranes') from which the Aztecs claimed to have started out when they made a southward pilgrimage to the Valley of Mexico. The story appears to express the tribes' feeling that they were born from and belong to the mother goddess. However, some historians suggest that the myth is symbolic of the transition from a nomadic hunting lifestyle to a more settled lifestyle of farming supplemented by hunting; a change that equated to a rebirth and gave the former nomads a new connection to the land.

Left: This Codex Durán *image depicts Moctezuma leaving on a retreat after hearing of the Spanish landing.*

TOLTEC WANDERINGS

The Toltecs, so revered by the Aztecs as the builders of the wondrous city of Tollán, were probably the first of many tribes who travelled southward from the wasteland of the north, beginning as nomads but settling in the more fertile lands further south and learning the skills of settled life. According to one account given by the chronicler Fernando de Alva Ixtlilxóchitl, the Toltecs came south by sea, following the coastline presumably in large sea-going Mesoamerican canoes, until they came to the mythical land of Tlapallán ('Land of Bright Colours'). Scholars regard this version of events as highly unlikely, preferring a more probable land route, but they do note that in some traditions the god Quetzalcóatl was regarded as an expert in navigating a canoe and that on the eastern edge of Mesoamerica Maya traders proved themselves capable of covering large distances by sea canoe.

DISPLACEMENT OF A PEOPLE

The Toltecs began their journey because they were displaced by a stronger, better-equipped or more warlike people, setting the pattern for generations of brief

Below: The Aztecs looked back to the Toltecs with the awe they felt for the grave offerings of Teotihuacán. This stone mask was placed on the face of a buried Teotihuacán noble.

Above: The Toltecs' travels to find a homeland lasted more than 100 years and included 13 brief periods of settlement.

settlements and enforced migrations. Ixtlilxóchitl's chronicle records that the Toltecs landed in Tlapallán in the year 1-Técpatl, identified by scholars as AD387. The chronicle then suggests that they were driven out from Tlapallán around 50 years later, in AD439, after rebelling against the king's authority. They settled nearby for eight years, then travelled to Tlapallantzinco, where they

rested for three years. Afterwards they began a long migration along the Pacific coast and across northern Mexico. According to Ixtlilxóchitl's chronicle, the Toltecs at last found the appointed place to establish their wondrous city of Tollán in AD566.

FOUNDING OF A CITY

The myth of Tollán is based on the history of the city of Tula, which lies around 80km (50 miles) north of Mexico City. The date of Tula's founding is not certain. It may have been as late as the 10th century AD, more than four hundred years later than the date given in Ixtlilxóchitl's account.

The location for the city was chosen by the Toltecs' priest-leader Hueymatzin ('Great Hand'). In that place he saw the future; the wonderful era of peace and self-expression that would come to the Toltecs in Tollán; but also the ineffably sad departure of the priest-king Topiltzin.

The site to which Hueymatzin gave his blessing lay in a valley that was so fertile that it became known as 'The Place of the Fruits'. The Toltec people were very glad to end their migrations, and they poured all their energy into building a truly magnificent city. For six long years they laboured, laying out the most luxurious palaces, expansive plazas and towering temples with great pillars honouring brave Toltec warriors. In the seventh year they elected a king named Calchiuh Tlatonac ('Bright Precious Stone') who ruled for 52 years. Under his wise governance, in an era of peace and prosperity, the Toltecs developed great artistic skills.

The stonemasons of the Toltecs were to produce carving of the very finest quality and they raised walls literally covered in sparkling gems. The Toltecs were famed for the temple complex in their capital. The inner sanctum contained four rooms of astonishing beauty. One had walls covered with gold, the second used precious jewels for decoration, the third was covered with seashells and the fourth was carved from a red stone and also had delightful shell ornaments.

Travellers from near and far were also astonished to see the Toltecs' House of Feathers. This magnificent building also had four main rooms, each decorated with hangings and tapestries woven from feathers of different colours. In the first room these feathers were yellow, and in the second they were made from the precious blue-green feathers of the quetzal bird. The third room in the House of Fearthers was decorated with pure white feathers, not a grubby or misshapen one among them, while the fourth was hung with cloths made from red plumage. So delicate and finely wrought were their artistic creations that their neighbours began to use the term *toltec* to mean an artist.

Above: Magnificent Toltec warrior figures stand on the Temple of Tlahuizcalpantecuhtli or Venus the morning star at Tollán.

Left: Toltecs believed that warrior-gods like this used their strength to support the universe.

THE GOLDEN REIGN OF TOPILTZIN

One body of stories concerning the wondrous age of the Toltecs in Tollán celebrates the golden achievements and eventual decline of their priest-king Topiltzin. He was one of a succession of priestly rulers dedicated to the cult of the Plumed Serpent, Quetzalcóatl. This group were known after their divine inspiration as 'the Quetzalcóatls'.

A TIME OF PLENTY

Topiltzin's reign, like that of Calchiuh Tlatonac before him, was remembered as a time of great plenty. Nobody needed to go without in the Toltec realm: ears of maize were so heavy and long that farmers had to use their arms to cradle them, while calabashes were the size of a man's lower leg. There was no need laboriously to dye cotton, for it grew in all the colours of the rainbow. The songs of brilliantly feathered birds hung sweetly in the clear air. A walker in the hills could easily gather gems and pieces of gold and silver, for they were as plentiful as flowers. People picked up the sparkling stones if they wanted to set them in a necklace or make an offering to the gods.

The people of Tollán pioneered all the great arts in this wondrous era. They understood mining, stone cutting and masonry and developed delicate skills as carpenters. They were the first in America to practise weaving, painting, music and writing. The priests invented the ritual calendar, so the passing of time could be measured and marked in the gods' honour. They were to develop the secret science of divining the future, the throwing of seeds

Right: This magnificent feathered fan is thought to have once been used by Moctezuma II.

and the interpretation of day-names and year-names to discover the hidden destiny that governed an individual's life.

The Toltecs built observatories and watched eagerly at night to plot the movements of the stars and planets. They were rewarded for their devotion with hidden knowledge. On shamanistic

Above: A carving of the birth of Topiltzin emphasizes the king's association with the Plumed Serpent Quetzalcóatl.

journeys they encountered the creator himself, lodged both beyond the farthest star and deep in their own hearts, and they understood the secrets of the ever-changing universe. They discovered the religious uses of such alcoholic drinks as *pulque* and of mind-altering substances such as the psychedelic mushroom *Psilocybe aztecorum* and the morning glory flower.

TOPILTZIN'S ORIGINS

There are several accounts of Topiltzin's origins, some of which seek to establish his divine status or to identify him as an incarnation of the god Quetzalcóatl. In one of these, his mother gave birth to him after she swallowed an emerald. His miraculous birth associated him with Huitzilopochtli, born after a ball of birds' down landed in his mother's bosom. According to another account, he was the son of the earth mother goddess, just as Quetzalcóatl was.

RELIGIOUS REFORM

Yet another version emphasized Topiltzin's human origins. According to this account, Topiltzin was originally a warrior, brave in battle, but he was drawn away from the cult of violence and of human sacrifice to the worship of the benevolent Quetzalcóatl, provider of

Below: The Toltec potter who made this ceramic Tláloc emphasized the god's curling snake 'moustache'.

good things to the human race. At this time the Toltecs' chief god was Tezcatlipoca, a patron of war and sower of disharmony. Topiltzin, it is said, undertook seven years of penances to cleanse his soul of the stain of other men's blood. He then established a religious community in a Toltec city named Tulantzinco. He taught that the gods did not require the slaughter of victims on the sacrificial stone, but were far happier with the pious and peaceful offering of animals or of a worshipper's own blood drawn from the earlobes, tongue, cheeks or penis.

The Toltecs asked him to become their ruler and to bring his religious reforms to Tollán. He became a deeply loved ruler and the cult of Quetzalcóatl increasingly eclipsed that of Tezcatlipoca. However, the remaining core of the war god's followers rose up to reassert their religious tradition and its dominance. Their approach was more forceful than that of the peace-loving Quetzalcóatl priests and Topiltzin was driven from Tollán, accompanied by a band of his followers.

Above: The Aztecs honoured the Toltecs and other ancestors during the Festival of Huey Miccailhuitl's pole-climbing ceremony.

Just as their distant ancestors had done, Topiltzin and his loyal followers embarked on a nomadic voyage of discovery. They may have settled on the Mexican Gulf Coast. In one account, they stopped for a while at Chapultepec ('Hill of Grasshoppers') near the site on which the Méxica/Aztecs would later build Tenochtitlán. They may have gone as far as the northern Maya city of Chichén Itzá and made it a major centre for the worship of the Plumed Serpent (who was known as Kukulcán to the Maya).

There is certainly evidence of Toltec/Mexican influence in Chichén Itzá. Traditional histories put this down to the migration of Toltec groups driven out of their Mexican homeland, but some scholars now argue the Toltec elements found in the city may be the result of trading contacts and cultural influence.

THE DIVINE PRINCE

The Aztecs, like their Mesoamerican contemporaries, were keen to associate themselves with the achievements and history of the Toltecs.

When the Aztecs first settled in the Valley of Mexico they made many marriages with noble Culhúa women of Toltec descent and told elegaic legends about the lost glory of the priestly prince Topiltzin. Over the course of time, this semi-historical figure became identified with the god he worshipped.

The story of Topiltzin's religious reforms, his conflict with the warrior elite who worshipped Tezcatlipoca, his defeat and exile all became part of the cycle of legends that describe the conflict between the god Quetzalcóatl and his dark brother Tezcatlipoca.

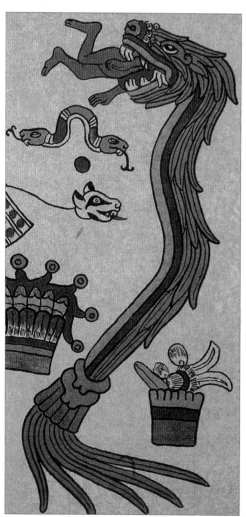

Left: The often peaceable Plumed Serpent Quetzalcóatl did take pleasure in human sacrifices from time to time.

THE FALL OF QUETZALCÓATL

According to these stories, Tezcatlipoca was jealous of the glory of Topiltzin-Quetzalcóatl's reign in Tollán and was angry that his own cult was being marginalized by the priest-king's religious reforms. Tezcatlipoca appeared in Tollán and began his shadowy scheming to unseat Topiltzin-Quetzalcóatl from the throne.

In one account, Tezcatlipoca descended from the thirteen heavens in the form of a spider on a dark thread. He came into Topiltzin-Quetzalcóatl's chamber and offered the Plumed Serpent a drink of *pulque*. One drink became many and, in time, Topiltzin-Quetzalcóatl became confused, then angry, then wild. In his drunkenness he forgot himself and violated his sister Quetzalpetlatl. The following day Quetzalcóatl felt his disgrace very keenly and declared that he would leave the city he had governed so well. After banishing the bright-voiced, brilliantly feathered birds of Tollán, burning his palace complex and burying his silver and gold for future generations of miners to find, he departed in the company of a select band of mournful followers. He either sacrificed himself on a great pyre or set sail into the Gulf of Mexico on a raft of serpents.

In another version, Tezcatlipoca persuaded Topiltzin-Quetzalcóatl to play the Mesoamerican ball game. They played long and hard, astounding the people of Tollán who had gathered to watch, delivering impossible balls from end to end through the ring mounted high on the side of the court. Topiltzin-Quetzalcóatl, though a peace-loving and retiring man, was at least the equal of his dark adversary on the ball court. At the height of the match, however, Tezcatlipoca used his dark arts to

Above: An alabaster disc from Teotihuacán represents the planet Venus, a key aspect of Quetzalcóatl, as a deity controlling waters.

transform Topiltzin-Quetzalcóatl into an ocelot, a smaller cousin of the jaguar, and drove the creature out of the city of Tollán.

Yet another account explains how the Lord of the Smoking Mirror, Tezcatlipoca, used the device with which he is associated. He gained access to the inner chamber of Topiltzin-Quetzalcóatl and showed the prince his reflection in the dark shadow-mirror. The power of this mirror was extraordinary: it provided both deceptive and unpleasantly truthful reflections, giving access directly to the dark side. The distortion of his image that Topiltzin-Quetzalcóatl saw in the mirror unnerved him. He wandered all night long, plagued with doubt and driven by a desire to return home to the place from which he had come to bring knowledge and culture to Mesoamerica. In the morning he left.

Still another account has it that Tezcatlipoca came to visit Topiltzin-Quetzalcóatl on his sickbed. For this purpose the Lord of the Smoking Mirror had transformed himself into a kind-faced elderly man. At first, Topiltzin-Quetzalcóatl's palace staff turned the

Above: This detail of a Quetzalcóatl head is from Xochicalco, a city at its peak in the early Postclassic Period.

visitor away but he used all of his dark trickery to gain admission. He found Topiltzin-Quetzalcóatl was seemingly exhausted, as if his life energy could no longer support him. 'My body is unwound, undone,' the king said. 'My hands and feet are weak. Getting up to attend to my business is too much for me. I cannot do it.' The disguised Tezcatlipoca came gently to the ruler's bedside. 'Try this potion,' he said in a soft voice. 'It brings fire to your veins and restores vitality. You will feel strong enough to spring up and don your ball game equipment. Nothing will seem impossible any more.'

At first Topiltzin-Quetzalcóatl resisted the drink, but at last he gave in. The potion was in fact the strong alcoholic drink *pulque* and as Tezcatlipoca plied the aged ruler with it, Topiltzin-Quetzalcóatl became drunk. In his drunkenness he was lost and the aftermath of the incident was that he no longer had any appetite to govern. He felt he must return whence he had come. The era of his glorious governance could not endure, for the world cannot support timeless perfection. Quetzalcóatl-Topiltzin had grown old.

ALL GOOD THINGS MUST END

The elegiac note in the legend of Topiltzin-Quetzalcóatl in Tollán captures the human sense that nothing good can last. Both in the account of Tezcatlipoca's visit to Topiltzin-

Above: An image of Quetzalcóatl from the Codex Durán (1579–81) shows him in human form with a warrior's shield.

Quetzalcóatl's sickbed and in the tale of the god-king's departure from Tollán, there is an awareness that the goodness of his blessed reign has been exhausted. The king is worn out; his youthful vigour has gone and death looms. The myths embody the experience of ageing and the need for reconciliation with mortality.

Some scholars argue that the legends also embody a celebration of the martial vigour and physical force of the bands of Chichimec ('Sons of the Dog'), invaders who swept away the Toltecs in the mid- to late-12th century. The priest-king is exhausted because his time, like that of the Toltecs, is up: a new force has arrived. The elegiac note appears because the invaders who developed the myths were aware of the greatness of Toltec culture and were keen to build on it.

HOW THE TOLTECS FELL

Left: The Toltecs' Chichimec enemies were as fierce as the jaguar. This painted creature is from Chichén Itzá in Yucatán.

The legends of Topiltzin and Quetzalcóatl account for the decline of the Toltec state following the abdication of its divine ruler. Another body of legends describes the same events from a different perspective, portraying the Toltec fall as a divine judgement on a king, Uemac or Huemac II, who had fallen into wicked ways.

According to this account, Huemac II became Toltec ruler in AD994. In his first years on the throne he was an exemplary king and a pious worshipper of the great Mesoamerican pantheon of gods. However, he was tempted into wrong-doing and the vices he acquired gripped his soul so tightly that he could not find his way back to virtue. The provincial cities under the rule of Tollán rose in a weak and finally inconsequential revolt. Although it came to nothing, the revolt was a sign that his stature as king was badly diminished by his sins and that his subjects neither honoured nor feared him.

A SORCERER ARRIVES

The arrival in Tollán of a great sorcerer named Toveyo made matters worse. This expert in the dark arts caused havoc among the people. On one occasion he lured a great number of Toltec people on to a stone bridge high above a riverbed. Then, using shadowy invocations, he made the bridge crack, tremble and collapse, causing the people to tumble to their deaths far below.

The story was also told that Toveyo invited the populace to a dance in the city's main plaza, but maddened the people by making the music swirl faster and faster. He finally drove the crowd into such a frenzy that the people rushed from the square into a nearby crevasse. They died as they bounced off the sides of the ravine and their corpses turned to stone when they finally came to rest at the bottom of the incline.

Toveyo appears to be a thinly veiled version of Tezcatlipoca, who was the dark hero in a whole range of tales of Tollán's downfall. The myth of the maddening music was also told of Tezcatlipoca.

Terrible apparitions began. The volcanoes visible from the city began to growl and belch flames in which the Toltec priests saw wild, threatening figures. When Huemac ordered a great sacrificial offering to the gods, a blood-chillingly awful portent was seen. At the climax of the ceremony, the priests bent the chief victim, a high-ranking noble from a rival city, over the sacrificial stone and opened his chest cavity with the sacred flint knife. But inside they could find no heart. For a few terrible moments, in chill silence, they patted at his chest and innards looking for the heart. They realized that his veins were dry and empty and that no precious blood was spilling on to the stones of the temple pyramid. Yet just a few seconds before the man had been walking and talking. In that terrifying moment a terrible stink began to rise from the body. The priests and people fled from the temple, but many were killed in an epidemic of foul wasting diseases seemingly caused by the stench of bloodless death.

PUNISHED FOR SELF-INTEREST

While out hunting in the forest, Huemac encountered the divine *tláloques*, the rain god's fleet-footed helpers. He fell on to his face, but not to honour them. Rather, he begged to be spared and to be allowed

Below: The myth tells that Huemac was punished by the rain god's helpers. This clay image of Tláloc is from Teotihuacán.

HOW THE TOLTECS FELL

to maintain his position of wealth and importance. The *tláloques* were enraged by his rank self-interest and declared that six years of plagues would punish the Toltec people. They were as good as their word. Huemac's unfortunate subjects endured terrible, crop-killing frosts followed by summer droughts, then destructive floods and wild storms. They were plagued by thousands of toads and locusts that poured across the fields and swamped the city markets.

Huemac abdicated and placed his illegitimate son Acxitl on the throne. Like his father, Acxitl began his reign well but soon slipped into decadence and corruption. The austere city of Tollán became known as a city of vice.

Below: To the west of the Temple of Tlahuizcalpantecuhtli at Tollán are rows of columns, probably part of a palace.

Two outlying provinces rose in revolt, and they sent an army led by a nobleman named Huehuetzin to attack the city of Tollán. The soldiers and their leader were bought off with the city's great riches, but by now it had become known far and wide across Mexico that the Toltec people did not have a leader worthy

Left: This terracotta brazier from Teotihuacán represents quetzal birds, which were associated with royal authority.

of the name and that their power was on the wane. The northern nomads, who were known as the Chichimec ('Sons of the Dog') began to make raids into Toltec lands. Huehuetzin attacked again, this time with the backing of groups of Chichimec. The Toltec people, once the most widely feared warriors of the region, now had to patch together a makeshift defence force that included a company of the women of Tollán. For three years, a Toltec army led by Huemac and Acxitl held the invaders at bay. Finally, the defences broke and the Toltecs fled.

The empire was broken. The Chichimecs flooded across the land, occupying and rebuilding Toltec cities.

243

THE ORIGIN OF THE MÉXICA

The México/Aztecs claimed that they originated on an island surrounded by reeds in a lagoon, in a place called Aztlán ('Land of the Cranes') somewhere in the far north. Its location was never identified, even by the Aztecs. (They themselves were curious and sent an expedition to attempt to find the lagoon-island in the 15th century.) From this unknown place they set out on a long and circuitous migration in search of a land in which to make permanent home. The journey, like that of the Toltecs before them, lasted more than 100 years.

The Aztecs also said they emerged from the womblike caverns of Chicomoztoc ('Seven Caves'). According to the account given by Fray Diego Durán in *The History of the Indies of New Spain*, the seven caves were in the region of Aztlán. Other accounts suggest that the México/Aztecs came to the place of the seven caves in the course of their lengthy migration.

MAN OR GOD?
Seven tribes emerged from the seven caves and left the region one by one. The first six tribal groups to depart were the Alcolua, the Chalca, the Tecpaneca, the Tlalhuica, the Tlaxcalteca and the Xochimilca. The México/Aztecs remained

Below: This intricate wooden carving of a prone Aztec warrior was used as a drum. It was found at Tlaxcala.

behind, instructed to do so by a divine vision. Diego Durán reports that the Aztecs left the caves 302 years after the last of the other tribes had departed. They set out to look for a fertile land in which, their god had promised, they would flourish.

A number of scholars believe that Huitzilopochtli, revered as the Aztecs' tribal god, might originally have been a historical figure, a leader who inspired the Aztecs to leave their original home and travel south. He may have been deified after his death and his cult promoted to a position where it rivalled that of much more ancient Mesoamerican gods. In Diego Durán's account, however, Huitzilopochtli was an idol carried by the Aztecs on their migrations. Durán reported the priests were custodians of the idol and relayed the god's pronouncements to the tribe. On Huitzilopochtli's orders, the Aztecs carried the characteristic tools of nomads; nets, bows and arrows. However, they were not always on the move. In some places they stayed for as long as 20 years and built temples and even ball courts. They laid out fields and raised maize, squash, beans, chillies and chia. They also hunted in the hills and valleys around their settlement to supplement their diet with meat. However, they did not put down permanent roots and when the god told them to move on, they obeyed. Often the old and sick members of the tribe were left behind when the more vigorous set off.

Above: Aztec carvings represent the cihuateteo, *spirits of women who had died in desperate or prolonged childbirth. They became the goddesses of crossroads.*

SPIRIT VOYAGE

According to the chronicler Fray Diego Durán, Moctezuma I, *tlatoani* of Tenochtitlán, dispatched an expedition sometime in the 1440s to try to find the Méxicas' original tribal home in Aztlán.

The exploratory group consisted of 60 shaman-priests who were equipped by their supernatural shape-shifting powers to see to the very heart of whatever they encountered. They headed north, past the Toltecs' great city of Tollán, and came to the mountain they knew as the birthplace of the tribal god Huitzilopochtli. Here they met a shrouded divinity who transformed them into birds for the next stage of their journey.

They arrived by air in Aztlán, where they returned to human form. Here they were introduced to an ancient relative of Huitzilopochtli who observed these formerly tough nomads had allowed themselves to be softened by their settled life in the comfortable surroundings of Tenochtitlán. He brought them to see Coatlícue, Huitzilopochtli's mother. They made obeisance before her and presented gifts they had carried from their capital, proudly telling her of the extent of the Aztec empire and the vast amount and wide variety of tribute they received each year from subject peoples. In reply, however, she prophesied that the conquering Aztecs would themselves be conquered. The travellers thus returned with unsettling news for Moctezuma. The fact that this adventure was presented as a spirit voyage to a place inhabited by the gods betrays the fact that the Aztecs considered Aztlán, their mythical place of origin, to be less a physical location than a place of spiritual birth.

Some scholars believe that the seven caves of Chicomoztoc can be identified as Mount Culhuacán ('Curving Mountain'), one of the Aztecs' most important stopping points on their journey. This peak may be a mountain near San Isidro Culhuacán. From ancient times, Mesoamericans understood caves to be holy places and believed life could be brought forth from the heart of the sacred mountain. In one myth, Quetzalcóatl discovers the maize plant in the heart of Mount Tonacatépetl. One theory says the Aztecs came to an existing ancient cave shrine in Mount Culhuacán and performed religious rites there. Perhaps they already shared the common Mesoamerican origin myth of emerging from the place of seven caves.

Above: Ancestors are honoured in this Mixtec codex, which records the genealogies of a place called Belching Mountain.

Below: This mural of deities in procession is from the Palace of Tepantitla at Teotihuacán.

THE CACTUS AND THE EAGLE

The México/Aztecs made many stops before they found the ordained site for a permanent settlement, the place in which their god Huitzilopochtli had promised they would find wealth and glory.

They came to an island in Lake Texcoco after fleeing the fury of the Culhua. On Huitzilopochtli's orders, the México/Aztecs had taken the daughter of the Culhua king and sacrificed her in a fertility rite, provoking the rage of the king and his warriors. The México had retreated from the place near Culhuacán where they had made their home and were hiding in the marshes and reed beds around Lake Texcoco.

FOUNDING TENOCHTITLÁN

Before sunrise the next morning, they canoed across the lake to the islands they could dimly see in mid-water. As they reached land, a priest of Huitzilopochtli had a blinding vision of his god declaring that the México should look for a place where an eagle perched on a large cactus holding a writhing snake in its talons. This would be the spot where they should build their permanent home. Although it was still just before sunrise, light was blazing in the priest's vision; he was trembling, and collapsed into a pool. His assistants hauled him back to safety, but he appeared oblivious to their attentions, jabbering, 'This is the spot, this is the spot!'

The settlers looked around and a cry went up. Sure enough, there was an eagle perched on a cactus holding a snake at its mercy. At that moment the sun rose and its light caught the eagle's feathers as the bird extended its wings. The Aztecs saw the light of the sun fall on the spot like a blessing from their sun god and leader, Huitzilopochtli. They ran to the place and threw themselves down, praising and thanking the god. They built a platform around the cactus and raised a temple house in which they placed their idol of Huitzilopochtli. From these humble beginnings rose the Great Pyramid at the heart of Tenochtitlán's temple precinct. While they were seeking building materials for the platform they found springs of blue and red water; to Mesoamericans, this was a well-known sign that a place was blessed.

THE DEFEAT OF COPIL

The priest's vision indicated that the cactus on which the eagle alighted was growing in the place where Huitzilopochtli had flung the heart of Copil after defeating and sacrificing him. The reference to Copil is to an earlier episode in the foundation legend. According to a mythologized account, the Aztec group had quarrelled and split in the years when they were making their first settlements near Lake Texcoco. One group of Aztecs remained under the

Below: Once the Aztecs had found the right place, they set to work to build their capital. This illustration is from the Codex Durán.

A MESSAGE FROM THE RAIN GOD

This proclamation from the war god was backed up by a message from the rain god. A priest maddened by religious ecstasy impulsively leapt into a pool nearby, where he sank to the murkiest depths. There he encountered Tláloc, god of rains, and received the word of the deity that the place was blessed and that any who built there would receive glory, a great empire and the tribute of countless subject peoples. In some versions of the story, the cactus on which the eagle perched bore red fruit. This symbolized the many human hearts that would be torn from their bodies and offered to Huitzilopochtli in the years after the establishment of Tenochtitlán.

Below: The eagle was a symbol of the sun, of human sacrifice and of the military prowess embodied by warriors.

guidance of Huitzilopochtli, here cast as a historical leader of the tribe, while a rival faction went their own way under the control of Huitzilopochtli's sister, Malinalxochitl. The breakaway group left the area of Lake Texcoco altogether and settled in mountains to the southwest. However, Malinalxochitl's son, Copil, returned to lead a force against the México when they encountered trouble during their stay at Chapultepec.

On that fateful day, Copil's army was triumphant but he himself was waylaid in the marshes by the invincible Huitzilopochtli. The war god trounced Copil, then took his still-living body and performed a brisk ritual sacrifice. He tore the heart from Copil's chest cavity and hurled it out across the water. It landed on the island in Lake Texcoco where Tenochtitlán would later be built.

A number of variant foundation stories were told. In one version, Copil had been put to ritual death on a sacrificial stone on one of the islands in Lake Texcoco. When the Aztecs came to the island, they found a nopal cactus growing from the spot in the stone where Copil's lifeblood had been spilled. They saw the eagle, symbol of Huitzilopochtli himself, alight on the cactus, seize a serpent from the ground nearby and proceed to tear the creature to pieces. In some accounts the people all heard Huitzilopochtli's voice crying from the spirit realm that this was the place to build their city.

THE QUICHÉ MAYA SEEK A HOME

Like their Aztec counterparts, the Maya told of an epic migration by their ancestors. The Quiché Maya *Popol Vuh* recounts how the early men and women lived in perpetual darkness and prayed devoutly to the creator gods Huracán and Gucumatz to provide a sun to give them light and to make their world safe.

The first created men and women – Jaguar Quitze and his wife Celebrated Seahouse, Jaguar Night and Prawn House, Mahucutah and Hummingbird House, True Jaguar and his partner Macaw House – had many children and grandchildren. They lived expectantly, facing to the east as often as possible, watching for the rising of Venus the morning star and the sun that would follow shortly afterwards.

When the sun did not rise, they began a pilgrimage that took them to a great city called Tulan Zuyua, ('Seven Caves, Seven Canyons'). Scholars note that this may have been the revered Tollán built by the Toltecs at Tula or the older city of Teotihuacán. The Maya thus shared the Aztecs' reverence for a place of seven caves that played an important part in the early lives of the first tribal ancestors.

GIFT OF FIRE

In the city of Tulan Zuyua, the main Quiché lineages were given the gods that they were to worship. The principal one was Tohil, who gave human beings fire. He has been identified as the Classic-Period deity Tahil

Right: The head of a Maya ceremonial spear found at Copán is carved with the heads of seven kings.

Above: In the Quiché story, the sudden appearance of Tohil froze the creatures of the forest to stone. This animal's head decoration adorns a pot found at Tikal.

('Obsidian Mirror'), who is represented in carvings at Palenque with a 'smoking mirror' in his head; a Maya equivalent of the Aztec god Tezcatlipoca.

In the very first days, people had all spoken a single language, but while the Maya ancestors were living in Tulan Zuyua, different groups began speaking in different tongues. The Maya had great need of the fire given to them by Tohil, for it was cold in the time before the sun rose and they would huddle around bonfires to try to keep warm. It so happened that a hail storm swept across the dark sky, drenching the people and putting out all the fires. Tohil relit the Quiché fire by rotating on the spot inside his sandal so as to make a spark of fire, rather in the way that a fire can be started by rotating a fire drill in its base.

A DARK PACT

The other Maya groups now clamoured to Tohil to renew their fires. He agreed to supply the golden flame on condition that, at a future date, they would embrace him and allow themselves to be 'suckled by him'. It seemed a harmless request and the other Maya agreed, little realizing that the hidden meaning of being 'suckled' was that they would one day be sacrificed to the god by the Quiché and have their hearts torn from their chests in his honour.

Tohil instructed the Quiché to leave Tulan Zuyua. They were greatly saddened that they would not be in that wonderful city when the sun finally rose, but they obeyed the divine command.

The Quiché resumed their pilgrimage, visiting a place named Rock Lines, Wrinkled Sands and then the Great Abyss, where One Hunahpú and Seven Hunahpú had their ball court. They eventually arrived at a mountain named

Place of Advice in the Guatemalan highlands, where they halted and awaited the dawn once more.

At last their patience was rewarded. They saw the morning star rise and they rejoiced. They burned sacred incense to honour Tohil and the other gods. Then the sun climbed into the sky. His first appearance was unlike any other. He was seen in his full body length and gave off so much heat that he scorched the surface of the earth and turned the idols of the Quiché and the snakes, jaguars and pumas of the forest to stone.

One god named White Sparkstriker escaped the effect of the sun by hiding among the trees. Ever since, White Sparkstriker has been known as a divine gamekeeper, the patron of the wild beasts of the forest. The Quiché were filled with joy at the sunrise. Then they recalled their brothers among the Maya, the groups from whom they had been separated, and this caused sadness in their hearts.

The Quiché settled at this place and they built a fortified settlement. While they were there, they began to sacrifice humans to Tohil and their other principal gods, catching their victims on the mountain roads and offering their hearts and lifeblood to the stone idols of their gods in the jungle. Then they rolled the heads of the dead strangers on to the lonely roads. The local peoples attacked the Quiché stronghold, but they were foiled by a combination of Tohil's magic and the martial force of the Quiché.

Left: This Maya noble wearing body armour with large ear decorations and helmet is part of a ceramic lid from Copán.

Above: With Tohil's blessing, the Quiché established a great settlement and dynasty. At Copán, a sculpted bench panel marks the accession of King Yax-Pac. He called his nineteen predecessors back from the afterlife to honour his occupation of the throne.

In the aftermath of this triumph the great ancestors Jaguar Quitze, Jaguar Night, Mahucutah and True Jaguar removed themselves to the land of the dead. Their sons led another great pilgrimage to the east, in the course of which they met a being named Nacxit, who was a form of the Plumed Serpent. Nacxit honoured them with gifts and titles indicating their high rank and they returned to the highlands in great splendour.

VISIONS OF TRIUMPH AND DOWNFALL

metztitlan.

Stirring visions of future glory and ominous warnings of impending disaster are common occurrences in the mythical history of the Aztecs and the Maya. The visions clearly bear the sign of having been inserted into narratives or added to traditions at a later date in order to provide a justification or celebration of particular events. Some narratives, which celebrate Christianity or use Christian imagery, were added by Spanish priests or by converts to the new religion.

DIVINE PROPHECIES

One of the most celebrated of these visions was the god Huitzilopochtli's prophecy of greatness for the Aztec people. As the México/Aztecs made their southward voyage in search of a place to build a great settlement, they were driven on by the urging of Huitzilopochtli. According to chronicle accounts, he promised the México that they would conquer all the peoples of the world and be blessed with subjects beyond counting. The tribute from these subject tribes would be in gold, coral, emeralds,

Above: The key reason for Spanish success was that Cortés was able to persuade native soldiers to fight against the Aztecs.

multicoloured cotton and magnificent quetzal feathers, and would allow the conquerors to dress in utmost splendour. They would also receive abundant supplies of rich-tasting cacao beans. They would be kings of the world.

However, others knew, even if Huitzilopochtli did not, that the Aztecs' time was limited. According to Diego Durán's account of the tribe's search for Aztlán, their mythical place of origin, Huitzilopochtli's mother Coatlícue troubled her listeners by prophesying a terrible and humbling end for the empire.

A RESURRECTION

In the months before the arrival of the Spanish invaders under Hernán Cortés, there were many troubling omens and portents. Not the least of these was the return from the land of the dead of Moctezuma's sister Papantzin and her prophecy of the Spaniards' arrival.

Papantzin was a dearly loved princess who was married to the governor of Tlatelolco. When she died she was mourned by Moctezuma and the extended family and laid to rest in a tomb of magnificent splendour with many supplies for her journey through the land of the underworld lord Mictlantecuhtli. However, early the next morning she was seen back in Tenochtitlán, awaiting the dawn in the gardens of the *tlatoani*'s residence. There was no doubt in anyone's mind that she had been dead and her body prepared for the afterlife, yet here she was, returned to earth.

When she walked into her brother's chamber he needed the support of his aides to prevent him collapsing. He tried to speak, but she held up her hand to silence him and told her remarkable tale. In a steady voice she reported that after she died she went from Tenochtitlán to a wide valley flanked by tall mountains. She saw a river to the east and approached it because she knew that the underworld must lie beyond the water

Below: By the time of the Spanish Conquest, the war god Huitzilopochtli was worshipped mainly by members of the Aztec elite.

Above: Troubling portents of Aztec decline and ruin included a dazzling comet witnessed by Moctezuma himself.

crossing. However, a youth with fair skin and emerald eyes stopped her. He was wearing a long cloak fastened by a diamond brooch and had an upright cross marked on his forehead. From his back sprouted great wings that glowed with myriad colours.

The youth led her around the valley, in which lay the disjointed remnants of many human skeletons, and showed her a site nearby where men with cloven feet were building a house. On the river she saw several white-skinned sailors voyaging in boats, carrying banners and wearing battle helmets. Then the young man explained all that Papantzin had seen. It was not time, he said, for her to cross the river to the land of the dead. Her destiny lay back in Tenochtitlán where she would witness the arrival of the bearded men and take pleasure in the blessing of the god they worshipped. The bones she saw were the sad remains of her countrymen

who rejected the new religion and so died without the blessing of the new god. The house being erected was for the many Aztecs who would die at the hands of the newcomers. She must return and tell her people of the coming events; the joyous arrival of the word of God in Tenochtitlán.

Moctezuma was greatly troubled by his sister's tale. She was certainly no ghost, for having returned from the land of the dead, she remained in the *tlatoani*'s palace. When the white-skinned men arrived and began to preach the good news of their religion – as she had foretold – she was one of the first Aztecs to convert to Christianity.

MAYA FOREBODING

The *Books of Chilam Balam* – an unsettling mix of prophecy, mythology and history kept by members of the Yucatec Maya – also appeared to prophesy

Right: Very few surviving solid representations of Huitzilopochtli survive, so scholars must rely on codex images.

the Spaniards' victory. One of the books declared that 'bearded men of the east' would arrive with violence but carrying the 'signal of god', and that they would impose their will on the Maya. The natives would lose touch with their own culture and have to speak the language and wear the clothes of the invaders.

AN EMPIRE LOST, AN EMPIRE WON

Both native and Spanish accounts of the Conquest mythologize events in order to suggest that the Spanish victory was preordained and so explain the Aztecs' less than vigorous response to the conquistadors' arrival.

The accounts claim that many portents and omens troubled Moctezuma and his people in the years before the Spaniards' arrival. A full decade before Cortés and his troops arrived, they say, a brilliant comet lit the skies.

Tzocoztli, who was the earthly representative of Huitzilopochtli and who lived in his temple, was first to see it. He was greatly amazed and informed Moctezuma, who waited up the following night to witness it. When Moctezuma saw the celestial phenomenon, his blood ran cold, for Netzahualpilli, the sorcerer-visionary *tlatoani* of Texcoco, had warned him that the Aztec people would be overcome and their ruler would see 'signs in the sky' when the catastrophe was near.

In a frenzy, Moctezuma called Netzahualpilli into his presence to ask what the omen might mean. The sorcerer-prince could give him no comfort. He said that death was coming to sweep them all away, and that the Aztecs' land would be filled with misfortunes.

Below: An image from the Codex Tlaxcala *depicts a clash of warring cultures as Spaniards and Aztecs compete for glory.*

Above: A Codex Durán *image shows Moctezuma briefing ambassadors before sending them to greet the invaders.*

Neztahualpilli declared that he himself was to travel very soon to the land of the dead, for he wanted to escape the terrors that were to come. After he left, Moctezuma was plunged into a deep depression. When Moctezuma heard, shortly afterwards, that Netzahualpilli had indeed died, his spirits fell lower still and he expected the worst.

AN ATTEMPT TO AVERT DISASTER

Moctezuma now decided that it was not too late to make lavish sacrifices to the gods in the hope of averting the predicted calamities. He sent for a new and larger sacrificial stone, but when his men found a suitable rock they were unable to move it. Reinforcements were sent for and at last they were able to shift the great rock. After many hours of hauling they stopped for the night and slept very deeply after their labours. However, in the morning they were once again unable to move the great boulder. For many hours they tried until finally the stone spoke, in a grating voice that struck fear into the hearts of all who heard it. The labourers must abandon their efforts and go and tell their ruler that it was indeed too late. The stone

would not come to Tenochtitlán, it said, because it wanted to avoid the terrible events about to hit that city. Moctezuma was to be swept away, the stone said, because the ruler, in his vanity, had wanted to claim more adoration than the living God.

Moctezuma's men finally got the rock moving again and carried on hauling it towards Tenochtitlán. However, when they came to a wooden bridge across a canyon, the rock broke the timbers and tumbled into the river far below. Many of the rock-cutters, stonemasons and porters were killed. When Moctezuma heard the news, he ordered divers to look for the great boulder in the water, but they found nothing. Eventually they heard a report that the stone had miraculously returned to the place in which it had first been found. Moctezuma himself went to see the rock and was astounded to find it there. He returned to Tenochtitlán even more badly shaken than before.

UNSETTLING EVENTS

Terrifying occurrences came thick and fast. A fire exploded in the temple of the tribal god Huitzilopochtli, high on the Great Pyramid. Bystanders reported that it had been started by a lightning strike from a clear sky. On a still day waves arose on Lake Texcoco and threatened to engulf the city, while at night the people of Tenochtitlán were awakened by wailing voices, the shrill cries of supernatural women telling of impending death and the demise of the empire. One day it snowed in Tenochtitlán, which it had never done before. A man was seen with two heads. A pillar of fire arose from the land, sending a host of new stars up into the heavens and the volcano Popocatépetl began erupting after long years of quiet.

Below: With an interpreter at his left hand and armed men at his back, Cortés meets the ambassadors sent by Moctezuma.

As well as all these unsettling events, a year of great import was approaching. By tradition, when Quetzalcóatl departed to the east on a raft of snakes he prophesied that he would return in the same year as his birth (1-Reed). According to the Aztec calendar, 1-Reed could fall in 1363, 1467 and 1519.

Moctezuma was thrown into fearful confusion as the year approached and the omens piled up. He increasingly neglected his state duties and spent his time in the company of priests and shamans, seeking reassurance and advice on ways to win the gods' favour. It did not help that when he performed a rite involving a mirror-headed bird, he saw a vision of unfamiliar armed men bearing down on his lands.

Scholars have established that the prophecy of Quetzalcóatl's return in the year 1-Reed was not originally part of native accounts of the Topiltzin-Quetzalcóatl legend and that it appears

Above: Between mountains to the lake city – this schematic map shows the route taken by Cortés from the coast to Tenochtitlán.

Xaltelolco.

to have been added after the Conquest to explain away the Aztecs' defeat by the small Spanish invasion force. The argument was that the Aztec collapse was inevitable because it was part of a divine plan and, moreover, part of a repeating pattern of history set in motion in the hallowed era of the Toltecs. History moved inexorably on. The great Aztecs were humbled, not by the European invaders but by the great Mesoamerican gods who had granted life, land and maize to Moctezuma's distant ancestors and who now chose to withdraw their gifts.

PART 2

ART, ARCHITECTURE AND SOCIETY

The peoples of Mesoamerica knew that death was never far away. Their lands could be inhospitable – with smoking volcanoes able to deliver sudden destruction, fierce predators such as the kingly jaguar on the prowl, and the threat of drought or flooding to destroy the staple food of maize. The gods seemed angry: priests and people believed it necessary to propitiate them with human blood, through ritual sacrifice and wars often fought largely to provide sacrificial victims. Life was often short and hard, but it was lived with skill, inventiveness and a fierce joy. This part of the book reveals the secrets of survival in Mesoamerica: how people grew food, created trading networks, served the state and the army; how men and women married, raised their families and relaxed with music, dancing, gambling and the ball game; and how artisans made the first metal weapons, fashioned exquisite work in gold, silver and precious stones, painted their sublime wall paintings and cut their magnificent statues and stone pillars. This section also considers how the great cities of Mesoamerica – places of resonant fame such as Teotihuacán, Tikal and Tenochtitlán – were planned and built, and examines the intense religious life that inspired such a wealth of architectural, artistic and practical achievements.

These huge warrior figures once supported the temple roof on top of a pyramid sacred to Quetzalcóatl in the Toltec city of Tollán. At some point in the past they suffered from attack by vandals, but have since been reassembled and returned to their place of duty.

LOST CIVILIZATIONS

An expedition of 600-odd adventurers from the Spanish colony of Cuba dropped anchor off the beaches of San Juan de Ulúa, on the Gulf coast of Mexico, close to where the port of Veracruz would later be established. Under the command of Hernán Cortés, the men came ashore with their horses and exchanged gifts with the Totonac inhabitants of the region. About 300km (200 miles) inland, in the capital of the Aztec empire, the *tlatoani* (ruler) Moctezuma II received reports of the fair-skinned sailors, of the ships – which the trader-spies who were his informants saw as mountains floating on the sea – and of the Spanish cavalry or 'man-beasts'.

The landing, which took place on Good Friday, 21 April 1519, was not the first meeting between Europeans and the peoples of what became modern Mexico and Guatemala. There had been a number of brief encounters, including one in 1502

Below: Chacmools *received offerings of human hearts. This* chacmool *stood before the temple to Tláloc in Tenochtitlán.*

between Christopher Columbus and traders from the lands of the Aztecs' Maya neighbours. Yet this momentous day in 1519, which was the first step in an invasion that would bring the Aztec empire to its knees, inaugurated the first prolonged contact between two very different and essentially alien cultures: the European and the Mesoamerican.

PAINTERS AND METALWORKERS

Human activity in the region of Mexico and neighbouring Guatemala dates back 20,000 years or more, to the time when the first hunter-gatherers settled in the area. In the period between that time and the height of the Aztec empire, in the 14th–16th centuries AD, a number of civilizations rose and fell in the locality.

Historians apply the name 'Meso-america' both to these civilizations and to the area in which they arose. This ran southwards from the desert regions of north-central Mexico, then eastwards to include the Isthmus of Tehuantepec, the Yucatán peninsula, Guatemala, Honduras, western Nicaragua and north-western

Above: A carving of an enigmatic quetzal-butterfly adorns the elegant Quetzalpapálotl Palace in Teotihuacán.

Costa Rica. Among these civilizations were the Olmecs, carvers of magnificent stone monuments and creators of a vast trading network in the 2nd millennium BC; the Zapotecs, builders of a mountaintop settlement at Monte Albán in Oaxaca, who may have been the first people in the region to develop written communication c.500BC; and the builders of the mysterious monumental city of Teotihuacán in highland Mexico c.100BC–c.AD500, who excelled in trade, the manufacture of enigmatic masks and the painting of evocative murals.

Others included the Maya, who in the period c.AD250–900 raised magnificent temples and palaces in the jungles of Guatemala and in parts of eastern Mexico, and who continued to thrive until the Spanish Conquest; the militaristic Toltecs, who built their capital Tollán north-west of Teotihuacán c.AD950 and developed bloodthirsty religious rites involving human sacrifice; the Mixtecs, who succeeded the Zapotecs in Oaxaca and

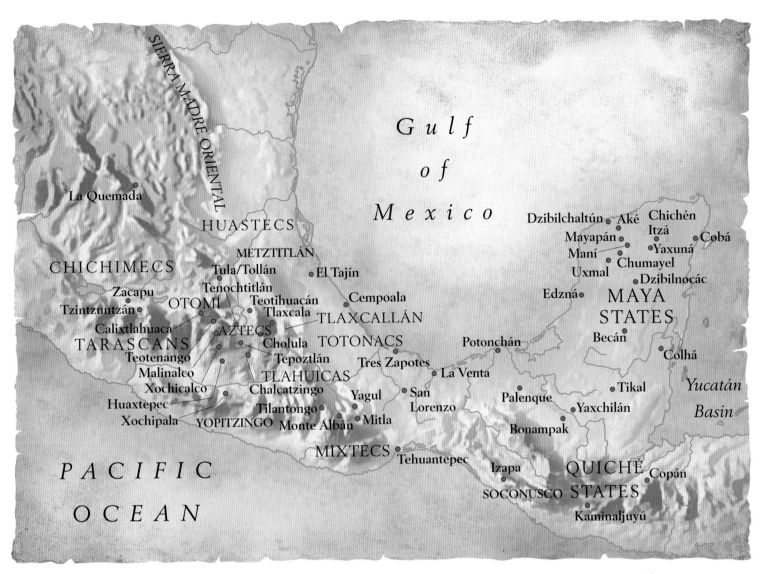

Map labels:

SIERRA MADRE ORIENTAL

Gulf
of
Mexico

La Quemada

HUASTECS

METZTITLÁN

CHICHIMECS · Tula/Tollán · El Tajín

Zacapu · Tenochtitlán
Tzintzuntzán · OTOMÍ · Teotihuacán · Cempoala
Calixtlahuaca · Tlaxcala · TLAXCALLÁN
TARASCANS · AZTECS · Cholula · TOTONACS · Potonchán
Teotenango · Tepoztlán
Malinalco · Tres Zapotes · La Venta
Xochicalco · TLAHUICAS · San
Chalcatzingo · Yagul · Lorenzo · Palenque
Huaxtepec · Tilantongo · Yaxchilán
Xochipala · YOPITZINGO · Monte Albán · Mitla · Bonampak
MIXTECS · Tehuantepec
Izapa
SOCONUSCO · Kaminaljuyú

Dzibilchaltún · Aké · Chichén
Mayapán · Itzá · Cobá
Maní · Yaxuná
Uxmal · Chumayel
Edzná · Dzibilnocác
MAYA
STATES
Becán
Colhá
Tikal
Yucatán
Basin
QUICHÉ · Copán
STATES

PACIFIC
OCEAN

---

who excelled in metalworking and hand-painted screenfold books; the Tarascans of Michoacán in western Mexico, highly skilled metalworkers who forged an empire after 1200; and the México, or Aztecs, who in the years after founding their capital of Tenochtitlán in 1325 built a vast empire encompassing 150,000sq km (58,000sq miles).

ALIEN CULTURES

Both the Mesoamericans and the Spanish invaders found plenty to marvel at and to disapprove of in the behaviour of their opponents. For example, it would appear that the Mesoamericans were shocked by the poor hygiene of the Spaniards. The conquistadors' accounts of the invasion tell of many occasions on which the locals doused them with incense. The invaders took this as a mark of respect, but historians suspect that the nobles of Tenochtitlán, who kept themselves very

Above: Mesoamerican cultural sites ranged over the years from San Lorenzo to Tenochtitlán and over miles from Tikal to La Quemada.

clean, were attempting to keep the stench of the unwashed soldiers at bay. On the other hand, the Spanish conquistadors were both attracted and repelled by what they found in Tenochtitlán when, after marching inland, allying with locals in Tlaxcala and defeating the lords of Cholula, they entered the Aztec capital on 7 November 1519.

The conquistadors were captivated by the beauty of the vast city laid out on islands in Lake Texcoco, by the elegance of the palaces and gardens inhabited by the ruler and nobility and by the astonishing range of goods for sale in the city's vast

Right: Aztec pilgrims took this greenstone mask from Teotihuacán and offered it in the Templo Mayor, Tenochtitlán.

market. However, they were equally shocked by the temples and ceremonial areas laid out to celebrate rites of human sacrifice, by the sight of priests with blood-matted hair and smoke-blackened skin, by images of Aztec gods and by blood-spattered reclining stone figures known as *chacmools* into which the still-warm hearts of sacrificial victims were placed.

CULTURE CLASH

The Spanish did encounter certain elements familiar from their own European culture. As in Europe, the warriors' achievements were lauded and military might enforced political power, networks of trade and tribute were vibrant and a strong sense of the sacred informed all parts of life. However, other elements of Mesoamerican civilization were bafflingly strange or broke European taboos. For example, while the conquistadors were certainly not unfamiliar with torture and slaughter, nor squeamish about the sight of blood or even the display of prisoners' remains, they were unprepared for the Aztecs' ritual celebration of slaughter, in which human hearts were torn out as a key element of public religious ritual. They were shocked by the vast numbers of victims sacrificed and by the gods and goddesses honoured. They were horrified to learn that certain Aztec religious rites included cannibalism. Nobles and priests shared the flesh of victims who had earlier been sacrificed on the steps before the temple and whose hearts were displayed on the *chacmool*.

This cannibalistic rite was informed by the Aztecs' understanding that a sacrificial victim impersonated and finally became the god to whom he was sacrificed. The elite members of Aztec society admitted to the feast were thus able to share in the divine essence. Aztec worshippers frequently understood several distinct performers of and elements in ritual to share the identity of a god or goddess. This included priests and victims dressed in honour of deities as well as natural elements used in dedication or worship. At the blessing of a new aqueduct carrying water into Tenochtitlán during the reign of the Aztec *tlatoani* (ruler) Ahuítzotl (1486–1502), priests, dressed in the jade skirt associated with the water goddess Chalchiúhtlicue, offered incense and precious turquoise (a stone linked to the goddess) as the aqueduct was opened and the waters ran for the first time. The goddess, the priests

dressed as the goddess, the turquoise and the water itself were all understood to be one in a concept typical of Mesoamericans but different to Western thought.

CYCLES OF TIME

Another key element of Mesoamerican culture that was immediately alien to the Europeans was the idea that the gods made time move in cycles. The Aztecs believed that the current world was the fifth in a succession of creations and that, within the current world age, events were destined to be repeated in a way which followed large, cyclical patterns.

Mesoamericans had a very deep respect for the past. In both Aztec and Maya lands, worshippers made respectful journeys to the great cities built by their ancestors such as Teotihuacán and Tollán for the Aztecs and Tikal and Chichén Itzá for the Maya. Indeed, the desire to recreate in the present the glories of the past was one of the driving forces behind the Aztec empire. The Aztecs wanted to honour the achievements of the Toltec founders of Tollán. They were also keen to celebrate the sacred city of Teotihuacán, which they viewed as the birthplace of the gods. Here, according to Aztec religious narrative, on the very ground and before the very buildings still visible today, the gods had gathered in the primordial past to create the sun and moon and set them in motion in the sky through offering their own divine blood.

Aztec builders and stonemasons made reverent use of architectural and sculptural styles from these ancient cities in creating the sacred precinct of Tenochtitlán. Aztec

Above: In observatories such as the Caracol at Chichén Itzá, the patterns of the night sky were interpreted.

pilgrims took masks and other sacred items from graves in Teotihuacán and Tollán to reuse them in their own temple offerings in Tenochtitlán. Aztec priests and worshippers enthusiastically practised the rituals of human sacrifice which (although they had ancient beginnings in the Mesoamerican past) had been decisively escalated by the honoured Toltecs.

Below: Maya sculptors reached great heights of artistic expression. This head represents King Pacal of Palenque in middle age.

At Chichén Itzá in northern Yucatán, a group of Maya, also influenced by the Toltecs, similarly used *chacmools*, arranged the skulls of victims on skull racks and held vast public rites of human sacrifice.

DUALITY AND CHANGE

The Mesoamericans' understanding that time moved in cycles governed by the gods was balanced by an acute awareness of patterns of change and structures of duality. The Aztecs and the Maya understood the universe to be structured according to a divinely ordained duality: life and death, day and night, light and darkness, wet and dry, the celestial realm and the underworld realm all balanced one another. They also tended to succeed one another. Day was followed by night, the rainy season alternated with the dry season, life was followed by death – and then by new life. A king's death was the prelude to his voyage to the underworld, land of the dead, and followed by his ascent to the celestial realm. However, the gods could break this sacred pattern of alternation at any time.

Left: Sacred symbols in nature. This Maya vase from the Sula valley, Honduras, shows a divine monkey-spider and a bird-man.

Each night, the sun took the form of a jaguar and had to fight its way through the underworld during the hours of darkness before it could be reborn in the eastern sky. A day might come on which the gods withdrew their favour and the sun did not rise.

Within the complex patterns of years created by Mesoamericans' use of twin 260-day and 365-day calendars, the period of 52 solar years had great sacred significance. It measured the time that elapsed before a day in the 260-day calendar would coincide with a day in the 365-day calendar. The end of a 52-year cycle was also viewed as a time of particular danger, when the gods might be particularly inclined to break the patterns of succession and bring the world to an end. Priests ensured that the sacred calendars of ritual were observed with particular care at such times of risk.

FATE AND FATALISM

Across Mesoamerica, astronomer-priests made observations of the cycles of planets and movements of stars, while shaman-priests interpreted the ritual calendars and performed rites of divination using psychotrophic substances.

Those who relied on the statements of these experts believed that the diviners had the power to identify sacred influences on human activity in the

Above: Serpent imagery abounds in this Mixtec representation of water goddess Chalchiúhtlicue. The snake was associated with water, fertility and the earth.

patterns of the sky and in the cycles of time. Some historians argue that beliefs in divination, the power of omens and the inevitability of time's repeating patterns made Mesoamericans more fatalistic than they would otherwise have been when faced with a challenge.

The so-called 'Maya collapse' – when in the 9th and 10th centuries AD a series of powerful cities across Guatemala stopped erecting dated monuments to the glory of their kings and fell into rapid decline – had many causes, principally environmental degradation, but was possibly also encouraged by a fatalistic belief among some Maya that the decline could be predicted from the patterns of time, that, by the gods' choice, these events mirrored others many centuries earlier and so were not worth resisting.

Equally, there were many practical causes for the defeat of the mighty Aztec empire by a small band of Spanish invaders fighting in alliance with local peoples, but historical accounts reveal that Aztec leaders were aware that the omens were bad and appeared to prophesy their downfall. Some in Tenochtitlán thought Cortés was destined for victory, and some Aztecs even believed that Cortés was the Mesoamerican god Quetzalcóatl making a long-promised return to claim his rightful inheritance in Tenochtitlán.

DISCOVERING THE PAST

Mesoamericans themselves were Central America's first archaeologists. The Aztecs and Maya had a deep reverence for their own shared past and the achievements of their forebears, and investigated the evocative ruins of once majestic cities such as Tollán, Teotihuacán and Tikal.

Both Maya and Aztecs engaged with the ruined cities as religious centres rather than as historical sites. They came to satisfy a religious and cultural yearning to touch and be touched by the past. They saw nothing wrong in entering monuments and tombs to gather funerary masks and golden grave offerings for their own religious use, or in adding offerings of their own to a temple cache.

The Aztecs carried artefacts back from Teotihuacán and Tula to Tenochtitlán for use as temple offerings in the great Templo Mayor, where later generations of archaeologists would discover them. In Maya lands, pilgrims from Chichén Itzá may have travelled to the ruins of Tikal to perform religious ceremonies; in later times both Uxmal and Chichén Itzá were pilgrimage sites. The Aztecs also carried out sacrifices and sacred rites at the city of Teotihuacán.

The Spanish invaders of the early 16th century treated the great architectural achievements of Mesoamerica with scant respect. They set out to destroy the temples and religious statuary of the Aztecs, which they believed to be touched by evil. They erected the capital of their colony, New Spain, atop the rubble and shattered remnants of the Aztecs' great metropolis of Tenochtitlán.

Left: This view of the archway at Labná is by English artist Frederick Catherwood who, with American author John L. Stephens, was a pioneer of Maya exploration in the 1830s–40s. It is taken from their 1841 book on Maya ruins.

WONDERS IN THE JUNGLE

The first organized archaeological investigation of Mesoamerican ruins took place in the 17th century. A Mexican Jesuit priest called Carlos de Siguenza y Gongora (1645–1700) led a dig at Teotihuacán which mainly focused on the Pyramid of the Moon, as part of a lifelong attempt to research and write a history of ancient Mexico.

The 18th century saw the modern rediscovery of important Mesoamerican relics and sites, notably of Maya cities that had been abandoned and overgrown by tropical jungle. Palenque, in the densely forested foothills of the Chiapas mountains and overlooking the coastal plain that stretches 128km (80 miles) to the Gulf of Mexico, was rediscovered in 1746 by Padre Antonio Solis.

The first excavation of the Palenque site, which began in May 1786, was carried out by Spanish artillery captain Don Antonio del Río, who had orders from King Carlos III of Spain to search for gold and other valuables. Del Río left with a stucco head, the carved leg of a throne and other pieces of decorative carving, which he sent to Spain by way of Guatemala. Many years later, the captain's report of his excavations was published in English in London in 1822 with copies of del Río's sketches reproduced as lithographs by Johann-Friedrich Maximilien von Waldeck. The book generated interest in further investigation of Maya cities. It was followed by the publication in Paris in 1834 of *Antiquités Mexcaines*, the account of an 1805–6 visit to Palenque by Frenchman Guillaume Dupaix in the company of Mexican artist Luciano Castañeda. Waldeck himself visited the site in 1821 and published his own meticulously rendered images in 1865.

GODDESS IN THE EARTH
An important discovery had occurred at the site of the former Aztec capital Tenochtitlán in 1790. Workmen laying paving stones discovered a 2.5 metre (8ft)-tall stone statue of the Aztec earth

Above: Désiré Charnay, first to conduct archaeological excavations at Tula, made this engraving of Palenque in 1887.

goddess Coatlícue, together with a 3.6 metre (almost 12ft) diameter carved stone monument that commemorated the five suns or world ages of Aztec belief (later known as the Sun Stone). The finds were the first evidence of the wealth of archaeological remains that lay directly beneath the surface of Mexico City. The Sun Stone was placed on display on one of the towers of the city's Metropolitan Cathedral, while the statue of Coatlícue was given to the Royal and Pontifical University of Mexico.

THE TREASURES OF THE JUNGLE
In the 19th century, many of the great abandoned cities of the Maya civilization were rediscovered among dense jungle foliage and explored. An important catalyst for the surge of interest in central American ruins was the publication in 1841 of the two-volume *Incidents of Travel in Central America, Chiapas and Yucatán* by American traveller John Lloyd Stephens (1805–52). This work was based on an 1839–40 voyage to Honduras, Guatemala and Mexico, which was undertaken by Stephens in the

Left: This romanticized view of the Temple of the Cross, at Palenque, was made by Johann-Friedrich Maximilien von Waldeck.

company of English architect and artist Frederick Catherwood (1799–1854). Stephens and Catherwood visited the magnificent site of Copán, which Stephens was able to buy for $50, discovered Quiriguá and also examined Palenque and Uxmal. On a second voyage in 1841–2, the two men explored sites including Chichén Itzá, Cozumel, Tulum, Dzilam, Izamal and Ake. They published another two-volume survey, *Incidents of Travel in Yucatán*, in 1843. Sites they publicized include Copán, Palenque, Chichén Itzá, Tulum, Uxmal and Quiriguá.

TOWERS AMONG THE TREES

The remains of the great Classic Period Maya city of Tikal, in the northern part of the Petén region of Guatemala, were also rediscovered in the mid-19th century. They were first noticed by a local gum-sapper named Ambrosio Tut, who saw the roofcombs of the city's soaring pyramid temples while working at the top of a sapodilla tree.

Tut reported the finding to Modesto Méndez, Governor-Magistrate of the Petén region, and a six-day exploratory expedition was despatched by the Guatemalan government under Méndez and Tut in 1848. Méndez's report, with fanciful images by artist Eusebio Lara, was published that year in the Guatemalan newspaper *La Gaceta* and in 1853 in the magazine of the Berlin Academy of Sciences.

Significant later 19th-century expeditions to the site included that of the Swiss botanist Gustave Bernoulli, who removed carved sapodilla-wood lintels from Temples I and IV and carried them off to the Museum für Völkerkunde in Basel. They also included that of the English archaeologist-explorer Sir Alfred Percival Maudslay (1850–1931), who visited in 1881 and 1882. Using recently invented camera equipment, Sir Alfred took the earliest photographs of the city of Tikal's magnificent monuments.

Above: This Catherwood engraving, from the 1841 Incidents of Travel in Central America, Chiapas and Yucatán, *is of the partly overgrown Castillo in Chichén Itzá.*

Other cities were being rediscovered in the jungle. In 1882, Sir Alfred led an official Guatemalan government expedition to a major but little known settlement on the Usumacinta river. Then known as Macanche, the riverbank city was later renamed Yaxchilán.

With official approval, Sir Alfred removed the superbly carved lintels from Yaxchilán to prevent their loss to less scrupulous visitors. In the same year, the French explorer and archaeologist Désiré Charnay visited and photographed the site. At Copán, George Gordon of Harvard University's Peabody Museum led a three-year investigation in 1891–4.

In the 1880s, Désiré Charnay also conducted the first archaeological dig at the site identified as the capital of the Toltecs, near the modern town of Tula in Hidalgo State, Mexico. In 1873, Antonio García Cubas, a member of the Mexican Society of Geography and History, had published a written description of the site. Charnay went on to excavate two houses and the structure known as the Adoratorio, in the middle of the main square. Later archaeologists were less than impressed by his unsubtle methods. These included the use of dynamite for clearance. Charnay did, however, also take some of the earliest photographs of ancient Mesoamerican ruins. He also experimented with papier-mâché to make impressions of ancient hieroglyphs.

Below: Beneath ground level in modern Mexico City archaeologists uncover Aztec remains. This is part of the Templo Mayor.

PAINSTAKING EXCAVATIONS

Throughout the 20th century, extensive and painstaking archaeological programmes gradually uncovered more and more evidence of how Mesoamericans lived, fought and worshipped.

CARNEGIE EXCAVATIONS

A pioneering archaeological project at Chichén Itzá in north-central Yucatán was led by Sylvanus Morley of the Carnegie Institution, Washington DC, for 20 years from 1924. The project excavated and restored many buildings, in the process discovering beneath them several almost intact constructions. These provided important evidence of the typical Mesoamerican building practice in which new structures were erected on top of their predecessors on sites already sanctified by ritual use. The work led to the scholarly division of Chichén Itzá's buildings into two groups. Those in the local 'Puuc style' from the end of the Classic Period and those exhibiting a Toltec-Mexican influence in the first years of the Postclassic Period.

The Carnegie Institution also conducted archaeological investigation at Uaxactún, 40km (25 miles) north of Tikal, in the years 1926–37. From the calendrical carvings, ceramic remains and buildings at Uaxactún, the Carnegie scholars plotted a chronology of cultural development for the region in the Classic Period that is still widely used by archaeologists today.

NEW MAP OF AN ANCIENT CITY

At Tikal, the combined efforts of Teobert Maler, Alfred Tozzer and R.E. Merwin led to the publication by Tozzer and Merwin of the first map of the site in 1911. Sylvanus Morley made a detailed study of Tikal's monuments and inscriptions on four visits in 1914, 1921, 1922 and 1928, while in 1926, Edwin Shook of the Carnegie Institution found a previously undiscovered group of buildings (now known as Group H) and two *sacbeob* or sacred causeways (now named in honour

Above: A corner of one of the painted rooms at Bonampak depicts the members of the royal court enjoying a lavish feast.

of Maudslay and Maler). Shook became the first field director of a major 14-year survey, the Tikal Project, which was conducted by the University Museum of Pennsylvania University 1956–70.

Major programmes were also carried out at Tula. In the 1930s, the work of ethnologist Wigberto Jimenez Moreno established that the site excavated by the Frenchman Désiré Charnay in the 19th

century was the Toltecs' celebrated city, known also as Tollán. Subsequently, Jorge Acosta of the Mexican National Institute of Anthropology and History (INAH) led a 20-year archaeological programme at Tula in 1940–60, during which his teams

investigated and partly restored one of the site's ball courts (now known as Ball Court 1), Temples B and C, the Coatepantli and the Palacio de Quetzalcóatl. Based on pottery remains, Acosta also worked out a chronology of events and occupying groups for the site. His work was extended through joint excavations by the University of Missouri, Columbia (UMC), under Richard Diehl and an INAH team under Eduardo Matos Moctezuma in 1966–76.

The second INAH team conducted a major survey of the surrounding land and restored a second ball court. Together with that of the UMC, their work established that Tula was a large and lively city, at its peak and that, for a period, it was Mesoamerica's prime power.

PAINTED WALLS
About 30km (18 miles) to the south of Yaxchilán, in the densely forested valley of the Río Lacanha in Chiapas state, a Maya site previously known only to locals was revealed to the wider world in 1946. American photographer Giles Healey was on a field trip looking for picturesque ruins when his guides led him to a small settlement they called Bonampak ('Painted Walls'). Healey found a three-roomed building containing vivid, brightly coloured images of court life in a Maya

Above: The ball court at Palenque lies to the north-east of the imposing Palace and the celebrated Temple of Inscriptions.

city during the 8th century AD. His report and pictures naturally provoked wide interest and the Carnegie Institute organized an archaeological programme at the site, which also contains an acropolis, a large plaza and a number of stelae. As at some other major Maya sites such as Palenque, there are buildings still unexcavated in the surrounding forest.

PALENQUE'S STEPPED PYRAMID
At Palenque, Sylvanus Morley, Oliver LaFarge, Franz Blom and Edward Seler all carried out work in the early part of the 20th century. In 1952, Mexican architect Alberto Ruz Lhuillier discovered the magnificent royal tomb of King Pacal, Palenque's ruler in the 7th–8th

centuries AD, in a crypt beneath the Temple of Inscriptions. Historians had believed that Maya stepped pyramids were used only as temple platforms; that is, to lift their temples above other buildings; Lhuiller's find was the first indication that the pyramids were in some places built primarily as royal funerary monuments.

TENOCHTITLÁN
In the centre of what was once Tenochtitlán, a major excavation of the Aztecs' great temple, the Templo Mayor, began in 1978. The programme was inspired by a chance find, when an electrical company worker digging in central Mexico City uncovered part of a clearly remarkable sculpture. The team of archaeologists who took over to clear away debris uncovered a vast monolith, 3.25m (10ft) in diameter, representing the dismembered form of the goddess Coyolxauhqui who, in Aztec creation narrative, was cut up by her brother Huitzilopochtli in the first moments of his life.

Excavation revealed that the Aztecs built the Templo Mayor in layers, each new construction enclosing an earlier structure. Archaeologists uncovered the successive constructions back to c.1390, showing the twin shrines to rain god Tláloc and Lord Huitzilopochtli.

Left: The Group of the Thousand Columns is one of the imposing structures in Chichén Itzá reflecting later, Toltec, influence.

TRANSLATING AN ANCIENT WRITING

The first modern visitors to Maya sites such as Yaxchilán or Copán were enthralled by tall stelae elegantly carved with inscriptions in artistically arranged picture glyphs. Historians were also deeply intrigued by the writing in four surviving Maya codices and by a list of glyphs presented as the 'Maya alphabet' by Bishop Diego de Landa in his 16th-century work, *Relacion de las Cosas de Yucatán*. Historians were frustrated that they could not read this ancient writing and so glean invaluable information about the Maya way of life.

DECIPHERING THE PAST

In the years up to the 1950s, linguists made slow but steady progress in interpreting Maya writing. Figures such as Léon de Rosny, Ernst Förstemann, Sylvanus Morley and J. Eric Thompson catalogued the glyphs and successfully identified some. Förstemann and Rosny, for example, translated the glyphs for 'north', 'south', 'east', 'west', 'zero' and 'twenty'. However, the entire world of Maya scholarship laboured under two misconceptions. The scholars wrongly believed that the inscriptions on Maya stelae contained religious and astronomical information, but no historical facts. Historians were also mistaken in their belief that the glyphs were logographic. The pictures represented whole words or ideas and did not stand for spoken sounds.

The first misconception was removed by the work of Heinrich Berlin and Tatiana Proskouriakoff in the 1950s. Berlin, a German-Mexican scholar, first identified an emblem glyph specific to each of several Maya sites and suggested that it recorded the place name or the name of the ruling dynasty. Proskouriakoff, a Russian-American expert on Maya art, then showed that carved inscriptions on stelae at Piedras Negras celebrated the birth, accession to the throne and other life events of a series of rulers of that city. In her work on Piedras Negras and then Yaxchilán, she identified glyphs for 'was born', 'acceded to throne', 'captor', 'captured' and 'died'.

Above: Stela 6 from Piedras Negras shows the king seated cross-legged in a recess with glyphs dating the monument to AD687.

The second misconception was laid to rest, also in the 1950s, by the Soviet linguist Yuri V. Knorosov, who demonstrated that, alongside their function as logograms, the glyphs had a 'phonetic' element; they represented spoken sounds. Working with the de Landa 'alphabet', Knorosov saw that many of the elements of the list were not letters but syllables combining a consonant and a vowel. There were no signs for a single consonant. When writing a word with the pattern consonant-vowel-consonant, he argued, a Maya scribe would use two of the combined signs, consonant-vowel plus consonant-vowel. The vowel in the second sign would match that in the first, but would be read as silent. For example, to write the word *cutz* ('turkey'), a scribe

Left: 'Emblem glyphs' specific to particular cities were identified by Heinrich Berlin in 1958. The symbols identifying the cities were written with a pair of affixes (appended signs) meaning 'holy king of'.

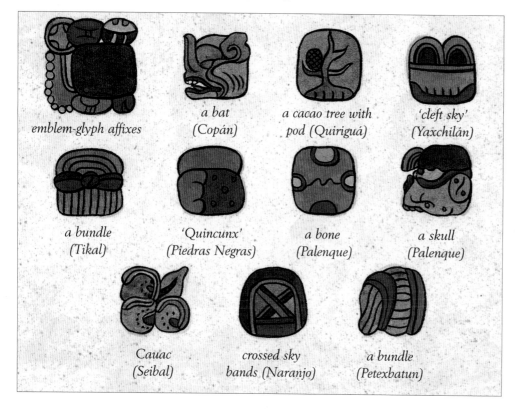

emblem-glyph affixes

a bat
(Copán)

a cacao tree with
pod (Quiriguá)

'cleft sky'
(Yaxchilán)

a bundle
(Tikal)

'Quincunx'
(Piedras Negras)

a bone
(Palenque)

a skull
(Palenque)

Cauac
(Seibal)

crossed sky
bands (Naranjo)

a bundle
(Petexbatun)

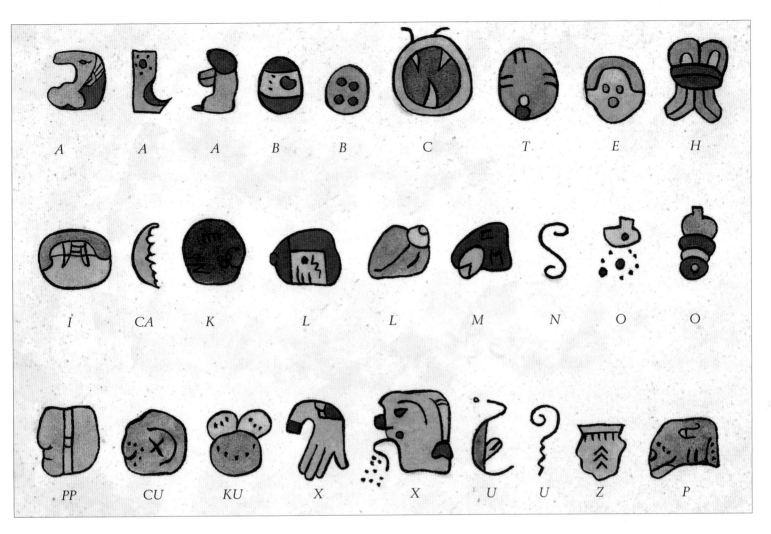

A	A	A	B	B	C	T	E	H

I	CA	K	L	L	M	N	O	O

PP	CU	KU	X	X	U	U	Z	P

Above: Bishop Diego de Landa's 'alphabet' of Maya writing was dismissed by scholars until linguist Yuri Knorosov showed that it was a list of syllables rather than an 'abc'.

Left: In a detail from Piedras Negras Stela 40, an individual performs a sacred rite of scattering in honour of an ancestor.

would write the signs *cu* and *tzu*. The two *U*s would agree, and the word would be read 'cutz' (with the last u silent.) The idea that the vowels would agree was dubbed 'synharmony' by Knorosov.

Knorosov's theory provoked outrage among many Maya scholars, but has proved to be largely correct. As Knorosov argued, Maya script contains both logographs and phonetic elements. The latest thinking is that the script, which was in use for more than 1,500 years, was originally mainly logosyllabic (pictures stood for syllables or words), but over time increasingly included more phonetic elements. However, further progress in deciphering Maya script has partially undermined Knorosov's idea of synharmony. When words were spelled phonetically, they often did not have the matching vowels that his theory suggested they should.

REINTERPRETATIONS

Historians have continued to make breakthroughs in interpreting glyphs, often with important implications for our understanding of the Maya. In 1979, Peter Matthews showed that an ear spool found at Altun Ha in Belize was labelled *u tup* ('his ear spool') with the name of the owner. Several other writers have since shown that the practice Matthews termed 'name tagging' was used by the Maya on bowls, plates and carved bones.

David Stuart and Stephen Houston have identified a glyph used to describe the spirit familiar or companion that Mesoamericans believed accompanied each of us. The discovery has led to the reinterpetation of many scenes on Maya pots or stelae, where figures once thought to be gods or rulers can now be positively identified as spirit familiars.

Linguistic work has also revealed that the Maya referred to stelae as 'stone trees' and to the objects historians generally label 'altars' as 'stone thrones'.

THE MESOAMERICAN WORLD

In a time before time, Huitzilopochtli, tribal god of the México/Aztecs, sprang from his mother fully armed to defend her against his jealous siblings on the sacred heights of Mount Coatepetl. In the mature years of the fifth sun or world age of the Aztecs, in the ceremonial precinct of the imperial capital Tenochtitlán, the great mass of the Templo Mayor was celebrated as a recreation of the mountain where the tribal god was born and was called Coatepetl or Coatepec. Both Aztec and Maya architects intended their temple-platforms to represent sacred mountains as part of a wider desire to honour and recreate in their cities and social organization the holy patterns of the natural world.

Mesoamericans saw divine meaning threaded through all natural phenomena. Theirs was a sacred universe, whose rules were established in the 'holy time' of religious narrative. They performed sacrificial ritual in obedience to demands established in this holy time, as a way of honouring the creative sacrifice of the gods.

This survey of the Mesoamerican world begins with a look at its terrains and wildlife, then examines the spread of human settlement across Middle America. It then proceeds to describe the vibrant trade that fuelled much of this expansion and to investigate Mesoamerican patterns of daily life and work, before concluding with a description of the ways in which Mesoamericans celebrated the sacred patterns of their universe in religious life and culture.

Maya warriors attack a village in Yucatán. As among the Aztecs, successful warriors were rewarded with social prestige and preferential treatment in the afterlife.

TIMELINE: ART AND ARCHITECTURE OF MESOAMERICA

PRECLASSIC PERIOD TO AD250

Above: Olmec stone heads may have been used in rites honouring royal ancestors.

3114BC The start date of the Maya Long Count dating system is equivalent to 13 August 3114BC.

2300BC Artist at Tlapacoya makes the oldest surviving ceramic figurine.

1400BC Oldest known ball court constructed at Paso de la Amada, Chiapas.

*c.*1400BC Potters in highland Mexico, fashion many ceramic figurines, probably for use as grave offerings.

1250–900BC Olmecs lay out pyramids and courts in their holy town of San Lorenzo.

1200BC Coapexco becomes a centre for the growing trade in obsidian.

1100BC Olmec influence seen in rock carvings at the trading centre of Chalcatzingo.

800–500BC Olmec stone heads set up in La Venta. Maya settlers build the pyramid Mound 30a at Izapa.

500BC The Zapotec city of Monte Albán is established in Oaxaca.

300BC Zapotec builders construct the main plaza of Monte Albán.

250BC Building of the North Acropolis begins at Tikal.

*c.*200BC Carvings of war prisoners added to Building L at Monte Albán.

200BC–AD300 Building J, an astronomical observatory and military conquest monument built at Monte Albán.

150BC–AD150 Vast El Tigre monument built in the Maya city of El Mirador.

100BC–AD150 Teotihuacán established as a sacred city and a major population centre. The Pyramid of the Sun is built and the Street of the Dead laid out.

31BC Stela C at Trez Zapotes, on the Mexican Gulf Coast, is carved with a date in the Maya Long Count equivalent to 3 September 31BC.

AD36 Stela 1 at El Baúl, Guatemala, is carved with a standing figure and the date AD36.

AD100 A ball court is built at Monte Albán.

AD156 Stela 1 at La Mojarra in Veracruz is carved with a standing figure and the dates AD143 and AD156.

*c.*AD200 The *talud-tablero* architectural feature is used on the Temple of the Feathered Serpent in Teotihuacán's Citadel area.

*c.*AD250 Artists decorate Teotihuacán temples with wall paintings.

C.AD250–900 CLASSIC PERIOD

Above: Tikal was a major city by AD300 and at its zenith in the 8th century AD.

AD300 The Zapotecs of Monte Albán establish the nearby settlement of Mitla, which contains many tombs. They call it Lyobaa ('Site of Burials').

AD400 Teotihuacáno influence is seen at the Maya site of Kaminaljuyú, where buildings begin to use the *talud-tablero* architectural feature.

AD426 The first ritual buildings are erected at Copán in the reign of King Yax Kuk Mo' (*r.* AD426–37).

AD647 King Pacal (*r.* AD615–83) begins a major building programme at the city of Palenque, with the construction of the Olvidado temple ('Unnoticed Shrine') to the west of the main plaza.

AD650 Potters at Remojadas and other sites in Veracruz produce ceramic figures for use in religious ritual.

AD692 At Palenque the temples of the Cross Group are dedicated.

*c.*AD700 El Tajín, in Veracruz, contains 12 ball courts and the remarkable Pyramid of the Niches, which contains 365 openings, one for each day of the solar year.

C.AD250–900 CLASSIC PERIOD

AD726 In Yaxchilán Lord Shield Jaguar (*r.* AD681–742) dedicates Temple 23 (Queen's House) to his wife, Lady Xoc.

AD734 Tikal's King Ah Cacau (*r.* AD682–734) buried beneath Temple I, which he built as his funerary monument.

AD738 King 18-Rabbit (*r.* AD695–78) completes building work on the Great Ball Court at Copán.

AD749 Copán's King Smoke Shell (*r.* AD749–763) completes the Hieroglyphic Stairway.

*c.*AD750 Builders erect Tikal's Temple VI (Temple of the Inscriptions) and the city's tallest building, Temple IV – 70m (230ft) tall.

*c.*AD750 Artists at Cacaxtla paint a series of magnificent murals.

AD775 At Copán, King Yax Pac (*r.* AD763–820) dedicates the monument known as Altar Q, which bears portraits of all 16 kings of the dynasty founded by Yax Kuk Mo'.

*c.*AD800 Tula/Tollán is laid out, like Teotihuacán, on a grid pattern.

*c.*AD900 Builders at Chichén Itzá erect the Caracol, perhaps as a temple to the wind god, but more likely as an astronomical observatory.

*c.*AD900 The Pyramid of the Feathered Serpent is built at Xochicalco.

POSTCLASSIC AND MODERN PERIODS AD900–2005

AD909 Monument 101 at Toniná is last carving with date in the Maya Long Count.

*c.*1230 The *Grolier Codex*, a calendar of the cycles of the planet Venus, is written.

*c.*1325 The México/Aztecs build the Templo Mayor in Tenochtitlán.

*c.*1345 The *Dresden Codex* is made.

*c.*1390 A larger pyramid-temple is constructed over the original Templo Mayor.

1431 The México/Aztecs build a third and much larger version of the Templo Mayor on the same site in Tenochtitlán.

1450–1500 A series of fine murals are painted in the Maya city of Tulum.

*c.*1450 The *Paris Codex* is compiled, perhaps in the Maya city of Mayapán.

1469 México/Aztec artisans carve a stone image of Coyolxauhqui to place at the foot of a staircase on the western face of the Templo Mayor pyramid.

22 Aug 1700 Death of Carlos de Siguenza y Gongora, Jesuit priest, pioneering historian and the first to lead archaeological investigations at Teotihuacán.

1746 Ruins of Palenque discovered.

May 1786 First archaeological investigations at Palenque.

1840 John Lloyd Stephens finds Quiriguá.

1848 First expedition to explore Tikal.

1853 Report on Tikal by Modesto Méndez published by Berlin Academy of Science.

Above: The first archaeological investigations at Palenque were in 1786.

1882 Sir Alfred Maudslay leads an official exploration of Yaxchilán.

1924–44 The Carnegie Institution (Washington DC) carries out an archaeological programme at Chichén Itzá.

1940–60 Acosta leads dig at Tula/Tollán.

1946 Giles Healey discovers Bonampak.

1971 Ancient sacred cave found beneath Pyramid of the Sun, Teotihuacán.

1978 Electrical worker discovers vast carving of Coyolxauhqui in Mexico City.

1997 'Codex' murals found at Mayapán.

1998 Archaeologists discover the oldest known Mesoamerican ball court at Paso de la Amada, Chiapas, *c.*1400BC.

2002 Guatemalan Maya jade artefacts found in an elite ceremonial burial at Teotihuacán's Pyramid of the Moon.

2003 Finds at San Andrés suggest the Olmec used a logographic writing system.

CHAPTER 13

LAND OF DANGER AND REWARD

The Aztecs and Maya made their home in an unstable and unpredictable physical environment. They feared the sudden shiftings of the 'earth monster' when earthquakes struck. They dreaded the onset of drought, the tightening of the dry earth that squeezes life out of the withering crops. They were wary of the beasts of jungle and plain, not least the majestic jaguar; in coastal regions they fled the onslaught of hurricanes and violent storms.

They saw the gods and goddesses everywhere. Partly because the world could turn on them suddenly and destructively, they became convinced of the need to honour the gods. The Aztecs, following long-established Mesoamerican practice, believed that the cycle of the sun's morning birth following death at evening might suddenly stop if blood sacrifices to the gods were not maintained. Equally, Mesoamericans celebrated the gods for the glory of divine energy and the pattern of sacred meaning they saw in all things.

Life in Mesoamerica, lived in the presence of death and catastrophe, was keenly experienced. Mesoamericans entered an intense relationship with their land, a region of rich contrasts – from the mountains of highland Mexico to the plains of the Pacific and Gulf Coasts, from desert and semi-arid landscapes to river valleys, lake shores and the dense jungles of lowland Guatemala.

Left: Aztecs and Maya feared the anger of the region's many volcanoes. The oval crater of Popocatépetl has near-vertical sides. Poisonous volcanic gases erupt from vents in the walls.

HIGHLAND AND LOWLAND

Mesoamerica's first settlers in the second millennium BC could choose between living at sea level along estuaries rich in marine life, in well-watered lowland tropical forests teeming with animals or on dry, elevated plateaux surrounded by rocky uplands well provided with minerals and other resources. Their choice of altitude would largely have determined the climate they would have experienced.

ALTITUDE VARIATIONS

From sea level up to altitudes of about 900m (3,000ft), in lands dubbed *tierra caliente* ('hot territory'), average temperatures were high, with little seasonal variation. In these low-lying tropical regions today, the temperature variation between summer and winter months is generally as little as 5°C and winter is marked by the coming of the rains. In Veracruz, the region on the Gulf of Mexico where the Olmec civilization emerged in the second millennium BC,

Below: Pine forests occupy elevated tierra fria *('cold territory') beneath the peak of Nevado de Toluca, 4,577m (15,016ft) high.*

the average year-round daily temperature is 25°C (77°F). Average temperatures of 24–28°C (75–82°F) hold in the Yucatán peninsula, which was home to many northern Maya settlements.

At altitudes of 900–1,800m (3,000–6,000ft), in *tierra templada* ('temperate territory'), average temperatures are about 5°C lower. The mountaintop Zapotec city of Monte Albán sat at an altitude of 1,600m (5,200ft); average temperatures in the region today are around 18°C (64°F). At 1,800–3,400m (6,000–11,000ft) or *tierra fria* ('cold territory') an average temperature is 5°C or lower, with much greater seasonal variation than at higher altitude. Mexico City, which arose on the ruins of Aztec Tenochtitlán, lies at 2,300m (7,500ft) and has an average daily temperature of 15°C (59°F). Temperatures there can rise to 26°C (78°F) in the hottest month (May) and may fall to a low of 12°C (54°F) in the coldest month (January).

With experience, Mesoamericans discovered that the deep-coloured highland soils of the Valley of Mexico or the Valley of Oaxaca were extremely

Above: Parched highlands such as this sweep of desert north of Chihuahua, Mexico, are typically rich in minerals.

mineral-rich and could be farmed intensively and on steep slopes. By comparison the earth in such lowland areas as El Petén in Guatemala often needed to be left fallow for prolonged periods to safeguard its fertility. Here farmers developed slash-and-burn agriculture, in which land was cleared with fire then used for perhaps three seasons before being left for as many as ten to recover its richness.

RAINFALL VARIATION

In parts of Mesoamerica drought was a persistent threat. Today, the Valley of Mexico receives as little as 600mm (23in) of rain in a year. However, other regions receive such abundant precipitation that they can support the vibrant growth of tropical rainforests. The Gulf coastal plain as far east as Tabasco, adjoining the Chiapas highlands, in whose foothills the great Maya city of Palenque arose, generally receives an annual average of 2,000mm (78in) of rain. To the southeast, in the jungle region of El Petén, average rainfall is around 1,350mm (53in) each year.

Above: Swamplands on the Mexican Gulf Coast made a resource-rich home for the earliest Mesoamerican settlers.

DROUGHTS OF THE 1450s

In the first years of rule by the Aztec *tlatoani* Moctezuma I (1440–69), a series of terrible calamities befell the peoples of the Valley of Mexico. In 1446 their harvests were lost to a plague of locusts, then in 1449 the island city of Tenochtitlán was flooded. Frosts and drought struck the crops for four consecutive years in 1450–4.

Chronicle accounts suggest that at the close of the 16th century – 150 years afterwards – people still told breathless tales of the privations of these times, when the weak and starving went hopelessly in search of food and watched with despairing eyes the circling shadows of vultures on the bone-dry ground. Sacrifices were urgently offered to the gods and finally, in 1455, the goggle-eyed rain god Tláloc returned with drenching rains. The people rejoiced in a bumper harvest of maize.

Across Mesoamerica the rainy season generally occurs between June and October. Rainfall can be very strong at the height of the season. Mexico City typically receives almost one third of its annual rainfall of 160mm (6in) in July alone, while Tabasco may be hit by 300mm (11in) in its wettest month (September). In El Petén the rainy season runs from June to December.

FLOODS AND HURRICANES

The Mesoamerican region was also vulnerable to storms, hurricanes and flooding. The Aztecs in their island city of Tenochtitlán were subject to periodic flooding, when the waters of Lake Texcoco rose with the spring rains. The east coast of Mexico adjoining the Gulf of Mexico and the eastern edge of the Yucatán peninsula frequently lay in the path of hurricanes. The Aztec god Tezcatlipoca had special power over hurricane winds, as did the Palenque god Tahil (Obsidian Mirror) and the Quiché Maya sky god Huracán.

The land was young: the great peaks of Citlaltépetl and Popocatépetl were recent outcrops in geological terms, having been driven upwards in the late Tertiary period (as little as 1.6 million years ago).

Mesoamericans must have felt deep respect for the untameable power of nature. They lived in one of the most dynamic areas of the Earth for volcanic and seismic activity and were familiar with the shudderings of the earth monster and the periodic explosions of the volcanoes that spotted the landscape.

Below: Tezcatlipoca, Lord of the Hurricane, was feared for his capricious nature. The Aztecs called him called Yáotl ('Adversary').

SACRED HEIGHTS

The Aztec territories in the Valley of Mexico are surrounded by mountains. The Aztecs and their forebears watched rain clouds gather around the great peaks before being blown by sweet winds to water the maize crops. Their priests taught that the rain god Tláloc stored his life-giving waters on the mountainsides and sent his assistants, the *tlaloques*, to gather the water and pass it to the lord of winds, Éhecatl-Quetzalcóatl. The great peak of Popocatépetl, part of the transverse volcanic axis that cuts across the southern part of the Mesa Central plateau, was sacred to Tláloc.

MOUNTAIN PERSONAE
Popocatépetl, whose name means 'Smoking Mountain' in the Aztecs' Nahuatl language, lies 72km (45 miles) to the south-east of the centre of Mexico City, in full view of the spot where the people of Tenochtitlán once raised their great temple pyramid to the glory of

Below: Popocatépetl is still an active volcano, belching smoke and gas as recently as 2000.

Tláloc and their patron deity Huitzilopochtli. Permanently snow-capped, it climbs to 5,465m (18,000ft), its height second only to Citlaltépetl (or Orizaba) in Mesoamerica. Offerings were made to Popocatépetl in Aztec times and shrines to Tláloc were built on its slopes. Popocatépetl remains active. The smoking peak erupted in 1947 and in 1994 it emitted a vast cloud of ash and gas that scientists feared was the prelude to another major eruption. It belched smoke and gas in 2000, but the volcano has since remained quiet.

The great mountain's twin, Ixtaccíhuatl ('White Lady' in Nahuatl), has three snow capped peaks that are said to resemble the head, feet and chest of a reclining woman. An Aztec folk tale cast Ixtaccíhuatl as a princess mourning the loss of her lover, who had been dispatched by her jealous father to a war in Oaxaca. The volcano is dormant.

The steep cone of Citlaltépetl ('Star Mountain'), Mexico's highest mountain, rises to 5,700m (18,700ft) about 80km (120 miles) to the east of Tenochtitlán

Above: A snow-covered plateau lies beneath one of the three peaks of Ixtaccíhuatl. Now dormant, the volcano last erupted in 1868.

and 40km (60 miles) from the Gulf of Mexico. The snowcapped peak of this volcano is also known as Pico de Orizaba. It held a significant place in Aztec religious narrative, for it was in the crater of Citlaltépetl that the revered prince-god Quetzalcóatl was said to have died after his retreat from the Toltec city of Tollán. He then reappeared in human form and departed into the Gulf of Mexico on a raft of snakes. An Aztec garrison named Ahuilzapán ('Pleasant Waters') lay at the foot of Citlaltépetl, on the site of the modern settlement of Orizaba. The volcano was active in Aztec times, but it has been dormant since 1687.

Another peak sacred to the Aztecs was Nevado de Toluca, Mexico's fourth-highest mountain, which rises to 4,577m (15,016ft) above the valley that bears its name to the west of Tenochtitlán. Nevado de Toluca was known as Xinantecatl in Nahuatl. Natural lakes in its dormant crater were used for religious rites and sacrificial offerings in Aztec times.

In the south-western Valley of Mexico rose the Xitle volcano, whose eruption in *c*.50BC devastated the developing ceremonial centre of Cuicuilco, at that time the arch-rival of Teotihuacán. Mesoamerican history in the Valley of

Mexico might have taken a very different course had this catastrophe not occurred, and ceremonial centres might have been flanked by round stepped pyramid-platforms like the one built at Cuicuilco rather than the square or rectangular platforms developed at Teotihuacán and elsewhere. The builders of Teotihuacán laid out their city to align with another very important Mexican peak, Cerro Gordo ('Fat Mountain'), which formed a

MYTHICAL PEAKS

Mountains play a key part in Aztec and Maya religious narratives. The Aztecs' tribal god Huitzilopochtli was born on the slopes of Mount Coatepetl (Serpent Mountain), while the Aztecs reported that they travelled to Culhuacán (Curving Mountain) on their southward migration from the barren north to the Valley of Mexico. The account of Huitzilopochtli's birth tells that his mother, the serpent-petticoated earth goddess Coatlícue, served as a priestess at a mountain shrine high on the slopes of Coatepetl.

Historians are agreed that this peak had no counterpart in reality, but report that the Aztecs applied the name Coatepetl or Coatepec to their great pyramid in Tenochtitlán, the Templo Mayor, which bore a shrine to Huitzilopochtli in its upper reaches. Culhuacán might also have been a mythical site, although some authorities have suggested a peak near the modern Mexican town of San Isidro Culhuacán as a possible location. An illustration in the *Historia Tolteca-Chichimeca* (1550–70) suggests that the curved mountain was also the setting of the seven sacred caves from which the Aztecs emerged, reborn from the earth, at a key point of their southward journey.

northern backdrop for the Pyramid of the Moon and the Street of the Dead. Cerro Gordo was itself the site of a temple and small ceremonial plaza.

MAYA MOUNTAINS

Large numbers of Maya lived far from mountains, in the jungled lowlands of El Petén or in the low-lying scrub of northern Yucatán. However, they shared the reverence of their Mesoamerican cousins for the sacred heights: the towering stone temples of cities such as Tikal were recreations in stone of the mountains that they believed were home to their ancestors after death. Sacred buildings such as those in Group E at Uaxactún were adorned with stucco masks signifying that they were holy mountains.

In the southern Maya territories of eastern Mexico and the southern highlands, which run from the border of the Chiapas region across Guatemala and into north-eastern Honduras, lay the mountains of the Sierra Madre de Chiapas. Of the Chiapas peaks, the volcano Tacana ('Fire House') rises to 4,050m (13,290ft).

The mountains of the southern highlands are mostly young and active volcanoes. The highest is the twin-peaked Tajumulco, which rises to 4,220m

Above: Four tectonic plates – Pacific, Cocos, Caribbean and North American – clash in Mesoamerica, pushing up great mountain chains and causing frequent earthquakes.

(13,845ft) and is dormant. In central Guatemala the extinct San Pedro volcano and the still active 3,535m (11,600ft) Atitlán volcano rise majestically above the waters of Lago Atitlán. The 3,158m (10,358ft) Toliman and the 3,763m (12,340ft) Fuego volcanoes, which are also in Guatemala, have been active as recently as 2002 and 2004 respectively.

Below: Beneath the Atitlán volcano in Guatemala, the waters of Lago Atitlán fill a large crater formed by volcanic subsidence.

LIFE-GIVING WATERS

The lakes of the Valley of Mexico were formed in prehistoric times when the sacred heights of Popocatépetl, Ixtaccíhuatl and other peaks of the transverse volcanic axis rose, damming the south-easterly drainage of the region's waters. Lake Texcoco, site of the Aztecs' island capital, was one of five expanses of water. It lay between lakes Zumpango and Xaltocán to the north and Xochimilco and Chalco to the south.

Lake Texcoco was the lowest of these in altitude. In the rainy summer season the other lakes would rise beyond their normal extent and flow into Lake Texcoco, creating one single expanse of water that the Aztecs dubbed Moon Lake. In the dry season, however, the two northern lakes, which lay 3.5–6m (11–19ft) higher in altitude than Lake Texcoco, would effectively disappear. The southern lakes of Xochimilco and Chalco,

Below: Mesoamerican rivers, notably the long Usumacinta in Yucatán/Guatemala, were major facilitators of trade.

3m (10ft) higher than Lake Texcoco, were fed by freshwater springs and remained, although they were separated from the central lake.

Scholars believe that farming using *chinampa* or artificial islands was pioneered in the Classic Period *c.*AD800 by the people of a settlement named Xico by Lake Chalco. By the time of the Aztec empire, Lakes Chalco and Xochimilco were the setting for great expanses of *chinampa* fields.

FROM HIGHLANDS TO SEA

To the west of the Valley of Mexico, the Lerma river rises in the region of Nevado de Toluca and flows north-westward to create Lake Chapala. From here, the Santiago river flows south down across the Sierra Madre Occidental into the Pacific Ocean. To the south of the Valley of Mexico the major river is the Balsas, which runs west into the Pacific Ocean and gives it name to the low-lying region known as the Balsas Depression. A second waterway, the Papaloapan, flows

Above: The Sacred Cenote at Chichén Itzá is around 30m (100ft) across. There is a drop of 22m (70ft) from the rim.

at a stately pace eastward into the Gulf of Mexico. Archaeologists believe that it was in fertile lands near the Balsas that early Mesoamerican farmers succeeded in domesticating maize from the wild grass known as *teosinte*.

To the east, beyond the low-lying Isthmus of Tehuantepec, the major rivers are the Usumacinta and the Grijalva, which together drain the waters of the Chiapas highlands. The Grijalva forms from headstreams that arise in the Sierra de Soconusco in Mexico and the Sierra Madre of Guatemala. It flows in a north-westerly direction through the state of Chiapas. The Usumacinta, formed in the Chiapas highlands by the combination of the Pasión and Chixoy rivers of Guatemala, flows north-westward towards the region of Tabasco and the Bay of Campeche. One of its three branches combines with the Grijalva before flowing into the Bay of Campeche near the modern town of Frontera, while a second, now called the San Pedro y San Pablo, feeds into the bay near the settlement of San Pedro. A third, now known as the Palizada, flows into the Términos Lagoon in the state of Campeche. The Usumacinta was an important 1,000km (600 mile) trading route.

WATERWAYS AND SETTLEMENT

Several important Maya settlements grew up close to these waterways. The ceremonial centre known as Altar de Sacrificios was founded at the very point where the Pasión and Chixoy rivers join to form the Usumacinta. A carved stela of AD455 shows the site was occupied in the early-to-mid Classic Period, while later evidence shows that it reached a peak of prosperity after AD600 for around two centuries. Farther west, Bonampak was built on the banks of the small Lacanja river. Around 80km (50 miles) down the Usumacinta from Altar de Sacrificios, Yaxchilán was founded on a terrace overlooking the river after AD300. A further 50km (30 miles) downstream, the Maya city of Piedras Negras was built on a hill in a bend of the Usumacinta. Still farther north-west, Palenque was built on the Otulum River, a small tributary of the Usumacinta, and overlooking the Usumacinta floodplain that runs down to the Bay of Campeche.

In the south-eastern Maya region the river Motagua rises in the central Guatemalan highlands in the region occupied by the Quiché Maya and runs for 400km (250 miles) eastwards to empty into the Gulf of Honduras. It was a major route for trade moving from highland Guatemala to the Caribbean. The Maya city of Quiriguá was established

close to the river by the 5th century AD. Copán drew much of its wealth from trade in obsidian and other natural resources on this river before it lost control of the trade to Quiriguá in AD738.

UNDERGROUND WATERS

On the Yucatán peninsula of Mexico, towards the northern edge of the Maya realm, there are no significant rivers. Rainfall drains away underground through porous limestone rock and there are very few surface streams. In places, this rock collapses to expose underground stores

Left: The Aztecs held the waters of lakes, rivers and sea sacred to Chalchiúhtlicue. This image is from the Codex Vaticanus.

Above: This drawing of the Bolonchen cenote is from Incidents of Travel in Central America, Chiapas and Yucatán *(1841).*

of water in natural wells named *cenotes* – from the Yucatec term *dz'onot*. *Cenotes* can be very large, measuring up to 60m (200ft) across and 30m (100ft) deep. There are around 6,000 *cenotes* in north-eastern Yucatán.

Cenotes were important sources of water for the Maya. They were also used for religious sacrifice and were understood to be entrances to the underworld. Of the two *cenotes* at Chichén Itzá, one was reserved for religious offerings and one was used for water supply. *Cenotes* were sacred to the rain god Chac.

TOWERING TREES, ROCKY SANDS

Many Maya made their living among dense jungle forests, tracking game or the rare quetzal bird, cutting back and burning the dense growth to fashion fields to grow crops and raising great stone temples that rivalled the height of the towering jungle trees. The wide variety of terrains, altitudes and climates encompassed by the Maya territories produced a range of distinct forests.

In the Alta Verapaz of Guatemala, at the northern edge of the southern Maya highlands, stand the highland rainforests, home of the rare and sacred quetzal, whose brightly coloured tail feathers were a valued item of trade among the Maya and other Mesoamericans. These humid

Below: The partly ruined Nohuch Mul pyramid rises 24m (80ft) to imitate a natural mountain at the Maya city of Cobá.

greenlands, sometimes called cloud forests, are dense with tropical growth of evergreens, lichens and mosses, delicate wild orchids, bromeliads and astonishing ferns that reach a height of 15m (50ft). Here professional hunters would track the quetzal in order to capture it alive, pluck its wondrous tail feathers and then set it free once more. In the wild the bird would grow new feathers after moulting.

STOREYED FOREST LIFE

In the lower altitude and denser rainforests of the southern Maya lowlands, different types of plant life thrive at distinct levels above ground. At the topmost level, perhaps 70m (230ft) above ground, towering mahogany and ceiba, a form of cottonwood, predominate. At a lower level, up to 50m (165ft) above ground, Spanish cedar, sapodilla, bari and

Above: The Lacandón rainforest in Chiapas, an ancient Maya homeland, is today under threat from farmers and loggers.

American fig trees grow densely. A third level, at up to 25m (80ft) in height, is vibrant with palms, avocado trees, rubber trees, breadnut trees and others. Vines, bromeliads and lianas climb their trunks. Beneath, at ground level, in dense shade, young trees and ferns are found.

TREE OF LIFE

The majestic ceiba, or silk-cotton tree, was sacred to the Maya and identified by them as the cosmic tree or tree of life. They believed that it linked the levels of the universe, sinking its roots through the earth to the lowest of the nine levels of the underworld and sending its towering branches to the topmost of the 13 levels of heaven. In some versions of their cosmology, the Maya told that five great trees supported the heavens, one in each of the four points of the compass and a fifth, the green ceiba, in the centre.

The vines that hang far down from the great ceiba's branches may have symbolized a spirit voyage from the ground level of earthly reality to the heights of heaven in the tree's great umbrella-shaped canopy. There, far above the forest floor, both epiphytes (aerial plants) and many species of animal make their home;

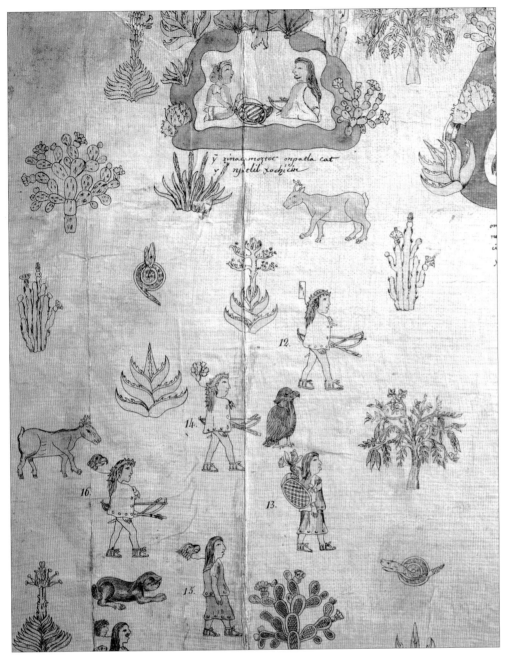

Above: Dry lands. Hunters cross a stretch of desert in a detail from the Mapa Tlotzin, *a genealogy of the governors of Texcoco.*

10m (30ft), palms, allspice and other species predominate. The growth of ferns and young trees at ground level is less vibrant here than further south. Here and there the forest gives way to seasonal swamps and grasslands. Tikal, Uaxactún, El Mirador and Calakmul all arose to glory in the central lowlands.

A PLACE OF NO CULTURE

At the other extreme of Mesoamerican terrains lay arid or semi-arid regions such as the wide plateau where the Toltec capital of Tollán was founded in highland Mexico and regions in Guatemala such as the Motagua Valley in the Maya highlands. In such areas the cult of the rain god was prominent and knowledge of irrigation techniques was key to agricultural success. Desert lay to the north in the northern part of the Mexican plateau, a region characterized by the Aztecs and their fellow inhabitants of the Valley of Mexico as a place of no culture, the place from which they had escaped in moving south. In the *Historia Tolteca Chichimeca*, an image of the seven caves from which the tribes were said to have emerged depicts several types of cacti, indicating that the primal landscape of origin in the first days was a sunblasted desert.

Below: At Labná in Yucatán, trees crowd close to the palace arch. To either side are stone representations of Maya village huts.

birds nest, mammals move about along the great branches, even frogs raise their young in the pools that form on branches and in tree trunks.

The ceiba blooms in the evening, producing tiny flowers very reminiscent of the ear flares worn by kings in Maya carving and ceramic images. Some authorities suggest that the king dressed himself as the silk-cotton tree, to signify that he was blessed like the holy ceiba and that he anchored the kingdom in sacred order. The carving on the lid of the sarcophagus in which King Pacal of Palenque was interred shows the king descending into the spirit realm of the underworld along the length of the cosmic tree. The Maya carved great canoes from the vast trunk of their sacred tree.

SEASONAL RAINFOREST

Farther north, in the region known as the central lowlands, the jungle is described as 'seasonal rainforest' because each year extended dry periods interrupt the supply of rainwater. The upper canopy of American fig, ceiba and mahogany is lower and often less complete, but still climbs to 50m (165ft) above ground. Beneath, a thick growth of fig, sapodilla and other trees form a very dense canopy, while lower still, at a height of around

LIFE IN THE WILD

The lands of the Aztecs and Maya were teeming with animal life. Mesoamericans so revered these creatures for their energy and marvellous abilities that they cast many of them in religious and creation narratives and even saw some, such as the jaguar and eagle, as principal physical forms of great gods.

KING JAGUAR

Throughout the region, the jaguar was king. The largest member of the *felidae* family of cats, the jaguar (*Felis onca*) can thrive in scrubland and desert as well as in its preferred habitat of dense forests and swamps. It can climb with ease and track prey along branches tens of metres above ground, but is also happy to leap into water and is a strong swimmer. The male, which is significantly larger than the female, can grow to 2.7m (9ft) in length and weigh up to 160kg (350lbs.) The jaguar hunts alone. It prefers to stalk

Below: Bird sacred to Huitzilopochtli. This detail of a stone carving on the Platform of the Jaguars and Eagles at Chichén Itzá depicts an eagle eating a human heart.

peccaries (pig-like mammals) and the capybara (a large rodent), but will also kill and eat deer, sloths, monkeys, anteaters, alligators, birds, turtles and even fish. The jaguar does not usually attack humans, unless cornered, when it is a savage opponent.

The jaguar played an important role in Mesoamerican religious life from early times. In the second millennium BC, Olmec craftsmen were carving intriguing jaguar-faced figures resembling human babies. The jaguar was associated with the ancient practice of shamanism (spirit travel) and was adopted by shamans as one of their animal forms.

Because of its fearsome capacity to hunt in darkness, it was an animal aspect of Tezcatlipoca, the Aztec lord of night and of dark fate, while elsewhere in Mesoamerica it was associated with the god of the underworld and with the realm of darkness. When the sun visited the underworld by night, it took the form of the jaguar. Like the lion in Europe, the jaguar became a symbol of royalty and bravery in Mesoamerica: Maya kings wore its pelt and were named after the jaguar, while in the Aztec army the two elite groups of fighters were called eagle and jaguar warriors.

The Aztecs called the jaguar *océlotl*. The smaller cat now known as the ocelot was known to the Aztecs as the *tlacaoocélotl* (literally, 'little jaguar'; *Felis pardalis*).

HUNTING ANIMALS AND BIRDS

When Mesoamericans went hunting they most commonly killed rabbits and white-tailed deer. Rabbits, perhaps because of their skittering speed of movement and rapid rate of reproduction, were associated by the Aztecs with drunkenness and with the alcoholic drink *pulque*. Maya and Aztec people also killed and ate ducks, geese, swans and other birds. The Hero Twins of Mayan mythology were celebrated for their skill in hunting birds using blowpipes.

Above: Ocelots, known to the Aztecs as 'little jaguars', were common in the fertile lowlands of Mesoamerica along with opossums and tapirs.

Mesoamericans also hunted the rare quetzal bird, which was tracked and captured for its magnificent tail plumes, but never killed. The quetzal is found in the highland cloud forests that run from Chiapas to western Panama. Just 35cm (14in) long, it has tail feathers of up to 1m (3ft 3in) in length. These plumes change colour in the light, a shimmer of gold, emerald green and blue that sets off the bird's bright red breast.

Only the male bird possesses the iridescent tail feathers that are so highly prized: as with the peacock and peahen, the female bird is much plainer in appearance. The quetzal was an animal form of the great Plumed Serpent

Quetzalcóatl and the feathers of the sacred bird were, like the jaguar pelt, symbolic of kingly authority.

Probably the most revered of birds was the eagle. An animal form taken by the Aztecs' tribal god Huitzilopochtli, it was central to Aztec origin narrative: the México/Aztecs founded their city of Tenochtitlán at the place where they saw an eagle destroying a snake upon a cactus, in fulfilment of a prophecy of Huitzilopochtli. The harpy eagle was found in the jungles of Maya lands while the golden eagle was known in central Mexico.

Other notable birds included parrots, macaws and toucans, falcons, owls, hawks and other birds of prey and, in estuaries and along coastlines, herons, giant storks and egrets. In the *Popol Vuh* of the Quiché Maya, the scarlet macaw, a vividly coloured species of parrot, attempted to set himself up as the pre-eminent god and to take the place of the sun, but he was outwitted by the Hero Twins. The hummingbird was another bird associated with Huitzilopochtli by the Aztecs.

BATS

The bat was also widely found. In the jungle bats nested beneath the vast roots of the ceiba that was viewed as the tree of life and understood to link the earth with the underworld and the heavens. Partly for this reason, and partly because of their natural associations with darkness, bats were linked to the underworld. The Zapotecs of Monte Albán associated the bat god with maize and fertility.

SNAKES AND MONKEYS

The snake was a complex and central religious symbol, associated with Tláloc and the rain, with the fertility of the earth, with the sun and heavens, with sacrificial blood and with religious and visionary experience. Mesoamericans also revered turtles and crocodiles: they sometimes said that the earth took the form of a crocodile or was resting on the back of a giant turtle. The Maya also identified the constellation Orion as a celestial turtle.

Monkeys were common in the lowlands. Species included howlers, spider monkeys and marmosets. Howlers, stocky, bearded monkeys up to 70cm (28in) long, live mainly in the upper branches of trees and would rarely have been seen. However, they would certainly have been heard: they take their name from the extremely resonant howl that they emit at dawn and dusk and during storms. The howler's cry can be heard more than 5km (as much as 3 miles) away. Marmosets are small, long-tailed monkeys that move quickly along branches, while spider monkeys are much larger with pot bellies. They forage in small groups among the very highest jungle branches. They rarely descend to the ground, but can be seen leaping from one tree to another. The Quiché Maya creators of the *Popul Vuh* narrative, which imagines a series of failed creations before the current one, told that monkeys were the descendants of a failed race of wooden people fashioned in early days by the creators.

Above: The jaguar is the largest New World cat. Like the lion in Europe, it became a symbol of royalty and bravery in Mexico.

Below: The intricate decoration in the Nunnery Quadrangle, Uxmal, contains twin images of the sacred rattlesnake.

FRUITS OF THE EARTH

The first humans in Mesoamerica were hunter-gatherers who survived on a diet of seeds and plants supplemented both by mammoths and mastodons and by smaller game, birds and fish. They lived in this way for many millennia before beginning to domesticate plants such as avocados, squash, beans and chilli peppers and turning to a settled, agricultural way of life.

PEOPLE OF MAIZE

The plant that would become their descendants' staple food – maize – was probably first domesticated from a wild cereal grass called *teosinte*. Archaeological evidence from the Tehuacán Valley in the Puebla region to the south-east of the Valley of Mexico suggests that, in the wild, the grass produced cobs that were no more than 2.5cm (1in) long: at this size, they could be an addition to a diet but not a staple food. In domesticating the plant, the first Mesoamerican farmers

Below: Images of the revered maize plant were carved on the sides of this basalt block used as an altar by the Aztecs.

succeeded in enlarging the cobs. In the wild, beans and squash grew alongside *teosinte* and other grasses, climbing up the grass stalks in the protection of the shade provided by the leaves. The first farmers, who had already domesticated varieties of squash and beans, might have copied this method of planting.

Archaeologists report that the first cereal domesticated in Mesoamerica was not *teosinte* but another, related to modern grain millet (*Setaria geniculata*). *Teosinte* itself was probably first domesticated in the lands adjoining the Balsas river of western Mexico some centuries before 5000BC. From archaeological remains we know that its use spread slowly eastwards, reaching the Tehuacán Valley by *c*.5000BC, Oaxaca by *c*.4000BC and Veracruz by *c*.2250BC. Its first cultivators perfected the making of stone mortars and used them to grind the maize ears.

Mesoamericans saw themselves as people reliant on, dedicated to and even made of maize. The word used by the Aztecs for the maize dough from which

Above: Xilonen, the Aztec goddess of young maize cobs, was worshipped in the form of a virginal adolescent girl.

they made tortillas is *toneuhcayotl* ('our flesh'). In some versions of both Maya and Aztec creation narratives, the first people were fashioned from a soft maize dough. In the *Popol Vuh*, the creators Huracán and Gucumatz gave ears of maize to a grandmother goddess Xmucané who ground them to flour, made a paste by mixing it with water and then moulded the first people.

According to Maya folk tradition, the first Mesoamericans were led to identify *teosinte* as a food source when they saw its grains in the dung of a wild cat. The *Popol Vuh* also recorded this debt to animals: Huracán and Gucumatz were led to the discovery of maize by four corn-eating creatures – a coyote, a fox, a parrot and a crow – who had tasted the maize

Above: In a detail from one of the murals in Building A at Cacaxtla, a bird swoops to seize a cocoa pod from a sturdy cacao tree.

THE SEARCH FOR FOOD

Mesoamerican creation narratives proposed that before the current world age began there were a number of previous creations. The Aztec account of the five suns or world ages revealed that in each of the five creations the earth's inhabitants found a more satisfactory staple food than eaten by their predecessors.

In the era of the first sun, which was governed by Black Tezcatlipoca, the world was inhabited by a race of giants who lived on acorns. The second sun, whose presiding god was Quetzalcóatl, saw the emergence of a race of primitive humans who lived on the seeds of the mesquite tree.

After the third age, which was ruled by Tláloc, in which people lived on plants that grew on water, such as the water lily, people returned to a diet of wild seeds in the fourth age of Chalchiúhtlicue. It was only in the fifth and current age, an age subject to the sun god Tonatiuh, that the peoples of Mesoamerica learned how to plant and harvest maize.

and found it good. In Aztec religious narratives, the god Quetzalcóatl – in some accounts, also a culture hero who taught people how to sow and harvest crops – discovered maize deep in the heart of a mountain, where it had been hidden by ants. He was unable to split the mountain to bring the maize to humans, but the god Nanahuatzin – who at the beginning of the current world age rose in the sky to become the sun – broke the peak apart with a thunderbolt.

FIELD AGRICULTURE

Mesoamericans developed different methods of field agriculture in the varied parts of their region. In arid and semi-arid areas fields were laid out where they could be watered by diverted springs and rivers, while in the region of Lake Texcoco farmers developed the technique of building *chinampa*, artificial islands, to reclaim land from the lake. In the dense jungles of the lowlands, fields were cut and the soil enriched by burning vegetation, while in the highlands further south, terraces were carved from the steep slopes.

By 1300BC, the four foods that would become the staple plants of the Mesoamerican civilization were well established in the fields of the pioneer farmers. Together they provided a balanced diet: carbohydrates from maize, protein from beans and squash, oils and fats from avocado. They could be supplemented with meat from rabbits, deer, ducks and geese and with fish.

Below: Cocoa beans are found within cocoa pods, the fruit of the cacao tree. The pods grow on the tree trunk and branches.

CREATING A SACRED WORLD

The oldest religion in Mesoamerica was the cult of the earth's fertility. At the very beginnings of settled life in central America, settlers were fashioning clay female figurines, believed to be representations of an archaic fertility goddess.

MOTHER AND MONSTER

From prehistoric times, Mesoamericans revered the earth as a mother with the capacity to gestate the seeds of domesticated plants and bring forth food. The ancient 260-day ritual calendar celebrated a sacred timespan that was possibly derived from both the lapse between planting and harvest in the Mesoamerican agricultural cycle and the time from conception to

Below: The duality of life and death is represented in a man/skeleton figure made by an Olmec craftsman c.500BC.

birth in a human pregnancy. The earth was a mother, but also a monster. In Aztec religious narrative, the earth monster Tlatecuhtli spread terror in the first days of the current era, when there was nothing but water. She was tamed by the gods Quetzalcóatl and Tezcatlipoca who tore her in two, making the sky from one half and the earth from the other.

OPPOSITES IN BALANCE

Mesoamericans believed the universe to be patterned by duality. Tlatecuhtli consumed the sun god each dusk, consigning him to the underworld for the hours of darkness, but the earth mother then gave birth to the sun once more in the redness of dawn. The earth goddess gave life in the form of crops but also demanded life in the form of sacrificial blood. Mesoamericans saw opposites held in balance. Darkness balancing light, death opposing life, dampness countering dryness, weakness balancing strength.

Duality also structured the divine sphere and was the hidden power of creation. The primal Aztec god Ometeotl ('Lord of Duality') took twin male and female forms, as Tonacatecuhtli ('Lord of our Sustenance') and Tonacacíhuatl ('Lady of our Sustenance') joined in a creative embrace. In Quiché Maya creation narrative, the earth was made when two gods, the sky god Huracán and the sea god Gucumatz came together in discussion. The gods had both benign and threatening aspects: the Maya rain god Chac or the Aztec rain deity Tláloc could deliver drought or lifegiving waters, destructive storms as well as the light moisture falling gently on crops.

The gods also had both spirit forms and physical forms, and most had animal aspects: Mesoamericans viewed the many powerful creatures of their landscape with deep reverence. In one version of the Aztec religious narrative

describing the creation of the sun and moon, the assembled gods who gave of their own blood to set the sun in motion afterwards became the animals of the plains, hills and jungles. The earth was opposed by the heavens, and also balanced the underworld.

In the Mesoamerican vision, the flat earth was both the lowest of the thirteen levels of heaven and the topmost of the nine levels of the underworld. The earth also gave access to the spirit realms of the underworld – the land was marked with sacred caverns that opened the way. The earth was also associated with snakes. According to the Maya, those in a state of religious ecstasy might be delivered

Below: The eagle, symbol of the god Huitzilopochtli and of warrior might, is celebrated on an Aztec wooden drum.

Above: Zoomorph P at Quiriguá shows a young ruler in the jaws of a monster, representing the entry to the underworld.

into the presence of ancestors or the gods by following the coils of a great snake known as the Vision Serpent.

SACRED PATTERNS

For Mesoamericans, the universe was structured according to sacred patterning. One of the forms of this patterning was that of the cyclical movement of time. Mesoamericans believed that everything happened in regular, periodic timespans. For this reason they structured their lives and religious ceremonies around the 260-, 365- and 584-day cycles of the moon, the sun and the planet Venus. Both the Maya and the Aztecs saw the current world as one of a series of creations, subject to periodic destruction and renewal.

In the Aztec view, the present age was the fifth sun or era, and this fivefold pattern was seen also in that of the five directions on the flat earth – north, south, east, west and the centre. In the centre was the great cosmic ceiba tree, and – for the Aztecs – the Templo Mayor of Tenochtitlán. The earth itself was also the centre point of creation, for Mesoamericans believed the earth to be surrounded by water. This gave sacred meaning to the island setting of the Aztecs' imperial capital of Tenochtitlán. The physical characteristics of Mesoamerica informed the range of associations that clustered around the directions of north and south.

To the north of the Valley of Mexico lay desert lands, inhospitable regions from which many nomads, including the Méxica/Aztecs, had escaped. The Aztecs saw the north as a place of dryness and death. It was the direction of the lord of deception and fate, Tezcatlipoca, and was linked to his colour, black – the hue of death. It was associated with xerophyte plants such as the Joshua tree that are adapted to desert climates. In the opposite direction, the south was said by the Aztecs to be the land of dampness, and of their tribal lord Huitzilopochtli, master of the arts of war through which they gathered sacrificial victims. In some versions, the south was the land of the rain god Tláloc, and like his heaven Tlálocan, a place of ease and lifegiving waters.

North and south appear to have been pre-eminent among the four directions. From at least Olmec times in the second millennium BC, many Mesoamerican sites were laid out on a roughly north–south plan. The same pattern was applied in Maya cities such as Tikal and Copán. For the Maya, north was the direction of the celestial realm, home of the gods, and south the way to the underworld. East and west were associated with the daily path of the sun.

Above the earth was the sacred sky, home of the sun god to whom the Aztecs, the people of the sun, dedicated themselves. By night, the movements of the stars followed paths established by the gods in religious and creation narrative. For example, the Great Bear constellation was identified with Tezcatlipoca and its dipping into the sea re-enacted the moment during his struggle with the earth monster at which he lost a foot. The cycle of the planet Venus eternally celebrated the achievements of the Aztec god Quetzalcóatl or the Maya Hero Twins in confronting the lords of the underworld.

In the sacred arenas of their cities, Mesoamericans created idealized versions of their world. Stone pyramids stood for mountains, wide plazas for lakes. Carved stone stelae – known to the Maya as stone trees – honoured the great trunks of the forest. Many scholars believe that the ball court was like a sacred cavern.

Below: This tiny Olmec female figurine was one of many Preclassic Period figures thought to have been used in fertility cults.

CHAPTER 14

FROM VILLAGE TO METROPOLIS

In the great northern Yucatán city of Chichén Itzá, probably in the 9th–10th century or a little later, labourers raised the Temple of the Warriors, a four-level pyramid with a wide central stairway leading to a *chacmool* sacrificial figure and beyond it a square *cella* or temple. This awe-inspiring sacred building appears to be a copy of or tribute to the main pyramid-temple at Tollán in highland Mexico, the capital of the revered Toltecs. At one time scholars thought that Toltecs conquered Chichén Itzá, but most now agree that Toltec architectural features are present in the Yucatán city as a result of the peaceful spread of Toltec influence.

The debate over Chichén Itzá is typical of the many difficulties in tracing patterns of influence through Mesoamerican history. In attempting to make sense of the spread of settlements, we will rely on the conventional division of the region's history introduced elsewhere in this book, into the Preclassic Period (20,000BC–AD250), the Classic Period (*c.*AD250–AD900) and the Postclassic Period (AD900–1521). This tripartite division is certainly useful but the labels must not be applied too rigidly, for the divisions can fall at different chronological points in different areas of Mesoamerica: for example, in Belize and arguably northern Yucatán, historians agree that the Classic Period continues past AD900 until as late as 1200.

Left: The Great Plaza was the heart of the mountain-top settlement of Monte Albán, one of Mesoamerica's first cities.

THE BEGINNINGS OF SETTLED LIFE
7000–2000BC

In Mesoamerica, hunter-gatherer bands of humans first began to domesticate wild plants *c.*7000BC. Over 5,000 years they gradually became more successful at growing crops, little by little abandoning their nomadic pattern of existence and establishing permanent settlements, which were supported mainly by farming. Archaeological evidence suggests that the first settlements were established in two areas of Mesoamerica – in highland Mexico and along the coasts of the Gulf of Mexico, the Gulf of Tehuantepec and the Caribbean. Archaeologists suspect that in other areas, such as the central Maya region, people may have been following the same long, slow path from nomadic life to settled farming at the same time but the evidence has not been found in these places.

BEFORE FARMING
The evidence from highland Mexico shows that before humans first experimented with domesticating plants they were living as nomads in small bands of up to eight, hunting, trapping and gathering. They hunted species of antelope and horse that are now extinct, as well as rabbits, rats, birds, gophers and turtles. They used knives and sharpened points of chipped flint. They sometimes

Right: Mesoamerica's first hunter-gatherers trapped birds and other prey. This Totonac stone axe-shaped head is from after AD900.

drove mammoths and other large creatures into marshy land, where they killed them with sharpened flints. Archaeological finds show that two mammoths were killed in this way at the edge of Lake Texcoco in the Valley of Mexico some time around 7700BC.

THE FIRST CROPS
Over the following two millennia, *c.*7000–5000BC, the nomads of highland Mexico began to domesticate avocados, chillis and squash. They also ate the black seeds of a weed called amaranth, which were probably gathered in the wild, and chewed a wild cereal grass named *teosinte* that would become the staple food of Mesoamerica in the form of maize.

In this period, humans were living in the Tehuacán Valley in the south-eastern part of modern Puebla province, at an altitude of around 1,400m (4,600ft). They made milling stones as well as mortars and pestles and began to experiment with weaving and woodworking. Groups settled in seasonal camps, but in spring left on nomadic trips. They killed cottontail rabbits and deer for meat. They buried skulls in baskets – perhaps as a rite of human sacrifice.

People were also living in the Infiernillo complex of caves in a desert environment in the south-western part of modern Tamaulipas province. They made fire-sticks, traps, rods and darts from wood and pioneered the making of mats and bags from yucca and agave plants. They ate wild runner beans, agave and prickly pear cactus and domesticated the bottle gourd and the chilli pepper.

At the same time, people in the Balsas region of western Mexico succeeded in domesticating *teosinte*. Another group made their living in caves near Mitla in Oaxaca. Like their cousins elsewhere, they hunted cottontail rabbits and deer, made flint tools and weapons and experimented with domesticating squash.

In 5000–3400BC, the inhabitants of the Tehuacán Valley began to establish semi-permanent camps that they inhabited for parts of the year, probably splitting into smaller nomadic groups only in the dry season. They succeeded in domesticating more plants, including *teosinte*, as well as

Left: From early days, Mesoamericans made alcoholic drinks from the maguey agave plant, which grew in Oaxaca.

the common bean, the crookneck squash and the bottle gourd. They cultivated sapotes, plum or apple-sized fruits with a sweet flavour. At another site in Oaxaca, Gheo-Shih, people were living in a semi-permanent site through summer and autumn, hunting but also raising maize.

From 3400 to 2000BC, the people of the Tehuacán Valley built larger settlements on river terraces they probably occupied all year round. They domesticated new plants, including the pumpkin, and began to keep and eat dogs. They made bowls from stone and long blades of obsidian. They trapped small animals such as foxes, turtles and birds rather than larger creatures such as puma or deer. However, as before, some members set off in nomadic hunting groups during the dry season and left evidence of their passing in highland caves.

A LAKESIDE HOME
In the more fertile setting of Lake Chalco in the Valley of Mexico, people began to live in permanent settlements much earlier, perhaps c.5500BC. At Zohapilco, near the volcano of Tlapacoya to the east of Lake Chalco, settlers had a wide choice of foods: molluscs, turtles and fish from the lake; water lentils and other plants from the marshy shoreline; wild fruits and

deer, rabbits, dogs, coyotes and rodents from the forested hills. The soil was rich and they grew amaranth and early domesticated forms of *teosinte*. Each winter they could also hunt or trap any of a large number of migratory birds such as Canada geese, teals, pintails and mallards. They made tools from locally available andesite and obsidian. However, this attractive setting had its drawback in the form of the nearby volcanoes. Some time before 3000BC, major eruptions devastated the area and people were not able to resettle the lakeside for about 500 years.

COASTAL SETTLEMENTS
At the eastern edge of Mesoamerica, on the Caribbean coast of Belize, groups of people were living in permanent settlements by 4200BC, eating shellfish, fish, turtles, seabirds and reptiles. On the Pacific coast, south of the Sierra Madre del Sur, groups lived at sites near Acapulco in Guerrero and Matanchén in Nayarit. The remains suggest that they lived there at least semi-permanently from as early as 3000BC, eating shrimps, clams and fish. In Veracruz on the coast of the Gulf of Mexico, people lived at Santa Luisa on the Tecolutla river

Above: The countryside of Oaxaca was the setting for an early Mesoamerican cave settlement near Mitla in 7000–5000BC.

in the years 3500–2000BC, by hunting, fishing and gathering wild foods. They left no evidence that they had even begun to experiment with farming. Farther east, beyond the Isthmus of Tehuantepec, the ancestors of the Maya were making a living on the Pacific coasts of Guatemala by c.2000BC. People were also settled very early in north-western Yucatán, in the region of the later settlement of Dzibilchaltún, about 20km (12 miles) inland from the coast.

Below: Copper axe heads like these were not made in Mesoamerica before the 9th–10th centuries AD.

URBAN CEREMONIAL CENTRES
c.2500–300BC

In slightly over 2,000 years from *c*.2500 to *c*.300BC, Mesoamericans laid the foundations of a great civilization. Larger settlements increasingly reliant on farming rather than hunting, gathering and fishing developed. More efficient ways of irrigating and using land meant farmers were able to produce surpluses of food.

Populations rose rapidly and people began to specialize in small industries and crafts, such as producing pottery, tools or items valued for their use in religious ritual. Social divisions emerged and, in some areas, elite groups took control. Public buildings such as temples were raised and large ceremonial centres laid out.

There was busy interaction between population centres, as people shared or swapped products, raw materials, plants and ideas. This enabled the development of a unified Mesoamerican culture and was a precursor of the long-range trade that was later one of the key defining features of Mesoamerica. Stonemasons began to use basic hieroglyphic signs. The first great Mesoamerican culture, that of the Olmec people, emerged about 1500BC in southern Veracruz and grew to a peak between 1100–600BC.

Below: At Izapa on the Pacific coastal plain of south-east Mexico, Maya settlers built a pyramid (Mound 30a) in 800–500BC.

Above: The image of the ruler in a monster's mouth representing the entrance to the spirit world was established by the time of the Olmec.

A major Olmec centre was established at San Lorenzo, at a spot advantageously situated where the Coatzacoalcos and Chiquito rivers meet and close both to lowland forests and resource-rich highlands, overlooking the fertile flood-plain. San Lorenzo was at the height of its power and influence in the years 1150–900BC. Its people established exchange or trading links with sites in Oaxaca, Guerrero and highland Mexico, and Olmec influence spread far and wide.

Between 900 and 700BC, the era of San Lorenzo came to an end: the Olmec monuments were attacked, defaced and buried. However, the centre was not abandoned until 400BC. A second major Olmec centre at La Venta, in Tabasco, was constructed from 1150BC onwards and reached its peak in the years 800–500BC. It grew up in a region where villagers had been living and raising maize since *c*.2250BC, supplementing their diet with crocodiles, toads and aquatic birds. The Olmec centre at La Venta was a large ceremonial site containing several platforms and pyramids generally oriented north–south, but set at 8 degrees west of true north – as at San Lorenzo. It also contained carved colossal heads, whose individuality suggests that they might be portrayals of rulers, and other monuments. The main Olmec sites were probably independent of each other. There was certainly no Olmec empire and there is no real evidence of military conquest – although Altar 4 at La Venta and Monument 14 at San Lorenzo bear carvings of one figure leading another by a rope, suggesting a captor and his captive and indicating there were inter-city rivalries.

OAXACAN HIGHLANDS
In the area of the modern Mexican state of Oaxaca, San José Mogote became an important centre. From a few simple public buildings *c*.1350BC, the settlement grew to cover 20ha (50 acres) by 1000BC,

with splendid stone temples and platforms. Its creators were independent of, but influenced by, the Olmec. San José's public buildings, like those at San Lorenzo, were oriented 8 degrees west of north. Craftsmen lived in quarters according to their speciality – for example, tool manufacturers, jade workers and basket-makers lived in separate areas.

Around 500BC the great Zapotec city of Monte Albán was established nearby in a hilltop position dominating the three valleys of Zaachila to the south, Etla to the north and Tlacolula to the east. The hilltop, 400m (1,300ft) above the floor of the valleys, was a strategic position that would have been easily defended in conflict, but there is no archaeological evidence that the city was ever attacked. This inspires historians to argue that the hilltop may simply have been chosen by competing Zapotec valley groups as a neutral setting for a central ceremonial and administrative settlement.

Left: This stone pillar is one of the few pieces of Olmec monumental art to represent a woman. It was found in 1925.

ABOVE THE VALLEY OF MEXICO

The village of Coapexco, perched at an altitude of 2,600m (8,500ft) on the side of Mount Ixtaccíhuatl, appears to have been a centre for trade in the highly prized volcanic glass obsidian c.1200BC, or it was perhaps the home to manufacturers of obsidian blades – archaeologists have found obsidian from distant and exotic sources at the site. Below in the Valley of Mexico villages established at Tlatilco on the western edge of Lake Texcoco and at Tlapacoya on the shore of Lake Chalco left remarkable stores of skilfully hand-modelled ceramic figures dating from c.1100BC. They represent mothers with babies, ball players, dwarfs, musicians, shamans, acrobats, hunchbacks and musicians. Some were found in house-hold waste, but others were placed in graves: as many as 60 were interred in a single grave at Tlatilco.

A ceremonial centre was constructed at Cuicuilco to the west of Lake Xochimilco in the Valley of Mexico c.400BC. Labourers raised a pyramid in four stages, from a circular base, finally facing it in stone and building two stair-cases climbing 27m (90ft) to a platform that held twin shrines. This is the earliest

Above: Olmec centres existed at Tres Zapotes, Río Chiquito, Portero Nuevo and Laguna de Los Cerros as well as at La Venta and San Lorenzo. Olmec influence spread as far as Chalcatzingo and Guatemala.

known pyramid-platform supporting two shrines. This feature would be adopted by many Mesoamerican peoples including the Aztecs, whose Great Pyramid in Tenochtitlán bore twin shrines to Tláloc and Huitzilopochtli. Cuicuilco rose to become a major population centre covering 400ha (1,000 acres) and home to 20,000 people. Just 1km (0.6 miles) to the east lay a collection of 11 sacred mounds at Peña Pobre.

CENTRAL AND SOUTHERN MAYA

The site of Nakbé in the lowlands of Guatemala was one of the pioneer centres of Maya civilization and was well established by 600BC. Public buildings included temples dedicated to the gods rather than individual rulers.

In southern Maya lands by c. 1800BC, people along the Pacific coast of Guatemala were living in permanent villages of 400–1,000 inhabitants, a size that suggests that a chieftain or leader was in control of the village. He might have established pre-eminence by giving gifts. The people of these settlements began to specialize in making salt, in fishing and in pottery.

THE RISE OF THE GREAT CITIES
300BC–AD250

The 500-odd years from 300BC to AD250 saw the emergence of great cities ruled by a king or members of a powerful elite. In the central highlands of Mexico, the most important was Teotihuacán, in the north-east part of the Valley of Mexico. In Oaxaca, Monte Albán was dominant. In the central Maya region, several significant centres emerged, including El Mirador and Tikal, where large stucco masks carved on temples and pyramids celebrated powerful royal dynasties.

A vibrant trade and exchange network arose and the elite groups clearly possessed great wealth. This is evident from the richness of palaces and other upper-class residences, the construction of lavish tombs and the laying out of wealthy grave offerings. The people of Teotihuacán prospered by trade rather than war, but the other major cities were built with the spoils of conquest. The Zapotecs of Monte Albán made a number of conquests and forced several communities to pay tribute. The cities of the central Maya region waged bitter war. Many centres – including Tikal, Monte Albán, Calakmul and Edzna – erected defensive walls and dug moats. Carved images of the period depict prisoners of war and sacrificial victims.

Above: The Zapotecs of Monte Albán had laid out their ball court on the north-eastern corner of the Great Plaza by AD100.

THE HOLY CITY

At the start of the period, Teotihuacán in the north-east part of the Valley of Mexico began to emerge as a centre to rival Cuicuilco in the southern part of the valley. Villages had existed in the Teotihuacán region since c.900BC.

The area was an ancient religious centre because of its network of caves and tunnels. (Mesoamericans viewed caverns as sacred places providing access to the underworld.) By c.300BC, Teotihuacán was growing, with evidence of obsidian workshops and other craft centres.

Both Cuicuilco and Teotihuacán drew people from throughout the Valley of Mexico; the two centres may have been rivals and perhaps even foes, as fortified and hilltop sites developed around the lakes of the Valley of Mexico in this period. However, an eruption of the Xitle volcano near Cuicuilco c.50 BC decided the matter. The area around Cuicuilco was devastated and the city abandoned in favour of Teotihuacán. The latter expanded rapidly: by AD150, it covered 20km (12 miles) and was home to around 80,000 people. Elsewhere in the Valley of Mexico settlers established villages for the first time on the eastern edge of Lake Texcoco. They could not farm these lands, so must have made their living from the waters of the lake.

OAXACA

In Oaxaca, Monte Albán established itself as the capital of the whole region, powerful in trade. Population rose from around 7,000 in 300BC to as many as 17,000 inhabitants one hundred years later, living in three distinct communities. As the centre of Monte Albán grew in importance and wealth, so did the area's previously pre-eminent community, San José Mogote, gradually become abandoned.

Like the Olmec before, the ruling elite in Monte Albán was able to command a vast labour force. Around the city's western and northern edge, 3km (2 miles) of defensive walls up to 4m (13ft) high were erected in a massive building project.

Left: This pyramid (E-VII) at Uaxactún is part of the Group E sacred complex aligned to solar and astronomical events.

Above: The Pyramid of the Moon, which is 46m (151ft) high, was built in Teotihuacán in the 1st century AD.

Another Oaxaca people, the Mixtecs, built hilltop centres at Yucuita and Monte Negro at the two ends of the Nochixtlán Valley in this era. Both featured ceremonial buildings laid out on an L plan, rather than around a plaza. Both sites were at their apogee c. 200BC.

SOUTHERN AND CENTRAL MAYA

In contrast to the far-reaching centralized powers of Teotihuacán and Monte Albán, in Maya territories several small, competing kingdoms developed.

In the southern Maya region, Kaminaljuyú was established in the Valley of Guatemala. In the years 400BC–AD100 its people laid out a large ritual centre, with several temple-pyramids – some containing burials – on either side of a long rectangular plaza or ceremonial way. Surviving statues depict rulers with divine characteristics – some wear a bird mask. These, together with lavish elite burials, suggest that the Kaminaljuyú nobility ruled with absolute authority. Izapa – on the Pacific coastal plain below the Sierra Madre de Chiapas – underwent a great expansion: more than 250 stone stelae, altars and carved boulders were added in 300–50BC. The style of carving on these stelae, which reveals some Olmec influence, would become highly influential, spreading as far to the east as the settlements of Belize and as far to the west as Tres Zapotes and Veracruz. Other expanding sites in the Pacific coastal region included Abaj Takalik, El Baúl, Monte Alto and Santa Leticia.

In the central Maya region, El Mirador was the largest city of this era, built c.150BC–AD150. It was at the hub of a system of causeways that linked it to several other cities, including Nakbé. Its central area was 2km (1⅕ miles) across and contained the vast El Tigre monument, which consists of a central pyramid with two smaller adjoining structures, all erected on a single base – and has a surface area six times larger than that of Temple IV, the largest building at nearby Tikal. Some historians believe that, alongside the settlement at Calakmul in the Campeche region of Mexico, El Mirador governed a state encompassing 10,000km (6,200 miles); monuments at Calakmul and El Mirador celebrated the same ancestral gods.

Tikal grew from a village in 300BC to a major dynastic city by AD300. Its oldest ceremonial structure, the North Acropolis, was begun c.250BC. The Mundo Perdido ('Lost World') complex was rebuilt many times up to AD300. A stela celebrating King Jaguar Paw I (r. AD278–317) erected in AD292 is the oldest known stela marked with a date in the Maya Long Count in the lowlands.

At Uaxactún, four temples were laid out according to precise astronomical alignment, in a pattern copied in many other cities, known to archaeologists as Group E. In this arrangement, three temples on the eastern side of a court were aligned so that at solstices and equinoxes the sun would rise above one of them when viewed from a fourth building erected to the west. Using these sightings, priests could keep precise track of time by pinpointing the year's shortest and longest days.

Río Azul in north-east Guatemala was established on the banks of the river Azul. Two temple platforms were built there in this era. In Belize, pyramids and plazas were laid out to celebrate the power of the king of Cerros beginning in 50BC.

THE GLORY OF TEOTIHUACÁN
AD300–500

Teotihuacán continued to expand in size and influence. Thousands of apartment buildings were constructed in the years AD300–500. They were built in compounds, each with room for 60–100 people, probably grouped by kin relationship or craft specialization. Elite dwellings alongside the Street of the Dead were built for higher social groups. The city reached its peak c.AD500, with a population of 125,000–200,000. This made it the sixth largest city in the world at the time.

GROWING SPHERE OF INFLUENCE

Some members of this vast population were incomers from other parts of Mesoamerica. One area in the north-eastern part of the city was dubbed the Merchants' Barrio by archaeologists because a large amount of pottery from other Mesoamerican regions was found there. Historians now believe that people from the Gulf coast and the central Maya region made their home there in the years AD300–500. Farther west, another part of the city was home to Zapotec incomers from the Oaxaca region.

Teotihuacán was a major religious centre, built on an ancient sacred site. More than 1,000 shrines and temples lined the Street of the Dead. A large number of full-time priests and temple staff must have resided in the city. Nevertheless, two-thirds of the population were farmers, primarily raising crops of amaranth, maize and squash. Some 9,700 hectares were irrigated, stretching to a distance of around 15km (9 miles) from the city centre. Many artisans and traders lived and worked in the city and its influence – so significant and far-reaching that one could almost speak of an empire – was spread by trade and exchange rather than by war or threat of military force.

The Maya city of Kaminaljuyú in the Guatemala Valley was drawn into Teotihuacán's sphere of influence through trade, probably in obsidian from the

Left: Clay figurines, such as this warrior, were used in religious rites in Teotihuacáno homes.

Guatemalan site of El Chayal. In this period, Kaminaljuyú's ceremonial centre was remodelled in the *talud-tablero* (sloping apron/vertical panel) architectural style of Teotihuacán. There might even have been intermarriage between the elites of the two cities. Teotihuacán traders also established a centre at Matacapan in Veracruz in AD400–500.

Monte Albán also continued to thrive, and its population grew. Farmers began to specialize, promoting the growth of a market in agricultural goods. The Zapotecs established a sacred site at Mitla in the Oaxaca region after c.AD300. Its name comes from its Aztec Nahuatl name *Mictlan* ('Realm of the Dead').

CENTRAL MAYA REGION

In the central Maya region, the population reached a maximum of about a million by c.AD300, after 600 years of steady growth since 300BC. Tikal rose to a pre-eminent position, eclipsing the power of El Mirador.

Many buildings in the North Acropolis were built over earlier constructions between AD250 and AD550. The area was a necropolis celebrating the city's ruling dynasty: eight funerary temples were laid out in a symmetrical pattern on a vast platform of 80m (260ft) by 100m (320ft). Like the structures at Kaminaljuyú, Tikal's buildings show evidence of the influence of Teotihuacáno *talud-tablero* architectural style.

A ruler named Yax Moch Xoc was afterwards celebrated at Tikal as the founder of this dynasty. He laid the foundations of Tikal's greatness by establishing the city as an independent ruling centre either through political acumen or military might. His early successors included Moon Zero Bird (whose accession c.AD320 and might are celebrated on the jadeite celt known to scholars as the Leyden plaque) and the great king Stormy Sky, whose mortuary shrine was built in Tikal's North Acropolis.

Lowland rivals Tikal and Uaxactún were drawn into increasingly fierce competition that culminated in AD378 when Tikal took control of its rival. A member of the Tikal dynastic elite named Smoking Frog – perhaps the brother of King Great Jaguar Paw – was either installed on the throne at Uaxactún or led a successful war against the city and seized power there. Two carved monuments at each site commemorate the event: bodies found in a tomb at Uaxactún near one of these monuments may be those of the Uaxactún king's family, buried there while the defeated king himself was taken to Tikal for ceremonial slaughter. In the reign of Smoking Frog's successor, Curl Nose, Tikal appears also to have conquered Río Azul c.AD385: altars at Río Azul commemorate the execution of eight local rulers, and Tikal kings are commemorated elsewhere at the site.

Tikal maintained close links to southern Mayan centres, notably Kaminaljuyú. The tomb of the Tikal king Curl Nose, who died c.AD425, contains offerings that prove links with elite burials at Kaminaljuyú. Some scholars have suggested that Curl Nose was a native of Kaminaljuyú who married into the ruling Tikal dynasty. By this route, the influence of Teotihuacán, which was strong at Kaminaljuyú, might have reached Tikal and can be seen in the style of carvings during the reigns of Curl Nose and his son and successor Stormy Sky.

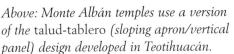

Above: Monte Albán temples use a version of the talud-tablero *(sloping apron/vertical panel) design developed in Teotihuacán.*

Alternatively, there might have been direct trading contacts between Teotihuacán and Tikal. In Stormy Sky's reign, Tikal's power spread further still, to reach Yaxchilán, Quiriguá and even Copán in modern Honduras. A Tikal emblem was carved on a lintel at Yaxchilán c.AD504 and a style associated with Tikal appeared in the carving of monuments at both Copán and Quiriguá during this period.

SOUTHERN MAYA REGION

In the south-east Maya lowlands, Copán in western Honduras became a major centre in the 5th century AD. People had lived in villages in this fertile valley setting since c.1000BC, but the settlement began to expand significantly from c.AD250 onwards. The great dynasty of Copán was founded by Yax Kuk Mo' in AD426. In his reign, the first ritual and administrative buildings were erected at Copán.

Left: Tikal's North Acropolis is one of the city's oldest parts. The towering Temple I (right) was built in the 8th century AD.

POWER CHANGES HANDS
AD500–700

Teotihuacán continued to thrive until c.AD550–650, when its vibrant trading network began to fail in the face of competition from the east. In the period up to c.AD750, the city maintained a prosperous appearance, despite the fact that decline had set in. The palace of Quetzalpapálotl in the south-west of the Plaza of the Moon, was built after AD500 and the magnificent murals in the Techinantitla apartment building were painted c.AD650–750.

Monte Albán expanded greatly in the years AD500–750, covering 6.5km (4 miles) and supporting a population of as many as 24,000.

There were friendly relations between the Zapotec capital and Teotihuacán. Not only were Zapotecs resident in Teotihuacán but, according to carvings on stelae at the South Platform of the Main Plaza at Monte Albán, Teotihuacáno diplomats paid a state visit to the Oaxacan capital.

Above: This figurine, found in Palenque, represents one of the members of the city's elite group of astronomer-priests.

Below: The Palace of Quetzalpapálotl is an example of the high-status residential and public buildings that continued to be erected in Teotihuacán, despite the city's continuing decline.

CENTRAL MAYA REGION

Population of the Maya lowlands in AD500 was an estimated one million, but by c.AD600, numbers of people began to climb very significantly, reaching a peak c.AD800 of 2.6–3.4 million.

In the first part of this period Tikal continued to thrive. Its success throughout this early-to-mid Classic Period was derived partly from its position: the site was rich in the highly prized natural resource of flint (needed for making chipped stone tools), and lay close to two seasonal swamps or lakes that could be used for intensive farming. The swamps, situated to east and west, helped to make the site easily defensible in times of conflict. Close to rivers that connected it ultimately both to the Gulf and to the Caribbean, Tikal was ideally situated for trade and commerce.

The city appears to have had a vibrant society, with potential for upward movement through military or trading success and this probably helped to inspire its rise and expansion. Tikal was also a major religious centre and place of pilgrimage. It was, finally, one of the pioneers of dynastic kingship in the Maya world. When places such as Calakmul, Yaxchilán, Caracol and Copán were rising to prominence, Tikal was revered as a divinely inspired forerunner.

However, from c.AD530, Tikal's position was eclipsed by rivals for a period and its wealth declined severely for about 150 years. Following an attack on Caracol in AD556, in the reign of the Tikal king Double Bird, Tikal was defeated by its rival. A carved ball game marker at Caracol, which archaeologists used to believe was an altar and therefore labelled Altar 21, celebrates the victory of King Lord Water over Tikal in AD562. This probably led to the sacrifice of Double Bird. Tikal entered a period in which its royal burials were far less rich and no significant stelae were erected. The city might well have been diverting much of

Above: Caracol was a major Maya city in Belize. Its core contained 128 plaza groups; the site covered 50sq km (19sq miles).

its wealth to Caracol, which expanded greatly, and Tikal's rulers may have been forbidden by Caracol to erect any stelae.

Refugees from Tikal travelled southwards to the rainforested Petexbatun region close to a major tributary of the Usumacinta river named the Pasión river, where they founded twin capitals at Dos Pilas and Aguateca. The first ruler, Flint Sky, was in power in Dos Pilas in AD647. His emblem glyph was almost identical to that of the Tikal dynasty. Meanwhile, Calakmul in the south-eastern Campeche region of Mexico rose to prominence in the years after AD600 and was an ally of Caracol in wars in the Maya lowlands. With Calakmul's backing, Caracol defeated Naranjo in AD631. Calakmul also entered into alliance with Dos Pilas.

Dos Pilas went on to challenge the formerly mighty Tikal and fought several campaigns, culminating in the defeat of the Tikal ruler Shield Skull by Flint Sky of Dos Pilas in AD679. Flint Sky celebrated his victories in a hieroglyphic stairway at Dos Pilas. However, Tikal's pride was to be reborn. In AD695, King

Ah Cacau of Tikal captured and sacrificed Jaguar Paw-Jaguar of Calakmul. Meanwhile, in the south-western Maya lowlands, Palenque established itself as a major power and the dominant force in the region in the early 7th century AD. Inscriptions at the site provide a long dynastic list, going back as far as the probable founder, Balam Kuk, who came to the throne in AD431 and even further beyond to an assuredly mythical figure named Kin Chan, who was said to have come to the throne in 967BC. However, the city's great success coincided with the long and stable reign of King Pacal, whose splendid tomb would be laid beneath the Temple of Inscriptions in his city. Pacal came to the throne in AD615 and the earliest surviving use of the Palenque emblem glyph is dated to his reign.

SOUTHERN MAYA REGION

Kaminaljuyú thrived greatly by trade in obsidian, but began to decline after AD550, perhaps because the waning of Teotihuacán affected trade. The settlements of the Guatemala Valley became markedly less prosperous and were abandoned altogether by c.AD800, as their inhabitants retreated to more easily fortified and defended hilltop positions.

Copán greatly expanded its sphere of influence, particularly in the long reigns of Butz' Chan (AD578–628) and Smoke Jaguar (AD628–95). In this time of great dynastic strength and stability, Copán took control of Quiriguá in AD653 and of much of the valley of the Motagua river, and thus of the trade in jade and obsidian that travelled down that corridor from the highlands to the Caribbean sea.

Above: Stelae celebrate rulers of Calakmul in south-eastern Campeche. Calakmul was at least as large as its famed rival Tikal.

299

THE COLLAPSE OF SOCIAL ORDER
AD700–900

In the years after AD700, Teotihuacán continued its slow collapse in prestige and power as the city's merchants endured the decay of the trade network that had once connected them to Veracruz, Tikal, the Guatemala Valley and beyond. After a fire c.AD750, the centre was abandoned, but about 40,000 people continued to live in outlying parts of the city. Monte Albán declined at the same time, beginning c.AD750, as the people of the Oaxaca valleys turned to local centres such as Lambityeco and Jalieza rather than the regional capital for the focus of their ritual life and work. Monte Albán's hilltop was abandoned and its population declined to about 4,000 by AD900.

The collapse of the centuries-old social order embodied by large centres such as Teotihuacán created a period of flux and of military conflict between small kingdoms. Peoples competed for trade and pre-eminence: many groups were on the move in the 7th, 8th and 9th centuries, leading to shifts in balance of

Below: Xochicalco and El Tajín were among the centres that rose to prominence with the decline of Teotihuacán and Monte Albán.

power and the emergence of new settlements. A Maya group named the Olmeca-Xicalanga travelled westwards from southern Veracruz and Tabasco to establish their capital in the fortress of Cacaxtla, on a hilltop dominating the Tlaxcala Valley, some time after AD650. The city, renowned for its murals, was at its peak until AD900. Settlements were established at Azcopatzalco, Cerro Portesuelo, Xico and Cerro de la Estrella in the Valley of Mexico.

To the south of the Valley of Mexico the fortified city of Xochicalco, in the western part of the Morelos region, won itself a regional state reaching west into the Balsas Depression, north into the Ajusco Mountains and south-west into the region known as Mixteca Baja. Xochicalco, although occupied in the previous centuries, was at its height in the years c.AD700–900.

In the tropical rainforest of northern Veracruz, El Tajín became an important centre. The site had been settled as early as c.AD100 and had thrived by contact with Teotihuacán: as Teotihuacáno influence waned, El Tajín began to assert its authority over its region. The same

Above: Carved columns on the roof of the Temple of the Warriors, Chichén Itzá, once supported the roof. The Castillo is beyond.

process – of increasing independence following the decline of Teotihuacán – applied to Cholula (in modern Puebla) and other city-states.

THE RISE OF THE ITZÁ
Other Maya groups known as the Chontal-speaking Maya, the Putún and the Itzá spread out from a base in the region of Chontalapa, in northern coastal Tabasco and south-western Campeche, at the western edge of the Yucatán peninsula. They were warrior-merchants, seeking political control and wealth through trade. Some established themselves at Palenque in the 7th to 9th centuries, others moved inland along the Usumacinta river to Yaxchilán, Altar de Sacrificios and Seibal. Putún Maya may have travelled into the southern Maya region along the upper reaches of the Usumacinta in the northern highlands.

The Itzá moved up the western coast of the Yucatán peninsula, then went inland towards the cities of Uxmal and Chichén Itzá. Most historians believe that the Itzá were established in Chichén Itzá by AD850. Inscriptions on important buildings at Chichén Itzá raised in the years AD869–81 praise an early Itzá leader named Kakupacal, who claimed to be related to the dynasty of Palenque.

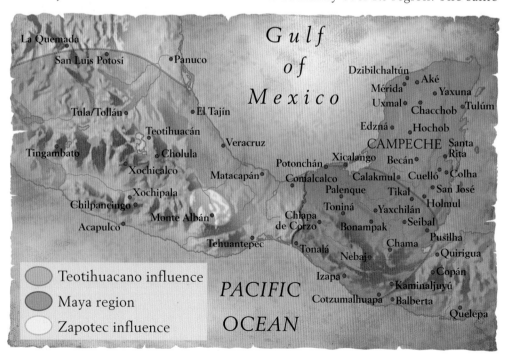

La Quemada
San Luis Potosí
Panuco
Gulf of Mexico
Dzibilchaltún
Mérida • Aké
Uxmal • Yaxuna
Chacchob • Tulúm
Tula/Tollán
El Tajín
Edzná • Hochob
Teotihuacán
Veracruz
CAMPECHE Santa Rita
Tingambato
Cholula
Xicalango Becán
Potonchán
Xochicalco
Matacapán
Comalcalco Calakmul • Cuelló • Colha
Xochipala
Palenque Tikal • San José
Chilpancingo
Toniná • Yaxchilán Holmul
Acapulco
Monte Albán
Chiapa de Corzo Bonampak • Seibal
Tehuantepec
Chama Pusilha
Tonalá
Nebaj Quirigua
Izapa • Copán
PACIFIC
Kaminaljuyú
Cotzumalhuapa • Balberta
OCEAN
Quelepa

○ Teotihuacano influence
● Maya region
○ Zapotec influence

CENTRAL MAYA REGION

In the Petexbatun region, Dos Pilas built a short-lived empire through warfare and diplomacy. After the death of the city's founder, Flint Sky, his son – known to historians as Shield God K – took power in AD698 and entered an alliance with Naranjo. His successor, who is known only as Ruler 3, defeated Seibal in AD735, made a marriage alliance with Cancuén and was also allied to the great power of Caracol. His successor, Ruler 4, extended the empire to cover c.4,000km (2,500 miles), but in AD761 he was captured and beheaded by a rival lord at Tamarindito. The power at the centre was gone and the area plunged into bitter conflict. Dos Pilas was largely abandoned after the AD761 war.

Palenque was at war with the city of Toniná in the Ocosingo Valley in the early 8th century. King Kan Xul II of Palenque was captured and beheaded by the ruler of Toniná in AD711.

In the Maya lowlands, Tikal enjoyed a great renaissance after more than 150 years in which it had erected no stelae and apparently suffered a severe decline in wealth. King Ah Cacau restored the city's military and political standing abroad by defeating the rival city of Calakmul and embarked on major building projects at home, including the erection of Temples I and II.

THE MAYA COLLAPSE

In the late 8th and 9th centuries the city-states of the Maya lowlands one by one stopped erecting stelae celebrating their divine kings. The cities fell into decline before being finally abandoned altogether. Historians believe that the decline was caused by a chain of events kick-started by overpopulation in the region, which led to ever more intensive farming and the degradation of the environment, matched by a fiercer form of warfare that focused less on raiding for prestige and more on territorial expansion. The result

Above: A Cacaxtla mural figure showing a man transformed into a jaguar, c.AD900.

was population decline – numbers in the southern lowlands fell by one-third in the century after AD830. Several sites – including Piedras Negras, Quiriguá, Naranjo and Calakmul – erected their last stela in AD810. The last carved stela was raised at Caracol in AD859 and at Tikal in AD869.

At Tikal, as at Dos Pilas and many other formerly magnificent centres, the cities were invaded by squatters who eked out a living in thatched homes on the great ceremonial plazas: they were not afraid to move monuments and even break into the tombs of once great kings in search of riches. However, this collapse did not take effect farther east in coastal or riverside settlements in Belize, where Rita Caracol, Lamanai and other sites continued to thrive after AD900.

Quiriguá in the Motagua Valley had been subject to Copán since AD653, but rose to challenge its overlord. In AD738 Cauac Sky of Quiriguá beheaded King 18 Rabbit of Copán. In this way, Quiriguá gained control of the lucrative trade in obsidian, jade and other items passing from the Guatemalan highlands along the Motagua valley.

THE TRIUMPH OF THE TOLTECS
AD900–1200

The city of Tollán (modern Tula) in the state of Hidalgo took over from Teotihuacán as the pre-eminent centre of highland Mexico c.AD950. It stood on a ridge overlooking a tributary of the Pánuco river named the Tula, near to the northern limit of Mesoamerica. It ruled for more than 200 years.

HOME OF THE TOLTECS
The Aztecs and early chroniclers wove a web of religious narrative around the origins of this city, home to the Toltecs so revered by the México of Tenochtitlán and also to the great feathered serpent god, Quetzalcóatl. According to this narrative, Quetzalcóatl or Ce Acatl Topiltzin was the son of a leader of the Chichimec people, who left his home at

Above: Each of the temple-top figures at Tollán (Tula) wears warrior garb: a butterfly breastplate and feathered headdress.

Culhuacán in the Valley of Mexico to assume leadership of the Toltec community of Tollán. Here he presided over a wondrous age of artistic expression and scientific achievement, but a Toltec named Huastec – in conjunction with Tezcatlipoca, god of darkness and fate – brought disgrace upon Ce Acatl Topiltzin, who departed from the city. Different versions recount that he either cast himself on a sacrificial pyre and rose into the heavens as the planet Venus or that he sailed away to the east on a raft of snakes, promising to return.

Historians do not know for sure who the Toltec founders of Tollán were. The evidence suggests that they were warlike incomers from the north.

The city they built covered 13sq km (8sq miles) and was home to a population of up to 60,000 people. It was a centre for craftspeople working obsidian, making pots, stoneware and tools from chert. The ritual centre – consisting of two plazas, two pyramids, meeting halls and two ball courts – was oriented precisely 18 degrees east of true north.

From Tollán the Toltecs exerted control over – and probably received tribute from – a sizeable area, incorporating the northern part of the Valley of Mexico, the region of modern Hidalgo state as far east as Tulancingo, plus the Toluca Valley, areas of the Bajío and territories around the Lerma River. The empire's days of glory were numbered, however, and the city was overrun and burned c.1150–1200.

In the period of Tollán's pre-eminence, the settlement of Cholula in the Puebla region of Mexico was also thriving. The town's wealth and prestige were such that its pyramid was rebuilt to a height of 55m (180ft). Historians are uncertain whether Cholula was a rival or an ally of Tollán.

CHICHÉN ITZÁ
Another legend concerning the Toltecs suggests that a group from Tollán led by Quetzalcóatl travelled to the Gulf Coast in the 10th century and then under the

Below: Towering carved warriors facing west atop the Temple of Tlahuizcalpantecuhtli at Tollán (Tula) proclaim Toltec might.

Above: The six tiers and crowning temple of the Pyramid of the Niches, El Tajín, were built over a similar earlier version of the building.

leadership of Kukulcán (the Maya form of Quetzalcóatl) made their way to northern Yucatán, where they settled in Chichén Itzá. Many elements of Toltec/Mexican style in architecture and religious iconography appeared at Chichén Itzá; these were most likely spread through trade.

Chichén Itzá was by now the heart of a growing tributary empire. The Tutil Xiu, an Itzá elite and ruling dynasty, grew wealthy by trading in salt from the Yucatán salt beds, in obsidian, which they imported from Mexico, in ceramics and in basalt. They developed port facilities on Ilsa Cerritos, an island just off the northern coast of Yucatán. They ruled through a group of nobles rather than through a single, divinely blessed king. However, the Itzá apparently made many enemies, for native chronicles contain many slighting references to these successful incomers. Around 1100, the city of Mayapán was founded around 100km (80 miles) to the west of Chichén Itzá and quickly became its principal rival.

A NICHE IN VERACRUZ

El Tajín continued to thrive in northern Veracruz. Its six-tier Pyramid of the Niches is an elaborate variation on Teotihuacáno *talud-tablero* architectural style. The site also contains no fewer than 12 ball courts: the city may have been a centre for playing the game and could have hosted regional competitions. There is even the possibility that many centuries before El Tajín's independent glory, the ball game could have been developed in this part of Mesoamerica.

SOUTHERN MAYA LANDS

In the period of Chichén Itzá's glory, northern raiders appear to have brought terror to Southern Maya regions, where many settlements on valley floors were abandoned as people moved to easily defensible hilltop settings, and built ditches, walls and other fortifications. These incomers came either from northern Yucatán or from the Gulf Coast region of Chontalapa. They brought their architectural style and warrior imagery along with them.

A settlement at Chuitinamit-Atitlan on Lake Atitlan has a carving of a feathered serpent mouth opening to release human heads that is reminiscent of imagery at Chichén Itzá. Another at Chalchitan, on the Uscaminta tributary the Chixoy, contains a platform that may be a Chichén Itzá-style skull rack or *tzompantli*, on which skulls were displayed.

LAND RAIDERS
1200–1325

Tollán was sacked by raiders in c.1150–1200. The city's violent demise was followed by 150 years of turmoil in the central highlands of Mexico, as warring groups of nomads known collectively as Chichimecs ('Sons of the Dog') spread through the Valley of Mexico and beyond, scrambling for control of the strategic settlements and well-watered agricultural land. All claimed descent from the Toltecs and a link to the glory that had been Tollán.

RICH PICKINGS
One powerful Chichimec leader, Xólotl, founded the settlement of Tenayuca, to the west of Lake Texcoco, then later transferred his capital across the water to establish Texcoco. Another group, which claimed to have the closest links to the Toltecs, settled at Culhuacán, south of the lake. The Tepanecs settled at Azcapotzalco, which had been founded towards the end of Teotihuacán's era of

Below: The fortress-town of Tulum, above the Caribbean Sea, was protected by cliffs and an 800m (half-mile) wall.

glory c.AD800–900. Lands all around Lake Texcoco were settled by Chichimecs and descendants of survivors from the fall of Teotihuacán and Tollán: towards the northern end were Tenayuca and Azcapotzalco; to the east lay Huextola and Coatlichan; to the south was Chalco, Cuitláhuac, Xochimilco, Xico, Mixquic

Above: Five circular platforms supported temples and might have housed elite burials in the Tarascan capital, Tzintzuntzan.

and Amecameca as well as Culhuacán. A tribe calling themselves the México, who were destined to establish the Aztec empire, came into the region after all the best land had been taken, probably towards the end of the 13th century.

THE FIRST AZTECS
Historians cannot easily supply an accurate account of the early years of the tribe, for the México/Aztecs later embellished their history in an attempt to justify their standing and to emphasize their links to the Toltecs of yore. It appears that they came into the region under the leadership of Tenoch, and settled near Chapultepec to the west of Lake Texcoco. When they were attacked by the Tepanecs of Azcapotzalco and the people of Culhuacán, the México cast themselves upon the mercy of Culhuacán. They settled nearby at a place named Tizapán and proved themselves capable agriculturists, adapting swiftly to the lakeside setting. They married into local families

and began to call themselves the México-Culhua. They fought alongside the Culhua against Xochimilco and also served the Tepanecs of Azcapotzalco. Then, after a dramatic dispute with the leaders of Culhuacán – in one account after they sacrificed the daughter of a leading Culhua lord – they moved on to the south and established their own city, named Tenochtitlán in Tenoch's honour, on an island in Lake Texcoco. This probably occurred in 1325. Tenoch was the first leader of Tenochtitlán, and was celebrated as *tlatoani* ('He who Speaks'), the title given to the ruler of the city, until the collapse of the Aztec empire in 1521.

POWER STRUGGLE IN YUCATÁN

The Tutul Xiu rulers of Chichén Itzá were driven from power in the 13th century by the Cocoms, a rival group of Itzá from Mayapán. According to the chronicles, the Cocoms hired a mercenary named Hunac Ceel from Tabasco who, by trickery and military force, forced the

Below: This haunting shell carving was made by a craftsman from Mayapán, rising power and controller of coastal trade.

Tutul Xiu from power and seized control of the city. The chronicles set these events c.1221 or 1283. There is archaeological evidence that Chichén Itzá was sacked in the early 13th century, but there are also signs that it was gradually abandoned. The Tutul Xiu might have been unable to maintain the elite that gathered around them and the city may also have suffered from drought and starvation.

Whether gradually or at a stroke, Mayapán became the major city of the area and took control of the lucrative coastal trade. It founded a league of city-states in northern Yucatán – itself, Chichén Itzá and Uxmal – that built a tributary empire. In the new capital at Mayapán, the Cocom built a smaller-scale version of the magnificent Temple of Kukulcán at Chichén Itzá. Mayapán was a city of around 15,000 people at its height. As a way of maintaining central authority, the Cocom rulers brought in the heads of tributary-paying states to reside in the capital city, as the Aztecs would later do.

On the east coast of Yucatán the fortified clifftop settlement at Tulum was established c.1200, probably by the rulers of Mayapán, as a coastal trading centre. At Tulum, and nearby Xelhá and Tancah, on the Isla de Cozumel, and farther south on the east coast of Yucatán, several settlements grew prosperous under the rule of the Mayapán alliance.

Above: Mayapán's principal sacred building is the nine-tiered Temple of the Feathered Serpent, now called Kukulcán's Castle.

Some of the survivors of the fall of Chichén Itzá headed south into the rain forests of El Petén and founded a new capital called Tayasal on Lake Petén Itzá in north-western Guatemala. There they would thrive until 1697, when they were finally conquered by the Spanish.

HIGHLAND KINGDOMS

In southern Maya lands, another wave of 'Mexicanized' Putún Maya warriors established kingdoms in the highlands. They arrived from the Gulf Coast lowlands c.1200 and set up mountain-top fortresses from which they brutally subjugated the local people. By c.1350, one group, the Quiché, had established rule over the central highlands. They established their capital, Ismachi, on a narrow piece of land between two ravines.

THE TARASCANS AND TZINTZUNTZAN

At Lake Patzcuaro in Michoacán four communities were established by c.1200: Tzintzuntzan, Ihuatzio, Pátzcuaro and the island settlement of Pacanda. The king of Tzintzuntzan, Tariácuri, took control of the four local powers and set out to forge an empire. This Tarascan kingdom became an arch rival of the México/Aztecs.

THE MÉXICA FORGE AN EMPIRE
1325–1517

On Lake Texcoco, the México/Aztecs founded a second settlement, named Tlatelolco, on a nearby island in 1358. They won acclaim as mercenaries, fighting for Tezozómoc, the Tepanec leader of Azcapotzalco, in wars against Texcoco and Culhaucán, as he built up a great empire.

The México/Aztecs expanded their territorial holdings by gaining *chinampa* agricultural fields in the region of Lake Xochimilco, to the south of Lake Texcoco. However, they came increasingly to resent their subject position and the Tepanecs warily watched their neighbours straining at the leash.

Below: The Selden Codex, *probably written in the Nochixtlán valley, Oaxaca, contains Mixtec genealogies covering* AD794–1556.

In 1428, following the death of Tezozómoc, the México/Aztecs rose up in alliance with Texcoco and Tlacopán to defeat the might of Azcapotzalco. The victorious members of this Triple Alliance divided the Tepanec empire three ways. Tenochtitlán took land to the north and south of Lake Texcoco. Land to the east went to Texcoco and territories in the western part of the Valley of Mexico went to Tlacopán. The Triple Alliance held sway over the Valley of Mexico and beyond until the arrival of the Spanish in the early 16th century. It was the basis of the Aztec empire.

The Aztec *tlatoani* Moctezuma I (*r.* 1440–69) led a great campaign of expansion, extending territorial holdings as far as the Gulf Coast. His successor and

Right: This jade funerary mask was made by a México artisan at the height of the Aztec empire.

grandson Axayácatl (*r.* 1469–81) led campaigns towards the west but was defeated by the Tarascans of Tzintzuntzan, and towards the east where he established control in central parts of Veracruz. He also took control of neighbouring Tlatelolco for Tenochtitlán in 1473. After Axayácatl was succeeded briefly by his undistinguished brother, Tízoc (*r.* 1481–6), a third of Moctezuma's grandsons, Ahuítzotl (*r.* 1486–1502), took power. He gained control over the basin of the Balsas river and coastal lands in Guerrero, as well as much of the Isthmus of Tehauntepec. After several attempts, the Aztecs conquered the sacred site of Mitla, in the Oaxaca region in 1494, and forced the Mixtec residents to pay tribute to Tenochtitlán. Under Moctezuma II in 1519, Aztec imperial holdings covered 150,000sq km (58,000sq miles).

POWER SHIFT IN YUCATÁN
Mayapán was sacked and burned *c.*1450. The nobles of the Tutul Xiu dynasty ousted at Chichén Itzá in the early 13th century had been living in exile among the ruins of Uxmal, a site sacred to them. One of their number, Ah Xupán, led a rebellion against Mayapán's ruling Cocom elite, slaughtering all of the city's rulers bar one, who was on a trading mission.

Above: A coatepantli ('serpent wall') encloses three sides of the Aztec pyramid at Tenayuca, near modern Tlalnepantla in Mexico City.

Most of the larger cities of northern Yucatán entered a decline following the fall of Mayapán. Survivors established new cities: one noble family, the Chels, founded Tecoh; the one surviving Cocom ruler made a new start at Tibolon, close to Sotuta. And the Tutul Xiu, glorying in revenge, founded a new settlement at Mani.

In this period, Chichén Itzá and Uxmal were pilgrimage sites, often visited as shrines. Times were hard in northern Yucatán. A hurricane struck in 1464 and the people were severely reduced by a plague in 1480. This was followed by an epidemic of smallpox in 1514.

In the wake of Mayapán's collapse, a settlement was founded at Santa Rita Corozal on the eastern coast at Chetumal Bay. Known as Chetumal, the city was the capital of a state of the same name. Chetumal/Santa Rita Corozal and other settlements in coastal regions of eastern Yucatán continued to thrive until the arrival of the Spanish in the 16th century.

At Tulum and Santa Rita Corozal, delicately rendered murals were painted in the second half of the 15th century in the Mixteca-Puebla style familiar from centres in Puebla and Oaxaca, such as Mitla. A wealthy elite in eastern Yucatán was rich enough to be able to pay for renowned artists from Mexico to produce these splendid wall paintings.

SOUTHERN MAYA LANDS

The Quiché abandoned their capital of Ismachi and founded another, Gumarcaaj or Utatlan, in the early 1400s. They subjugated other peoples and established a Quiché realm, but in 1470 one of these peoples, the Cakchiquels, rebelled and created a rival state. They set up their own capital at Iximche. The two groups fought fiercely. The Cakchiquels held the ascendancy when the Spanish arrived in the region. Other highland city-states included one established by the Pokomam, with a capital at Mixco Viejo; one built by the Mam, with a stronghold at Zaculeu; and the territory of the Tzutuhil at Atitlan, on Lake Atitlan. All these peoples claimed to be descended from the Toltecs.

WESTERN MEXICO

In Michoacán, the small empire of the Tarascans, based at Tzintzuntzan on Lake Pátzcuaro, was strong. They succeeded in holding the Aztecs at bay. Neither the efforts of Moctezuma I nor the expansionist campaigns of Itzcóatl succeeded in bringing the Tarascans into the Aztec empire. The Tarascan army maintained tight control over a small area in the basin of Lake Pátzcuaro within the boundaries of the modern state of Michoacán.

Below: The Mixtecs, Zapotecs, Totonacs and Huastecs were within the Aztec empire, but the Tarascans held imperial forces at bay.

CHAPTER 15

INFINITE RICHES

All principal Aztec towns in the Valley of Mexico contained a bustling marketplace, located close to the main temple. Merchants were required by law to take their goods to this commercial centre and were forbidden to attempt to sell elsewhere – buyers and sellers risked incurring the wrath of the market god if they did business away from the official place of commerce. On a busy day, 60,000 people might be crammed in the Aztec empire's marketplace in Tlatelolco, Tenochtitlán's twin settlement in Lake Texcoco – making it the largest market in the world at the time. The Aztecs relied on trade – and on goods from an extensive network of tribute-paying areas within the empire – to provide them with foodstuffs, military equipment and other necessaries and with the rare and exotic goods used in their colourful religious ceremonies.

Long-distance trade was a key element of Mesoamerican life, with beginnings in the Olmec civilization of the 2nd millennium BC. Throughout the region's history, trade links between far-flung communities provided conduits along which religious practices, political ideas and artistic styles could pass. Trade was an alternative to warfare as a means of spreading dynastic and political influence, so much so that it is often difficult to establish whether architectural features or religious imagery from the city of Teotihuacán, for example, reached Guatemalan sites such as Kaminaljuyú and Tikal through conquest or trade.

Left: These columns, carved in the Toltec style, stand in the area of Chichén Itzá believed to have been the marketplace.

FIRST TRADERS

Trade flourished in Mesoamerica from early times because of the region's great geographic diversity across relatively short distances. The wide variety of terrain, soil and climate – from tropical jungle to river valley, coastal estuary to highland lake – meant that materials could be found and items manufactured in one setting that were much in demand in a nearby region. Trade networks were established by at least the 2nd millennium BC; they might have grown from a pattern of exchange and gift-giving between elite groups at different sites.

FIRST SETTLEMENTS

The first large Mesoamerican settlements arose in the Gulf Coast lowlands because the productive coastal land allowed its Olmec settlers to produce agricultural surpluses. Elite groups emerged with the power and resources to construct ceremonial and ritual centres. They were also well situated to import raw materials from highland areas inland. At San Lorenzo, on a plateau raised around 50m (164ft) above the surrounding land, settlers built a ritual centre after c.1250BC.

Below: Trade promoted political contact. This Olmec carving from La Venta is thought to be of a visiting ambassador.

Using earth and coloured clay, labourers erected platform mounds around rectangular courts arranged on a north–south axis, but oriented 8 degrees west of true north. They arranged colossal carved stone heads and altars or thrones in the ritual centre.

The basalt for these sculptures was imported from the Tuxtla mountains 70km (40 miles) away; the blocks were carved at the mountains and then floated on rafts by sea and up the Coatzacoalco river to San Lorenzo. Historians believe that the heads were images of Olmec rulers and the large 'altars' were their thrones. A remarkable buried basalt drain was 170m (550ft) long and with three branches, connected to fountains and ponds, which might have been used either functionally or in religious ceremony.

TRADING NETWORKS

The Olmec established centres – such as Chalcatzingo in the valley of the Amatzinac and Teopantecuanitlán rivers close to the Amacuzac river – to trade with and exploit the resources of less developed local cultures. Olmec trading networks extended over very long distances – there is evidence of contact with the valley of the Motagua river in Guatemala and as far as Chalchuapa in El Salvador. The networks distributed goods manufactured in the large Olmec centres in return for minerals and rare stones. In this period the Olmec were probably importing obsidian from or through the village of Coapexco. This clung to the side of the Ixtaccíhuatl

Left: Demand for elite goods propelled the growth of trade. This mask of c.AD200 is made of precious jade.

volcano at a height of 2,600m (8,500ft) and seems to have been a centre for trading in or manufacturing blades of obsidian. Archaeologists have found Olmec pots, grinding tools, ritual figurines and stamps at the site, but they cannot be sure whether these finds are evidence of Olmec trade with local people or of communities of Olmec living in Coapexco.

At Tlatilco on the western shore of Lake Texcoco, people buried their dead with Olmec pots and clay figurines. Here and elsewhere in Oaxaca and Puebla large numbers of Olmec 'dolls' – small hollow clay figures with chubby, outspread legs and baby faces – were collected. Las Bocas in Puebla has yielded a number of these baby figurines and it must have had significant contact with Olmec traders.

TRADING CENTRES

In the Morelos region, Chalcatzingo grew wealthy as a trading centre. The village lies in the valley of the River Amatzinac at the foot of a cliff and would have been well situated as a centre for three trade routes: one heading north to the Valley of Mexico, one going south towards Guerrero and a third running south-east to the Olmec region of the Gulf Coast and the Zapotec sites of Oaxaca. From the Amatzinac valley came cotton, hematite, lime and kaolin; from the region of the Valley of Mexico traders arrived carrying salt and obsidian; while from

Above: Zapotec artists painted this mural in Tomb 105, one of the best-preserved tombs in Monte Albán, c.AD200.

Guerrero merchants came bearing loads of hematite, jadeite and magnetite. Before 1100BC, Chalcatzingo was equipped with a stone-paved public area and two stone-covered platforms about 2m (7ft) in height. Olmec-style monuments were carved in the period 1100–700BC. One, called El Rey by archaeologists, depicts a king or ruler seated in the mouth of a monster that experts identify as the entrance to the underworld; above him are carved rain clouds and three descending raindrops identified as a symbol of authority. This image presents the king as the link between the underworld and the heavens of the rain clouds, like the cosmic tree or world axis. In his person he ensured fertility (rain) and order.

In 700–500BC, Chalcatzingo rose to its highest point of prestige. Many monuments were carved in the style of the Olmec centre at La Venta, which was also then at its peak. The elite rulers of Chalcatzingo, who may have been merchants themselves,

established trading contact with La Venta and elsewhere on the Gulf Coast, with Monte Albán and other Oaxacan sites and with Izapa, far away on the Pacific coastal plain of south-east Mexico.

Another major trading centre of the Olmec era lay in the Guerrero region at Teopantecuanitlán. The site was linked to Chalcatzingo by the Cuautla and Amacuzac rivers, and itself provided

access to the great Balsas river, which could carry loads all the way to the Pacific Ocean. Trading in precious stones, tin, copper and highly prized jade from Guerrero, Teopantecuanitlán became a major centre by 600BC. A pyramid and two ball courts were built and finds of marine shells there suggest that the town was linked to marine trading networks.

In Oaxaca, San José Mogote and other developing villages were trading with San Lorenzo from c.1150BC onwards. Two main lineages or family groups grew prominent, both associated with Olmec motifs. One was linked to the image of the jaguar-faced human or were-jaguar, thought by scholars to represent the earth, while the second was connected to a fire-serpent image thought to be the sign for lightning.

San José Mogote became a great craft centre, with craftsmen housed in one of the four quarters of the settlement according to their speciality.

Left: Spring god Xipe Totec, represented in this Zapotec brazier, may have derived from an Olmec deity known as God VI.

A CITY OF MERCHANTS

The great city of Teotihuacán was a beacon for merchants. It was a major centre for Mesoamerican trade in obsidian, the volcanic glass. This was in demand because craftsmen could fashion it into mirrors, dart-tips for weapons and cutting edges used both in everyday activities and in sacred ritual for letting blood and dispatching sacrificial victims.

Teotihuacán grew up on an ancient site of pilgrimage, and could support a rising population because its position on the San Juan Teotihuacán river made irrigation of farm fields easy. It thrived because it was close to sources of obsidian and because it lay on a major trade route running from the Valley of Mexico to the Gulf Coast.

OBSIDIAN AND OTHER GOODS

In the city's workshops, workers manufactured stone masks, ceremonial tripod vessels, obsidian blades, household furnishings, clay figurines, stone and basalt tools, stonework in shell, serpentine and jade, domestic pots and ornaments of slate. Merchants sold a range of manufactured goods to the large population or organized their export far and wide. Teotihuacáno interests also controlled a

Below: Teotihuacán was renowned from ancient times as a sacred site as well as a major trade centre.

Right: Quetzalcóatl's head adorns the staircase of the Temple of Quetzalcóatl at Teotihuacán.

major obsidian-processing site at Tepeapulco, to the north-east of the city. Obsidian forms when igneous volcanic flow cools rapidly and is only found in highland areas with active volcanoes. The glass appears black, but when some varieties are fashioned into flakes or a transparent edge, the colours grey and green are visible. Minerals in the molten matrix can also produce green obsidian, and because this form was much rarer in Mesoamerica than black-grey obsidian it was consequently much more highly valued. Near Teotihuacán, there was only one source of green obsidian, Cerro de las Navajas at Puchuca, in modern Hidalgo state, but there were at least 15 sources of black and grey obsidian.

By performing trace-element analysis, geochemists have established the source of the obsidian worked in or around Teotihuacán. In workshops at Tepeapulco, workers manufactured items from obsidian which were delivered by footpath from sources at Cerro de las Navajas, at Tulancingo, Paredón and Barrance de los Estetes. From here blades, darts, sacrificial knives and other artefacts were transported to Tulancingo in the Metztitlán Valley and from there to sites such as El Tajín.

Tepeapulco was the centre of Teotihuacán's obsidian industry, but there were also obsidian craftsmen within the city. One group near the Great Compound, for example, specialized in working high-status green obsidian.

Teotihuacán also controlled trade in and distribution of fine-paste pottery bowls and effigy jars known to archaeologists as thin orange pottery. As many as eight settlements in the region of Tepexi, in Puebla state, specialized in the manufacture of these pots, which were distributed far and wide via Teotihuacán.

Teotihuacán's marketplace was probably situated in the Great Compound, on the opposite side of the Street of the Dead from the Ciudadela or Citadel in the centre of the city. Here merchants from near and far dealt in locally manufactured and imported goods, as well as raw materials such as marine shells, rubber, luxury feathers, cotton, magnetite, hematite and chert.

Groups of foreign merchants made their homes in this great metropolis. One part of the city has been dubbed the Merchants' Barrio by archaeologists, who found large amounts of pottery there from Veracruz and from Maya lands in northern Belize and the Yucatán peninsula. Another quarter was home to merchants from Oaxaca, who built tombs modelled exactly on those in their ancestral home of Monte Albán.

THE TRADE ROUTE

A major trade route, dubbed the Teotihuacán corridor by historians, connected the city to markets and sources of raw materials to the east and south. It left the city via its East Avenue and headed to Calpulalpán, in Tlaxcala, then south-east to Huamantla. Two branches left Huamantla, one heading east to Veracruz and the second turning south by way of Teotihuacán. On the route, passes and gateways allowed officials to regulate the movement of raw materials into Teotihuacán and manufactured artefacts on the way out of the city.

Farther afield, Teotihuacán set up a trading centre in Matacapán, situated in fertile land in southern Veracruz between the volcano of San Martin Tuxtla and the waters of Lake Catemaco. It was close to the coast and to rivers leading inland, and might well have controlled trade by sea for Teotihuacáno merchants. Matacapán, a source of kaolin, became a major production centre for fine paste pottery. Artisans also made elite products of the kind made in the 'mother city' of Teotihuacán. They lived in an apartment compound of the sort built in Teotihuacán. Farther south, Teotihuacán had prolonged trading and diplomatic links with Monte Albán in Oaxaca. Carvings at Monte Albán, including four stelae erected around the Main Plaza's South Platform, depict figures that scholars interpret as a record of peaceful visits by high-ranking Teotihuacános.

Teotihuacán had trading contacts as far afield as Kaminaljuyú in the Guatemala Valley and Tikal in the central Maya region. Archaeological evidence suggests

Right: This evocative Teotihuacáno mask has survived intact with its mould.

that traders from Teotihuacán may have become well established in an enclave at Kaminaljuyú. Some scholars have suggested that Teotihuacán used force against Kaminaljuyú, which sat on a trade route for valuable cacao beans and was situated close to a major source of obsidian. Perhaps the Teotihuacános attempted to gain a monopoly over mining and distribution of obsidian. A central area of Kaminaljuyú was reconstructed in Teotihuacáno architectural style.

Settlements to the west of Kaminaljuyú on the Pacific coastal plain probably also had close links with Teotihuacán in the cacao trade and may have been home to Teotihuacáno merchants. One settlement produced Teotihuacán-style ceramic ritual vessels. There was probably also direct trading contract between Teotihuacán and Tikal. After Tikal's victory over Uaxactún in AD378, the Maya of Tikal adopted the style of warrior-costume associated with Teotihuacán, and began to plan battle campaigns according to the cycle of Venus, following the Teotihuacáno tradition.

In other directions, Teotihuacán dominated the Valley of Mexico to the south-west, while to north and west the city's interests were confined to sourcing raw materials. Far to the north-west, the city established a settlement at Alta Vista, in the modern state of Zacatecas, to exploit its sources of jadeite, turquoise and precious green stones, flint, chert, hematite and malachite. The raw materials were taken back by porters to be worked in the city's workshops.

313

TRADING OVER GREAT DISTANCES

The pattern of long-distance trading established by the Olmecs and Teotihuacános continued into the era of the Aztecs. Throughout this vast time span, trade and exchange networks were also vibrant over small distances within the many regions of Mesoamerica. Short-range trade tended to be in foodstuffs and other everyday commodities such as clothing and household pottery, while long-range trade was in rare commodities highly prized for their use in religious ritual or as status symbols by members of the elite. Quetzal feathers – used in priestly and royal costumes – jaguar skins and sacred greenstones used for divine effigies and masks all commanded a high value at market.

MAYA CONNECTIONS

The Maya, who were in the path between the markets and raw materials of Central America and Mexican sites such as San Lorenzo, Teotihuacán, El Tajín or Tenochtitlán, played a crucial role in long-distance trade connections. Maya lands were also sources of prized commodities. Quetzal feathers, jadeite, serpentine, pyrite and obsidian were exported from the southern Maya highlands. Jaguar skins and teeth, valued for use in royal ceremonial, were exported from the lowlands of the central Maya region, together with parrot and macaw feathers. From coastal areas of the southern Maya region came sharks' teeth, coral, shells and sting-ray spines used for bloodletting in rites of autosacrifice, as well as cacao. Salt was traded from the coasts of Yucatán.

Below: Tarascan artisans made these lip ornaments from gold, obsidian and turquoise before 1500.

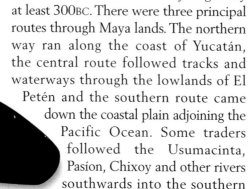

Merchants were trading over long distances from the central Maya region by at least 300BC. There were three principal routes through Maya lands. The northern way ran along the coast of Yucatán, the central route followed tracks and waterways through the lowlands of El Petén and the southern route came down the coastal plain adjoining the Pacific Ocean. Some traders followed the Usumacinta, Pasíon, Chixoy and other rivers southwards into the southern

Above: Many goods travelled long distances on the Aztec tribute network. This codex page lists tribute from 16 imperial towns.

Maya highlands, and they were able to make their way through to the Motagua Valley and its path to the Gulf of Honduras. Within Maya territories, trade routes linked the northern parts of Yucatán with their salt industry and with the southern regions that were the important source of obsidian and quetzal feathers.

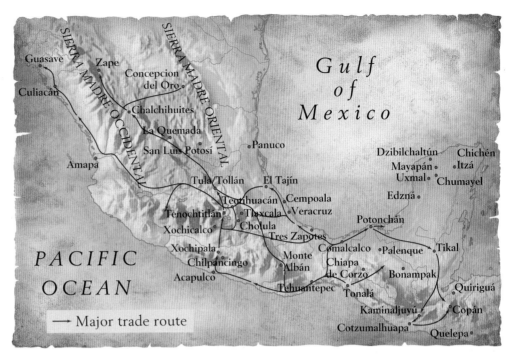

Guasave
Zape
SIERRA MADRE OCCIDENTAL
SIERRA MADRE ORIENTAL
Concepcion del Oro
Culiacán
Chalchihuites
La Quemada
San Luis Potosí
Panuco
Amapa

Gulf of Mexico

Dzibilchaltún · Chichén
Mayapán · · Itzá
Uxmal · · Chumayel
Edzná ·

Tula/Tollán
El Tajín
Teotihuacán
Cempoala
Tenochtitlán
Tlaxcala
Veracruz
Potonchán
Xochicalco
Cholula
Tres Zapotes
Comalcalco · Palenque · Tikal
Xochipala
Monte
Chiapa
Bonampak
Chilpancingo
Albán
de Corzo
Quiriguá
Acapulco
Tehuantepec
Tonalá
Copán
Kaminaljuyú
Cotzumalhuapa
Quelepa

PACIFIC OCEAN

→ Major trade route

Goods were laboriously transported by porters. Mesoamericans certainly knew how to make wheels, for they left wheeled toys in tombs, but they did not make wheeled vehicles for transport. In part this was because they lacked large traction animals but, in addition, many parts of Mesoamerica were unsuited to wheeled transport and more easily traversed on foot or by boat. A porter secured a load around his head or chest using rope and often travelled in convoy with several colleagues. In Aztec times the maximum load permitted was about 22kg (50lb) per person. Goods were also packed in great canoes and taken to sea or along rivers.

NORTHERN TRADE

In the north of Mexico, La Quemada (in modern Zacatecas state) lay in a good position for north–south trade, including turquoise from what is now the US state of New Mexico, and throve throughout the Classic Period until c.AD850. It is part of the Chalchihuite culture, whose remains provide early evidence of religious and military iconography (skull racks, *chacmools* and symbols of the god of the north, darkness and fate, Tezcatlipoca), which would become very important in Aztec times. In the far north, Casas Grandes, in modern Chihuahua state, was a major centre from c.1050, part of an important trading network linking Mesoamerica to sites in the south-west USA. Marine trade across the Caribbean also linked the islands and the south-east USA.

AZTEC TRADE ROUTES

In Aztec times, merchants doubtless operated from Tenochtitlán to the north, in the modern states of Zacatecas and Durango, and to the north-west in Querataro and Hidalgo, but historians know more about trade towards the

Right: Chachihuite settlements in northern Mexico combined fortified trading sites with farming villages and religious centres.

south. Routes from Tenochtitlán led down to Tuxtepec, where they divided, with one path leading into Oaxaca and on into the Isthmus of Tehuantepec and Soconusco, and one leading to the coast of the Gulf of Mexico and the towns of Coatzacoalco and, inland a little way, Cimatan.

From Cimatan traders could follow the River Grijalva into the Chiapas Highlands, where amber was to be found, or travel east into the region of Chontalapa, where there were no fewer than 25 Aztec trading posts with warehouses to store goods.

Beyond, on the Gulf coast, the port of Xicalango at the western edge of the Laguna de Terminos was almost certainly an Aztec trading centre, although it was peopled by Chontal-speaking Maya. From Xicalango, merchants could follow tracks

Above: Wherever possible, traders chose to follow low-lying routes through river valleys or along coastal plains.

and waterways down to the forests of El Petén in the central Maya region and beyond to trading posts on the coast of the Caribbean Sea.

From Tenochtitlán, merchants exported luxury goods manufactured in the imperial capital from raw materials brought in by trade or as tribute from subject regions of the empire, as well as obsidian, bells and ornaments of copper, combs and herbs. Slaves were also exported to areas needing cheap labour such as cacao plantations on the coasts of the Gulf, the Pacific and the Caribbean. They imported cacao, gold, animal skins, precious stones and brightly coloured feathers.

BY CANOE AND PADDLE

In the 10th century, the powerful merchants of Chichén Itzá built a trading post on Isla Cerritos, a small island just off the coast of northern Yucatán and about 90km (55 miles) from their capital city. They built or improved existing piers and docks, together with a 330m (1,000ft) sea wall to guarantee calm waters for unloading from large seagoing canoes. These vessels, recently developed, transformed seagoing trade. At 15m (50ft) long and 2m (6ft 6in) wide, they were far bigger than earlier canoes and able to voyage into far rougher waters.

SEA TRADE

Through Isla Cerritos, Chichén Itzá imported basalt from Belize, gold jewellery from Central America, pottery from Guatemala and obsidian from sites in Mexico. Itzá sea traders travelled as far as the ports of Naco and Nito in Honduras.

Coastal settlements were probably operated in this way as trading posts for powerful inland cities or states throughout Mesoamerican history. For example, Cerros, on a peninsula of coastal Belize

Below: Caribbean waves wash the shore by the trading centre of Cozumel. Goats were traded by canoe along the coast and among offshore islands.

Above: Members of the merchant elite lived in the Palace of the Kings, a sumptuous residence in the trading city of Mayapán.

that projects into Chetumal Bay, was transformed from a small village into a significant settlement with large pyramids, public buildings and platforms in the period 50BC–AD100, probably at the behest of an inland centre seeking an outlet into the Caribbean Sea. The style

and appearance of the stucco deity-masks on these buildings suggest links to nearby Lamanai or, farther afield, to Tikal. Archaeological evidence has led historians to suggest that Cerros operated in tandem with Komchen, far away in northern Yucatán, as a trading partner, probably in the movement of salt from the northern region. Jade and obsidian from the southern Maya region were also traded at Cerros.

Mesoamericans carried on sea trade from earliest times. The peoples of western Mexico were in contact along the Pacific coast with tribes in Ecuador as early as 1500BC – as suggested by the appearance of Ecuadorian-style chamber tombs. In the Olmec centre at Teopantecuanitlán, in the Guerrero region, a workshop produced elite items using marine shells from distant points on the Pacific Coast.

TRADING POSTS

Many sites along the coasts of the Yucatán peninsula and Belize thrived through seagoing trade for many centuries. Jaina Island, the settlement off the west coast of the peninsula celebrated for its cemetery and the clay figures left in its graves, was a thriving trading and fishing port for at least 700 years. Tancah, a fortified town on the eastern coast of northern Yucatán,

Above: The elite of Yucatán combined warfare with trade. This is a mural in the Temple of the Warriors in Chichén Itzá.

appears to have been a centre for trade in the *Strombus gigas*, a type of conch shell used in religious ritual from at least the time of Teotihuacán, where the shells are depicted in murals. Tancah was a trading post from the last centuries BC onwards, handling obsidian, jade, pyrite, granite and slate vessels exported from the Maya cities of the Puuc region inland. The neighbouring coastal settlement of Xelha was a port for the inland city of Cobá from at least the 10th century. A *sacbé* or raised causeway left the main square of Xelha and ran inland to Cobá.

CONTROL OF SEA TRADE

Around 6km (3½ miles) south along the coast lay Tulum, which was founded on the cliff top overlooking the Caribbean Sea in 1200 at a time when maritime commerce was a source of great wealth and prestige for the merchants of the northern Yucatán peninsula.

A cliff-top beacon guided sailors through a gap in the reef that runs parallel to the shore and on to a safe landing on the beach beneath the town. At this time, the cities of the League of

Mayapán – Mayapán, Uxmal and a Chichén Itzá much reduced from its former independent glory – had control of seagoing trade, and probably built Tulum.

The League's merchant elite also maintained an offshore trading centre on the Isle of Cozumel, a little further north opposite the mainland settlement of Xcaret. On Cozumel, large platforms right across the island were used as seasonal stores for products such as honey, cacao and salt. The island traded all year in obsidian and building stone. The western part of Cozumel was the site of one of the region's most important religious shrines, to the Maya Moon Goddess Ix Chel.

Below: Lying in the sacred east, Tulum – together with Xelhá and Tancah – was a religious as well as a trading site. This structure is a clifftop temple to the wind god.

TRADERS, SPIES, PROTECTORS

Long-range trade in the Aztec empire was handled by professional merchants called *pochteca*. Working both on their own behalf and as emissaries of rulers and members of the nobility, they specialized in importing luxurious materials such as animal skins, rare feathers, precious shells and stones used in religious ritual. The Aztec word *pochteca* is derived from their name for the *Bombax ceiba*, the great tropical tree that was viewed by the ancient Mesoamericans as the tree of life that linked the terrestrial realm to heaven and to the underworld. The tree of life was an image for the king or rule, and the association of *pochteca* with the tree suggests that merchants were viewed – like kings – as protectors or guarantors of stability and fertility.

MERCHANT WARDS

Pochteca were an elite hereditary group, whose members lived together as a *capultin* kin body in a part of the city reserved for them. Such was the size of Tenochtitlán and the number of *pochteca* serving the empire that there were six wards for merchants in the capital: Amachtlan, Atlauhco, Itztotolco, Pochtlán, Tepetitlán and Tzonmolco.

Ten other towns in the Valley of Mexico were renowned for their communities of professional merchants. These were: Azcapotzalco, Chalco, Coatlinchán, Cuauhtitlán, Huexotla, Huitzilopochco, Otumba, Mixcoac, Texcoco and Xochimilco.

There was a strict hierarchy among *pochteca*. The *pochtecatlatoque* were the most senior merchants, handpicked by the *tlatoani* and his advisers to organize

Left: This exquisite jade ear ornament, carved delicately with Maya glyphs, was found by archaeologists at Pomona, Belize.

trading expeditions and to supervize the activities of younger traders. They were proven merchants with wide experience of travel, usually drawn from the 'aristocracy' of trading families. The *pochtecatlatoque* stayed in Tenochtitlán and followed the progress of an expedition through reports sent back by the travelling merchants; both overseer and trader took a share in the profits. Perhaps most prestigious of all the responsibilities of the *pochtecatlatoque* was to ensure that the capital's markets were orderly and honest places. They sat in judgement on dishonest *pochteca* and customers in special merchants' courts and no other authority could interfere with or challenge their judgements. A trader found guilty of cheating or selling stolen goods or a person caught trying to steal would be sentenced to death.

SLAVE TRADERS

Second in the hierarchy of *pochteca* were traders in slaves. They were called *tlaltlani* ('washers of slaves'), a reference to the ritual bathing that slaves underwent before they were taken to be sacrificed. Bernardino de Sahagún recounts in his *General History of the Things of New Spain* that *tlaltlani* were the wealthiest of all merchants. By tradition they were particularly devout and were treated with the greatest respect as providers of sacrificial victims.

Beneath them were the travelling *pochteca*, the veterans of long-range expeditions who brought luxury produce back to Tenochtitlán's eager markets. They were sometimes called *oztomeca* ('front-line merchants'). Those among the *oztomeca* who worked only for the *tlatoani* were called *tencunenenque* ('king's voyagers'); they often worked as collectors of tribute from subject states within the empire.

Pochteca held a special position of privilege. Unlike their fellows, they were not required to perform personal services for the *tlatoani*. Instead they provided elite goods as tribute. In 1500, as a reward for the role played by *pochteca* in the military conquest of Soconusco, the *tlatoani* Ahuítzotl (*r.* 1486–1502) made a proclamation praising long-range merchants and granting them the right to wear loincloths and capes that were normally reserved for the nobility on special occasions.

SPIES BEHIND ENEMY LINES

One group of merchants, the *naualoztomeca* ('traders in disguise'), performed a vital function for the *tlatoani*, his military advisers and the army commanders. Wherever they went, ostensibly travelling as merchants, they were working as spies, looking for signs of potential unrest and listening for mutterings of discontent against the Aztec rulers. When the military elite in Tenochtitlán was planning a military campaign, it would send *naualoztomeca* into the region to seek useful preliminary information.

In the early Aztec era, traveller-spies went through the empire disguised as locals in order to learn what they could from gossip in the marketplace. However, later the travellers began to take the guise of merchants. It was a dangerous occupation; if caught, a spy was likely to be slain and perhaps cooked. Upon landing in Mexico, Hernán Cortés made first contact with a group of *naualoztomeca*. It was these trader-spies who carried the first news of strange bearded beings in 'flying' ships back to the court of Moctezuma II in Tenochtitlán.

NOBLE MAYA TRADERS

The Aztecs' Maya contemporaries did not have professional merchants comparable to the *pochteca*. Among the Maya, long-distance trade was carried out by rulers and members of the nobility. At Chichén Itzá and Mayapán, the rulers appear to have been merchants. One account of the fall of Mayapán recounts that all the city's rulers were slaughtered in an attack, save one who was away from the city on his travels, seeking trade.

In both Maya and Aztec lands, short-distance trading was performed either by small-scale entrepreneurs, peddlers who bought and sold as they travelled hither and

Right: Danger on the road. A detail from the Codex Mendoza *shows Aztec trader-spies being attacked by lawless locals.*

thither, or by the producers and manufacturers of the goods – the farmers, weavers, toolmakers and potters. From ancient times, across Mesoamerica, long-distance trade was the preserve of a wealthy ruling elite. Trade was the lifeblood of development: because they brought wealth to the community, and because they traded in

Above: The largest of these vases from Tikal shows a fat Maya merchant who was clearly wealthy enough to indulge himself.

elite goods such as feathers, jaguar skins and sacrificial knives that were needed for religious ceremony, traders began to enjoy religious prestige.

MARKETS LARGE AND SMALL

The Aztec capital contained several outdoor markets of various sizes. (The outdoor marketplace was called *tianquiztli* in Nahuatl.) In addition to the justly celebrated marketplace in Tlatelolco, there was another substantial market in Tenochtitlán proper, alongside the ceremonial precinct. There were also many smaller places of sale scattered throughout the city in its various wards.

WHO SOLD WHAT, WHEN

The sale of elite goods that had been transported from distant parts of the empire was probably restricted to the Tlatelolco and the main Tenochtitlán market. Sales in the different wards were probably of local agricultural produce brought in from *chinampa* fields or of craft products made at workshops in the vicinity. Transactions at these markets were not purely economic, but were bound into the fabric of life and

Above: The walls, steps and frieze carving are part of the vast Pyramid of Quetzalcóatl in Cholula, a town sacred to that god.

Right: These steps and walls are another part of the pyramid remains at Cholula, a major trading as well as a religious centre.

intimately connected with entertainment, socializing, politics and religion. Markets were places where people made friends, swapped news and gossip, perhaps hatched plots and formed alliances, places through which people made their way to the temple.

It is possible that market days were scheduled to coincide with important days in the ritual calendar. Pilgrims would have travelled to a town to make offerings at its shrine and then gone on to the marketplace. Merchants would have taken part in the pilgrimage.

RELIGION AND COMMERCE

Above: The Descending God, Tulum.

Many Mesoamerican trading settlements were also important religious centres. In the highlands of Mexico, Cholula's marketplace was thronged with people while the city's great Temple of Quetzalcóatl was a major draw for pilgrims.

Several trading sites on the eastern seaboard of the Yucatán peninsula were believed to have sacred power because of their position towards the direction of the moon's rising and the reappearance of Venus. The Isle of Cozumel, an important trading port for the League of Mayapán, contained a shrine to moon goddess Ix Chel on its eastward-facing shore; the goddess was believed to speak through an oracle there. On the mainland, the fortified trading centre at Tancah was the site of a *cenote* or large natural well with a holy cave lying on an east–west axis and painted with murals delineating the fearful power of the sea. At nearby Tulum, the Temple of the Descending God was adorned with a carving of a creature diving towards earth; the curious image, only found at Tulum and Cobá, is thought to be associated with the cult of the planet Venus in the form of Xux Ek, the Maya 'wasp star' god.

It is likely that the holy day was enjoyed as a holiday, with entertainments and perhaps a ball game tournament.

Some markets specialized in local produce. Cholula, for example, won a wide reputation for the excellence of its chillies, while Coyoacán was known for the wood grown near the town. Fine gourds, cloth and ceramics were the speciality of Texcoco market. The best places to go for slaves were Azcapotzalco and Itzocán, and the best dog market was at Acolman. In the Mixtec area, the market at Miahuatlán was widely renowned, not least for its sale of exquisite local gold work. Smaller markets were usually held each day or sometimes on a rota with other nearby centres.

MAYA MARKETS

Many Maya towns and cities also held centralized markets in open squares. There is little archaeological evidence of marketplaces, however. Commercial activity usually took place in the open, with perhaps a few pole-and-thatch buildings to provide shade or to keep the rain off, that have since decayed. There is evidence that Classic Period Tikal had a permanent central marketplace. Archaeologists believe that the commercial zone was probably an enclosed area of the city's East Plaza, containing buildings with many doorways. We know that in the post-Classic Period, Iximche in the southern Maya region had a market plaza with overseers to settle arguments, ensure that regulations were observed and levy taxes. As at Tlatelolco, Maya markets were efficiently organized, with different types of goods laid out in separate areas.

Markets contained areas for visiting and foreign merchants, but rival controlling interests sometimes came into opposition. For example, Aztec *pochteca* trading in elite goods were not welcome in areas where Maya nobles ran long-distance trade. Where necessary, representatives of the two sides met in neutral areas.

Below: At Tollán, the remains of the Palacio Quemado lie to the west of the raised temple platform sacred to Quetzalcóatl.

THE GREAT MARKET AT TLATELOLCO

The greatest marketplace of the Aztec empire was at Tlatelolco, the island city that adjoined the imperial capital of Tenochtitlán. Even on a quiet day, 25,000 people would throng the Tlatelolco marketplace, according to the conquistador Anónimo, while every five days a special market attracted more than double that number. Hernán Cortés declared that he saw around 60,000 people in the market. His colleague Bernal Díaz reported that even in the course of two days a curious person would not be able to see the vast range of produce sold there.

The market square at Tlatelolco was surrounded by a covered arcade. In its centre stood a raised platform from which officials made public pronouncements and where thieves and dishonest merchants were shamed and put to death by stoning. The traders' stalls were arranged in a grid pattern around the central platform. At one corner of the market square was the court of the *pochtecatlatoque*, the most senior merchants whose responsibility was to levy sales taxes, to maintain order in the marketplace and also to sit in judgement on those who broke the law.

Above: This illustration, from the Florentine Codex, *is of Aztecs storing amaranth.*

The goods were laid out in areas according to type. The *pochtecatlatoque* organized the market, ensuring products were sold in the right area and at the right price. Every raw material and product imaginable, the produce of a great empire, was available in the Tlatelolco market.

ANCIENT CORNUCOPIA

A canal ran down one side of the marketplace, and a stream of heavily laden porters carried goods from canoes to market stalls. In one area were farmers and merchants selling fresh

Left: These jewellery pieces are typical of the artefacts the elite could buy at Tlatelolco.

produce: beans, vegetables, herbs and fruits. In another were turkeys, deer, ducks, rabbits, dogs and hares. Elsewhere, a customer could find fish and all kinds of marine life; in another place, tortillas, honey cakes and other cooked foods were on offer, including, according to the conquistador Bernal Díaz, cakes with the flavour of cheese made by fisherwomen using a weed that grows in Lake Texcoco.

In another part of the market, shoppers could browse among a vast range of pots, plates, water jars and bowls before moving on to look for bark paper and inks, then to seek out reeds filled with tobacco. A person could buy sandals, coloured robes and lengths of plain cloth. Another could buy timber or pine torches. Those seeking elite items would find them in plentiful supply: feathers of many colours, including the magnificent quetzal tail feathers of up to 1m (more than 3ft) in length; the skins of jaguars, lions and deer; magnificent gold masks and jewellery fashioned by the best Mixtec goldsmiths; delicately finished mosaic masks; elegant sacrificial knives; statues, and other stone carvings; turquoise, jade and other precious stones. A warrior could find all kinds of military equipment, including padded cotton armour, leather shields, the sharpest *atlatl* darts of obsidian and splendid ceremonial cloaks and shields decorated with feathers and mosaic.

Slaves were also for sale. Merchants fitted them with collars and bound them to a long pole to prevent them running away. Any slaves who did escape could gain their freedom if they managed to reach the palace of the *tlatoani* without being caught. Only the merchant who owned them could give chase. Some merchants bought slaves to offer as sacrifices, particularly for the festival of Panquetzalíztli ('Lifting of the Banners'), which was held after the harvest each year. Others purchased strong male slaves to transport and sell to cacao plantations or as canoe oarsmen in coastal regions. Some female slaves were sold as prostitutes. The going rate for a slave was 25 cotton cloaks, rising to 35 cloaks for one who was skilled in dancing.

All goods were counted out or sold by measuring their size, never by weight. Customers usually bartered with merchants, although some products, such as cacao beans, cotton mantles, pieces of tin, copper axe-blades, transparent quills full of gold dust and the feathers of tropical birds, were used as forms of currency.

PUNISHMENTS AND PROCESSIONS

Cheats sometimes got away with making counterfeit cacao beans from amaranth dough and wax. When the *pochtecatlatoque* found a merchant guilty of trying to cheat his customers they sentenced him to be put to death on the platform in the centre of the square. The merchant's goods were confiscated and his dishonest measures smashed. A person caught stealing from a stall or storehouse would be similarly sentenced to death.

The marketplace was a vibrant place where people gathered to chat, street performers entertained the crowds and drummers set bystanders dancing. Religious processions passed through the market from the ceremonial precinct of Tlatelolco nearby. Priests waving smoking censers, their bodies painted black and long hair matted with sacrificial blood, made an unnerving spectacle. Sometimes they were at the head of a procession of victims bound for sacrifice in the temple.

Below: Today office buildings crowd close to excavated ruins of Tlatelolco platforms in the heart of the Mexican capital.

A NETWORK OF TRIBUTE

Large quantities of produce entered Tenochtitlán in the form of tribute payments from provinces within the Aztec empire. The activities of tribute collectors complemented those of *pochteca* merchants in providing sumptuous goods to please the nobles of the imperial capital and to supply the materials used in the city's magnificent religious ceremonies.

A TRIBUTARY EMPIRE

Some *pochteca* worked as itinerant tribute collectors, but generally collectors were appointed to reside in a conquered territory to ensure payments were made. The Triple Alliance of Tenochtitlán, Texcoco and Tlacopán built its tributary empire through military might: its armies pursued battle to the point at which a conquered state or city agreed to pay tribute, when the conquerors imposed a schedule of amounts and timings. The rulers of the defeated state remained in power, and the collector made sure that they honoured the tribute agreement, under threat of further military action.

Tribute payments maintained the infrastructure and daily operations of the empire. Some provinces were required to send labourers for construction projects, others tools and building materials, some

Below: The Zapotecs of Monte Albán celebrated their conquest-led tribute network in carvings on the arrow-shaped Building J.

sent soldiers, others military equipment such as shields and padded cotton war jerkins. Many areas sent maize, beans and other basic foodstuffs, while others provided firewood for the braziers of the nobility. Certain states were contracted to send local products such as obsidian or cacao, fine metalwork or ceramics, jaguar skins or colourful feathers. One of the most highly prized Aztec tributary provinces was the resource-rich region of Soconusco, defeated after four years' conflict by Ahuítzotl in 1486; it provided tribute of jaguar skins and jewellery.

RECORDS OF PAYMENT

Details of the tribute network operated by Texcoco are found in the 16th-century document the *Mapa Quinatzin*. They show how meticulously tribute operations were planned. There were eight tributary regions, each with its own tribute collector required, among other responsibilities, to furnish the administrative buildings, city temples and royal palaces in Texcoco with foodstuffs and wood for braziers. In particular, two groups of 13 tributary towns were arranged in a rota to provide firewood for the *tlatoani*'s main palace throughout the year. The *Codex Mendoza* (*c*.1541) contains a lengthy tribute list detailing the responsibilities throughout the year of various tributary towns and states. Cuauhnahuac is listed as one of 16 towns contracted to dispatch a consignment of cotton skirts, loincloths and robes to Tenochtitlán twice a year, supplemented by an annual delivery of shields and war equipment. With so many tribute payers required to provide materials according to a regular schedule, there must have been a steady stream of porters and canoes bringing deliveries from far and wide, which would have required detailed administrative control.

Before the Triple Alliance, other cultures – including the Zapotecs of Monte Albán and the Toltecs of Tollán – established tributary empires. At Monte

Above: Portable wealth. This pendant earring of solid gold was one of the pieces found in Monte Albán Tomb 7 in 1932.

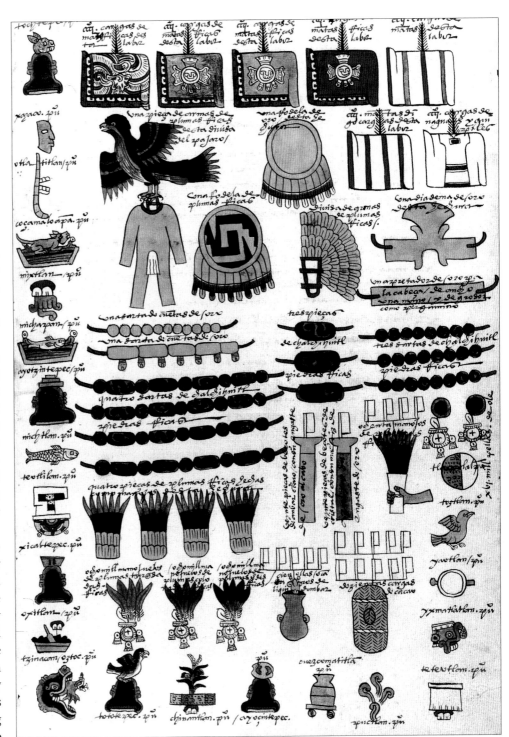

Right: A page from the Codex Mendoza *shows the tribute collected by Aztec civil servants from the province of Tochtepec.*

Albán, the curious arrow-shaped structure known to archaeologists as Building J, erected between *c.*200BC and AD300 in the Main Plaza, bears about 50 carvings that appear to represent areas conquered or required to pay tribute to the Zapotecs. Some carvings specify the kind of tribute that must be paid.

They included Cuicatlán, a mountain settlement on the border between Oaxaca and the Téhuacan Valley, and Tututepec on the coast of the Pacific Ocean. At Cuicatlán the Zapotecs acted with great ruthlessness: they destroyed entire villages, moved other settlements, established military strongholds and terrified surviving locals by building skull racks in their villages to display the heads of their conquered menfolk.

In many areas they did not need to use military force, however. In return for supplying elite goods from Monte Albán to the leading figures of a village, the Zapotecs exacted an agreement that they would receive tribute of agricultural produce. Many centuries later, the warriors of Xochicalco, in the western part of Morelos, established a tributary empire in the period AD700–900, as evidenced by glyphs of tribute-paying towns carved on the upper part of the Pyramid of the Feathered Serpent there.

The Putún Maya traders who ruled Chichén Itzá and later Mayapán both built tribute networks. At Mayapán, cotton, copal, cacao, honey and turkeys were among the forms of tribute received. In the southern Maya realm the warlike Quiché Maya also exacted tribute payments from those they conquered. However, the Quiché did not allow local leaders to remain in place, as the Aztecs did; instead, triumphant warlords had their enemies executed and took the dead men's wives into their own families.

THE GIVING OF GIFTS

From earliest times goods moved across Mesoamerica in the form of gifts between elite groups in different areas. Such gift-giving was a mark of mutual respect between rulers and a way of sharing resources between regions rich in different source materials – for instance, a highland group might make a gift of obsidian cutting blades in return for surplus maize or cacao grown by another group in the coastal lowlands. The gift of sumptuous and prestigious materials was also a statement of power on behalf of the giver, an attempt to demonstrate status. Moctezuma II attempted to prove his divine grandeur and magnificence by making splendid gifts of gold, silver and magnificent featherwork to Hernán Cortés and the conquistadors in 1519.

THE SACRED WAY

The Maya built raised causeways known as *sacbeob* (singular: *sacbé*) between settlements. These paved roads eased communications and passage for merchants while giving solid form to political alliances among cities.

GREAT CAUSEWAY

The greatest of these roads was built *c.*AD800 in Yucatán, and ran for 100km (60 miles) from the Castillo pyramid at Cobá to Yaxuná. Cobá lay at the intersection of some 43 roads. It was also connected, for example, to its seaport at Xelhá. Some scholars believe that the rulers of Cobá embarked on this remarkable feat of engineering in an attempt to consolidate their power at a time when the aggressive Putún Maya incomers at Chichén Itzá were making unwelcome intrusions into the region. The attempt may have succeeded: the Itzá attacked and defeated Yaxuná in *c.*AD850, but there is no evidence they overcame Cobá. Its people maintained their independence, although the city's trading success was limited, its ambitious building programmes were curtailed and various outer parts of the settlement were gradually abandoned.

Several *sacbeob* were constructed in northern Yucatán. Typically they were elevated 2.5m (8ft) above the surround-

Above: Several causeways were in use at the fortified trading centre at La Quemada in Zacatecas state, Mexico.

Left: A sacbé *connects a small group of buildings to the two-storey palace at Labná. The palace is similar to that at Sayil.*

ing land, were around 4.5m (15ft) wide and covered with lime cement. Labourers used a 5-ton roller to finish the surface; this would have needed 15 workers to push it. The roads did not curve: they ran perfectly straight, then made a sudden turn to change direction if necessary. One – 4m (13ft) wide – ran for 18km (11 miles) between Uxmal and Kabah. At Kabah it passed through a remarkable stone corbelled arch with a span of 5m (16ft) and led to the central civic area. Another ran for 18km from the settlement at Ucí. It was a remarkable 8m (26ft) wide.

The Maya built *sacbeob* from the time they erected their first monumental buildings in the lowlands. The earliest known system links El Mirador to Nakbé, 13km (8 miles) away, Tintal and other nearby sites. These roads were built in the Late Preclassic Period (*c.*400BC–AD250). The *sacbeob* between cities were expanded versions of the sacred ways that the Maya built to link areas within their

cities. At El Mirador, causeways connected different parts of the city centre. A series of *sacbeob* ran from the Great Plaza in the centre of Tikal. One led north, to the buildings labelled Pyramid Group 3D-2 and Group H by archaeologists. Another went directly west to Temple IV and a third ran south-east to the Temple of Inscriptions. At Chichén Itzá a stone *sacbé* 6m (20ft) wide and 300m (985ft) long connected the Temple of the Feathered Serpent to the Sacred cenote.

SACRED SYMBOLISM

The causeways in cities such as Tikal were integrated into the sacred symbolism of the site layout. The arcane meaning of the layout was that the north was the realm of supernaturals, glorious deceased ancestors who had risen to the heavens, while the south was the region of the Underworld. A ball court was often built between north and south to represent an entrance to the Underworld. Buildings to the east and west suggested the east–west passage of the sun and the rule of the king, whose symbol was the sun.

Causeways were used to link different symbolic areas and to emphasize the unity of the design. At Tikal, for example, the sacred north position was filled both by the North Acropolis, which contained many tombs of ancestors, and further out by the Pyramid Group 3D-2. South was the South Acropolis, west was Temple IV and east was the Temple of the Inscriptions. The three causeways completed the design. A ball court in the East Plaza was an additional way into the Underworld between north and south.

In many cities, for example Yaxhá and Caracol, causeways were built to lead out from the centre to outer settlements. At Caracol there were no fewer than seven causeways providing access from the centre to living areas and plazas, with one running for 8km (5 miles) to the allied smaller settlement at Cahal Pichik. At Seibal the three main groups of buildings were laid out on a cluster of hilltops and connected to one another by causeways. A few *sacbeob* were built in other parts

Below: Archaeologists have dated this well-preserved roadway at Cantona in Puebla state to AD700–950.

Above: The carving on the façade of the Governor's Palace at Uxmal is reproduced in Catherwood's 1841 drawing. From Uxmal a sacbé *ran directly to Kabah, where it passed beneath an archway.*

of Mesoamerica. At Xochicalco, paved causeways like *sacbeob* were the connecting link between different parts of the ancient city. In northern Mexico the trading settlement of La Quemada, in southern Zacatecas state, also used causeways to link different parts of the settlement.

AZTEC ROADS

There is little archaeological evidence of Aztec roads. Whereas in Maya lands labourers built paved *sacbeob*, in southern and central highland Mesoamerica there was generally no need to build formal roads between settlements. However, scholars know that a network of routes carried trade within the Aztec empire.

There are references in post-Conquest accounts to roads, roadside gods, rest houses and teams of couriers and there was certainly a road inland from Veracruz to Tenochtitlán, for Cortés followed it in 1519. Aztec *pochteca* followed well-trodden paths with their long caravans of human porters, heavily laden with goods, or had their loads transferred to canoes for transport by river and in coastal waters. Aztec garrisons were established at vulnerable points on the trade routes.

CHAPTER 16

THE WORLD OF WORK

Opportunities for Mesoamericans were limited by birth. We know this from Spanish records about the Aztecs, their contemporaries and the Maya in the 16th century. Also, because the archaeological record of preceding Mesoamerican cultures is similar to that of the Aztec and Maya and indicates that there was continuous development, we can project the nature of Aztec society back into pre-Aztec times. The top military, legal, administrative and priestly positions were open only to members of the hereditary nobility; among the middle class of skilled artisans and merchants, most were probably glad to follow their family profession, since it could provide sufficient wealth to secure a good level of comfort. Most people had their living from the land, the men working as fishermen, hunters and farmers.

In terms of food and basics, common people could be self-sufficient. They grew most, if not all, of the food they ate. They often had sufficient skills to produce pots, clothing, basketwork and tools for their own use. Some might produce a surplus of cloth or tools that could be bartered for luxury items – a turkey, some meat or extra vegetables, decorated clothing and so on – at market. They were also connected to the wider world of religious life, ceremonial centres and military campaigns through their responsibilities to pay taxes or tribute to their rulers and to serve in the army or as labourers in construction projects when required.

Left: A codex scene depicts the harvesting of cacao. Farming was the principal livelihood of most Mesoamericans.

RAISING CROPS ON LAND AND WATER

At Tenochtitlán farmers relied on *chinampa* fields in Lake Texcoco. The first *chinampas* were constructed along the shore or around islands, but by the reign of Moctezuma I, water control techniques made it possible to reclaim fields from the lake.

CREATING CHINAMPAS

A farmer building a *chinampa* plot would ideally use a shallow or swampy part of the lake. First he would mark out a rectangular area around 30m (100ft) long and 2.5m (8ft) across with four corner posts, then build fences around the area with wattles, vegetation and mud. He or a member of his kin group could make another *chinampa* directly alongside the first, with a canal running between the two, and proceeding in this way the farmers of Tenochtitlán could create large areas of *chinampas* on a grid pattern. In some areas the *chinampas* were laid out in pairs between canals, with a footpath running between the two *chinampa* 'fields'. Some *chinampas* were very much

Above: One of several scenes of agricultural life in the Florentine Codex *of c. 1570 depicts Aztec farmers harvesting maize.*

bigger than the plot of 75sq m described, and could be as large as 850sq m (9,000sq ft); plots such as this supported as many as 15 farmers.

Farmers would plant willows at the edges of their plots. Their roots grew down into the lakebed and strengthened the walls. The trees required regular pruning to prevent them casting shade on the crops. The 'fields' within the fences were built up with layers of fertile sediment dredged from the lakebed. Farmers turned the earth with a hand-held implement and planted seeds in holes made with a planting stick or *coa*. In the dry season, farmers lifted water in a container from the canal onto the *chinampa* alongside. To fertilize the earth they used human excrement, which was carried by canoe from the city along the network of canals. Springs from the Ajusco mountains fed into lakes Chalco and Xochimilco, where great expanses of *chinampa* fields lay. The Aztecs needed to control the supply of water to prevent flooding in the wet season or drought in the dry period. They created a system of dams, canals and sluices – channels with end-gates that could be lifted or dropped to control the flow of water.

The main crops grown by the Aztecs were maize, beans, squashes, tomatoes and chillies. Farmers in Chalco and Tlaxcala grew large amounts of maize, and these areas became associated with the staple crop in Aztec times. Elsewhere other *chinampa* farmers in the Valley of Mexico grew vegetables and flowers.

BURNING FIELDS

In other parts of Mesoamerica, farmers used a range of agricultural methods, according to local conditions. In highland areas, which usually had mineral-rich soil, they cut terraces from the steep hillsides

Left: Chinampa *fields at Xochimilco, constructed by Aztecs in the 15th century, are still in use by Mexicans today.*

Above: The method of building up a chinampa field using stakes and mud is seen in this painting based on a 16th-century manuscript.

and built aqueducts to irrigate the fields from mountain streams. In the tropical lowlands of the central Maya region, where soils were poorer, farmers practised 'slash-and-burn', first cutting down the dense jungle growth with stone axes, then leaving the plants to dry before burning them to enrich the soil and recover its fertility. They could use a field so made for perhaps three years, but then had to leave it fallow for as long as eight years to allow the soil to become enriched with minerals once more. Many farmers using this method then moved on to clear another area.

Where possible, lowland and other Maya agriculturalists also cut terraced fields, which helped to prevent water draining from the soil. They also made raised fields in swampy ground. The farmers cut channels in the wet ground and piled up the cleared earth, creating raised fields intersected with waterways for irrigation. Maya farmers were growing food on raised fields beside the Hondo river in Belize as early as 1100BC. The method was also used in the Quintana Roo area of Yucatán and alongside the Candelaria river in Campeche. In Belize, humidity and high rainfall allowed farmers to grow highly valued crops of cacao, as well as cotton. At Pulltrouser Swamp in Belize, locals grew cacao, cotton, amaranth and maize on their raised-field agricultural land.

In the Maya lowlands, farmers planted maize, squash and beans together. The squash vines helped to prevent soil erosion, while the beans climbed the tall stalks of the corn. As in Tenochtitlán's *chinampa* fields, farmers turned earth using hand-held implements, then used a planting stick to make holes and dropped five or six seeds into each hole.

People kept kitchen gardens close to their houses: here they planted vegetables and the breadnut tree, which yields a fruit high in vegetable protein that can be stored without decaying for as long as 18 months. They may have grown fields of ramon, sapodilla, avocado and cacao.

FEEDING AN EXPANDING CITY

By the mid-1400s Tenochtitlán's population had grown to upwards of 150,000 – five times larger than its lakeside near-neighbour Texcoco, which had some 20–30,000 inhabitants. The Aztec capital, which did not have its own zone of *chinampa* fields, had a pressing need for more agricultural land. The *tlatoani* or ruler Itzcóatl seized control of the *chinampa* zone in the southern lakes, Chalco and Xochimilco. In the reign of Moctezuma I, sizeable new areas of *chinampa* were created in the lakebed. Imperial conquests also helped, by bringing substantial quantities of staple and luxury foods in the form of tribute payments from conquered regions.

GARDEN EXPERTS

In Aztec Tenochtitlán there was a hierarchy among agriculturalists. The men who worked the fields had a wide variety of skills and knowledge: they took responsibility for turning the soil, weeding, levelling land, measuring out fields, planting, watering by hand and using irrigation systems, harvesting and storing produce. However, there was also a group of experts in horticulture, widely respected for their knowledge in seeding and transplanting. These men were valued for their skills by members of the nobility and the political and priestly hierarchies. Combining their knowledge with information from the sacred *tonalamatl* calendar books, the garden experts decided the most propitious and the most practical times for sowing crops and harvesting them.

PLEASURE GARDENS

Garden experts were also much in demand for planning and maintaining the gardens of the empire. Many of the villas of Tenochtitlán had splendid pleasure gardens. Moctezuma II kept three: at his palace in Tenochtitlán, at Chapultepec and at Ixtapalapa. When the conquistador Bernal Díaz visited Moctezuma's garden at Ixtapalapa, he was astonished by the variety of trees, fruits and flowers and their captivating aromas. He declared there was probably no land on earth to match the one that contained such a garden. Hernán Cortés also visited the garden and described it in a 1520 letter to Carlos V of Spain as containing many trees, flowers and places for bathing, with an orchard and areas of aromatic herbs and a wide walkway around a central pool containing fish and visited by waterfowl.

At Texcotzingo, Netzahualcóyotl of Texcoco followed an established Aztec tradition in keeping a botanical garden. The most splendid of these botanical gardens was that founded in 1467 by Moctezuma I of Tenochtitlán in a warm, fertile spot at Huaxtepec, beneath Mount Popocatépetl in the modern Mexican state of Morelos.

When the Aztecs discovered an ancient garden created by their forerunners at Huaxtepec, Moctezuma appointed an official named Pinotetl to upgrade and revamp the already elaborate irrigation works, which included springs, reservoirs and fountains. Then the *tlatoani* ordered the transport from Cuetlaxtlán in Veracruz of cacao trees, vanilla orchid plants and other rare species and for herbs, cypresses and other plants from far-flung parts of the Aztec empire. The plants were carefully dug up, wrapped in cloth and sent to Huaxtepec along with experts in their cultivation.

Religious ceremonies were held to bless the plants and the enterprise. The specialist gardeners from far and wide joined in an eight-day fast before taking part in a bloodletting ceremony in which they pierced their earlobes and sprinkled the blood over the plants. Priests made offerings of incense and sacrificed a large number of quail in order to bless the earth with the birds' blood. These ceremonies must have won the gods' approval for

Left: Tribute sent to Tenochtitlán by Cihuatlan, on the coast, included cacao beans and rare seashells used in ritual.

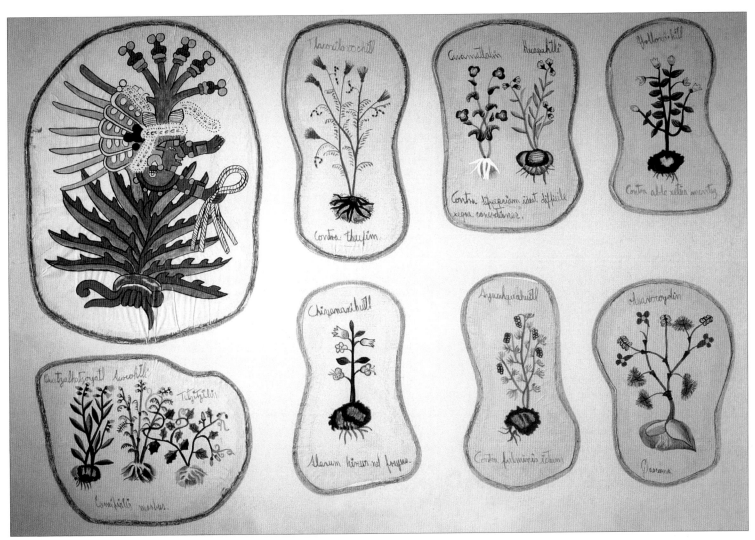

Above: This 16th-century manuscript juxtaposes drawings showing the medicinal uses of various plants used by Mesoamericans with a picture of an Aztec god.

the plants took to their new home and grew fast and strong. When finished, Moctezuma's gardens – 11km (7 miles) in circumference – contained more than 2,000 species of herbs, shrubs and trees. It also contained an aviary and a zoo.

HEALING HERBS

In the botanical gardens at Huaxtepec and Texcotzingo, the garden experts grew a wide range of medicinal herbs. The use of healing herbs was an ancient Mesoamerican art. Most people knew enough to treat themselves and grew herbs among the vegetables on their garden plots. Some of the herbs grown in the botanical gardens were used in doctors' experiments. Members of the nobility paid for the experiments, in return for medical treatment when needed. Ordinary citizens were able to volunteer as guinea pigs, receiving free experimental treatment on condition that they return to report the results to the doctors and planting experts.

THE MAYA AND CACAO

Foremost among elite crops grown by the Maya was cacao. To flourish, cacao needs a thick layer of good soil and humidity in all seasons. One of the prime exports from Maya lands to Mexico, it was grown in plantations, primarily in Soconusco (the Pacific coastal region of Guatemala and Chiapas), in the valley of the River Motagua and at sites in Belize.

The Maya merchant god Ek Chuah – known as god M by some scholars – was lord of cacao and the owners of plantations made offerings to him in the 15th month, Muan. According to the account given by

Right: This Maya chocolate pot was made c. AD300–900. It was used to pour the chocolate drink to generate a pleasing froth.

Diego de Landa of Maya religious festivals in 16th-century Yucatán, the plantation owners found a dog with cacao-coloured dots on his coat to kill and, amid the burning of incense also offered sacrifices of blue bird feathers and blue-coloured iguanas. To conclude the rite, each plantation owner was given a cacao pod to hold.

FRESH FROM THE WILD

Throughout their history Mesoamericans supplemented their diet with meat and fish. In the earliest days, hunting-gathering groups were self-sufficient, but as village life developed, people increasingly had specialized occupations and markets sprang up at which villagers could barter and exchange foods and other necessities. Skilled hunters doubtless brought their meat to market. Fishermen or traders carried dried fish from coastal, riverside or lakeside areas to inland settlements.

MAYA HUNTERS

Among the Maya, hunters used snares and traps to catch deer for their meat. They also hunted rabbits, pig-like mammals called peccaries and rodents – including squirrels, porcupines, agouti and paca. They were skilled with the blowpipe, sending tiny clay pellets at velocity to kill monkeys, macaws, raccoons and other animals in their habitat in the branches. In coastal, lakeside and riverside areas Maya fishermen thrived, using dugout canoes, nets and lines with bone fishhooks. All around the coasts of Maya lands and inland on freshwater lakes and rivers, fish and shellfish were an important part of the diet.

The Maya also domesticated and raised some animals. They kept dogs as guards and hunting companions and may also have fattened some for food. They also kept turkeys, doves – and perhaps

Above: Mesoamericans knew the coyote for its cunning and ability as a night hunter. This statue was made c.1250–1450.

the Muscovy duck – to eat. According to some authorities, the Maya raised herds of domesticated deer in large fenced areas for food. Describing the Maya of Yucatán in the 16th century, Bishop Diego de Landa reported that the women made a habit of breastfeeding young deer, who became entirely tame. In areas such

as the lands beside the Candelaria river in Campeche, the Maya might also have 'farmed' fish and molluscs in the waterways between their raised fields and in artificial ponds. They might have introduced freshwater fish into these enclosed areas of water and caught the excess produced by breeding.

De Landa also reported that Maya hunters in Yucatán believed that success in tracking, catching and killing animals was in the gift of the hunting gods Acanum and Suhui Dzipitabai. He reported that in the second and third month of the year, Uo and Zip, hunters partook in ceremonies honouring the gods. In waterside areas they were joined by fishermen praising the fishing deities Ah Kak Nexoy, Ah Pua, Ah Cit and Dzamal Cum. They prayed for success in the field. In the eleventh month, Zac, hunters celebrated another festival in honour of Acanum and Suhui Dzipitabai, this time seeking forgiveness for the blood they had spilled in the hunt. To the Maya, shedding blood was always a wicked act, for which a man or woman must seek forgiveness. Sacrificial offerings of one's own or a victim's blood were excepted.

IN HIGHLAND MEXICO

In Aztec times, the inhabitants of Tenochtitlán and other cities around the lakes of the Valley of Mexico had easy access to fish, shellfish and aquatic birds. Boys often hunted for birds with nets on the end of long poles while their fathers fished with canoes and nets on the waters of the lake. The men were also skilled in catching frogs and iguanas, a kind of lizard, for food. They collected *axolotl* newts, which were abundant in the lakes and were highly prized as a food and medicine. Many people kept small, hairless dogs as companions and pets – and as a

Left: In a scene from the Florentine Codex, *an Aztec seated on a reed mat eyes the turkey and dogs he keeps for meat.*

Above: A detail from a Maya mural depicts scenes of village life including fishing, hunting and digging the house garden.

source of food. Otherwise, animal meat was available at market, from local hunters, from traders and as part of the regular and substantial deliveries of tribute from around the empire. Diego Durán's account of the myriad kinds of tribute delivered to Tenochtitlán listed deer, rabbits, quails, weasels, moles, snakes and rats as well as larger animals including jaguars and ocelots.

From ancient times, the Aztecs' forerunners and ancestors in Mexico had hunted in small bands by tracking and trapping. They used chipped flint and obsidian weapons such as spears and *atlatl* darts to kill mammoths and other large game, but also trapped and hunted many other small creatures including turtles, birds, rabbits and gophers. The Aztec god of hunting, Mixcóatl, probably originated in these archaic times as a hurricane or storm god. His name means 'Cloud

Serpent' and he was associated with lightning, thunder and tempests – his followers saw lightning bolts as the hunter god's darts. He appeared as a deer or rabbit or as a hunter carrying a bundle of arrows. He was also identified as the father of the Feathered Serpent god Quetzalcóatl. In the account of the Toltecs' southward migration from the northern deserts, Mixcóatl was their leader and his son was Topiltzin-Quetzalcóatl the revered ruler of Tollán. In another narrative, Mixcóatl took the form of a deer to chase the fertility and earth goddess Cihuacóatl ('Female Serpent'), and – catching her at last – fathered the Feathered Serpent god.

In the Aztec era, Mixcóatl and fellow hunting god Camaxtli were honoured in Tenochtitlán

Right: This ceramic vessel in the form of a duck is decorated with jade and shells. It was made in Teotihuacán c.AD500.

in the festival of Tóxcatl ('Drought'), when impersonators of these gods and of the dark lord of fate Tezcatlipoca were put to death, and in that of Quecholli ('Treasured Feather'), when hunting contests were held and prisoners of war dressed as deer were sacrificed. The Aztecs also made offerings to Opochtli ('Left-handed'), the god of bird-catchers and fishermen, praising him as the inventor of the nets used for catching birds and the harpoon with which eagle-eyed fishermen speared fish in the waters.

SKILLED IN ANCIENT CRAFTS

The skilled craftsmen and women of the Aztec empire were a discrete class who could claim social status partway between the common folk and the *pipiltin* nobility. Workers such as basketmakers, potters and weavers were the inheritors of ancient Mesoamerican tradition and passed their skills down the generations.

AZTEC ARTISANS

From the time of San José Mogote *c.*1350BC, craftworkers traditionally occupied their own quarters of a settlement. In the Aztec era, most lived in the large cities of the Valley of Mexico, although there were concentrations of artisans in other parts of the Aztec domain.

Below: The intricate patterns of relief brickwork at sites such as Mitla might have been inspired by designs on woven robes.

Right: Scholars believe that traditional weaving in Mexico today follows patterns established in ancient times.

The *amanteca* or feather-workers were based in their own quarter in Tlatelolco, where they elected officials from their number to govern craft business and worshipped their own patron deity in a local temple. The *amanteca* made clothing, dancing costumes, bracelets, banners, magnificent headdresses and ceremonial military items such as shields. Theirs was painstaking work. When they were making feather-decorated clothes, they tied the feathers' stems one at a time into the fabric when weaving. When they were making a banner or a shield, they sewed the feathers individually on to a backing, usually made of paper attached to reeds and covered in leather. They used a

mixture of feathers from local birds and brightly coloured plumage brought by traders from the tropical rainforests of the Maya lowlands. Friar Bernardino de Sahagún describes their craft, adding that the use of tropical feathers was a recent innovation among the Aztecs.

ROBES, BASKETS AND POTS

Weavers made cloth of plant fibres from maguey agave or henequen for the clothes of the common people and spun cotton cloth for the nobility. Women performed the spinning and weaving of the cloth. Cotton was imported into highland Mexico from lowland areas of Mesoamerica. The fineness of the material was the sole difference between the clothes of rich and poor: weavers produced the same range of clothes – loincloths, capes, skirts and large cloaks called *huipiles* – for both nobles and commoners. These often bore embroidered, woven, painted or dyed decorations to signal social class or region of origin.

Like their forebears for thousands of years, Aztec basketmakers made use of the reeds that grew thickly around the lakes of the Valley of Mexico. They also used the leaves of maguey agave, palmleaf and several cacti in their work. They made a wide range of baskets, from compact, tightly woven containers for small valuables to large lidded chests for use as clothes baskets. They also made containers for grain and foodstuffs. The reed craftsmen also made mats and simple stools. Mats

TOOLS AND TOOLMAKERS

For many thousands of years, artisans, soldiers and farmers used tools of obsidian, flint and wood developed in the earliest days of Mesoamerica. Only in the last few centuries of the region's history did its people – notably the Tarascans – begin to make and use metal weapons.

Among the oldest known tools in Mexico is a collection of obsidian scrapers, knives and weapon points, together with some flint blades, made in the region of Lake Texcoco c.7700BC. Prehistoric hunter-gatherers also made cutting tools from the volcanic rock andesite. The first farmers developed the use of a sharpened wooden planting stick. With some improvements, these basic tools remained in use across the millennia. Elite soldiers in the Aztec army were still using weapon points of obsidian in their wooden *atlatl* dart-throwers some 9,000 years later. Generations of Mesoamericans made their livelihood from mining and trading in obsidian, or fashioning it into tools, weapons and other items in workshops.

Metal weapons and tools were not made in Mesoamerica until after c.AD800. The necessary skills were passed along trade routes from South America, probably by sea to western Mexico and overland to the Maya regions of Guatemala, Belize and Mexico. However, it is striking that in western Mexico comparatively few metal tools or weapons were made. Most production was of bells, pins, figurines and jewellery for the elite. The quality of stone and shell tools must have been high enough to prevent their being superseded. In addition to copper, gold and silver were also worked.

Above: This richly coloured painted bowl, probably made for a Maya nobleman or prince, has been dated to c.AD600–900.

were in particularly high demand both for common houses and royal residences, since the Aztecs rarely used furniture.

Potters made a variety of ceramic wares for home cooking and storage, for decorative use by the wealthy and nobility and for ritual use in temples. Without the use of the potter's wheel, they made all their containers and figurines by hand moulding. One favoured method was to build up coils of clay then use a scraping tool to thin out the walls of the pot. Both Aztec and Maya potters produced work of great delicacy and expressiveness.

MAYA CRAFTS

In Maya lands, as in Aztec cities, it was common for craft specialists to live grouped together in a residential area. The craft was probably handed down through the generations, so a craft living unit might also have been a family group. As among the Aztecs, weaving was performed by women. As a spindle they used a thin stick weighted at one end with a ceramic disc. Resting the heavy end on a gourd on the ground, the spinner twirled the spindle to spin the cotton thread. Her companion worked a simple loom on her lap to produce a cloth around 1m (3ft)

wide. The goddess of weaving, Ix Chebal Yax, gave her blessing to this method and was shown using this type of loom in an image in the *Madrid Codex*. The weavers produced different types of cloth and traditional designs in different areas.

Maya basketmakers created containers of intricate and varied weave. None has survived to be examined by archaeologists, but a representation of a basket on Lintel 24 at Yaxchilán shows a complex pattern and indicates the quality of Maya basketwork.

Feather-workers produced a magnificent range of headdress decorations, capes, ceremonial shields and weapons, fans and fringed cloth. They also decorated wicker frames that dancers wore on their backs and protective canopies for royal thrones. In some areas, for instance among the Quiché Maya, birds were bred in captivity for their plumage. Hunters and trackers brought back the feathers of the macaw, the quetzal and other birds from tropical forests. The quetzal was sacred, its feathers symbolic of royal authority.

MASTERS OF THE PAINTED WORD

Scribes were talented, highly educated individuals who combined the skills of painter and writer. In the Aztec empire they were trained in the elite *calmecac* schools at which the children of the nobility and a few precociously talented commoners learned the use of the sacred calendar, the timing of religious festivals, temple rituals, history, astronomy, arithmetic, oratory and the art of *tlacuilloli* or how to 'write-paint'. They were known as *tlacuiloque* or painter-writers. The script they used, which combined pictures that stood for ideas, words and numbers with others that represented a sound from spoken language, was closely derived from ancient Mesoamerican writing systems developed by the Olmec and Zapotecs. It was read in the Aztec tongue Nahuatl, but would have been largely comprehensible to the Maya and to other peoples. This made it highly suitable for keeping records of trade and tribute among the many ethnic and linguistic groups of the empire.

WRITTEN FORMS

The Aztec literate elite produced many different types of book, and scribes probably specialized in one kind. In addition to manuscripts on the ritual calendar and astronomy used for telling fortunes and predicting the future, Aztec scribes made maps, genealogies, histories or annals, law books, tribute lists and documents on dreams. They made ritual

Above: The Maya logograph for 'book', pronounced hun, *represents leaves of bark paper pressed between jaguar-skin covers.*

books or *tonalamatls* and annals or *xiuhamatls* in the form of screenfolds, often from pieces of deerskin stuck together with glue and covered on both sides with white lime. Scribes fashioned some screenfold books from *amatl* paper, produced from the bark of the wild fig tree. They also used *amatl* paper to make long pull-out scrolls or *tiras* and also, one piece at a time, for legal and administrative documents. They painted genealogies and maps on *lienzos*, large pieces of cotton.

KEEPER OF THE BOOKS

Among the Maya of the Classic Period, scribes were treated with great respect as men of genius. Here too, scribes were both writers and artists. Yucatec-speaking Maya called a scribe *ah ts'ib* ('He who Performs Writing and Painting'). From post-conquest accounts, we know that the Maya, like the Aztecs, wrote and kept a wide range of books, including maps, genealogies, medical treatises, books on healing plants, documents about the animals of the wild, as well as priestly

Left: Frederick Catherwood's 19th-century drawing is of a head of Itzamná, inventor of writing, carved in a wall at Izamal, Yucatán.

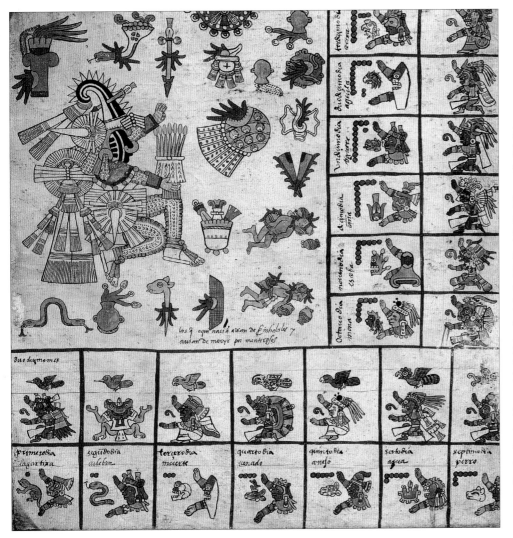

Left: Aztec scribes wrote the Codex Borbonicus *around the time of the Spanish Conquest to delineate divine influences.*

In representations of high-ranking groups on vases, in murals and in relief carvings, Michael Coe has identified that a batch of sticks worn in the headdress was intended to represent scribal pens and was a sign that the individual either held the position of a scribe or, while occupying another court position, was proud of his ability to read and write. Even kings were depicted with the scribal pens in their headdress.

It is indicative of the high regard for individual scribe-artists and their work among the Maya that the scribes who decorated and wrote on the beautiful ceramic products of the Classic Period signed their names on the pots as they finished them. A city-state's chief scribe appears to have lived in the utmost splendour. At Copán, a magnificent building known to archaeologists as the House of the Bacabs has been identified as the home of Max Chanal, chief scribe in the reign of King Yax Pac (AD763–820).

textbooks on the ritual calendar and the movements of the stars. Unfortunately these books were almost all destroyed in the frenzy of book-burning unleashed by Spanish administrators and churchmen who considered them to be idolatrous.

The scholar Nikolai Grube showed that the highest-ranking Maya scribes were also known as *ah k'u'hun* or *ah k'un* ('Keeper of the Sacred Books') and suggested that they were in charge of the king's library. Fellow Maya expert Michael Coe then demonstrated that the *ah k'un* was a key senior administrator who served as master of ceremonies for state and religious ritual, a marriage negotiator and as the writer of royal genealogies and keeper of tribute lists.

In the Classic Period, Maya scribes were educated in scribal schools close to the palace in the centre of Maya cities. The schools were open to the elite, to the offspring of rulers and the upper nobility. Eldest sons would probably have been destined for military training and power, but younger sons, and probably also sons by less senior wives or concubines, would have entered the schools, happy to take the first steps in the prestigious life of the scribe. Women could also be scribes among the Maya and the schools must have taken princesses and the daughters of the nobility.

LITERARY ELITE

Scribes' work was performed by the elite for the elite. In Classic Period Maya cities, an estimated one-quarter of the population could read and write. A larger number, perhaps, could read inscriptions on stelae without being able to write and many more again could admire the artistic achievement of the *ah ts'ib* while having the meaning of the words explained. Among the elite, it was a matter of great pride to be literate.

Right: This figure of a seated Maya scribe was displayed in one of the houses of the elite quarter of Las Sepulturas in Copán.

A SOLDIER'S LIFE

The attractions of a soldier's life were many. In Aztec society members of the army were respected as paragons of courage and fortitude. They were understood to be fulfilling Tenochtitlán's sacred destiny as an imperial power and to be following divine orders to bring prisoners home for sacrifice. When they died, their souls would travel to the east and be made honourable companions of the great sun Tonatiuh himself. Moreover, the military offered one of the few avenues by which a commoner could climb through the ranks of Aztec society. Success in battle, particularly the capture of many prisoners, won a war hero many coveted privileges, such as the right to wear more elaborate clothes, to partake of the alcoholic drink *pulque* in public or even to join the elite military cadres of the jaguar- and eagle-warriors. These top-ranking figures wore magnificent battle costume to go to war and to take part in ceremonial dances and sacred rituals.

A successful warrior won acclaim and seniority within his own *capultin* or clan. Because he had brought glory on the

Below: The soldiers shown in this mural may be mythical figures representing the forces of night taking on the armies of day.

Above: The Atzecs inherited from the Toltecs the ideal of warriors as embodiments of manly vigour and defenders of divine order.

group, he was awarded extra portions of land, or a larger share of any imperial tribute accorded them. He might be named *tecuhtli* ('Grandfather') and in meetings of the clan council his views were respected.

AZTEC RANK AND FILE

Most soldiers were conscripts called up for a campaign by the military establishment in units of around 400 from each *capultin*, or units in a tribute payment of fighting men supplied to the army of the Triple Alliance by one of the empire's subject cities. They would have had a good military training as part of their education in the *telpochcalli* school attached to the local temple. Many also took part in ceremonial military activities as part of religious festivals. Where possible, inexperienced men fought behind veteran warriors. Sometimes novice fighters wore no protective armour, as the wearing of quilted cotton body armour was often restricted to warriors who had achieved glory by killing or capturing many victims. Clan group members wore tribal symbols.

INJURED IN BATTLE

Most Aztec battles were over swiftly, with prisoners of war often far outnumbering battlefield casualties and fatalities. Nevertheless, Mesoamerican armies contained skilled doctors, who accompanied soldiers on campaign equipped with herbs and other natural materials and a wealth of traditional medical knowledge. Army surgeons used obsidian knives to make surgical cuts and human hair to sew up wounds. They even made plaster from tree sap and feathers to set broken bones.

When a soldier was injured by a sharp obsidian *atlatl* dart, the doctor would first clean the wound with whatever sterile liquid was available – if necessary, by using his own urine. Afterwards he looked in his medical bag for a little of the herb he called *coapatli* (a wild form of the common dayflower) to stop the soldier's bleeding. The sap of the maguey agave, which when fermented made

Above: A detail from the Mixtec Codex Zouche-Nuttall *depicts warrior leaders crossing a river in order to take an island.*

the favoured drink *pulque*, was an effective dressing. The doctor gave a herbal painkiller to soldiers who were in terrible pain.

ESCAPING ONE'S ORIGINS

Among the Maya, those who won status as warriors rose from the mass of farmer-commoners to a position halfway up the social pyramid, on a level with artisans and administrators. As among the Aztecs, successful warriors were rewarded with social prestige. Any killed in battle would receive preferential treatment in the after-life, for they were earmarked – along with sacrificial victims, priests, rulers, those who died giving birth and those who hung themselves – for a heavenly place of rest, while the unhappy majority of humankind went down to the dark place of trials, Xibalba. Maya rank and file

Below: Wielding spears, Maya warriors sweep resistance aside as they capture a village in Yucatán.

soldiers fought in cotton jerkins or simple loincloths and cloaks, while nobles and elite warriors wore feather-bedecked helmets and jade jewellery. The king went to battle magnificently attired in a jaguar tunic, a symbol of royalty and of ferocious martial strength. He must have been more of a figurehead than a combatant

and was protected by a group of elite fighters. The capture of a king was a tremendous coup and ended any battle. In Aztec and Maya realms, the warrior was an ideal, a role occupied or assumed by the ruler. The images of kings carved on the stelae erected in Maya cities from the late Preclassic Period onwards presented the king as warrior and priestly sacrificer, imbued with divine power. The king received this power from his predecessor and passed it on to his successor. He was the link – like the great ceiba tree – between the terrestrial plane of daily life and the heavenly realm of the ancestors.

Martial vigour and achievement was seen as proof of the king's stature and status. Newly elected Aztec *tlatoanis* were required to conduct a war as part of their extended coronation rites; the king of a Classic Period Maya city often undertook a military raid in order to obtain victims to be sacrificed as part of the king's own coronation ceremony. Shield Jaguar II of Yaxchilán took a notable local lord, Ah Ahau, captive in a raid of AD680 that scholars believe was a prelude to Shield Jaguar II's coronation the following year.

IN THE STATE'S SERVICE

The administration of the Aztec empire and its largely self-governing constituent units was a major task and provided employment for large numbers or people. All the most important and senior positions were filled by members of the *pipiltin* nobility. Nobles served as advisers to the ruler, as ambassadors, as governors of allied provinces, as judges, as collectors of tax and tribute, as leading members of the military hierarchy and as bureaucrats. Others joined the priesthood, where they had opportunities to pursue intellectual interests in, say, astronomy, mathematics or writing. All these men were graduates of elite *calmecac* priestly schools.

Commoners – whose living came from farming, fishing, hunting, soldiering, artisan work or mercantile activity – could rise to positions of authority within the *capultin* or tribal clans to which they

Below: A painted Maya pot of c.AD600–900, from the Motagua valley, shows a dignitary carrying shield and spear.

Above: Clay figurines from Jaina Island show the elaborate headdresses, jewellery and other adornments of the Maya elite.

belonged. One was elected *calpullec*, who oversaw economic matters, such as grants of land, within the clan; another was the *teochcautin*, the keeper of laws. At times of conflict, the *teochcautin* led the clan's conscripts to war.

THE KING'S MEN

Similarly, in Maya culture commoner-farmers, fishermen and soldiers could not rise to the most senior administrative and economic positions. In the Maya cities of the Classic Period, the top military staff, administrators and traders were all members of the upper nobility. The top military chief, *sahal*, was generally one of the king's closest relatives.

In Postclassic Yucatán, as described by Bishop Diego de Landa, the ruler of a regional state, called the *halach uinic*, appointed those who governed the towns

and villages of the region from the highest levels of royalty and the nobility, including his own nephews, cousins and brothers. Each of these men, who were called *batabs*, ruled through a council of two or three and decisions on regional matters had to be approved unanimously by all councillors.

The *batab* was the local judge and military leader. He ensured that his town or region was ready with its economic tribute when required by the *halach uinic*. The *batab* had two or three deputies called *ah kulelob* to perform his bidding. He worked closely with a military specialist called a *nacom*, a noble who served in this highly prestigious and

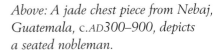

coveted position for three years. During this period, he was required to live a celibate and sober life, with no contact of any kind with women. Even those who waited upon him and served his food were required to be men.

Another group of senior administrators were the *ah holpopob* who ran the council meeting house and were well informed on matters of foreign interaction. Day-to-day matters such as village disputes or petty crimes were the province of the *tupiles* or local law officers.

THE QUICHÉ ARISTOCRACY

Among the Quiché Maya of highland Guatemala, once again, commoners were excluded from the highest levels of government and administration. The nobility or *ahauab* were descendants of the Quiché founders, who were probably originally Putún Maya merchants from the Gulf Coast lowlands of Mexico. The *ahauab* provided rulers, military leaders, priests and administrators.

Members of the middle class could find work as land managers, soldiers, traders and bureaucrats. The *ahauab* were organized into groups depending on descent from a common father. Members of particular kin groups specialized in serving as priests, warriors or administrators. The leaders of these kin groups governed their relatives and served as advisers to the Quiché ruler.

At the Quiché capital Utatlan in the 15th century, three lineages were pre-eminent and identified with gods: the Ahau Quiché were followers of the sky god, the Nihaib were dependents of the moon goddess and the Cawek were devotees of the sun god. Their elite members filled the top administrative posts of army captain, judge and other positions identified as 'speaker' and 'receiving officer', a kind of ambassador and master of ceremonies who received important visitors. Above them all was the ahpop ('Ruler or Mat Lord'). He was high priest, army leader and chairman of the ruling council.

Above: A jade chest piece from Nebaj, Guatemala, c.AD300–900, depicts a seated nobleman.

Below: A limestone carving from Palenque shows King Pacal, seated on a regal jaguar-head stool, receiving a headdress – and so divine authority to rule – from his mother Zac Kuk. Archaeologists found the relief inside House E of the Palenque palace.

COPÁN'S GOVERNORS

Archaeologists working at Copán have uncovered details of civil administrators in the reign of King Yax Pac (AD763–820). Leading nobles, who lived in the region of Copán called Las Sepulturas by historians, were members of Copán's ruling council and each headed a prestigious blood lineage. Their houses have been excavated and contain splendid carved benches that suggest that these men had significant independent authority and wealth.

One of these was the king's chief scribe, Max Chanal, whose house contains several portraits of him holding his tools. A delicately carved bench dedicated in AD781 celebrates his own rank, his proud descent and the might of his king.

Yax Pac's brothers, Yahua Chan and Yax K'amlay, were also important figures in the administration. Scholars believe that the king's authority was failing and that he attempted to bolster it by giving more power to his brothers and to leading nobles. However, the attempt was doomed to failure. After his death, the dynasty and Copán itself suffered the effects of a decline that had already begun some years earlier.

NOBLE SERVANTS OF THE GODS

In Maya lands, entering the priesthood was not generally an option for the sons of farmers, artisans or merchants: the most important priestly positions – like the top administrative and legal opportunities – were hereditary and passed down the generations by members of the nobility. Bishop Diego de Landa reported that in the 16th century the leading Maya priests trained their own sons or the younger boys of important lords, while the high priest was succeeded by his son or nearest blood relative.

SERVANTS OF THE SUN

De Landa wrote that the high priest was called *ahuacan* ('Lord Snake') and was kept in fine style by gifts and contributions from secular rulers. He was the final authority on arcane priestly matters concerning astronomy, divination, writing and record keeping, interpreting holy books, the setting of festivals and the ritual to be followed. He led sacrifices and ritual worship only on very important occasions and also oversaw the training and appointment of more junior priests.

The word for priest was *ah kin* ('Servant of the Sun'). One was appointed to discover and interpret the prophecies associated with each of the 13 *katuns* – periods of 7,200 days – that recurred in a cycle as part of the Maya Long Count. Other leading Maya priests at the time of Bishop de Landa were the *chilanes* ('Declaimers'), who functioned as oracles, passing on to eager listeners the decrees and warnings of the gods. These men were shaman-diviners, who reported on the reality they discovered during spirit voyages or in the course of religious visions inspired by mind-altering drugs.

Another priest was the *nacom*, who was entrusted with the crucial sacrificial task of slicing open the victim's chest and removing the heart. This skilled executioner's position was held by a man for his lifetime. His four helpers, who held down the writhing body of the victim on the sacrificial stone, were named *chacs* in honour of the rain god. They also had the task of lighting a new sacred fire at the beginning of each year.

Above: A fresco image from the Tepantitla apartment building in Teotihuacán depicts a priest making obeisance to the deities.

These roles certainly had their counterparts in Maya cities of the Classic Period, although the details of sacrificial practice and priestly hierarchy probably differed. From the very beginnings of settled life in Maya lands, it appears that priests specialized in knowledge of astronomic cycles and seasonal change. They became specialists in time, maintaining control over the recurring patterns of religious life by setting dates for festivals and becoming repositories of dynastic history. They developed the elite skills of writing and reading and, by the Classic Period, were closely associated, if not synonymous, with the scribes and stonemasons who were so revered for their written art.

Left: Wearing facepaint, elaborate costumes and headgear and carrying ritual staffs, Mixtec priests advance to sacrifice.

Above: The goggle eyes of the rain god can be seen on this ceramic figurine of a splendidly attired priest from Teotihuacán.

TEMPLE WOMEN

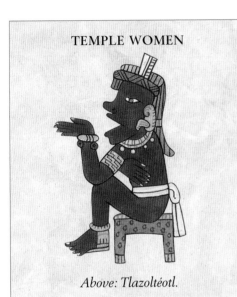

Above: Tlazoltéotl.

There were many opportunities for women in Aztec religious life. The major goddesses were served by cadres of female priests. For example, priestesses of the fertility goddess Tlazoltéotl heard confessions from those wishing to own up to sexual wrongdoing. The priestess of Chalchiúhtlicue, goddess of rivers and ocean, performed a rite of blessing for newborn babies, sprinkling the infant with holy water. Priestesses also represented and impersonated their patron during religious festivals. During the festival of Huey Tozoztli ('Major Vigil'), the priestess of corn goddess Chicomecóatl pronounced a blessing over farmers' supply of seeds.

In Ochpaniztli ('Clearing'), the harvest celebration, the Chicomecóatl priestess sacrificed and flayed a female victim and donned her skin as a suit. With another priestess, appearing as the fertility goddess Toci, she then hurled fistfuls of corn into the crowd. Farmers kept the seeds for planting next season.

Some priestesses, the *maqui*, served as temple prostitutes. They were visited by young warriors, travelled with the army on campaign and even marched into battle. Their divine patron was Xochiquetzal, goddess of flowers.

MANY PRIESTS, MANY TASKS

While the top-level priests were all members of the *pipiltin* nobility in Aztec society, members of any class could become rank and file priests. There was a range of opportunities for priests. Top-level sacerdotal administrators supervised the ranks of priests, the priestly schools, the performance of ritual and the practical management of temple finances and landholdings. Elite serving priests led worship in the Templo Major and main temples and performed major sacrifices on important religious feast days. Other sons of the nobility lived as monk-like attendants and celebrants in the great temples. Each painted his body black or wore a long, black-hooded cloak. They were celibate and often fasted for festivals. Their hair was matted with blood from the cuts they made to their head during rites of autosacrifice.

Right: The elaborate ritual costume, headgear and jewellery worn by Maya priests are depicted in delicate detail on a stela from the mid-8th century AD.

Some priests were members of the army and marched into battle alongside high-ranking soldiers in the centre of the army's battle line. They carried images of Huitzilopochtli and other deities. Others worked in *calmecac* schools, where all the teachers were priests. Some were the learned artist-scribes who expressed their vast knowledge of astronomical cycles and ritual worship in codex books. Others were shaman-diviners, gifted with spiritual vision, the capacity to interpret it and the gift of spirit and body healing.

CHAPTER FIVE

EVERYDAY LIFE

The day started early for Mesoamericans: the people of Tenochtitlán rose before dawn. When the morning star, Venus, appeared in the sky, drums and conch trumpets sounded from the Templo Mayor and the temples that were the focus of religious life in each locality. The *tlatoani*, his relatives and the nobles, priests, farmers, fishermen, hunters and merchants all awoke. Many took a steam bath to refresh themselves. For most, breakfast was a few tortillas or tamales, perhaps a cup of *atolli* or maize soup. Labourers carried a few more maize snacks to work for a midday meal.

In a Maya village or city of the Classic Period, the first hours of the day were markedly similar. The majority rose before dawn, took a steam bath, ate a maize breakfast and made their way to the fields, artisan-workshop or other place of work grasping a few tortillas for later sustenance.

After a long day's labour, most workers were home before dark. They ate their largest meal, again based on maize, at this time. Some accounts suggest that labourers, hungry from their labours in the fields, ate as many as 20 large tortillas at evening meal. Men and women usually ate separately, squatting or sitting on the floor. Afterwards, lighting their homes with pine torches, both men and women often settled down to craft-work, perhaps chipping simple tools from flint or making pots for their own use. Merchants, by contrast, sometimes hosted elaborate feasts, while in noble houses evenings of poetry and music might be laid on in gardens and patio areas giving on to luxuriously appointed dining areas.

Left: A page from the Mixtec Codex Zouche-Nuttall depicts the wedding of Lady 3-Flint to Lord 12-Wind.

LIFE IN THE HOME

In Tenochtitlán, the *tlatoani's* divine magnificence was reflected in the splendour of his elegantly decorated palace, surrounded by gardens containing ponds, walkways, an aviary and even a zoo. Members of the *pipiltin* nobility also had palatial residences with a *temazcalli* or steam bath and expansive gardens, while wealthy merchants and craftsmen expressed their social standing in fine, but much smaller houses. The home of a common family was a single-roomed hut, or a few rooms clustered around a courtyard. Walls were usually of adobe or wattle and daub, although some wealthier commoners lived in stone buildings.

Multiroom houses contained one or more bedrooms, a living room with a central hearth and perhaps a bathroom. Single-room huts provided little more

Above: This modern reconstruction of an Aztec working family shows a farmer bringing home crops while his relatives weave and attend to the children.

Below: Aztecs lived on or near the floor, sitting on reed mats to eat and work at weaving or toolmaking close to the hearth.

than a space for sleeping, with the family hearth often situated outside beneath a canopy. The family might keep a turkey or a small dog in a pen alongside the house or a few birds in a cage. Many households also had a small garden called a *xochichinancalli* ('flowerbed among the reeds') for growing vegetables, flowers and healing herbs. All houses had a shrine to the ancestors. The location as well as the size of a family's home depended on their wealth and social standing.

WORKING FROM HOME
Home was a place of labour for women, who spent long hours spinning, weaving and cooking. They span thread from maguey agave, henepen or cotton using a handheld drop spindle, working it into woven cloth using a loom strapped on the back and held in the lap. When not weaving or sewing, they ground maize for hours using a rolling stone or pestle at a low table called a *metatl*. With maize dough they made tortillas on a large clay disc laid over a fire on three hearthstones.

Poorer families generally lived farther away from the city centre. They often lived in single-room huts, whereas the better off families lived in stone buildings nearer the city's ceremonial precincts and major markets. Aztec houses had little or no furniture: people worked, sat and ate on the floor. They usually slept on woven reed mats.

The men worked in the *chinampa* fields or took their boats, nets and harpoons out fishing on the lake. They taught their sons how to fish and encouraged them to try their luck at catching birds. If the conscription call came, they could be forced to go on military campaign in the army or perhaps to serve as labourers in a vast building construction project designed to express the might and celebrate the religious devotion of the 'people of the sun'.

Left: The kind of thatched hut typically occupied by Maya peasants is depicted amid trees in a detail from a temple mural.

WITHIN THE CORNER POSTS

In the lowlands of the central Maya region, the typical commoner's house was built on a low platform of earth or rubble, with walls of stone, mud blocks or adobe built around four wooden corner posts and a roof of pole and thatch. Sometimes only the lower half of the wall was made of long-lasting materials such as stone or adobe, and the upper part was filled in with straw or reeds. The house contained one or two rooms at most.

Builders often laid out three or four of these small constructions around a central courtyard. According to Bishop Diego de Landa, the Maya of Yucatán split these houses lengthways by building an internal wall. In the rear, private part they built bed frames of branches and saplings over which they laid mats as mattresses. Here they slept, using cloaks as coverings.

The front part of the house functioned as a kind of porch, and provided a cooler place to sleep in hot weather. In some areas a family group might have used several small buildings arranged around a central yard: one for storing food, tools and equipment, one for sleeping, one as a living area, one as a shrine, one as a work-shop for making stone tools – and a small hut with a central fire heating stones for use as a steam room. Some Maya villagers stored food and water in pits called *chultunes* dug in the ground.

As among the Aztecs, the majority of men were away from home for long hours working in the fields or hunting. At home, the women worked ceaselessly spinning, weaving, grinding flour, preparing food, tending to the garden and the needs of the turkeys or dogs they kept for meat.

Any cloth that was not needed, together with surplus vegetables or other items that could be spared from the garden were taken to the nearest market to be sold or to barter for items which the family did not make themselves.

At times of sowing and harvest the division of labour shifted, so that women went out to assist their menfolk in the fields with the extra seasonal work.

FAMILY NETWORK

People tended to live in family or extended family groups. At Tikal, an extended family often lived in houses arranged on the north, south and west sides of a courtyard and facing east towards a fourth building on a higher platform. This probably contained a shrine to the ancestors and, beneath the floor, the graves of the most revered among past family members.

All members of Maya settlements lived in the same pattern of buildings. Wealthier members such as nobles, traders, military leaders and the king lived in increasingly splendid versions of the basic buildings.

Below: Carving on an archway in Labná depicts a simple, one-roomed thatched hut.

THE MATCHMAKER'S ART

Among the Maya of Yucatán at the time of the Spanish Conquest, girls and boys who reached puberty went through a ceremony named the Descent of the Gods. The sacred rite, performed by a priest with the help of local elders, set the young apart from their childhood. From that day onwards, they were considered to be members of the adult community.

Girls were then judged to be ready for marriage. Their mothers taught them the skills necessary for married life and instructed their daughters in modesty. This included showing her how, when she met a man on a path, she should turn away and present her back to him, so that he could pass easily and undisturbed. The young woman was also instructed that, if she came to the well with her cousin or another man, she should keep her eyes gently lowered as she brought him water.

In some Maya communities, sons left the parental house and moved into a communal building set aside for unmarried men. There they played dice and games with small balls and beans. It was not unknown for these young men to bring prostitutes home and they paid for their services with a handful of cacao beans. Unmarried men marked themselves out by painting their skin with black dye. They avoided tattoos, which were only permitted to husbands.

MARRIAGE PLANNING

Marriages were generally arranged, either by the father or by a professional matchmaker called an *ah atanzah*. The ideal wife would be a woman of the same social level and from the same village as the son. Marriage plans were often agreed between families while the son and daughter to be wed were still children; the families then began to live as in-laws even though the marriage might be some years off.

Before any marriage agreement was made, both families consulted the priestly astronomers who made sure that there was no ill omen attached to the prospective couple's dates of birth or to the day proposed for the wedding ceremony. Marriages were permitted between first cousins, but some unions were taboo. For example, a man could not marry a woman who carried the same surname or patronym.

Left: Xochiquetzal, ('Precious Flower') was honoured by the Aztecs as a goddess of love, domesticity and the flowers of the earth.

Above: Chalchiúhtlicue, who presided over the prolonged wedding ceremonies of the Aztecs, is usually shown wearing jade.

The marriage ceremony was held in the house of the bride's father. The couple wore new robes woven for the occasion by the two mothers. After the wedding the new husband and wife lived in the house or the group of houses occupied by the bride's family for about six or seven years. The husband's new in-laws benefited from his labour throughout this time and, indeed, by custom could evict him from their home compound if he refused to work.

After this the couple moved to live adjacent to the husband's father, often in a newly built house within the complex. Commoners had one wife, but wealthier men could wed several women. Members of the elite in Classic Period Maya cities such as Tikal took many wives and also kept women outside wedlock as concubines.

DEATH AND DIVORCE

A couple could divorce simply by one partner repudiating the other. Younger children of the wedding would remain with the mother, while older children tended to go with the same-sex parent.

A man might divorce his wife if she proved unable to have children or if she failed in duties such as making food or preparing his evening bath. Any remarriage took place without ceremony, as wedding rites were reserved for first marriages. A man seeking a new union would simply visit the house of the woman he had chosen. If she was agreeable she would prepare him a meal. Widows and widowers were expected to mourn the lost partner for a year before remarrying. A widower could not marry his dead wife's sister or mother.

CHALCHIÚHTLICUE'S BLESSING

Customs were not very different among the Aztecs. Weddings came under the protection of river and ocean goddess Chalchiúhtlicue. Young Aztecs married in their late teenage years or perhaps their early twenties. The young man's parents arranged his marriage after consulting with members of the extended family or kin group. They sent a professional matchmaker to the parents of the chosen young woman. The matchmaker presented his case on four consecutive days, after which the parents of the young woman were expected to announce whether they accepted the marriage offer or not.

The marriage ceremony lasted four days. On the evening of the first day, the bride was bathed and dressed in fine robes, before her kinswomen decorated her legs and arms with red feathers and painted her face with a paste containing tiny, shimmering crystals. They offered

Left: A scene from the Codex Becker *shows the wedding of a Mixtec noble couple. Faint footsteps lead to their future offspring.*

her words of wisdom about the life she was preparing to begin, then the strongest one lifted the bride on to her back and carried her through the streets to the house of the husband's parents.

Inside, amid scenes of celebration, the couple sat side by side on a marriage mat, while elders lit a fire in the family hearth and burned offerings of copal incense, which sent up sacred clouds of smoke to attract the gods' blessings. The groom's mother produced a wealth of robes and mantles as gifts for her prospective in-laws. Then a matchmaker approached the couple and tied the groom's cape to the bride's skirt and the groom's mother fed first the bride and then the groom with

four mouthfuls of tamales, a dish prepared of meat and corn husks. This ceremony marked the couple's union: next they were led into the bedroom to consummate their marriage, while the gathered relatives made merry.

Feasting continued for four days. At the end of this time, a series of formal speeches concluded the celebration. First, the most respected elder female on the new husband's side reminded the new wife of her duties and of the need to be trusting, humble and hard working. The mother of the bride spoke next, to her new son-in-law, asking him to remember that he owed his wife a duty of love, hard work and self-sacrificing attention.

Below: The bride arrives at her wedding on the back of her matchmaker (bottom centre) and is shown, later, seated on a mat.

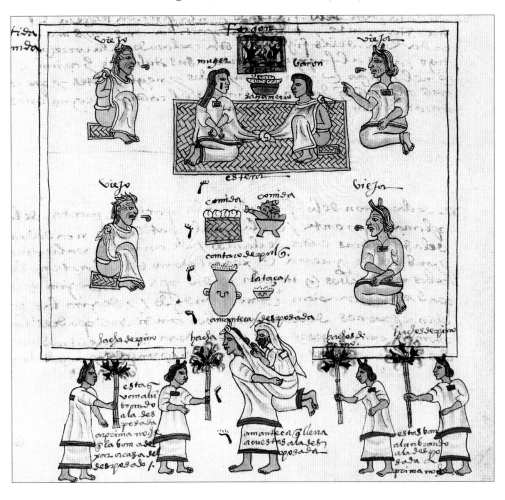

A CHILD IS BORN

When a pregnant woman went into labour, her midwife would lead prayers to the goddess of childbirth – Tlazoltéotl among the Aztecs and Ix Chel among the Maya – to ease the woman's pain and bring a healthy baby. The midwife mixed herbs and grasses to produce a sedative mixture that she fed to the mother. She then gently laid a warm stone on her straining belly. Among the Aztecs, when the baby was born the midwife would utter a series of battle cries in praise of the exhausted mother who had fought long and hard with her offspring in

labour. Then the midwife would speak to the baby, greeting the new arrival as if it were a voyager who had completed a long and difficult journey, encouraging the infant to settle among its family, declaring that life in the world was short but a man or woman had many duties, the most important of which were to work hard and to honour the gods.

The midwife would next cut the baby's umbilical cord and store it safely, before giving the baby its first bath, explaining in a reverent voice that pure and cleansing waters were the gift of Chalchiúhtlicue, the consort of Tláloc the rain god and goddess of springs, rivers and the sea. If the baby were a boy, he was expected to keep the umbilical cord until adulthood and carry it to a distant battlefield, where it was his duty to bury it; a girl would bury her umbilical cord beside the family hearth.

Left: Heavy with the power of fertility, this statue of a pregnant woman was made in Nayarit, West Mexico, c.200BC–AD200.

Above: Power over the beginnings of life. This almost abstract face is believed to be that of the Huastec goddess of childbirth.

After its first bath, the newborn was ready to receive visitors. Many members of the extended family came to pay their respects. One after another, they would make reverent declarations of respect for

A NOBLE WELCOMING
Among noble and wealthy Aztecs, a baby's arrival was celebrated with a lying-in that lasted up to three weeks. Visitors came from great distances – some important families even received ambassadors from foreign states. The hosts provided splendid gifts of the finest woven cloaks and embroidered skirts for their prominent guests. Food, *pulque* and other drinks were provided for all who came to pay their respects.

the mother, the midwife and the newborn baby. Visitors were greeted with food and drink. Priestly interpreters of the *tonalamatl* book of the sacred calendar would arrive to interpret the ramifications of the baby's precise minute, hour and day of birth for its prospects and future behaviour.

Much depended on which gods were influential at the child's birth. If the omens were bad, the interpreters offered advice as to how parents and baby could improve the infant's prospects. They also set the date for the baby's bathing ritual: this would normally be four days after the birth, but could be delayed or brought forward if the divine influences on that day were not good.

A BATHING CEREMONY

On the appointed day, the midwife conducted the bathing ceremony in the presence of parents and extended family. She laid a basin of water on a reed mat and surrounded it with miniature tools appropriate to the baby's sex and the family's standing and profession. If a boy child had been destined for the army by the *tonalamatl* priests, the midwife would lay out a small bow and arrow on top of an amaranth-dough tortilla intended to represent a warrior's shield. If he were the son of an artisan, then she would lay out tiny implements representing the father's profession, the path that lay before the boy as he grew. For a female baby, the midwife would place a tiny skirt together with spinning instruments to represent a woman's work.

The midwife then circled the basin in an anticlockwise direction as she spoke to the baby, before she bathed him or her and presented him or her four times to the heavens and to the cleansing water provided by blessed Chalchiúhtlicue. Any older children in the family were next sent out into the street to publicly announce the name chosen for the newborn. The baby was dried, dressed and laid in its cradle while the joyful mother, the father and the assembled relatives celebrated the birth with feasting and music.

Left: The young boy represented by this terracotta statuette, made in Veracruz c.AD550–850, learned to wear headdress, earrings and necklace before clothes.

A WEB OF DIVINE INFLUENCES

The Maya keenly believed the minute, hour and day of a baby's birth in the ritual calendar set the child's temperament, determined its prospects and brought with it religious and ritual responsibilities – acts that were necessary to limit or bring to fruition the divine influences at work in the moment of birth.

Among the Cakchiquel and other southern highland Maya, babies were given the name of the day in the 260-day calendar on which they were born. Among the Yucatec-speaking Maya at the time of the Spanish Conquest, each baby took four names: a name chosen by a priest following a divining ceremony; the father's family name; the family names of father and mother together; and lastly a familiar or nickname.

So developed was the shared aesthetic sense among the Maya that mothers and fathers were willing to work on the baby's body to make it conform to common ideals of beauty. To produce the flattened forehead that was widely admired they bound the baby's head between flat pieces of wood, one pressed against the forehead and one against the back of the skull. After several days encased in this way, a baby's skull was flattened for the remainder of life. The Maya also admired a cross-eyed look, so a mother would tie resin balls to the hairs that fell down towards the eyes of the growing baby to encourage the child to focus on the resin balls.

THE FIRST YEARS

Aztec parents brought their children up to be hardworking, dutiful and self-disciplined. As toddlers grew older, their parents taught them various domestic tasks. At around the age of three, daughters were taught by their mothers to spin and weave, to grind maize and to make tortillas. At the same age, boys began to help around the house, for example, by fetching and carrying water. When boys reached the age of six or seven years, they began to spend their days with their fathers at the lakeside, learning to fish and to gather reeds. If the family made their living by a specialized craft such as pottery or basketmaking, the mother or father would begin instruction in its techniques when the child was aged eight to ten years.

The Aztecs were not averse to using corporal punishment to bring their children into line, although codex accounts suggest that they avoided doing so until the child was around eight or nine years old. The Codex Mendoza shows parents punishing backsliding or lazy children by pinching them on the ears or arms, pricking their skin with the thorns of the maguey cactus, spanking them or binding them up and laying them in a cold, damp place. The most unusual punishment depicted was forcing a child to inhale the burning odours of roasting chilli peppers by holding him or her over a fire on which chillies had been scattered.

AZTEC SCHOOLS

Children progressed to school when they came of age. Scholars are uncertain whether this was at 7, 10 or 14 years. Children of commoners went to the *telpochcalli* ('young person's house') that stood beside their local temple. In sizeable cities there was a *telpochcalli* for each *calpulli* or residential ward. Girls and boys were taught separately. They learned history, public speaking, dancing and singing and received religious instruction. Boys also underwent rigorous military training, while girls learned to serve in the temples of the city. An Aztec education emphasized a young person's duties and responsibilities: he or she was encouraged to find fulfilment in serving the gods, the state, the *calpulli* and the family livelihood.

Sons and daughters of the nobility were educated separately from commoners, in establishments called *calmecac*. They received instruction in religious ritual, in following the sacred calendar and

Left: The Codex Mendoza *shows discipline of 7–10 year-olds. At 7, a boy is taught to fish while a girl learns to spin; beneath, the children are threatened with maguey spikes at age 8, then pricked with the spikes at 9, and bound and beaten at the age of 10.*

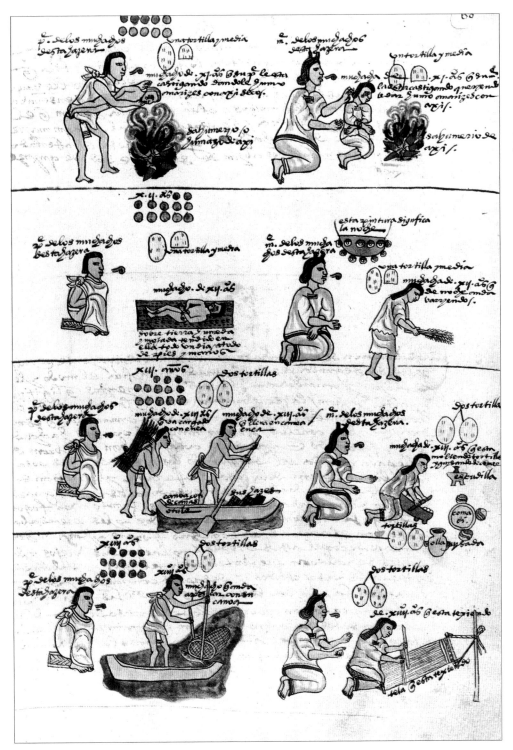

Above: The Codex Mendoza *depicts 11-year-olds being forced to inhale chilli smoke; at 13, the boy transports rushes by canoe while the girl grinds maize for tortillas.*

interpreting the *tonalamatl* and in understanding and conducting the main festivals of the Aztec religious year. They also learned military theory, agriculture and horticulture, astronomy, history and the skills of architecture and arithmetic. Students at *calmecac* were also taught and practised the skills of high oratory and of reading and writing. They graduated to become such leading figures of state as judges, military commanders, bureaucrats and priests in the most important temples. A few very able children of commoners were also selected to enjoy the benefits of this elite form of education. There was one elite school for girls and one for boys in each city. Students were expected to follow religious fasts, to perform penances and to take purifying sacred baths. Their teachers were priests.

LEARNING IN MAYA LANDS

The Maya of the Classic Period ran similar elite schools to train the younger sons of royalty and the highest echelons of the nobility as artist-scribes. Some elite Maya scribes were women, so these elite schools must either have accepted female pupils or have operated sister establishments for princesses and the daughters of the nobility.

Less privileged Maya were educated at home in the skills of domestic living and of the family livelihood. For the first three years both boys and girls spent their time almost exclusively with their mother, but from the age of four or five years they began a wider life. At this stage a boy would have a white bead tied in his hair as a sign that he was ready to accompany and begin learning from his father, while a girl had a red shell tied to a string around her waist. Boys went with their fathers to the fields and on hunting trips, day by day picking up the skills they would need in adult life.

Below: A potter in Tlatilco, Mexico, made this striking and well proportioned ceramic child's head c.400BC.

THE GIFT OF THE MAIZE GOD

Throughout Mesoamerica the staple food was maize. Its preparation was laborious: first it was soaked with lime or ash, then boiled until its skin could be pulled off; afterwards it was ground to a paste with a grooved rolling stone on a long flat stone the Aztecs called a *metatl*. This dough was baked as tortillas (flat, thin cakes) on a circular clay dish supported over the fire by three hearthstones. Maize was cooked with chilli pepper and honey in a soup-like stew the Aztecs called *atolli* and in tamales – mixed with peppers and vegetables or sometimes meat, then wrapped in corn-husks and baked on the cooking plate.

Below: A ceramic Zapotec funerary urn from a Monte Albán tomb depicts the corn god with an animal-mask headdress.

A Maya villager woke to a breakfast of maize water, then left for the fields carrying several balls of ground maize encased in leaves. At night, refreshed after his agricultural labours by a steam bath, he was served tortillas. In Atzec lands a peasant's midday meal consisted of the maize soup *atolli* and his reward for his work in the evening was to dine on tortillas topped with beans, other vegetables and chilli sauce.

FEASTING ON FLESH

Richer members of the Aztec community ate a more elaborate diet, but it was always based on tortillas and tamales. Successful merchants laid on magnificent feasts for their fellows to boost their professional standing. During the festival of Panquetzalíztli, held in honour of the Aztecs' tribal lord Huitzilopochtli, these feasts included the flesh of slaves provided by the merchants to be sacrificed at the temple – served with tortillas, tamales and other maize and bean delicacies. According to the records of the Spanish churchman Bernardino de Sahagún, the *tlatoani* or ruler of Tenochtitlán faced an array of 2,000 dishes every day. This combined basic and luxury foods – tortillas, tamales, turkey, venison, quail, rabbit, hare, rat and many fishes, plus fruits in great variety.

VEGETABLE VARIETY

To supplement their maize, Mesoamericans grew the grain amaranth, called *huautli* in the Aztecs' Nahuatl language. The Aztecs ate a wide range of vegetables including many types of bean, squashes, onions, sweet potatoes (called *camotli*) and a root vegetable

Above: The Tudela Codex *(1553) shows a woman pouring chocolate from a height to give the drink a frothy head.*

called *jicama*, which resembled the turnip. It was added to vegetable stews, steamed or thinly sliced and eaten raw with a spicy chilli and salt seasoning. They also added peanuts and popcorn to their diet. Among fruits they ate the green tomato (called *tomatl*) and the red tomato (*xictomatl*), the avocado (*ahuacatl*), the custard apple, the zapote, the guava and the chirimoya.

The poor ate whatever meat and fish they could add to their diet. The Maya ate deer, home-raised and wild turkeys, iguanas, armadillos, rabbits, peccaries (a pig-like mammal), squirrels, porcupines, monkeys, macaws and other birds and rodents including agouti, paca and doubt-less rats. Those among the Maya who lived in coastal, riverside and lakeside areas ate fish and shellfish while others

Above: On a painted plate from the region of Tikal, an enthroned ruler is being served a cup of the chocolate drink.

made do with dried fish transported by traders. In Tenochtitlán and other Aztec cities, the menfolk caught fish and birds, and they probably hunted rabbits and deer in the countryside. Families raised turkeys and dogs in small pens and birds in cages if they could afford to do so. Sometimes the women-folk traded home-woven cloth and flint tools or obsidian blades made at home by their husbands for deer or rabbit meat at the market.

SEASONINGS AND DRINKS

As well as chilli peppers, Mesoamericans used coriander, sage and the herb dogweed (*chenopodium*) for seasoning. Among other flavourings, they prized vanilla very highly, finding it in the pods of a species of orchid.

The wealthy greatly enjoyed the chocolate drink the Aztecs called *xocolatl*. A man making the drink would grind roasted cacao beans then sometimes mix the powder with dried corn. He would add cold water and beat the liquid until it foamed, then add pods of the vanilla orchid or spoonfuls of honey. The Maya also used a flower called the ear flower (identified by scholars as *Cymbalopetalum penduliflora*) as a flavouring for chocolate drink. In carved and ceramic representations of elite groups, one noble figure is often depicted holding a bundle of these ear flowers.

Xocolatl was a drink of rulers, princes and nobles: some sources suggest that Moctezuma II and his court consumed 50 jugs of the drink every day. The Maya served it in tall cylindrical vases from which they poured it into shallow calabash drinking cups from a great height to generate froth. In AD749, a king of Piedras Negras celebrated the 20th anniversary of his accession with a chocolate-drinking ceremony with leading members of the nobility and an ambassador from Yaxchilán. The event was commemorated in a carved wall panel. Chocolate was also drunk by Maya parents and matchmakers during elite marriage negotiations and it was served at high-class weddings.

Throughout Mesoamerica, people drank an alcoholic drink made from the fermented sap of the maguey agave together with a bush root called pulque wood. The drink was called *pulque* by the Aztecs. They celebrated the goddess Mayáhuel as the divine patron of the drink.

In Aztec lands, *pulque* was officially allowed only to nobles, the ill and the elderly and to warriors brave in battle. There were fierce laws against public drunkenness, enforceable by the death penalty if a person were discovered drunk three times.

Bishop Diego de Landa, describing religious ceremonies celebrated each month by the Maya, suggests that public drinking and intoxication was part of religious ceremonial. Celebrants indulged in a sacred wine called *balche* made from the bark of the balche tree together with water and fermented honey. It was left to steep for some time, during which a prayer was intoned to the spirits of all animals and plants in the surrounding wilderness. It was said to induce feelings of tribal unity and togetherness.

Right: A Huastec statue celebrates corn goddess Chicomecóatl. She was also known as Chicomolotzin ('Seven Ears of Maize').

CLOTHES AND HAIRSTYLES

In Maya lands, commoners, nobility and royalty all wore the same basic clothing but wealthier people possessed far more ornate and elaborate versions of the outfit worn by the peasants.

MAYA MALE WARDROBE

The male Maya peasant wound a cotton loincloth between his legs and several times around his waist. The cloth, called *ex* in the Yucatec tongue, was woven on the home handloom and was around five fingers in width. More elaborate versions of the *ex* were decorated with feathers at each end and, when worn, these hung down colourfully before and behind. Elite men wore loincloths embellished with geometric designs and the heads of deities. Nobles often wore a belt from which they hung jade deity masks and plaques. They might also have worn a god mask on the chest together with a jade-bead necklace.

When he needed protection from the elements, a man wore a square cotton robe over the loincloth. It was held up by knots on the shoulders. This piece of clothing, called a *pati* in Yucatec, was worn plain by the poorest, but was decorated with elaborate embroidery when worn by wealthier members of the community. Rulers often wore a jaguar skin or a *pati* sewn with quetzal feathers to signify their exalted status.

Maya peasants wore deer-hide sandals (*xanch*) tied between the toes and around the ankles with cords of hemp. Nobles wore extremely elaborate sandals with long ties and large heel covers decorated with images of ancestors and deities.

Above: The magnificence of a Maya lord's headdress and chest plate is recreated in this terracotta figure, made c.AD100–650.

Left: Twin statuettes made in Oaxaca AD1150–1250 represent Mixtecs wearing elaborate ear and face jewellery.

MAYA FEMALE WARDROBE

Women in Maya communities wore a loose cotton garment called a *huipil*. In some communities, the *huipil* was a waist-length blouse, worn with a skirt; in others it was a loose, untailored shift-like dress with head and armholes. The *huipil* blouse is worn to this day by Maya women in the mountains of Guatemala: each community has its own distinctive embroidered geometric design. The loose-fitting *huipil* dress is still worn by Maya women in Yucatán, where traditional embroidered designs decorate the hem and the area around the arms and neck. The 16th-century authority Herrera, who reported on the Maya for the Spanish crown, wrote that in his era women wore a loose sack-like dress like the Yucatán *huipil*, together with a cotton headdress. Bishop Diego de Landa wrote that Maya

Above: Musicians and court attendants at Bonampak wear relatively simple costumes but extravagant masks and headdresses.

women wore a simple skirt and a cotton cloth wound around the torso to cover their breasts. Women sometimes also wore a petticoat beneath the *huipil* or skirt, and a shawl over it.

HAIRSTYLES AND BODY ART

Men shaved a small area at the crown of the head, but otherwise kept their hair long, winding it in a plait around the head with the 'tail' dangling down the neck. Luxuriant tresses of black hair were the pride of Maya women, and mothers instructed their growing daughters in caring for their hair and in the many different hairstyles worn. Men and women experimented with body paint and tattoos: the designs worn by women were more delicate than those sported by their husbands and brothers. The colour of body paint could be significant: black indicated that a man was a bachelor, black and red meant a warrior, while black and white was reserved for prisoners. A prayer would be offered for men painted turquoise blue, for they were bound for a fate of ritual slaughter under the priest's sacrificial knife.

Low-ranking men and women wore simple loop earrings made from stone, shell, bone or wood. They embellished their appearance with lip and nose plugs. Elite figures, on the other hand, wore lip plugs, earrings and nose plugs made from obsidian, jade or stone. They also wore a variety of necklaces, collars, bracelets and knee or ankle bands made of jade, feathers, sea or river shells, crocodile teeth and the teeth or claws of the majestic jaguar. After the arrival of metalworking among the Maya in around the 9th century AD, the elite began to wear ornaments and decorations of copper or gold.

ONE ROBE FITS ALL

Among the Aztecs, clothing was also similar among all classes, with the higher social ranks wearing more elaborate garments. Peasant farmers and fishermen often went barefoot and wore a simple loincloth or *máxt-latl*, adding a cloak or *tilmatl* that was knotted over the

Right: Just 14cm (6in) tall, this figurine shows the headdress in great detail.

shoulder when necessary. Among the poor these items were woven from maguey agave fibres, but the wealthier wore cotton. The *tilmatl* might be decorated with animal designs or geometric patterns or have a coloured border. Leading nobles' robes were sometimes feather-covered, bordered with rabbit-fur, dyed turquoise or decorated with jade beads, seashells and pieces of gold. Those in highest authority were permitted to wear a richly coloured waistcoat or *xicolli*.

Nobles wore sandals (*cacli*) usually made of animal skin or woven plant fibres. As among the Maya, these had pronounced heel covers to protect the back of the foot. They also had rubber boots.

Aztec women wore a skirt called a *cúeitl*, wound about the lower body and tied at the waist with a fabric belt. There were regional variations in upper garments. In Tenochtitlán, women wore a waist-length shirt called a *huipil*: the word that is used for the similar Maya garment by scholars is in fact from the Aztecs' Nahuatl tongue. Elsewhere, women tended to wear a cape called a *quechquémitl*.

359

BEATING THE ODDS

According to Spanish chroniclers, the Aztecs were devoted gamblers. All Mesoamerican games had religious overtones because they saw the entire universe as structured by and charged with divine meaning. Even the apparently chance events of a sporting contest or a gambling pastime were open to interpretation and might provide guidance from the gods.

THE BALL GAME

By far the greatest devotion was reserved for the ball game. It was played in various forms from at least the mid-second millennium BC in Mesoamerica. Two teams of players on an I-shaped earth or stone court tried to send a hard rubber ball through a stone loop set high on one or both walls – or in some versions into the 'end zone' behind their opponents – using elbows, hips and legs. The game was rich in religious symbolism. The ball might be identified with the sun, or the match interpreted as a re-enactment

Left: On the feast of Xocotluetzi, young men competed in climbing the pole to be first to take hold of symbols hanging there.

Above: The test of daring called voladores. *Later, the men will swing upside down around the pole on the end of the ropes.*

of sacred battles between the Aztec gods Quetzalcóatl and Tezcatlipoca or between the Maya Hero Twins and the lords of the underworld. Spectators gambled on the outcome of matches. The game must have been an exhilarating spectacle, played at high speed by very skilled and brave performers wearing elaborate protective costumes. Nevertheless, the ball game was so deeply coloured by its many religious overtones that it was more a religious ceremony than a public sporting contest.

THE BEAN GAME

Another ancient Mesoamerican game of chance and skill, called *patolli* by the Aztecs, was played on the ground using a cross-shaped board of 52 squares painted on a mat or scratched into plaster or clay. Players moved blue and red pieces around the board according to the throw of dice, with the aim of moving all one's pieces to the centre of the cross. The game that developed into *patolli* was played at least as early as the 7th century AD, when a board was marked out on the floor of the Zacuala residential building in Teotihuacán. About 100–200 years later, no fewer than three boards were marked on the plaster floor of the Palacio Quemado at Tollán.

The cross-shaped Aztec board appears to have been a simplification of an older design incorporating a cruciform shape and squares. *Patolli*, like the ball game, was played throughout Mesoamerica. The Maya marked out playing boards at many ancient sites including Tikal, Uaxactún, Piedras Negras, Chichén Itzá, Palenque and Dzibilchaltún.

In their version of the game, the Aztecs used inscribed kidney beans as their dice – their name *patolli* derives from the Nahuatl word for kidney bean. Both players and onlookers placed wagers: according to a report by Diego Durán, a noisy group would gather around the game and bet on the players. Wealthy merchants and members of the nobility risked large amounts of gold and precious jewels on the outcome; others bet what they could afford. Desperate gamers are said to have bet their house or even their freedom on the result. Durán's report indicated that the game was called *totoloque* and that both playing pieces and dice were made of gold, but scholars believe he must have been mistaken on this last point.

Winning or losing was in the hands of the gods. Durán wrote that players would pray to Macuilxóchitl, god of pleasure and of games, and cast incense into a nearby brazier before making a throw. Sometimes priestly diviners would be asked to interpret the outcome of a throw or of a game. The mat was portable, so the game could be played anywhere, even in the streets. Spanish chroniclers' accounts suggest that *patolli* was played with remarkable and noisy fervour at all hours of night and day in Tenochtitlán.

The Aztecs also played a game resembling checkers on a mat or board marked with squares, using black and white pieces.

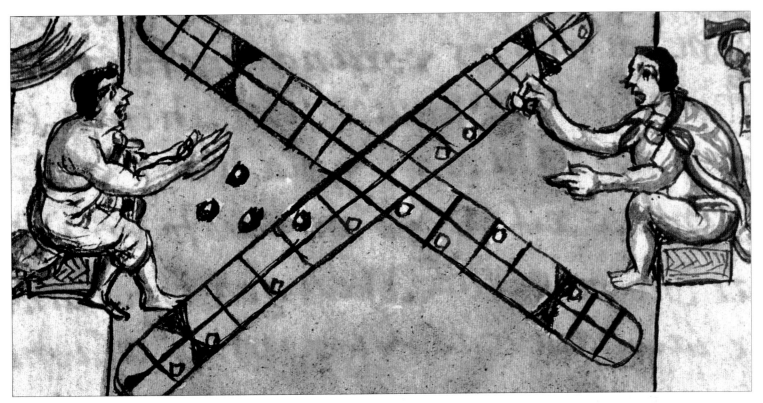

POLE GAMES

Two remarkable tests of skill and strength centred on descending or climbing a tall pole. One was a contest associated with the festival of the god Huehuetéotl. Several men competed to be first to reach the top of a very tall pole and grasp an icon of Huehuetéotl that had been placed there.

Another game, dubbed *voladores* ('flyers') by the Spanish conquistadors, involved five men. The five players clambered to the top of a pole. Four attached themselves by one ankle to ropes that were wound elaborately around the pole while the fifth settled himself with flute and drum on a wooden platform at the top of the pole.

As the drummer-flautist played his musical instruments, each of the four flyers leapt headfirst from the pole. Falling upside down, the men would swing round and round by the ankle very fast and getting closer and closer to the ground as the rope unravelled. Just before the flyer smashed his head on the ground, the man would pull himself up on the rope with his hands. This meant that he landed feet-first on the ground – and the momentum then carried him forward at a fast pace. An image from the *Codex Borbonicus* depicts the men circling the pole on ropes to the beat of the drum, while a priest standing on the steps of a nearby temple pyramid calls down a blessing on the proceedings.

This test of skill as performed by the Aztecs is still attempted in the early 21st century in the Gulf Coast region of Mexico.

Above: Diego Durán gave a full account of patolli *in the* Codex Durán. *This image, from that codex, is of a variant of the game.*

Below: These columns are all that remains of Tollán's Palacio Quemado, where three patolli *boards were marked on the floor.*

THE BEAT OF THE DRUM

For the Aztecs, music, dancing and singing were among the highest arts. Musicians aspired to be like the great Toltecs of Tollán, masters of every craft and creative art who were celebrated for composing from the very deep places of their hearts and so making music divine. The Aztecs valued dance and music both in profane and sacred contexts, not only as a form of recreation and communal celebration such as in naming ceremonies for children or at marriage feasts, but also as an act of religious devotion, an integral part of ceremonies honouring the gods.

Below: Dressed for ceremonial performance. This carved whistle is from Nebaj, Guatemala, c.AD300–900.

THE SONG HOUSE

Both these forms of music and dance were taught to the young. In the *calmecac* schools of the nobility – where the teachers were priests and where pupils were fledgling rulers, scribes and men of religion – sacred music and ritual dances were taught. In the *telpochcalli* schools frequented by commoners, the future workers of the empire were instructed in love songs, war songs and profane dances. Each of the *telpochcalli* was equipped with a special area called a *cuicalli* ('song house'), consisting of a courtyard surrounded by rooms. The school's highly respected music teacher would place his drums in the centre of the yard and the children would be put through their paces as he played and instructed them in the steps of the dance.

The Spanish churchman Gerónimo de Mendieta, writing in the 16th century, reported that Aztec nobles kept a composer as part of their domestic staff. The composer would write new songs and dances for religious festivals, but also to mark secular events such as a war triumph, a noble wedding or the accession of a new ruler.

DRUMS AND PIPES

Aztec music was stronger on rhythm than on melody: musicians created a strong beat on drums, rattles and rasps. There were two main types of drum: the *huehuetl*, which stood upright, consisted of animal skin stretched over the ends of a carved wooden frame and was played with the hands, while the *teponaxtli*, which was laid horizontally on a circular base, was split to form a double tongue that the drummer hit with rubber-headed hammers to produce a two-tone note. Other musicians complemented the drummers' rhythm with rattles and scrapers made from notched human or animal bone. Wind instruments included conches (large seashells) and flutes, whistles and trumpets (usually made of

Above: This impressive example of the Aztec huehuetl *('vertical drum') or war drum is carved with warrior imagery.*

clay). Dancers contributed to the music with hand-held gourds filled with seeds, or with anklets of seashells.

The Maya also led their music with rhythm. They had a wide variety of drums. The *tunkul* was, like the Aztec *huehuetl*, an upright drum: the Maya version was made from a hollowed tree trunk and was often as tall as the drummer's chest, with a deerskin stretched over the end. A second Maya drum was identical to the Aztec *teponaxtli*, with two wooden tongues played with hammers, while

Right: Sacred steps in the round. Aztec dancers encircle a minimalist orchestra in this image from the Codex Durán.

another was made from a tortoise shell and played with the palm. Bishop Diego de Landa reported that this tortoise drum gave issue to a very doleful sound. A fourth drum was made from clay and shaped like two vases set base to base, with a membrane at each end. Musicians also played panpipes, conch shells and trumpets of clay or wood. They also had flutes carved from hollowed human leg bones, deer bones and reeds or fashioned from clay. Dancers tied copper, gold or silver bells to their wrists, legs and waist and played a small hand-held drum, called a *pax*, as they danced.

STREET ENTERTAINERS

Music and singing accompanied street entertainments provided by jugglers, acrobats and clowns. Troupes of entertainers laid on dances and comic entertainments for the elite at the courts of rulers and on the spacious patios of noblemen's houses, but also for the commoners in marketplaces, on streets and even outside the cities in small villages. Since trade was performed by barter and currency was little used even at market, they doubtless performed for their supper or for a supply of tortillas, beans and vegetables to take away for later consumption. Hernán Cortés took a troupe of acrobats with him back to Europe, where they performed at the imperial court of Charles V in Spain.

Right: A Mixtec figurine celebrates Macuilxóchitl, patron of the ball game and of the board game patolli, *and god of music.*

FESTIVAL OF THE MUSIC GOD

Macuilxóchitl, who was associated with gambling in his guise as god of pleasure and of games, was also considered to be the patron deity of musicians. He was connected to flower god Xochipilli and to the calendrical day-name '5-flower'.

Macuilxóchitl was sometimes shown with a symbol like a butterfly in place of his mouth. In his role as music god, he might take the form of a turtle. Before his feast day in Tenochtitlán, devotees fasted then covered themselves with jewellery and symbols of the god. According to Bernardino de Sahagún, the ceremony included songs and dancing to the resonant beat of a drum, before worshippers made offerings of animal blood and specially baked cakes to Macuilxóchitl. At the climax of the feast-day celebration, Sahagún reported, priests put a company of slaves to death to satisfy the music god's thirst.

LYRICS AT THE FEAST

Aztec poets found an enthusiastic audience for their work at elite banquets in the leading cities of the empire. Rulers, princes and nobles shared a love of metaphorical language and lyrical self-expression. Masters of verse and philosophical reflection recited their poems in the patio areas of palaces and noble homes, to the accompaniment of music on flutes and drums, while stars danced overhead in the deep blue of night. Most members of the elite classes, including rulers such as Netzahualcóyotl of Texcoco and Tecayehuatzin of Huexotzingo, were poets.

GENRE POETRY

The verses came in a range of genres. One group, known as *xochicuicatl* ('flower songs'), focused on the pleasures and consolations of nature's beauty for those afflicted by suffering. Another group was

THE POET NEZAHUALCÓYOTL

Nezahualcóyotl, ruler of Texcoco, was celebrated as a warrior, wise king and writer of laws. While his forebears and contemporaries were devoted to many gods, he built a temple to a single deity he called Ipalnemoani ('The One By Which We Live') or Tloquenahuaque ('The One Who is Always Near'). He was also a celebrated and sensitive poet, who often examined the pain humans feel due to the changes brought about by the movement of time – which was called *cahuitl* ('the power that departs from us') in the Nahuatl language.

One of his poems declared: 'What can put down lasting roots in this place of change? Everything here is only passing. Even the most precious creations, of jade and turquoise, end in pieces, crumbling to dust.'

yaocuicatl ('war songs'), which expressed a fierce joy in conflict and traced the movements of the mind and heart in battle. *Xopancuicatl* ('spring songs') celebrated the new life of the fields in spring, reminding listeners of the spirit's quickening when maize shoots return after winter. A fourth type were *icnocuicatl* ('orphan songs'). They described the pleasures of life, while recalling the ephemeral nature of all pleasures. One declared: 'The time will come for us all to go, by day or by night, down into the mysteries of death. Here on earth we have time to know ourselves, briefly we pass over the earth's surface.'

The language of the Aztec poets was rich in metaphor. Their poetry was 'song and flowers' bloom'; when a poet

Left: Xochipilli, god of poetry, flowers and souls, was also a symbol of summer. This image is from the Codex Vaticanus.

Above: An unusual portrait of a standing coyote, this stone carving was made by a Totonac sculptor and found at Ihuatzio.

stepped forward to speak he entered into the 'flowering space', the 'spring arena' or the 'house of blooms'. He called political and temporal power 'the place on the mat'.

Tenochtitlán was 'eagle and cactus place' because the México/Aztecs had traditionally founded the city at the spot where they saw an eagle on a cactus, in fulfilment of their god Huitzilopochtli's promise. The city was also 'home of white willows' in reference to the trees that grew there and 'place of darts' because of weapon production in the city.

Poets celebrated warfare as 'shield and dart', 'a singing of shields', and as 'the place where the shields' mist clears'. Poets often spoke of self-knowledge in terms of 'knowing his face'. In Mesoamerican philosophy, the face was seen as the place in which the self resided. Aztec poets could find employment within the religious establishment, as composers of the many hymns – in honour of gods such as Huitzilopochtli, Centéotl, and Tláloc – sung as part of the great religious ceremonies. They also wrote epic poetry, for example the narratives of the birth of the god Huitzilopochtli, of the creation of the world and succession of five world eras, of the many gifts to humankind and the heroic actions of the god-prince Quetzalcóatl.

PUBLIC DEBATE

Another body of literary figures, who may also have been poets, were the *tlamatinime* ('the Ones who Know'). They produced prose works called *huehuehtlahtolli* ('statements of ancient knowledge') that contained philosophical questions, along with statements about duty, death and honour. Sometimes these works were read and debated in public ceremonies. One takes the form of an address by a father to his daughter, in which he warns his offspring that the world is a place of suffering, exhaustion and disappointment, of pain caused by burning sun and winds sharp as obsidian blades. However, he adds that the bitter taste of life is sweetened by compensations such as sensory pleasure, laughter, physical strength and bravery.

A VOICE AT COURT

We have little evidence of the role of Maya scribes in producing poetry and secular writing other than official documents such as the tribute lists, marriage papers or the genealogical histories. However, we know from reports by Diego de Landa and other post-Conquest sources that the Maya enjoyed communal celebrations involving both sacred hymns and secular music with dancing.

The revered *ah ts'ib* or *ah k'u'hun* of Classic Period Maya cities, who proudly wore his pens in his long hair as a status symbol and badge of office, was celebrated for his facility both with language and with images. This exalted figure sat with rulers and their intimates at great state occasions and must surely have given right expression to the feelings of the group in songs and poems. A people that so appreciated the visual arts and music are likely to have been an appreciative audience for the skilful use of words.

Below: This chocolate goblet is decorated with an image of a Maya prince enjoying the drink.

CHAPTER 18

SACRED CULTURE

Teotihuacán's Temple of Quetzalcóatl, adorned with vast heads of a feathered serpent, was set in a compound containing a plaza large enough to hold a significant proportion of the city's 100,000-plus population. At Chichén Itzá, the Pyramid of Kukulcán also gave on to a vast plaza and was aligned in such a way that thousands of spectators could watch the sun create an astonishing serpentine pattern of light and shadow at spring and autumn equinox. Throughout Mesoamerica, sacred centres were laid out with spectators in mind. At the top of steep steps, positioned scores of metres above the crowd, priests and rulers in bright costumes celebrated the gods in choreographed acts of sacred theatre.

Often this theatre presented acts of sudden or extreme violence – such as slicing open a victim's chest and wrenching out his palpitating heart. However, the sacred drama of religious life also included gentler elements such as dances in celebration of ancestors during the festival of Tlaxochimaco or making corn effigies of the god Xiuhtecuhtli and eating tamales with greens during the festival of Izcalli. Equally, many acts of religious celebration centred on astronomical and seasonal events and effects (as in the equinoctial light show at Chichén Itzá) or on marking the passage of time. Festivities accompanied the end of each *katun* of 7,200 days in Maya cities of the Classic Period such as Tikal and Uaxactún.

Left: The great palace at Palenque commanded views of the city's sacred buildings and ceremonial areas.

THE GAME OF THE GODS

The ball game called *tlachtli* by the Aztecs and *pok-a-tok* by the Maya goes far back into the Mesoamerican past. By the time of the Aztecs it was already at least 2,000 years old, for it was played in Mexico in the mid-second millennium BC. An earthen ball court, 80m (260ft) long and 8m (26ft) wide, at Paso de la Amada in the coastal region of Soconusco, Chiapas, was in use *c.*1400BC and is the oldest court yet discovered in Mesoamerica.

Scholars believe that the game, which was played with a rubber ball, may have originated in the coastal lowlands adjoining the Gulf of Mexico. This was the land of

Below: The ball game's connection to blood-letting fertility rites is plain in this carving from Veracruz depicting a player decapitated after losing a match, with snakes of lifeblood coming from his neck.

rubber and the area in which the Olmec civilization developed in the second to first millennium BC, named in later years from the Nahuatl word *olli* ('rubber'). The design of courts changed over time. The ball court was usually shaped like an 'I', with a thinner central section between two wider end zones. Raised walls usually ran down the sides of the central section and, in many courts, a stone hoop was set in each side wall.

RULES OF THE GAME

Two teams of between two and eleven men each played with a hard, solid rubber ball about 15–20cm (6–8in) in diameter – slightly smaller than a human head.

Players tried to keep the ball moving using only the head, hips, elbows and knees. A team scored points – or in some variants won the match – when one of its players sent the ball through the hoop on the side wall. Stone markers were set at various points of the court, and in some versions players could also score points by hitting these markers or by sending the ball into their opponents' end zone.

The rules must have varied a good deal in different eras and various types of court. In the murals of the Tepantitla residential building in Teotihuacán, artists depicted both the traditional ball game and players competing with hand bats, so the city's residents must have known a bat-and-ball variant of the sport.

Archaeologists also report that at Teotihuacán teams played the traditional ball game on open ground with a few markers to indicate the limits of the pitch and the end zones. The courts had no sidewalls or stone rings and so players

Left: This ceramic figure, found at a site in Nayarit, Mexico, takes part in a variant of the ball game played using hand-held bats.

cannot have scored points by putting the ball through the hoop. Few pitches dating from before AD1100 have been found with side rings on the walls. This element of the game appears to have been an addition of the Postclassic Period.

The ball game was always a great spectacle. The oldest known court, at Pasa de la Amada, was laid out between banks of benches for spectators. In the Aztec era it was customary for the winners of the game to seize the belongings of the watching crowd – rich pickings, given that the elite turned out bedecked in jewellery and fine robes. There must have been quite a scramble to escape from the seats when the ball passed through the hoop on the side wall and the winning players suddenly poured into the crowd.

A SACRED NARRATIVE

From ancient times the ball game had major religious and ritual significance. Scholars report that the game represented a sacred narrative of the sun god's descent into the underworld, victory there and subsequent ascent as the maize god. Some suggest that a match was played as part of the fertility rites after crop planting, to bring on the rains that fed the maize plants. Carved panels on ball courts often represented maize or cacao plants.

Above: El Tajín had no fewer than 12 ball courts. One court had walls carved with a defeated ball player awaiting death, the sacrificial knife poised above his head.

In Aztec lands, the game was associated with the divine history of Quetzalcóatl, the Plumed Serpent god, his descent into the underworld of Mictlán, his out-witting of Mictlantecuhtli and his ascent as the planet Venus. In one version of the myth of Quetzalcóatl-Topiltzin in Tollán, the god played an epic ball game against the god of darkness and fate, Tezcatlipoca, only to lose when the dark lord transformed him into an ocelot.

In Maya regions, the game was an enactment of the exploits of the Hero Twins Hunahpú and Xbalanqué, who played the ball game in the underworld Xibalba against the lords of that place before rising to the heavens as the sun and the planet Venus. It celebrated the divine twins' defeat of the powers of death. Some writers suggest that the ball represented the sun and that the players' attempts to keep it off the ground were part of religious rites designed to honour the sun and maintain its life-giving position in the sky. The ball game represented the ongoing struggle between the powers of light and those of darkness.

SACRIFICIAL GAMES

The ball game was also associated with blood sacrifice. Among both Maya and Aztecs, defeated players could be put to death at the end of the match. Some Maya court complexes included stair-cases: the defeated captain was tied in the shape of a ball and hurled down the steps to death, in celebration of the gods' descent to the underworld. Some author-ities suggest that battles may have been re-enacted through the ball game and that kings or nobles among the prisoners of war were sacrificed at the close of the proceedings.

Rulers either played the game or donned the protective clothing worn by the players for ritual performance. A panel at La Amelia in Guatemala shows the King of Dos Pilas wearing a ball game outfit of kneepads and belt, while a ball court carving at Copán represents the king as a ball-playing Hero Twin. Like the board game *patolli*, the ball game could be an act of divination. In some accounts, Moctezuma II was defeated in a match against Netzahualpilli, the ruler of Texcoco, who had prophesied that a foreign race would govern Tenochtitlán. Moctezuma's defeat was one of many ill omens that unsettled the ruler before the arrival of Hernán Cortés.

Below: Players face up for a round of the ball game in an image from the Codex Borbonicus. *The Nahuatl word* tlachtli *also meant the I-shaped court on which it was played.*

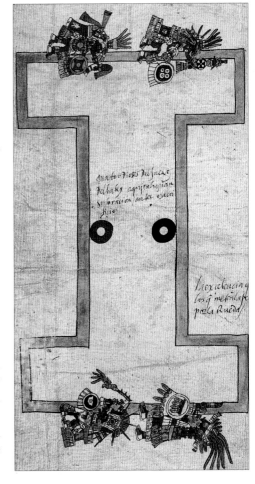

CYCLES OF TIME

Mesoamericans believed the universe was constructed according to a sacred pattern that could be read in the movements of the stars, and of time through its units of hours and days. Priests and astronomers kept astonishingly accurate track of time using the movement of the stars as their measure. The long, recurring patterns of the night sky provided a physical template of the invisible patterns of time.

OBSERVING TIME IN THE SKIES

These highly skilled astronomers apparently used the simplest of observational equipment, judging the movements of the stars with the naked eye against

Below: One of the windows in the Caracol tower at Chichén Itzá is aligned to the setting of the sun on the vernal equinox.

notches cut in a pair of crossed sticks. Sacred structures and complexes of buildings were laid out to honour celestial and calendrical events such as solstices and equinoxes and to aid in their observation. For example, the Pyramid of the Sun at Teotihuacán was aligned to mark the sun's daily east–west passage and the equinoctial rising of the Pleiades constellation on the horizon.

At Uaxactún the pyramids and temples labelled Group E by scholars were precisely arranged to enable astronomical observation to be made and celebrated. On the western side of a plaza stood a single pyramid, while opposite, on top of a platform on the eastern side, were three temples – E-I (at the platform's northern edge), E-II (in the platform's centre and so due east of the pyramid) and E-III (at

Above: A detail of a stone carving from Chichén Itzá represents Noh Ek (Great Star), the symbol of the planet Venus.

the platform's southern edge). An astronomer standing on top of the pyramid on the western side of the plaza would have viewed the sun rise directly above temple E-I on the June 21 solstice, directly above temple E-III on the December 21 solstice and precisely over temple E-II on the midpoints of 21 March and 23 September. This remarkably precise layout was the prototype for other building complexes in Maya cities of the Classic Period.

INTERSECTING CYCLES

Astronomers plotted the 584-day cycle of the planet Venus and its interaction with the 365-day solar pattern and calculated that the two intersected every 2,920 days – equivalent to eight solar years or five Venus cycles. Occasions on which holy cycles interconnected in this way were doubly sacred and were the occasion for grand ceremonies. Another example is the intersection once every 52 solar years of the *tonalpohualli* day count and the *xiuhpohualli* year count. The end of a 52-year cycle – called a 'bundle of years' by the Aztecs – was a time of potential

calamity, with the prospect of universal dissolution should the gods choose not to inaugurate a new bundle of years. The new cycle in turn was a time of renewal and optimism, in which pyramids and ceremonial buildings might be refaced with stone and householders rebuilt or refurbished their homes.

THE MAYA LONG COUNT

The Maya also marked time using a longer-running measure that scholars label the Maya Long Count. Dates were marked on stelae, stone thrones and other monuments in Maya cities of the Classic Period to commemorate royal births and accessions to the throne, battle victories, ritual sacrifices of rival leaders and so on.

Time was counted forward from a date zero that corresponds to 11 August 3114BC in the Gregorian calendar and dates were carved in five units of decreasing size: 144,000 days (*baktun*), 7,200 days (*katun*), 360 days (*tun*), 20 days (*uinal*), and 1 day (*kin*). Kings set up monuments to mark the end of each *katun*, which was a time of public festivity. The elite and people of Uaxactún held a *katun*-end festival in AD357 – or 8.16.0.0.0. in the Long Count. Rulers also erected monuments to mark the halfway point in a

Below: This pyramid is one of the temple-observatories of Group E at Uaxactún, aligned to view sunrise on the solstices.

Above: The four-storey tower in the Palace complex at Palenque was probably used as an observatory by the king's astronomers.

katun – a period of 3,600 days known as a *lahuntun*. At Piedras Negras and Quiriguá, rulers even marked the passing of the quarter-*katun* timespan of 1,800 days (*hotun*).

Katuns came in cycles of 13, totalling 93,600 days or around 256 years. Each *katun* of the 13 was identified by number and associated with a set of prophecies: diviners, rulers and ordinary people expected a *katun* to contain events and conditions similar to those in a past *katun* of the same number.

This temporal repetition could be bad or good, unwelcome or welcome. Kings at Tikal in particular went to great lengths to emphasize their connection through the cycle of *katuns* to an earlier period of material wealth.

THE HOLY COUNT

Certain numbers had profound religious symbolism. Three was a holy number because the universe had three layers: the heavens, the terrestrial plane and the underworld. Thirteen, the number of planes in the heavens, was also sacred, as was nine, the number of layers in the dark underworld. Divine figures had power over each of these layers. According to Yucatec-speaking Maya, the gods of heaven were *oxlahuntiku* (combining the words for 'god', *ku*, with that for 'thirteen', *oxlahun*) and the lords of the underworld were *bolontiku* (from 'nine', *bolon*).

HOLY WORLD, SACRED SKY

Ancient religious life in Mesoamerica was focused on the fertility of the earth and led by shamans who assumed animal form to undertake spirit voyages. In the religious tradition that grew from these roots, the earth and heavens were sacred, patterned with divine meaning.

NATURAL AND SUPERNATURAL

Mesoamericans saw no clear distinction between the material world in one place and the spirit world in another. The physical world of deserts, rivers, seas, mountains, storms, maize plants, great trees, wild animals and people was built according to the sacred template that also structured the movements of celestial planets and the cycles of time. Diviners could interpret earthly events and celestial movements in terms of time's patterns and future events. The movements of celestial bodies such as the sun and Venus gave sacred meaning to the physical forms of the earth. For example, some Maya traditions understood the four directions in terms of the movements of the sun. The east was the place of

Above: This stone turtle was carved by an Olmec craftsman before 200BC. The Maya believed the earth rested on a turtle's back.

the sun's morning emergence from the underworld and the west the place of its evening descent to the dark Xibalba, place of death. The north was the sun's full power at the zenith, its position at noon, while the south was identified with

Below: Mesoamericans saw sacred wells, such as this one at Chichén Itzá, as an opening into the underworld of the spirits.

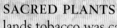

SACRED PLANTS

In Aztec lands tobacco was called *yetl*, and was said to have been created in the celestial realms for the gods' enlightenment. Priests smoked the plant in animal-headed clay pipes in an attempt to call on the god whose animal form was depicted by the pipe bowl. For example, a pipe with a dog's head might be used to summon Xólotl, the twin form of Quetzalcóatl, who took the shape of a dog.

In Maya ceremonies in Yucatán, priests rolled great cigars of tobacco and drank a wine made from the bark of the balche tree. Experts report that they used wild tobacco with a nicotine content of 16 per cent, a full 16 times stronger than that smoked in typical Western cigarettes.

Mesoamericans also held holy a number of hallucinogenic mushrooms (for example, *Psilocybe aztecorum*) as well as the maguey cactus, whose fermented sap was made into the alcoholic drink *pulque*.

Above: A wall painting at Chichén Itzá, c. AD900, depicts the ancient plumed serpent god known to the Maya as Kukulkán.

the darkest hour of midnight, when the sun fights for its very life with the lords of the underworld.

In the night sky, the Maya saw the Milky Way as a vast two-headed sky serpent, with one head giving issue to life and the other the source of death. The serpent appears to have been an embodiment of the supreme Maya god Itzamná or Hunab Ku. In this form, Itzamná gave issue from one mouth in the east to the rising sun, bringer of life, while from his second mouth in the west death came with the swallowing of the sun. The Milky Way was also a pathway to the underworld. In Yucatec it was called *Zac Beh* ('The White Path') and was understood to be the road followed by the spirits of the deceased as they travelled to the underworld to face a series of demanding tests.

Mesoamericans saw mountains as sacred; a physical form for the celestial home of ancestors according to Maya traditions, a source of life according to Aztec beliefs. The Aztecs identified mountains as the places of the rain god Tláloc's stores of water, the origin of the maize plant discovered in the mountain's heart by Quetzalcóatl and the place of the tribal lord Huitzilopochtli's birth. A cave in a rocky, dusty mountainside was

a place of burial, an entrance to the sacred earth and a place of access to the land of the revered ancestors.

Aztec and Maya cities replicated these sacred physical forms in stone. The temple was a holy mountain and its entrance was a sacred cave. The ball court, also like a holy cavern, represented an entrance to the underworld.

ANIMAL ALLIES

The sacred patterning extended to the world of animals. Many creatures were held to be holy because they were forms of the gods. Tezcatlipoca might be the majestic jaguar or the cunning coyote; Huitzilopochtli was eagle, hummingbird or macaw, Quetzalcóatl – or Kukulcán in Maya lands – was quetzal as well as divine serpent. The turtle, the crocodile and the snake were images of the fertile earth.

Mesoamericans also believed that humans had animal protectors or familiars known as *nahual* in the Aztec language and as *way* by many Maya groups. These were

Right: This figure made by a Remojadas potter in Veracruz, c.600–900AD, wears a jaguar-head belt and may represent a shaman.

the creatures whose forms shamans might adopt. They would do this upon entering a state of instructive spiritual ecstasy under the influence of one of the plants held to be sacred for their power to transport seekers beyond the boundaries of everyday consciousness.

THE HEALING ARTS

To the Aztecs healing was sacred: their main word for doctor, *teopati*, combined *patli* ('medical arts') and *teo* ('holy'). Aztec creation narrative explained the cause of sickness. At the start of the fifth or current world age, the existing race of humankind was made from the bones of the men and women who had lived in the fourth world age. These bones had been languishing in the underworld, but the Feathered Serpent god Quetzalcóatl ventured into that dark realm to rescue them. However, the Feathered Serpent was tricked during his escape from the underworld and dropped the bones, which broke into many pieces. He carried the remains to the home of the gods, where all the divine lords and ladies agreed that the bones should be ground to a powder, then moistened with the gods' blood and mixed to a paste. From this paste the first people of the fifth world age were made. People suffered illness, old age and death because they were originally made from broken bones. However, they had a special calling to serve the gods because they were fashioned from the gods' blood.

THREE SPIRIT CENTRES

People were made according to the same divine template that structured all parts of the universe. Just as the universe had a tripartite structure – with the heavens above, the terrestrial plane in the middle and the underworld beneath – so three spirit centres existed within the human body. The first, residing in the head, was *tonalli* ('hotness'). This was the counterpart of the soaring heavens.

When a body lost *tonalli*, death followed – and so a corpse was cold. People dissipated *tonalli* by self-indulgence in sex or drunkenness. They could boost it by bravery in battle and by living an austere, self-restrained life. Doctors sometimes prescribed herbal fragrances to increase a patient's *tonalli*. In the natural way of things, *tonalli* increased with age and old people were respected for having a strong *tonalli*. When a shaman or diviner embarked on a spirit voyage, it was his *tonalli* that left his body and entered another realm.

The second spirit centre, *teyolia*, was the counterpart of the terrestrial plane and was situated in the heart. *Teyolia* was the source of our thoughts, creative impulses and human personality. Tenochtitlán's noble poets were rich in the quality of *teyolia*. This, too, was weakened by sensual indulgence. The *teyolia* was akin to the Western idea of the soul in that it departed the body at death and travelled to its fate in the afterlife – the underworld for most, but one of the levels of heaven for those who had been sacrificed, killed in battle, died giving birth or suffered various watery deaths associated with the rain god Tláloc.

The third spirit centre, *ihiyotl*, situated in the liver, was the counterpart of the underworld. Energy, life's breath and

Left: The Florentine Codex *(1575–77) depicts various Aztec medical procedures, including a cure for haemorrhoids, treating a fever and the binding of a broken leg.*

passionate desire were the products of *ihiyotl*. Lazy people, who lacked drive and the power to achieve things, were understood to have a badly functioning *ihiyotl*.

A HEALTHY BALANCE

The three parts of the universe were perpetually held in balance by natural order, by the four cardinal directions and by the tree of life that majestically rose in the centre of the universe connecting heaven, earth and underworld. Doctors taught that the way to health lay in safeguarding the good functioning of the three spirit centres of the body and ensuring a natural balance between them. An unexpected reverse or accident might damage one of the centres and cause illness or disturbed behaviour. For example, a shock resulting in emotional turmoil would be expected to damage a person's *ihiyotl*.

SPIRITUAL HEALING

Throughout Mesoamerica healing combined knowledge of herbal remedies with trust in the power of shamans and diviners to seek and remedy the causes of health problems. In addition, all peoples of Mesoamerica put faith in the power of public bloodletting and sacred ritual to satisfy the gods and avert disease, famine, earthquake and other natural disasters. Physical and spiritual were intertwined: illnesses or disturbances might have physical or spiritual causes and could be treated with spiritual or physical means, or both. A doctor might tell a woman with a severe cold that she had suffered damage to her *tonalli*. He could use his knowledge of herbal medicine to prescribe a fragrance to boost her *tonalli*. Equally, he might seek out the spiritual cause of the malaise by sending her to a diviner.

Above: A Mixtec codex celebrates the god of medicine. Aztecs revered Patécatl, who was also god of drunkenness, as lord of medicine.

The diviner would seek to discover whether the damage to the woman's *tonalli* was caused by a curse from one of the gods. Sometimes the diviner might take hallucinogenic mushrooms, peyote or morning glory seeds to bring on a trance in which he could discover the cause and find a way to appease the god in question. He might throw coral seeds and seek answers from the movement of sensations in his body.

Aztec doctors were divided broadly into those treating physical symptoms, the *teopati*, and those seeking and addressing spiritual causes, *tictli*, men who could read the divine patterns and structures of the universe. The medical specialists were expert in herbal medicine, the *tlametpatli*, who drew on their ancient healing art to treat problems including heart trouble, stomach sickness and breathing disorders. In markets across the empire, *panamacanis* sold mixed herbal remedies.

Left: A detail from the Florentine Codex *shows a plant used to treat fever. Healers administered bitter medicines wrapped in chocolate paste to patients.*

SACRED THEATRE

Large-scale public sacrifices on the steps of temple pyramids made a powerful statement of secular power as well as of religious devotion. In Tenochtitlán, visiting dignitaries witnessed an over-whelming proof of the city's great power, which was sufficient to build the vast sacred arena, mobilize a cadre of magnificently attired priests and musicians and bring to sacrifice a vast army of prisoners.

RITES OF SACRIFICE

The crowds which gathered for the ceremony celebrated the power of the gods who demanded and were worthy of such ritual; the glory of the ruler who could command such a display; and – a central

Above: At Chichén Itzá the Temple of the Feathered Serpent – viewed here from the top of the Temple of the Warriors – was an awe-inspiring setting for sacred ritual.

mystery of their religion – the fact that life was dependent on sacrifice. Just as, in Aztec belief, the gods had sacrificed their blood to the creation of humans in the current age and then again to set the sun moving in the sky, so human blood was a necessary offering to maintain sacred order and balance in the cosmos.

Public rites of sacrifice brought the gods to visible life on the temple steps or in sacred processional. A priest or ruler dressed as the god or goddess honoured became that divine form. A priestess wearing a jade skirt was Chalchiúhtlicue in Tenochtitlán, while a Maya ruler might embody the maize god or Chac, lord of rains. Equally, victims destined for sacrifice were considered by the Aztecs to be *ixiptla* ('in the gods' image'). They were believed to contain within their frail human bodies the awesome power of creation and destruction that belonged to the gods,

Right: A detail from the Codex Mendoza *(c.1541) shows part of a sacred ritual as a priest plays drums and sings hymns.*

making possible the re-enactment of the primal scenes of divine sacrifice through which this world's sun and people were brought into being.

The Toltecs and their followers in Tenochtitlán and Chichén Itzá greatly escalated the use of ritual slaughter in religious ceremonies. From the era of Tollán onwards, human sacrifice had a much greater role.

RITUAL SONGS

The Aztecs sang hymns to honour their gods during religious ceremonies. Sacred songs have survived to the goggle-eyed rain god Tláloc, to flower god Xochipilli, to strong-limbed maize deities Chicomecóatl and Centéotl and to the war lord Huitzilopochtli. The hymn in praise of Xochipilli declares that the sacred quetzal bird sings its joy in the flower lord during the dark hours of midnight, while the worshipper makes his song at dawn, adding that praise will rise to Xochipilli from Tláloc's temple.

Tláloc's hymn praises the god as a magician and envisages ancestors at rest or playing at ball in the misty paradise of Tlálocan. Huitzilopochtli's hymn celebrates him as the sun god, who lives among the clouds and the cold air, who as he spreads the brilliance of light stirs a passion for war in the hearts of men. The song, which was probably declaimed by two singers in a stirring answer and response, hails Huitzilopochtli as the instigator of sacred conflicts that result in the defeat and capture of many prisoners for holy sacrifice.

particular musical ceremonies in which they specialized. De Landa described one dance in which two men led the steps. One hurled reeds at the other, who exhibited great skill in catching them, all the while following the steps of the dance. Another dance witnessed by de Landa was a sacred war dance, in which as many as 800 men carrying small banners followed a complex pattern of steps in perfect unison. In Tenochtitlán, the leading warriors, priests and members of the *pipiltin* nobility engaged in a sacred dance with their divine ruler at the climax of enthronement ceremonies that began the rule of a new *tlatoani*.

Below: In the gods' image. A Maya funerary urn, c.AD250–900, represents a fearsome-looking priest dressed in ritual costume.

Above: Offering plate. A chacmool from Tenochtitlán holds the hollowed dish used to display the hearts of sacrificial victims.

INCENSE AND DANCING

Ceremonies were accompanied by the burning of incense, usually copal resin, but also the resin of the rubber and chicle trees. Worshippers believed that as the smoke rose it became food for the gods and goddesses. In sacrifices to placate the rain god, his human petitioners told that the clouds of incense had the power to attract the dark, rain-heavy clouds for which they prayed. Before burning, cakes of resin were painted turquoise blue, the colour of sacrifice. When worshippers could not provide a jaguar or alligator for animal sacrifice, the incense was sometimes moulded into the shape of an animal heart. In the Cenote of Sacrifice at Chichén Itzá, a worshipper made an offering of an incense ball containing a cake of vegetable material in the shape of a human heart.

Music played an important role in the theatre of the sacred. Large bands of musicians took part in sacred processions and sacrificial ceremonies, playing clay and shell trumpets, drums and rattles, and creating a mournful howl with conch shells. The celebrated murals at Bonampak represented a 12-man orchestra as part of a procession: they played tortoise-shell drums, ceramic trumpets and seed-filled gourds.

Among the Maya, group dances were very serious and highly sacred. According to Bishop Diego de Landa, groups of men and women danced separately and had

THE ROUND OF FESTIVALS

The Aztecs believed that they were dependent on the gods for the sun's rising every morning, and wove rites of religious observance into the very fabric of daily life. Each of the eighteen 20-day months had at least one festival honouring the gods. These were not all of equal importance to an individual. People with skilled occupations, for instance, had their patron gods and observed ceremonies with particular attention at the time

Left: A statue of Xipe Totec from Veracruz c.AD900–1200 shows a priest who is wearing a flayed skin.

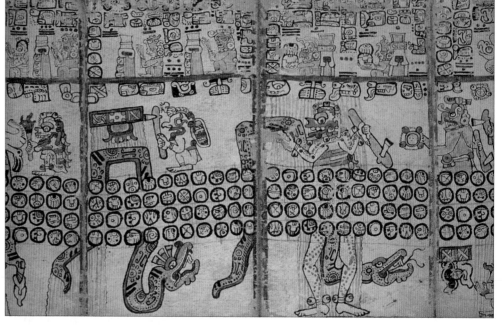

Above: Sacred serpents and presiding deities are detailed in one of the 56 almanac pages of the Maya Madrid Codex.

when their patron was celebrated. Among the people of the empire, so many of whom worked on the land, the more ancient fertility-based cults of such gods and goddesses as Tláloc, Chalchiúhtlicue and Centéotl would probably have had more impact than the newer cult of Huitzilopochtli, which was associated with the elite.

CYCLE OF AZTEC FESTIVALS

For a farmer in the Tenochtitlán *chinampa* fields, the festivals associated with the stages of the agricultural year loomed largest. In the first month of the Aztec year (14 February–5 March), worshippers at the festivals of Atlcaualo ('The Ending of Water') and Cuauhitleua ('The Lifting of Trees') made offerings to maize goddesses Chicomecóatl and Xilonen. These included sacrifices of children.

In the second month (6 March–25 March), during the festival of Tlacaxipehualiztli ('Skinning of the Men'), sacrificial victims were killed and skinned in honour of Xipe Totec, god of spring and germinating seeds. The god's priests wore the skin of a victim over their own face and body. In the fourth month

(15 April–4 May), as part of Huey Tozoztli ('Major Vigil'), priestesses of Chicomecóatl performed rites to bring the gods' blessing on farmers' seed supplies.

In the eighth month (4 July–23 July), the festival of Huey Tecuilhuitl ('Major Festival of the Lords') celebrated the appearance in the fields of the first shoots of maize and particularly honoured Xilonen, the goddess associated with these shoots. Offerings were made to a young woman who took the form of Xilonen for the duration of the festival.

Harvest was celebrated in the eleventh and twelfth months (2 September–21 September; 22 September–11 October), in the festivals of Ochpaniztli ('Clearing') and Teotleco ('Coming of the Gods and Goddesses'). In the first of these, a female victim was killed and flayed in honour of Xilonen-Chicomecóatl and her skin worn by a priestess of the goddesses, in grim echo of the festival of Tlacaxipehualiztli. The second festival was a simpler celebration of the harvest.

No doubt overshadowing all these festivals in the mind of the farmer was the one that marked the end of a 52-year cycle of the 260- and 365-day calendars and the beginning of a new cycle. It usually occurred once only – if at all – in a lifetime. On the night in question, the most senior priests sacrificed a victim on Mount Huixachtlán ('Place of the Thorn Trees'), cut his chest, then tore out his heart and in his gaping chest cavity lit a new fire signifying the new cycle of years. If the new fire did not take, according to religious teaching, it showed that the gods did not consent to allow a new cycle to commence and the current age of the world, in which the Aztec empire had grown to glory, would end.

Below: A deity consumes the flesh of a sacrificial victim in a detail from an Aztec tonalamatl *book of days.*

CYCLE OF MAYA FESTIVALS

The Maya laid out large and important complexes of buildings in major cities of the Classic Period to celebrate equinoxes and solstices. Occasions such as the year's shortest and longest days were charged with sacred meaning and were the focus of ritual public celebration.

Our main source for detailed knowledge of the festivals of the Maya year is the account given by Bishop Diego de Landa of religious ceremonies in 16th-century Yucatán. As with the Aztec calendar, the year ended with five days of ill renown when people tried to avoid activity. The new year and beginning of the first month, Pop, was celebrated by sweeping houses and replacing all household tools and utensils. The second month, Uo, was the time for fishermen, hunters, doctors

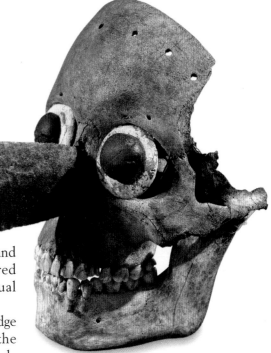

Above: A flint sacrificial knife symbolically stops the life breath in a ritual victim's skull. This offering is from Tenochtitlán.

and priests to celebrate their patron gods; the priests performed acts of divination using the sacred books to read the fates for the coming year. In the fifth month, Tzec, beekeepers made offerings to Hobnil, one of the four *bacabs* said to support the creation in the four cardinal points. They burned incense and prayed to be granted large amounts of honey. In the sixth month, Xul, offerings were made to Kukulcán, the Feathered Serpent. A great procession with feather banners culminated in offerings of food at Kukulcán's temple; devotees stayed at the temple for five days, while jesters toured the town putting on performances and collecting contributions that were then divided between the nobility, the priests and the jesters themselves.

During the eleventh month, Zac, hunters made offerings to atone for the blood they had spilled as they went about their work. In the thirteenth month, Mac, a large-scale sacrifice of animals was performed in honour of Itzamná and the four rain gods or Chacs to ensure plentiful rainfall to feed the maize plants in the approaching rainy season. In the sixteenth month, Pax, a war ceremony was held that culminated in feasting, drinking and sacred dances.

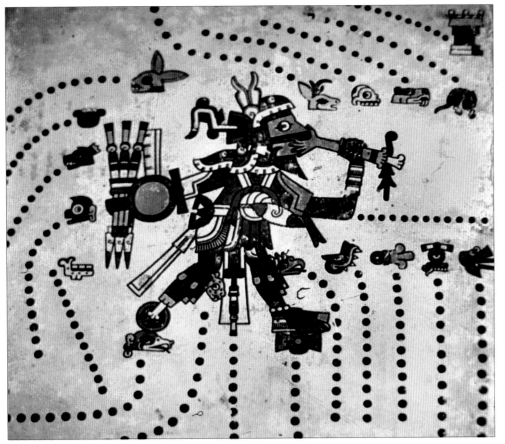

THE CULT OF VIOLENCE

Mesoamericans saw conflict as a sacred and ubiquitous element of life. As the sun rose each morning, it slaughtered the moon and stars that had proudly ruled the night sky just as, the Aztecs said, proud Huitzilopochtli had killed the moon goddess Coyolxauhqui and his four hundred brothers in the first moments of life. The shedding of sacrificial blood was a sacred duty; a way of maintaining universal order by honouring the blood sacrifice offered by the gods that had brought the current world age into being.

Sacrifice and warfare were intimately connected; indeed, military conflict was a sacrament. Warfare was celebrated as an opportunity to demonstrate character, bravery and power and as a means of feeding the gods' thirst for blood. A major impetus for warfare was the need for sacrificial victims.

Below: A detail from the late 16th-century Codex Magliabechano *shows a bloody sacrifice in honour of Tezcatlipoca during the Aztecs' 13th month, Pachtontli.*

Among the Maya, commoner prisoners may have been made into slaves, but nobles, leading warriors and – most significantly – rival rulers were destined for ritual public sacrifice. The Maya considered human sacrifice to be a necessary rite for major events such as the inauguration of a new king's reign, the first use of a new temple or building and the announcement, birth or blessing of an heir to the throne.

KILLING KINGS

In Classic Period Maya cities, a special decapitation ceremony was reserved for the despatch of captured kings and rulers. Such a sacrifice was recorded in carving by a glyph called the 'axe event' by scholars. A ball court marker erected by King Kan II of Caracol commemorates the sacrifice by 'axe event' of a Caracol ruler in AD556 in the rival city of Tikal, a sacrifice that sparked a conflict between Caracol and Tikal. The

Below: Sacrificial ritual mirrored the ferocity of the wild. This jaguar statue is from Chichén Itzá.

conflict ended in a Caracol victory in AD562 and, probably, in the sacrificial beheading of Tikal ruler Double Bird. The decapitation sacrifice may have occurred as the climax of a ritual enactment of the ball game, which celebrated the triumph of the Hero Twins in defeating the lords of Xibalba.

Among the Maya of the Postclassic Period in cities such as Chichén Itzá, victims were painted turquoise blue, the colour of sacrifice, and led up the temple steps to the sacrificial platform wearing peaked headgear. There, high above the crowds watching in the plaza below, the sacrificial stone was painted turquoise and four assistant priests, also dressed in this brilliant colour, held the victim over the stone while the main priest or *chilan* carved open the victim's chest and wrenched out his heart. The *chilan* then smeared statues of the gods being honoured with the heart blood of the sacrificial victim and wiped the blood on his own skin. He cast the body down the steep steps into the plaza, where it was skinned by helpers. The skin was given back to the *chilan*, who put it on as a 'suit' and danced before the crowd.

The Maya of Chichén Itzá had adopted the Mexican sacrificial practice, presumably the one followed by the Toltecs. Aztec priests of this era also tore the heart from the chest of a sacrificial victim. After

Above: A ritual victim's death was highly honourable. The Codex Durán *(1570–81) shows a team of Aztec priests extracting a human heart on the sacrificial stone.*

holding it up in offering to the sun god Tonatiuh, they threw it at the image of the god being celebrated, Huitzilopochtli or Tláloc, which in time became covered with the blood of the victims. In the plaza below, the audience in this theatre of sacred violence watched the rite and saw blood run down the steps of the temple platform while the bodies of the victims were cast down to tumble over the slick steps until they reached bottom.

DEATH BY RITUAL CONFLICT

Both Maya and Aztecs also performed sacrifices through ritualized conflict. In the Aztec festival of Tlacaxipehualiztli ('Skinning of the Men'), held in the second month in honour of Xipe Totec, Aztec warriors bearing clubs fitted with razor-sharp obsidian blades attacked victims tied to a sacrificial stone who were armed only with a club decorated with feathers. The warriors slashed at the defenceless 'combatants' until their blood ran freely into the earth.

A similar stylized conflict was performed as a rite of sacrifice by the Maya. The victim was stripped naked, painted turquoise blue and dressed in the peaked headdress associated with sacrifice. He was tied to a post while warriors danced around him, each bearing a bow and arrows. A priest took blood from the victim's genitals and made offering of it to the gods. Then the warriors began to shoot, sending a hail of arrows at the chest of the victim until he slumped lifeless on the spot.

A graffito drawn in Temple II at Tikal depicts a similar sacrifice of a victim tied to a sacrificial post and slain by a magnificently attired warrior-priest who is using either an arrow or a spear.

REVERENCE FOR ANCESTORS

Long after its decline from power, the city of Chichén Itzá was a major destination for pilgrims from throughout Maya territories. They came to offer sacrifices in the great Cenote of Sacrifice and to wonder at the magnificent temple of Kukulkán, the immense ball court and the vast hall of the thousand columns. Here, as in highland Mexico, the present seemed unable to match the achievements of the past.

The México/Aztecs who founded Tenochtitlán were part of a wave of incomers from the barren north. Insecure as newcomers and as nomads with no evidence of past achievement, they attempted to find glory by association through linking themselves to the Toltecs and Tollán, even claiming that they had spent some years among the holy ruins of that city during their southward migration; the older ruined city of Teotihuacán the Aztecs saw as a place of the gods, site of sacred events at the start of the current world age. They made pilgrimages to both Tollán and Teotihuacán, bringing offerings to place in the sacred spaces of those cities, adding their own religious structures on the hallowed ground and also removing items left by the ancestors and carrying these objects back to sanctify sacred buildings in Tenochtitlán.

Aztec mourners buried two people with pottery from Tenochtitlán and Texcoco in part of the Ciudadela at

Right: This stone mask was part of a noble burial in Teotihuacán c. AD400. Many masks were later reused by the Aztecs.

Teotihuacán; Aztec architects even built a pyramid-platform over and encompassing the pyramid-temple of Quetzalcóatl there.

At Tollán Aztec religious visitors made similar burials and ceramic offerings, and also built residential quarters and sacred structures on top of the ceremonial centre of the Toltecs. Funerary masks from Teotihuacán graves were laid as offerings within the Templo Mayor in Tenochtitlán.

Left: The scale of Teotihuacán's sacred architecture overawed later Mesoamericans. Surrounding the Plaza of the Moon, once a scene of ritual worship, are eleven temples.

SACRED GIFTS
Throughout Mesoamerica, people of the Post-Classic Period performed religious rites and made offerings before or within great sacred sculptures of earlier times. In Morelos in the 13th century pilgrims made offerings before the great 2,000-year-old Olmec carvings at Chalcatzingo: local Tlahuica builders erected stairways and platforms to a height of 30m (100ft) to create a sacred space before the carving known as Monument 2, which represents a reclining figure with two people wearing elaborate ceremonial garb approaching him and one moving away. At Monté Albán, Mixtec pilgrims buried their rulers and in the grave known by archaeologists as Tomb 7 left magnificent offerings of gold and silverwork. Maya pilgrims conducted religious ceremonies and left ceramic effigies in the ruined temples at the Classic Period site of Dzibanché, Quintana Roo.

A SACRED TRADITION

In venerating ancient objects, reusing them and making offerings of them in tombs and temples, the peoples of the 12th–15th centuries AD were following a very well-established Mesoamerican religious tradition. Many centuries earlier, at Classic Period cities such as Tikal, Uaxactún and Cozumel, devotees made offerings of Olmec figurines, masks, plaques and objects used for drawing one's own blood. Maya nobles or rulers in this era wore Olmec greenstone pieces as sacred amulets.

A PILGRIMAGE GONE WRONG

In 1536 Ah Dzun Xiu, descendant of the Xiu dynasty that had been ousted by their rivals the Cocoms at Chichén Itzá in the 13th century, determined to lead a pilgrimage to make human sacrifices at the Sacred Cenote in the city of his ancestors. The king, who now ruled in the city of Mani, had been convinced by a recent hurricane, plague and smallpox epidemic that there was a pressing need to appease the gods. He asked for a guarantee of safe passage through the lands of his traditional enemy, Nachi Cocom. The lord of the Cocoms granted the request but plotted violence. When Ah Dzun Xiu, his son, nobles and trains of sacrificial victims arrived in Cocom lands, they were lavishly welcomed with feasting and entertainments that lasted for four whole days. But on the fourth evening, the hosts turned suddenly and viciously on their guests and slaughtered every last one. The gods had their sacrifice, but without the ceremony that had been planned. The episode served further to divide the Maya of Yucatán and paved the way for victory in the region by a force of Spanish conquistadors.

PILGRIMS TO THE PYRAMIDS

Surviving documents from the 16th century indicate that the Aztecs used the Teotihuacán pyramids not just for reverent worship, making offerings and blood sacrifices, but also as a dramatic setting in which to execute criminals. One account reports that on the Teotihuacán pyramids Tenochtitlán priests set up images of the underworld god Mictlantecuhtli, of the moon goddess Coyolxauhqui and of Tonacatecuhtli (Lord of our Sustenance), the male aspect of the primeval god of duality Ometéotl. The priests came in the company of the *tlatoani* once every month in their calendar – that is, every 20 days – to seek the gods' continued blessings on the growing empire. Priests and worshippers also sought guidance at oracle shrines in the ancient city. Aztecs deeply respectful of the achievements of the past also visited the ruins of the fortified city of Xochicalco, in western Morelos, where they reverently viewed the carvings of serpents, hieroglyphs and humans on the Pyramid of the Feathered Serpent.

Aztec potters and stonemasons expressed their devotion to the sacred power of the past and respect for the achievements of their ancient forebears by imitating bygone styles. At Tenochtitlán a group of heads of the *xiucóatl* ('fire-serpent') accompanied by calendrical dates is a homage to Xochicalco's Pyramid of

Above: Many generations of Mesoamericans revered their Olmec forebears. This head of an Olmec king is now at Villahermosa.

the Feathered Serpent. Sculptors also produced statues celebrating sacred images from Teotihuacán, while builders copied the proportions, murals and decorative style of Teotihuacán when constructing the five diminutive buildings in Tenochtitlán called the Red Temples. The nearby House of the Eagles, which lay just to the north of the Templo Mayor, was a detailed celebration of the achievements of Toltec stonemasons, sculptors and woodworkers.

Below: Many sacred structures at Chichén Itzá were built to honour the architecture and religious culture of the Toltecs. This is a detail of the Platform of the Eagles.

WHERE THE ANCESTORS GO

The Aztecs were taught not to fear death. Life and death were one aspect of the sacred duality that structured the universe, a duality also expressed in oppositions such as day and night, hot and cold, light and darkness.. Life was not easy, suffering was inevitable and death was inescapable. Many deaths were celebrated as honourable, for example, dying in giving birth, in battle or in a rite of human sacrifice. For the Aztecs it was a matter of honour to embrace death with equanimity and with a certain pride.

DAY OF THE DEAD

The Aztecs' positive attitude to death has carried through into modern Mexican celebrations on the Day of the Dead.

The Day of the Dead is celebrated on the Roman Catholic Church feasts of All Saints' Day (1 November) and All Souls' Day (2 November). The first day is usually set aside to remember those who died in childhood and infancy, with departed adults celebrated on the second day.

At home people build small altars in memory of the dead and load them with food, drinks, cakes and sweets – including sweet rolls called *pan de muerto* ('death bread') adorned with dough pieces shaped like bones, and breads called *anima* ('souls'), as well as a cup of the traditional maize soup (*atole*) and for adults beer, tequila and cigarettes. The altars are lit by candles and perfumed with traditional copal incense. The dead are expected to return to share once again in the sensual joys of life on earth. At the family burial plot, relatives gather to hold celebrations including dancing, singing and feasting at the graves of their departed. These festivities are complemented by an open-air Roman Catholic mass.

FLOWERS BLOOM

Each year the people of Tenochtitlán held the festival of Tlaxochimaco ('Coming Forth of Flowers') in honour of ancestors and, in particular, in celebration of the lives of those who had died in the last year. In the first days of the festival, the people gathered wild flowers in the fields near the city and carried them to the temple as an offering to the ancestral tribal god Huitzilopochtli and to Tezcatlipoca, one of the gods of death. They performed ritual dances in memory of the deceased.

The Maya, by contrast, were profoundly fearful of death despite the fact that it was as frequent a visitor among them as it was among the Aztecs. Far from celebrating those who had departed the earth, the bereaved made great demonstrations of their grief with wails of despair by night and floods of tears by day.

Funerary customs also varied among the cultures of Mesoamerica. The ancient way, which was followed widely in the

Above: These figures are part of a procession of gods and goddesses painted on the walls of a noble burial chamber (Tomb 105) in Monte Albán, probably in c.AD500–750.

Below: A skull decorated with shell and jade was laid in the tomb of an Aztec noble who went fearlessly to the spirit world.

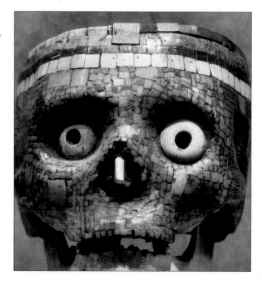

settlements of Oaxaca, in Teotihuacán, in Veracruz and throughout Maya regions, was to bury the body in a shroud with a funerary mask for the wealthy and a range of offerings connected to the person's livelihood when alive. The Toltecs and their followers in the Postclassic Period, including the Aztecs, preferred cremation. The body was wrapped in bandages and tied in an upright, seated position before being burned; the resulting ashes were then buried with funerary offerings. Some members of the Aztec elite, however, were granted burial.

RICH AND POOR BURIALS

The burials of rulers, nobles and the wealthy were considerably richer than those of commoners. Elite graves in Classic-Period Maya cities were rich in offerings of jade and serpentine, in funerary masks, jewels and splendid clothes.

In some special cases a pyramid-temple might be erected or an existing structure refashioned to encompass a tomb for the deceased king. A high-ranking scribe would be buried with the pens and other equipment he used to ply his elite trade.

Commoners were generally buried beneath the floor of their houses. In time, as relatives died and were buried alongside them, the house would be abandoned and used as a family shrine. According to Bishop Diego de Landa, a commoner in Yucatán would be buried in his cotton robe with a few grains of maize or jade beads in his mouth. These would sustain or support him on his voyage along the white road of the Milky Way to the underworld.

Above: Zapotec nobles were buried. Urns such as this one, found in Tomb 113 in Monte Albán, were not used to contain ashes and must have had a ceremonial use.

SACRIFICED IN DEATH

From the 10th century on, the Mixtecs broke open the graves of Monte Albán's former Zapotec rulers and used them to bury their own elite. They left magnificent grave offerings in gold and silver. Slaves and dogs were killed and interred to mark the rank of their former master.

Sacrificial burial appears to have been a Mesoamerican practice as far back as the time of Teotihuacán. A series of burials beneath the Pyramid of the Feathered Serpent contain 137 bodies with hands tied behind the back. Scholars believe they were killed as an offering to the gods upon the completion of the pyramid *c.*200AD.

Left: The snake, a complex symbol of new life and of the earth, is depicted consuming a human skeleton in a carving from Tula.

ART AND ARCHITECTURE

A carved bone found in the tomb of King Ah Cacau (*r.* AD682–734) beneath Temple I at Tikal depicts the hand of an artist-scribe emerging from a gaping monster's mouth. This monster-mouth was an established Mesoamerican image for the entrance to the spirit realm of the underworld – and the carving indicates that the Maya believed artistic ability and inspiration to have a divine source. Certainly the Maya of the Late Classic Period, in which this bone and the great majority of delicately painted polychrome vases were produced, celebrated their artists as a gifted elite. These exquisite vases – some of the finest produced in any world culture – were often signed by the artists who painted them.

The México/Aztecs, too, revered their artists, whom they called 'Toltecs' after the founders of the city of Tollán/Tula. In the Aztec Nahuatl tongue *tolteca* meant 'artist', and the word for artistic ability was *toltecayotl*. In the years of the Aztec empire, there was no distinction between artists and craftsmen: *tolteca* included artisans such as carpenters and weavers. They were seen as divinely blessed: their task was to seek sacred meaning in their heart and express this truth in their work. If they worked in this way, they would truly be like the Toltecs, whose city of Tollán was remembered as place of beauty and artistic excellence.

This survey of arts and crafts begins with a discussion of the main styles of architecture and a survey of the great cities. It describes the work of potters, weavers and featherworkers, then looks at stone and wood carving, metal-work, jewellery-making, mural painting and the production of painted codex screenfold books. It ends with a discussion of Mesoamerican aesthetics.

Temple I or Great Jaguar Temple, from the terrace of the northern acropolis of the Maya city of Tikal, was once painted red and adorned with moulded plaster masks.

CHAPTER 19

PALACES, TEMPLES AND SACRED CENTRES

Archaeologists generally distinguish between two types of Mesoamerican public building: 'palaces' and 'temples'. Palaces are usually long, low residential and administrative buildings that contain many rooms, small windows, niches above doorways and carved benches. Temples are usually built on top of tall stepped pyramid-platforms, with very limited interior space, and are topped with tall roof combs masonry structures that support a decorative façade. Scholars see palaces as utilitarian, and temples as sacred spaces reserved for ritual activity.

The distinction is helpful, but must be used with some caution since these words are only labels applied retrospectively by historians. Many palaces were used for administrative functions – such as meetings of council groups, or collection and storage of tribute – in addition to being the residences of kings or leading nobles. They contained shrine rooms and areas used for religious ritual such as autosacrifice – the letting of one's own blood. 'Temples', meanwhile, were used for varied purposes in different places and at different times. Some buildings, such as the five-storey palace in Edzná or the Great Palace of Sayil, appear to have combined sacred and utilitarian functions.

Left: In the middle of the three levels of the Palace at Sayil, a pair of columns divides each of the wide chamber doorways.

FROM HUTS TO TEMPLES

A decorative frieze on the Nunnery Quadrangle at Uxmal gives a stylized representation of a simple hut, the kind of dwelling inhabited by millions of Maya householders. A similar image was carved on an ornate archway leading to a group of palace buildings at Labná and was represented in murals painted at Chichén Itzá. The images depict the front of a single-storey oblong dwelling with a square central doorway and a thatched roof.

The Maya generally erected buildings on raised platforms: even the tall pyramids constructed to support temples can be seen as building platforms functionally. For a simple dwelling, however, the platform was low, built of earth or rubble covered in adobe plaster (a thick mixture of mud and straw). The great majority of Maya houses were built mostly

if not entirely of perishable materials and so did not survive to be examined by historians. However, archaeologists can trace the remains of domestic building platforms and so plot the arrangement of houses within settlements. However, the actual building methods used by the Maya to raise their houses remain a matter of educated conjecture, based on the frieze and mural images described above and on the building methods employed today by modern descendants of the ancient Maya.

MAYA BUILDING METHODS

Scholars believe that ancient Maya house builders first set up four sturdy corner posts, then created a lattice of thin sticks between them and covered the latticework with adobe plaster. In hot regions,

Above: This Aztec terracotta model represents the 'sacred mountain' of a steeply stepped pyramid topped with a temple.

builders might well have left the walls unplastered, allowing breezes to pass through and cool the inhabitants. The shape of the plot was usually rectangular, but could have rounded ends. In some areas, where building stone was readily available, builders laid stone building platforms for houses, or even built the lower parts of the walls in stone before covering them with adobe or lime plaster.

This tried and tested design was the template for all Maya buildings. Stone temples were more elaborate and permanent versions of the ancestral hut. Elements of the primitive house were reproduced in palace and temple: for example, builders in stone used the same square-shaped door with wooden lintel

Left: Maya dwellings often consisted of small buildings arranged around a central courtyard. This example is in Honduras.

that had been developed over generations by house builders. The sinuous lines of rope or creeper that tied the straw wall-padding in place in the family hut were reproduced in the ornamental carving on the friezes of sacred buildings and palaces.

TEMPLE MOUNDS

The earliest temples, of c.2000BC, were probably almost indistinguishable from ordinary dwellings – the gods naturally lived like humans. However, priests and their builders set the gods' buildings apart from village dwellings by raising them on higher platforms than those used for domestic structures. The platforms grew higher and higher over time. The practice of rebuilding temples on the same spot, over and encompassing their predeces-

sors, became a hallowed architectural custom. As the temple mound or platform grew taller and taller, builders had to add a new architectural element – one or more access stairways to enable priests and other ritual contributors to reach the temple at the top of the platform. The temple-platform began to resemble a great hill, entirely appropriate for a people who regarded mountains as sacred.

AZTEC BUILDING

Houses varied from simple, single-room huts with wooden walls and a straw thatched roof to large and elaborate stone mansions with flat stone roofs supporting herb gardens. Remains indicate that walls were made of wooden planks, latticework plastered with adobe, sun-dried adobe bricks or stone. In the marshy lakeside terrain of Tenochtitlán, even basic houses were often raised on stone building platforms to provide firm foundations

The design of the simplest housing similarly remained the template for palace buildings and the temples atop the steep pyramid-platforms. Images drawn for Friar

Above: The Aztec Temple of the Eagles at Malinalco was cut c.AD1500 from mountain rock near modern Tenancingo.

Bernardino de Sahagún's *General History of the Things of New Spain* (completed 1569) depict an Aztec house made of wood and straw, one built from stone with a straw roof and one built entirely of stone. Another shows a nobleman's house with an elaborate decorated frieze.

Left: The simple thatched hut occupied by Maya peasants was celebrated in stone in the archway at Labná (c.AD600–900).

RAW MATERIALS

Builders made use of locally available stone and other materials. In the southern Maya region, there was generally a shortage of easily worked rock for construction. Even major buildings were often made from adobe blocks, although at Copán labourers quarried and used local trachyte and at Quiriguá they worked with marble, sandstone and rhyolite.

In the central and northern Maya regions, builders had access to large amounts of limestone that was easy to cut into blocks. The limestone could also be burned to produce lime for making plaster.

BUILDING STYLES
FROM TEOTIHUACÁN TO TIKAL

The architectural style of Teotihuacán was widely influential across Mesoamerica for many hundreds of years. In particular, the city was known for its *talud-tablero* construction, which alternated an upright rectangular section (*tablero*) with a sloping section (*talud*). The *tablero* had a recessed central part.

In Teotihuacán, the style was particularly developed in the Ciudadela or Citadel area of the city, which included the Temple of Quetzalcóatl and 15 other stepped pyramids, as well as two elite residential buildings and an 11-hectare (4.4-acre) open plaza. The Teotihuacános used *talud-tablero* construction only for sacred buildings. At Teotihuacán, the upright *tablero* was always larger than the sloping *talud*, but elsewhere these ratios varied.

Archaeologists do not know for sure where the style originated, although some

Below: Architectural styles such as 'Puuc', 'Chenes' and 'Usumacinta' take their names from the regions in which they developed. This map also shows the main mining areas for certain raw materials.

suggest that immigrants to Teotihuacán from Tlaxcala might have brought a taste for and expertise in this type of building with them. Tlaxcalans, who also brought agricultural expertise in cutting terraced fields and irrigation with dams and canals, were using a form of *talud-tablero* construction in their civic and ceremonial buildings before 300BC, well in advance of the first major sacred buildings at Teotihuacán.

VARIATIONS ON A STYLE
The *talud-tablero* style was used very widely. At Kaminaljuyú *c.*AD200–400 builders either from or influenced by Teotihuacán built a ceremonial centre using *talud-tablero* construction. The style was also used in the Lost World complex at Tikal. At Xochicalco the Temple of the Feathered Serpent played a unique variation on the style by reducing it to the single component of the design: in profile, the temple presents one large sloping *talud* topped with a single *tablero*. Another variation on *talud-tablero* was developed by the builders of the Pyramid of the Niches at El Tajín in Veracruz:

Above: The archway at Kabah, Yucatán, is a good example of the corbelled vault or 'false arch' which looks like an inverted V.

there are six *talud-tablero* levels, with each sloping *talud* topped with a vertical *tablero* containing several niches, and at the top of each *tablero* there is an additional 'flying' reverse *talud*. At Tollán the El Corral temple consisted of two *talud-tablero* levels. The style was revived in the Temple of the Feathered Serpent at Chichén Itzá, which has nine *talud-tablero* tiers. The Aztecs built two small *talud-tablero* buildings in their sacred precinct at Tenochtitlán as an explicit tribute to the sacred city of Teotihuacán.

RAISING THE TEMPLE PLATFORM
In Maya lands builders usually constructed pyramid-platforms from earth and rubble and faced them with cut stone. These platforms usually had four faces with either one stairway or four stairways, one on each face, providing access to the temple on the summit. In some sites, several buildings were built on a single platform, in which case archaeologists usually call the platform an 'acropolis'. The platforms rose from generation to generation, for it was customary to build new platforms and temples over and enclosing the existing sacred structures. The roofs of Maya temples were typically decorated with tall facades of stucco

La Quemada
San Luis Potosí • Panuco

Gulf of Mexico

POST-CLASSIC
Dzibilchaltún • TOLTEC
Mayapán • • Chichén Itzá
Tula/Tollán
Uxmal •
• El Tajín
PUUC Tulum
Edzná •
Teotihuacán • Cempoala
Tenochtitlán • • Tlaxcala • Veracruz
CHENES
Cholula
Xicalango RIO BEC • Becán
Xochicalco
Potonchán •
Tres Zapotes Comalcalco
USUMACINTA Colha
Xochipala Palenque • • Tikal
Chilpancingo •
• Monte Albán • Yaxchilan
Acapulco • • Chiapa Bonampak
de Corzo
Tehuantepec • Quiriguá
COPAN
Precious metals
Jade and jadeite *PACIFIC* Kaminaljuyú • Copán
Serpentine
Cinnabar mining *OCEAN* Cotzumalhuapa
CHENES **Architectural style** Quelepa

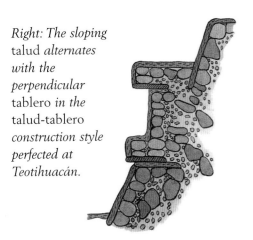

Right: The sloping talud alternates with the perpendicular tablero in the talud-tablero construction style perfected at Teotihuacán.

moulding or mosaic sculpture, usually supported from behind by masonry structures called roof combs. In the mortuary temples of Tikal, the roof comb element contained a portrait of the king buried in a vault beneath the temple platform.

Maya builders of the Classic Period generally relied on the corbelled vault – called the 'false arch' by architectural historians – to support the roof. This structure, which resembles an upside-down V, is created by laying inward-projecting blocks on top of one another: the blocks successively narrow the gap between walls until a single stone can bridge the gap at the top of the arch. (This contrasts with a true arch, whose use was never developed by the Maya, in which the keystone at the top anchors the other stones and creates a structurally much stronger unit.) Corbelled vaults need the support of thick walls beneath them. Maya buildings with false arches had severely reduced interior space given their outer size. Walls were generally made of rubble covered with stone.

BUILDING STYLES

A number of regional styles developed in Maya lands. The sacred buildings of Tikal epitomize the central Petén style, which is characterized by vertiginous pyramid-platforms each topped by a temple with a tall masonry roof comb, a single doorway and thick rubble-filled walls.

At Palenque, Yaxchilán, Piedras Negras and Bonampak the Usumacinta style was characterized by buildings with thinner walls and three or more doorways. At Palenque, for example, builders could erect thinner walls with several doorways

Above: Stucco carving on vertical temple-top roof combs was used to convey dynastic information, as here at Palenque.

because they had replaced the tall vertical facades used in the Petén style with inward-sloping facades that were partly supported by the vaulting of the roof. They also made lighter latticework roof combs rather than the solid masonry ones of the Petén region. Within, the buildings often had two parallel rooms divided by a wall that also helped to bear the roof's weight. A benefit of using thinner walls was that the buildings were considerably lighter and more airy within.

Another regional style of monumental architecture developed at Copán and Quiriguá, where temples, palaces and platforms were decorated with elaborate stucco modelling. A distinctive feature was the building of 'reviewing stands',

which were large platforms with wide access stairways. In the reign of King 18-Rabbit (AD695–738) at Copán, artisans began to create carved stone decorative elements in place of stucco; these were generally painted over with plaster.

Below: From the time of the Toltecs onwards, chacmool sacrificial figures were placed outside pyramid-top temple sanctuaries.

A LOVE OF DECORATION: YUCATÁN

The ornate modelling and façades at Copán had counterparts in styles developed farther north in the Maya region. In the Río Bec style, used in the southern Yucatán peninsula in the late Classic Period, builders put decoration and style before function. They erected vast constructions that were essentially reverent imitations of the great pyramids at sites such as Tikal: lofty towers with non-functional steps, doorways that led nowhere and 'false temples' built of solid rock for appearance only. Their buildings had elaborate façades incorporating mosaic masks, which often featured a long-snouted deity believed to be the rain god Chac.

Examples of the style are found at Becán, Xpuhil and Río Bec, in the region north of Calakmul. For example, the building known to archaeologists as Structure 1 at Xpuhil has towers supporting solid temple-like structures with roof combs. Buildings with the appearance of monumental sacred architecture clearly brought prestige to settlements such as Xpuhil or Becán, even if the temples and pyramids could not be used.

The related Chenes style took decorative elements a stage further, creating building façades dominated by decorative masks. In some of these, the entire façade represented a divine face with the doorway as the god's mouth. Chenes-style buildings were raised in the late Classic Period at sites slightly farther north in the

Above: Intricate decorative patterns and masks of the Maya rain god Chac on the upper walls of the Nunnery Quadrangle at Uxmal are typical of the Puuc style.

Yucatán peninsula. On the building known as Structure II at Chicanná, the façade represents the face of a god; perhaps the primordial creator Itzamná. The doorway is a serpent mouth, with two stylized eyes and fang-like projections above the opening. The structure gave its name to the settlement, for Chicanná means 'house of the snake's mouth'.

PUUC ELEGANCE

Further north again, the Puuc style developed in the Puuc region in north-western Yucatán. Builders preferred to limit decoration to the upper façade and to keep the lower half of walls plain. They built walls of lime concrete and faced the lower part with limestone veneer. Craftsmen applied pre-cut decorative elements to the upper façades in a repetitive pattern, whose elements were sometimes divine masks or serpents, but were more often abstract patterns such as lattices, fretwork and columns. In developing this style, which appeared at the close of the Classic Period (*c.*AD800–1000), Puuc

builders may been influenced by the repetitive decorative patterns used by their counterparts at Mitla and other sites in Oaxaca.

Splendid examples of the Puuc style are found at Uxmal in the Governor's Palace and the buildings of the Nunnery

Left: The Temple of the Magician, Uxmal, rises to an imposing height against the night sky. Its western stairway climbs to a sanctuary whose entrance is a god's mask.

> **'THE MAYA REVIVAL'**
> The US architect Frank Lloyd Wright was greatly impressed with the elegance of Puuc structures and applied the style in several public buildings erected in the 1920s. These created a vogue for a Maya Revival movement in architecture that encompassed other architects including Robert Stacy-Judd, Alfred Bossom and Richard Requa. Stacy-Judd used Maya inspiration in building the ironically named Aztec Hotel in Monrovia, California, in 1924–25. Requa's Maya Revival buildings included the Federal Building in San Diego (1935).

Quadrangle, both of which combine a plain lower wall with intricate decorative designs in the upper façade. The city of Uxmal demonstrates that these architectural styles developed alongside one another and were not mutually exclusive, for the shrine on the first terrace of the Temple of the Magician, at the top of a steep west-side storey, presents its west-facing entrance as the mouth of a divine mask in pure Chenes style.

At Kabáh, which was connected to Uxmal by an 18km (11-mile) *sacbé* causeway, the Temple of the Masks uses masks of the rain god Chac as the repetitive element on the façade. The building is identified as Puuc style by archaeologists, although its façade is entirely covered

Below: The Castillo and Group of the Thousand Columns typified the Chichén Itzá style copied in later Yucatán cities.

with the pattern of masks and so does not feature the plain lower half and decorated upper half typical of pure Puuc. The Great Palace at Sayil and the Palace Arch at Labná are other fine examples of the Puuc style.

TOLTEC ARCHITECTURE

At Chichén Itzá, archaeologists identify two main groups of buildings, with largely distinct styles. The southern group – which includes the Nunnery buildings, the Akabdzib, the House of the Deer, the Red House and the celebrated circular Caracol – is built largely in the Puuc style. The northern group – which includes the Temple of the Warriors, the Group of the Thousand Columns and the great Castillo or Temple of the Feathered Serpent – pioneered a new architectural style in the Maya region, featuring buildings with colonnades. The style exhibited a strong

Above: Sacred entrance. The creator god's face – with fangs and eyes above the door – sanctifies Structure II at Chicanná.

influence from the monumental architecture of sites such as Tollán (Tula) in highland Mexico.

This style became the prototype for building in the Postclassic Period that followed the collapse of Chichén Itzá. The Chichén Itzá style was influential, for example, in the construction of building at Mayapán and Tulum, although the 'copies' were of much poorer quality than the magnificent originals at Chichén Itzá.

HIDDEN MEANINGS IN SACRED BUILDINGS

At the heart of Tenochtitlán, the Aztecs built up the Templo Mayor over many years on the same sacred site, each new pyramid-temple encompassing its forerunner. The first temple on the site was raised as early as the city's foundation *c.*1325, while improvements and enlargements continued until 1502. This was in line with hallowed Mesoamerican building practice. The great Pyramid of the Sun at Teotihuacán was built in the 1st–2nd centuries AD over a sacred underground cavern and a ground-level shrine, while builders at Tikal, Uaxactún, Chichén Itzá and countless other ceremonial centres followed the same custom, raising their ceremonial structures ever higher, like great mountains, as they built over and on the temples of their ancestors.

In Tenochtitlán, the Aztecs identified the Templo Mayor as a recreation of the holy mountain of Coatépetl on which their tribal god Huitzilopochtli was born. In a number of Maya cities, also, temples were explicitly identified as holy mountains. Stucco masks representing mountains (called *witz*) often flanked the stairways on these structures. Just as a cave in a mountainside was a point of access to the spirit world, so the temple entrance high on a sacred mountain gave access to the supernatural regions.

SACRED TEMPLATE
In Tikal and other cities, architects of ceremonial centres followed a template based on the four cardinal points and three levels of the universe: earth, heaven and underworld. While north was associated with the celestial realm, south was the way to the underworld. East was the place of the rising sun and west, the place of its descent into darkness, represented the earthly realm, governed by time cycles such as the daily pattern of the sun's rising and setting. Buildings in east, west and north were often placed to form a triangle, with the fourth, southern position in the sacred pattern implied.

The scholar Clemency Coggins showed how at Tikal the Twin-Pyramid groups erected to celebrate the end of a *katun*

Above: Holy mountain top. Rising 42m (138ft) above the forest floor, Tikal's Temple II outreaches even the towering treetops.

(7,200-day period) were laid out according to this template. These groups consisted of pyramids with four stairways at east and west, with a building containing nine doors lying to the south and a roofless enclosure containing a stela and 'altar' or 'throne' to the north. While the east and west pyramids celebrated the sun's daily cycle, the nine-door southern building represented the underworld, which had nine levels. The northern building was uncovered and so gave access to the sky, the celestial realm of the ancestors. In this place, as if connected to and blessed by his dynastic forebears, the king stood – represented by the stela that named him and the throne stone that celebrated his power.

HOLY NUMBERS
The numerical patterning of Mesoamerican cosmology was regularly celebrated in architecture. Just as the southern

Left: Worshippers gather in the plaza for a katun-ending ceremony at one of the Twin-Pyramid Groups in Tikal.

building of the Twin-Pyramid groups at Tikal contained nine doors to represent the nine layers of the underworld, so the 50m (164ft) Temple I at the same site had nine levels. So did the 30m (98ft) Temple of the Feathered Serpent at Chichén Itzá.

The numbers of 365-day and 260-day calendars similarly gave sacred meaning to ceremonial buildings: the Temple of the Niches at El Tajín in Veracruz had 365 niches, while the four staircases of Chichén Itzá's Temple of the Feathered Serpent each contained 91 steps which, when added to the single continuous step at the base, made 365. The Temple of the Masks at Kabah had 260 masks.

RITUAL FURNITURE

In Tollán, Chichén Itzá and Tenochtitlán, adaptations of sacrificial ritual called for specialized pieces of sacred furniture. One was the *chacmool*, carved in the form a reclining figure thought to represent the god Tláloc, with a receptacle on his chest

into which a sacrificial victim's heart could be deposited. Another was the skull rack on which the heads of decapitated victims were displayed. These pieces of ritual furniture were used, and might indeed have been invented, by people in

Above: In Frederick Catherwood's engraving Chichén Itzá's Temple of the Feathered Serpent is notable mainly for its mountain-like bulk. But archaeological clearing revealed its intricate design, with 365 steps to match the days of the solar year.

the northern reaches of Mesoamerica at La Quemada and Alta Vista in Zacatecas state and at Cerro de Huistle in Jalisco. This people, identified by scholars as belonging to the Chalcihuites culture, built a court with colonnades, using both square and round columns, a plaza with pillars and a very large I-shaped ball court. They carved militaristic images of warriors with shields and weapons and they used skull racks as well as – at Cerro de Huistle – an early form of the *chacmool*.

Scholars believe that the sites predated the rise of Tollán and the Chalcihuites culture might therefore have been the precursor of many of the militaristic sacrificial rituals of the Toltecs and their followers at Chichén Itzá and Tenochtitlán.

Below: Twin shrines occupied the summit of the Templo Mayor in Tenochtitlán. This chacmool *demanded sacrificial blood outside the shrine of rain god Tláloc.*

THE IMPACT OF COLOUR AND SOUND

To a worshipper in the Great Plaza of the Citadel in Teotihuacán, the Pyramid of the Feathered Serpent rose vast against the blue sky, presenting a great wall of red, its moulded plaster decoration depicting snakes, feathered serpent heads and goggle-eyed, fanged masks picked out in green, blue and white.

At Tikal, a nobleman in the Great Plaza gazing up at the great temples of the North Acropolis would see towering red-painted buildings adorned with moulded plaster masks. Mesoamerican sacred buildings, which are today remarkable for their size, structure and setting, in their prime also created a major impact with bright colouring and detailed stucco decoration.

The Pyramid of the Niches in El Tajín makes an extraordinary impression because of the contrast of light and shadow in the 365 apertures of the structure. Archaeologists report that its appearance in its prime would have been even more remarkable, for they have found traces of the dark red paint that originally coloured the interior of each niche and of the bright turquoise that bordered each one. Colour played a crucial role in the theatre of the sacred that Mesoamerican ritual centres generated. Priests, and sometimes victims, donned

Above: Traces of wall colouring remain on one of the palaces at Kabah. The city was linked to Uxmal by a sacbé *roadway.*

brilliant plumage and costumes. Among the Maya, victims destined for sacrifice were painted turquoise. Their blood splashed brilliant red on the *chacmool* or sacrificial stone.

COLOURED MESSAGES
The use of coloured paints enhanced the messages of divine, dynastic or military power represented by sacred and other ceremonial buildings. The twin temples atop the Templo Mayor in Tenochtitlán were painted in bright colours as a way of identifying their divine patrons. The northern shrine to Tláloc was painted blue and white to signify his powers over water, while the southern shrine, to Huitzilopochtli, was red to celebrate his control of war and sacrifice.

At Palenque, the detailed stucco images in the roof comb of the shrine that tops the Temple of the Inscriptions pyramid were painted in bright colours to make them clearly visible to crowds in the plaza below.

At Kabah, near Uxmal, each of the myriad repeating heads of the rain god Chac that adorn the 50m (150ft) length of the Temple of the Masks was originally painted in turquoise, green and red, creating what must have been an overwhelming impression.

At Tollán, the great carved warriors that once supported the temple roof atop the Temple of Tlahuitzcalpantecuhtli were painted in bright colours to emphasize their bulk and power.

Left: Uaxactún's Pyramid E-VII-sub was originally decorated with red stucco and large masks, perhaps of the underworld god.

SOUND EFFECTS

Recent scholarly work has suggested that ritual complexes and sacred arenas might have been designed with acoustics in mind. The architecture of the Temple of the Feathered Serpent at Chichén Itzá appears to reinforce the sound of a voice declaiming at the top of the building: a

Below: A modern reconstruction of Teotihuacán's Temple of Quetzalcóatl shows the colours that greeted worshippers.

crowd watching and listening in the plaza beneath would have been able to hear the words of a priest making a ritual speech in praise of the gods or celebrating the undying power of the state. If so, the builders would have had knowledge of a building acoustic science that is now lost among architects.

David Lubman has reported that when a person standing in the plaza before the pyramid-temple claps his hands, the pyramid steps reflect back a sound like a descending bird-call – a sound that is a remarkable imitation of the primary call of the sacred quetzal bird. The quetzal was associated with the god Quetzalcóatl/Kukulcán, who is celebrated in the temple. Lubman argues that the steps were carefully designed to produce this echo. The lower steps combine a narrow tread and tall back, making a high-pitched 'chirp' echo, while the upper steps create a deeper echo like a whoop. Together they form a descending sound highly reminiscent of the quetzal's call. Lubman adds that the echo is a little ragged

Above: Solar blessing. At winter solstice the setting sun's rays lit on dynastic carving in Palenque's Temple of the Sun (right).

because the pyramid steps are no longer covered with plaster, as they would have been in ancient times. When the pyramid was newly built, the echo effect would indeed have been striking.

LIGHT EFFECTS

The Temple of the Feathered Serpent possessed another remarkable secret. Its builders positioned it so that at spring and autumn equinox, sunlight creates an undulating pattern of light and shadow on the steps, a celebration in light of the divine serpent in whose honour the temple was raised.

Alignments at Palenque produce light effects that celebrated the divine standing of the ruling dynasty. The Temple of the Cross is aligned so that at winter solstice, the setting sun will illuminate carved scenes and appear to bless the dynasty they honoured.

399

ARENAS FOR A SACRED CONTEST

The magnificent Great Ball Court in Chichén Itzá is Mesoamerica's largest, measuring 68m by 166m (225ft by 545ft) including the surrounding structures. Its pitch is I-shaped, opening out into wider end zones. The playing surface, 36m by 146m (120ft by 480ft), is enclosed by vertical sidewalls 8m (26ft) in height, each of which bears a circular ring halfway up its surface.

Chichén Itzá's Great Ball Court was part of the city's northern complex of ceremonial and sacred buildings, which archaeologists have dated to AD900–1200. The city contained no fewer then 13 ball courts, the largest number at any Maya centre and more even than at the other great Mesoamerican centre of the game, El Tajín in northern Veracruz, where there were 12 ball courts.

As elsewhere, the game at Chichén Itzá had important ritual and sacrificial elements. Relief sculptures on the walls of the court depict a newly victorious ball player who has just decapitated his defeated opponent: he holds the victim's

Below: The ball court at Monte Albán is an example of the earlier court design, with sloping sidewalls and without wall rings.

head aloft in triumph, while blood cascades from the headless corpse. The Great Ball Court carvings depict a total of 14 ball players, each with a skull attached to his belt. This iconography identifies them as lords of the underworld, Xibalba, against whom the Hero Twins played ball in Maya religious narrative.

SACRED IMAGES

Similar bloodthirsty rituals were carved in stone at Yaxchilán, where relief images on the steps of the structure known as Temple 33 depict King Bird Jaguar, his father and predecessor Shield Jaguar and his grandfather, another Bird Jaguar, playing the ball game with balls made from the bound bodies of captives. Scholars suggest that the images refer to an ancient Maya religious narrative known as *Ox Ahal* ('The Three Victories'), which told of human heroes who in time immemorial defeated and beheaded three lords of the underworld. The panel depicting Bird Jaguar playing the ball game makes reference to the narrative, which survives in the Quiché Maya *Popol Vuh*. One of the courts at El Tajín had vertical walls carved with a defeated ball player awaiting death, the sacrificial flint knife poised.

Above: Points were scored by hitting the ball through the ring. This court is at Uxmal, where – as in many cities – the court was positioned to connect north and south.

WATCHING THE DEADLY GAME

Ball courts usually provided seating for spectators. The oldest known ball court in Mesoamerica – found in 1988 at Pasa de la Amada in Chiapas, Mexico – had side-banks with benches 30cm (1ft) tall and 2.4m (8ft) deep. Thousands of years later, the Aztecs also built their courts with spectator seating.

Many courts had rings mounted on the walls. Sidewall rings were found on courts at Tollán, and in many highland Mexican sites of the Postclassic Period, including Tenochtitlán. This contrasts with most earlier courts – for example, at Monte Albán, Copán, Cerros and Tikal – that had low sloping sidewalls and no surviving wall-mounted rings.

The earlier courts often had markers indicating the centre of the playing area, so dividing the pitch into two equal halves. Some courts had niches at the ends in diagonally opposite corners. These were found, for example, in the courts at

Right: Copán's Great Ball Court – dedicated in 18-Rabbit's reign (AD695–738) – linked the Great Plaza to the north with the palaces and temples to the south.

Monte Albán and at Tollán. Scholars are unclear of their purpose. The rules of the ball game clearly varied in different eras and locations. At Chichén Itzá and in other courts of the Postclassic Period, the object appears to have been to score points by driving the ball through the sidewall rings. On other courts, players may have scored points by making the ball bounce in their opponents' endzone.

Below: The Great Ball Court at Chichén Itzá, seen here from the south, was overlooked by the Temple of the Jaguars.

IMPORTANCE OF POSITION

The ancient ball court at Pasa de la Amada was unusual in that it was not linked to a ceremonial centre: it appears to have been built in the heart of an elite residential area with no temples or ritual areas nearby. In many later settlements, the ball court played an important role within the sacred patterning of a city's ceremonial centre. A court was often placed between the northern realm of the celestial ancestors and the southern region associated with the underworld. The court, like the open plaza and the mouth of the pyramid-top temple, represented an entrance to the underworld. A ball court in Tikal's East Plaza performed this function in a three-point north-west-east design based on the North Acropolis and Temples I and II. At Cerros, in Belize, the ball courts (dating to 400–150BC) were positioned to consolidate the north–south alignment of the ceremonial centre.

THREE PARALLEL GAMES

Tikal's oldest ball court, laid out in the Great Plaza's south-east corner, contained a unique triple court, which had three pitches within a single complex. This was built to the south-east of the Great Plaza, beyond a ravine. It stood beside a sweat-bath. These buildings, called *temescals*, were closely associated with the ball game. They might have been used for cleansing rites as part of sacred ceremonial connected with the game.

PALATIAL STYLE OF MAYA RULERS

Palenque is unique among the Maya cities of the Classic Period in giving a central position in the city to the royal palace and administrative area. In most cities, the 'sacred mountains' of temple-platforms and mortuary monuments took pride of place, adjoining or enclosing plazas and open spaces that held stelae celebrating the achievements of royal rulers. At Tikal, for example, the central structure was the ceremonial Great Plaza bounded by royal mortuary shrines, to the north in the form of the North Acropolis and, to east and west, in the form of Temple I and Temple II respectively. The palace buildings were situated to the south of the main plaza in the Central Acropolis and farther south again in the buildings known to archaeologists as Group G, which lie alongside the causeway laid to connect the centre to the Temple of the Inscriptions.

HOME OF A KING

At Palenque, the palace stood on a raised platform, 10m (33ft) in height and measuring 80m by 100m (260ft by 320ft). It commanded views of the city's sacred buildings and ceremonial area and looked

Above: The square four-storey palace tower at Palenque had no counterpart elsewhere in the world of the Classic Maya.

beyond them across the river plain of the Usumacinta down to the Gulf of Mexico. The palace was home to King Pacal (r. AD615–83), whose ornate tomb was dug beneath his funerary monument, the Temple of the Inscriptions. His accession

was marked by a carved panel in the palace representing his royal mother, Lady Zac Kuk, in the act of passing the crown to him.

Pacal greatly expanded and improved the existing palace complex, which had been built by his predecessors from the 5th century onwards. Beginning in AD654, he laid a higher platform in the centre of the palace area and on it erected the structure called House E. This building later served as a throne room, in which three or more of his successors held ritual coronation ceremonies. Pacal constructed House C, to the north of House E, in AD661. Another palace building, House C, rose between two plazas, the East Court and the West Court, in the northern part of the palace. Directly south of the East Court the king raised another palatial dwelling, House B, also c.AD661, and directly to the east of the East Court he added House A around seven to ten years later.

Below: King and courtiers enjoyed elegant privacy in the interior courtyards of the palace complex at Palenque. The concrete roof rested on strong beams of sapodilla.

DYNASTIC BUILDING

Pacal's successors continued his work. His son Chan-Bahlum II (AD684–702) might have added Houses A and D at the far eastern and far western limits respectively of the building complex. Another building, House A–D, was probably added at the northern limit of the complex by King Kan-Xul II (AD702–711). He also built the rooms at the southern edge, including the remarkable four-storey tower that may have been an astronomical observatory.

The palace is luxurious throughout. Not only is it decorated with elaborate modelled stucco inside and out, but its builders used a modified arch that allowed spacious interiors, in marked contrast to the corbelled arch and narrow rooms found in many other Maya palaces and cities. When in use, the building was also brightly coloured. House E was painted white and also known as the

Right: Carving on the second storey of the Palace at Sayil features monsters and a rare deity known as 'the descending god', found only here and at Cobá and Tulum.

White House but the other parts of the complex were coloured a dark red with details in blue, green and yellow. The complex contains 85 'windows' in the T-shaped form of a Maya calendrical daysign that scholars call 'IK': its translation is 'wind-breath' or 'breath of life'. The 'windows' might not have been built for the usual purpose, for they were generally set rather too high in the wall for people to look through them comfortably. Nevertheless, they allowed light to enter and also had a decorative function. In the East Court, the king received

Above: This view of Palenque's palace is from the top of King Pacal's mortuary monument, the Temple of the Inscriptions.

ambassadors and fellow rulers. Its walls were decorated with carved inscriptions detailing Pacal's military successes and representing the many foes and rivals he had humbled and made captive.

A PALACE-TEMPLE

At Copán, King 18-Rabbit (AD695–738) erected a building that archaeologists believe was a combined palace-temple complex – known to archaeologists as Temple 22 – on the northern edge of the East Court of the Acropolis, the southern part of the city centre. Like many Maya temples, it was adorned with *witz* (sacred mountain masks) at the corners. In the Maya city of Edzná in Campeche, builders raised a pyramid temple platform that was also a palace: the five-storey structure had lower levels designed with many rooms, doorways and windows like a palace, but also a temple building on the flat fifth level that was accessed by a frontal staircase.

THE AZTEC PATTERN OF ELEGANCE

Aztec rulers lived in splendour, at a very great remove from the humble dwellings of their subjects. Their palaces were large and splendid, but took the same basic form as the dwellings occupied by the nobles and the middle classes: several rectangular rooms arranged around a courtyard or patio. They were unusual, however, in having a second floor: only nobles and rulers were permitted to build two-storey dwellings. Palaces contained administrative and storage rooms as well as living quarters for the ruler, his wives, concubines, guards and servants. Royal residential areas in Aztec palaces were generally reserved for the upper storey, while council rooms, courts, war chambers, arsenals, storage rooms and other administrative buildings were laid out on the ground floor. Extensive patios and pleasure gardens, well planted with trees and watered by streams and fountains, stocked with abundant wildlife, covered vast areas.

Below: Many of Teotihuacán's elite residences were decorated with murals. This owl fresco is from the Tetitla complex.

Above: In Teotihuacán the Quetzalpapálotl Palace, at the south-west corner of Plaza of the Moon, may have been priestly quarters.

A PICTURE OF ROYAL LIFE

According to Fernando de Alva Ixtlilxóchitl, writing in the early 17th century, the palace of Netzahualcóyotl, ruler of Texcoco, covered an area of more than 80 hectares (200 acres). A celebrated image from the 16th-century *Mapa Quinatzin* depicts the palace complex in Texcoco. Netzahualcóyotl holds court with his son Netzahualpilli in the throne room overlooking a large patio-courtyard

DESIRE FOR PRIVACY

Although an Aztec palace contained many public rooms such as stores and courtrooms that could be accessed even by commoners, the *tlatoani's* own quarters were reserved on the upper storey and contained many secluded outdoor patios and gardens in which the ruler and his intimates could associate with their noble peers in quiet and privacy. The divine aura of the ruler, which dictated that he must eat alone and could not be addressed with full eye contact, needed to be protected.

There were certainly ancient Mesoamerican prototypes in Teotihuacán and Tollán for setting the palace alongside centres of public life such as the marketplace and ceremonial area, but equally in the 'palaces' of Monte Albán, there was a prototype of an elite building with many stairways, corridors and secluded patios – a design intended to safeguard the privacy of rulers and nobles.

in which several men – either allied rulers or the leaders of Texcoco's communities – are in earnest discussion. Behind them on one side is an extensive network of rooms for storing imperial tribute, while on the other side of the patio are temple rooms containing shrines. On either side of the throne room are administrative chambers, one used for counting and storing military supplies and the other a courtroom for the city's judges.

Opposite these rooms at the far side of the patio is a splendid area for receiving ambassadors from rival and allied cities and a large meeting house set aside for discussing matters of war. This pattern is typical of Aztec-era palaces and similar to the design of Moctezuma's splendid building in Tenochtitlán.

Above: A fresco detail from the Tetitla residence in Teotihuacán contains a floor plan for a palace building.

PALACE PROTOTYPE

The unknown builders of Teotihuacán, who exercised such an enduring architectural influence on later Mesoamericans, constructed a palace compound in the 1st–2nd century AD of the kind built about 1,200 years later by the Aztecs. The palace at Teotihuacán was part of the great Ciudadela or Citadel complex that also contained a vast plaza and the Pyramid of the Feathered Serpent. It lay at the junction of the main thoroughfares that divided the city into four and sat directly opposite a large marketplace. Similarly, in Tenochtitlán the *tlatoani's* palace occupied a position adjoining the main square and temple precinct in the heart of the city.

The Ciudadela palaces lay on the north and south sides of the great Pyramid of the Feathered Serpent. They consisted of groups of low-lying apartment buildings gathered around open patios – the very pattern that Aztec builders would later use in their own designs.

Opposite the Ciudadela, the open space that archaeologists believe was a marketplace was flanked by other low-lying palace-style buildings that were probably administrative buildings needed to monitor and control the vibrant trade on which the city thrived. By the era of Tenochtitlán, the two 'palace' functions – ruler's residence and administrative compound – had been combined.

The monumental Ciudadela complex built *c.*AD100–200 was a new departure for the Teotihuacános, who had previously laid out buildings in groups of three on an ancient sacred pattern. Scholars believe that the new style might have marked the beginning of a new political era, an attempt by a powerful new leadership in the city to distance themselves from a possibly despotic former regime.

The Ciudadela celebrated the authority and power of the state, with its palaces adjoining open spaces for the gathering of residents and centralization of trade. Later Mesoamericans learned a great deal from this association of elite residences with monumental architecture.

THE BURNT PALACE

At Tollán, the Toltecs erected twin palace-administrative buildings adjoining the Temple of Quetzalcóatl. To the east was the Palace of Quetzalcóatl and to the west was a much larger three-halled structure, now known as the Burnt Palace because much of it was lost to a fire. Like its predecessor at Teotihuacán and its successors at Texcoco and Tenochtitlán, the palace building probably hosted meetings, was used to greet notable visitors and was a state storeroom for items of trade and tribute. Once again, the building adjoined both a plaza and a large area that scholars believe was a marketplace.

Below: At Tollán these pillars are remains of the colonnades that once graced the Palacio Quemado or 'Burnt Palace'.

THE MAGNIFICENCE OF MOCTEZUMA

Moctezuma's palace in Tenochtitlán was a statement in stone of the *tlatoani's* divine magnificence. Surrounded by extensive gardens containing ponds, courtyards, an aviary and a zoo, the palace was a residence fit for a ruler so magnificent that none of his subjects were permitted to look him in the eye.

ROYAL CITY WITHIN A CITY

Spanish accounts report that Moctezuma's palace had more than 300 rooms, which were arranged around internal courtyards. Legal documents concerning landholdings suggest that the emperor's city complex covered 4 hectares (10 acres). An administrative building as well as a royal home, the palace contained military council rooms, a throne room and reception areas for greeting ambassadors and political visitors, legal apartments used by judges as courtrooms, two armouries and large areas for storing

Below: A reconstruction of Moctezuma's two-storey palace in Tenochtitlán reveals extensive courtyards and gardens within.

tribute from around the empire. According to an account by the conquistador Bernal Díaz del Castillo, the palace contained extensive areas for storing cacao, feathers, gold, jewels, cotton and foods that had been received as tribute payments. There were also rooms for accountants managing the wealth generated by tribute and taxation.

The vast building contained libraries, music rooms and areas for craftsmen retained to work for the emperor. There were also permanent quarters for the rulers of Texcoco and Tlacopán, the Aztecs' allies in the Triple Alliance, together with guest rooms for visiting notables from states within the empire. The importance of the lakeside town of Chiconauhtla, derived largely from its control over the straits connecting the lakes of Zumpango and Xaltocán with Lake Texcoco, was reflected in the fact that the ruler had the right to keep an apartment in the imperial palace

The Tenochtitlán palace complex was arranged over two floors, with the *tlatoani's* quarters on the upper floor and

Above: A serpent-head Tenochtitlán foundation stone was uncovered by archaeologists in Mexico City.

state or administrative rooms and servants' living space on the gloomier ground level. An image from the *Codex Mendoza* (*c.*1541) represents the two-storey building with a courtyard and steps leading to an upper-floor reception room in which the dazzling Moctezuma himself sits in state. On either side of his quarters stand apartments for leading allied rulers. Below on the ground floor lie two meeting rooms, in one of which four judges discuss an important case, while the other is kept for councils of war.

PALACE COURTROOMS

Friar Bernardino de Sahagún's description of the palace in Tenochtitlán indicated that legal administration worked on three levels for nobles, military and commoners. In one room of the palace court, legal experts heard noble disputes and complaints of wrongdoing. Their sanctions included banning an offender from the palace complex, banishing a person from the city or ordering his execution by stoning, hanging or beating; chopping off the hair was a lesser punishment, but greatly feared because it

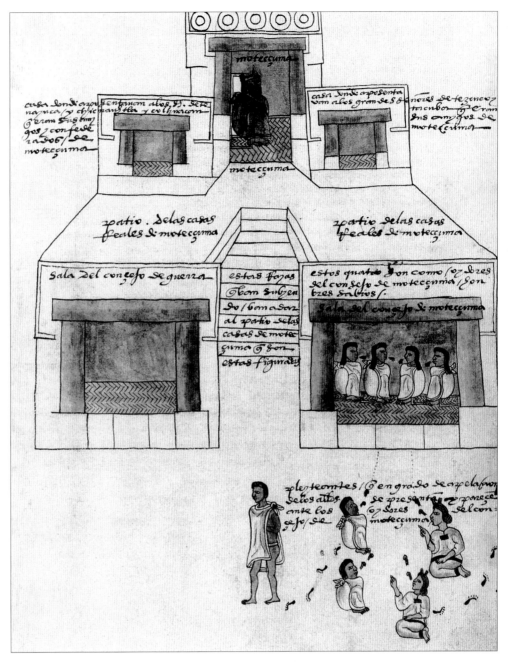

would make a leading member of the *pip-iltin* nobility look like a shaven-headed *macehual* or commoner.

In a palace room named the *tecpilcalli*, leading members of the military dispensed their own justice. In the *teccalco* chamber, commoners could bring disputes and complaints to judgement. The *tlatoani* himself heard difficult cases and took advice from the three most senior judges or *tecuhtlatoque* before passing judgement. Judges faced the strictest sanctions – including execution – if they were found to be corrupt.

ANCIENT AMENITIES

There were more than 100 bathrooms in the *tlatoani's* palace. Several times a day the ruler washed and changed his clothes: he discarded his garments after wearing them once. He lived in great splendour on the palace's second floor, with his two wives and 150 concubines, together with legions of guards and attendants. His servants were housed in their own luxurious apartments.

A large part of the palace was given over to kitchens and food stores. At every meal some 300 guests were served from an extensive menu designed to stimulat-

Below: This stone, once part of Moctezuma's elegant Tenochtitlán palace, shows evidence of having been worked by an Aztec mason.

ing the most jaded palate. Such was the *tlatoani's* splendour that dinner guests were forbidden to watch him engage in activities such as eating: he consumed his food in isolation behind a golden screen. Delicacies to tempt the royal diners included frogs served with green chilli peppers, sage-doused locusts and a helping of prickly pear served with fish eggs from the great lake of Texcoco.

In the patios of the royal palace complex, acrobats and musicians practised. The gardens contained ten pools stocked with waterfowls that feasted on fish. Hernán Cortés wrote to King Carlos V of Spain that these birds were so numerous they required 110kg (250lb) of fish each day. In the zoo, royal jaguars, coyotes and

Above: The Codex Mendoza *(c.1541) shows Moctezuma sitting on the upper floor of his two-storey palace, between apartments for visiting dignitaries. Before the building, one man departs while four litigants present a case to the judges in the lower right-hand chamber. The lower left-hand chamber is identified as the war council room.*

serpents were kept in regal luxury. Some were fed on human flesh carried from the temple complex nearby.

Throughout the palace, servants, guards and administrators burned incense and sweet-smelling woods in their braziers to mask the smell of decaying body parts that the breeze sometimes carried across from the temple quarters.

CHAPTER 20

BUILDING THE CITIES

The builders of great Mesoamerican centres looked for inspiration in the cities and sacred buildings of the past. They paid homage to the achievements of their ancestors by reproducing their styles: Teotihuacáno *talud-tablero* construction spread across Mesoamerica – being used, for instance, in Tikal, Kaminaljuyú, Xochicalco, El Tajín and Chichén Itzá. Great cities of the past were also places of pilgrimage or sacred occupation.

Cities had a unifying function, linking cultures and peoples across centuries, but also connecting people within a region. A city was the focus of its area, providing employment in outlying artisanal areas or an outlet for the excess agricultural produce of the region's farmers. For instance, Tikal provided a means of living for a vast outlying population of some 60,000; Teotihuacán similarly supported a large outer area of rural settlements, some growing food, others working local flint or obsidian; Tenochtitlán was the focus of an extensive area of *chinampa* farmlands.

A city also created connections between areas across great distances: from before the start of the Classic Period, Mesoamerican trade was driven by the needs of wealthy city populations and religious elites for rare or exotic products. Long-distance trade driven by the vast population of Teotihuacán, for instance, forged links across many thousands of kilometres between the Mexican highlands and settlements such as Tikal or Kaminaljuyú.

Left: The North Platform bounds the northern edge of Monte Albán's Plaza, at the heart of Mesoamerica's first true city.

SACRED TOWNS:
SAN LORENZO AND LA VENTA

Settlers first occupied the plateau that became the Olmec centre of San Lorenzo, near the Gulf Coast of Mexico, *c.*1500BC. Their descendants began public building works about 250 years later. A group had grown wealthy and powerful controlling the farming of fertile lands alongside the local Coatzacoalcos and Chiquito rivers and perhaps by managing trade in obsidian, greenstone and basalt from resource-rich uplands nearby. The leader of this group was able to command and reward the labour needed to build a sacred ceremonial centre.

Below: Stela 2 at La Venta shows an Olmec monarch dressed as a player with the bat used in some versions of the game, after c.1000BC.

SACRED CENTRE
Beginning *c.*1250BC, hundreds of workers built up and levelled the plateau. On its top, 50m (160ft) above the surrounding countryside, they laid out a series of pyramids and rectangular courts on a north to south alignment, oriented precisely 8 degrees west of true north – probably to line up with the rising of a star or planet at a ritually significant time such as an equinox. They used clay and earth to make these buildings, but imported basalt from the Tuxtla mountains 70km (10 miles) away to line a remarkable series of drains that were connected to fountains and artificial ponds. These were made from skilfully shaped interconnecting pieces of basalt.

Above: On Altar 5 at La Venta, a king or shaman-priest wearing a jaguar headdress holds a 'were jaguar' baby – an infant with snarling jaguar features.

SACRED FIGUREHEAD
The king may have been worshipped. Eight colossal basalt carved heads erected at San Lorenzo were probably portraits of the settlement's rulers. Some of the heads were more than 3m (10ft) tall and weighed 20 tons. The king's power derived not just from his wealth, but also because he was a sacred figurehead, guarantor of his people's safety and of the

> ### RELIGIOUS PIONEERS IN TWIN OLMEC SETTLEMENTS
> Olmec remains at San Lorenzo and La Venta suggest that the inhabitants of these temple towns were pioneers in many facets of Mesoamerican religious life. The Olmec worshipped a feathered serpent deity together with a rain god and revered jaguars and eagles as well as crocodiles and sharks. They also practised the rites of autosacrifice, in which a worshipper expelled his or her own blood: stingray spines and other items – perhaps including shark's teeth – were used to induce blood flow. Generations of Mesoamericans would follow the Olmec lead in these matters.

continued fertility of their maize fields. The buildings and monuments of San Lorenzo were erected before 900BC. While the site appears to have been a busy trading settlement after that date, its people did not feel the need to raise further pyramid-mounds or to carve new stone thrones or heads. Some time during the years 900–700BC, axe-wielding men smashed the Olmec heads and thrones of San Lorenzo and buried the remnants in ditches. The violence done to the statues suggests that this was an act of vandalism by invaders, but the careful collection and hiding of the remnants in ditches might indicate that it was a piece of elegiac destruction by Olmec who wanted to set their own age apart from the past.

Pottery remnants from the years after 700BC suggest that at this time San Lorenzo was occupied by people originating in Maya regions of Chiapas and Guatemala. In the years 600–400BC, the inhabitants of the settlement probably built a ball court. Archaeologists have discovered two elongated mounds running in parallel that they believe are the side walls or spectators' stands of a ball court.

Above: The four sides of La Venta Altar 5 are carved with shaman-kings holding 'were jaguar' babies. The 'were jaguar' may have been venerated as an image of the rain god.

AMID THE MARSHES: LA VENTA

From *c.*1150BC onwards, Olmec builders constructed another centre at La Venta, about 60km (35 miles) north-east of San Lorenzo and just 12km (7 miles) inland from the Gulf coast. They chose a salt mound amid freshwater marshland, in an area where villagers had already been living for more than a millennium, supporting themselves by fishing, hunting, gathering and growing maize in the fertile soil.

La Venta's builders raised a ceremonial centre of mounds and plazas, aligned like those at San Lorenzo precisely 8 degrees to the west of true north. The tallest of these, called Complex C by archaeologists, is an earthen mound 32m (105ft) high. Some scholars have suggested that it was intended as a recreation of a sacred volcano. Others have likened its shape to that of the pyramid in the Group E complex at the later Maya city of Uaxactún, which may have been structured in four quadrants to celebrate the cardinal points and which was aligned precisely to the sun's rising on sacred equinoctial dates. In front of the mound, running northwest, lay an elongated plaza. Beyond the plaza lay a further sacred arena (named

Left: Olmec religious life appears to have centred on worship of the ruler and his ancestors. This colossal basalt head, from La Venta, may represent a departed king.

Complex A by archaeologists) containing a court enclosed on two sides by basalt columns, ten further mounds, several platforms and a buried serpentine mosaic pavement measuring 4.5 by 6m (15 by 20ft) and representing the face of a jaguar, beneath which many sacred offerings were laid. Above the pavement, at ground level, lay a sarcophagus of sandstone carved to represent the earth monster in the form of a crocodile floating on water.

Both La Venta and San Lorenzo were relatively small in size. With around 1,000 people resident in each at their peak, the settlements are perhaps better called towns than cities. For many years archaeologists concentrated on the ceremonial role of La Venta and San Lorenzo, but recent work has established that the sites were residential as well as religious centres. At La Venta, living quarters lay to the north-east of the main ceremonial complex. At San Lorenzo the network of drains may have been used functionally by the town's inhabitants, or may have played a role in religious ceremonies celebrating the life-giving power of the waters that fed the maize plants.

CITY OF THE ZAPOTECS:
MONTE ALBÁN

An elite group among the Zapotec inhabitants of the highland Valley of Oaxaca founded the settlement of Monte Albán c.500BC. It was located in a dominant position on a flattened mountain ridge between two peaks, with good views down all three arms of the valley. In its early years, the settlement consisted of three residential districts and contained up to 7,200 people. The ridge had no agricultural land, and Monte Albán's residents lived on the produce of the three arms of Oaxaca valley: Tlacolula to the east, Etla to the north and Zaachila

Below: A plan of Monte Albán's Main Plaza. The plaza was laid out and paved in white stucco by Zapotec labourers c.300BC.

to the south. Produce was distributed at a market on the flattened ridge. The settlement grew rapidly. Home to 15,000 people by c.200BC, Monte Albán had become Mesoamerica's first city.

Major building works had begun about a century earlier, c.300BC. An army of labourers flattened the uneven mountaintop and laid out a plaza paved in white stucco.

The Temple of the Danzantes, adorned with carvings of defeated war captives, arose in the south-west corner of the plaza. The city's elite commissioned stone tombs for their burials and builders produced increasingly elaborate masonry graves, some of which were distinguished by corbelled roofs.

Above: Looking north across the expansive Main Plaza at Monte Albán, Building H looms in the foreground.

A MATURE CITY

Monte Albán was a thriving city for several centuries. In the period AD500–750, its population rose as high as 24,000. The city spread over two adjacent hilltops, covering 6.5km (4 miles), and contained 14 residential areas. Each had its own plaza, while the city's elite rulers and administrators lived in 14 'palaces' arranged around the city's main commercial plaza. In these years, labourers erected a great pyramid 15m (50ft) in height and more than 100m (325ft) in length at the south end of the main plaza. Carved stelae at the four corners appear to commemorate a state visit by emissaries from Teotihuacán, perhaps on the occasion of the building's ceremonial dedication. At the northern end of the plaza, builders constructed a hall with fine colonnades that gave on to a low-level patio backed by tall pyramids.

The city specialized in crafts, making elite produce from obsidian and seashells: The workshops lay to the north-east of the main plaza in an area of noble dwellings. The elite of Monte Albán appear to have valued seclusion and privacy. Noble dwellings were secluded, with central patio areas sometimes accessed by long corridors and through a number of intervening rooms. The main plaza was largely cut off from other parts of the city.

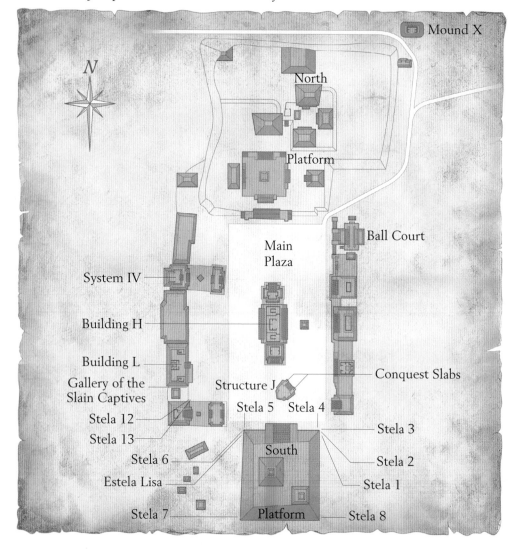

CAPITAL OF THE BALL GAME:
EL TAJÍN

The settlement of El Tajín in the Gulf Coast region of northern Veracruz was established in the early Classic Period, when it had trading links with the great metropolis of Teotihuacán. The celebrated remains, which include the Pyramid of the Niches and no fewer than 12 ball courts, date from much later – the 9th–11th centuries AD. These remnants are a small part of the city that once stood here: ruins untouched by archaeologists and so still covered in foliage stretch for 5km (3 miles) into the low hills of the surrounding tropical rainforest.

PYRAMID OF THE NICHES
Builders erected the ceremonial centre that contains the Pyramid of the Niches in the flat southern part of city. The six-tier pyramid supports a temple on its flat top, making seven levels in all, with progressively fewer niches in each level. The bottom tier contains 88 niches, the second has 76, then the levels contain 64, 52, 40 and 28 while the temple has 17 – making a total of 365, one for each day of the solar year. Close by, the builders set out two ball courts. One is decorated with bas-relief carving depicting the sacrificial slaughter of a ball player.

Below: Building 3 stands directly west of the Pyramid of the Niches in central El Tajín. It makes use of niches and Teotihuacáno talud-tablero architectural elements.

Above: The buildings of El Tajín were at one time covered with polychrome stucco. The niches of the Pyramid of the Niches were painted red with turquoise borders.

Labourers cut terraces into the small hills to the north of the ceremonial centre and laid out an extensive residential area. They raised elite homes or palaces with colonnades, rooms with corbelled vaults and fine roof combs. They built walls to separate the residential district – known as Tajín Chico – from the ceremonial area to the south and from the king's palace complex to the west.

HOME FIT FOR A KING
Skilled stonemasons cut splendid ornate reliefs in the Building of the Columns, one of the main structures in the royal complex, depicting images of military conquest and sacrificial ritual. The ruler shown most frequently in this area is King 13-Rabbit. Images represent toads as well as sacred serpents and royal jaguars. Glyphs indicate that the people of El Tajín followed the 260-day cycle as well as the calendar of 365 days celebrated in the niches of the main pyramid. The wet season in this part of Mexico hits hard: to prevent flooding and conserve water, builders dug elaborate drains, underground waterways and tanks for storage. The city's 12 ball courts have led scholars to speculate that it might have been a centre for playing the ball game – perhaps a site used for grand enactments of sacred ritual linked to calendrical observations.

CAPITAL OF THE TOTONACS?
El Tajín might have been an early capital of the Totonacs, a people who rose to greater prominence in the Postclassic Period in Veracruz and the northern part of Puebla. In the 16th century, the Totonacs – who by then had their capital at Cempoala, some 150km (90 miles) south of El Tajín – had the distinction of becoming the first Mesoamerican people to join Hernán Cortés in his military action against Tenochtitlán.

THE PLACE OF THE GODS:
TEOTIHUACÁN

The great city of Teotihuacán – named 'the place of the gods' by the Aztecs – was laid out from *c.*100BC onwards, on an ancient sacred site in a region of highland Mexico where villagers had been living since *c.*900BC. Builders erected the first buildings in an area now called Oztoyahualco ('Old City'), in the northern part of the valley about 1km (⅝ mile) to the west of the land on which the Pyramid of the Moon was later built. They chose the Old City site, which had little water, because it gave access to a network of sacred caves and tunnels.

UNDERGROUND RITUAL

In the period AD1–150, the city's builders reverently enlarged a natural cave beneath the ground on which they would later build the Pyramid of the Sun. They created an underground ritual site 100m (325ft) long, with basalt roofing, walls covered with mud plaster and water channelled in for ritual use via a covered drain made of stone. It led into four small chambers. Next they built a small shrine of stone and adobe bricks at ground level.

In the northern, original area of the settlement, the builders laid out a series of small plazas, each enclosed by three temples. Archaeologists report that these

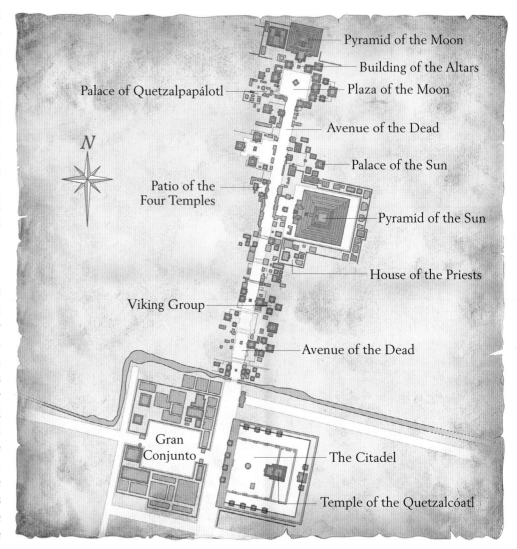

Above: The city's axis, the 2.4km (1.5-mile) Street of the Dead, runs 16 degrees east of true north, linking the Pyramid of the Moon and the Ciudadela complex in the south.

Below: Looking south from the Plaza of the Moon, the Pyramid of the Sun rises on the east side of the Street of the Dead.

sacred constructions were associated with access to caves and suggest that a series of plaza-temple complexes, running roughly south-west, probably followed the line of the ancient subterranean caverns and tunnels. In all there are 20 of these plaza-temple units, which have been left largely untouched by archaeologists. Each might have been the original settlement of 20 tribal or kin groups who possibly united to found the city. In the same period (AD1–150), farmers dug the city's first irrigation system, a network of simple canals excavated to spread the waters of the Barranca de Cerro Colorado among the farmlands at the western perimeters of the expanding settlement.

CITY PLANNING

From the start the city was laid out according to a clear design, divided into quadrants by wide thoroughfares running roughly north–south and east–west. The north–south axis was oriented 16 degrees to the east of north to align both with the peak of Cerro Gordo and, according to some scholars, with the point at which the Pleiades set at that time. The Pyramid of the Sun, located on the east side of this north–south line, was the first sacred

building erected in Teotihuacán, in the 1st century AD. The original structure was later rebuilt, but archaeologists report that in its first version the pyramid was very nearly as tall as the majestic final building, which rose to a height of 66m (216ft). The original pyramid might have supported twin temples, as did the pyramid built at Cuicuilco, also in the Valley of Mexico, and many later Mesoamerican pyramid/temple-platforms.

The city grew very fast. In AD150 it was home to as many as 80,000 people and covered 20sq km (7sq miles). The population continued to grow – reaching a peak of 100,000–200,000 by AD500 – although the city did not expand far beyond this ground area. Large numbers lived in and farmed outlying rural areas beyond the city limits.

When finished, the north–south thoroughfare was 40m (130ft) wide and 2.4km (1½ miles) long. It was lined on both sides with low-lying buildings identified by archaeologists as elite residences or palaces, but which the Aztecs believed

Below: The small stepped pyramids flanking the Plaza of the Moon are dwarfed by the 66m (216ft)-tall Pyramid of the Sun.

were the tombs of their ancestors – leading them to call it the Street of the Dead. At the northern end of the street lay the Pyramid of the Moon, 43m (140ft) in height. It faced and gave on to an open square known as the Plaza of the Moon. In its south-west corner the elite residential building known as the Palace of Quetzalpapálotl was built in AD500–750. One of Teotihuacán's plaza-temple groups, the Plaza of the Columns, lay to the west of the Street of the Dead, a little to the north and on the opposite side to the imposing Pyramid of the Sun. Both the Sun and Moon pyramids were flanked by smaller pyramids and gave on to plazas, which might also have been intended to form plaza-temple groups of the kind typical of Teotihuacán.

Heading south, the street is flanked by palace buildings and sacred structures and gives access via side streets to areas of residential apartment buildings. An extensive collection of apartments, temples, plazas and platforms on both sides of the street is known as the Street of the Dead Complex. These were magnificent buildings, constructed of the finest materials and provided with mica floors.

Above: At the southern edge of the city centre, a serpent's head honours the Feathered Serpent Quetzalcóatl on the god's temple in the Ciudadela complex.

IN THE CITADEL

Further south, the Street of the Dead gave to the east on to the city centre, the Ciudadela, a vast, enclosed square structure of platforms, roughly 400m (1,300ft) square and incorporating 15 pyramids, two palaces, a 4.4-hectare (11-acre) plaza and the magnificent stepped pyramid-platform Temple of Quetzalcóatl. Opposite the Ciudadela, on the west side of the Street of the Dead, was another vast enclosed area called the Great Compound that was probably the city's main market place. Its northern and southern edges consisted of long platforms supporting apartment buildings thought to have been the homes of the city's administrators and bureaucrats. The large western avenue led directly out of the compound heading west, while the eastern avenue began at the eastern edge of the Ciudadela, behind the Pyramid of Quetzalcóatl. The Street of the Dead continued southwards beyond the Ciudadela and the Great Compound for 3km (2 miles).

TOWERING MONUMENTS:
TIKAL

In the dense jungle of the Petén region, Tikal began to expand from a village *c.*500–300BC. By 300AD it was a major city, celebrating in stone the achievements of a great dynasty of kings. At its greatest extent in the 8th century AD, the city – with extensive environs covering about 16sq km (6sq miles) – was home to a population of 60,000.

CYCLICAL REBUILDING

The building of Tikal was a massive feat of construction. The main temples, tombs, ceremonial buildings and elite residences covered 2.5sq km (1sq mile). Moreover, most of the city's main buildings were refashioned and reconstructed many times. By Mesoamerican tradition, new structures were erected directly above and encompassing their predecessors. In Tikal, the building of the North Acropolis, a collection of pyramid temple-tombs, began as early as 250BC. Over the centuries the Acropolis floor was re-laid 20 times, so that the final layer was a full 10m (33ft) higher than the first. Scholars believe that the city must have supported a full-time force of stonemasons, sculptors, painters and labourers to carry out this cyclical building and rebuilding.

The centre of the ceremonial complex was the Great Plaza. To its north lay the North Acropolis, burial ground of kings. Many times rebuilt, it consisted in its final form of a large rectangular platform, 100m by 80m (325ft by 260ft), supporting eight royal temple-tombs built *c.*AD250–550. Subsequently, four further temples were built on a second platform along the southern extremity of the North Acropolis, giving via stairways on to the Great Plaza.

TWIN MORTUARY MONUMENTS

Facing one another on the eastern and western sides of the Great Plaza rose Temple I and Temple II. Temple I, which climbs in nine terraces to a height of 50m (164ft) on the eastern side, was built as

the funerary temple of King Ah Cacau (AD682–734). He was the first member of Tikal's dynasty to be buried outside the North Acropolis. Temple II, rising in three levels to a height of 42m (138ft), supports a sacred building that might have been set up to honour Ah Cacau's queen: the remains of a wooden lintel from this temple bear a portrait of a royal woman.

To the west and east of the Great Plaza lay other plazas. Behind Temple I lay the East Plaza, containing a ball court and a rectangular collection of buildings thought to have been used as a market. From the East Plaza, a *sacbé* known to archaeologists as the Mendez Causeway

Above: The stairs leading to the summit of Temple I rise at an angle of more than 70°.

led south-east past a collection of palaces now called Group G for 0.5 km (0.3 miles) to Temple VI. This temple is also known as the Temple of the Inscriptions because stonemasons carved a record of Tikal's dynastic history on the rear and sides of the roof comb that rose above its summit temple. Labourers built Temple VI during or just after the reign of Ah Cacau's son, Yax Kin (AD734–46). A stela celebrating Yax Kin's accession was erected at the foot of the great pyramid. South of the East Plaza was the Central

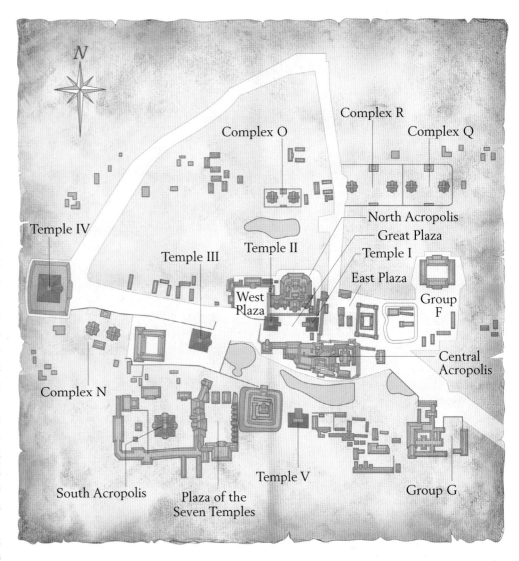

Acropolis, a vast palace containing buildings arranged around courtyards. This was probably the official residence of Tikal's ruling dynasty. Farther south beyond one of the city's many reservoirs rose Temple V, Tikal's second tallest structure at 57m (185ft), the temple-tomb of an as yet unidentified ruler. This southernmost region of the ceremonial centre also included another area of royal tombs, the South Acropolis, and the Plaza of the Seven Temples, which in addition to seven temple-shrines gave on to numerous palaces to south and west. It contained a triple ball court, with three pitches, which is unique in Mesoamerica. Beyond this plaza to the west, labourers built the Lost World complex, which contained a platform on its western edge and three platforms on its eastern side aligned with equinoctial sunrises – like the Group E arrangement of pyramids in the Maya city of Uaxactún.

Behind Temple II, a *sacbé* now known as the Tozzer Causeway led westwards to Temple IV, 70m (230ft) high and the tallest building in Tikal. This structure was built for King Yax Kin (AD734–746). Two surviving wooden lintels above the

Below: This view of the North Acropolis is from the heights of Temple I.

doorway to the temple-shrine on the summit of the artificial mountain record the date 9.15.10.0.0. in the Maya Long Count (AD741). A *sacbé* now called the Maudslay Causeway ran north to a collection of twin pyramid groups.

Temple III, which lay to the south of the Tozzer Causeway, was the last pyramid temple erected at Tikal. It was probably the mortuary shrine of King Chitam (AD768–794). A stela erected at its base was carved with the date 9.19.0.0.0. (AD810). Only one later dated monument was raised at Tikal, a stela of 10.2.0.0.0. (AD869) in the Great Plaza. By the end of the 9th century the city had been abandoned to the encroaching vegetation and to groups of squatters.

TWIN PYRAMID GROUPS

At Tikal, several rulers erected twin pyramid groups to mark the close of a *katun* or period of twenty 360-day years (a total of 7,200 days). The groups consisted of

Above: Four sacbeob *(causeways) link groups of sacred buildings in central Tikal.*

two pyramids, each with a flat top and four access stairways, symmetrically arranged on the west and east edges of a plaza, with an enclosure containing an altar and a stela on the plaza's northern edge and a building with nine doorways on its southern edge. These groups have been found only at Tikal, save examples at Yaxha and Ixlu. The first at Tikal was erected in the early years of the 6th century AD in the East Plaza and reused several times. In the late 7th century AD, King Ah Cacau (AD682–734) erected a twin pyramid group to celebrate the end of the first *katun* following his accession. Its altar was marked with the date 9.13.0.0.0. (18 March AD692). From this occasion until AD790, a new group was erected for each *katun*-ending. The largest (known as Twin-Pyramid Group 4E-4) was built in AD771 by King Chitam.

PACAL'S GLORY:
PALENQUE

The city of Palenque at the northern edge of the Chiapas highlands in Mexico, site of the ornate 7th-century tomb of King Pacal that is one of the glories of Mesoamerica, was distinctly different from Tikal and other great Maya cities of the Classic Period.

It contained no forests of carved stelae, no wide ceremonial plazas, no great *sacbé* or causeways, no acropolis of royal tombs. Its buildings were adorned with stucco sculpture and carved reliefs that pioneered naturalistic portraiture of royal figures. It gave pride of place at the centre of the city to the royal palace, home of the living king, rather than – as at Tikal – to temple-tombs housing the remains of divine ancestors.

Palenque appears to have risen to a position of power in the reign of King Pacal (*r.* AD615–83). Most of the surviving parts of the city date from his reign or later and the oldest surviving use of the city's emblem glyph was cut during his time.

PACAL'S PIONEERS
Pacal began a major programme of building in AD647, raising the temple Olvidado ('Unnoticed Shrine'), around half a kilometre to the south of the palace in the city centre. His architect-builders pioneered the use of the thin walls and numerous wide doorways that would become a distinctive feature of Palenque architecture. The temple, standing on an

Above: The lid of Pacal's sarcophagus shows the king falling down the cross-shaped Tree of Life into the underworld.

escarpment and reached by four stretches of stairs linked by platforms, had three doorways giving on to two inner rooms. Inscriptions on the north façade, carved within round cartouches, identified the king as the son of his father, Kan-Bahlum Mo', and of his mother, Lady Zac-Kuk.

THE KING'S PALACE
Pacal proceeded to develop the palace complex. On the large palace platform originally constructed by his predecessors, he built the royal residences identified as Houses E, C, B and A and laid out the expansive East Court. He commissioned sculptors to decorate the palace walls with stucco portrait masks, hieroglyphs, supernatural symbols and sacred scenes. To the south he began work

Left: In the eastern part of the city centre, the temples of the Cross, the Foliated Cross and the Sun celebrated Pacal's dynasty.

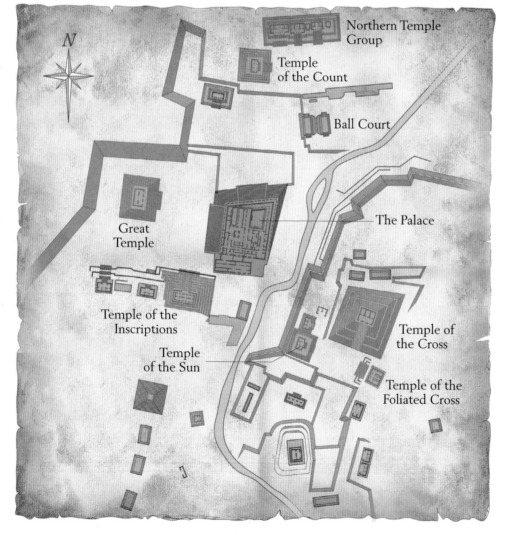

Northern Temple Group

Temple of the Count

Ball Court

Great Temple

The Palace

Temple of the Inscriptions

Temple of the Sun

Temple of the Cross

Temple of the Foliated Cross

Above: The Palace tower at Palenque commands wide-ranging views of the green Chiapas countryside.

on the great Temple of the Inscriptions, beneath which his tomb was prepared, ready for his eventual death in AD683.

Pacal's son Chan-Bahlum (r. AD684–702) completed the Temple of the Inscriptions, which rose to a height of 25m (82ft) and was topped with a temple containing five wide doorways and a roof comb. The portions of the temple facing the court were decorated with painted stucco reliefs that depicted the new king receiving his divine sanction to rule from great Pacal.

POWER OF THE ROYAL LINE

Next, Chan-Bahlum erected three shrines – the Temple of the Cross, the Temple of the Foliated Cross and the Temple of the Sun – facing one another across a plaza in the eastern part of the city centre. They each represented one of the three levels of the Maya universe. The Temple of the Cross, situated in the north, was linked to the heavens; the Temple of the Foliated Cross, in the easterly direction of the rising sun, was associated with the earth; and the Temple of the Sun, in the westerly direction of the setting sun, was identified with the underworld. They contained carvings celebrating Chan-Bahlum's links to his divine father.

A panel in the Temple of the Cross showed Pacal and Chan-Bahlum on either side of the ceiba world tree that the Maya believed connected the three levels of the universe. The carving in the Temple of the Foliated Cross depicted the pair on either side of a giant cob of maize bearing human heads, a reference to the Maya creation myth in which the gods Huracán and Gucumatz made the first humans from maize. The image in the Temple of the Sun presented Chan-Bahlum and his father adopting a martial pose, one to each side of a battle shield adorned with spears and the jaguar god of the underworld.

Archaeologists have not found Chan-Bahlum's tomb, but many believe it may lie beneath the Temple of Cross since this was the northern member of the group and burials were generally laid in the direction of the north.

Chan-Bahlum II's brother, Kan-Xul II, rebuilt the palace complex and may have erected the curious four-storey tower that was probably an astronomical observatory. This structure has no counterpart anywhere else in the Maya realm. Scholar Linda Schele has suggested that the tower was built as a tribute to King Pacal. An observer standing at the top of the tower at the winter solstice would see the sun set directly on to the Temple of the Inscriptions, thus going down into the underworld by way of Pacal's tomb.

With Kan-Xul II's reign the great building work of Palenque came to a close: the king was captured in AD711 by the rival city of Toniná and, after a long captivity, was beheaded there. Before the century was out, Palenque became one of the first Maya cities to cease cutting dates in inscriptions and so enter the historical silence of the celebrated collapse of the 8th and 9th centuries. The last inscribed date at Palenque was AD799.

CITY OF THE JAGUAR KINGS:
YAXCHILÁN

Yaxchilán was built on a hill overlooking a bend in the Usumacinta river in Chiapas, Mexico. The city's origins lie in the 4th century AD, when it may have been founded as a satellite of Tikal, but it was developed primarily by two kings of the 8th century: Lord Shield Jaguar (*r.* AD681–742) and his son Bird Jaguar (*r.* AD752–68). From the date of its investigation by Sir Alfred Maudslay, the British gentleman-scholar hailed as the 'father of Maya archaeology', Yaxchilán has been celebrated for its magnificently carved door lintels, some of which have been on display in the British Museum in London since Maudslay had them shipped to Europe in 1882.

TOMB FOR A QUEEN
The city's main ceremonial area lies on an artificial terrace above the Usumacinta. The large plaza runs parallel to the river. On its south side, Lord Shield Jaguar built a structure known to archaeologists as

Below: A detail shows the stone lintels of Yaxchilán's palaces. The remains of a stone throne lie before the building.

Above: Stucco sculptures once decorated the roof of Temple 33. Standing on high ground, the vast temple dominates the city centre.

Temple 23, or the Queen's House, that was dedicated to his principal wife, Lady Xoc, in 9.14.14.13.17 (726AD), the 45th year of his 61-year reign. This building contains celebrated door-lintel carvings of Lady Xoc performing rites of ritual bloodletting by running a spiked cord across her tongue; of Lady Xoc having a sacred experience through the Vision Snake of King Yat Balam, founder of the dynasty; and of Shield Jaguar, accompanied by his wife, donning battle garb as he prepared to set out in search of sacrificial captives. Temple 24, erected on the western edge of the Queen's House, recorded her death in AD749 and almost certainly contains her grave.

Earlier, in AD732, the king dedicated Temple 44, also known as the War Memorial as it commemorated a series of noble captives taken by Lord Shield Jaguar. Among other sacred structures erected by Shield Jaguar was Temple 41, at the summit of the hill that rises behind the ceremonial terrace. This structure commemorated celebrations of a sacred solstice in 9.15.9.17.16 (AD741).

STRUGGLE TO SUCCEED
Lord Shield Jaguar was succeeded by his son Bird Jaguar. The succession was not without its difficulties. Bird Jaguar was not the king's son by his principal wife, Lady Xoc, but by another royal bride, Lady Evening Star, who is thought by scholars to have come originally from Calakmul. Whether because the succession was contested by a son of Lady Xoc, or because Bird Jaguar's connection to the royal line of Calakmul made him unpopular, there was a gap of ten years between the death of Lord Shield Jaguar in AD742 and the coronation of Bird Jaguar in AD752. Afterwards these difficulties contributed greatly to construction in Yaxchilan's ceremonial quarter: Bird Jaguar erected many buildings and stelae promoting his right to the throne and, once his position was secure, poured his construction efforts into securing the succession of his son Chel Te.

In the course of these projects, Bird Jaguar III rebuilt most of the ceremonial centre and also extended the city to the south-east. Before his time the main plaza was crossed by gullies, but he had the area flattened and smoothed. In a reign of 16 years, he built 12 sacred buildings and raised 33 monuments. Much of the work complemented that of his father. He built a new hilltop structure, Temple 40, alongside Shield Jaguar's Temple 41 and in front raised a carved stela that celebrated both his father and mother and made reference to the solstice celebration of

Below: Bird Jaguar wears an elaborate costume and headdress and holds the manikin *sceptre, symbol of royal authority.*

AD741 in which, as a prince, Bird Jaguar had shared duties with his father. Alongside Temple 23, which his father had built to honour Lady Xoc, Bird Jaguar erected Temple 21, which was adorned with lintels representing Bird Jaguar and his wife enacting the same scenes celebrated in the lintels of the earlier temple. One showed Bird Jaguar watching a wife letting blood from a tongue, another showed a wife encountering the Vision Serpent and a third showed Bird Jaguar in his military glory.

LINTEL RECORDS

Behind Temple 23, Bird Jaguar built another sacred building, known as Temple 33, where the steps were carved with scenes of rituals involving the ball game: one showed Bird Jaguar enacting a sacrifice with noble victims bound in the form of balls from the ball game. On the lintel above the temple doorway, Bird Jaguar rose in his full glory at his accession, dressed in the costume of a Maya king and holding the *manikin* sceptre. Other lintels at the temple depict Bird Jaguar and his son performing a ritual and Bird Jaguar again in the company of a leading noble. Many of the nobles of Bird Jaguar's reign are represented in door-lintel carvings and on stelae: scholars suggest that the king may have needed support in order to consolidate his position and so was forced to share status with these lords by including them in the historical record.

THE ELEGANT CITY:
COPÁN

The great Maya city of Copán in western Honduras – celebrated in particular for the ornate, almost florid style of its sculpture – lay at an altitude of 700m (2,296ft) in a river valley surrounded by mountains. This attractive, well-watered, fertile spot alongside the river Copán was the site of villages from at least 1000BC.

FIRST STAGES OF THE ACROPOLIS
The city developed and rose to prominence in the 5th–8th centuries AD, when it became capital of the most powerful state in the south-eastern Maya region.

Below: The city's extensive ceremonial centre was laid out on a north–south axis on the west bank of the River Copán.

The ceremonial and sacred centre of the site measured some 300m by 600m (984 by 1,968ft). In the southern half was a raised platform known to archaeologists as the Acropolis, built up over generations and incorporating two great courts and a number of temples. In the northern part lay a ball court, a celebrated stairway carved with hieroglyphs detailing dynastic history and the vast Great Plaza, site of numerous stelae and carved 'altars' or thrones. *Sacbé* or causeways left the great plaza running north-east and west: to the north-east lay an elite residential area known to archaeologists as Las Sepulturas.

Copán's kings in the 8th century claimed to be part of an unbroken dynastic succession of 18 monarchs running

Above: A decorative mask, perhaps of the sun god, adorns the Stairway of the Jaguars (AD200–900) in the East Court.

back to the founder they identified as Yax Kuk Mo' (c.AD426–37). In his reign, the buildings of the Acropolis structure – first laid out before AD400 – were added to and expanded.

SHRINE TO THE CITY'S FOUNDER
One of the Acropolis buildings, subsequently built over and called the Papagayo, appears to have been a shrine to Yax Kuk Mo': it contained a stela that identified the dynasty's second king as the son of the founder and recalled rites performed by Yax Kuk Mo' on an auspicious date in 9.0.0.0.0. (AD435). Contemporary with the Papagayo structure, the first of several version of the Copán ball court was laid out to the north of the Acropolis.

The Acropolis was established at its final size by as early as c.AD450–500. At this time, a higher platform occupied the south-eastern quarter of the Acropolis, while the northern part consisted of a lower area of elite residential and administrative buildings arranged around three adjacent courtyards.

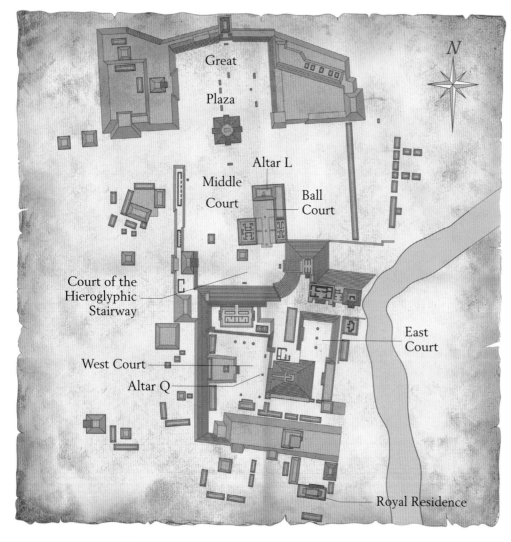

Great
Plaza

N

Altar L

Middle
Court

Ball
Court

Court of the
Hieroglyphic
Stairway

East
Court

West Court

Altar Q

Royal Residence

The seventh king of the dynasty, Waterlily Jaguar, may have built a two-level platform that arose in the mid-6th century AD at the eastern edge of the Acropolis's East Court. Hieroglyphs on one of its stairs named the king and reported that he built a palace, called the House of Mah Kina Yax Kuk Mo, on the southern edge of the Great Plaza.

Also around this period, builders on the Acropolis raised a two-storey temple with many rooms known to scholars as Rosalila. Its façade was covered with brightly painted stucco carving of birds and the god Itzamná.

Almost the whole of the 8th century AD was taken up with the reigns of two kings, Butz' Chan (AD578–628) and Smoke Jaguar (AD628–95). In their reigns, Copán developed into a powerful city state with wide influence.

Smoke Jaguar may have begun the final restructuring of the Acropolis. To celebrate the calendar period-ending of AD652, he erected a series of stelae at both the eastern and western limits to the valley of Copán. These may have been intended to mark the limits of his territories or may have been aligned with astronomical events.

CLAIM OF GREATNESS

Smoke Jaguar's successor King 18-Rabbit (AD695–738) carried out a great deal of construction work in the central part of the city. King 18-Rabbit erected a great temple-palace, identified by *witz* ('sacred mountain') masks in its decorative carving as a holy peak, on the northern edge of the Acropolis East Court. This was the last of several royal structures on the site. He laid out a series of stelae bearing his portrait in the Great Plaza. One of these, Stela A of AD731, was inscribed with the emblem glyphs of Tikal, Calakmul and Palenque as well as that of Copán and has been interpreted as a statement of Copán's status as an equal among these illustrious states.

King 18-Rabbit also built or completed the building of the Great Ball Court, the final version of several courts constructed on a site north of the Acropolis. An inscription on its eastern wall recorded the ball court's completion as 9.15.6.8.13 – a day in AD738. Just 113 days after this date, the king was captured and executed by

Left: Temple 22. The main door was carved to represent the mouth of the Witz or sacred mountain – and so was seen as an entrance to the spirit realms of the underworld.

Above: The Hieroglyphic Stairway contains 63 steps carved with 2,500 glyphs recording the history of Yax Kuk Mo's dynasty.

King Cauac Sky of Quiriguá. The scholars Linda Schele and David Friedel have suggested that 18-Rabbit probably met with disaster during a campaign intended to furnish him with sacrificial victims for the ritual dedication of the ball court.

To the south of the ball court, the later King Smoke Monkey (AD738–49) began the Hieroglyphic Stairway that recorded the kings of the dynasty to that date. He also built a council house, believed to have been used for meetings of lineage officials, which was dedicated in AD746. His successor Smoke Shell (AD749–63) completed and dedicated the Hieroglyphic Stairway in the first year of his reign.

The 16th king Yax Pac (AD763–820) commissioned and dedicated the monument known as Altar Q, which bore the images of all 16 kings of the dynasty and featured the first king, Yax Kuk Mo' handing the sceptre of power to Yax Pac. He also built the structure known by archaeologists as Temple 11 facing north across the plaza bounded by the Hieroglyphic Stairway towards the Great Plaza.

PRIDE OF THE TOLTECS:
TOLLÁN

The celebrated home of the Toltecs was an extensive city encompassing some 13km (8 miles). Its population of up to 60,000 was spread out in outlying areas and lived by farming, mining basalt, making chert tools and working obsidian. The ceremonial area at the centre was precisely laid out 18 degrees east of north. It contained two pyramids, two plazas, a council hall and two ball courts.

The most important structure, facing on to the main plaza from its eastern edge was the one known as Building C. This was once a pyramid temple platform, but Aztec pilgrims dismantled the temple and removed the stone facing. All that remains is the small mountain of rock and earth that formed the core of the pyramid, together with a few pieces of carved stone. Scholars believe that the temple would have been a modest two-room building with an antechamber and a shrine, but do not know which god was honoured there.

Below: Sacred snakes feast on human skeletons on the coatepantli *or serpent wall that runs along Building B's north side.*

IN QUETZALCÓATL'S HONOUR

To the north of the plaza, Toltec builders erected a five-stepped temple pyramid sacred to Quetzalcóatl. On the top of the pyramid the temple roof was supported by columns, some in the shape of warriors 3.5m (11ft) tall. Before the temple, a reclining *chacmool* would have been placed. The warrior figures were broken up and cast into a ditch, perhaps by looters, but have been reassembled and returned to their place of duty on the top of the pyramid.

Stonemasons cut panels to face the tiers of the pyramid. They represented a human head emerging from a monster's jaws, an image tentatively identified as Quetzalcóatl Tlahuizcalpantecuhtli, the god in his form as Venus the Morning Star. They also showed eagles, jaguars and coyotes consuming human hearts. Traces of paint sometimes show that these would have been painted bright colours.

THE BURNT PALACE

To the east of the temple lay a secular building that archaeologists call the Palace of Quetzalcóatl or Edificio 1, while to the west was a vast building measuring 59m

Above: Atlantean figures on the Temple of Quetzalcóatl. Their eyes and mouths were probably inlaid with obsidian or shell.

by 91m (200ft by 300ft) and called the Palacio Quemado – or 'Burnt Palace', because it was largely consumed by flames. Its builders set it out in three halls with colonnades that face south on to a long gallery. The Burnt Palace was probably an administrative building used for meetings, receptions and storing trade and tribute items. Gamblers would have gathered there to play *patolli*: three boards for the game are marked on the floor.

In the west of the central area lay a ball court and the space between the main plaza and the court was probably the marketplace. In the centre of the main plaza stood a square shrine around 1.7m (5ft 6in) tall, built in the *talud-tablero* style of Teotihuacán and with one staircase on each of its four sides.

TWIN STYLES:
CHICHÉN ITZÁ

The main buildings of Chichén Itzá were laid out in two styles in different areas of the city. Three structures, mainly in the Puuc architectural style, later called the Nunnery, the Annex and the Iglesia occupied the southernmost part of central Chichén Itzá. The Akabdzib, a building in similar style to the east of this group, has been dated to *c*.AD869. To the west lay the Casa Colorado or 'Red House', with a frieze commemorating noble bloodletting ceremonies in AD869 and AD870.

North-east of the Nunnery group, lay the curious circular building later called the Caracol (from the Spanish for snail) because the spiral staircase within it was held to resemble a snail's shell. A stela found on the building's upper platform dated it to AD906. It may have been a circular temple or an observatory.

THE NORTHERN COMPLEX

A *sacbé* ran northwards from the Caracol to the northern group of buildings, comprising the Temple of Kukulcán, the Temple of the Warriors, a ball court and the Group of the Thousand Columns. The complex was arranged precisely 18 degrees east of true north.

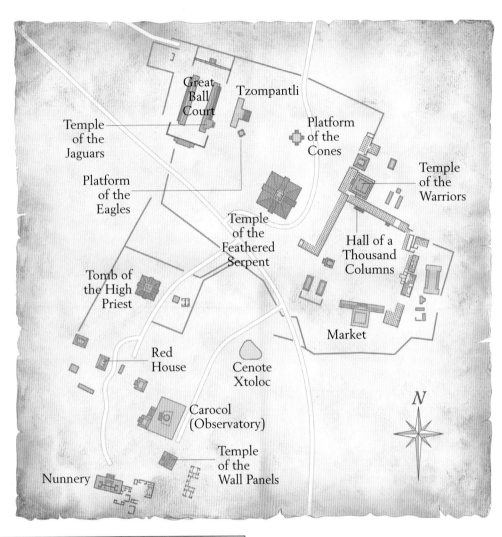

Above: Puuc-style buildings were in the south, Toltec-style structures in the north.

HOLY WATERS

The city made use of two major *cenotes* or natural wells formed when the limestone rock in the area collapsed to reveal water gathered beneath. One, the Xtoloc *cenote*, lay in the centre of the city, to the east of the causeway linking the Caracol to the northern platform. The second, the *Cenote* of Sacrifice, was the site of human sacrifice and other ritual offerings and lay to the north of the northern platform.

Left: Puuc-style carving on the façade of the Nunnery represent the the earth monster and the long-nosed rain god Chac.

HILL FORTS:
CACAXTLA, XOCHICALCO AND TEOTENANGO

In the central highlands around the Basin of Mexico, three fortified hilltop settlements flourished from the 7th and 8th centuries AD onward, at the time that Teotihuacán and Monte Albán were in decline. Historians believe that as the powers of Teotihuacán and Monte Albán waned, the highland cities began to reassert their influence. The cities of Cacaxtla, overlooking the Tlaxcala valley, Xochicalco in western Morelos and Teotenango in the Toluca valley exhibited a common style in the use of glyphs and counting systems. The first two cities largely faded from prominence after AD900, but Teotenango was an important independent centre until its conquest by the Aztec *tlatoani* Axayácatl in 1476.

CACAXTLA

Celebrated for its mural paintings, Cacaxtla rose to prominence after *c.*AD650 in a well-appointed hilltop location that had been occupied since the Preclassic Period. The hill on which Cacaxtla stood

Below: The South Plaza at Teotenango appears to have been laid out as a homage to the Ciudadela or Citadel in Teotihuacán.

would have been an obvious choice for settlement, for it enjoyed a plentiful water supply from its own springs and was an easily defended position commanding views of the Tlaxcala valley and beyond.

Archaeologists have discovered that there were at least five stages of construction at Cacaxtla. Its builders laid out the ceremonial site on the hilltop on a rough north–south axis. They erected a palace, temple-shrines, altars and several corridor-like structures. The corridors were part of a distinctive construction thought to be associated with the system of defences: a series of long, low buildings arranged around patios over several levels and joined by staircases, which would have been easily defended in times of conflict.

Cacaxtla's patios and doorways were the sites of human offerings, mainly of babies and children: 208 skeletons have been found, including those of 199 infants. These scores of young lives were probably offered as dedication sacrifices when the buildings were completed. In the sacrifices the bones were scattered randomly, together with obsidian points and scrapers, shells, figurines of animals,

Above: On Xochicalco's Temple of the Feathered Serpent, Quetzalcóatl is represented with consuming jaws.

bone needles and jewellery such as ear spools and nose plugs. From the main patio of the ceremonial area, steps led up to an elongated chamber with seven entrances painted with vividly coloured murals depicting battle scenes. The conflict might portray a ritualized blood-letting. Warriors wearing Teotihuacán-style outfits defeat others identified as Maya by their deliberately deformed heads. Some of the Maya are naked and painted turquoise blue, the traditional colour of sacrifice.

A stairway from the chamber led to a structure now called Building A by archaeologists, which was dominated by four large painted figures on either side of the doorway. One figure, believed to represent the moon, is depicted as a jaguar-man releasing drops of life-giving water from a sceptre on to the prone body of a jaguar-serpent. Another figure, in similar costume, pours water from a pot marked with symbols of the rain god Tláloc.

In the south-west of the ceremonial centre builders erected what appears to be a temple to Venus the Morning Star (Tlahuizcalpantecuhtli). On either side of a doorway artists painted two large figures, each wearing a five-pointed half-star that was a well known symbol of Venus.

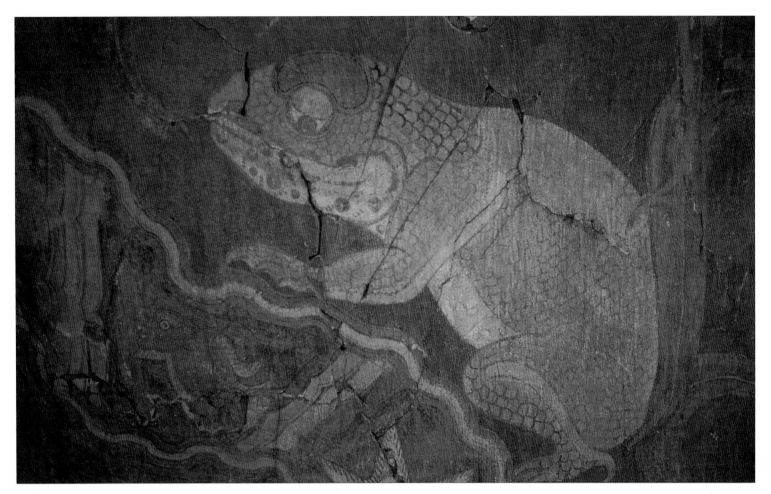

XOCHICALCO

At Xochicalco, builders cut deep ditches, walls and ramps to fortify much of the lower part of the hill and laid out the residential and ceremonial areas of the settlement on terraces cut into the upper slopes. They built causeways to connect areas of the site and to link the city to

Left: The Temple of the Feathered Serpent stands in the centre of the main square in Xochicalco, laid out on a terraced acropolis.

Above: This blue-skinned toad appears in Cacaxtla's Red Temple. The plant behind him bears 'fruit' of human heads.

nearby settlements. One connected the ceremonial and residential hilltop to the ball court, which was laid out on the lower hill with rings on the side walls.

In the main ceremonial area, artisans carved the Pyramid of the Feathered Serpent with images of high-ranking warriors and lists of places that paid tribute to the city's military hierarchy, together with Feathered Serpent reliefs and glyphs relating to fire ceremonies and to the ritual calendar. About 30m (100ft) south of the pyramid, workers built a sacred structure now called the Temple of the Stelae, because it contained three expertly carved stone posts, each bearing a human face and a set of glyphs. Scholars still debate the meaning of these stelae. Some suggest that they represent sky and fertility deities and were used in

agricultural rites. Others claim that they were, like the carving on the pyramid, a celebration of Xochicalco's military might. The stelae were deliberately damaged and broken, then buried in pieces, but scholars have gathered the fragments and put them back together.

TEOTENANGO

At Teotenango the land falls away sharply from the hilltop on three sides, while on its northern edge labourers erected a vast defensive wall. On the hilltop, from about AD750 onwards, settlers laid out a large ritual and civic area with a number of plazas, altars, temple platforms, a ball court, residential areas, streets and markets. The builders were clearly influenced by Teotihuacán and paid tribute in their own construction to the architecture and sculptural achievements of that great city. In particular, the South Plaza at Teotenango, enclosed by low buildings with stairways, appears to be a reproduction of the great Citadel at Teotihuacán. Teotenango's highest building was the Temple of the Serpent, adorned with serpent carvings.

TARASCAN STRONGHOLD:
TZINTZUNTZAN

The Tarascans laid out their capital, Tzintzuntzan, beneath wooded highlands on the shores of Lake Pátzcuaro in Michoacán, western Mexico, at an altitude of 2,130m (7,000ft). An army of labourers, probably prisoners or workers provided as tribute by peoples humbled in the course of the Tarascans' empire-building wars, created a vast east-facing terrace measuring 440m by 260m (1,440ft by 850ft). Here they built, in line, five temples on terraced circular platforms. The temples have been destroyed but the platforms, called *yácatas*, remain. They were faced with great slabs of stone.

Nearby, the Tarascans' labour force raised a building now known as El Palacio, with many rooms arranged around a patio together with a roofed, narrow gallery defined by rectangular pillars. This might have been a royal palace or a residential area for elite priests, conveniently situated close to the temples supported by the *yácatas*.

A KING'S TEMPLE BURIAL?

The *yácata* temple mounds might also have been mortuary monuments. Archaeologists found graves they believe to be sacrificial burials of servants in the mound they call Yácata V. One grave, in the south-east corner, contained five women, buried with copper ornaments,

Below: The yacátas *were faced with stone veneer, which does not survive here. Some 40,000 people once lived in Tzintzuntzan.*

bells and ritual vessels. Another, in the north, contained nine women buried with arms linked together and accompanied by rich deposits including obsidian lip plugs, turquoise ear plugs, silver tweezers and gold earrings, along with copper bells and axes. The burials might have been made to accompany one of the Tarascan kings on his voyage into the afterlife. The royal grave probably lies nearby, but has not yet been found.

HOME OF THE HUMMINGBIRDS

The Tarascans were skilled producers of gold and silver jewellery and of copper axe heads. They and their predecessors in western Mexico were the pioneers of metalworking techniques in Mesoamerica, using knowledge and skills passed along trade routes into western Mexico from Colombia and Peru. They were the only Mesoamericans to use metal weapons.

The Tarascans were also known for their high level of skill in weaving, in particular for making mosaics of feathers using the plumes of local hummingbirds. Their capital's name, Tzintzuntzan, meant 'home of the hummingbirds'.

Above: Circular platforms or yacátas *survive at Tzintzuntzan without the temples that once stood on top of them.*

TARASCANS DEFEATED

Tarascan skill in making weapons, together with great martial spirit, kept all-comers at bay. Even the imperial Aztec army in the reign of Axayácatl (1469–81) did not succeed in defeating the people of Tzintzuntzan in 1479. However, in 1522 the Spanish adventurer Captain Olíd, who had served under Cortés in the siege of Tenochtitlán, took the Tarascan capital without a struggle.

When Cortés had been marching on Tenochtitlán in 1519 he had sent emissaries to Tzintzuntzan asking for military help. Rather than send a reply, the king ordered his priests to sacrifice the Spaniards to the gods. However, the Europeans had unwittingly brought a hidden weapon, for a smallpox epidemic swept through the ranks of the Tarascans and carried off the king. When the Spanish returned three years later, the new king did not dare to fight the soldiers who had brought down the Aztecs.

CITY OF PRIESTS:
MITLA

The elegant palaces of Mitla, which lie at an altitude of 1,480m (4,855ft) on the eastern edge of the Tlacolula valley in Oaxaca, were built on an ancient settlement inhabited by Zapotecs from as early as 1200BC. Mitla rose to prominence in the Postclassic Period following the decline of nearby Monte Albán. From c.AD900 the Mixtecs left their mark on the site. Archaeologists have found numerous Zapotec tombs at the site, which they believe was a sacred burial place. Its Zapotec name was Lyobaa ('Site of Burials'), while the name of Mitla was Nahuatl for 'Realm of the Dead'.

A CITY LAID OUT

The city was laid out in five groups of thin, elongated structures arranged around rectangular courtyards. Beneath the South Group, which was on the southern bank of the Rio Grande de Mitla, archaeologists found a collection of cruciform tombs with elite burials in them. The

Below: The Hall of the Columns still bears traces of its original colour. It takes its name from the stone pillars standing within it.

other buildings were arranged on the rocky hillside opposite. To the west lay the Arroyo Group and the Adobe Group, while the Group of the Columns sat in the east and the Churches Group occupied the north-east of the settlement. Gravediggers laid out more tombs beneath the Group of the Columns.

INFLUENTIAL MOSAICS

At Mitla, Zapotec craftsmen arranged cut stones in a mosaic to form a decorative fretwork and other geometric patterns on façades and door frames. Architectural historians believe these designs might have been influenced by the development of geometric decoration patterns in the Puuc style of north–central Yucatán.

The Zapotec builders used beams to support the roofs, which were gently sloping, so that rainwater would drain off into the courtyards. They made the walls of mud and stone and covered them with plaster or trachyte.

The Group of the Columns was divided into north and south courtyards. From the North Court there was access through a hall named for its six huge

Above: The intricate geometric carving on the outer walls of the Hall of the Columns is remarkably well preserved.

columns to an enclosed courtyard surrounded by four rooms. Historians believe this was the residence of Mitla's priestly elite. The courtyard decorations represent Quetzalcóatl in the form of a stylized celestial serpent. Some of Mitla's rooms were decorated by Mixtec painters.

CENTRE OF THE WORLD:
TENOCHTITLÁN

Like the Teotihuacános before them, the Aztecs laid out their capital in four quarters – according to legend, on the command of the tribal lord Huitzilopochtli himself. At the centre stood the vast ceremonial precinct containing the Templo Mayor. Nearby was the great imperial palace and the vast market square of Tlatelolco. Causeways 3.5m (12ft) in width left the island city to north, west and south, connecting the mainland. On the island the causeways became great thoroughfares that terminated in the sacred complex at the city's heart. Fresh water was carried into the city by aqueduct from Coyoacan.

Each of the *capultin* or tribal groups had its own land, with sacred precincts and temple. There were 12–15 *capultin* in each of the four quarters. Major rites and important celebrations were held in the main ceremonial precincts. People moved about on foot or by canoe along the canals that crisscrossed the city.

THE TEMPLE GROUNDS

The sacred quarters of Tenochtitlán were enclosed by a wall in a large square area about 365m (1,200ft) on each side. The wall was known as the *coatepantli* ('Serpent Wall'), because its outside was carved with snake images. At the eastern end the Templo Mayor rose to a height of 45m (150ft), supporting twin temples. On the northern part of the temple platform stood a shrine to Tláloc, with a *chacmool* before it, while on the southern part was the holy place of Huitzilopochtli, before which stood a blood-drenched sacrificial stone.

THE IMPORTANCE OF CLEANLINESS

Aztec cities were kept extremely clean. In Tenochtitlán no fewer than 1,000 workers swept the city's public places daily and public toilets were built on the impressive causeways that led into the city. Aqueducts carried clean drinking water into the teeming capital from springs in the hills around. The Aztecs took a bath every day – which would have been unheard of in Europe at the time – and used herbal preparations as deodorants and to sweeten the breath. At every meeting with the conquistadors, the *tlatoani's* courtiers sprinkled the Europeans with incense – which the Spaniards took as a mark of respect, but which might have been a way of fumigating the air. Richer inhabitants of Tenochtitlán had their own steam bath in or alongside their home, and there were many public steam baths for poorer citizens.

Climbing towards these temples from ground level, a priest first took a staircase decorated with painted stucco designs honouring the Feathered Serpent Quetzalcóatl and with frogs, which were symbols of Tláloc. The steps led him to a lower platform, on which a vast stone carving of moon goddess Coyolxauhqui was set in the floor before the steps to the Huitzilopochtli shrine. From this place steps rose steeply to the temple above. When a victim's body was cast down from the shrine of Huitzilopochtli, it would fall on the features of the god's mother, Coyolxauhqui. The Templo Mayor was flanked by other sacred structures. To the north were the military

Left: Scholars now believe the temple north of the Templo Mayor to have been the warriors' quarters, the House of Eagles.

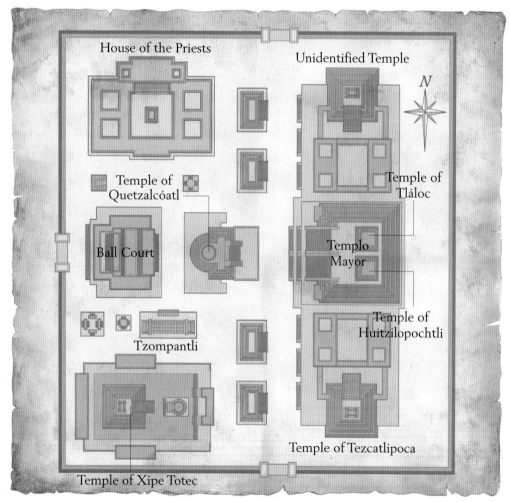

House of the Priests

Unidentified Temple

N

Temple of Quetzalcóatl

Temple of Tláloc

Ball Court

Templo Mayor

Temple of Huitzilopochtli

Tzompantli

Temple of Tezcatlipoca

Temple of Xipe Totec

quarters of elite warriors, called the House of Eagles, while to the south rose a temple to Tezcatlipoca. West of the Templo Mayor stood a circular temple holy to Quetzalcóatl in his guise as wind god Éhecatl and beyond that, at the western limit of the ritual enclosure, was a ball court.

THE TEMPLO MAYOR OVER TIME

The first temple was built c.1325, the year of the city's establishment. According to the foundation legend, the México/Aztecs built a rudimentary platform and temple from wattle and daub to honour Huitzilopochtli in the very spot at which they saw an eagle consuming a snake on a cactus, in fulfilment of a divine prophecy. Archaeologists have not been able to uncover evidence of this lowest-level structure. They do know that by c.1390, a temple building about 15m (50ft) tall stood on the site. It already supported twin temples to Huitzilopochtli and Tláloc, approached by twin staircases.

Around 1431, three years after the foundation of the Triple Alliance of Tenochtitlán, Texcoco and Tlacopan, the Aztecs built a much larger temple on the same site, entirely enclosing the previously existing structure.

They made further improvements in 1454, under the rule of Moctezuma I (1440–69), adding decorative elements and making many offerings. In particular, builders added a new staircase to the western face of the pyramid and skilled

Above: The vast Templo Mayor, 45m (150ft) tall, dwarfed the rounded temple of Quetzalcóatl-Éhecatl that stood before it.

craftsmen laid a greenstone sculpture of Coyolxauhqui at its foot. This was the forerunner of the celebrated Coyolxauhqui stone, which artisans carved in 1469 under the rule of Axayácatl (1469–81).

Later rulers Tizoc, Ahuítzotl and Moctezuma II demonstrated their devotion by making improvements and additions to the temple in 1482, 1486 and 1502 respectively.

A SACRED SPOT

The México/Aztecs built up their capital in a sanctified setting on twin islands in Lake Texcoco. Setting the city on an island had great religious significance, for it made Tenochtitlán a recreation of the México/Aztecs' legendary northern place of origin, Aztlán, which they believed was

land surrounded by water. It also meant that the city was a microcosm of the earth itself, a tribute to the gods' creation, for in Aztec cosmology, the earth was surrounded, like a great island, on all sides by water.

WATERWORKS

Tenochtitlán's development was due in no small part to their success in reclaiming the marshy shallows of western Lake Texcoco for *chinampa* fields, and later taking control of the established fields in the southern lakes of Chalco and Xochimilco. In the reign of Moctezuma I (1440–69), labourers built a vast 15km (10-mile) dyke to prevent the salt waters of the northern and eastern part of Lake Texcoco from polluting the freshwater areas that they were farming.

Left: The Codex Durán *represents the twin shrines, to Tláloc and Huitzilopochtli, that occupied the top of the Templo Mayor.*

Right: Sacred precinct in the heart of the city. Hernán Cortés drew this map of Tenochtitlán to send to Charles V.

CHAPTER 21

POTTERS AND WEAVERS

As royal wife Lady Xoc knelt before her kingly husband Shield Jaguar, drawing a spiky rope across her tongue to make a sacred offering of her blood, she wore an exquisitely decorated *huipil* cotton garment. The carver of this celebrated 8th-century scene on a limestone door lintel from Temple 23 in Shield Jaguar's city of Yaxchilán paid great attention to detail – and gave a tantalizing glimpse of the highly developed art of Maya weaving.

Of the work of Mesoamerican potters, weavers, basket-makers, mat-makers and feather-workers covered here, only pots survive in large numbers. This is partly because woven textiles and basket-work naturally decay while ceramic products survive unless smashed, but also because many pots were saved from everyday breakage by being put to sacred use as temple or tomb offerings. Yet although most Maya and many Aztec creations in cloth and basketwork have not survived, we know that they were intricately made and decorated. We have evidence of carved and painted images – both of people wearing woven textiles and of decorative schemes derived from textile and basket patterns. A basket shown in a mural in Chichén Itzá's Temple of the Jaguars, for example, was highly elaborate in construction and decoration. Clothes represented in carvings on Classic Period Maya stelae, in the Bonampak murals, on painted Maya pots, in Aztec statuary and in painted codices give an idea of the range and quality of Mesoamerican woven materials.

Left: The musicians shown taking part in a procession at Bonampak wear elaborate headdresses and costumes.

MILLENNIA OF POTTERY

Mesoamericans produced pottery for 4,000 years, from the beginnings of settled life in villages c.2500–2000BC until the Spanish Conquest of 1519–21. They made a variety of wares in many different finishes, reaching the apogée of their craft in the delicate portrait plates and vases made in the Maya cities of the late Classic Period. As Mesoamerican artisans produced such a range of pots, plates, cups, vases and ritual vessels, this survey is only able to select a few highlights and distinctive developments.

Below: Sea hunter. A cormorant closes in on a fish in the decorative scheme of this Maya cylinder vase (c.AD700–900).

BEGINNINGS

The first Mesoamerican potters might have picked up the necessary skills from South American incomers, for people in Ecuador and Colombia were making ceramic pieces about 1,000 years earlier than their counterparts in Mexico and Guatemala.

Early potters might have taken their basic forms from those of everyday containers . For example, neck-less jars with wide, globular bases were probably based on the shape of gourds.

From these first days in c.2500–2000BC (during the early Preclassic Period), Mesoamerican potters experimented with decoration. They added colour-slips (additional layers of clay) and polished the surface. They made incised patterns of dots and lines and used hand-modelling, adding faces or heads to the shoulders of jars. They experimented with painting pottery and using 'resist' or negative patterns to provide a contrast to the main colour and they tested the effects of different firing techniques.

In these early times, potters began to make anthropomorphic figures that probably represented the gods in rites at the household shrine. These figures were produced in considerable numbers right through to the Spanish Conquest.

A DEMAND FOR RITUAL WARES

By c.1000–400BC (the middle Preclassic Period), potters were producing tripod bowls, spouted vessels, tall-necked jars sometimes bearing handles on the neck, and cylindrical incense burners.

Artisans first produced polychrome (many-coloured) vessels by applying coloured paints in yellow, red, white and black after the vessels had been fired. They also used bichrome (two-coloured) slips or additional layers of clay on vessels. Incense burners were the first Mesoamerican ceramics to have a specialized ritual function.

Around 400BC–AD250 (the late Preclassic Period), pottery decorated with sinuous parallel lines negative to the main colour – known as Usulutan ware – was popular in Maya lands. Artisans made the pattern by applying parallel lines of wax to the pot. These melted away during firing to reveal a secondary colour beneath. Potters further developed the use of modelled decorations on vessels and their handles, particularly on incense burners. Bowls with toad decorations and clay models of mushrooms are identified by scholars as celebratory of mind-altering substances ingested by shamans, who valued a secretion of toad glands as well as certain mushrooms for their capacity to

METHODS OF PRODUCTION

From the first days of Mesoamerican pottery onwards, many householders who lived by farming probably made simple pots for their own use at home. If they developed their skills, they may have produced extra pots or plates to be sold at market. Around 250BC–AD1, towards the end of the Preclassic Period, some of these home potters began to specialize in particular forms such as vases, plates or pots. By the start of the Classic Period c.AD250, certain skilled artisans had become specialist potters who, while working from their home, made their living entirely by ceramic production and no longer worked the land. Soon after this time, elite groups appear to have established workshops of potters in cities, to supply wealthy and royal circles with the elegant handmade pottery they admired. From c.AD800–900 onwards, light-industrial centres were established to produce wares using moulds for distribution across wide areas. All these methods of production coexisted.

transform consciousness during spirit adventures and acts of divination. During the years c.AD250–550 (the early Classic Period), polychrome decoration became dominant in Maya lands. Artisans used geometric designs or bands of diminutive images in red and black on an orange/cream background. The potters of Teotihuacán were influential at this time: their small containers and brightly painted cylindrical pots with tripod legs were widely traded and copied.

PORTRAIT PLATES AND VASES
Around AD550–800 (the late Classic Period), potters and scribe-artists in city workshops of the central Maya region produced justly celebrated vases, tripod dishes, cups, pots and incense burners painted with portraits, scenes of court life and glyphs. Then in AD800–900 the spread of militaristic Putún Maya merchants from their homeland in Tabasco was accompanied by the fine-grained pots known to historians as Fine Orange Ware.

Right: This flanged and lidded bowl (c.AD250–550) is typical of Maya vessels with geometric decoration produced in the early Classic Period.

These appear to have been early examples of light-industrial production, for they came in standard sizes and with decoration produced using moulds.

In AD900–1250, artisans in the Pacific coastal regions of south-western Guatemala began to fire pots in pit kilns that were able to generate high enough temperatures to produce a glazed finish. The pots, decorated with moulding and carving, are known by historians as Plumbate Ware. They were the only glazed pots produced in Mesoamerica, although from the Classic Period on, potter-artists in Maya cities had been able to achieve a glaze-like finish. They did so by painting pots after firing and decorating them with a clear, unknown wash – perhaps a kind of resin – that scholars call 'Péten gloss' due to its use by potters from cities in the Péten region.

In 1250–1521 Maya artisans in the southern highlands made and traded simple wares decorated with black and red designs on a cream or white base colour. Scholars call these pots 'Chinautla Polychrome'. Another distinctive development was the mixing of talc in clay, which produced a slightly reflective sheen and a

Above: Rain and lightning god Cocijo was a favourite subject for ceramic funerary urns among the Zapotecs who worshipped him.

cooking surface – on, for example, *comales* (tortilla griddles) – with certain non-stick qualities. Products made with this mixed clay were found throughout the highlands of the southern Maya region, where the Quiché and Cakquichels rose to prominence at this time.

IN AZTEC LANDS
One of the many aspects of the market in Tlatelolco that astonished the Spanish conquistadors was the vast display of beautifully finished ceramics. In the Aztec era, craftsmen produced a wide range of pottery for use in both sacred and utilitarian contexts. For sacred use they made incense burners, braziers, censers, urns, figures of gods and goddesses, goblets, votive vessels and model temples. For everyday use they made plates, cups, bowls, jugs, pitchers and other vessels.

Many of these utilitarian objects could also have had a sacred function, since they were included in offerings at the Templo Mayor, in graves at Teotihuacán, at Tollán or in other temple settings. The elite polychrome ceramics used in the *tlatoani's* palace and by members of the nobility were made in Cholula and parts of Oaxaca. Aztec-era potters also made fired-clay flutes and ceramic rattles.

FIGURES OF CLAY

Potters at Remojadas in the region of Veracruz produced very distinctive hollow clay figurines in the 8th–9th century (the late Classic Period). These craftsmen, part of the 'Veracruz culture' associated with the city of El Tajín, were inheritors of an ancient Mesoamerican tradition. From as early as *c.*2500BC, at the beginning of settled village life in Mesoamerica, early craftsmen and women were making female figurines associated with cults of the land's fertility. One of these figures, dating from 2300BC, was found in a household fireplace at Zohapilco at the eastern end of Lake Chalco in the Valley of Mexico.

In the 2nd millennium BC, Olmec craftsmen made baby-face figurines called 'dolls' by some early archaeologists. These were beautifully produced hollow figures, with a surface coating of white, representing chubby figures with legs outspread and the face of a baby. The figures probably had some religious use associated with Olmec cults seemingly focused on the were-jaguar, a jaguar-faced human – often resembling a baby – thought by scholars to stand for the earth.

Olmec baby figurines were exported far and wide from centres such as La Venta and San Lorenzo using the Olmecs' extensive trading networks.

SHAMANIC RITES

About 1100BC, craftsmen made and used large numbers of handmade ceramic figures in the Valley of Mexico, in the villages of Tlatilco on the western side of Lake Texcoco and Tlapacoya beside Lake Chalco. Some were clearly used in association with shamanistic rites: they represented shaman-priests and weird two-headed creatures or three-eyed monsters that were perhaps the product of ecstatic visions and spirit-journeys following the consumption of mind-altering substances. Others were caught in such scenes of home life as mothers nursing babies or religious

Above: This smiling boy (c.AD750–900) is typical of 'Remojadas figurines', with outstretched arms and wide, ecstatic grin.

festivities and other celebrations involving cavorting acrobats, musicians and players of the sacred ball game.

Figurines such as this were produced in all parts of Mesoamerica in the Preclassic Period, but their use appears to have gradually died out towards the end of that era before reappearing in the mid-to-late Classic Period. Scholars have suggested that since the figurines were probably used in pre-temple religious rituals, they would not have been needed or welcome when formal religious life centred on temples became the norm. The new religious elite would probably

Left: These figurines made in Veracruz c.AD1200–1520 may represent ritual victims. The man (right) seems to be taking a hallucinogenic substance. Victims were drugged so that they seemed calm when going to their deaths.

have been keen to destroy all materials connected with rituals which they would have seen as outmoded. Archaeologists at Monte Albán, for example, report that hand-modelled figurines associated with household shrines disappeared from residential remains about the time that the building now called Mound X, identified as the city's first public temple, was erected some time after *c*.300BC. It is unclear precisely how and under what conditions the practice of making and using figurines resurfaced.

STYLIZED TEOTIHUACÁN FIGURES

In Teotihuacán *c*.AD400, craftsmen used moulds to make articulated figures about 25–30cm (10–12in) in height. In stark contrast to the highly naturalistic representations of the later creators of the Veracruz Remojadas figurines, the Teotihuacános produced stylized figures with triangular-shaped faces, which generally have openings in the top of their heads. They also made non-moveable figures set in unusual postures. Scholars have not established a context in which these figures could have been used, beyond suggesting that they might have played a role in survivals of ancient village-based fertility celebrations in the wide spread of village communities around the metropolis of Teotihuacán. Then about AD650–700, Teotihuacáno craftsmen began to produce larger mould-made figurines representing nobles and deities on thrones.

RELIGIOUS ECSTASY

There was certainly significant Teotihuacáno influence in the Veracruz region, so the tradition of mould-made ceramic figurines in the great metropolis of highland Mexico might well have fed into the marvellous flowering of clay-figure moulding represented by the late Classic Period Remojadas craftsmen.

The gifted modellers at Remojadas made clay images of men, women and children, some attired as ball game players, some dressed as warriors. One distinctive form represented men – and more often women – with

Left: Veracruz figurine c.AD250–500 represents a club-wielding warrior with skin blackened for battle.

Above: A Veracruz potter of c.AD500–950 fashioned this statue of a priest wearing a jaguar god headpiece and costume.

outstretched arms and elegant, wide-faced features, their mouths open and drawn in a broad smile or laugh, their teeth visible within their mouths.

The Remojadas potters produced highly naturalistic work. They decorated some figures with black asphalt paint to emphasize the features and details of the figures' often elaborate dress; other figurines they painted in many colours. Some scholars argue that the figures are in a state of religious ecstasy, having taken mind-altering substances. Others suggest that the laughing individuals are sacrificial victims whose unusual demeanour has been produced by swallowing hallucinogenic drinks intended to enable them to hide their terror and assume a joyful demeanour as they go to their deaths. The figures are typically about 30–45cm (12–18in) in height. The Toltecs at Tollán also produced mould-made clay figurines of people and animals, as did craftsmen at Xochicalco.

RULERS' GRAVEYARD?

Maya potters developed great artistry in moulding clay figurines in the middle to late Classic Period (c.AD400–900). A large collection of exquisitely modelled figures was found in graves on the limestone Island of Jaina, just off the west coast of the Yucatán peninsula.

The island was a flourishing sea-trading and fishing centre for many centuries. In addition to its port and trade facilities, it contained two modest ceremonial centres named El Zacpool and Zayosal, together with a ball court and cemeteries in which the clay figurines were found. The buildings were simple, made of an earthen core that was faced with an irregular pattern of stones, then plastered with stucco and painted.

Scholars are uncertain whether the splendid clay figures and wealthy grave offerings were laid in the tombs of rich local merchants, of priests and sacerdotal assistants at the ceremonial centre or

Below: This kneeling figure, 15cm (6in) in height, is one of many Jaina Island models that represent ball players.

of nobles and rulers from inland cities such as Uxmal and Kabah. Because the island's ceremonial buildings were modest, it would appear most likely that cemeteries were the graves of elite groups from the mainland rather than of locals. Jaina lay just off the coast and could be reached by foot through swamps at low tide. Because the island was on the western coast of the peninsula, the sun dropped behind it each night as it sank into the underworld Xibalba. Accordingly, some scholars argue that Jaina might have been chosen as the site for an elite cemetery because symbolically it lay on the path to the underworld.

Older figures found at Jaina, dating from before AD650, are generally solid and hand-modelled. After c.AD650, potters began to produce hollow figures made using moulds, perhaps in emulation of the Teotihaucáno craftsmen who were making hollow-mould figures from c.AD400–500 onwards. Some of the later Jaina artisans were not happy to rely solely on moulds and combined the new technique with older traditions producing, for example, a figurine with a mould-made torso but a handmade head. Many of the figures are musical instruments. Some, with holes bored in the back, are whistles. Others contained clay pellets and could be used as rattles.

PORTRAITS IN CLAY

The Jaina figures are generally 20–30cm (8–12in) tall. Some figures are highly naturalistic portraits – perhaps of the nobles in whose graves they were buried. They depict proud warriors with scarred or tattoed skins, wise old men, beautiful maidens and elderly matrons. Other statuettes represent less than idealized figures taken from life such

Below: The potters who made the Jaina Island models worked with great skill and delicacy, as evidenced in the attention to detail in the feather headdress, necklace, bracelets and ear decoration on this figurine.

Right: The Jaina Island tomb figures give us an invaluable insight into the clothes and headgear worn by Classic Period Maya.

as invalids, dwarfs, drunks and hunchbacks. One 7th–9th-century figure represents an old man who has lost his wits to drink. He holds a flask beneath his arm and has a look of unseeing stupefaction on his face.

Some of these models are careful representations of figures involved in religious ritual. One such 7th–9th-century figure represents a naked man with his hands tied behind his back, who would appear to be a noble prisoner bound for ritual sacrifice following capture during a war campaign launched by a rival city against his own. Another figurine depicts a ball player wearing protective belt and holding the ball prior to the start of a ball game. Other Jaina Island figures represent a shaman or priest in a trance.

IMAGES OF GODS

Some figures show gods and goddesses – usually divinities associated with the underworld. One such statue-pair from the 8th–9th century AD represents an elderly, lecherous man who is trying to raise the skirt of a beautiful maiden: scholars identify the man as a treacherous underworld lord and his consort as the moon goddess Ix Chel.

Another statue-pair represent a woman who is standing behind and over a seated male, almost enveloping him in her cloak. This may be a celebration of the protective power of Ix Chel in her role as mother goddess. A deity who is represented several times among the Jaina models is a figure called the Fat God, a squat full-faced man with a feathered headdress and very tall helmet.

The Jaina Island figurines were painted in bright colours. Curiously, the potters did not work hard on reproducing the feet or hands of their subjects, which were often finished without attention to detail, but they put great effort into reproducing individual physiognomies and styles of clothing as well as adornment with jewellery, headdresses and body art such as tattoos.

The figures have been an invaluable source for historians seeking information about details of Maya court life – such as elite clothing. The finest of the figurines are the older, solid ones made before *c.*AD650. Experts declare them to be among the finest pieces of their kind in all the Americas. Because so many of the figures were of warriors, some argue that the island cemetery might have been reserved for members of the military elite, or for rank and file members of the army who had won particular glory in battle.

Below: Scholars believe that this cloaked Jaina Island figure with mysterious headdress may represent an elite priest.

CERAMIC CULTURES

Fragments of pots, plates, bottles and jars generally provide the bulk of remains discovered by archaeologists when investigating living areas such as house platforms or household waste areas. In graves and temple offerings elite pottery forms are also well represented. The distribution of types of pottery and methods of decoration in different regions across spans of time gives a clue to the movements of people and influence. For this reason, archaeologists and historians often identify cultures by the type of pottery remains they left.

MANY-COLOURED SCENES OF COURT LIFE

The painted vases, plates, incense burners and drinking vessels produced in the Maya cities of *c.*AD550–800 in the late Classic Period were probably decorated by the highly educated noble artists usually referred to as scribes. Many of these vessels bore glyphic writing that gave the names and titles of the people represented and identified other elements of the image. Sometimes the glyphs provided an entire dynastic history for the ruler who was depicted sitting in state, conferring with his scribes and advisers, celebrating an anniversary of his accession or enjoying the chocolate drink.

EXPERT POTTERS

Some vases were incised with images and glyphs rather than painted, and in these cases the delicate lines were almost certainly cut by the same artists who were such skilled carvers of stelae and lintels.

We do not know whether specialist potters created the plates, cups and vases and then handed them over to be decorated

Below: Ceramics such as this painted vase from the Sula Valley, Honduras, accompanied elite burials in their tombs.

Above: Deities were often shown in attendance at the scenes of religious ritual and court life represented on vases.

or whether the scribal artists were also responsible for making the pots. Some of the surface effects and colouring on painted vessels were achieved by expert manipulation of oxygen levels during the firing of the pottery and in these cases the scribal artists responsible for the final appearance of the vessel must have been involved in its firing.

Scholars believe that many of the scenes depicted on pictorial vases were taken from screenfold books. The scribal artists must have developed an expert judgement in order to transfer the elegant proportions of composition and neat glyph-work to the curved surface of the vase being worked.

There is very little evidence that the scribes first marked out the designs before painting over them, for this would have left visible marks beneath the final design.

Scholar Michael Coe has suggested that the artists might have marked out the design in charcoal, which would have disappeared when the vessel was fired, but this can be no more than speculation.

ROYAL FUNERAL RITES

Examples of elegantly painted Maya ceramics of the late Classic Period include the vessel known to archaeologists as the Altar Vase, found in the Usumacinta-region city of Altar de Sacrificios. According to scholar R.E.W. Adams, the image painted on the vase represents a funeral held in AD754 following the death of a royal woman of middle age.

Six dancing figures on the vase are believed to represent three visiting dignitaries from other cities, each accompanied by a *way* or spirit companion. The visitors, who had travelled from nearby Yaxchilán, from mighty Tikal and from an unidentified city in the highlands of the southern Maya region, laid offerings of fine ceramics in the royal tomb. The Altar Vase itself was laid in the grave of a young woman sacrificed in honour of the deceased princess or royal wife.

An image on the vase of a young woman performing rites of autosacrificial blood-letting might be a portrait of this young victim, who was herself probably a junior royal.

At Uaxactún archaeologists found a magnificent cache of painted ceramics in a stone tomb containing the corpse of an elite figure, probably a king. The corpse, buried in the building known as Structure A-I, was laid along the sanctified north–south axis used for ceremonial centres, with its head to the north. Next to the skull was a vase painted in the 8th century AD with a scene of court ritual using black and yellow against a red-orange base colour. The scene shows a king enthroned beneath a feathered shade held by an attendant. The king faces two elaborately dressed visitors, their visible skin painted black, one carrying a spear and one holding a ritual object with three spikes that scholars call a 'knuckle duster'. A seated jaguar, mouth open in a roar or snarl, accompanies the two visitors.

In all, the tomb contained eleven exquisite pottery pieces, nine of them painted. A beautifully painted tripod plate depicting a dancer had a small hole bored in it – the result of a ceremony performed to free the soul of the plate so that it could travel with the spirit of the deceased king as he made his way to the underworld. Many other delicately painted ceramics were left as grave offerings in Tikal, Seibal, Altun Ha, Tayasal and other settlements.

HIGHLAND VASES

Painted vases of very high quality were also produced in the highlands of the southern Maya region. A vase found at Chama in the valley of the river Chixoy, Guatemala, depicts seven individuals in red, brown and black against a pink base.

Right: Elaborately attired priests, warriors or gods ring a beautifully finished vase from Honduras, made c.AD600–900.

Two main figures face one another, both painted black, one wearing a jaguar skin. Individual features are represented in detail, suggesting that these were portraits executed from life. The black paint on the main figures might be intended to identify the two main figures as merchants by linking them to Ek Chuah, the patron god of that group.

Many vases, plates and cups were signed by the artists who painted them. For example, a cup for drinking chocolate was signed by Ah Maxam, the noble scribe from Naranjo who decorated it. The glyphs he inscribed in black paint on a cream base describe the function of the vessel and identify Ah Maxam as scribe and member of the royal household.

POTTERY FOR BANQUETS AND TEMPLES

México/Aztec potters specialized in a range of fired-clay braziers sanctified by the images of gods and goddesses. They were positioned outside temples or before the altars of the gods and used for burning aromatic copal incense, a form of rubber latex called *hulli* and body parts of animal and human sacrifices.

SMOKE GUIDE

The braziers were painted in bright colours. One splendid painted clay brazier of *c.*1500 found in Tlatelolco celebrated male and female vegetation deities Xiuhtecuhtli and Chalchiúhtlicue.

A set of five braziers of *c.*1500 commemorated warriors who had perished in battles or been sacrificed and whose souls were believed to accompany the sun god in his daily passage across the heavens.

Hulli was burned particularly in rituals honouring the rain god Tláloc, for worshippers believed that the dark smoke it produced would summon dark, rain-laden clouds. Some authorities taught that the smoke from ceremonial braziers could

Below: These elegant goblets are typical of the high-quality wares imported to Tenochtitlán from the Aztec empire.

lead the soul of a deceased person to the afterlife. Large braziers measuring 40–100cm (16–40in) or more in height were made to be placed on the ground, but smaller versions about 20cm (8in) long were threaded with cords through the handles and waved by priests to spread sweet-smelling copal incense around the temple.

Potters also made long-handled painted clay censers, with a round fretwork head that contained coals and incense. Priests waved the censer to perfume images of the gods and goddesses.

Potters produced goblets for use in temple rites. The sacred vessels were filled with blood and connected by straws called *pópotl* to the mouth cavities of god and goddess statues.

Two imported Mixtec goblets of *c.*1500, decorated with skulls and three painted bands (representing the night sky), were found in a burial cache of ceramics laid beneath an area of Tenochtitlán known as El Volador, thought to be the southern part of Moctezuma II's great palace.

Above: This lidded vessel decorated with images of the rain god Tláloc was made by potters in Tikal in the early Classic Period.

Aztec worshippers created a large demand for votive vessels decorated with images of gods and goddesses such as Tláloc, Chalchiúhtlicue, Chicomecóatl and Xilonen to be placed in temple offerings. Potters also produced clay plaques which were perhaps intended for temple display or for use as offerings. One, dating from *c.*1500 and found in Culhuacán, represented the rites of the festival of Ochpaniztli, in which a priestess of the maize goddesses Xilonen and Chicomecóatl wore the flayed skin of a sacrificial victim.

TINY TEMPLE PRECINCTS

Clay-modellers produced miniature temple structures, typically 30–40cm (12–16in) tall, for use in home shrines. They were detailed reproductions of Aztec Postclassic Period pyramid-temples, complete with balustraded stairways on all four sides of the pyramid, a sacrificial stone at the top of the steps and a simple temple building, perhaps with decorated roof. One of three such temples found in Calipan, modern Puebla state, was even painted with a red line down one stairway to represent the blood of sacrificial victims. The temples were probably placed on home shrines alongside small

Above: An architectural decoration representing a forerunner of Tláloc was made in Teotihuacán c.AD100–500.

clay figures of corn, rain and fertility deities and used in rites linked to the festivals of the agricultural year. However, the temples were also used to honour other gods: the three models found in Calipan were made in honour of the fire god Xiuhtecuhtli, the earth mother goddess Toci and the war god Huitzilopochtli.

Potters in Puebla and Oaxaca specialized in large painted funerary urns with side handles. An important centre of production was the area known to historians as Mixtequilla Veracruzana in the south of modern Veracruz state where it borders Oaxaca.

These large vessels were also used to contain drink at ceremonial feasts. A mural at Cholula known as 'Los Belsilores' shows drinkers dipping their tankards into the large urn-like vessel. After being used in this way, they would probably have been placed in a temple offering.

Below: Small clay models of deities and of temple-pyramids were used in home worship until Aztec times.

BANQUET WARE

The ruler and nobles of Tenochtitlán imported their high-quality ceramics. Potters in Texcoco produced a polished red ware that was used by the nobility at banquets, to make offerings in the temple and to accompany high-ranking individuals in their graves. In Cholula and in Mixtec crafts centres in Oaxaca, potters produced polychrome ceramics that were also popular in Tenochtitlán.

Many examples of Texcocan polished red wares were put in tombs or survived. A splendid red-ware vessel with painted black designs now in the St Louis Museum is typical of the style. Art historian John W. Nunley has interpreted the shell-like black markings as representations of the maguey cactus leaf and suggests that the vessel was intended for serving the alcoholic drink *pulque*, which was made from the fermented sap of the maguey. He adds that the phallic outline of the vessel's spout was intended to emphasize and celebrate the drink's reputed qualities as an aphrodisiac.

The nobles favoured painted tripod plates with elegant decoration in many colours. The legs of the plate often represented snakes, eagle heads or jaguar claws. A delicate cup made *c.*1500 for noble enjoyment was fashioned in the likeness of a flower, its long stem like four intertwining flower stems, and its bowl in the shape of a cluster of petals. Flowers were associated with the noble life: *pipiltin* nobility routinely held small bouquets of flowers to enjoy their scent and keep troubling smells at bay.

TENOCHTITLÁN'S LIFE-SIZE CERAMIC FIGURES

Aztec craftsmen produced remarkable fired-clay statues about 1.7m (5ft 4in) tall for the House of Eagles, a sacred precinct north of the Templo Mayor in Tenochtitlán. This was a notable development of the Mesoamerican tradition of making small clay figurines for use in worship. Aztec potters also followed this more modest path, making figures of deities such as Xipe Totec, perhaps 20cm (8in) tall, for use in domestic religious ritual and in temple offerings.

SUN COMPANIONS

A pair of life-sized statues representing eagle-warriors were mounted on a bench in the House of Eagles, which was used for penitential retreats and rites of autosacrificial bloodletting in which worshippers cut ears, cheeks or penis to offer blood to the gods. The statues were originally covered with stucco and decorated with a design in white paint that reproduced the eagle feathers worn into battle by these elite warriors. Each statue was made in four segments – the head and helmet; the torso and arms; the groin; and the lower legs. Archaeologists report that the eagle-warrior statues might have been images of the sun at dawn.

LORD OF THE UNDERWORLD

The House of Eagles also contained a pair of statues of Mictlantecuhtli, lord of the Aztec underworld Mictlán, also mounted on benches. One of the statues – 1.76m (5ft 7in) tall and 80cm (2ft 10in) wide – represented the hideous form of Mictlantecuhtli as a near-naked man with decaying flesh, bony torso and protruding liver, wearing a meagre loincloth, his hands vast claws, his mouth a terrifying grimace. Holes in the statue's skull would have held the dark curly hair associated with Aztec earth and death deities. Like those of the eagle-warriors, the statue was made in five pieces.

SKINNING OF THE MEN

Like their counterparts elsewhere in Mesoamerica during the Postclassic Period, Aztec craftsmen generally made smaller ceramic pieces using moulds. Four

Left: One of a pair of ceramic figures (c.1480) of underworld god Mictlantecuhtli, shown with exposed liver and grimacing mouth. Traces of the original white stucco covering are still visible. Like the warrior figure, above right, he stood in the House of Eagles in Tenochtitlán's sacred precinct. Here he stands on a tzompantli *(skull altar).*

Above: One of two life-size ceramic figures of eagle-warriors who stood in the House of Eagles, this was made c.1440–69.

figures found in Tlatelolco in 1968 celebrated the gruesome rites of the festival of Tlacaxipehualiztli ('Skinning of the Men') held to honour Xipe Totec, god of vegetation and germinating seeds.

The clay statues, each about 15cm (6in) high, represented priests and worshippers. Two warriors were seated on a bench, while two priests or other participants wore the skins of flayed sacrificial victims. An intermediate-sized statue, 97cm (3ft 2in) tall, of a Xipe Totec priest wearing the puckered skin of a victim was found in 1975 in the fortified city of Tepeji el Viejo in the mountainous southern part of modern Puebla state. The sacrificial statue, which was very beautifully made, had in its turn been sacrificed by being smashed. Archaeologists have reassembled the pieces to recreate the work.

BASKETWORK, MATS AND FURNITURE

The lakeside reedbeds of Mexico and Guatemala kept Mesoamerican basket-workers well supplied with raw materials. The makers of baskets and reed mats were practitioners of an ancient craft tradition and users of skills developed thousands of years earlier. Archaeological evidence shows that even before the beginnings of village life in Mesoamerica, hunter-gatherer groups made baskets, mats and sandals from reeds. In the Classic and Postclassic Periods, most working householders probably knew enough about reed-weaving to make their own simple mats and baskets for everyday use, just as they had sufficient rudimentary pottery skills to make their own pots, plates and cups.

NAPATECUHTLI, PATRON GOD OF REED WEAVERS

The Aztec reed-weavers' patron god, Napatecuhtli, was represented wearing a tall headdress crowned with a *quetzalmiahuayo* ('gathering of sacred quetzal feathers'). A band of the bark paper used to soak up blood in rites of autosacrifice was wound around his head, with bark-paper ornaments suspended from it.

Doubtless because reed-weavers gathered their raw materials at the lakeside, Napatecuhtli was also a god of water and was associated with the rain deity Tláloc. For this reason Napatecuhtli's face was generally covered with a serpentine Tláloc mask, in which curling snakes formed eyes and upper lip. His robes were also made of bark paper and hung to his feet. He carried a reed sceptre or *oztopilli* in his left hand and sinuous snake-staff in his right hand. A delicately rendered fired-clay vessel of *c.*1500 representing Napatecuhtli was discovered in 1996 in Tláhuac, Mexico Federal District.

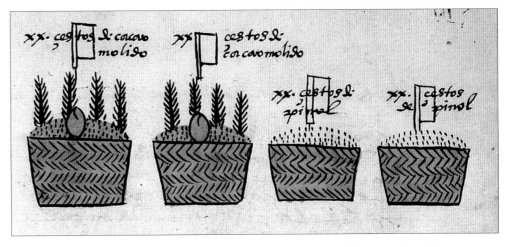

Above: A detail from the list of Aztec tribute due from Tlatelolco to Tenochtitlán shows woven baskets of cacao and chia.

Specialist basket-makers made and supplied finer quality goods to those who could afford to barter for them at market. In the Aztec era, the reed-workers also made use of palm leaf, slats of cane and the leaves of the maguey cactus. They fashioned baskets in many sizes and shapes that could be used on *chinampa* fields, in the marketplace, in the household and even in the temple precincts for moving goods, storing food, secreting valuables or ritual items and keeping clothes away from dust and dirt. Other reed-weavers made *petlatl* mats and seats in fine weave for supply to nobles. Seats and low tables were generally restricted to wealthy households, while other folk used mats on the ground.

MAYA MATS AND BASKETS

The Maya of the Classic Period certainly used mats and baskets, but none has survived. An image of a basket carved on Lintel 24 in the city of Yaxchilán reveals how intricate Maya baskets could be. It combines three decorative schemes – a featherwork pattern, a twill design and a combination of frets and small squares – in a single item. The imprint of a Postclassic Period mat has been found on the floor of the shrine discovered beneath the Temple of the Feathered Serpent at Chichén Itzá. The pattern of its weaving is the same as that of mats still produced in the locality.

Mats were conceptually associated with political power. In Aztec society the *tlatoani* was known as 'the one who takes this place upon the mat'. For the Maya, too, the mat was the locus of authority. The title *ahpop* assumed by Maya rulers meant 'the one who sits on the mat'.

Below: A typically wide-eyed and grimacing Veracruz clay figurine of c.AD600–800 holds a woven basket full of produce.

RICHLY DECORATED ROBES

From sculptures such as door lintels and stelae we know that the rulers and noble elite of Classic Period Maya cities wore cotton fabrics with a rich weave and elaborate embroidery. Weavers made large amounts of cotton cloth in a variety of patterns. Only a few fragments of cloth produced by the ancient Maya have survived. A cache of chipped flints buried in the 6th–7th century Copán temple known to archaeologists as the Rosalila structure was wrapped in disintegrating fabric. A few pieces of white cotton cloth were discovered with late Postclassic pottery of *c*.1250–1500 at Tenam, a site in the eastern part of Chiapas. When archaeologists dredged the *Cenote* of Sacrifice

Below: Toltec warriors wore quilted cotton battle dress. This stone soldier, carved at Tollán, reproduces the costume in detail.

Above: Used by Zapotec artisans, these loom shuttles carved from bones of the regal jaguar were placed in Monte Albán Tomb 7.

at Chichén Itzá, they found among the multitude of gold, silver and other precious offerings a few pieces of carbonized fabric with complex weaves.

AZTEC DESIGNS

In the Aztec empire, as in Maya lands, few pieces of cloth survived, but images in codices, in sculptures and in ceramics – together with the descriptions of Spanish invaders – reveal the rich variety of cloth and elegant decorative designs that were available.

As among the Maya, there were regionally distinctive designs. These were generally embroidered, woven, dyed or even painted on to the cloth. They were usually geometric designs, although some regions specialized in decorating with images of local animals or plants. The empire's finest textiles were those

imported to Tenochtitlán from Veracruz. Huaxtec weavers, who were based in that region, produced highly prized white cotton cloth decorated with animal motifs.

Weavers made dyes from minerals, plants and animals. Red came from cochineal insects gathered in groves of nopal cacti – a useful sideline for agriculturalists. Blue clay and yellow ochre were other sources.

Purple came from the sea snail *Purpura patula*, found around the shores of Yucatán (see box). This snail was related to the Murex mollusc, found in the Mediterranean, from which the ancient Phoenicians made the 'royal purple' dye in classical Europe.

MAYA COLOUR CODE

Highland communities in modern Guatemala still follow ancient traditions in weaving practice, as far as historians can tell. These communities use handlooms to make cotton cloth and embroider this with cotton thread that has been dyed the required colour. Different communities have traditional designs. No two designs are identical, but they adhere to distinctive local patterns closely enough to be immediately recognizable. The meaning of the colours used also follows time-honoured ways. Red stands for blood, and blue sacrifice. Green-turquoise, the colour of the quetzal bird's magnificent tail plumes, is symbolic of royalty. Yellow, as the colour of maize, suggests food, while black stands for weapons – because it was the predominant colour of the obsidian used to make cutting blades for weapons. A deep purple colour derived from the sea snail *Purpura patula* found on the Pacific coast and carried inland by traders was highly esteemed.

COLOURFUL BATTLE DRESS

A celebrated portrait in the 16th-century manuscript *Codex Ixtlilxochitl* of Netzahualcóyotl, ruler of Texcoco, shows the colourful costumes available to the noble elite in Aztec Mexico. The portrait shows Netzahualcóyotl in ceremonial battle garb, bearing a blue shield, with long red tassels, on his left arm and on his head a blue headdress with white and red horizontal bands. These colours were matched in the blue of his tunic and the red of the protective binding on his upper arms. On his lower half he wears a flowing kilt in horizontal colour bands of white, red, green, yellow, red and green once more.

A page from the *Codex Mendoza* (*c*.1541) also made clear the bright colours worn by elite warriors for ceremonial dress. It depicts a selection of colourful outfits with elaborate feather headdresses and coloured shields decorated by *amanteca* feather workers.

Below: A modern Mexican hooked rug uses an Aztec design, incorporating images of birds and animals, and plant motifs.

FESTIVAL COSTUME

Clothes played an important role in religious ceremonies. At festivals, priests and priestesses, prisoner-sacrificial victims or commoners selected for sacrifice wore costumes that identified them as the god or goddess being honoured.

The costumes were often elaborate and highly coloured and so added to the spectacle and drama generated by these

Above: In August 2000, archaeologists excavating the Templo Mayor found this Aztec cloth in an offering to Tláloc.

public enactments of religious ritual. Colours and design elements added layers of religious meaning, a process well suited to representations of deities with many complex attributes, several of which they might share with other gods and goddesses.

For example, a celebrated statue of water goddess Chalchiúhtlicue (dated *c*.1500) found in Mexico City in 1824 wore the headdress that identified her as Chalchiúhtlicue, while her cape was embroidered with *chalchiuhtil* or jade symbols that were also essential elements of the goddess's outfit. However, she also wore a rattlesnake sash to hold up her lower garments and these associated her with maize goddesses and also with the earth goddess Coatlícue.

Statues like this one of Chalchiúhtlicue might have represented a deity or a priest/priestess impersonating a deity and showed details of festival dress. A few statues are naked or barely dressed figures and might have been dressed in brightly coloured real clothes as part of festival rites.

A GATHERING OF FEATHERS

Images in the *Florentine Codex* (1575–77) of Friar Bernardino de Sahagún depict skilled Aztec *amanteca* feather-workers at their job, sewing green quetzal feathers into elaborate headdresses for royal and priestly costumes, on to ceremonial shields and across temple banners. The emerald-green tail plumes of the male quetzal, gathered by specialist hunters in the tropical forests of Maya lands and imported to highland Mexico, could be 1m (3ft 3in) long. It made a great visual impact when sewn around a headdress or added to its crown to make a tall *quetzalmiahuayo* (gathering of quetzal feathers). The feather-workers also used feathers from macaws, parrots, spoonbills and other birds and made elite items of clothing, bracelets and costumes for dancing.

From at least the prime of Teotihuacán, in *c.*AD500, the transport of feathers was a major component of Mesoamerican trade. Other images in the *Florentine Codex* depict Aztec traders at market sitting alongside brightly coloured feather displays. Feathers and feathered items were suitable offerings in temples because of their rarity and great worth. Quetzal feathers were additionally valued because of their length and because their colour resembled that of precious jade – the green of maize shoots and water, associated with Chalchiúhtlicue ('Mistress of the Jade Skirt'), and symbolic of life itself.

FEATHER-WORKING DEITY

The Aztec feather-workers, gathered in their own quarter of Tlatelolco, worshipped Coyotlinahual as their patron god. This deity was associated with Tezcatlipoca. In one version of the myth of Quetzalcóatl-Topiltzin as ruler of Tollán, when Tezcatlipoca arrived in the city of the Toltecs to bring about the fall of the Feathered Serpent through trickery and deception, he was accompanied by Coyotlinahual, who was identified as a magician.

EUROPEAN ADMIRATION

Feather-work was an unfamiliar craft to the Spanish invaders and one of the artistic achievements of the Aztecs and Maya that made the greatest impression on Europeans. (Although the conquistadors were keen to collect and send home Mixtec work in gold and silver, they admired it for its monetary rather than artistic worth and melted it down on its arrival in Europe.)

A magnificent example of the work of the most skilled *amanteca* was a *quetzalapanecayotl* ('quetzal-feather headdress') sent to King Charles V of Spain by Hernán Cortés in 1519 and now part of the collection of the Museum für Völkerkunde in Vienna, Austria. The vast headdress, which measures 1.16m by 1.75m (3ft 10in by 5ft 9in), contains 450 quetzal feathers adorned with gold appliqué and turquoise. It would have made a great impression, even from afar, when worn by priests of Quetzalcóatl in

Below: Feather birds. These creatures on a painted terracotta brazier from Teotihuacán are stylized images of the sacred quetzal.

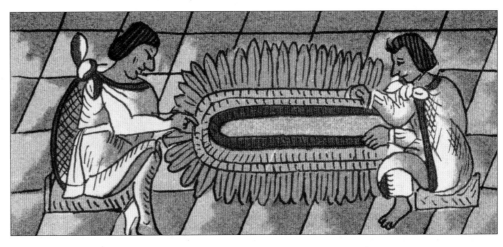

Right: The Florentine Codex *depicts highly regarded* amanteca *craftsmen lavishing attention on a feather costume.*

processions and sacrificial rituals. Cortés collected a good number of featherwork items and sent a large consignment of them to Spain in 1522 but the precious cargo was seized by pirates.

NOBLE ADORNMENT

The Museum für Völkerkunde also contains a large fan, 1.19m tall and 68cm in diameter (3ft 10in by 2ft 2in), made from quetzal feathers and gold appliqué in the last years of the Aztec empire. Fans were used by rulers, nobles and elite *pochteca* merchants. These most elegant of Tenochtitlán's citizens provided a regular demand for the feathered fans produced by the *amanteca* of Tlatelolco. Nobles could be seen carrying a brightly coloured fan – feathered, for example, with the plumage of parakeets and hummingbirds – in one hand, and a bunch of flowers in the other. The fans were usually made with carved wooden handles.

Another fine survival of Aztec featherwork was a striking ceremonial shield, 70cm (2ft 3in) in diameter of *c*.1500, that depicted a creature some scholars identify as a long-tailed water beast called an *ahuítzotl* ('water-prickle creature'). Aztec legend had it that the *ahuítzotl* lay in wait for an unwary wanderer on riverbanks and lakesides, caught the wanderer in its tail and pulled him down to the depths of the water where he drowned. The beast's name was taken by the *tlatoani* Ahuítzotl (*r*. 1486–1502), who led vast sacrificial rituals for the dedication of the rebuilt Templo Mayor in Tenochtitlán in 1487.

Other historians have suggested that the beast on the shield is a coyote, an animal

Right: Amanteca *had many commissions from Tenochtitlán's religious hierarchy for feathered costumes worn in sacred ritual.*

form of the god Tezcatlipoca who was one of the patron deities of war, and that it might have been the mascot-symbol of an elite military order. The shield was made of reeds strengthened with lengths of wood and covered with animal hide. The craftsman stuck feathers of the spoonbill, oriole, macaw and cotinga to pieces of agave paper and glued these to the shield to create the design, adding quetzal plumes and more spoonbill and cotinga feathers around the rim. Strips of sheet gold emphasized the design.

MAYA FEATHERWORK

No examples of Maya feather-work have survived, but carved and painted images reveal the splendour of the capes, shields, headdresses, fans, spear pendants and other ornaments made by the Maya counterparts of the *amanteca*. At Piedras Negras, for example, Stela 12 depicts a ruler wearing both feather headdress and feather robe. Similarly, in Chichén Itzá's Temple of the Jaguars, wooden door lintels were carved with images of featherwork. The murals at Bonampak also provide evidence of elegant Maya featherwork designs.

IN THE CHRISTIAN ERA

The native craft of feather-work survived the Spanish Conquest, after which featherworkers' expertise in making priestly headdresses and costumes led to their contributing to the wardrobe and paraphernalia of Christian priests. The Bishop of Michoacán's remarkable mitre was made in *c*.1530–60 from maguey paper and cotton cloth with a delicate mosaic of feathers from hummingbirds, macaws, parrots, cotingas, spoonbills, tzinitzans and starlings depicting events from Christ's Passion and the Last Judgement.

CHAPTER 22

THE CARVER'S ART

The monumental carved heads of Olmec kings in the 2nd–1st millennium BC were raised in rows in plazas or ceremonial areas, where their steady, inscrutable gaze would fall on any who approached. Likewise the carved stone pillars or stelae of Maya cities in the Classic Period stood in great public spaces, a statement of dynastic power. Sculpture in Mesoamerica took two main forms: free-standing monuments, such as Olmec heads or Maya stelae, and decorative elements on buildings.

In many cases carving on buildings was also for public consumption – for instance, the stucco deity masks that flanked access stairs on Maya pyramid-temples and the dynastic scenes carved on temple roof combs were both visible from the plazas below. In other cases – such as carving on door lintels at Yaxchilán or Piedras Negras or on stucco panels within temples at Palenque – these carved elements were intended for viewing close up and would have been seen only by members of the priestly and ruling elite. They still celebrated divine blessing on royal achievement and consolidated the standing of the dynasty, but did so by what historians call 'horizontal propaganda' within a single social level as opposed to 'vertical propaganda' from a higher level (of the rulers) to a lower level (of the commoners).

Left: The Toltecs developed the coatepantli *or serpent wall. At Tollán, it limited access to the main ceremonial area.*

THE KING'S HEAD:
OLMEC MONUMENTAL CARVING

The craft of Olmec stonemasons appears to have burst fully formed into the history of Mesoamerican carving. Scholars know no precedent in the region for the monumental heads, three-dimensional figures, colossal royal thrones and early forms of stelae or pillars that the Olmec produced from the 2nd millennium BC onwards. The only three-dimensional representations in Mesoamerica before the rise of the Olmec in the Gulf Coast region were the small clay figures found at many sites including the villages around the lakes of the Valley of Mexico.

SYMBOLS OF ABSOLUTE POWER

Seventeen Olmec monumental heads have survived. They are remarkably similar, with fleshy faces and foreheads gathered in a frown. All wear a tight helmet or cap that comes down to just above the eyes. Some 2–3m tall (6ft 6in–10ft) and weighing up to 20 tons each, their size alone makes

Below: Scholars believe that the Olmec could identify individual kings or the dynasties to which they belonged by interpreting emblems in their headdresses.

them deeply compelling, but they are also arresting in their naturalism; in the lifelike detail of thick, slightly separated lips, the pupils of the eyes and the folds of flesh on the cheek. Simultaneously, their emotionless gaze makes them seem withdrawn and superior and is expressive of authority and absolute power.

MONUMENTAL FEAT

The heads were carved from large, smooth basalt boulders that occur naturally in the Tuxtla mountains around 80km (50 miles) from the Olmec temple towns of La Venta, San Lorenzo and Laguna de Los Cerros. The boulders were probably carved *in situ* in the mountains, then carefully wrapped and transported by river-raft to the ceremonial centres of these settlements, where hundreds of labourers assembled to move and erect the vast structures in rows.

Scholars believe that the heads were portraits in basalt of Olmec kings, perhaps the reigning lord or his most recently deceased ancestor, probably commissioned to mark funerals, coronation rites or important anniversaries of these

Above: La Venta Altar 5, marked with images of helmeted adults bearing 'werejaguar' babies, was probably a royal throne.

Below: Olmec kings had power to deliver fertility, represented in this La Venta carving by the turtle shown above the ruler's head.

events. The headdresses are all different, marked with emblems that might have represented the king's name or that of the dynasty to which he belonged.

KNEELING BALL PLAYER?

Other notable Olmec stonework included a kneeling figure known as Monument 34 from San Lorenzo. Carved from basalt *c*.1100BC, the figure is 79cm (2ft 7in) high, with sockets cut at the shoulder that once held moveable arms and a carving of a concave mirror on his chest. Some scholars suggest that this kneeling male represents a player of the Mesoamerican ball game.

A statue carved at Laguna de Los Cerros *c*.1100BC is the only known standing figure carved by Olmec sculptors: the caped figure, nicknamed 'Superman' by scholars, stood 1.5m (5ft) tall.

More typical was a large greenstone statue of a seated man holding a baby that combined the features of a human infant with the square snout of a jaguar, an example of the 'were-jaguar' image commonly used by the Olmec and tentatively identified by scholars as an image of the rain god. This statue, found at Las Limas in Veracruz in 1965, is 55cm (22in) in height. On the knees and shoulders of the seated figure, the sculptor carved four profiled faces with distinctive features that may represent either four aspects of a deity or four distinct divinities.

Olmec craftsmen also carved several large stone thrones, which were once believed by archaeologists to be altars used in sacred ritual. Of these thrones, the most celebrated is the La Venta monument, which is known to archaeologists as Altar 4. This depicts a seated ruler in a bird headdress emerging from an opening in the front of the throne, holding a rope that connects him to a bound figure on one side of the stone. The same rope probably originally connected him to another figure on the other side, but this carving has been defaced. The

rope might indicate that the king had taken the other figure captive, or that the two were bound by dynastic links.

Archaeologist David Grove identified a buck-toothed ruler portrayed on Head 4 at La Venta as one of the bound figures represented on a throne at San Lorenzo. This suggests either that the two sacred towns had been at war and that a San Lorenzo king had captured a La Venta king, or that the monument celebrated

the kinship ties between the two ruling dynasties. On the La Venta Altar 4, a gaping jaguar's mouth was carved above the king suggesting that, in emerging from the niche in the stone, the king was coming forth from the heart of this regal predator.

Below: The posture and hand positions of this Olmec volcanic-stone statue led scholars to label him the 'standard bearer'.

FROM THREE TO TWO DIMENSIONS:
THE FIRST STELAE

After *c*.500BC, Mesoamerican craftsmen moved away from the three-dimensional carvings of heads and seated or kneeling figures produced by Olmec artisans to concentrate largely on relief carvings in two dimensions. For more than 1,000 years, although potters continued to make clay figurines, relief carvings on panels, and thrones, slabs attached to buildings and stone pillars or stelae were the norm.

From the 6th century AD onwards, sculptors at the Maya city of Toniná created an unusual group of stelae that were carved on all four sides of the block, almost like a statue. Then in the 9th century AD, with the rise of the Toltecs – and perhaps in the Chalcihuites culture of northern Mexico, which some scholars now identify as a source of many Toltec practices and motifs – craftsmen returned to making this kind of monumental three-dimensional statue.

The Toltec-Maya at Chichén Itzá and the Aztec inheritors of Toltec power at Tenochtitlán were also enthusiastic practitioners of three-dimensional sculpture.

Below: The skeletal figure on this late Preclassic stone fragment from Izapa represents the underworld god of the dead.

Above: The deep relief carving of King Curl Head on Stela 10 (c.AD527) from Tikal has been eroded by time. Stela 10 stood on the North Terrace facing the Great Plaza.

CHALCATZINGO CARVINGS
The Olmecs had already demonstrated a great capacity for relief carving, evidenced in their high-relief work on stone thrones, in rock carvings and also in stone pillars or stelae. As early as 1100BC, craftsmen who were themselves Olmecs or who were working in the Olmec style cut elaborate reliefs in rocks at the trading centre of Chalcatzingo in the Amatzinac valley, to the south-east of the Valley of Mexico. One, dubbed 'El Rey' by historians, represents a king wearing an elaborate headdress, seated on a throne and holding a bar bearing a scroll design identical to the one carved on his throne, within a monster-mouth or cave believed to represent the entrance to the underworld. Art historian Esther Pasztory notes that the focus is on the importance of costume, equipment and location, as distinct from the monumental heads, which celebrated the power of the physical form.

Above: Some Monte Albán stelae celebrated the achievements of individual rulers. They were carved with dates believed to be birth-dates taken by the kings as their names.

Olmec stelae similarly celebrated rulers in elaborate costume. The monument labelled Stela 2 at La Venta, for example, represents a figure in ceremonial attire apparently holding a sceptre, weapon or bat. Historians suggest that the image may depict a player of the ball game – perhaps a royal ball game player. The stela, 2.46m (8ft) tall, was carved *c*.1100BC.

RECORDING THE CYCLES OF TIME
The Olmecs' contemporaries in Oaxaca also excelled at relief carving. At San José Mogote, Zapotec craftsmen carved a stone slab representing a fallen figure and set it in the doorway of a ceremonial building where people would tread. In the carving, known to archaeologists as Monument 3, skilled and learned stonemasons cut the day sign 1-Earthquake from the 260-day ritual calendar between the feet of the figure, perhaps to record the name of the person represented or the date on

Above: Danzantes. Some 300 carvings of ritual victims or prisoners – once thought to be dancers – were displayed on Building J as a statement of Monte Albán's might.

which he was killed or sacrificed. Cut *c.*700–500BC, this is the oldest evidence we have for the use of the 260-day calendar in Mesoamerica.

Shortly afterwards, in *c.*500–200BC, Zapotec artisans at nearby Monte Albán carved loose-limbed figures on the structure now called Building L or the Temple of the Danzantes. Slabs bearing these carvings were probably arranged along the side of the building. The fluid carving of these figures – believed to be prisoners of war or sacrificial victims – includes scrolls emanating from the groin, probably representing the flow of sacrificial blood after the priests had mutilated the victims' sexual organs, or possibly celebrating rites of autosacrifice in which the depicted figures had cut their own sexual organs to offer their blood. Scholars note that the stonemasons here represented victims rather than rulers, and as at San José Mogote, exhibited a concern with marking the place of the images within the cycles of time.

STELAE IN MAYA LANDS

At Izapa on the Pacific coastal plain of Chiapas, in the southern Maya region, craftsmen developed a highly influential style in carving stelae from *c.*300BC onwards. They cut images of scenes from religious narratives, in which human-animal figures interact in making offerings.

Scholars identify Stela 21 at Izapa (cut *c.*100BC–AD100) as the first representation in Mesoamerican carving of the act of sacrifice. The pillar depicts a standing figure holding the head of a newly decapitated victim, whose lifeblood pours forth in long scrolls both from the head and the prostrate body, while in the background a ruler or noble passes by in a sedan chair carried by two porters. Another roughly contemporary stela, number 25, represents a man or hero from religious narrative standing on the ritually important right-hand side of a scene, holding a staff on which a magnificent bird perches and facing a crocodile with its nose in the ground and tail vertically in the air. The stone-carver gave the crocodile an explicit likeness to a tree and indeed added a bird in the 'branches' of its tail. Scholars cannot fully explain the scene, but the crocodile, normally an image for the earth, may be a representation of the ceiba cosmic tree connecting underworld and heavens through the terrestrial plane.

Craftsmen also cut stelae in this period at Kaminaljuyú in the Guatemala valley. They carved rulers, generally portrayed walking in profile wearing elaborate garb and headdress and holding objects of ceremonial or ritual significance.

SET IN STONE:
THE POWER OF MAYA KINGS

Craftsmen in settlements such as Izapa, Kaminaljuyú and Abaj Takalik in the southern Maya region were cutting glyphic inscriptions that probably included calendrical dates in the years *c*. 100BC–AD250 (the late Preclassic Period). Fragments of what might originally have been dated monuments survive, but none of the dates themselves have been found.

CHANGING PERSPECTIVE
In these early years, Maya sculptors represented rulers with feet, legs and head in profile, but the torso turned towards the viewer with both arms visible. At Tikal, sculptors began to experiment with the position of the figure. Stela 4, dated AD378 and recording the accession of King Curl Nose, is the oldest known pillar to show a figure turned entirely towards the viewer. Another Curl Nose monument, Stela 18 of AD396, is the oldest known Maya image of a seated figure facing the viewer. Another early carving of a figure looking straight out of the pillar, Stela 26 at Uaxactún, is dated AD445. This position was then found on stelae throughout the Classic Period, at sites including Palenque, Yaxchilán, Piedras Negras and Seibal.

Above: At Quiriguá, Stela D is one of several in the Main Plaza bearing the face of King Cauac Sky (r. 724–84).

Below: Intricate Puuc-style carving surrounds a standing figure of the king on this monument from Kabah in Yucatán.

KINGS AND QUEENS OF CALAKMUL
The city of Calakmul, in south-eastern Campeche, contains 113 stelae – more than at any other Maya city. Some of these are unique in the Maya world in that they were raised in pairs that bear male and female portraits, understood to be the king and his queen. The first of these paired portraits were Stela 29 and Stela 28, raised by the city's second king in AD623. Another set, Stela 24 and Stela 23, were erected in AD702 by Calakmul's fifth king on the western edge of the city's Central Plaza.

Four stelae at Piedras Negras depict a newly inaugurated king in the position adopted on the celebrated Olmec Altar 4: seated cross-legged in a recess, facing the viewer. These four stelae were Stela 25 (dedicated in AD608), Stela 6 (AD687), Stela 11 (AD731) and Stela 14 (AD761). Each was an advance on its predecessor in terms of the success with which the carving was achieved, using progressively deeper recesses that permitted fuller development of the seated figure.

DEEP RELIEF
Images of kings facing out of the stela were most successfully developed by craftsmen at Copán and Quiriguá. At Copán, the carving on Stelae H (AD730)

Above: Quiriguá. The image of Cauac Sky on Stela E – which stands 10.7m (35ft) tall – is more than three times life size.

and Stela A (AD731) is extremely ornate and in very deep relief. At Quiriguá, Monument 5 (also known as Stela E and dated AD771) bears a splendid high-relief portrait of King Cauac Sky commemorating his victory over Copán. The largest known Maya stela, it measures 1.5m (5ft) wide by 10.7m (35ft) high and has an estimated weight of 65 tons.

CARVING THE GODS

Sculptors at Quiriguá moved on from stelae to carve large, unquarried sandstone boulders, subsequently known as zoomorphs, with images of sky divinities, earth creatures and kings.

One of these, Zoomorph P (also known as Monument 16), depicts a young ruler seated in the open jaws of a serpent representing the underworld and holds a shield with a sun god portrait and a sceptre of rulership. More than 3.4m (11ft) wide and 2.1m (7ft) high, the vast structure was typical of Maya sculptural aesthetics in its combination of natural and grotesque supernatural figures and the refusal to leave any space plain. The zoomorph was dedicated in AD795 and might have been cut to celebrate the accession of King Jade Sky.

ALL-ROUND CARVING AT TONINÁ

The stelae at Toniná, a city 50km (30 miles) south of Palenque, were unique in the Maya world in that they were carved in the round like statues. They were also unusually small, about 2m (6ft 6in) tall rather than the average for Maya stelae of 2.5–3m (8–10ft). Another carved structure at Toniná, known as Monument 122, features more conventional carving. It bears an image of King Kan Xul II of Palenque as a captive. Toniná's third ruler, who acceded to the throne in AD688, achieved a great coup in capturing Kan Xul II in AD711. Art historian Linda Schele suggests part of the tribute involved the despatch to Toniná of an elite sculptor from Palenque who was forced to carve an image of his defeated king.

Below: Many believe the deep-relief carving on Copán stelae to be the finest in the Maya world. Animal masks and complex regalia contrast with the serenity of the face.

THE WORK OF MAYA STONEMASONS

Maya carvers worked the rock that was locally available. For most this was limestone. At Quiriguá, Altar de Sacrificios, Toniná and a few other sites, stonemasons had access to sandstone, while at Copán they used a volcanic rock called trachyte. With a fine grain and predictable texture, trachyte was easy to carve and its availability at Copán was one important reason why that site rose to such prominence as a centre of the sculptor's art. The only drawback of trachyte was that it sometimes contained very hard flint

THE RULER'S ORNATE SCEPTRE
Maya kings were often represented on stelae and in other carvings holding 'the manikin sceptre', an ornately decorated staff symbolic of royal power: an example can be seen on Monument 16 at Quiriguá (carved in 795). Some centuries earlier, the influence of Teotihuacán on Maya sites had been seen in part by the carving of a Teotihuacano-style weapon, the spear thrower, on royal images: Stela 4 at Tikal celebrated the accession of King Curl Nose in 378 by depicting the king holding a spear thrower on his left arm beneath an image of the divine Maya patron of royalty, Bolon Tza'cab. Scholar Clemency Coggins demonstrated that the manikin sceptre symbol was formed by combining an image of Bolon Tza'cab with a carving of a spear-thrower.

Above: Manikin sceptre.

lumps. These were either hacked off, creating small depressions in the monument's surface, or left in place, forming small lumps. Elsewhere, stonecutters needed to work limestone and sandstone shortly after it had been quarried, for the rock was soft when first exposed but grew harder the longer it was in contact with the air.

ANCIENT QUARRYING
Labourers quarried rock by digging along the sides and ends of an oblong shaft of stone suitable for a stela. Then, probably using tree trunks as rollers and creepers as ropes, they hauled the shaft to the site where it was to be erected. There they dug a receiving hole and lined it with masonry, then pulled the shaft upright into the hole, probably by building a ramp of logs behind the shaft and using an A-frame fashioned from wooden beams to raise it. Once the shaft was in place, they built platforms around it on which skilled carvers set to work. They used round-handled, single-edged stone chisels 5–15cm (2–6in) and hammer stones up to 7cm (2¾in) across.

After the carvers were finished, their work was rubbed smooth using sand and water, then plastered and painted. Most stelae were painted a dark red or blue mixed with copal resin. This produced a long-lasting coating with a varnish-like finish. In some places, particularly where the relief carving was deeper, the paint remains visible, more than 1,000 years later.

WALL PANELS AND LINTELS
In addition to stelae, Maya sculptors excelled in cutting wall panels, thrones, stone lintels and decorative elements on buildings. Some of the finest examples of wall panels and thrones were carved at Piedras Negras, roughly midway between Yaxchilán and Palenque on the river Usumacinta. A wall panel carved in the year 9.16.6.9.16 (AD757) adorned a nine-

Above: Serpent warrior. On the Temple of the Warriors at Chichén Itzá, a soldier emerges from the jaws of a sacred snake.

level mortuary monument now called Structure O-13 by archaeologists. The panel represents the fourth king of the Piedras Negras dynasty making a ritual designation of his son as the royal heir.

Below: This limestone chacmool, *inlaid with shell and obsidian, was originally painted. He performed service as an offering stone for ritual victims' hearts at Chichén Itzá.*

Above: Delicate limestone carving of courtly consultation adorned the back of a royal throne dated AD747 and found in Chiapas.

The king is depicted on his throne, with his son and two other boys standing on his left and three elite visitors from Yaxchilán, including King Bird Jaguar, on his right. Piedras Negras stonecarvers also created a magnificent, bench-like throne that was placed in the main room of the palace in a position where it could be seen by subjects standing in the courtyard before the palace. The stonemason-scribes carved glyphs on three sides of the throne's front legs; the inscriptions reveal that the piece was dedicated to royal use in 9.17.15.0.0. (AD785).

The finest carved stone lintels in the Maya world were the depictions of King Shield Jaguar and his wife Lady Xoc on Lintels 24, 25 and 26 at Yaxchilán. These images of Lady Xoc performing autosacrifice by drawing a thorn cord across her tongue, of Lady Xoc experiencing a vision and of the king dressing for battle ,were raised in Temple 23, dedicated to the queen and the gods in AD726.

At Copán, stonemasons excelled not only in carving stelae and altars or thrones, but also in providing elaborate decoration for architectural elements such as stairways and a platform with monumental stairway that archaeologists call a 'reviewing stand'. On the Hieroglyphic Stairway, which was dedicated in AD756, they cut more than 2,000 glyphs recording the city's dynastic history. The 63-step structure stood more than 20m (65ft) high and was 10m (33ft) wide, including its balustrades.

THE SEAT OF THE JAGUAR

In the 9th–10th centuries AD, rulers in the cities of the northern Maya region stopped commissioning carved monuments, instead employing stonecarvers to make decorative elements for sacred buildings. Artists at Uxmal produced an image of a head emerging from a serpent's jaws that was mounted in the façade of the base of the pyramid known as the House of the Magician. They also carved a new type of royal seat, the jaguar throne: a life-sized jaguar with flattened back on which the ruler sat. A jaguar throne has also been found at Chichén Itzá. Also at Chichén Itzá, under Toltec influence,

Right: This standard bearer was made for the Temple of the Warriors in Chichén Itzá.

stonemasons carved the reclining *chacmool* figures that were set before temples. The arched figures each include a vessel into which the heart of a sacrificial victim was placed.

The carvers also made standard bearers, seated figures about 1m (3ft 4in) tall that held a feather banner, and the upright warriors that archaeologists now call 'Atlantean figures'. These were used to provide the support necessary for door lintels and daises.

459

INTRICATE CARVING IN STUCCO

There was a long tradition in Maya lands of carving in stucco or plaster. From the late Preclassic Period (400BC–AD100), builders used carved stucco as a decorative element on sacred buildings.

PLASTER MASKS

At Cerros, in Belize, a temple-platform known as Structure 5C-2 and built c.50BC included a long stairway flanked by four large painted plaster masks, one pair representing the rising and setting sun and the other depicting the planet Venus as morning and evening star.

At Uaxactún, a temple platform (H-sub 3) erected about the same time had a similar decorative layout. Four large masks representing the sacred mountain monster of Maya belief flanked the central stairway on the western face of the platform. In the lower two, the mountain was shown rising from the waters. The upper pair showed the mountain giving issue to the Vision Serpent that the Maya

Below: Awe-inspiring lord of day. This stucco mask from Kohunlich is of the sun god Kinich Ahau, a form of Itzamná.

believed conducted shamans and initiates on spirit journeys along its many coils.

At the same site, the modestly sized platform known by archaeologists as E-VII-sub had a total of 16 stucco masks on its four faces. These masks represented the sun and Venus, as at Cerros. The platform served as an astronomical observatory in an arrangement of sacred buildings that historians call Group E, laid out to align with sunrise on winter and summer solstices. Similar masks were carved on sacred buildings at Tikal, Kohunlich, Lamanai and El Mirador in the late Preclassic Period.

RELIEF AT PALENQUE

The Maya tradition of decorative stucco carving continued into the Classic Period. It probably reached its apogée in the elegant relief panels and heads carved at Palenque in the 7th century AD. Here,

Above: Best known for murals, Bonampak also provides evidence of the well developed Maya art of stucco carving. A series of 130 stucco glyphs, like this one at Bonampak, were carved in Temple 18 at Palenque.

FROM STUCCO TO STONE

In the reign of King 18-Rabbit of Copán (695–738), when the centre of the city was transformed with the rebuilding of many structures and the erection of several monuments and much of the Acropolis took its final form, the king ordered the transition from stucco to carved stone for decorative elements on buildings. In their original form the stone carvings were covered with plaster and then painted. The underlying stone proved a much more durable material than plaster.

relief panels and other decorations took on the role, played by stelae in many other cities, of recording royal history and transmitting dynastic propaganda. The Group of the Cross temples built by Chan-Bahlum, son and successor of the great King Pacal, contained three large stucco relief panels. These represented scenes rich in religious detail celebrating the transfer of power from the deceased king to his son. On the roof of the Temple of Inscriptions, beneath which King Pacal was buried in a hidden crypt, stood a wide, five-doored temple. On its roof comb were stucco reliefs that similarly portrayed the new king being granted the right to rule by his father.

Right: A noble profile carved in stucco at Bonampak shows the nose built up to join the forehead in line with the Maya ideal.

STUCCO MASTERPIECES

The crypt in which King Pacal was laid to rest was adorned with beautiful stucco reliefs representing nine figures variously identified by scholars as the nine lords of the night, the nine gods of the under-world or nine of the king's divine ancestors. On the crypt floor beneath the king's sarcophagus were two masterpieces of stucco carving: life-sized twin portraits of the king, one in his youth and the other in mid-life maturity. The heads, about 40cm (16in) high, portray an idealized image of the king. In line with Maya ideas of youthful beauty, the bridge of the nose of the youthful portrait is built up to connect to the forehead. However, the second head, of the middle-aged king, elegantly combined the ideal with the truth, for it reproduces the long face that the king had in other representations.

Scholars believe that Pacal's successor, Chan-Bahlum, probably ordered his carvers to produce actual rather than idealized portraits. An image of Chan-Bahlum on a stucco tablet from Temple IV shows him with a thick lower lip, an outsized nose

Left: The ancient sculptor who moulded this melancholy portrait for Palenque's Temple of the Sun achieved a moving naturalism.

that went far beyond the Maya ideal and an expression of nervousness that is far different to the serenity accorded to Pacal. Similarly, fine stucco panels carved in House D in the Palenque palace complex during Chan-Bahlum's reign appear to show more realistic than idealized portraits.

ROSALILA MASKS

At Copán, stucco carvers reached great heights of achievement. Early buildings in the area later called the Acropolis were covered with elaborate stucco masks, but these were destroyed when the buildings were enclosed by later development. Nearby in the mid-6th century AD, a temple now called Rosalila by archaeologists was erected, its façade covered with fine stucco carvings. When, after many years, the building was encased by the next phase of construction, the masks and other elements were carefully preserved.

MEN AND GODS IN STONE:
AZTEC STONE CARVING

The years after c.AD900 in Mesoamerica saw a return to free-standing sculpture, an art that had not been practised since the time of the Olmec. Peoples of the northern Mexican Chalcihuites culture, the Toltecs of Tollán and those influenced by them at Chichén Itzá and elsewhere made three-dimensional Atlantean figures that supported temple roofs and door lintels, seated standard-bearer statues and reclining *chacmool* figures which were used to display and store human hearts in sacrificial ritual.

The Huastecs, a Maya-speaking people who inhabited the Gulf coast in northern Veracruz, also made monumental seated and standing statues that were a major influence on Aztec sculptors. Many of these anthropomorphic stone statues bore a second figure on its back, thought by scholars to represent an ancestral spirit companion. The Huastecs, who were particularly associated with the worship of Quetzalcóatl in his form as wind god Éhecatl, also built circular temples that might have inspired the building of the

Below: The Tizoc stone celebrates the military triumphs of the tlatoani Tizoc, who *took 14 towns for the expanding empire.*

circular Caracol at Chichén Itzá and which were certainly forerunners of the circular Éhecatl-Quetzalcóatl temple in the Aztecs' main ceremonial centre in Tenochtitlán. Having conquered the Huastecs c.1400, the Aztecs imported these styles in sculpture and temple architecture among the spoils of war.

GODS IN STONE
The Aztecs carved many stone figures of gods and goddesses with detailed iconography. This served to identify the deities and to suggest the complex attributes that they shared with other gods.

An 80cm (2ft 6in) stone statue of Xiuhtecuhtli, patron of the rulers or *tlatoque* (plural of *tlatoani*), depicted him wearing the *tlatoani's* costume: a diadem, *xicolli* ceremonial waistcoat, triangular loincloth that signified warrior status and sandals adorned with sun-rays at the heels. His mouth gave issue to fangs that were a symbol of the god's great age: Xiuhtecuhtli was so old that he had lost his real teeth. Xiuhtecuhtli was also a god of fire and associated with the sun: he was the Aztec form of the ancient god Huehuetéotl ('The Old One').

Above: This Aztec sculpture of Quetzalcóatl in his form as a coiled rattlesnake was cut from a single block of stone.

Such statues combined inconographic detail with naturalistic verve and a mastery of the human form. Seated statues of flower god Xochipilli depict a near-naked youth wearing only mask, loincloth and sandals. One, 115cm (4ft) tall, had flowers cut as if tattooed on the arms and legs. Some scholars suggest that these were images of plants with mind-altering properties used in divinatory rites. The statue was found in the 19th century in the village of Tlamanalco on the side of the sacred volcano Ixtaccíhuatl.

THE HUMAN FORM
Aztec sculptors also made beautifully realized statues of ordinary men and women. A female nude statue dated

Right: This cuauhxicalli *or eagle vessel, used for storing sacrificial victims' hearts, was sacred to Huitzilopochtli.*

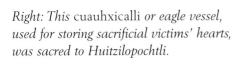

*c.*1500 found in Texcoco and once called the 'Venus of Texcoco', together with several seated and standing statues of *macehualtin* commoner young men either naked or wearing loincloths, celebrated the youthful human form. Such statues might have been dressed in ritual costume that identified them as particular deities at festival time. A seated 33cm (13in) statue of a hunchback made *c.*1500 exhibited the sculptors' delight in naturalism and might also have been a tribute to Nanahuatzin, the disfigured and deformed god who rose to become the sun in the religious narrative of the first days at Teotihuacán. Hunchbacks and other people with physical deformities were well cared for in Tenochtitlán, but at times of solar eclipse might be chosen for human sacrifice because their bodies marked them out as the children of the sun god.

ANIMAL CARVINGS

Sculptors also represented the natural world, producing statues of dogs, coyotes, rabbits, jaguars, insects, lizards, fish, snakes, eagles, toads, pumpkins, squash and cacti. Many, while exhibiting the craftsmen's great naturalistic skill, had powerful sacred symbolism, since many gods and goddesses took animal form. Stone solar discs were carved and celebrated as symbols of the sun god Tonatiuh and of the current world age, which came under his rule and protection.

Aztec craftsmen reproduced Toltec forms such as Atlantean figures and *chacmools*. Archaeologists found a sculpted *chacmool* figure in front of the Tláloc shrine atop the early version (*c.*1390) of the great pyramid of the Templo Mayor in Tenochtitlán. The rather crude effigy was carved with Tláloc symbols, as was a later and more expertly carved *chacmool*

*c.*1502–20. A series of five stone warrior figures roughly 1.2m (4ft) tall found in Tenochtitlán possibly functioned as roof supports in the style of Toltec Atlantean figures. The five statues represented four male soldiers clutching spear throwers and wearing the triangular loincloth of the warrior and one female, wearing a skirt of arrows. Scholars suggest that they might have stood in the four cardinal points: males at east, south and north and the female in the west, a direction associated with women. The fourth male would have stood in the centre, the position of the world tree and the current world age, the spot occupied in Aztec cosmology by the great Templo Mayor itself.

TRIUMPHAL MONUMENTS

The Aztecs also produced monumental stone carving that celebrated the power of the gods, of the *tlatoani* and of the state. The celebrated Sun Stone, carved from basalt in the reign of Axayáctal (1469–81) with a diameter of 3.6m (12ft), commemorated the myth of the five world ages, the glory of the sun god and the power of the *tlatoani*. The Tizoc stone, a great cylinder 2.65m (8ft 8in) across and carved in 1481–86, celebrated the military triumphs of the Aztec army and in particular the *tlatoani* Tizoc (*r.* 1481–86) was depicted 15 times around the stone gripping a battle-weary victim by the hair, with a glyph beside each victim identifying the place of conquest. Another similar stone, 2.24m (7ft 4in) in diameter, was carved to celebrate the victories of Moctezuma I (*r.* 1440–69).

The Teocalli stone, carved in the shape of a pyramid-temple with front steps flanked by date glyphs, bore a 'temple' at the top carved with a sun disc and images of Huitzilopochtli to the left and Moctezuma II (*r.* 1502–20) to the right, both preparing to offer their blood in rites of autosacrifice. The stone, 1.23m by 92cm by 99cm (4ft by 3ft by 3ft 3in), was probably used as a royal throne. It was carved to celebrate the new fire ceremony that marked the beginning of a new 52-year cycle in 1507.

CARVING IN WOOD

The Maya called their stelae 'stone trees', suggesting that in the great cities of the Classic Period, dynastic monuments might once have been carved from tree trunks. There was certainly a flourishing Maya woodcarving tradition, as is evidenced by the few examples of wooden door lintels and beams that have survived.

DOOR LINTELS

The temples of Tikal were once graced by wooden door lintels. One of the surviving lintels, which once spanned a doorway in the building known as Temple IV, was carved from sapodilla wood with an arched serpent in the mid-8th century AD. From the serpent's mouth emerged an ancestral spirit, who might represent the dynastic founder, while above the serpent was the sacred quetzal bird of the Maya, its wings outstretched. Beneath the serpent's arched back was King Yax Kin (*r.* AD734–46), enthroned in splendour. The glyphic inscription declares that the king was shown celebrating a military triumph for Tikal on 26 July AD743. A slightly older lintel survives from Temple I, depicting King Ah Cacau (AD682–734) on the throne of Tikal, with a deity – perhaps his ancestral spirit – above him and a glyphic text celebrating military triumph over Calakmul on 5 August AD695.

Later wooden lintels survived in temples at Chichén Itzá and Uxmal. In the Temple of the Jaguars at Chichén Itzá, a carved lintel depicts a human figure surrounded by a feathered serpent and another figure within a spiked circular design representing the sun. US traveller John Lloyd Stephens (1805–52) discovered a carved sapodilla beam in the Governor's Palace at Uxmal and took it with him when he returned to the USA. Unfortunately, it was destroyed in a fire, much to the dismay of later scholars, who

might have been able to use the beam to date the beautiful building in which it was found.

SKILL OF THE WOODCARVERS

The beauty, detail and precision of the glyphic carving in wood was remarkable. The scribes carved the hard sapodilla wood while it was still green, for once

Above: A detail of an Aztec wooden drum of c.1500 shows an eagle-warrior who stands for the sun god Tonatiuh.

Below: Woodcarvers received military commissions for ceremonial weapons, such as this gold-covered spear-thrower.

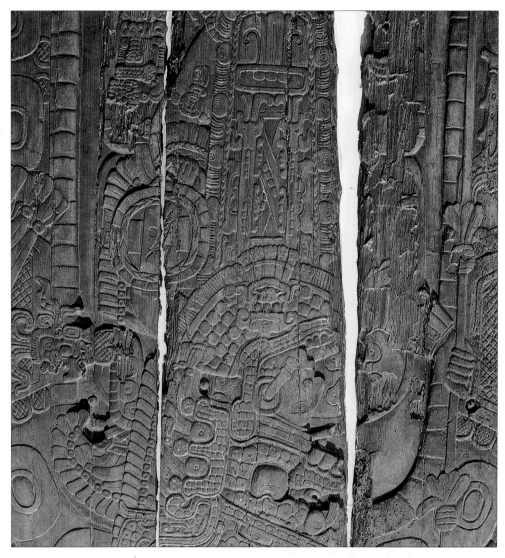

cured it became as hard as metal. Scholar Michael Coe has suggested that the scribes first painted the symbols on the wood before cutting them with obsidian blades. Another surviving piece that demonstrates the skill of Maya glyphic carvers is a wooden box celebrating the memory of a late 7th century AD king of Tortuguero, a settlement near Tikal. The style of the glyphs closely resembles that on the Tikal lintels.

Maya woodcarvers almost certainly also made figures of gods and goddesses from wood, but none have survived, for they would have been easily and enthusiastically destroyed by Catholic churchmen. Images in the *Madrid Codex* depict the gods themselves at work fashioning masks and figures from wood. This would seem to provide evidence that the craft was practised in Maya workshops.

A few examples of wooden figures of Aztec deities have survived. A seated statue of Macuilxóchitl of *c*.1500 depicts the god of music and gaming wearing his trademark crested headdress. Traces of paint show that the statue was originally red, but the inlay from the eyes and the ornament that once adorned his mouth are missing.

The statue was found in a cave, where atmospheric conditions were favourable to its survival. The same was true of a cedarwood fertility goddess figure of *c*.1500 which was discovered still in use for worship in a cave near the Toluca valley, Veracruz, in the 19th century. The figure wore the hairstyle which was conventionally adopted by married women and held her hands up to support the weight of her breasts, emphasizing her maternal role. Wooden statues of deities were called *cuauhximalli* by the Aztecs.

WOODEN DRUMS
Elaborately carved examples of both *huehuetl* upright drums and *teponaxtli* oblong drums have survived. A *huehuetl* drum, 98cm (3ft 2in) tall and elaborately carved with war symbols, was found in Malinalco

– one of the mountain-top temples of the eagle- and jaguar-warrior elite – in the latter part of the 19th century. The carver cut the symbol for the current world age, Nahua Ollin (4-Earthquake), between an eagle-warrior and a jaguar-warrior. The glyph for war, *teoatl-tlachinolli* ('fire water') arises from the warriors' mouths. On the opposite side of the round drum the craftsman cut an image of an eagle-man that was almost certainly intended to be the sun god Tonatiuh himself. The lower part of the drum base was adorned with images of eagle- and jaguar-warriors in warlike procession.

A *teponaxtli* drum of *c*.1250 carved in the form of a jaguar was found in Puebla state in the late 19th century. Making these drums was the work of highly skilled specialists, who first hollowed the wood by burning, then

Above: A sapodilla-wood door lintel from Tikal Temple IV celebrates a military victory of King Yax Kin in July AD743.

finished the interior with chisel work. The top of the horizontal drum was split into two tongues and played with a hammer to produce a two-tone note.

Yet another example of a beautifully finished drum of *c*.1500 was carved in the shape of a reclining warrior from Tlaxcala shown with a copper-bladed axe.

Left: Mixtec craftsmen carved this delicate wooden jaguar and encrusted it with fine mosaic in c.1400–1520.

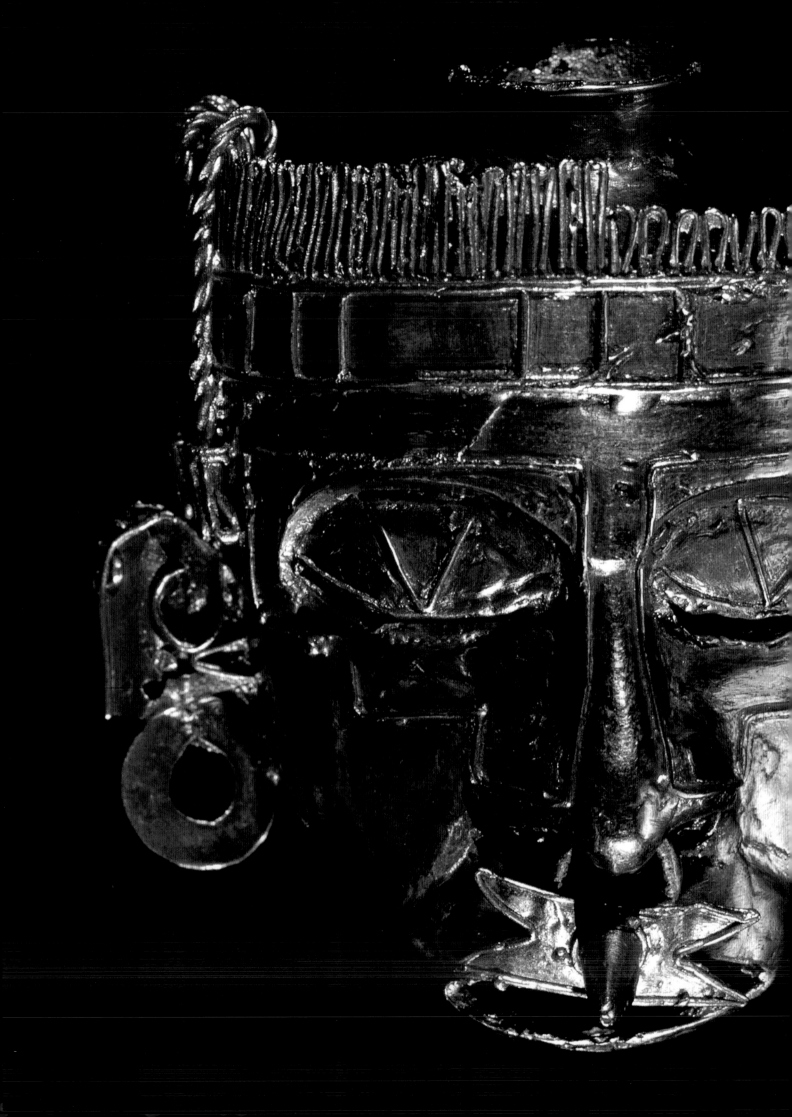

CHAPTER 23

PRECIOUS WORK

In April 1519 Moctezuma II sent magnificent gifts of gold and silver to Hernán Cortés and his conquistadors. The collection – which included a solid gold disc as big as a cartwheel, together with an even larger disc of silver – was intended to honour the newcomers and to impress the Aztec emperor's power and wealth upon them. The gift also made a religious statement, for the gold and silver discs represented the sun and moon and celebrated the pre-eminence of the Aztecs – self-styled 'People of the Sun'.

The Spaniards, versed in a different culture, could not be expected to understand the religious message: the gift served only to fan their lust for Aztec riches. Some members of the invading group, including Cortés himself, certainly admired the craftsmanship of the pieces – he wrote to Charles V about Aztec jewellery that 'nowhere in the world could a smith have done better'. But many Europeans could not see beyond the dazzling monetary value of the silver and gold; predictably, the discs did not survive – they were melted down for their metal, the fate that awaited the great majority of gold and silver ritual items, ceremonial jewellery and other pieces sent back to Europe by the conquistadors. Cortés despatched several loads of Aztec precious metalwork, and these were among the items that astonished German artist Albrecht Dürer, who declared them to be 'strange and wonderfully worked objects' that thrilled his heart.

Left: God of spring and goldsmiths. This exquisite gold mask of Xipe Totec was an offering in Tomb 7 at Monte Albán.

AN IMPORTED CRAFT:
METALWORK IN MESOAMERICA

On 6 January 1932 Mexican archaeologist Alfonso Caso made a breathtaking find in a tomb at the Zapotec mountaintop city of Monte Albán. The grave had originally been laid out c.AD 500–750 with a large fore chamber leading into two rooms aligned east–west. These contained a stone carved with Zapotec glyphs and a number of funerary urns. The grave had then been reopened in the late Postclassic Period (c.1250–1500) by local Mixtec mourners, who buried nine skeletons with a magnificent tribute-cache of metalwork and jewellery. The grave, known as Tomb Number 7, contained no fewer than 121 golden objects, 24 silver objects and a large number of rings, necklaces and pendants. This find provided ample evidence of the Mixtecs' astonishing skill in metalwork and making jewellery.

LATE STARTERS
When compared to their South American neighbours, Mesoamerican craftsmen were late starters in metalwork. Native Mesoamericans did not make jewellery, ritual items, weapons or tools from metal until after c.AD800. As early as 2000BC, the inhabitants of the Andes mountains in South America had begun to develop metalworking techniques that slowly travelled northwards along marine and land trade routes. These techniques took almost 3,000 years to reach Mesoamerica, probably arriving roughly simultaneously in two separate areas: the northern Maya region of the Yucatán peninsula and, hundreds of miles to the west, coastal settlements in western Mexico.

Among the oldest metal objects in Mesoamerica is a small claw, c.AD550 in Panama. It is made of the alloy of silver, copper and gold known as tumbaga, and was buried in the ceremonial centre of Altun Há, on the coastal plain north of modern Belize City. Later, a hollow figure of a gold-copper alloy was deposited as part of a cache of valuables beneath Stela H at Copán. The stela was dedicated in AD782, although archaeologists cannot rule out the possibility that the cache was buried after this or added to at a later date. Only the legs of the figurine remain, but expert analysis of the casting and alloy suggest that it was imported from a site in the southern parts of Central America such as Panama or Costa Rica.

BEGINNINGS IN MEXICO
Archaeologists have established that in the earliest days of Mesoamerican metalworking, during the 9th century, artisans working with copper in western Mexico were producing the same items in the same way as their counterparts in

Left: One of the finds in Tomb 7 was this Mixtec gold pectoral or breast ornament representing the 'old fire god' Xiuhtecuhtli.

Left: This Mixtec gold earring was one of the hoard buried in Tomb 7 at Monte Albán. The Mixtecs' exquisite gold jewellery and other fine metalwork was admired and highly influential across Mesoamerica.

Another metalworking centre was established at Amapa, Nayarit, about 50km (30 miles) inland from the Pacific coast, on the river Santiago. Here artisans made copper rings, knives, needles, pins, axe-heads, beads, plaques, bells and awls.

In Michoacán the Tarascans worked local copper to produce small ritual figures, tweezers, open rings, needles and a large numbers of bells. They also made copper axe-heads that were used as a form of money.

In Oaxaca the Mixtecs began developing their metalworking expertise after AD900. They became the pre-eminent metalworkers of the Aztec age, when some Mixtecs worked as producers of jewellery and precious-metal items in Tenochtitlán, while others worked in their own centres in Oaxaca. México/Aztec craftsmen centred in Azcapotzalco also produced metalwork in the Mixtec style. They worked in gold, silver and tumbaga.

In the northern Maya region, metalworkers developed great expertise in repoussé work, hammering designs into a sheet of metal from the reverse side. Many repoussé pieces hammered from both gold and copper were found among the objects cast into the *Cenote* of Sacrifice at Chichén Itzá. They depicted scenes of conflict between Maya soldiers and warriors of the invading wave of 'Mexicanized' merchants.

Ecuador. They were making needles, rings, tweezers, fishhooks, axe-heads for wooden-handled weapons and the sharply pointed pricking instruments known as awls. There is evidence that smelting and metalwork were carried out on the coast of Guerrero by *c*.AD900. In a settlement at Zihuatanejo, archaeologists uncovered slag pieces (the refuse separated from metal when it is smelted) and many bronze and other metal pieces in a find dated *c*.AD900–1100. The metal pieces included rings, bells and sheets of gold.

THE GODS' GOLD

Gold was identified as *teocuitlatl* ('the gods' excrement') in the Nahuatl tongue, probably because it was found in nuggets, like the droppings of animals. Its colour meant it was also associated with the sun. Images of the gods sometimes represented them wearing the gold jewellery worn by rulers, warriors, nobles and priests. A stone casket of the late 15th century that belonged to the *tlatoani* of Tenochtitlán, Ahuítzotl (*r*. 1486–1502), depicted the god Tláloc wearing a necklace carved with the symbol for gold. A statue of Xochipilli of *c*.1350–1500 shows the god of flowers and music wearing a gold necklace.

Below: This Mixtec painted vase is of a human head laden with jewellery with pierced earrings and an elaborate headdress.

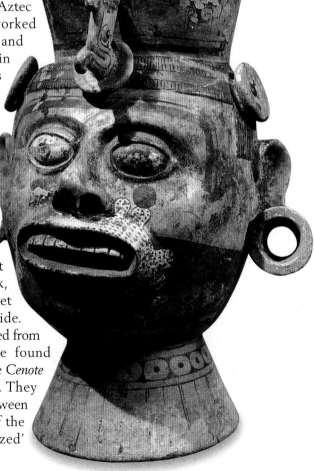

GOLDEN ORNAMENTS

Among the gold, silver and other precious items found in Tomb 7 at Monte Albán was a remarkable gold pendant, some 22cm (8.5in) long, made by Mixtec craftsmen *c*.1200–1500. This elaborate piece, an earring, was cast by the lost-wax process and consists of four detailed images set horizontally and beneath them four pendant elements. The four images represent, from the top: two gods playing the Mesoamerican ball game on an I-shaped court; a solar disc; a butterfly set in a square border that some identify as an image of a flint knife; and the crocodile earth monster. Some scholars interpret these as levels of the universe: the celestial realm of the gods, the sun, the moon (represented by the butterfly/knife) and the earth. Mixtec craftsmen were the masters of jewellery-making in the Aztec age.

JEWELLERY IN A SINGLE STYLE

The wearing of jewellery was strictly regulated in Aztec lands. Only elite warriors and members of the nobility were permitted to wear lip, nose, neck or ear ornaments in social intercourse, although gold and silver finery was also

Below: This Aztec butterfly nose-ring was probably worn by a statue of moon goddess Coyolxauhqui in the Templo Mayor.

Above: Aztec beaten gold arrows represent the xiuhcóatl *or fire snake wielded by Huitzilopochtli. They end in serpent mouths.*

used as part of the sacred costumes worn by priests. Jewellery was made in a single style across the Mesoamerican region – except among the Tarascans of western Mexico, who kept the Aztec world at bay. Scholars call this pan-Mesoamerican jewellery the South Mexican International Style. This style had three distinguishing features. First, its decorative elements were similar to the style of the codices or bark-paper books painted by the Mixtecs. Second, it was of very high technical quality, made by artisans expert in lost-wax casting and wirework. Third, its artisans favoured composite designs that combined metal and precious stones, more than one type of metal or that added pendant elements to pectorals or rings.

ANIMAL SIGNIFICANCE

A pair of 6cm (2.4in)-long ear ornaments, made by México/Aztec or Mixtec craftsmen *c*.1400–1521, represent bird heads emerging from solar disks and giving issue from their mouths to tassels and bells. Experts identify the birds as *coxcoxtli*, a woodland species associated with Xochipilli, god of flowers, music and games. A 15th-century gold finger ring made by Mixtec craftsmen is adorned with the head of an eagle crowned with an intricately reproduced feather diadem. The eagle's beak probably once held a pendant element or a bell. The body of the ring takes the form of a delicately imagined serpent. This ring is typical of

Mixtec output in representing common animals that had powerful sacred significance: the eagle is an image of Huitzilopochtli and the snake of Quetzalcóatl. Another Mixtec ring (*c*.1200–1521) represented both a jaguar head and a double-headed serpent, summoning the qualities of those powerful creatures for the wearer. Such rings were worn by members of the noble elite, in these cases perhaps by leading military figures, since the jaguar and the eagle both had important martial associations as the symbols of elite warrior groups.

Some jewellery represented the gods. A 6cm (2.4in)-long Mixtec gold pendant of *c*.1500 depicts Xiuhtecuhlti, patron of rulers and fire god, with the cylindrical elements in his headdress that were his

USING AND DISPOSING OF JEWELLERY

Jewellery was worn by members of the Aztec and Maya ruling and noble class for display and as part of ritual costumes in religious ceremonial. Precious items were offered in sacrifice, cast into the Sacred *Cenote* at Chichén Itzá, laid in a temple offering or provided as part of a cache interred during dedicatory rites for a building or stela. The best offering was the most precious: blood, the force of life. Jade, the colour of Chalchiúhtlicue and closely associated with life in the form of green maize shoots, was considered even more precious than gold or silver.

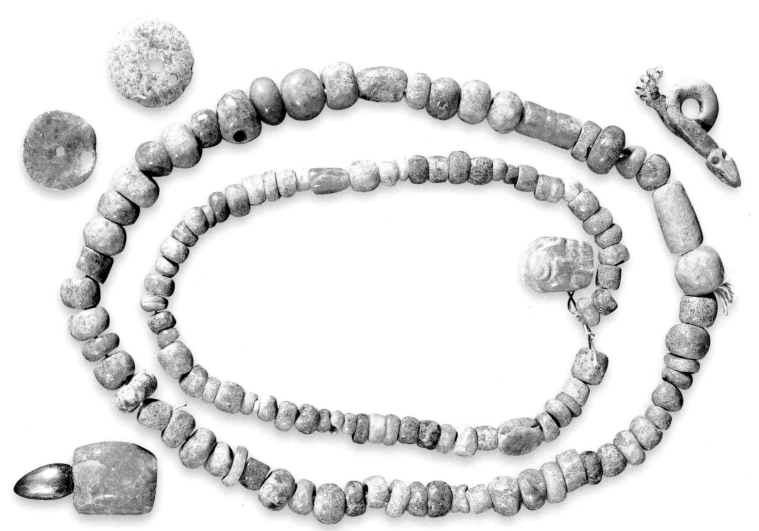

Above: Sacred jade had connections to fertility. These jade-bead jewellery pieces were found in a tomb at El Otero, Mexico.

trademark; such cylinders were the sticks used to start a fire. The god's face bears a beard and from his mouth emerge two fangs, features that mark him as a primordial deity who has lost his teeth through age. From his ears hang two large circular ornaments that end in solar rays. These are appropriate as Xiuhtecuhtli also had solar associations and was identified as the Aztec counterpart of the Mixtec sun god

Iha Ndikandii. A Mixtec pectoral brooch of *c*.1500 also depicted Xiuhtecuhtli/Iha Ndikandii with these characteristic elements of fangs, beard and headdress with vertical cylinders.

LIP ORNAMENTS

Mixtec goldsmiths made elaborate lip ornaments for the Aztec warriors and nobles. A cast-gold lip plug in the shape of an eagle's head made *c*.1500 shows remarkable detailing in the feathers and beak of the bird. The plug was worn on the

lower lip: its shaft was inserted through a hole in the skin and gum and held in place by a plate worn inside the mouth. Eagle lip plugs were probably worn by leading members of the eagle-warrior society. Such plugs must have been heavy. Another example, made *c*.1400–1500, had a cast-gold eagle head and gold plug for securing the ornament in the mouth, but the connecting piece was fashioned from rock crystal to make it lighter.

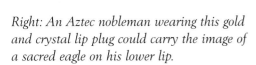

Right: An Aztec nobleman wearing this gold and crystal lip plug could carry the image of a sacred eagle on his lower lip.

WORK OF THE GOLDSMITHS

In his *General History of the Things of New Spain*, Friar Bernardino de Sahagún gave a lengthy inventory of the astounding wealth of gold, other rare metals and precious stones stored in Moctezuma II's treasury as items for ornamenting dancers and their costumes. These included gold models of plants, pelicans, sacred eagles and the *xiuhcóatl* fire serpent wielded by Huitzilopochtli. There was a turquoise disc set in gold, an eagle fashioned from greenstone and mounted in gold and a cylindrical crystal lip plug with feathers from the cotinga bird, also set in gold. The store also contained many articles made from jade and amber.

CELEBRATING WARRIORS

In wearing pendants or other images of warriors, an Aztec indicated that he or she was of good birth and a leading member of the nobility. A number of gold items have survived that celebrate or represent elite warriors. An exquisite pendant bell in the shape of an eagle warrior, made *c.*1500 by Aztec goldsmiths using the lost-wax technique, was worn on a chain or necklace. The bell, 9cm tall and 7.5 cm across (3.5in by 2.9in), consists of a hollow, pear-shaped gold vessel containing a copper pellet with eagle claws at the base. At the top of the pear shape, the warrior's head is enclosed in a battle helmet in the likeness of an eagle's beak, open to reveal the soldier's stern face. His arms are thin and feathered, giving them the appearance of wings. The left arms is bent to the front across his chest, where the soldier wears a pendant plaque in the warrior style. The right arm is raised beside his head and grasping a small, feather-trimmed shield, three dart-like spears and a staff – perhaps an *atlatl* (spear-thrower). Above the head there is a rectangular frame fashioned from gold wire. On the back of the helmet, two loops were used to mount the pendant on a chain when the piece was worn by a member of the fraternity of eagle-warriors in Tenochtitlán.

Right: A Mixtec pendant of c.AD1500 *(described on pages 220–221), represents fire god Xiuhtecuhtli. The projections in his headdress are firesticks; the earrings are solar rays. He is usually shown bearded.*

A Mixtec pendant of *c.*1200–1521 depicts another elite warrior in remarkable detail. The cast-gold figure, 8cm tall and 4.5cm across (3.1in by 1.7in), was worn on the chest or as a lip pendant. The figure wears a decorated headband and long, dangling earrings, together with a nose ornament, warrior-plaques on his chest and a lip plug from which a victim's head and three bells are suspended. His left hand holds a ceremonial shield, while his right grasps a pole that perhaps represents an *atlatl* spear-thrower or a staff of authority.

Another precious-metal warrior figure is a free-standing figurine made from tumbaga (a gold-coloured alloy of silver, copper and gold). The curious piece was found in a cache of gold objects in Texcoco. The figurine, made by Aztec metalworkers after 1346, stands 11.2cm tall and measures 6.1cm across (4.4in by 2.4in). The figure wears ornaments in the lip, ears and nose, together with a splendid headdress. His warrior's loincloth is covered with a skirt of pendant bells. In his left arm he carries a shield and weapons and in his right hand he holds a ritual object and another pendant bell. Cavities in his chest and the back of his head almost certainly once held precious stones. The eyes, now empty, were probably also inlaid with obsidian and shell. The glyphs 2-Rabbit and 3-Water, marked on his back, have puzzled scholars, for they have no obvious relevant meaning. Scientific tests on the metal suggest that it was cast in the period 1346–1570.

GOLD AS TRIBUTE

Mixtec and México/Aztec craftsmen used gold that had been supplied as tribute from subject regions of the empire. In regions such as Soconusco in western Chiapas, it was washed down from the hills and mountains in rivers and collected in the form of nuggets from the riverbeds. In workshops in the valley of Mexico, the metal was smelted at very high temperatures produced by craftsmen-labourers blowing through long tubes on to charcoal fires. Some goldsmiths worked in Moctezuma's palace in Tenochtitlán, producing goldwork exclusively for the *tlatoani* and his inner circle of nobles. These artisans were valued so highly that they were exempt from paying tax.

GOD OF THE GOLDSMITHS

Xipe Totec, worshipped by the Aztecs as the god of regeneration and of the green shoots of spring, was the patron deity of the Mixtec goldsmiths. Scholars believe that his cult, adopted by the Aztecs from the Mixtecs, had in turn been taken by the Mixtecs of Oaxaca from the region of Guerrero where some of western Mexico's very earliest metalworking centres were established in the 9th century AD. The breaking open of seeds in spring

Above: Golden deity. Mixtec goldsmiths produced delicate, lightweight pieces with intricate decorative and figurative elements. This breast ornament appears to make use of solar symbolism.

Xipe personified was perhaps considered to be like the breaking of moulds when goldworkers used the lost-wax method for casting.

Above: A delicately carved golden handle in the shape of a snake's head, made by a Mixtec artisan at Monte Albán, honours the sacred Mesoamerican serpent.

BELLS AND REPOUSSÉ DISCS

Among members of the Aztec nobility, metal bells with a good sound and a pleasing colour were highly prized. Many of the bells made by metalworkers were sewn on to nobles' outfits, so their resonance was highly valued. The creation of a good sound when walking was an important part of the overall impression that a nobleman made.

The colour of the bells was also significant, with silver and gold the preferred colours. The association of these colours with the moon and the sun had been established from ancient times among South American metalworkers and was passed into Mesoamerican belief and cultural patterns along with the metal-working techniques.

Metalworkers learned to make silver-coloured bells and other items by adding a little arsenic to copper and to make gold-coloured metal for artefacts by combining copper with tin.

Hernán Cortés reported on the widespread use of bells in costumes and other artefacts in his first despatch from Mexico. He described a bluestone mosaic headdress with many bells and gold beads, and a collection of animal heads with coloured skins that were hung with bells.

Small copper bells were widely made and distributed in Maya lands. They were worn by the death god Yum Cimil, who is also known to archaeologists as God A and are found on their own because they were probably hung on images of the god that have since been broken or disintegrated. The inhabitants of Quiriguá were using copper bells and ornaments in the period after c.AD800. These were almost certainly locally made.

SKILLED HAMMERWORK

Metalworkers in the northern Maya region developed particular skill in repoussé work, hammering intricate raised designs into copper, silver and gold from the reverse side of the disc. The work is stylistically close to the murals and carved

reliefs of the early Postclassic Period at Chichén Itzá (AD1000–1250). One repoussé disc bears the image of a ruler with elaborate nose ornaments seated on a stone. He is wearing a magnificent feathered headdress and leaning forward in the direction of his extended left hand, which holds a pair of darts or small spears, while his other hand holds a ritual object. Several repoussé discs portray scenes of conflict between defeated Maya warriors and victorious warriors wearing and using Mexican-style equipment. One, 22cm (8.75in) in diameter, depicts two Mexican or Toltec-styled warriors driving Maya footsoldiers forward at the point of a feathered spear. The Maya warriors have the built-up upper noses characteristic of

Above: The skilful repoussé work can still be seen in remains of a gold disc recovered from the sacred cenote at Chichén Itzá.

their people and wear long nose ornaments, together with elaborate feathered headdresses. On the ground by the feet of the Toltec warriors, a sacred serpent, perhaps a representation of the god Quetzalcóatl, rears to give his blessing while the outer rim of the disc is decorated with a serpentine motif that also appears to incorporate the goggle eyes of rain god Tláloc. Another disc represents the mouth of a sky-serpent yawning to give issue to a Toltec-styled warrior. Some discs show sacrificial scenes, representing the highland Mexican rite of tearing the

CASTING BY THE LOST-WAX METHOD

Mesoamerican metalworkers used the lost-wax or *ciré-perdu* method to cast objects. To cast a statuette, a craftsman would first make a clay model then, after dusting this with charcoal, he would brush the shape evenly with melted wax. Once the wax had hardened, he would dust the surface again with charcoal before adding a second layer of clay. He would invert the object and heat it until the wax melted and poured out. Then he would set the mould right way up before filling it with molten metal. He would set the whole aside to cool. Later he would break the mould to reveal the cast-metal object.

Some objects in two metals were produced by two-stage casting, An example is the ornament historians call the Pectoral of Teotitlán del Camino, which is now held in Mexico City's National Museum. This combines gold and silver. The gold segment was cast first, then the silver part afterwards.

victim's heart from his chest. These were made in northern Yucatán using metal reworked from imported items.

OFFERINGS IN THE CENOTE

Archaeologists found a large number of metal offerings in the Sacred Cenote at Chichén Itzá. These include bracelets, necklaces, pendants, rings, bells, beads, earplugs, masks and disks decorated with scenes in elaborate repoussé work. They are made of copper and gold. The archaeological team also uncovered decorative metal elements from wooden objects such as ritual masks and ceremonial shields, in

Right: This delicate beaten gold nose ornament was found at Colima, Meixco.

cases where the wood had rotted away leaving only the metal. Many items had been broken or damaged as part of a rite designed to free the spirit of the object before it was offered. One gold sheet was rolled into a ball, but through academics' painstaking work has been restored to a condition in which it can be viewed and copied. It is decorated with an image of a triumphant Mexican warrior defeating two hapless local Maya in the course of the invasion of the Yucatán peninsula.

Many of the metal objects found at Chichén Itzá were imported items made in South America, the southern countries of Central America and the metalworking regions of western Mexico. Scientific analysis of the items dredged from the Sacred Cenote revealed that some of the pieces were made in Chiapas, Oaxaca, and the valley of Mexico, in Honduras, Panama and Colombia.

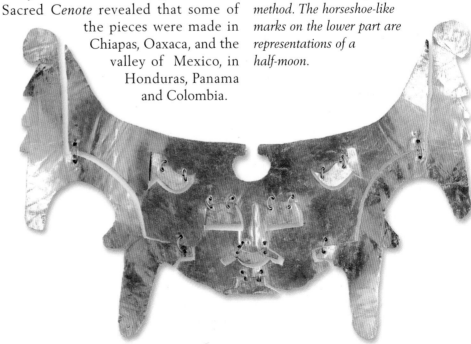

Above: Recovered from the waters. This gold shield pendant was part of a hoard of Aztec gold, probably looted by conquistadors from the palace of Axayácatl, then lost at sea and found in 1975 in deep water near Puerto de Veracruz. Eight bells hang from its base. It was cast by the lost-wax method. The horseshoe-like marks on the lower part are representations of a half-moon.

FACES OF GODS AND KINGS

An important strand of Olmec art was the carving of masks in greenstone, jade and other precious stones. Some have regular human features that scholars believe might have been portraits of rulers. Many others represent fierce animal faces with a snout. These may have been connected to the cult of the 'were-jaguar' that scholars identify as a possible image of the rain god. Members of the Olmec elite wore these fierce deity masks on their chests and in their headdresses during both religious and secular ceremonies. After death, rulers were laid to rest wearing these masks over their faces.

ANCIENT SHAMANIC RITES

Many scholars believe that the carving and wearing of animal-featured masks probably predated the Olmec to the people of the first villages in Mesoamerica. Shamans might have worn such masks during religious and divinatory ceremonies: the shamans were understood to take the form of fierce, snouted creatures such as the jaguar during their religious experiences. Perhaps the masks were worn more generally by the people during community festivities and gift-giving ceremonies in which wealthier members of the community – the members of a developing ruling class – redistributed some of their wealth as a way both of establishing their own status and satisfying the needs of the poor. The Olmec rulers apparently appropriated the tradition, commissioning and wearing masks of the most precious materials such as jade and greenstone. These were highly valued because of their green-turquoise colour, which had such powerful associations for Mesoamericans with fertility and life-giving waters.

MYSTERY OF THE MASKS

In Teotihuacán, carvers of serpentine, greenstone and other precious stones represented serene-looking human faces in masks. The masks often had eyes inlaid with shell, iron pyrite and other materials. They were certainly not portrait masks, for they had regular, slightly abstracted features.

Archaeologists have uncovered hundreds of these masks in the ruins of the ancient city. They were not worn during ritual or placed in graves, but might have been mounted on clay busts or bodies made of perishable materials. The busts or bodies were dressed in splendid costumes and worshipped as ancestors or as nature deities. Some authorities suggest that the masks were attached to corpse-bundles containing mummified bodies and venerated in a sacred setting.

In the same period, craftsmen in Maya regions were also carving masks of jade and other precious stones to be placed in elite graves. At Calakmul an elite figure identified from glyphs by scholar Joyce Marcus as Long-lipped Jawbone was

Right: Precious green. This Mixtec greenstone mask has undeniable power, although it does not aim for naturalism.

buried before *c*.AD500 wearing a jade-mosaic mask, with a second laid on his chest and a third worn on his belt. A life-sized jade mask with inlays of shell and pyrite was buried at Tikal in the grave known to archaeologists as Burial 160 in *c*.AD527. A jade mosaic mask was laid over the face of King Pacal's corpse in his tomb at Palenque (*d*. AD683). It was found in pieces but has been painstakingly remade by art historians.

OLMEC HEIRLOOMS

Many Olmec portrait and deity masks were placed in graves and preserved throughout Mesoamerican history. In Aztec times they were treasured possessions passed down the generations as heirlooms. The Aztecs also collected Teotihuacáno and other masks and often reused them as grave offerings, sometimes adding their own mosaic work to the original artifact before placing it in a tomb.

Some 88 painted greenstone masks carved in the abstract style identified by archaeologists as Mezcala were collected and

Right: Face beyond death. This image of Tezcatlipoca is a human skull inlaid with turquoise mosaic.

Above: Ceremonial jade. This mask of jade inlaid with shell was carved by a Maya artisan in the Classic Period.

placed in Chamber II of the Templo Mayor, Tenochtitlán. The style was associated with a culture that flourished near the Mezcala river in the region of the modern Mexican state of Guerrero from *c*.AD100–650, contemporary with Teotihuacán. Masks and figurines made by Mezcala craftsmen tended to have abstract features, indicated by circles, lines or depressions and raised areas in the surface. Some of the buried masks had the attributes of Tláloc, and scholars believe that the large offering was made to honour the rain god's helpers, the *tlaloque*.

The Aztecs themselves carved many masks in greenstone, obsidian, jade and other stones. Priests, priestesses and other impersonators of deities wore the masks in temple ceremonies.

Sometimes, as in Teotihuacán, the masks were attached to sacred bundles, to represent the face on the divine body. A splendid Aztec greenstone mask of Coyolxauhqui, moon goddess and sister of Huitzilopochtli, was probably decorated with ornaments and worn on the chest during ritual performances. The mask, made *c*.1500, was carved with images of bells on the cheeks that celebrated the goddess's name ('Lady with Bells on Her Face'). A diorite mask of Chalchiúhtlicue, carved *c*.1500, was probably attached to a sacred body. It included carvings of a quetzal-feather crown, marks representing face paint on the cheeks and, on the rear, an engraving of the glyph '8-Grass', one of the goddess's names in the ritual calendar.

DEATH MASKS

Craftsmen in Tenochtitlán and other cities also made masks that were buried with the deceased, presumably to provide individuals with a face for the spirit world after the cremation of the corpse. A very fine stone portrait mask carved *c*.1350–1500 and representing the features of a fresh-faced young man was dedicated to Quetzalcóatl in his guise as wind god Éhecatl by an image of the seated wind god together, with a carving interpreted as '9-Wind', one of the god's names in the ritual calendar.

SHELL AND PRECIOUS STONE DECORATION

Mesoamerican craftsmen excelled in fine mosaic work using turquoise, onyx, mother-of-pearl, malachite, jade, marine shells and other forms of inlay. From Olmec times, deity and funerary masks carved from precious stones were sometimes decorated with mosaic covering or inlaid with obsidian, onyx and shell to represent the eyes.

A magnificent Teotihuacáno mask of *c*.AD450 was covered with turquoise across most of the face, with inlays of shell for the eyes and obsidian for the eyeballs. Red spondylus or mollusc shell added a geometric nose ring, outlined the eyebrows and added a central forehead glyph that scholars believe once identified the person or deity celebrated in the mask itself.

This mask was found in an ancient grave in Malinaltepec, modern Guerrero province, in 1921. It was probably carried there by traders from Teotihuacán.

Below: At Palenque artists made exquisite mosaic masks, such as this late Classic Period jade piece (c.AD600–900).

TIKAL TREASURES

Two superb Maya jade mosaic vessels were buried at Tikal in the 8th century AD. One was laid with the body of King Ah Cacau (*r.* AD682–734) and a rich selection of jade jewellery, shells, pearls and jaguar skins in the grave known as Burial 116 beneath Temple I. The vessel was constructed from jade pieces tacked with jade pins around a cylinder of wood; its lid bore a portrait believed to be of the king himself. A second, similar vessel was laid in the grave now called Burial 196, within the comparatively modest Temple 73 at the south-western corner of Tikal's Great Plaza. Other items in the tomb, including the inscribed spine of a stingray and a named drinking cup, suggest that the tomb was associated with Ah Cacau's successor, Yax Kin (*r.* AD734–46). However, many scholars argue that the tomb is too modest to be that of so great a king as Yax Kin and that it might be that of his far less celebrated son (AD766–68), known to scholars only as the '28th Ruler'.

In the 14th–16th centuries, Mixtec craftsmen were renowned for their mosaic work as well as for their metalwork. One of Moctezuma II's tribute lists reveals that each year Tenochtitlán received ten turquoise-mosaic masks made by skilled artisans in Oaxaca. Tribute of turquoise-mosaic ceremonial shields was also sent from Oaxaca to Tenochtitlán each year.

FACE OF THE GODS

A number of Aztec-Mixtec mosaic-encrusted deity masks have survived. One celebrated example is a mask of the god of darkness and fate Tezcatlipoca. This

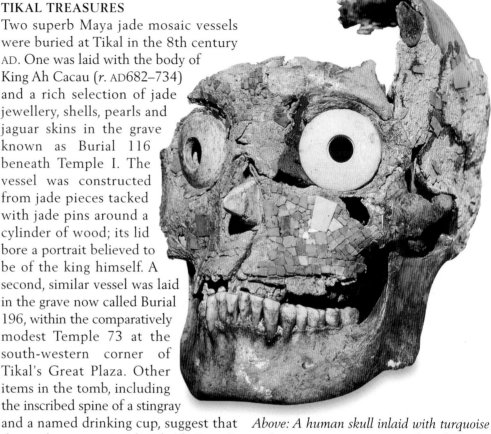

Above: A human skull inlaid with turquoise and ivory mosaic was among the gold offerings found in Tomb 7 at Monte Albán.

was fashioned *c*.1400–1521 from a human skull with a mosaic of turquoise and lignite inlaid in bands across the front, and eyes filled with white shell and black discs of iron pyrite. The inner part of the skull was lined with leather and the lower jaw hinged so that it could be moved when the mask was worn by a priest during religious ceremonial.

A turquoise-mosaic mask with serpents encircling the eyes and mosaic representations of feathers on either side of the eyes was made, probably by Mixtec specialists, on a cedar-wood base *c*.1400–1521. The mask was intended for priests of Quetzalcóatl or of Tláloc. The serpent eye-goggles were traditionally a symbol of Tláloc, while the feathers suggested the plumed serpent Quetzalcóatl. The mask, 17.3cm high and 16.7cm wide (6.8in by 6.7in), closely matches the description

given by Bernardino de Sahagún of a turquoise-encrusted mask despatched as a gift by Moctezuma II to Hernán Cortés in 1519. Sahagún reported that the mask would have been worn with a tall plume of quetzal feathers.

Another Tláloc mask, of *c.*1500, is made of turquoise, malachite, mother-of-pearl, jade and red and white shell laid on a wooden base. The mask, with the rain god's elongated snout and tall headdress, was 29cm (11.4in) tall. Scholars suggest that this sacred Tláloc likeness formed the top of a priest's staff or ruler's sceptre.

A magnificent Aztec wooden pectoral covered with turquoise mosaic and shell inlay represents the double-headed sky serpent that was one of the symbols of the feathered serpent god Quetzalcóatl. The pectoral, made *c.*1400–1521, measures 20.5cm by 43.3cm (8in by 17in)

Below: On this unique double-headed Aztec serpent pectoral, turquoise mosaic is attached to the wooden base using resinous gum. White and red shell mark the mouth.

Above: This Aztec helmet decorated with mosaic of precious stones was probably made by a Mixtec artist c.AD1400–1520.

and was worn by priests of the feathered serpent god Quetzalcóatl or by the ruler himself – Quetzalcóatl was one of the patrons of Mesoamerican kingship. Its eye sockets, now empty, were probably once inlaid with shell and iron pyrites. Some scholars suggest that the pectoral was worn during ritual celebration of the birth of the Aztecs' tribal god Huitzilopochtli, whose birthplace Coatepec ('Serpent Mountain') was represented by the towering bulk of the Templo Mayor in Tenochtitlán.

In the Aztec era, mosaic craftsmen also applied their expertise to the making of elaborate handles for sacrificial knives. The handle of one splendid knife depicts an eagle-warrior in a mosaic of turquoise, shell and malachite laid on wood; the blade is of chalcedony. The crouching warrior holds the handle or *ixcuac* between extended hands, while his face emerges from the open bird's beak.

MOSAIC ON WOOD

Throughout Mesoamerican history, artisans probably also cut deity and portrait masks from wood and then added fine mosaic overlay. Few of these precious objects have survived. Some, made by Aztec-Mixtec craftsmen in the 14th–15th centuries and preserved in desert conditions near Tehuacan in the modern Mexican state of Puebla, give an indication of the style and quality of the work.

One of the masks found in Puebla retains all its original turquoise covering, and part of the onyx inlay in the eyes and mouth. The find in Tehuacan also contained several once-splendid mosaic ceremonial shields, some with all the mosaic decoration now sadly worn off.

CHIPPED AND CARVED STONES:
ELABORATE OFFERINGS

Maya artisans chipped and cut stones, blades and flints with elaborate skill. Obsidian and flint blades and the remarkable decorative chipped flints known by scholars as 'flint eccentrics' were sacred objects, buried in large caches beneath temples and monuments.

Above: An Olmec jade piece was carved in the form of a canoe c.500BC. Sacred markings are visible at the ends.

FLINT ECCENTRICS
Some eccentrics are fashioned to represent human heads in profile. A number of chipped flints found at El Palmar, Quintana Roo, were probably once the heads of ritual staffs. One represents a human figure, with elaborate headdress, protruding lips perhaps intended to suggest a lip plug and a large ornament on

Below: This carved Maya jade pendant, 12cm (5in) across (c.AD850–1250), was found in the Sacred Cenote at Chichén Itzá.

the back. The 6th-century Copán temple that archaeologists call the 'Rosalila structure' contained a large cache of chipped flints, including a number of human profiles. Scholars believe that these may once have been the heads of the 'manikin sceptres' carried by Maya rulers as a sign of authority. Other flints are chipped to represent leaves or the form of the symbols of office called 'knuckle dusters' by scholars and held by notable court attendants in murals and painted scenes on vases.

CARVED FIGURES AND PLAQUES
From the days of the Olmec, Mesoamerican craftsmen cut small pieces of jade and other stones with remarkable delicacy and precision. An Olmec jade bead found in Chiapas was fashioned in the shape of a human head, while another small jade found at Necaxa in modern

WORKING JADE
Technically, Maya jades are jadeite, a very hard mineral with a chemical composition distinct from that of nephrite, the material carved in Chinese jades.

Mesoamericans gathered jadeite from streams and rivers in the form of pebbles, rocks and even sizeable boulders. Skilled craftsmen used a sawing motion with cords to cut and deepen lines in the hard rock, drilling holes with bones or pieces of hardwood, in both cases using water and sand or tiny stones to aid in cutting. The precision, delicacy and artistic flair of their work is astonishing.

Partly because the rock was found in streams, but more significantly because of its typical mottled green to blue-green colouring, jadeite was associated with water and fertility among the Aztecs, and with water and rain deities such as Chalchiúhtlicue and Tláloc.

Above: An Olmec jade figurine, found at La Venta and made c.1200–200BC, is believed to represent the god of the maize plant.

Puebla state was cut in the shape of a crouching tiger. In Maya lands, archaeologists found several delicately carved figurines in jade and other similar stones during excavations at Copán, Chichén Itzá, Uaxactún and other sites.

The small, carved heads were often worn as pendants. One found at Chichén Itzá bore a date in the Maya Long Count equivalent to AD674. Scholars believe that traders brought it to Chichén Itzá from Piedras Negras, its probable place of origin. A cross-legged human figure beautifully fashioned from fuchsite, a stone similar to, but softer than jade, was deposited in an offering at Uaxactún beneath a stairway at the structure archaeologists call Temple A-XVIII. The figurine had linked forearms, rounded belly, rectangular eye sockets originally painted red and a large left ear – its right ear was apparently damaged. Holes drilled in the stone probably gave such ornamental pieces ritual meaning.

At Palenque, a carved jade figurine of the Maya sun god Kinich Ahau was placed within King Pacal's sarcophagus in the royal tomb beneath the Temple of the Inscriptions. A substantial jade head of the same god, found in a king's tomb at Altun Há in Belize, weighed 4.42kg (9.7lb), making it the largest Maya sculpture in this precious stone.

CELTS, PLAQUES AND PECTORALS

A 4th-century jade celt or implement, probably worn as a belt decoration, was carved with the Maya Long Count date 8.14.3.1.12 (17 September AD320) and with a full-length portrait of Tikal ruler Moon Zero Bird. The celt, known by scholars as the Leyden Plaque, celebrated Moon Zero Bird's 'seating' or accession to the throne of Tikal on the marked date in AD320. It depicts the king, in full ceremonial costume with celts and deity masks hanging from his belt, trampling on a captive depicted in a style similar to that used for images of captives on Tikal monuments. The plaque, one of the oldest dated Maya artefacts, was probably taken from King Moon Zero Bird's tomb at Tikal in ancient times. It was found in 1864 at Puerto de Barrios near the river Motagua in Guatemala.

A blue-green jade plaque, 30cm (12in) tall, was carved by a leading jade-craftsman of the late Classic Period Maya world. It represents a king on a throne, his body facing forwards but head in profile, wearing a serpent headdress from which emerges a figure with an unsettling, grotesque face. Before the throne a second figure kneels in supplication, while

Right: An Olmec adze, or type of axe, from Veracruz is carved with the features of the sacred jaguar.

a speech scroll coming forth from the king's mouth indicates that he is declaring his identity and mighty achievements or else offering prayers to the gods on behalf of his people. The beautifully worked piece, found in Teotihuacán, was perhaps offered as an elite gift or else traded for valuable goods.

A splendid jade pectoral cut by Mixtec craftsmen c.AD1000 bears witness to the continued popularity of this precious stone for ceremonial and sacred objects.

CHAPTER 24

IMAGES, SYMBOLS AND WORDS

Mesoamerican wall paintings are filled with religious and political meaning. Sometimes accompanied by explanatory hieroglyphs, they are sacred statements, often dense with complex symbolism, intended to be 'read' and interpreted: celebrations of the gods' goodness in guaranteeing the fertility of the earth, of the power of the king and his ancestors or of the movements of time as evidenced by astronomical cycles.

Classic Period Maya-painted scenes include the humiliation or sacrifice of a defeated ruler, victory in battle, ceremonies of dynastic consolidation or acts of ritual bloodletting. Images represent action and carry narrative, while glyphs provide meaning and permanence by giving names and by setting the events in time.

In a parallel tradition, beginning in Teotihuacán and also finding expression in murals at Cacaxtla and in Caribbean Yucatán in the 13th–16th centuries, artists created symbolic religious scenes connected with the underworld, fertility and the cycles of the stars rather than dynastic or military events. In this tradition, glyphic writing played a much smaller role – there were no glyphic inscriptions at Teotihuacán. But scholars are convinced that religious symbols such as the five-pointed half-star Venus sign could be 'read' as part of a 'symbolic writing' by residents of Teotihuacán or Cacaxtla.

Left: Solar symbolism. A mural in Cacaxtla shows a man with eagle beak and wings who may represent the sun by day.

THE DATING OF EVENTS

The desire to record and celebrate the patterned movements of sacred time might have been the impetus that drove Mesoamericans to develop their glyphic system of writing. Many historians agree that the complex 260-day and 365-day calendars evolved before the earliest forms of writing, somewhere around the mid-first millennium BC.

CYCLES OF THE CALENDAR

As far as we know, written language was first used to identify people or to mark military triumphs by placing them within the cycles of the calendar.

The carvings often cited as the oldest piece of Mesoamerican writing are the hieroglyphs cut in the threshold of Monument 3 at San José Mogote c.600BC. These record the date 1-Earthquake from the 260-day calendar alongside an image of a prostrate figure.

The symbol is interpreted either as identification of the figure who, like many later Mesoamericans, had taken his name from the date of his birth, or as a

Below: Intricate calendrical hieroglyphs in the Palace at Palenque date the events depicted to AD644, during Pacal's reign.

record of the date of the victory in which he was taken captive or the day on which he was sacrificed.

Scribes or stonemasons using the dates of the 260-day and 365-day calendars could place an event precisely within a hallowed cycle of 52 years that the Maya called the Calendar Round. (This longer period represented the time that elapsed before a day in the 365-day year and a day in the 260-day year coincided: 18,980 days, or 52 solar years of 365 days.) Scribes who wanted to date events within longer spans of time needed a different measure. The dating system used on stelae of Maya cities in the Classic Period, known as the Maya Long Count, identified events both within the Calendar Round and within a span of years beginning on 13 August 3114BC. Historians do not know the significance of this date, but some have suggested that it marked the creation of the current world cycle, according to religious narrative.

The Long Count organized days in units of 20: *kin* (one day), *uinal* (20 days), *tun* (360 days), *katun* (7,200 days) and *baktun* (144,000 days). Given that the system was vigesimal – it used units of 20 rather than units of 10, as in decimal

Above: Stela at Sayil, dated AD800–950. Contemporaries could interpret details of the king's stance, costume and equipment.

calculation – the *tun* count should have been 400 (1 *kin* multiplied by 20 multiplied by 20), but the developers of the Long Count amended this to 360 to make it closer to the length of the solar year.

WRITING NUMBERS

Before creating the Long Count, the Maya must first have developed the concept of zero, so that some units in the count could be marked empty. Scribes and stonemasons indicated numbers by using dots for units up to four and a horizontal bar for the number five. They could write numbers up to 19 (three bars and four dots) using this system. For larger numbers they used the same symbols in horizontal layers, representing

Above: Divinely ordained cycles of time were plotted in calendrical charts. This is a modern reconstruction of an Aztec calendar.

units of 20. The lowest layer showed the number of units (1–19), the second showed the number of 20s, the third showed the number of 400s (that is 20 units of 20) and the fourth the number of 8,000s (20 units of 400).

same city, a mason cut the date 9.13.0.0.0. on the stone throne or altar associated with a twin-pyramid group set up by King Ah Cacau. This meant 9 *baktuns*, 13 *katuns*, 0 *tuns*, 0 *unials* and 0 *kins* after 13 August 3114BC: 18 March AD692.

Twin-pyramid groups were raised by Maya rulers in this period to celebrate the ending of *katun*-periods, which explains why the date in the inscription fell so precisely at the end of the 13th *katun*.

Below: Stela 9 at Tikal celebrates King Kan Boar. Both narrow edges of the monument are carved with an inscription that ends with his name glyph and that of Tikal.

On stelae, sculptors carved dates in vertical columns to be read from bottom to top, beginning with the largest unit.

The Long Count date on Stela 29 at Tikal used no zeros and was cut with the figures 8.12.14.8.15, meaning 8 *baktuns*, 12 *katuns*, 14 *tuns*, 8 *uinals* and 15 *kins* after the initial date of 13 August 3114BC, giving a date for the stela of 8 July AD292. Almost exactly 400 years later, in the

DID THE OLMEC USE WRITING?

A tall column of basalt known as the Ambassador's Monument was found at the Olmec holy town of La Venta. Some historians claim this bears the very first evidence of writing in Mesoamerica.

Some time between *c*.1150BC and 500BC, stonemason-scribes carved one end of the column with the image of a walking bearded man (likened by scholars to an ambassador) alongside three signs (which appear to be glyphs) and one of which, a bird's head, might represent his calendar name. Olmec potters and carvers of ceremonial implements in precious jade and serpentine also incised symbols which might be glyphs, but scholars have been unable to break the code of the symbols.

Linguists suggest that Mesoamerican writing probably originated in a lowland environment like that occupied by the Olmec or the people of the central Maya region rather than the highland surroundings of the Zapotecs in Oaxaca. The glyphs represent predominantly lowland creatures such as the crocodile, the jaguar and the monkey.

REFERENCE BOOKS FOR PRIESTS

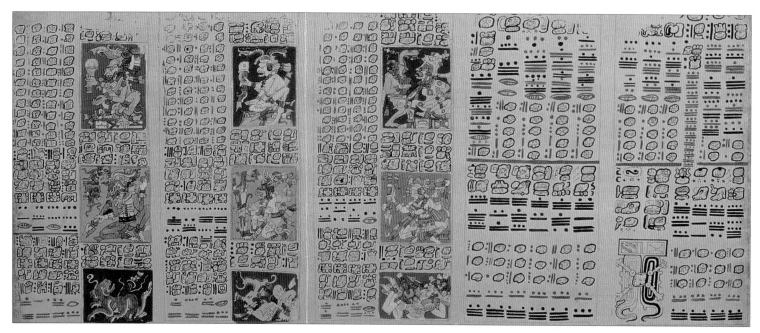

The chief scribes of Maya cities in the Classic Period were in charge of large libraries, containing a wide range of books written on bark paper or deer skin recording genealogies, arcane ritual and astronomical knowledge, medical information, and compendia of herbs, plants and animals. A mere handful of these books have survived natural decay over several hundred years and the book-burning zeal of the Spanish, who believed the sacred and even secular literature of the Maya and Aztecs to have been tainted by its association with sacrificial religion. Of the four surviving Maya codices, three date from the years before the Spanish Conquest, with one probably made in the 17th century. The finest of the three pre-Conquest books is the *Dresden Codex*, so named from its location, since 1744, in the Royal Library in Dresden, Germany.

THE DRESDEN CODEX

Consisting of 39 pages of *amate* paper, with writing and images on both sides, the *Dresden Codex* contains almanacs of the 260-day calendar, with details of presiding deities and appropriate rituals, mathematical tables, descriptions of new year ritual celebrations and detailed charts of solar eclipses and cycles of the planets

Above: Gods, days and rituals. The intricately covered almanac pages of the Dresden Codex *are dense with meaning.*

Venus and Mars. Its scribes used very fine calligraphy, particularly in the Venus chart, which has tiny, delicate glyphs as small as 4mm (0.15in) high and 5mm (0.19in) across. According to the scholar Michael Coe, this is the most delicate fine-line work of any world manuscript, and it was written with a quill or with a reed pen rather than with the brush used for other Maya manuscripts.

The book was written by more than one hand. Variant scholarly accounts identify five or even eight distinct calligraphic styles across the 39 pages. In particular, the section on new year ceremonies on pages 25–28 of the manuscript is in a quite distinct and 'broader-brush' style, with glyphs more than three times wider than those in the Venus Table. Some scholars date the *Dresden Codex* to as early as AD1250. Others place its composition in about 1345.

Some scholars believe the book to be a copy of a codex produced during the Classic Period. It was in Vienna in the 16th century, having perhaps been found

---

THE 'WRIGHT CODEX'

The earliest known codex is not a book at all, but a ceramic vase around 25cm (10in) in height, which was discovered in a private American collection in 1991. On each of the four sides of the rectangular vase an artisan incised hieroglyphs and religious figures that appear to be reproductions of pages from a codex. Probably made in Guatemala *c.* AD600–900, the vase – known to scholars as the *Wright Codex* – is as much as 700 years older than the most venerable existing Maya codex previously known. Its illustrations represent a man taking part in religious ceremonies, perhaps associated with his way or spirit companion. Scholars have hailed the vase as physical proof of their contention that the Maya used books throughout the Classic Period.

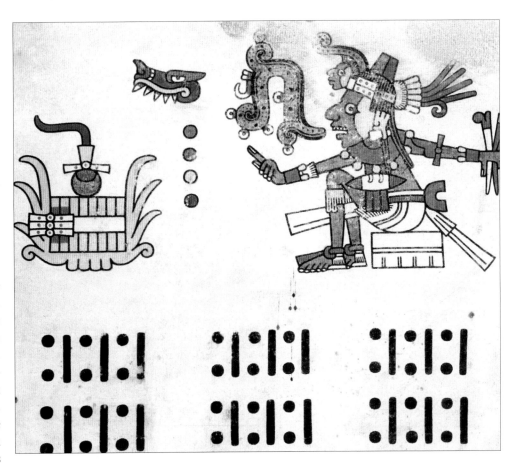

by Hernán Cortés in 1519 on the island of Cozumel. The shrine of moon goddess Ix Chel on Cozumel was an important pilgrimage site, and the book might have been brought there as an offering from an important city.

WORK OF A PROVINCIAL SCRIBE

The oldest surviving Maya codex is the *Grolier Codex* of *c*.AD 1230. It is so named because, following its discovery in Mexico in 1965, it was first exhibited at the Grolier Club in New York City in 1971. The codex is a 10-page section of an original, probably twice as long, dealing with the 584-day cycles of the planet Venus. Its screenfold pages are painted on one side only. It contains little information beyond details of the day signs and deities associated with each phase of the planet's cycle and it was written without great care, perhaps in haste or by an unskilled scribe in a provincial setting.

One account of its provenance suggests that it was found in a wooden box with a sacrificial knife and a mosaic mask in a dry cave near Tortuguero, in the modern state of Chiapas. The book might have been used for reference by a provincial priest in the region of Chiapas or Tabasco, some distance from such contemporary centres of ritual religion and learning as Chichén Itzá.

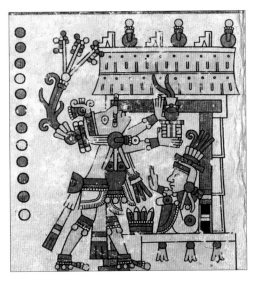

CEREMONIES OF YUCATÁN

The *Paris Codex*, which takes its name from the French capital where it has been stored since 1832 in the Bibliothèque Nationale, probably dates to *c*.1450. According to historian Bruce Love, it might have been produced in the Itzá city of Mayapán. Analysis shows that its 11 double-sided pages were all written by one scribe. It contains information on cycles of *katuns* (periods of 7,200 days) and of *tuns* (360-day years) and on the importance of the larger 13-*katun* period, (containing 93,600 days or roughly 260 years), after which a new cycle of history was expected to begin, probably bringing a repetition of events in the previous 13-*katun* period. It also provides details of the gods presiding over the *katuns*, of the Year Bearers in the ritual calendar and of new year celebrations, as well as almanacs of astronomical cycles.

The fourth Maya codex is the *Madrid Codex*, which was probably produced in the 17th century in Yucatán.

Left: In the Codex Fejérváry-Mayer, *a maize plant in the form of Chalchiúhtlicue is blessed by Tláloc, lord of the rains.*

Above: The Codex Fejérváry-Mayer *is one of only nine* tonalamatl *reference books to have survived the Spanish Conquest.*

CALENDAR OF FESTIVALS

In Aztec lands, some fifteen pre-Conquest codices survived destruction in the early 16th century.

One example is the *Codex Cospi*. Written by Mixtec scribes in the period 1350–1500, it takes its name from its later European owner, the Marchese Ferdinando Cospi. Its 13 screenfold pages, made of coated deerskin, are painted on both sides and contain details of the ritual calendar and the Venus cycle as well as of sacrificial rites appropriate to the worship of different deities.

The *Codex Fejérváry-Mayer*, made before 1521 and also named after later European owners, is a *tonalamatl* reference book on the 260-day and 365-day calendars. It contains 22 double-sided pages of animal skin covered in white lime and painted with interpretations of the calendars. It also contains accounts of variously presiding deities, including the nine lords of the night and details of tribute in goods and labour which were required at different times of the year.

A VANISHING CULTURE

The majority of surviving codices were produced after the Spanish Conquest in the 16th century either by Spanish churchmen or by Mexicans educated in colonial schools. Many of these were based on eye-witness accounts or were reworkings of pre-Conquest manuscripts. Among the most celebrated and useful to scholars is the *Codex Mendoza*. This

Below: Hieroglyphs are inscribed on the scales of the feathered serpent Quetzalcóatl in this detail from the Madrid Codex.

was composed in the period *c.*1525–41, following a commission by the first Spanish Viceroy, Don Antonio de Mendoza. It is made of European paper and contains 72 pages written by a Mexican scribe in Nahuatl. Translations and interpretations have been added in Spanish by a bilingual author.

The first section starts with the building of Tenochtitlán and then describes the lives of nine Aztec rulers up to and including Moctezuma II, ending with an account of the Conquest. The second part contains an exhaustive tribute list of goods claimed by Moctezuma II from the empire of the Triple Alliance. A third section details customs of daily life among the Aztecs, including birth, marriage, education, state obligations, law and justice.

COPIED MANUSCRIPTS

A number of post-Conquest books appear to be copies of Aztec manuscripts. The *Codex Magliabechiano*, produced *c.*1521–1600 on European paper, includes illustrations of ritual outfits, a *tonalpohualli* sacred calendar and details of the sacred monthly festivals, together with images of funeral and sacrificial rites, autosacrificial bloodletting and ritual cannibalism. The *Codex Telleriano-Remensis*, written and illustrated by Mexican scribes and artists in Tlatelolco in 1555–61, combines an account of sacred festivals, a *tonalamatl* book of days used for divination and a chronicle of Aztec history.

The *Codex Ríos*, written and illustrated by Mexican Dominican friar Pedro de los Ríos *c.*1570–95, contains additions in Italian by another author which explain the traditions of the Aztecs. Its first section retells religious narratives and gives accounts of Aztec cosmology, while the second includes a *tonalpohualli* 260-day ritual calendar with a *xiuhpohualli* 365-day solar calendar. The third part details sacrificial and mortuary rites and provides information about calendrical day-signs, while the fourth contains post-Conquest historical accounts.

The style of drawing in the Ríos and the Telleriano-Remensis codices is very similar. Scholars believe they were both copied from a single pre-Conquest source.

ACCOUNTS BY CHURCHMEN

Two other important post-Conquest books classified as codices are the accounts of Aztec history and customs written by Spanish churchmen, the *Codex Durán* and the *Florentine Codex*. The *Codex Durán* is the name applied to the *History of the Indies of New Spain*. This

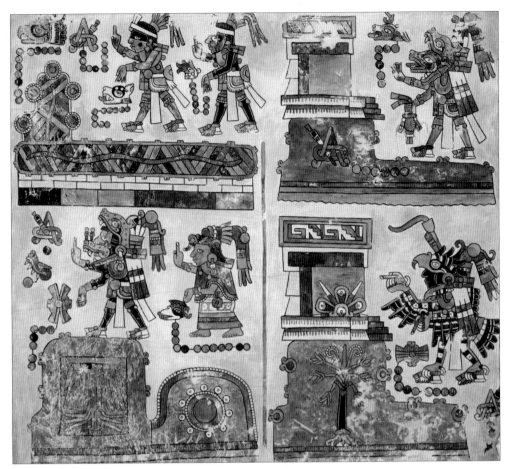

Above: A page from the Vienna Codex, *also known as the* Codex Vindobonensis. *Walking figures are gods or kings in action.*

('Book of Advice') contains a wealth of Maya religious narrative and astronomical knowledge including detailed accounts of the myth of the ball-playing Hero Twins. It was transcribed from sources written in hieroglyphs into the Roman alphabet by senior members of the Quiché Maya *c*.1554. It was then translated from the Quiché tongue into Spanish by Franciscan friar Francisco Ximenez in the 18th century.

The *Books of Chilam Balam* recorded the history and traditions of groups of Maya from north-western Yucatán and were named after a Maya shaman-seer of the late 14th century. They were written in the Roman alphabet and Yucatec tongue from hieroglyphic sources from the 16th century onwards.

was written in Spanish in 1570–81 by Dominican missionary Diego Durán. Spanish Franciscan friar Bernardino de Sahagún's *General History of the Things of New Spain*, also known as the *Florentine Codex* because of its association with libraries in the Italian city of Firenze (Florence), was written by scribes in Tlateloclo in 1575–77 in Spanish and Nahuatl. Both the Florentine and Durán codices contain detailed accounts of Aztec religious traditions, sacrificial rites, history and daily customs composed by their European authors on the basis of information gathered over many years among local survivors of the Spanish Conquest.

MAYA BOOK OF RITUAL

In Maya lands, one of the four surviving Maya codices is post-Conquest in date. This is the *Madrid Codex*, so called because it is kept in the Museo de América in the Spanish capital. It was long considered to be two separate manuscripts known as the *Troano* and the *Cortesianus*, but in 1880 Frenchman Léon de Rosny established that the two were sections of a single manuscript. The *Madrid Codex* contains 56 leaves, all except the first painted on both sides, making a total of 111 codex pages.

The *Madrid Codex* combines details of Maya beliefs about the four cardinal directions and their presiding deities with information about new year celebrations and detailed almanacs of the 260-day calendar. Like the *Grolier Codex*, it was apparently written in haste or by a lesser scribe, as it contains grammatical errors and careless penmanship. Scholar Michael Coe argues that as the *Madrid Codex* contains a piece of recycled Spanish paper among its bark-paper leaves, it must have been produced after the Spanish Conquest of Yucatán in 1542 that it was perhaps written in Tayasal, which retained its independence until 1697. Martin de Ursua, Spanish Governor of Yucatán, took Tayasal as part of a road-building project to link Guatemala and Yucatán.

Accounts of the history and religious traditions of particular Maya groups based on ancient sources were written down in the post-Conquest period. The *Popol Vuh*

Below: Stone workers hewing and crafting stone from Bernardino de Sahagún's General History of the Things of New Spain, *also known as the* Florentine Codex.

GLYPHS AND IMAGES

Sculptors of Maya stelae embedded their meaning in the image. Viewers were expected to understand the hieroglyphs in conjunction with the image portrayed. The image could be of a king with his defeated rival or of a ruler performing sacred rites of bloodletting. The hieroglyphs placed the event in the cycles of time and named the protagonists.

TYPICAL INSCRIPTIONS

A typical stela inscription began with detailed calendrical information, giving the precise day on which the event celebrated in the image took place. First it named the patron god or goddess of the month, then it gave the Long Count date and transcribed this same date into the

Above: Meaning in action. Divine rulers and gods adopt abstract postures in Mixtec-style codices. This page is from the Codex Zouche-Nuttall, *which may have been a gift from Moctezuma II to Hernán Cortés.*

Above: This cylindrical vase from Uaxactún is marked with a symbol and date that may record the owner's birth-date and name.

260-day ritual calendar, naming the god among the nine lords of the night who controlled that day and the phase of the moon that applied.

After this, an inscription might specify an event or anniversary of ritual significance that applied to the depicted activity, such as a *katun*-ending, then name the king and any other protagonist who had been involved.

Sometimes the glyphs giving the identity of the king would also name his ancestors or his offspring. At other times they would provide evidence of recent heroic activity. For example, various glyphs identified the king as lord of five, ten or even twenty captives. Following glyphs might give dates for subsequent events such as the king's partaking in ritual bloodletting or sacrificial worship. The second date in an inscription would be given only in the 260-day calendar, since the historical context within the Long Count had already been established.

Above: The Maya used these glyphs to convey historical and dynastic information. From top left – 'was born'; 'acceded to throne'; 'event of taking captive'; 'taker of captives'; 'taken captive'; 'he'; 'she'; 'wife'; 'ruler's number in dynastic line'; 'king or queen died'.

NAMING

Some scholars liken the glyphs naming kings and dating their stelae to the name tags that the Maya inscribed on sacred and everyday items such as incised bones, ear ornaments and drinking vessels.

The practice of name-tagging was discovered by scholar Peter Mathews in 1979 when studying an ear flare from Altun Há, Belize. The ornament was inscribed with the phrase *u tup* ('this man's ear flare'), together with the name of the owner, who was a member of the royal family. Name tags were subsequently identified on incised bones from the tomb of King Ah Cacau in Tikal, and on plates, dishes and vases.

Scholar Michael Coe found a repeating pattern of hierogylphs on elaborately decorated polychrome vases of the late Classic Period. This pattern, named the Primary Standard Sequence, amounted to a formula for naming and dating vases.

Generally painted around the outer rim of the vase or bowl or sometimes placed in a vertical column, it included up to 22 glyphs, always in the same order, but often with some missing and sometimes with as few as three glyphs. The sequence begins with several initial glyphs, sometimes including the head of the god Pawahtún, a four-fold god of the directions. This is thought to have functioned as a dedication of the vessel. Then came glyphs indicating whether the pot was carved or painted and identifying its shape, its use (perhaps for drinking or serving cacao), its owner and the artist who produced it. Sometimes the sequence also includes a date in the Calendar Round, which unusually referred to the date the object was made rather than the date on which the depicted events took place.

WORDS IN CODICES

In codices and in murals – just as in the inscriptions on stelae, stone thrones, zoomorphs and ceramics – words functioned to identify names and provide calendrical information, while images represented the activity that was being celebrated. In such pre-Conquest Mixtec books as the *Codex Zouche-Nuttall* or the *Codex Cospi*, illustrations were not designed primarily for aesthetic effect but to convey meaning.

Glyphs generally identified three key facts: dates, places and names. The human figures took a limited number of stylized postures, usually walking, standing or seated in profile and deity figures were usually shown in a flat, full frontal position. There was no attempt to achieve the naturalistic effects found in Classic Period Maya murals, stucco-work and polychrome vases and in Postclassic statuary.

Below: The highly prized role of the scribe could be taken by royal or noble women as well as by top-ranking men. This Maya ceramic shows a female scribe at work.

THE AGE OF BOOKS

In the Postclassic Period, the artistic style of Mesoamerica derived largely from that of codices. Ceramic decorations, mural images, representations on monumental state sculpture and decorative symbols in jewellery are all similar to illustrations in the codices. Because the largest number of surviving codices were written and painted by Mixtec scribes working near the city of Puebla, scholars call this the 'Mixteca-Puebla style'.

The style was not regional but far-reaching and even international. In Tenochtitlán, images carved on state monuments resembled pages from a codex. In Oaxaca, delicate jewellery figures and fine murals at Mitla had the 'codex style'. On the Caribbean seaboard at sites such as Tulum in eastern Yucatán and Santa Rita Corozal in northern Belize, 15th-century murals closely mirrored the appearance of Mixtec codices.

SACRED SYMBOLS:
OLMEC AND TEOTIHUACÁNO MURALS AND FRESCOES

Finds of superb murals in the sacred city of Teotihuacán, in Maya cities such as Bonampak and in highland Mexican settlements such as Cacaxtla provide evidence of a highly developed Mesomerican wall-painting art.

TRADITION OF WALL-PAINTING

The roots of this tradition date all the way back to the Olmec period, when artists decorated sacred caves with distinctive ritual imagery. In caves in the southern Sierra Madre mountains, modern Guerrero province, historians have found cave paintings representing kings, a stone throne, sacred serpents and a fierce jaguar.

The oldest of these paintings are probably those at Juxtlahuaca and Cacahuaziziqui, which date to *c*.1000–700BC. One of the images at Juxtlahuaca represents two men, one seated and the second standing in elaborate costume that includes a hooped tunic-skirt, jaguar skin and black cloak, together with a feather helmet. The standing figure holds a

Below: Were mural painters in Teotihuacán using a language of nature symbols? This strange bird adorned a residential complex.

serpent-like object in his left hand, while his right controls a ritual implement – perhaps a sceptre or a sacred tool like the 'knuckle-duster' seen in later Maya paintings. Other Juxtlahuaca paintings represent a jaguar with black outline and

Above: Sacred animals in the Jaguar Palace (c.AD400) in Teotihuacán were intended to bring bounty to the city's inhabitants.

a red-bodied serpent with fiery eyebrow and the distinctively Olmec cross (like the cross of Saint Andrew) on its face. Two figures painted at Cacahuaziziqui appear to have glyphs close to their mouths, as if representing speech.

At Oxtotitlán, near the town of Acatlán, artists created an intriguing set of cave paintings *c*.800–500BC. A large image of a ruler seated on a throne dominates the sacred cave. He wears an owl mask and feathered cape, together with a skirt bearing the Olmec claw-wing symbol. His left hand reaches vertically up, his right hand reaches down diagonally, while his left leg is drawn up and his right leg falls down before him. His throne represents a monster mask with open jaws.

A second image depicts a man, painted in black outline with outstretched right arm, standing behind and possibly performing a sexual act with a fierce-faced jaguar. A third mural at Oxtotitlán shows a four-petalled flower with a human face at the centre. This is suggestive of later cosmological images that represent the universe as a flower with a petal to north, south, east and west and the tree of life in the centre.

TEOTIHUACÁN MURALS

Among the people of Teotihuacán were skilled potters, makers of haunting masks and magnificent monumental architects. However, mural painting was without doubt the art in which they most excelled.

Teotihuacános created wall paintings from c.AD300 onwards, first decorating small structures lining the Street of the Dead. After c.AD500 they began to paint murals in the city's many apartment compounds and in the palace areas close to the Pyramid of the Moon and the Pyramid of the Sun.

Their style was almost abstract. They painted few narrative scenes such as battle victories or rites of sacrifice and no naturalistic portraiture, but used a wealth of stylized images and motifs taken from nature, such as shells, stars, coyotes, and jaguars. In recent years, scholars have argued that Teotihuacáno artists used these religiously charged signs as a form of symbolic written communication.

The artists first prepared the walls by applying a layer of clay, later adding a coat of lime mixed with sand and quartz. Once the surface was ready, the painters set to work, first applying a red background colour then drawing designs in black and a darker red. They filled in additional colours of blue, green and yellow as the last stage in the process.

THE GREAT GODDESS

Many murals contain images of the Teotihuacános' supreme deity, dubbed the Great Goddess by art historian Esther Pasztory. Like many Mesoamerican divinities, the goddess had dual aspects as both a beneficent giver of life and as an awe-inspiring force of evil. She was recognizable from her red and yellow zig-zag band, her nose bar and her bird headdress. The murals of the Tepantitla apartment building show the goddess in her lifegiving aspect in a river setting, with water creatures and abundant growths of flowers. In the Tetitla building, meanwhile, she is seen in her evil aspect, with fangs and bestial claws.

The goddess clearly possessed fertility aspects, but otherwise had little connection to other female deities of Mesoamerica – her cult was apparently unique to Teotihuacán. Other gods represented in the Teotihuacán murals have closer links to those of the wider Mesoamerican pantheon. One is the storm god, with strong links to lightning and thunder and to the god the Aztecs called Tláloc. Another is the feathered serpent god whom the Aztecs called Quetzalcóatl. A third, an aged god represented as a crouching man supporting a brazier on his skull, was later known to the Aztecs as Huehuetéotl.

THE TECHINANTITLA COMPOUND

These paintings, produced c.AD600–750, are unusual for Teotihuacán in representing scenes of military life. They include a long procession of figures wearing a tasselled headdress associated with warriors and positions of power. Above and below the figures, a border consists of footprints. Eight of the marching warriors have glyphs painted by them, probably representing their names. Another section represented trees.

Below: Water falls from the hands of an early version of the pan-Mesoamerican rain god in a mural from Teotihuacán.

SCENES OF RELIGIOUS LIFE

Murals were painted at Cholula in the Puebla region of Mexico *c*.AD100–400, when the settlement was pre-eminent in its area and had close ties to both Teotihuacán and Monte Albán in Oaxaca. The earliest images are similar to some Teotihuacán wall paintings. They represent stylized insects with very large heads painted in red and yellow against black and other backgrounds.

THE DRINKERS

A more significant Cholula mural is one known to scholars as 'The Drinkers' and apparently representing scenes of ritual intoxication. Some 60m (200ft) across, the painting depicts a succession of humans – all wearing loincloths and some with headdresses or masks of fabulous creatures – together with several large drinking jars.

The figures are painted a light-orange flesh colour against a red background and rest on a blue-green band, beneath which are decorative elements including rhombuses. Some of the figures lift the vases up as if to pour out libations for nobles at a banquet, others hold drinking bowls. The drinking was probably of *pulque* (maguey cactus liquor) as part of a religious ritual. The figures are in loose, relaxed positions, probably because of the

Below: Staple food. In the Red Temple at Cacaxtla the muralist painted a maize plant that gives issue to human heads.

effects of the *pulque*, while their masks might be intended to represent the animal spirit companions that a shaman or spiritual adventurer would expect to meet during spirit voyages facilitated by *pulque* or other psychotropic substances. The mural was painted on the west-facing façade of a mortuary pyramid in which archaeologists found the rich burial of a man with Maya facial features.

Another Cholula mural, in a structure known to scholars as Building 2, represented shells and five-pointed stars, imagery found both at Teotihuacán and Cacaxtla and thought to be associated with fertility and the planet Venus.

A SYMBOLIC BATTLE?

A magnificent series of murals were painted in the hilltop settlement of Cacaxtla, above the Tlaxcala valley, *c*.AD655–835. These remarkable pictures, some of the finest in Mesoamerica, were discovered by looters in October 1975.

Overlooking the ceremonial area, the elongated structure known as Building B contains brightly coloured murals of battles or perhaps ritualized conflicts between two groups of warriors, who are clearly identified by their battledress. Some scholars focus on the geographical and cultural affiliations of the two groups. They identify the first group as Mexicanized Maya, who exhibit the influence of Teotihuacán in their battledress and equipment and who probably come from the Mexican Gulf Coast. They identify the second group as warriors from Maya lands farther east.

Other historians suggest that the conflict might be symbolic. The Mexicanized warriors sport equipment with jaguar symbolism while the central Maya wear nothing except bird helmets and body ornaments. The clash might be between night (represented by the jaguar, fearsome night predator and the form taken by the sun when it journeyed through the underworld during the hours of darkness) and

Above: At Cacaxtla drops of rain fall from a serpent sceptre wielded by a jaguar man. He is thought to represent the moon.

day (represented by the birds of the air). The images exhibit great naturalistic skill and painstaking attention to detail in their depiction of headdress and costume.

GODS OF THE SKY

Murals with complex religious symbolism adorn Building A at Cacaxtla, which is reached via a short stairway from Building B. These images consist of four large standing figures. On the south doorjamb of the entrance looms a black-skinned man, apparently dancing, who holds a conch shell from which a head emerges bedecked in jewels. On the south wall, another black-skinned man in eagle costume stands on a blue-green feathered serpent, holding a bright blue-green serpent sceptre from which flames emerge. On the north doorjamb of the entrance is a man with jaguar paws and skin, his head emerging from the open jaws of the jaguar. He wears a serpent headdress and holds a serpent in his left hand while, using his right arm, he up-ends a large jar decorated with the symbols of the rain god from which life-giving blue-green waters fall. From his belly emerges a maize or water-lily plant, bearing flowers.

On the north wall of the building another jaguar man holds a brilliant blue-green rain sceptre from which waters fall on to the body of a creature that is both jaguar and serpent. The scholar Maria Teresa Uriarte has identified these complex figures as images of the night sun (or moon) on the north wall and the sun by day on the south wall, with images of the rain god Tláloc/Chac on the north door-jamb and of Pahuantún or god N, a deity with links to the four directions and the underworld, on the south doorjamb. The main north and south wall images might represent the Hero Twins of Maya reli-gious narrative as moon and sun, for in some accounts the twins rose to become these celestial bodies.

A third richly coloured mural adorns the structure at Cacaxtla dubbed the Temple of Venus by scholars. Artists painted a pair of blue-skinned figures, one to each side of the doorway. One badly damaged mural represents a female fig-ure, with one breast visible, and the wall disintegrated where the other breast and her head would be. The other depicts a standing male with black hair, large pro-truding eye and arms upraised. Both wear jaguar-skin skirts beneath large, five-pointed half-star symbols of the planet Venus that hang from their waists. Both have bare feet, with white cloths tied around their ankles. One of the man's hands is not visible due to wall damage, but the other is in the shape of a jaguar's paw and in it he holds a five-pointed half-star. Behind him a scorpion's tail is visible and his arms are segmented like the tail. The images represent dual aspects of the planet Venus. Maria Teresa Uriarte suggests they might celebrate an astro-

nomical conjunction between the planet Venus and the scorpion constellation. The visible part of the Venus cycle had asso-ciations with the rainy season, so the planet and its deity therefore had links to water and fertility.

GOD OF THE UNDERWORLD

Another remarkable set of murals adorned the building known as the Red Temple at Cacaxtla. The muralists deco-rated the east and west walls of the temple, either side of a staircase. On the east wall they painted a feathered serpent rising behind a human figure who stands

Above: The opposing Cacaxtla image depicts the sun – an eagle man holding a fire-serpent and standing on an earth-serpent.

against a terracotta background over a bundle that might represent the travel-ling pack of a merchant, while before him grow a cocoa plant and blue-green maize plants that give issue to human heads. Among the plants is a toad with a blue-green body. The mural's border consists of serpentine figures and watery images in turquoise and yellow. Scholars suggest that the figure might be god L or the Old Black God, lord of the Maya underworld.

THE BONAMPAK MURALS:
A PRINCE IN LINE

The famous murals in the Maya city of Bonampak, on the River Lacanjá in the Chiapas region, were painted in the building now known as Temple 1 in the late 8th century AD. They celebrated the designation of the royal heir to King Chan Muan, a prolonged ritual that took place over 20 months from 14 December AD790 to 6 August AD792. Bonampak was greatly influenced by the larger centre of Yaxchilán, 30km (18 miles) to the north. The two centres may have been connected by a *sacbé* (sacred causeway) that archaeologists have discovered departing Bonampak and heading north. Alongside King Chan Muan and his heir, Yaxchilán royals are depicted taking part in the ceremonies as allies or overlords.

The murals adorn three rooms in the temple. They are painted on both the walls and the inner roof, with a band of

Above: On the lower north wall of the first room, musicians and elaborately dressed gods or priests celebrate the heir's accession.

Below: A detail from the celebration scenes depicts senior figures from the court of King Chan Muan in intimate conversation.

hieroglyphs running between them. The hieroglyph section contains Long Count dates giving precise dates for the events depicted. The artists probably intended the images to be viewed from the benches that are laid out on the floors of these rooms.

PRESENTATION OF THE HEIR
In the first room, the painting on the vault of the west wall depicts the young royal heir being presented to 14 white-robed noblemen of the court while his royal father and mother look on approvingly from a wide throne-stone. The vault of the north wall shows the king wearing a vast feather headdress, a jade pectoral and ear plugs. He is accompanied by two splendidly attired lords, apparently preparing for a ritual held, according to the hieroglyphic inscription, 336 days later than the initial presentation of the prince. The lower walls appear to depict this celebration, showing a band of musicians playing a wooden drum, trumpets, flutes, turtle shells and rattles, as well as a procession of masked and elaborately costumed members of the court, or perhaps priestly figures. One figure

appears to have crayfish pincers in place of arms. One wears the costume of the maize god, while a third is robed to represent a crocodile. Two members wear flowers in their headdresses.

VICTIMS FOR SACRIFICE
The second room depicts a battle fought to secure prisoners for ritual sacrifice, an important part of the heir-designation ceremony. The south, west and east walls are covered with battle scenes that vividly depict the chaos and carnage of conflict, with elaborately dressed soldiers fighting hand-to-hand, grabbing one another by the hair and thrusting spears forward threateningly. King Chan Muan is shown holding a jaguar-skin spear and a prisoner by the hair while standing alongside an allied ruler that scholars identify as King Shield Jaguar II of Yaxchilán. Both kings sport magnificent headdresses, wear jaguar-skin clothing and are protected from possible injury by a cadre of proud warriors. On the vaults above these walls,

Above: A battle scene from the second room shows fierce soldiers with extravagant headdresses facing down the enemy.

images represent the astronomical alignments that were found to be propitious for this great battle. On the southern vault, a turtle with three stars on its shell stands for the constellation of Orion. Other images represent different stars and the planet Venus.

The north wall of the second room depicts King Chan Muan presiding over the painful torture of captives destined for sacrifice to sanctify the heir-designation. One prisoner has already been killed and decapitated; his head lies on one of the platform-steps. Several nobles and two royal ladies flank the king at the top of the steps, standing beneath glyphs of their names. One of the women is Queen Green Rabbit from Yaxchilán. At the foot of the steps, warriors stand guard over the prisoners.

SACRED BLOODLETTING

Unfortunately, the murals of the third room have sustained quite serious damage, but enough is visible to reveal that they represent further royal scenes in the heir-designation ritual. In one painting, king and nobles in elaborate costume stand on a pyramid while musicians and dancers perform sacred rites in the plaza below them. A second painting depicts the royal family on a throne or dais within the palace performing autosacrificial bloodletting as a way of seeking the gods' blessing on the prince of Bonampak. The king cuts his tongue with a spiked cord and collects the blood on bark paper. He will later burn the paper, both as an offering and as a way of summoning the Vision Serpent, along whose coils he might travel to encounter his way spirit companion, great royal ancestors or even the god and goddesses themselves.

The murals at Bonampak are valued for the insight they give, through their colourful and naturalistic representations of court ritual, into royal and religious life in Maya cities of the late Classic Period. Although they are an unusually complete survival, they are typical of the wall decoration used in many Maya palaces, religious and ceremonial structures. It was common practice to commemorate religious, dynastic and military events through wall painting.

Below: On the north side of the second room, King Chan Muan takes centre stage, wearing jaguar skin and holding a spear. At his feet prisoners of war endure torture at the hands of their captors.

WALL PAINTINGS AND MURALS

Fragments of murals survive at many Maya sites. At Tikal, small parts of murals dating to the 4th century AD have been found in the buildings architects call Group 6C-XVI, just to the south of the Lost World complex. One represents a human figure alongside a black circle marked with a glyph that has underworld associations. A second mural, known as 'The Mural of the Gamers', depicts eight human figures in two groups of four, walking in profile. Those whose heads are undamaged wear ribbon headdresses. Some authorities suggest that the figures in both murals are ball players.

At Xelhá near the coast of Quintana Roo, a mural in the substructure of the buildings called Group B depicts flying parrots and macaws. These images date to *c.*AD400–600. At Uaxactún, artists painted a mural *c.*AD450–550 to adorn a

Above: Mayapán's rulers commissioned murals in order to add to their city's status as it rose to eclipse Chichén Itzá.

room in the building called Structure B-XIII. They depict scenes of noble life, showing groups of standing figures with fine headdresses and adornment. One group is seated within a building. Associated hierogylphs probably provide dates or names.

At Palenque, in House E of the royal palace, mural images of four-petalled flowers and geometric decorative designs have survived, along with a profile head of a noble or king wearing a splendid headdress containing a fish. These date from the 7th century AD.

At Yaxchilán only a single figure in profile and a few patches of colour remain of wall-paintings that once covered the interior of Temple 40, built during the reign of King Bird Jaguar (*r.* AD752–68).

MAYA TOMB PAINTINGS

From an early period the Maya painted the walls of tombs. A tomb dated to *c.*50BC in the North Acropolis at Tikal (Burial 166) has a mural with a red background and black outlines depicting standing figures with feather headdresses and deity masks, probably representing divine ancestors of the king or nobleman buried in the tomb. These are identified as the most venerable painted images yet discovered in Maya lands.

Several other Tikal tombs had paintings and glyphic inscriptions: Burial 48 is dated to AD457. Near-contemporary images in Tomb 1 at Río Azul in Guatemala, represent deity masks, serpents and watery features, and they can be dated to AD417 by a Long Count date in the accompanying inscription. At the same site, Tomb 19 (*c.*450–550) bears paintings said to represent the Jester god linked to the ruler's glyph 'ahaw'.

Below: This damaged mural from Tulum appears to be an image of the rain god, worshipped as Chac by the Maya.

HIGHLAND MEXICAN STYLE

At Chichén Itzá, fragments of mural were found on rubble pieces that once formed the inner walls of the Temple of the Warriors. They have been reconstructed to form two murals, one representing a military attack on a town and the capture of prisoners, the other depicting life in a coastal village. These are painted in a quite different style to the fluid, expressive naturalism of Maya mural painting that reached its apogée at Bonampak; instead, they are flat, two-dimensional and almost schematic. They apparently form part of the wave of Mexicanized culture and artefacts also represented by the appearance at Chichén Itzá of sacred furniture such as *chacmool* sacrificial figures and skull racks, of serpent-columns on buildings and of atlante carved warriors. The same schematic style, though

Below: Murals at Tulum and other cities of Postclassic Yucatán apparently return to the style and subjects of Teotihuacán art.

with rather more movement, is apparent in murals of fighting soldiers painted within the Temple of the Jaguars.

Wall paintings were also commissioned by the rulers of the city of Mayapán, which succeeded Chichén Itzá as the pre-eminent city of northern Yucatán after *c.*1250. Fine paintings discovered in 1997 in the buildings known as Structure Q160 and Structure Q80 exhibit a style reminiscent of the codex art of contemporary Maya and especially Mixtec painter-scribes. In Structure Q80, serpents are combined with geometric designs while anthropomorphic figures adorn Structure Q160.

INFLUENCE OF BOOKMAKERS

Murals at many sites on the Caribbean coast of Yucatán – including Tulum, Xelhá, Cobá, Rancho Ina and Tancah – exhibit this same codex-influenced style in the years after *c.*1250. They are different from earlier Maya murals in subject matter as well as in style. They do not represent scenes of military glory, dynastic succession and ritual sacrifice,

Above: War machine. In a mural from the Temple of the Jaguars, Chichén Itzá, the city's rampaging army engulfs a village.

but focus instead on themes of agriculture and the fertility of the earth, rebirth and astronomic cycles in an apparent return to the mural subjects of Teotihuacán style.

At Tancah, for example, within the building called Structure 12, a mural represents seven deities performing an agricultural rite in the company of the young maize god, who wears an ear of corn as a headdress. In Structure 1 at Cobá, a mural of the Postclassic Period shows a similar agricultural rite performed by deities included the maize god, the rain god Chac and the creator god Itzamná. Murals at Tulum adorn the Temple of the Frescoes and the Temple of the Diving God. In the latter, another scene of agricultural ritual represents two pairs of gods separated by the linked bodies of serpents. The mural is divided into the three cosmic levels of heavens, terrestrial plain and underworld.

SYMBOLISM AND NATURALISM

The artists of Teotihuacán produced representations in murals, pottery, masks and figurines that exhibited little interest in naturalism and far more in religious symbolism. Humans were anonymous members of a mass group: in masks, human features were often reduced almost to geometric shapes or hidden behind nose bars. Murals tended to represent people in profile, often in procession, moving towards a goddess or god figure who was shown full frontal. Many scenes were of animals, plants and deities, often involved in rites associated with fertility. These images did not glorify the military and political achievements of rulers, apparently focusing instead on deities and religious symbols.

In contrast, many Maya muralists, stucco sculptors and ceramicists of the Classic Period (AD250–900) excelled in naturalistic representations of the human face and body. At Bonampak, for example, the suffering of prostrate prisoners of war was depicted with deft and feeling naturalism in Room 2 of Temple 1. Images of court life on polychrome vases

and stucco carvings of King Pacal or King Chan Bahlum at Palenque are accurate and fluid representations of human expressions and gestures. (This is distinct from the much more stylized representations of royal figures produced by stonemasons on stelae and stone thrones.)

Images in Maya murals, ceramics and stucco focused on the beauty of the human body and face and of ceremonial attire such as the headdresses and costumes that also glorified the gods through sacred symbolism. Artists celebrated an ideal of human beauty in the stucco heads of King Pacal at Palenque and in the young maize god at Copán; in images of kings and courtiers on polychrome vases and in murals. This ideal consisted of a serene face with wide eyes, the bridge of the nose built up to join the forehead, full lips and smooth cheeks.

ROYAL PORTRAIT CONVENTIONS

Maya muralists and other artists generally stayed within established conventions of representation. They usually showed royal figures as exemplars of ideal beauty, not prone to ageing, in elegant costume

Above: Stone beauty. Maya sculpture probably reached its apogée in work such as this elegant head found at Copán.

and standing formally or occupying a regal seat. Artists had more leeway when it came to scenes of battle or those involving prisoners. The muralists at Bonampak took full advantage in representing an intense battle and subsequent presentation of prisoners to King Chan Muan in Room 2 of Temple 1. They showed soldiers and prisoners in many lifelike postures and expressions, prone and sitting, striding and thrusting, grimacing with pain and rolling their heads as if about to lose consciousness.

THE SHAPE OF A KING

Artists at Palenque made a limited departure from the tradition of idealizing the physical appearance of the ruling family. Doubtless on royal orders, they appear to have emphasized physical abnormalities peculiar to the ruling dynasty of King

Below: Coiled force. One of many sculptures of the sacred serpent by Aztec artists illustrates the powerful naturalism they achieved.

Pacal. These included an outsized head and jaw, signs of the pituitary disorder known as acromegaly, seen in images of Pacal's mother Lady Zac-Kuk. Depictions of Pacal's son, Chan-Bahlum, on the Temple of the Inscriptions show him with six fingers on the left hand and six toes on both feet. One of Pacal's uncles had a club foot, and scholars believe that Pacal himself might have inherited this. In images Pacal's foot was stylized as a serpent, and from the early 10th century AD, a god with serpent feet, Bolon Dz'Acab, became established as patron of kings. King Chan Bahlum appears to have encouraged his sculptors and artists to pursue a more realistic style in portraiture, as evidenced by a portrait head of the king in Temple XIV which depicts him with natural features at odds with the Maya ideal.

These dual strands of Maya naturalism and Teotihuacáno symbolic art had a joint flowering in the remarkable murals of Cacaxtla, in Tlaxcala, which were painted in the 7th–9th centuries AD. Artists combined concern with representing the human body in action (for example, in the Mural of the Battle in Building B) with a commitment to near-abstract scenes dense with religious symbolism (such as the murals possibly representing the sun and moon in Building A).

Artists of the Aztec era enthusiastically pursued naturalism in some statuary, but in painted work on vases and in codices followed the tradition of Teotihuacán.

Above: The artists who painted this mural in Tomb 105 at Monte Albán used symbolism reminiscent of Teotihuacán.

The codex art of the Mixtecs and Aztecs was reminiscent of Teotihuacáno murals in representing humans in profile in flat, almost schematic scenes. It differed in that it was often focused on the recording of dynastic history and the achievements of rulers, while Teotihuacáno art was intent on celebrating fertility through religious symbols.

The murals of cities such as Tulum, Xelhá and Cobá on or near the Caribbean coast of Yucatán in the 13–16th centuries returned to the religious-artistic themes of the Teotihuacános. It used a decorative style that was close to that of the Mixtec codices to celebrate fertility and astronomic themes using images of deities and religious symbols.

Left: The evocative impact of Teotihuacáno art is evident in this jade mask, probably intended for funerary use.

INDEX

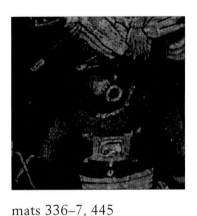

ACKNOWLEDGEMENTS

Ancient Art and Architecture Collection Ltd: 256t, 259t, 265b, 282b, 284t, 286l, 287b, 292t, 299t, 302b, 303, 312b, 321b, 333b, 334t, 337, 341t, 343b, 344b, 346–7, 352b, 357tl, 358b, 359b, 365b, 373t, 376t, 377t and b, 379b, 380t, 382b, 383b, 385b, 400t, 402t, 456t, 457t and b, 462t, 465b, 472, 473b, 477t and b, 479t and b, 485b, 490t, 500t and b; /Dr S Coyne: 372b; /Israel Museum: 373b, 378b; /J. Stevens: 312t.

Art Archive: 19t, 87bl, 187l, 192l, 193t, 204l, 209t and b, 210t, 212b, 218r, 230t, 236r, 245t, 252l, 348b, 374; /Antochiw Collection, Mexico/Mireille Vautier: 335t, 349t, 449t and b; /Archaeological Museum, Copan, Honduras/Dagli Orti: 339b; /Archaeological Museum, Teotihuacan, Mexico/Dagli Orti: 313, 492b; /Archaeological Museum, Tikal, Guatemala/Dagli Orti: 442t; /Archaeological and Ethnological Museum, Guatemala City/Dagli Orti: 343t, 362b, 332–3, 490b, 496b; /Biblioteca Nacional, Madrid/Dagli Orti: 361t, 363t, 381, 431bl; /Biblioteca Nacional, Mexico/ Dagli Orti: 260–1, 263t, 279t, 327t, 338b, 397t; /Biblioteca Nacional, Mexico/Mireille Vautier: 279b, 364; /Bibliothèque de l'Assemblée Nationale, Paris/Dagli Orti: 339t, 360b, 369b; /Bodleian Library, Oxford: 85b, 119b, 213r, 306b, 314t, 319b, 325, 332, 351b, 354, 355t, 376b, 407t, 445t; /British Museum, London/Eileen Tweedy: 359t, 481b, 506; /Album/Joseph Martin: 146l, 238t, /Joseph Martin: 350b, 358tr; /Museo de America Madrid: 191t, 232l, /Dagli Orti: 356t, 388; /Museo Ciudad, Mexico/Dagli Orti: 331, 431br, /Museo Ethnografico Pigorini, Rome/Dagli

Orti: 464b; /Museo de Jiquilpan, Mexico/Dagli Orti: 2721t; /Museo de Michoacan, Morelia, Mexico/Dagli Orti 314b; /Museo del Popol Vuh, Guatemala/Dagli Orti: 342b; /Museo Regional de Antropologia, Merida, Mexico/Dagli Orti: 370t, 459b; /Museo Regional de Oaxaca, Mexico/Dagli Orti: 324r, 446t, 466–7, 469tl, 478tr; /Museo Regional, Puebla, Mexico/Dagli Orti: 390t, 442b, 459t; /Museo del Templo Mayor, Mexico/Dagli Orti: 257b, 379t, 444l and r; /Museo de Teotenango, Mexico/Dagli Orti: 362t, 464t; /Museum of Mankind, London/Eileen Tweedy: 318; /Museum San Pedro de Sula, Honduras/Dagli Orti: 259b, 440b, 441; /Museum für Völkerkunde, Vienna/Dagli Orti: 471b, 476; /National Anthropological Museum, Mexico/Dagli Orti: 281t, 284b, 286r, 310t, 333t, 335b, 355b, 356b, 357r, 363b, 365t, 368t, 375t, 382t, 384t, 385t, 399b, 438bl, 439br, 443t, 446b, 448, 454b, 461b, 463, 469b, 470t and b, 473t, 474, 478b, 480t, 484t, 485t, 499t; /National Archives, Mexico /Mireille Vautier: 360t, 380b; /National Ethnological Museum, Mexico/Dagli Orti: 336t; /Dagli Orti: 3, 28t, 34b, 42t, 58t, 67l, 69b, 70t, 71b, 76, 85t, 86b, 87t, 89t, 92, 93t, 94b, 98b, 99b, 102l and r, 103b, 104l, 108l, 109b, 115b, 119t, 124b, 134r, 135l, 136b, 143t, 145t, 151b, 152t, 153b, 165l, 170t, 176t,

182bl, 188t and bl, 196r, 197b, 198r, 199t and r, 200l and r, 201t, 202r, 206t, 207l, 210l, 211r, 214–15, 218l, 219t and b, 220l, 222l and r, 223t and b, 224bl, 225t, 226t and r, 227l, 228t and l, 229l and r, 231l and r, 232r, 233b, 234–5, 237b, 239l, 240r, 241r, 242l and r, 243t and b, 244t and b, 245b, 246b, 247b, 248l and r, 249l, 251t, 252t, 253l and r, 254t, 255b, 256tl, 257t, /Dagli Orti: 278t, 281b, 287t, 310b, 321t, 323, 327b, 336b, 340b, 344t, 349b, 371b, 386–7, 391t&b, 392t, 393t, 395t&b, 397b, 399t, 401t, 404t&b, 405t, 410t, 413t, 417b, 422t, 423t&b, 424t&b, 428t, 429t, 450–1, 455, 458br, 484b, 492t; /Nicolas Sapieha: 164b, 413b; /Eileen Tweedy: 63b, 147b, 230b, /Mireille Vautier: 17t, 77b, 83b, 91t, 94t, 120–1, 143bl, 194–5, 203l, 205l and r, 208l, 217t, 233t, 239r and b, 240l, 250l, 251r, 256b, 259tr, 268–9, 290t, 291b, 317t, 328–9, 330t, 334b, 375b, 480b, 489b, 498t&b, 499b; /Francesco Venturi: 319t, 465t; /Xalapa Museum, Veracruz, Mexico/Dagli Orti: 353, 368b, 411b, 437t.

The Bridgeman Art Library: 43t, 69t, 83t, 90t, 110l, 111, 112t, 118l, 133t, 142l, 150t, 152b, 155b, 156b, 168l, 180l, 227l; /Archives Charmet: 72b; /Baluarete de Santiago, Veracruz, Mexico, Banco Mexicano de Imagenes, INAH 475t; /British Museum, London 475b; /Brooklyn Museum of Art, New York: 182br, /Giraudon: 417t, 130r, 147tr, 150b, 197tl; /Index: 108tr, /Lauros

/Giraudon: 106; /Ian Mursell /Mexicolore: 38t, 165t, 188br; /Banco Mexicano de Imagenes/INAH: 88, 113r, 144t, 163t, 166l, 171t, 176b, 178r, 181l and r, 187t, 189t, 192t; /Museo Nacional de Antropologia, Mexico City, Mexico/Giraudon: 481t; /private collection: 262t, 486; /private collection, Stapleton Collection: 262b; /Sean Sprague/Mexicolore: 174–5, /The Stapleton Collection: 107t and b.

Corbis: 122l, 421; /Archivo Iconografico, S.A.: 110r, 128–9, 158–9, 160, 162r, /Paul Almasy: 361b, 370b, 405b; /Artephot/Corbis Sygma: 378t; /Yann Arthus-Bertrand: 170b, 280b; /Bettmann: 5.4, 13t, 19b, 202l, 211t, 322b; /Bowers Museum of Cultural Art: 434, 435b, 436b&t, 437b; /Anna Clopet: 97t; /Richard A Cooke: 415t; /Sergio Dorantes: 427t; /Macduff Everton: 271t, 316b, 402b, 419, 427b; /Randy Faris: 22–3, 55t, 260; /Werner Forman: 342t, 401t, 407bl, 438r, 439t, 443b, 487t and b, 491b; /Arvind Garg: 49b, 277b; /Historical Picture Archive: 196l; /Angelo Hornak: 429b; /Jacqui Hurst: 447b; /Kimbell Art Museum: 105b, 155tr, 435t, 445b; /Robert Landau: 394b; /Otto Lang: 410b; /Danny Lehman: 10t, 72t, 326t, 400b, 411t, 428b; /Charles and Josette Lenars: 1, 20t, 21t and b, 36t and b, 82t, 177t, 258b, 383t, 396t, 406t, 412t, 420b, 454tr, 496t and b; /Craig Lovell 420t; /Macduff Everton: 109t, 138–9; /North Carolina Museum of Art: 272–3; Gianni Dagli Orti: 125, 30t, 37l and r, 56t, 57b, 68b, 89b, 98t, 99t, 116r, 117tr and b, 149b, 179, 184b, 191l, 264, 266t, 32b, 341b, 414b, 415b, 489t; Della Zuana Pascal/Corbis Sygma: 497b; /Reuters: 276b, 447t; /Enzo & Paolo Ragazzini:

48b; /Kevin Schafer: 371t; /Gian Berto Vanni: 12b, 403b, 454tl, 460b; /Vanni Archive: 403t; /Francesco Venturi: 394t; /Nick Wheeler: 90b; /Peter M Wilson: 388–9.

Werner Forman: 66b, 77t, 114tr, 126t, 132b, 162b, 189b, 217b, 258t; /Anthropology Museum, Veracruz University, Jalapa: 142l, 221r; /David Bernstein, New York: 66t, 115t; /Biblioteca Nacional, Madrid: 41t; /Biblioteca Universitaria, Bologna: 75, 84b, 122t, 127t, 180r; /British Museum, London: 42b, 62, 70b, 74b, 172b, 173b, 178l, 184t, 186r, 193l, 208t, 225r, 249r; /Dallas Museum of Art: 78l, 114b, /Field Museum of Natural History, Chicago: 84m; /Philip Goldman, London: 198t; /Liverpool Museum, Liverpool: 63t, 140–1, 144b, 157t, 207t, 213r; /Edward H. Merrin Gallery, New York: 104r, 156t; /Museo de America, Madrid: 131t; /Museum of the Americas, New York: 17b; /Museum of Fine Arts, Dallas: 112l; /Museum für Völkerkunde, Basle: 38b, 67r, 136t, 190r, 203r, 216r; /Museum für Völkerkunde, Berlin: 71t, 73tr, 130l, 145b, 167b; /Museum für Völkerkunde, Hamburg: 167; /Museum für Völkerkunde, Vienna: 39t; /National Museum of Anthropology, Mexico: 82b, 91b, 95b, 97b, 123tl and r, 137t, 148t, 149t, 155tl, 166r, 172t, 173t, 185l and r, 190l, 216l, 220r, 221l; /National Museum of Denmark, Copenhagen: 148bl; /Pigorini Museum of Prehistory and Ethnography, Rome: 41b, 68t, 86r, 161t; /Portland Art Museum, Oregon: 118t; /private collection: 34t; /private collection, London: 48t; /private collection, Mexico City: 103t; /private collection, New York: 16r, 95r, 104l,

132t, 134l, 153t, 182t, 236l; /St Louis Art Museum, MO: 171b; /Smithsonian Institution, Washington: 124t, 168t; /Sotheby's, New York, 146t; /Dr Kurt Stavanenhagen Collection, Mexico City: 59b, 164t, 212t.

N.J. Saunders: 12t, 24tr, 32t, 39b, 44–1, 49t, 50b, 169b, 183.

South American Pictures: /Fabienne Fossez: 460t, 461t; /Robert Francis: 24tl, 30br, 35b, 46t, 50t, 53t, 58b, 59t, 270tl and tr, 274t, 280t, 297t and b, 304b, 401b, 416, 452bl, 458t; /Tony Morrison: 2, 4.3, 10b, 11b, 14–15, 25tr, 26–7, 28l, 29b, 33t and b, 43b, 46bl, 51l, 54t, 55b, 60–1, 74t, 80–1, 100–1, 112r, 125t, 136r, 163b, 201l, 259tl, 256b, 263b, 274b, 275t, 288–9, 290b, 291t, 293b, 302t, 345b, 366–7, 452br, 453; /Iain Pearson: 18b, 276t, 292b, 299b, 315b, 320t and b, 426t and b; /Chris Sharp: 18t, 25bl, 29t, 30bl, 32b, 35t, 51r, 52l and r, 53b, 54b, 56b, 73tl, 78r, 79t and b, 93b, 96l and r, 116l, 137b, 154b, 186b, 237t, 241l, 258t, 265t, 283b, 285t, 294t and b, 295t, 296, 298t and b, 300t, 301, 304t, 305t and b, 306t, 308–9, 311t and b, 316t, 317b, 322t, 324b, 326b, 330b, 340t, 345tr, 352t, 369t, 372t, 384b, 390b, 408–9, 425b, 440t, 452t, 456b, 462b, 468, 482–3, 493, 494t and b, 495, 501t and b; /Kate Smith: 307t; /Karen Ward: 398t; /Rebecca Whitfield: 46br.

This edition is published by Hermes House,
an imprint of Anness Publishing Ltd
Hermes House, 88–89 Blackfriars Road, London SE1 8HA
tel. 020 7401 2077; fax 020 7633 9499

www.hermeshouse.com; www.annesspublishing.com

Anness Publishing has a new picture agency outlet for
publishing, promotions or advertising, please visit our website
www.practicalpictures.com for more information.

Publisher: Joanna Lorenz
Editorial Director: Helen Sudell
Editor: Joy Wotton
Project Editor: Molly Perham
Designer: Nigel Partridge
Maps: Peter Bull Art Studio
Illustrations: Vanessa Card
Production Controller: Don Campaniello

ETHICAL TRADING POLICY

Because of our ongoing ecological investment programme, you, as our customer, can have the pleasure
and reassurance of knowing that a tree is being cultivated on your behalf to naturally replace
the materials used to make the book you are holding. For further information
about this scheme, go to www.annesspublishing.com/trees

A CIP catalogue record for this book is available from the British Library.

Previously published in two separate volumes,
The Lost History of Aztec & Maya and
The Aztec & Maya: Life in an Ancient Civilization

p. 1. A fine mask of Xochipilli, the Aztec god of flowers.
p. 2. The Temple of the Count, Palenque.
p. 3. A golden Mixtec necklace.
p. 4 top. The Templo Mayor, Tenochtitlán.
p. 4 bottom. A Pre-Columbian figure from Oaxaca.
p. 5. A *chacmool* outside the Temple of the Warriors, Chichén Itzá.
p. 510. The Pyramid of the Sun, Teotihuacán.
p. 511. Musicians and court officials from a Bonampak mural.
p. 512. Clockwise from top left: Yacatecuhtli, Huitzilopochtli,
Quetzalcóatl and Chalchiúhtlicue.

PUBLISHER'S NOTE
Although the advice and information in this book are believed to
be accurate and true at the time of going to press, neither the
authors nor the publisher can accept any legal responsibility or
liability for any errors or omissions that may be made.